IDAHO HANDBOOK

IDAHO HANDBOOK

SECOND EDITION

BILL LOFTUS

MOON
PUBLICATIONS, INC.

IDAHO HANDBOOK
SECOND EDITION

Published by
Moon Publications, Inc.
P.O. Box 3040
Chico, California 95927-3040, USA

Printed by
Colorcraft Ltd., Hong Kong

Includes bibliographical references and index.
ISBN: 1-56691-061-7
ISSN: 1077-1905

Editor: Don Root
Copy Editor: Nicole Revere
Production & Design: Carey Wilson
Cartographers: Bob Race, Brian Bardwell
Index: Nicole Revere

Front cover photo: Ed King
All photos by Bill Loftus unless otherwise noted.

Distributed in the U.S.A. by Publishers Group West
Printed in Hong Kong

Please send all comments, corrections, additions, amendments, and critiques to:

IDAHO HANDBOOK
MOON PUBLICATIONS, INC.
P.O. BOX 3040
CHICO, CA 95927-3040, USA

Printing History
1st edition — February 1992
2nd edition — January 1995

For my parents,
Howard J. and V. Martha Loftus
And for Idahoans
who love a beautiful state

CONTENTS

MAPS

MAP SYMBOLS

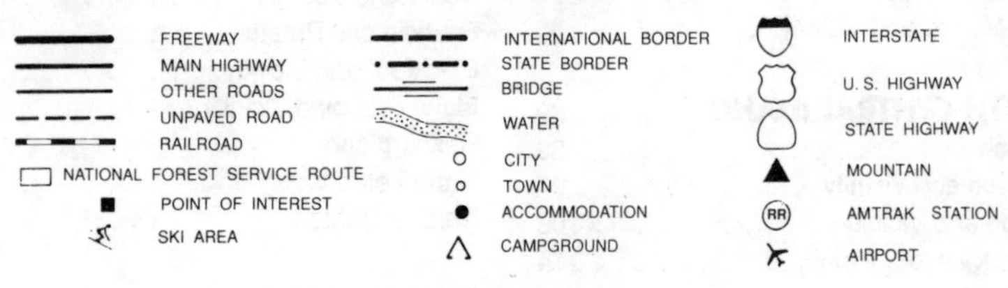

ABBREVIATIONS

B&B—bed and breakfast
BLM—Bureau of Land Management
d—double
Hwy.—highway
I-(with number)—interstate highway
INEL—Idaho National Engineering Laboratory
KOA—Kampgrounds of America
LCSC—Lewis-Clark State College
mph—miles per hour
NF—national forest
NRA—national recreation area
P.O.—post office
RV—recreational vehicle
s—single
UI—University of Idaho
USGS—United States Geological Survey
WW II—World War II

CHARTS AND SPECIAL TOPICS

ACKNOWLEDGMENTS

To my wife, Kelli, and to my children, Bob and Kate, thank you for your patience. To my colleagues at the *Lewiston Morning Tribune,* Idaho's best newspaper, bar none, thanks for your endurance. Some individual thank-yous to Rick Just of the Idaho Parks and Recreation Department; Tom Kovalicky, U.S. Forest Service, retired; Roberta Rene of the Idaho Department of Commerce; author Michael Frome and outdoor writers Tom Wharton and Rich Landers for friendship and support along the way. Thanks also to those throughout Idaho who provided information, food, and lodging for a family on the road.

IS THIS BOOK OUT OF DATE?

Travel information is continually changing, even in slow-paced Idaho. We have endeavored to make the information in this book as accurate as possible at the time it was published, and we will continue to update it. You can help. If you spot information that is no longer valid, please let us know. If you discover places that could have been included, share them with fellow travelers by informing us about them. We especially appreciate feedback from women travelers, local residents, outdoor enthusiasts, and special-interest or special-needs travelers. We also like hearing from experts in the field as well as local business owners who wish to serve travelers. Address your letters to:

IDAHO HANDBOOK
c/o Moon Publications
P.O. Box 3040
Chico, CA 95927-3040 USA

CATHY CARLSON

INTRODUCTION

Most people think of Idaho as a bucolic state filled to overflowing with potatoes—fields of potatoes stretching across the flatness of the Snake River Plain. Others more familiar with the state might envision cattle, sheep, or miners in the scene as well. Loggers in Idaho's mountain forests may hew their way into this mental sketch; as might the fruit orchards and vineyards of southwestern Idaho, or the golden wheat fields of the north state. Idaho is all those things, in part.

But for those who know the state well, all those images tend to wither and fade against the backdrop of the state's wilderness—its azure lakes, striking peaks of clean rock, startlingly fresh lava flows, and whitewater rivers. Wilderness is plentiful in Idaho. Six federally designated wilderness areas take up over four million acres of the state. One of these, the 2.3-million-acre Frank Church–River of No Return Wilderness, is the largest such preserve in the lower 48 states. Through its rugged landscape flows the famed Middle Fork of the Salmon River, a free-flowing stretch of Wild And Scenic whitewater that has carried two U.S. presidents—Jimmy Carter and George Bush—and countless other adventurers through Idaho's untamed outback.

In addition, the U.S. Forest Service manages 9.3 million roadless acres in the state's national forests; the BLM oversees millions more acres of open and unclaimed Idaho land; and the National Park Service preserves a modest 43,000-plus acres at Craters of the Moon National Monument near Arco.

With all this undeveloped land in the state, it's not surprising that land-use conflicts are almost a tradition here. Should the land be protected from development as a public recreation resource, or opened up to private development to benefit the state's economy? Recent debate has focused on the question of whether to designate more of the national forest lands as wilderness.

But while the debate rages, even ardent critics of additional wilderness saddle up their horses for fall hunting trips into pristine lands. Wilderness is still a way of life for Idahoans. And with urban areas in such close proximity to mother nature, most of the state's residents find plenty of places to relax—from community ski hills to excellent fishing streams—within minutes of work or home. Maybe that helps keep those smiles in place and explains Idaho's most effective marketing tool—its friendly populace.

Idaho's economy is still firmly founded on agriculture and supported by other jobs dependent on natural resources such as mining and logging. But the state has also worked hard to recruit light industry and other businesses from around the country, while encouraging the growth of new companies within the state. That's made Idaho a land of opportunity for residents of other states who find their surroundings fit a little too tight. The state's population is growing. But there's plenty of wilderness to go around here—wilderness that breathes life into the slogan that echoes through this state from time to time: "Idaho is what America was." Idahoans, for reasons sometimes aside from wilderness, like it that way.

THE LAND

Occupying the northeastern fringe of the intermountain West, Idaho lies west of the Rockies and east of Washington's Cascades. Girded by mountains, it was the last of the 50 states to be sighted by European descendants—the Lewis and Clark Expedition first topped the Beaverhead Mountains at Lemhi Pass near Tendoy in 1805.

Almost all of Idaho's eastern flank is mountainous—from the Bitterroot Range running along most of the Montana border, to the Tetons, just across the Wyoming border. A portion of Idaho's eastern border lies along the Continental Divide, and Idaho's highest point, 12,662-foot Borah Peak, is also on the state's eastern side, in the Lost River Range near Mackay. By contrast, about a third of the state's western border is formed by the lower reaches of the Snake River, which flows out of Idaho into Washington at the state's lowest point—738 feet near Lewiston. Between those two extremes, a generality can be drawn—that Idaho slopes downward from east to west.

Idaho stretches 479 miles north to south and 305 miles at its widest from east to west. With 83,557 square miles, it ranks 13th among the states in area. In the 1990 census, its population was estimated at 1,006,749 or 42nd among the states. That translates into lots of room to move for everybody.

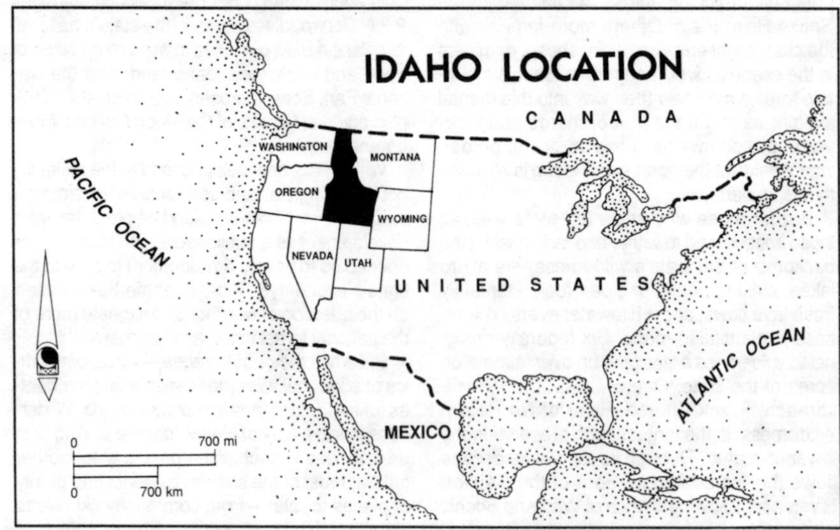

Mountains

Idaho's numerous mountain ranges are scattered over most of its area. In addition to the Bitterroots along the eastern spine, the Selkirk and Cabinet mountains rise up at the tip of the panhandle where it cozies up to Canada. Heading south, the high ridges that rumple north-central Idaho east of Grangeville are the Clearwater Mountains, which are mirrored by the Salmon River Mountains, just across the Salmon River to the south. To the west of those, looming above Hells Canyon, stands the high cordillera of the Seven Devils Mountains. And in the southwestern corner of the state are the Owyhee Mountains, famous for their mining history.

Southeastern Idaho also has its share of peaks. The weathered Pioneer Mountains slope toward the Craters of the Moon National Monument near Arco. The broad-shouldered slopes of the Albion Mountains impress visitors with their bulk which builds patiently toward the sky along the Utah border. The Portneuf and Caribou ranges anchor the southeastern corner of the state. The Grand Tetons dominate the state's border with Wyoming and give Driggs a boost (though they actually lie just across the border), and the Centennial Mountains tower above the upper reaches of the Snake River Plain near Henry's Lake.

But Idaho's middle holds its most dramatic ranges, the Sawtooths, Boulders, and White Clouds. These are the mountains that helped make Sun Valley famous, the ones that give Stanley its alpine appeal. If any mountains figure in Idaho's national image, these ranges qualify. And just east of the Sawtooths, the Lost River and Lemhi ranges thrust themselves forward with classic basin-and-range credentials. For sheer visual impact, these mountains are hard to beat. The Lost Rivers above Mackay, after all, claim Borah Peak among their company.

IDAHO'S RIVERS

Idaho's rivers have always been a thread in the fabric of the state's social and commercial life. The lure of a watery route across the continent to the Pacific Ocean led President Thomas Jefferson to dispatch the Corps of Discovery, with captains Meriwether Lewis and William Clark, across an unexplored continent in 1804. The explorers hastened out of the Rocky Mountains to the banks of the Clearwater River at their first opportunity in 1805, confident at last that they could make steady headway to the Pacific.

Waves of fur traders followed soon after, many of them inspired, even educated, to the ways of the West by the Lewis and Clark Expedition. David Thompson explored Idaho first in 1809, building Kullyspell House along Lake Pend Oreille's shoreline. Mountain men penetrated southern Idaho, looking for beaver streams. Because of the success they found there, the Snake River and its tributaries drew them back repeatedly, despite the dangers posed by hostile Indians.

The Snake River also funneled the next wave of settlers through the state during the great Overland Migration of the 1840s. And in 1861, it carried the tide of humanity that poured into Idaho with the discovery of gold along Canal Creek near Orofino. Columbia and Snake river steamers hauled most of the first miners. Miners also prompted the first damming of the Snake when **Swan Falls Dam** was built south of Kuna by A.J. Wiley to supply electricity to the Owyhee mines. A dozen dams now impound the Snake, holding its water for adjoining farm fields and stripping its energy for electricity to power the state. The Snake may have been dammed from its source to its mouth, but the Salmon River's 400-mile course within the state still flows unimpeded.

Rivers And Lakes

Although mostly an arid state, Idaho holds 880 square miles of water spread across thousands of miles of streams and more than 2,000 lakes. The rivers threading their ways through the mountains, plains, and deserts help give Idaho its character.

Nearly all of the state's waters find their way to the Snake River, which stretches nearly 1,000 miles from its headwaters in the heights of Yellowstone National Park to its confluence with the Columbia River in Washington. Along the way it crosses the width of Idaho, flowing westward across the Snake River Plain, turning north near Parma to form part of Idaho's border with Oregon, then leaving Idaho near Lewiston to eventually join the Columbia nearly 140 miles to the west.

Another of the state's major rivers is the Salmon, the nation's longest undammed river within a single state. It starts in the Sawtooth Mountains near Stanley and flows 420 miles through the state's wild heart before joining the Snake downstream from White Bird.

The Salmon is the most esteemed of the nine Idaho rivers having segments protected under the Wild and Scenic Rivers Act. Wild status means just that, with permanent and wide-scale development prohibitions—unless Congress changes its mind. Two wild stretches along the Salmon and its middle fork offer 185 miles of wild river crossed by only one road. There is a chance the state's congressional delegation may succeed in getting the final segment of the Salmon—from Long Tom Bar above Riggins downstream to its mouth—added to the Wild and Scenic list.

Other protected rivers, from south to north, include 67 miles of the Snake River and 24 miles of Rapid River and its west fork (near Riggins), all guarded by Hells Canyon NRA; the Lochsa and the Selway, which join to form the Clearwater River's middle fork, also protected (the three accounting for another 192 miles of protected river); and 67 miles of the St. Joe River, from its origin at St. Joe Lake to its north fork, near St. Maries.

The St. Joe and its Panhandle neighbor, the Coeur d'Alene, drain into Lake Coeur d'Alene, which in turn drains into the Spokane River that heads westward to its confluence with the Columbia in Washington. Other major rivers include the Bear River of southeastern Idaho, which feeds Great Salt Lake; the Moyie and Clark Fork rivers, which feed Lake Pend Oreille; and the Pend Oreille River, which gathers the waters of Priest River and heads west to its own union with the Columbia.

Lake Pend Oreille ranks as the state's largest lake with 180 square miles of water surface. Other major lakes include Priest Lake and Lake Coeur d'Alene, also in the Panhandle; Dworshak Reservoir in north-central Idaho; Payette Lake and Cascade Reservoir near McCall; American Falls Reservoir outside Pocatello; Island Park and Palisades reservoirs near the Wyoming border; and Bear Lake, straddling the Utah border in the southeast corner of the state. Many other smaller reservoirs are spread around the state, and hundreds of gemlike mountain lakes sparkle across Idaho's expansive backcountry.

Climate

Idaho's climate can be tough to figure out. The state's varied topography makes for a wide range of climatic extremes. Gooding, on the Snake River Plain, ranks as one of Idaho's warmest and driest locales. During its arid summers, 100-degree days are routine, and the annual precipitation averages just under six inches. Less than 40 miles away, as the crow flies, Anderson Ranch Dam holds the official state record for the most snow in a 24-hour period: 31 inches fell there on a December day in 1967. And in Stanley, little more than 133 miles north, snow routinely lingers until April and frosts can nip buds in any month of the year. Elevation makes the difference: Gooding hunkers down at 2,750 feet while Stanley looks into the Sawtooths from 6,198 feet.

A jetboat runs the Snake River where it separates Idaho and Washington

IDAHO CLIMATE

City	Elevation (feet)	January Mean High/Low Temps (°F)	June Mean High/Low Temps (°F)	Mean Annual Precipitation (inches)	Mean Season Snowfall (inches)
PANHANDLE					
Bonners Ferry	1,810	32/19	84/50	24.09	69
Coeur d'Alene	2,158	35/22	86/52	25.79	49
Sandpoint	2,100	32/20	81/49	33.33	80
NORTH-CENTRAL					
Grangeville	3,355	37/20	82/50	23.33	56
Lewiston	1,413	39/26	90/59	12.78	19
Moscow	2,660	35/22	84/49	23.96	50
BOISE AND SOUTHWEST					
Boise	2,842	37/23	91/59	11.71	21
McCall	5,025	30/12	81/45	28.06	151
Mountain Home	3,190	39/20	94/56	10.17	14
Weiser	2,120	36/20	93/55	11.61	21
SOUTH-CENTRAL					
Hailey	5,328	31/8	85/50	16.20	122
Rupert	4,204	35/15	90/54	8.30	26
Twin Falls	3,770	36/19	92/54	9.29	19
SOUTHEAST					
Idaho Falls	4,730	28/5	87/49	8.62	34
Montpelier	5,960	30/6	85/47	14.17	67
Pocatello	4,444	32/15	89/54	10.86	37
CENTRAL					
Challis	5,175	30/10	87/51	7.37	17
Salmon	3,949	30/9	89/49	9.93	20
Stanley	6,230	26/-1	78/34	16.20	94

Although Stanley routinely ranks as the state's (and sometimes the nation's) coldest spot, Island Park Dam near Yellowstone National Park holds the Idaho record of -60° F. At the other end of the thermometer, Orofino in the Clearwater River canyon is Idaho's hot spot with a record of 118° F set July 28, 1934.

Weather is important for travelers, whether they're in the backcountry or on Idaho's sometimes trail-like highways. During the winter months, anytime from November through March, sometimes into April, road conditions can be challenging with snow and ice. A particularly dangerous phenomenon for highway travelers is known as black ice. In cold spells, the snow can melt during the day, then refreeze at night into an all-but-invisible coating of ice on the roadway. A motorist's first warning that the road is icy can be the start of a spectacular spin toward the ditch. The Idaho Transportation Department maintains a telephone road report service at (208) 336-6600 for winter travelers. Carrying basic survival gear in the car with you is recommended while driving during cold spells, in case the car quits or the highway closes. Such gear would include a blanket or sleeping bag, some food, and candles. Hot weather travelers would be wise to tuck away a few gallons of water, extra food, and something to create some shade if venturing into remote areas, even for the day. Mechanical failures can change plans.

PRECIPITATION

10 - 20 INCHES
20 - 30 INCHES
30 - 40 INCHES
40 - 50 INCHES
50 - 60 INCHES
0 50mi
0 50km

Travel Seasons

Idaho's climate lends itself to two peak travel seasons: the summer season for campers, rafters, and others who like the state sans snow; and the winter season that attracts thousands of skiers and snowmobilers to the state. At Sun Valley or Coeur d'Alene, for example, these two basic dialects of Idaho tourism translate into high seasons that run June-August and November-March. The rates drop during the interim months, and many tourists, especially hunters and fishermen, prefer these slack times. In fall, hunters from around the nation come to the state for its elk herds and the chance to hunt the mighty bulls in undisturbed wilderness. And spring days in Orofino can see more Montana than Idaho license plates along the Clearwater River, as anglers try for truly big fish, sea-run steelhead that average 12-14 pounds.

GEOLOGIC HISTORY

During the Paleozoic era, 600 to 250 million years ago, much of Idaho was submerged. The end of this era also coincided with a mass extinction that wiped out 90% of all life on the planet. Most of Idaho as we know it took shape in the Mesozoic era between 250 and 65 million years ago. Dinosaurs roamed the earth, and during the Cretaceous period, at the end of the Mesozoic era, the intrusions of granite that formed the Idaho Batholith bubbled up and cooled. It was also during this period, about 100 million years ago, that islands from the south seas docked against the continent's western margin. One such island is now known as the Seven Devils Mountains, along the state's western border. About 50 million years ago, things began to heat up in earnest. Challis-area volcanoes began dumping a load of rhyolite ash all over the place. At that time Idaho's climate was mild and wet, evidenced by redwoods preserved in the hot ash. About 10 million years later, at the end of the Eocene period, the climate turned drier. Redwoods persisted in the mountains but no longer could grow in the valleys of the northern Rockies.

The mid-Tertiary period, roughly 17 to 20 million years ago, was notable in Idaho for the advent of a subtropical climate. In the Clarkia area, it is possible to find fossils that still preserve the colors of the original leaves and insects, for a few minutes at least. Pry apart a bit of rock and the blue or green iridescence of a beetle shell glimmers briefly before oxidizing to black. More remarkable is that scientists have been able to extract actual plant tissue and DNA from leaves that fell millions of years ago.

But the real fun started about 17 million years ago with the beginning of the massive lava floods that formed the Columbia Plateau and layered Hells Canyon like a torte. The basin and range geology of southern Idaho was formed by lava that lapped in waves over the terrain. And strangely enough, just a million years or so later, the Snake River Plain was formed by vulcanism as well. Geologists are beginning to think the three events developed because of a common catalyst, a giant meteorite that struck southeastern Oregon. The hot spot that resulted beneath the earth's crust created a string of volcanic eruptions. The continent has steadily drifted westward over the weak point, leaving the broad volcanic Snake River Plain in the hot spot's wake. The hot spot is now beneath the western edges of Wyoming and Montana, where

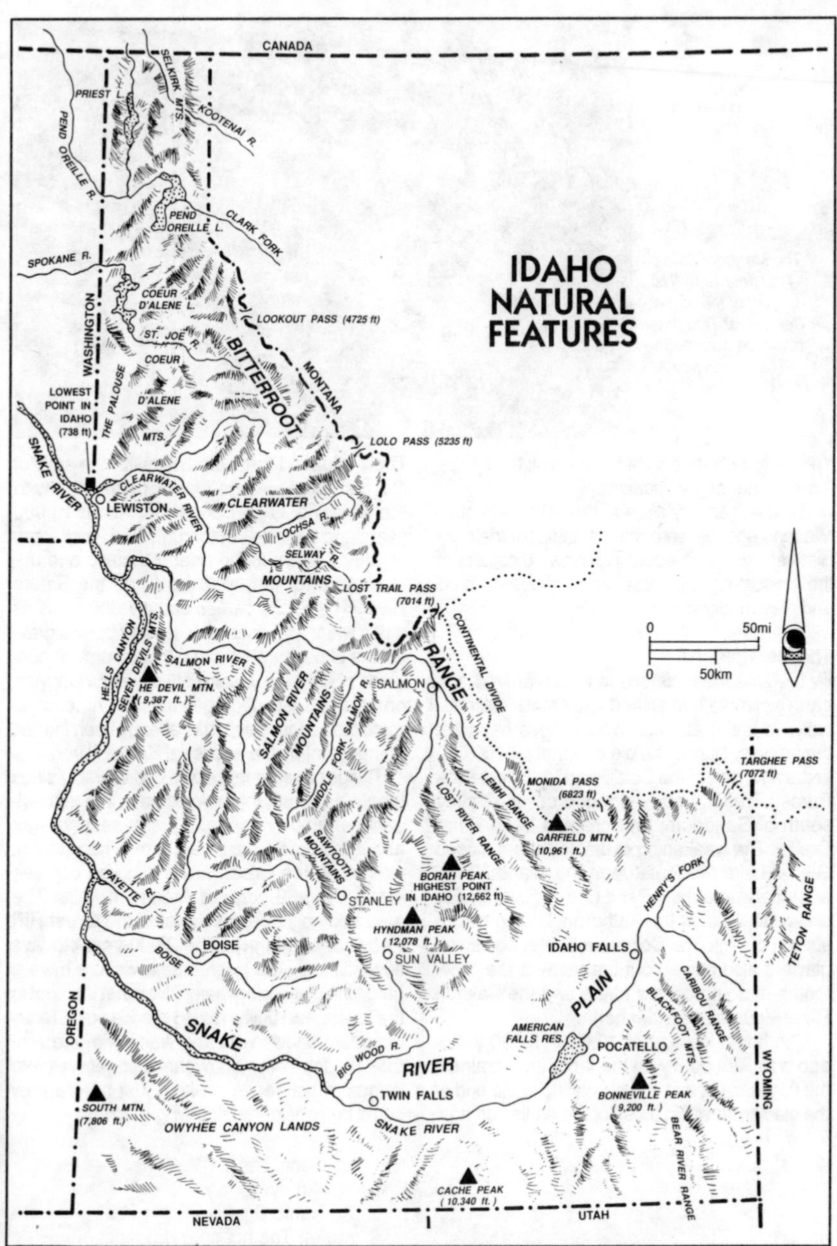
IDAHO
NATURAL
FEATURES
CANADA
PRIEST L.
SELKIRK MTS.
KOOTENAI R.
PEND OREILLE R.
PEND OREILLE L.
CLARK FORK
SPOKANE R.
COEUR D'ALENE L.
LOOKOUT PASS (4725 ft)
ST. JOE R.
BITTERROOT
MONTANA
WASHINGTON
THE PALOUSE
COEUR D'ALENE MTS.
LOWEST POINT IN IDAHO (738 ft)
LOLO PASS (5235 ft)
SNAKE RIVER
CLEARWATER RIVER
LEWISTON
CLEARWATER
LOCHSA R.
SELWAY R.
MOUNTAINS
LOST TRAIL PASS (7014 ft)
CONTINENTAL DIVIDE
RANGE
0
50mi
0
50km
HELLS CANYON
SEVEN DEVILS MTS.
SALMON RIVER
HE DEVIL MTN. (9,387 ft.)
SALMON RIVER MOUNTAINS
MIDDLE FORK SALMON R.
SALMON
LEMHI RANGE
LOST RIVER RANGE
MONIDA PASS (6823 ft)
TARGHEE PASS (7072 ft)
GARFIELD MTN. (10,961 ft.)
SAWTOOTH MOUNTAINS
BORAH PEAK HIGHEST POINT IN IDAHO (12,662 ft)
STANLEY
HENRY'S FORK
TETON RANGE
PAYETTE R.
HYNDMAN PEAK (12,078 ft.)
BOISE
SUN VALLEY
IDAHO FALLS
BOISE R.
CARIBOU RANGE
BLACKFOOT MTS.
PLAIN
OREGON
SNAKE
AMERICAN FALLS RES.
POCATELLO
BIG WOOD R.
RIVER
WYOMING
SOUTH MTN. (7,806 ft.)
TWIN FALLS
BONNEVILLE PEAK (9,200 ft.)
OWYHEE CANYON LANDS
SNAKE RIVER
BEAR RIVER RANGE
CACHE PEAK (10.340 ft.)
NEVADA
UTAH

The Meadow Creek Trail near Lowell is part of the Idaho Centennial Trail that stretches from north to south.

Yellowstone National Park shows all the symptoms of lingering vulcanism.

By the Tertiary's end, the Pliocene and Miocene epochs were most notable for their dry climates, the fossil record indicates. Ancestors of the modern camel, horse, and rhinoceros lived and died in Idaho.

The Ice Ages

By the time the Pleistocene epoch arrived, the earth's climate had shifted even more dramatically. In Idaho at least two ice ages have left their marks. During the big chill that hit 100,000 years ago, part of the Cordilleran Ice Sheet—the Purcell Trench Lobe—gouged out the valley south of Sandpoint and created Lake Pend Oreille. The weakening of that ice sheet loosed Glacial Lake Missoula upon the inland Northwest, carving out the Pend Oreille River Valley and washing over the Rathdrum Prairie before spilling out into the Columbia Basin. Localized glaciers also carved out the teeth of the Sawtooths of south-central Idaho and the Salmon River Mountains farther north.

The latest ice age of 10,000-15,000 years ago was less heavy on the land. Its moraines, the ridges of dirt and gravel piled up at the end of the glacier, lie within those of the earlier ice age. The wet period that coincided with the start of this last great ice age also flooded Utah with the waters of Lake Bonneville. About 15,000 years ago the lake cut through Red Rock Pass in southeastern Idaho near Pocatello and unleashed a torrent northward into the Snake River. The Snake carried about 1,000 times as much water as it does now, leaving behind gravel bars of bowling-ball-sized "melon gravel" hundreds of feet high. Geologists say Hells Canyon, one of the deepest gorges in North America at more than a mile deep, had already been formed at that point by the ancestral Snake River.

Things have calmed down considerably since then. Of course, in geologic time, the last volcanic eruption happened just a second ago, about the time Christ was born. The eruption was along the Great Rift, which you can see along Hwy. 39 north of American Falls. The area has now been designated the **Great Rift National Landmark.** The 2,000-year-old lava flow still looks so fresh, some visitors have a hard time convincing themselves that it is cool to the touch. And unlike during the ice ages, today mountain snows wax and wane with the winter—though some snowbanks linger well into August most years, melting just before they could be considered fledgling glaciers.

FLORA AND FAUNA

FLORA

Taiga And Tundra

Subarctic **taiga** dominates Idaho's landscape north of the Snake River Plain. The lower elevations and moist, cool climate of western Idaho support thriving Rocky Mountain montane forests—including thick stands of **western red cedar, hemlock, western larch, white pine,** and **Douglas fir.** Another common species here, the **ponderosa pine,** grows best in more scattered stands where its thick bark protects it from the occasional fires that sweep the countryside. Smokey Bear's fear of fire of any sort ironically put the big ponderosas in jeopardy by allowing young trees and brush to crowd in around their bases. These ladder fuels, as they're known, feed low-intensity ground fires and turn them into raging blazes that can climb into the crowns of giants.

The ponderosas, cedars, and white pines are the most valuable trees for the state's timber industry. The white pine suffered near devastation at midcentury when blister rust, an introduced pest, killed whole forests across northern Idaho. The Forest Service and timber industry landowners responded by logging thousands of acres and billions of board feet of the state's best timber. Major investments are being made now to return the white pine to its former place.

Idaho's central mountain ranges act as a rain shadow for points east. Vegetation is more sparse here, with **bunchgrasses and shrubs** dominating the lower elevations. Higher up, **aspen, subalpine fir, limber and lodgepole pine,** and **Engelmann spruce** cover the cool, moist north-facing slopes.

Low-growing **tundra** vegetation—mosses, lichens, sedges, shrubs, and the occasional stunted tree—inhabits mountaintops above 8,000 feet across the state.

Grasslands And Desert

Grasslands cover the semiarid regions between the taiga and the deserts of the Snake River Plain. Conifers, grasses, and desert shrubs commingle in a haphazard survival pact; juniper and sagebrush occasionally invade. Unlike the Great Plains' tallgrass prairie, Idaho's native grasslands were mainly perennial bunchgrasses, adapted to summer drought. Overgrazing and out-of-season fires have wreaked havoc, with sagebrush and cheatgrass invading disturbed sites. The greatest grasslands of the state have been converted to cropland. The Palouse and Camas Prairie of north-central Idaho yield rich crops of wheat, barley, peas, and lentils. Farther north the Rathdrum Prairie is a major producer of bluegrass seed.

Desert spreads across southern Idaho; plants here have extensive root systems to glean scarce water, and small, waxy or hairy leaves to reduce water loss. **Greasewood, saltbrush, bitterbrush, winterfat, sagebrush,** and **shadscale** dot the landscape, growing as thick as water supplies will allow.

WILDLIFE

Idaho has an abundance of wildlife. Some species are thriving in the state, while others are teetering on the brink of extinction. The great herds of buffalo that once roamed the Snake River Plain are long gone, and salmon runs today are seriously imperiled. But at least today, wildlife in general enjoys the most extensive human efforts to restore habitat and stop poaching since the northern Rockies were settled. As a positive example, steelhead runs returning to Idaho now rank among the most abundant since record keeping began on the Snake River three decades ago.

Much of the state's wildlife fails to see much distinction between life in the city and life in the country. And with the state trying hard to protect its wildlife, it becomes more and more likely that individuals of some species are going to find their way into town sooner or later. Idaho Falls may win the honors as the most popular among moose. Dozens have to be removed from the city during some winters. Elkhorn Village near Sun Valley has a regular feeding station set up for elk. Lewiston has been visited by bighorn sheep, a cougar, and a black bear in recent years. Such visits present great peril for the wildlife, but they symbolize how close Idaho residents are to nature. There are times, however (such as when a bear is in the backyard), that close is not all that comfortable.

The state's university system offers numerous opportunities to learn more about Idaho's natural world. The University of Idaho maintains field stations at Clark Fork and McCall through its College of Forestry, Department of Wildlife and Range Sciences, tel. 885-6441. The Clark Fork Field Station, tel. 266-1452, and McCall campus, tel. 634-3918, can furnish current information about their offerings.

MAMMALS

Hoofing It

Idaho's **elk and deer** herds have apparently never been more healthy. Across the length and breadth of the state, their ranges are expanding, in part because the fires that blackened millions of acres of Idaho's forests early this century turned northern Idaho hillsides into lush pastures. A rarity in the early 1800s when Lewis and Clark passed through, elk have now reached what may be their highest numbers ever in Idaho. Idaho licensed more than 100,000 elk hunters at last count. With a few herds showing signs of overhunting, the Idaho Fish and Game Commission has cast a wary eye toward too much of a good thing. Hunters themselves are complaining increasingly that the state needs to limit hunters to provide a quality experience.

BOB RACE

bighorn sheep

Flourishing also are mule and white-tailed deer, the former creatures of the open grasslands and river canyons, the latter creatures of the forests. The whitetail sticks mostly to the lush forests and stream valleys of the northern part of the state, almost vanishing from the landscape south of the Salmon River. Mule deer are found primarily in the arid lands of the state from the Salmon River south. North of the Salmon, smaller numbers of mulies inhabit the highest ridges.

The mighty **Shiras moose,** the biggest member of the deer family in the state, regularly makes forays to towns, and the **woodland caribou** roams the Panhandle's Selkirks in greater numbers now than in past decades. Once common across 11 northern-tier states, the caribou nearly vanished from Idaho. The herd dropped to 25 or fewer in the Selkirks, its last range in the lower 48 states. In the 1980s, federal funds allowed Idaho Fish and Game Department biologists to capture and import 60 caribou. The herd continues to struggle but now stands a better chance of reversing its past declines. **Pronghorn antelope** are the speedsters of the Idaho landscape, reaching speeds most drivers would shudder at trying to reach on secondary roads threading their way across the southern rangelands. As elegantly attired in their white and buff capes as penguins in their formal wear, the pronghorn herds are healthy in Idaho. Some farmers say herds in some locales are too healthy, eating their way through haystacks and crops.

Idaho is also home to two species of bighorn sheep that live in the rugged high country around the Selway River and in the remote Owyhee canyon lands in the state's southwest corner. The Owyhee area is the home of a seed herd of California bighorn sheep, used by government naturalists to repopulate herds in other states.

Canis lupus

Canis lupus, Canis latrans

The great hunters, always the first targets of modern man, are here but just barely, moving about the state as ephemeral as shadows. The **wolf** (*Canis lupus*) is here, undoubtedly. Modern technology allows biologists to track the animals even when their shyness veils their presence. A lone male wolf occupied the upper Kelly Creek country northeast of Pierce for several years. Collared near Glacier National Park in 1990, the male dropped from sight in January 1991. In January 1992, University of Montana wolf expert Robert Ream picked up the gray male's radio signal in Kelly Creek. For more than a year, the male roamed Idaho's rugged backcountry along the Montana border, ranging as far south as Lolo Pass, with no one reporting they'd seen a wolf in a place that matched his location. Another wolf was found fatally poisoned in the Bear Valley area of south-central Idaho in 1991. Efforts to locate other wolves have fallen short. But tracks of these wary hunters still appear as if by magic, and backcountry visitors still find the hair on the back of their necks lifting uncontrollably on occasion when a howl pierces the air. The wolf situation may change and soon. Efforts to restore wolves to Yellowstone National Park may lead to releases of the animals into Idaho wilderness as well, beginning as early as 1994.

Unlike the wolf, the **coyote** (*Canis latrans*), mythical trickster of Nez Perce legend, flourishes in Idaho despite decades of warfare among ranchers and government agents to wipe it out. Trappers and hunters have pursued the coyote with unrestricted ardor for sport or to capitalize on fur prices. The coyote lives on, still exacting his toll on livestock operations and singing to the full moon from across the state.

Grizzly Bears

Most grizzlies are in the country west of Yellowstone, where the great bear still finds country to its liking. They are also known to inhabit the Selkirk and Cabinet mountains in the Idaho Panhandle. The Interagency Grizzly Bear Committee has wrangled with plans to begin releasing grizzlies into the Bitterroot Mountains of north-central Idaho and adjacent Montana by the mid-1990s. Some residents object, saying they find offensive plans to restore an animal that occasionally considers humans part of the food chain.

the grizzly bear, Ursus arctos

FISH

Salmon

Three species of salmon—coho, sockeye, and chinook—were once prolific in Idaho's rivers. No more. **Coho** salmon died out long ago and man's efforts to restore their numbers failed miserably, victims of too little money and too little recognition of the problems too late. The coho once returned to the Clearwater River, but early this century their route was blocked by the Lewiston Dam. Although efforts were made to reseed the Clearwater with coho, they failed. Although some coho still linger in the lower Snake, none have been counted for years at Lower Granite Dam some 34 miles west of the Idaho line.

Unfortunately, the 1990s appear to be witnessing the last struggle of the **sockeye** salmon to perpetuate itself in the Salmon River's headwaters. Though they are now protected as an endangered species, in 1990 no sockeyes returned to Redfish Lake, the lake once named for the wanton abundance of the fish that colored the lake bottom red. Federal and state fisheries biologists have tried raising sockeye fry in hatcheries at Eagle and Seattle. But it remains to be seen whether the young hatchery-raised salmon, when released, will be able to find their way to ocean pastures and then return to Redfish Lake again in abundance. Hopes are slim.

With the sockeye down and the coho out, efforts for the next decade are being focused on saving the **chinook** salmon, which returns to Idaho waters in spring, summer, and fall. State biologists regard each season's run as distinct, and each run looks different from the others as well. Spring chinook are most prized because their flesh is the richest with fat. The spring chinook were greeted with the most enthusiasm by the Nez Perce and Shoshone tribes of Idaho. Special ceremonies were held each year to celebrate the catch of the first salmon of spring. Summer chinook are tawnier, slimmer fish than their spring cousins. Fall chinook can be the brawniest, the latest to arrive from the rich pastures of the sea. The most threatened with extinction of the chinook runs, the falls numbered fewer than 100 fish above Lower Granite in the early 1990s. Major efforts are being made to make the Snake River and its tributaries more hospitable for the chinook and for all anadromous fish—those that hatch in freshwater, migrate to sea, then return to freshwater to spawn.

Steelhead And Other Fish

The steelhead is an oceangoing trout, an anadromous cousin of the salmon. The Snake and Clearwater rivers both support healthy steelhead runs. A good-size steelhead can weigh 15 pounds and give an angler a challenging fight. Rainbow and brown trout are found across the state's waters, and some of the state's lakes harbor the kokanee, a small, landlocked variety of salmon that has evolved to live without life at sea. Other fish you might find at the end of your line here include the humongous sturgeon and the mighty mackinaw. For more information, see "Fishing" in the "Out and About" chapter.

BIRDS

The **whooping crane** was the focus of a novel experiment at Grays Lake National Wildlife Refuge that ended in failure. At their lowest ebb, an estimated 20 whooping cranes made up the last of their kind in Idaho. Biologists tried to establish a second wild flock of the endangered species with eggs they brought to Grays Lake from Canada's Wood Buffalo National Park and Maryland's Patuxent National Wildlife Research Center. Unfortunately, a string of droughts made it nearly impossible for enough young whoopers to survive to adulthood and the program was discontinued.

Birds Of Prey

Birds of prey in general have enjoyed a rebound after people began to appreciate their nobility rather than shooting them on sight as competitors for gamebirds or as "chicken hawks." **Bald eagle** numbers have increased dramatically in recent years. More than 800 birds now winter in Idaho and more than 100 pairs nest here. The **osprey** or fish eagle has shown a similar rebound. Its nests are now a familiar sight along most of the state's waterways. The **golden eagle,** once reviled as a livestock killer and even a baby snatcher, has had its image reformed largely through the efforts of Boise's Morley Nelson. Nelson can also be credited with helping attract the World Center for Birds of Prey to Boise. The center is the home of the Peregrine Fund, the nation's most successful example of an effort to restore a vanishing species. **Peregrine falcons** are also beginning to nest in greater numbers in Idaho. Several pairs have been spotted nesting on downtown buildings in Boise, and Nampa's sugar refinery supports another pair.

The most grand display of birds of prey in Idaho is at the **Snake River Birds of Prey natural area.** In 1993 the Idaho Congressional delegation united behind the leadership of Rep. Larry LaRocco to expand protection for the 482,640-acre area. More information about the Birds of Prey area south of Kuna along the Snake River is available from the BLM's Boise office, tel. 384-3015.

REPTILES

Western rattlesnakes inhabit much of the state, but they are seldom seen and rarely bite. Should you come across one, keeping a cool head should allow you and the snake to get out of each other's way with neither the worse for wear. Idaho's reptiles can actually be a lot of fun to watch, if you leave them alone. The sagebrush desert is alive with **lizards,** especially the quick little side-blotched lizard. Western fence lizards can be comical when they display their electric blue bellies to ward off intruders. The truly lucky will find a larger collared or leopard lizard to watch for a while.

WILDLIFE REFUGES

The U.S. Fish and Wildife Service maintains seven national wildlife refuges in Idaho. In the north, the **Kootenai National Wildlife Refuge,** tel. 267-3888, near Bonners Ferry is a popular haunt for waterfowl throughout the year and for hunters during the duck- and goose-hunting seasons. In southwestern Idaho, **Deer Flat National Wildlife Refuge** surrounding Lake Lowell south of Caldwell provides a popular recreation retreat for fishermen, hunters, and others throughout the year. Like Kootenai and the other refuges, it is also open to waterfowl hunting. Near Rupert is the **Minidoka refuge,** tel. 436-3589, the central Snake River Plain's major waterfowl center. Southeastern Idaho holds several refuges including the **Southeast Idaho Refuge Complex,** headquartered at Pocatello, tel. 237-6615. The **Grays Lake refuge,** tel. 574-2755, near Wayan, is home to a major flock of sandhill cranes. It is where efforts were made to establish a second migratory flock of whooping cranes. The **Camas refuge,** tel. 662-5423, near Hamer, is a wild oasis at the edge of the farm fields and desert in the upper reaches of the Snake River Plain. **Bear Lake refuge,** tel. 847-1757, lies beside the incredibly blue waters of Bear Lake on the Idaho-Utah border.

BOB RACE

bald eagle

HISTORY AND PEOPLE

PREHISTORY

Idaho's first residents arrived somewhere between 11,000 and 15,000 years ago. The only remnants of their culture are stone tools, often little more than scrapers formed by breaking river cobbles. The native people's sophistication with tools and weapons increased through the millennia. Perhaps as long as 5,000 years ago, a rocky outcrop above what is now Midvale served as a quarry for fine-grained basalt. Evidence shows that the **Weiss rock shelter** near Cottonwood dates back to about the same time. While the evidence of these earliest Idahoans' presence is convincing, it is subtle. Along the state's major rivers, dimples mark where pit houses once sheltered the hearth and early inhabitants.

More impressive are the pictographs (rock paintings) and petroglyphs (rock carvings) scattered across the state from north to south. One of the most impressive displays of both kinds of rock art is at Buffalo Eddy along the Idaho shoreline of the Snake River south of Lewiston. The best way to see the Buffalo Eddy art is by tour boat. Some petroglyphs can be seen along the Washington shoreline of the Snake by driving south from Clarkston. The Hells Canyon NRA office along Washington Hwy. 129 can direct visitors to Buffalo Eddy or provide a list of tour operators. Pittsburg Landing in the Hells Canyon NRA west of White Bird also has impressive petroglyphs. Another group of drawings adorns the Bruneau River Canyon near Hot Creek, and hundreds of other sites with drawings are known along the Salmon and Snake rivers. Hundreds more, no doubt, remain to be found. Some drawings recount hunting expeditions, showing buffalo, bighorn sheep, elk, or other prey. Others portray strangely equipped beings. During the UFO craze, petroglyphs along the Snake River shoreline at Buffalo Eddy south of Lewiston were presented as evidence of alien influence on our prehistory.

Idaho's native peoples had a flourishing culture for thousands of years. Archaeological excavations show a well-developed trade that brought obsidian from the area that is now Yellowstone National Park, northwest to the Nez Perce people of north-central Idaho. Shell beads from Pacific Ocean tribes were traded eastward as well.

INDIGENOUS PEOPLES

The Nez Perce

Idaho's most famous tribe was the Nez Perce, a people known for their friendly greeting of whites, for their breeding of the Appaloosa horse, and for staging one of the last Indian wars (1877).

The Nez Perce were named for some tribal members' penchant for wearing nose pendants. The fashion apparently was never widely adopted, however. The tribal members referred to themselves as the Ne-Mee-Poo, simply "The People." The Nez Perce were one of the Sahaptin-speaking tribes of the Columbia River Basin. In Idaho, they lived in the valleys of the Snake and Clearwater rivers, with the largest bands based in the Lapwai Valley and near Kamiah. Another important band lived in the high valleys of northeastern Oregon's Wallowa Mountains. The Nez Perce lived well by digging camas bulbs and other roots, catching the abundant salmon and steelhead that filled the streams nearly year-round, and hunting big game.

The arrival of the horse among the Nez Perce in the early 1700s soon altered their lifestyle dramatically. The tribe adapted to the horse quickly, using the new mobility it offered to strike out westward hundreds of miles to the Columbia River and traditional fishing grounds there, and eastward to the plains of Montana to hunt buffalo. They adopted some of the nomadic characteris-

BOB RACE

petroglyphs at Pittsburg Landing in Hells Canyon NRA

tics of Plains tribes in the process. The tepee became commonplace, replacing their earlier nonportable longhouses and A-frame communal lodges that could hold as many as 30 families. With this increased mobility, the Nez Perce were also said to become more warlike.

The Nez Perce excelled in their understanding of the horse. They are widely credited with becoming the tribe that best understood the principles of horse-breeding, selectively producing horses that had the traits they wanted. They also get credit for either producing the Appaloosa horse or strengthening the traits of the earliest lines of Spanish horses. The Appaloosa, a breed known for its endurance and good disposition, is distinguished by the presence of dark spots on its light coat. The spots may be confined to a circular white blanket over the horse's rump or spread across its body in a leopard pattern. According to the National Park Service, which operates the Nez Perce National Historical Park visitor center at Spalding, "horses of this color are rare and first appeared in 14th-century Persian art and in Chinese art dating to 500 B.C. They are believed to have been imported into the New World from the Near East or Spain along with shipments of goods to Mexico in the 1600s. These Old World horses gradually moved northward to the high plains and reached the Nez Perce people about 1730. Early explorers observed that the Nez Perce had large numbers of Appaloosas . . ."

The Shoshone-Bannocks

Idaho's most populous native people are the Shoshone. The Shoshone and the Bannock peoples occupied southern Idaho's desert from western Wyoming to eastern Oregon. The area offered difficult living conditions at best. The salmon runs that fed the Nez Perce also provided for the Shoshone and Bannocks. Southwestern Idaho, especially Salmon Falls, was a favorite fishing ground where Shoshone, Bannock, Nez Perce, and Paiute peoples would mingle in the late spring.

The Shoshone and Bannock tribes also made trips to higher areas to harvest camas roots and berries. Before the arrival of the horse in the 1700s, the Shoshone-Bannocks (a later amalgamation of the two tribes) relied on small game extensively, though remaining rock blinds near antelope or deer trails show that the ancient hunters were also skilled at taking larger game. Bighorn sheep were a prized quarry.

Although originally separate tribes, the Shoshone and Bannock peoples began to cooperate more and meld together after the arrival of the horse. Like the Nez Perce, the Shoshone-Bannocks turned to hunting buffalo as their skills as horsemen increased. By the 1840s, however, their efforts and those of white hunters and settlers had essentially eradicated the buffalo from Idaho.

The Shoshone-Bannocks provided a well-used trade link among the region's native peoples by exporting obsidian found in the Yellow-

William Clark

INDEPENDENCE NATIONAL HISTORICAL PARK / 2

stone area for arrowheads and knives. The Shoshone-Bannocks were also skilled at making baskets to store and carry the seeds they harvested.

The Shoshone have been called the more peaceable of the two, although both belonged to the same group and were united by language and customs. Their pride in their fighting abilities led the Bannocks to fight the Overland migration by frequenting the California and Oregon trails through southern Idaho. The Ward and Otter massacres that occurred near Boise and Murphy are regarded as the results of Shoshone and Bannock unhappiness with the emigration west.

Northern Tribes

In Idaho's Panhandle, native peoples included the Kootenai, Coeur d'Alene, and Kalispel. The Coeur d'Alene people were known mostly for their willingness to receive missionary Jesuits (whom they knew as the "Black Robes") and for their sharp trading skills. So difficult was it to deal with the Coeur d'Alenes that early traders called them the sharp-hearted people, the people with hearts like an awl. The Kootenai and Kalispel were more peaceable and tractable to the incursions of whites into their territories and so have maintained a lower profile.

EXPLORATION

Lewis And Clark

Idaho was the last of the United States to be seen by white explorers. The Lewis and Clark Expedition was the first group of European-Americans to cross the continent in search of an overland route to the Pacific Ocean. President Thomas Jefferson dispatched them west soon after the Louisiana Purchase in 1803. That purchase of the lands west of the mighty Mississippi River inaugurated nearly a century of interest in, and shifting boundaries for, Idaho.

The "Corps of Discovery," as the Lewis and Clark Expedition was called, first ventured into Idaho in August 1805 at Lemhi Pass. Idaho would prove to be the harshest part of their journey across the West. First, the expedition tried unsuccessfully to find a way across the state by way of the Salmon River. Convinced that they could not survive the River of No Return, they backtracked into Montana over Lost Trail Pass, turned north, and eventually found a better but still difficult route across the Bitterroots via the Nez Perce's Lolo Trail. Back on the Idaho side of the mountains, the expedition encountered the Nez Perce, who greeted with friendship and generosity this first party of explorers to reach their territory. The explorers stayed with the Nez Perce for nearly a month to rest, cache supplies, and build canoes for their trip downriver to the sea.

Mountain Men

The next wave of explorers came for fur. David Thompson swung south from Canada in 1808 while exploring the Kootenai River country for the Northwest Fur Company. He returned the following year to found **Kulyspell House,** the first European-built building in Idaho, along the shore of Lake Pend Oreille. The native tribes Thompson and his party encountered traded obsidian, buffalo robes, bitterroot tubers, dried salmon, and beads among themselves, and traded furs to the Europeans for ribbons, knives and other useful items. The mountain men in turn traded the pelts they collected to the fur companies for whiskey, powder, lead, and other items they needed to keep going.

By 1810, the Missouri Fur Company headed by Manuel Lisa established Fort Henry, the first American trading post in Idaho, near Elgin. The Astorians, the fur company founded by John Jacob Astor of New York, traipsed through Idaho the following year and, led by Wilson Hunt, reconnoitered the Snake and Boise rivers. Until the 1830s, when silk top hats took over the London fashion scene and demand for beaver felt hats fell flat, the mountain men were Idaho's main visitors. Jedediah Smith, Peter Skeen Ogden, Kit Carson, and Capt. B.L.E. Bonneville were some of the most famous mountain men and explorers to venture through. The trappers gathered annually for lusty, drunken hurly-burlies in the state's southern valleys. The Teton River Valley and Pierre's Hole near Driggs provided two of the liveliest trading locales.

Meriwether Lewis

Missionaries

By 1836, the fur market had ebbed and the tide was shifting. Henry Harmon Spalding and his wife Eliza, pioneer missionaries, ventured to the land of the Nez Perce and established a mission and school along the Clearwater River. The Nez Perce welcomed these white visitors with friendship as well. Henry taught the Nez Perce about the Bible and farming, and built a sawmill and gristmill at Lapwai. Eliza bore a daughter in 1837, the first white child born in Idaho. The Jesuits were not far behind in establishing a base in Idaho. Friar Pierre Jean deSmet began missionary work in the Panhandle among the Coeur d'Alene people in 1840 and founded St. Joseph Indian Mission along the St. Joe River in 1842.

SETTLEMENT

The Oregon Trail

Idaho started out as part of the vast Oregon Territory that spread from the Continental Divide westward to the Pacific Ocean, and from the 49th parallel dividing Canada and the United States to the 42nd parallel that marked a similar treaty line established between the fledgling nation and Spain. The Oregon country had at one time or another been claimed by Spain, Great Britain, Russia, and the United States.

Beginning around 1843, Oregon country started to become a mecca for Easterners who envisioned themselves as overcrowded and unable to find good farmland in their home states. The emigrants of "The Great Overland Migration" wound their way across Idaho from Montpelier to Fort Hall to Fort Boise. The two forts were major resting points for the wagon trains. The surge of emigrants was impressive: by 1849, 20,000 had passed through southeastern Idaho on the California Trail. As the influx of settlers began to encroach on native territory, tensions increased and clashes began. In 1847, the Nez Perce protected the Spaldings when the neighboring Cayuse tribe of eastern Washington rebelled and killed Marcus and Narcissa Whitman near Walla Walla. In 1853, Idaho was divided between the newly formed Washington and existing Oregon territories, and Washington Territory governor Isaac Stevens began campaigning to end the Northwest tribes' wanderings and create reservations for them.

Cultures Clash

On Aug. 20, 1854, one of the first of Idaho's confrontations between native peoples and whites began just west of Boise when a member of a Snake River tribe tried to steal a horse from a wagon train. The would-be thief was killed. In the battle that followed, 18 of the 20 men, women, and children in the train were killed. Of the two survivors, Newton and William Ward, one had feigned death after being knocked out and the other escaped after he was shot with an arrow. They were the sons of Alexander Ward of Missouri, the apparent leader of the party and patriarch of a large family that comprised half its members.

When news of this and other clashes reached and inflamed newspaper editorialists in Oregon and back East, it was the beginning of the end for the traditional freedoms of the Nez Perce and other native peoples. The Portland *Oregonian,* outraged by reports that women had been grotesquely assaulted, children buried alive, and other atrocities committed, screamed for vengeance and demanded, "Either exterminate the race of Indians, or prevent further wholesale butcheries by these worthless races resembling the human form . . ."

The push to force the tribes onto reservations continued, and by 1855, the Nez Perce and other tribes in the region were signatories to the first general treaties. One of these, the Stevens Treaty, created the Nez Perce reservation. Although Nez Perce chiefs signed the treaty, many among the tribe disputed their authority to represent them. Some of the tribe moved onto the reservation peacefully . . . some did not.

In 1859, Oregon was admitted as a state and Idaho remained part of Washington Territory. But changing political boundaries didn't affect the intercultural tensions. The next conflict took place Sept. 9, 1860, when the Otter-Van Orman wagon train came under attack southeast of Murphy. Eighteen emigrants were killed. Abigail Van Orman was raped and killed. Four of her children, including three girls, were kidnapped. Reuben, the boy, was recovered in 1862 from Bannock and Shoshone people, but the three girls were never seen again. The emigrants abandoned their wagons as the attack continued. Sixteen of them wandered 90 miles through the Owyhee Desert before rescuers found them in late October. By then, the 12 who remained had traded their clothing to other native peoples for food and had fallen to eating their dead.

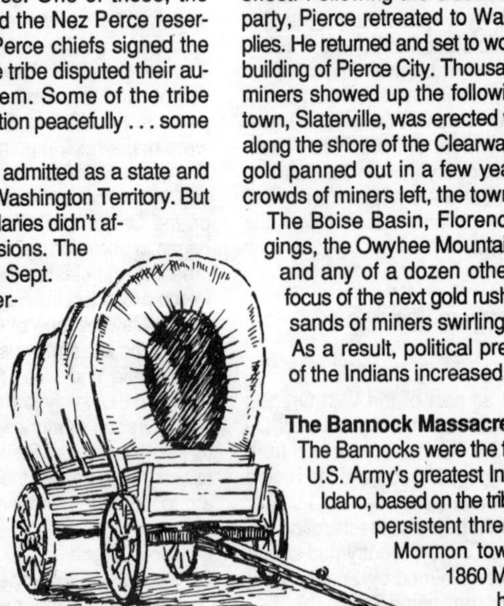

White bandits, who sometimes posed as tribe members, preyed on the Overlanders as well, even surpassing the tribes in their cruelty. Some 25 miles west of Fort Hall along the Lander Cutoff, a party of Iowans was attacked and eight were killed. The dead, scalped and butchered, included a five-year-old girl who had been horribly mutilated. The three "Indians" who led the attack wore beards, had light brown hair, and spoke perfect English.

Gold!

The first discovery of gold in Idaho was made on the Nez Perce Reservation on Sept. 30, 1860 by a party of prospectors led by Elias D. Pierce, one of the original Overlanders who most likely passed through southeastern Idaho on the California Trail in 1847. Pierce had been ordered to stay out of the reservation in the past with no effect. Following the discovery of gold by his party, Pierce retreated to Walla Walla for supplies. He returned and set to work supervising the building of Pierce City. Thousands more hopeful miners showed up the following spring. A tent town, Slaterville, was erected virtually overnight along the shore of the Clearwater River. Pierce's gold panned out in a few years, but while the crowds of miners left, the town remained.

The Boise Basin, Florence, Warrens Diggings, the Owyhee Mountains, Yankee Fork, and any of a dozen other spots were the focus of the next gold rushes that sent thousands of miners swirling across the state. As a result, political pressures to get rid of the Indians increased.

The Bannock Massacre

The Bannocks were the target of one of the U.S. Army's greatest Indian massacres in Idaho, based on the tribe's reputation as a persistent threat to the fledgling Mormon town of Franklin. In 1860 Mormon leader Brigham Young had dispatched a party north from Utah

ROB RACE

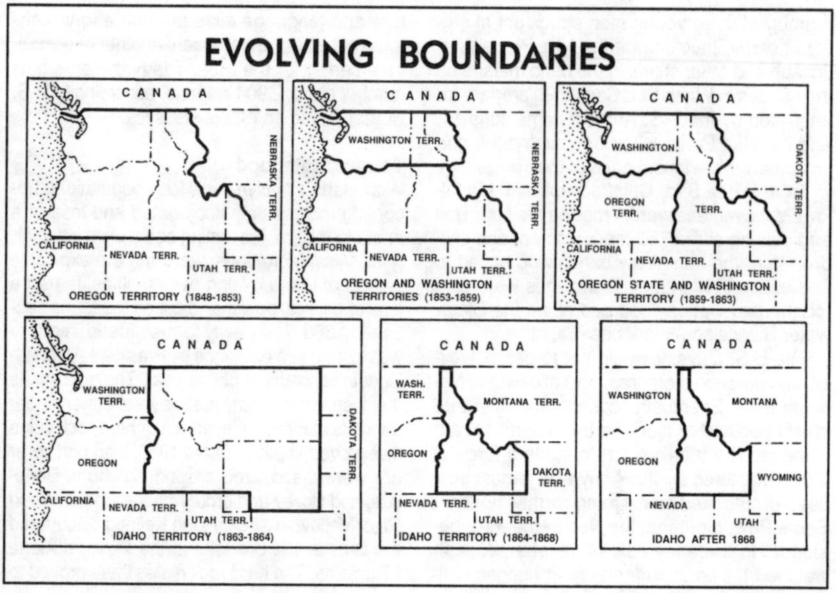

EVOLVING BOUNDARIES

CANADA
NEBRASKA TERR.
CALIFORNIA
NEVADA TERR.
UTAH TERR.
OREGON TERRITORY (1848-1853)

CANADA
WASHINGTON TERR.
NEBRASKA TERR.
CALIFORNIA
NEVADA TERR.
UTAH TERR.
OREGON AND WASHINGTON TERRITORIES (1853-1859)

CANADA
WASHINGTON
DAKOTA TERR.
OREGON TERR.
TERR.
CALIFORNIA
NEVADA TERR.
UTAH TERR.
OREGON STATE AND WASHINGTON TERRITORY (1859-1863)

CANADA
WASHINGTON TERR.
DAKOTA TERR.
OREGON
CALIFORNIA
NEVADA TERR.
UTAH TERR.
IDAHO TERRITORY (1863-1864)

CANADA
WASH. TERR.
MONTANA TERR.
OREGON
DAKOTA TERR.
NEVADA TERR.
UTAH TERR.
IDAHO TERRITORY (1864-1868)

CANADA
WASHINGTON
MONTANA
OREGON
WYOMING
NEVADA
UTAH
IDAHO AFTER 1868

to establish Franklin, which prospered and ranks as Idaho's oldest town. Young had sought to develop peaceful relations with the Bannocks, intoning to his followers that it was better to feed them than fight them.

Things soon began to go bad, however. By January 1863, Franklin's residents had turned against their native neighbors. While the Mormons themselves took no action against the Indians, they watched the arrival late that January of a cavalry and infantry company of California volunteers led by Col. Patrick Connor. Connor had come to discipline the Shoshone after a party of miners had suffered one death in a brush with the tribe in the Bear River Valley. What followed was perhaps the West's bloodiest single moment and the greatest massacre of native peoples.

Connor found the Indians at Battle Creek's confluence with Bear River. With at least 200 cavalrymen and 60 infantry soldiers, Connor charged across the river, then positioned his forces so the Shoshone were trapped in a crossfire. The Mormons, anxious for relief, watched the battle unfold. Witnesses said they counted some 400 men, women, and children killed on the battleground. One witness estimated that two-thirds of the Shoshone killed were women and children.

In the aftermath, the Boise and Bruneau bands of the Shoshone were assigned to the Fort Hall Indian Reservation in 1867; in 1869, the Fort Hall Shoshone-Bannocks were assigned to the reservation as well. In 1873, the reservation boundaries were further reduced. The Native Americans were losing the fight, but would put up one last heroic battle.

Nez Perce War

In 1863, the Nez Perce Reservation was trimmed dramatically by another treaty that divided the tribe further. The Nez Perce leader known as Lawyer accepted the new treaty, but many did not. The internal factions remained at odds until the government ordered the so-called non-treaty Nez Perce to report to the Lapwai Valley or be forced there by the U.S. Army. Young Chief Joseph persuaded his band in the Wallowa Mountains to undertake the move themselves peaceably. The trip across the spring runoff-swollen Snake and Salmon rivers went well until the band was within a few days' travel of the Lapwai Valley. On June 13, 1877, the day before the bands' deadline for entering the reservation, a group of three young men struck out at settlers nearby, touching off the Nez Perce War. Joseph and other chiefs in the band marshaled their forces in White Bird Canyon to prepare for retaliation by the U.S. Army. It came June 17, and the Nez Perce killed 34 cavalrymen and volunteers while losing none of their own.

From White Bird, Chief Joseph and his followers moved eastward, crossing the Lolo Trail and gaining some 750 men, women, and children from the non-treaty bands who hoped to find peace in Montana. Skirmishes were also fought near Cottonwood and along the Clearwater River's south fork near Stites.

The U.S. Cavalry would not forget, however, and pursued them through Yellowstone National Park. Eventually, Joseph and the other chiefs decided to lead the band north toward Canada. The tribe's effort to elude a force of 2,000 mustered by the Army was almost successful. Blocked from going farther north at Bears Paw, Montana, the Nez Perce were besieged. In the early cold of October, Joseph watched his band suffering from hunger, children dying from the cold, and warriors dying from attacks by a superior force. Forty-two miles short of Canada and escape from a war he had hoped to avoid, Joseph surrendered.

Joseph's closing words, reported by a *Harper's Magazine* correspondent who may or may not have taken liberties, have survived as one of the most eloquent speeches of surrender and appeals for peace: "Hear me my chiefs, from where the sun now stands I will fight no more forever."

Contrary to the terms of surrender, the non-treaty Nez Perce were banished to Oklahoma, a malarial country far from their homeland. Pleas by the tribe and by others finally led the government to relent somewhat. Joseph was allowed to return to the Northwest, to the Colville Indian Reservation in northeastern Washington, but not to the Nez Perce homeland.

In 1965, Congress recognized the tribe's pivotal role in the nation's history by creating the Nez Perce National Historical Park. The park's 24 sites are scattered throughout north-central Idaho, with a headquarters at Spalding, near Lapwai, the site of Nez Perce tribal government. The park and other developments have helped awaken tribal members to their heritage. Tribal leaders are trying to keep the Nez Perce culture and language alive through efforts centered at Lapwai and Kamiah, another major cultural center for the tribe. The Nez Perce now number about 2,900 in Idaho, according to U.S. Bureau of Indian Affairs statistics.

Toward Statehood

With Idaho's Native American populations becoming increasingly subjugated and less of a threat to miners, the mining boom went into high gear. Washingtonians, watching the explosive growth of Idaho mining communities, feared a loss of political power and cut off the Idaho section in 1863. The newly formed Idaho Territory was signed into existence by President Abraham Lincoln on March 4 of that year. The gold mines that inspired the early rushes were either placer deposits that soon played out or hard-rock veins that proved shallow. But in 1880, lead and silver ore were discovered around Ketchum, Bellevue, and Hailey and brought a rush to the Wood River Valley. In 1884, Noah Kellogg discovered the Bunker Hill ore lode in the Coeur d'Alene Mountains. The hard-rock mines there proved to

WHERE IDAHO GOT ITS NAME

Generations of Idaho schoolchildren learned that the state's name derived from "E Dah Hoe," meaning "Gem of the Mountains," or "Light Coming Down From the Mountains." In the late 1960s, however, new light from historians showed the true origins of the name. They found the name Idaho had been proposed but rejected for Jefferson Territory in favor of Colorado (for the river). However, the arguments for Idaho caught the fancy of some and became the name of a settlement, Idaho Springs, in the territory. From there Idaho became the name of a steamboat launched on the Columbia River in June 1860. The steamer hauled freight up the Columbia and Snake rivers to mines farther upstream on the Clearwater and Salmon rivers. The mines came to be called the Idaho mines. Sen. Henry Wilson of Massachusetts argued for naming the new territory Idaho in March 1863, saying that the name meant "Gem of the Mountains" and so meant as much or more than the other proposal, Montana. An ironic twist here is that Wilson had torpedoed a proposal to give Colorado the name Idaho, arguing the name had "nothing in it."

have staying power, yielding some $5 billion in gold, silver, lead, and zinc.

Idaho Territory stretched across Montana and Wyoming to the Dakota Territory for a year, when it was trimmed back to essentially its present boundaries. From the beginning, the territory had a rough go of it politically. Sixteen territorial governors were appointed between Lincoln's signature and statehood in 1890; five of them never even visited the territory. Others made what amounted to little more than cursory visits and then headed elsewhere. For a year and a half, the territory didn't even have a governor. The worst territorial governor, hands down, was the second, Caleb Lyon, who proved himself not only incompetent but a thief as well by stealing $46,418 destined for native peoples. Idaho's politics could only improve from its territorial track record. Idaho became a state on July 3, 1890, the 43rd to enter the Union.

GOVERNMENT AND ECONOMY

Politics

If one word could describe Idaho politics, possibilities would include quirky, volatile, conservative, liberal. An example: although Mormons have long been a dominant social and political force, the first Mormon governor wasn't elected until 1945. The first Jew elected as governor in the United States was Moses Alexander, who won the position in Idaho in 1916. And Idaho politics have been fragmented at best, with politicians tinkering with radicalism, liberalism, libertarianism, radical conservatism, and even socialism throughout the state's history.

In its century of statehood, Idaho has seen some of its political leaders rise to power and prominence in Washington. The state has elected two U.S. Senators who rose to the chairmanship of the prestigious Foreign Relations Committee. The first was progressive Republican William E. Borah, the "Lion of Idaho," who gained international stature for his statesmanship while serving Idaho in the Senate from 1907 to 1940. The second was Frank Church, a liberal Democrat who idolized Borah and who served Idaho in the Senate from 1956, when he was elected as the youngest senator, until 1980. Church campaigned for the Democratic nomination in the 1976 presidential race and won four state primaries before losing out to Jimmy Carter. Idaho's most successful politician is Gov. Cecil D. Andrus, who won an unprecedented fourth term as governor in 1990. Andrus left office in the middle of his second term in 1977 for Washington, D.C., to serve as Secretary of the Interior during the Carter administration. He returned in

QUEST FOR THE MOTHER LODE

The great gold rushes of the West hit paydirt in Idaho on Sept. 30, 1860, when W. F. Bassett, a member of a party led by Capt. Elias D. Pierce, struck gold along Canal Gulch north of the Clearwater River. Bassett found the color in diggings along the stream. The gold dust was very fine, leading the party to name the stream Oro Fino Creek. Captain Pierce returned to Fort Walla Walla to resupply. Word spread quickly and about 60 men returned to winter in the area. The lust for gold started a stampede the following spring and Lewiston was born.

For the next decade the mines of fabulous Florence in the Salmon River country east of Riggins, Warrens Diggings northeast of McCall, and the Boise Basin drew their own tides of the hopeful. Silver City, south of Murphy, reigned for her day as the queen of Idaho's mining scene and remains today as the queen of Idaho's ghost towns.

In 1885 Noah Kellogg found an outcropping of galena, a rich lead ore, in the mountains of the north state. Out of this find grew Idaho's richest mining district, the Coeur d'Alenes. The galena find led to the discovery of rich veins of silver ore. The gold here is a by-product of the primary ores. The Coeur d'Alene mines, particularly Bunker Hill, which Kellogg discovered, produced more than 28 million tons of lead, silver, and zinc during operations.

Gold can still be found along Idaho's streams in placer deposits. In some areas, notably near Elk City and in the Owyhee Desert near Silver City, a controversial new method of extracting gold is practiced. Cyanide heap leaching removes gold too fine for older methods. A solution of deadly cyanide is sprayed on a pile of gold-bearing earth and gravel, dissolving the gold. The cyanide is then chemically processed to strip it of the gold. Potential environmental drawbacks to the process include contamination of the water table and poisoning of wildlife.

er then and a landslide four years later. He did not run for reelection in 1994.

Mining

Mining, which boomed following the discovery of gold by Elias D. Pierce's party near present-day Pierce, provided the spark that ignited Idaho's modern-day economy. Hundreds of millions of dollars worth of gold, silver, lead, zinc, and other resources have come from Idaho's hills.

The Coeur d'Alene Mining District, also known as the Silver Valley, produced much of the nation's silver for decades. The metals are still there, but cheaper silver from foreign sources has tarnished the district's glory in recent years. Idaho still ranks first in the production of antimony, vanadium, and garnet. It holds onto second place for silver and also for phosphate, a fertilizer that led the pack monetarily with a value of $464 million in 1991. Other minerals produced in the state include lead, molybdenum, and perlite, a pumicelike horticultural product. In 1989, mining accounted for 1.36% of the gross state product.

Farming And Ranching

Agriculture got off in fits and starts in Idaho. The Spaldings' mission to the Nez Perce near Lapwai in the 1830s began the push toward farming, which grew from those mission days to supply the thousands of miners coming into the state. Cattle and sheep operations grew as well, to supply the hunger for beef and mutton, and provide wool. While cattle remain a major industry, wool growers feel the same sorts of pressures that have hampered the mining industry.

Idaho's potato crop was its most valuable, bringing in $446 million in 1991, and supplying 29% of the nation's production—enough to win top spot among the states. Potatoes may have the image of being king of the economy here, but livestock operations bring in far more money to the state, almost as much as potatoes and all other crops combined. Farming (all crops) contributed over $1.5 billion in receipts in '91, while livestock contributed nearly $1 billion. Cattle is the largest single source of value, contributing $705 million.

Nuclear Idaho

In 1949, the Atomic Energy Commission cast about for the most remote, uninviting, and so least popular, corner of America. The bureaucracy found a blank spot on the map within the borders of Idaho near the Lost River Mountains. The 572,000 acres appropriated for the National Reactor Testing Station have since become the home for 51 nuclear reactors, the largest concentration and greatest variety of nuclear reactors in the world. Now called the **Idaho National Engineering Laboratories** and managed by the U.S. Department of Energy, the site retains its heritage.

The EBR-1 reactor was the first to harness the nuclear reaction, using heat to generate electricity. By 1953, a reactor prototype for the first nuclear-powered submarine, the *Nautilus,* was operating in the Idaho desert. In 1955, a reactor supplied all the electricity needed for nearby Arco. In 1956, nuclear scientists showed nuclear heat could power a turbojet engine, and in 1958 a reactor suitable for a large ship was demonstrated.

The white buildings of the nuclear reactors now stand like gleaming cities in the sagebrush. But while the laboratories employ more than 5,000 workers, no one lives at the site itself. Most INEL workers, from scientists to maintenance workers, live in Idaho Falls to the east and commute to work aboard buses.

Logging And Other Industries

Timber also ranks as a major industry in the state, producing lumber, plywood, pulp, and residual products with a market value of $1.15 billion in 1990. Idaho ranked seventh among lumber-producing states in 1990 by milling nearly 2.1 billion board feet. The debate about how the national forests will be used, whether as timber-producing tree farms or wilderness preserves, carries major implications for the industry.

Other key contributors to Idaho's gross state product as of 1989 included manufacturing, 18.4%; services, 15.8%; financial elements, 14.1%; and government and military, 11.9%. In addition, tourism has now become the state's third-biggest revenue producer (after manufacturing and agriculture), bringing $1.7 billion to the state in 1992. All in all, Idaho's economy has remained stable, even vibrant, compared to the economies of many other states.

LITERARY IDAHO

Idaho can't claim the Bard, but some plenty famous poets and writers have called the state home at some point in their lives. The list includes:

CHRIS PARMENTIER / 2

Ezra Pound was born in Idaho . . .

Ezra Pound

Ezra Pound, the eccentric poet, was born Oct. 20, 1885, at Hailey. His family left for Wyncote, a Philadelphia suburb, when he was two. Pound left the United States in 1908 to win a place in Europe's literary circles. He was credited with discovering both James Joyce and T.S. Eliot. As an expatriate in Paris, he met Ernest Hemingway and coached him as a writer. An outspoken supporter of Italian dictator Benito Mussolini, Pound was arrested for treason in 1945 but was later found unfit for trial because of insanity. After 12 years in St. Elizabeth's Hospital in Washington, D.C., he returned to Italy in 1958 where he died in Venice on Nov. 1, 1972.

Ernest Hemingway

Idaho had a similarly short-lived claim to Ernest Hemingway. The state, Sun Valley in particular, was a familiar stomping grounds for the writer, who, as an avid sportsman, loved Idaho's exceptional hunting and fly fishing. From 1939 to 1940, Hemingway worked on portions of *For Whom The Bell Tolls* in Ketchum. In 1952, Papa won a Pulitzer Prize for his writing and in 1956, the Nobel Prize. He lived in Cuba for a time, but in 1960, after Fidel Castro overthrew Fulgencio Batista and turned the country to communism, Hemingway left the island and moved to Ketchum, where he and his wife, Mary Welsh Hemingway, had purchased a house.

Hemingway moved back to Idaho depressed by the deterioration of his writing and health. Suffering from alcoholism and diabetes, he was hospitalized and underwent extensive medical treatment. Convinced he could not recover his health or his talent, Hemingway ended his own life as his father had, with a shotgun, on July 2, 1961. He is buried in the Ketchum Cemetery.

A memorial in a grove overlooking Trail Creek near Sun Valley commemorates one of the 20th century's greatest writers with a passage Hemingway wrote as a eulogy for a friend of his who died in a hunting accident:

Best of all he loved the fall. The leaves yellow on the cottonwoods, leaves floating on the trout streams and above the hills, the high blue windless skies. Now he will be part of them forever.

Vardis Fisher

Vardis Fisher was born and lived his life in Idaho. His best-known books included *Children of God,* a 1939 history of Mormonism, and *The Mothers,* a 1943 account of the Donner Party's descent into cannibalism when stranded in the Sierras. Fisher also wrote the 12-volume *Testament of Man,* an encyclopedic exploration of humanity's spiritual and intellectual development. Fisher was the Idaho director for the Federal Writer's Project in 1935 and produced the *Idaho Guide* and *Idaho Encyclopedia,* books that are still found on library shelves.

. . . Ernest Hemingway died there.

Edgar Rice Burroughs
One of the world's most popular writers formed many of his ideas about adventure in Idaho. Edgar Rice Burroughs, the creator of *Tarzan* and *John Carter of Mars,* among other heroic characters, got his start as a young man in the mid-1890s on a Raft River ranch owned by his brothers. After an unsuccessful bid to attend West Point and a stint in the U.S. Cavalry, Burroughs returned to Idaho in 1898. He bought a cigar and stationery store at 233 W. Center St. in Pocatello in 1898 and sold it back to its former owner in 1899. He turned to creative writing after that and later worked on a Snake River ranch and as a dredge operator. He tried politics in Parma in 1904 but lost. His failures in Idaho convinced him to move to the Southwest, where he began writing, and later to California. His book *Tarzan of the Apes* first appeared as a serial in 1912. His adventure books have sold more than 100 million copies and have been printed in 56 languages.

Women Writers
Women writers also won their place in Idaho's literary circles. **Carol Ryrie Brink** grew up in Moscow and attended the University of Idaho from 1914 to 1917. Her book *Caddie Woodlawn* won the Newberry Medal for children's literature in 1936. She wrote some 30 books for adults and children between 1936 and 1977. Seven of her books deal with life in Idaho.

Mary Hallock Foote earned a national reputation as a Western novelist, essayist, and illustrator. She lived in Boise 1884-95 with her mining engineer husband, Arthur De Wint Foote. Her novels, *The Chosen Valley* and *Coeur d'Alene,* focused on men at work. Her stories were also published in *Century* magazine, as were her illustrations.

Outdoors Writers
One of Idaho's best-known authors is **Patrick McManus,** whose humorous tales of the great outdoors regularly find their way onto the best-seller lists. His books include *A Fine and Pleasant Misery; They Shoot Canoes, Don't They?; The Night the Bear Ate Goomba; Never Sniff a Gift Fish;* and *The Grasshopper Trap.* McManus humor appears each month in an *Outdoor Life* magazine column. McManus grew up near Sandpoint and now makes his home across the state line in Cheney, Washington.

Outdoor Life also published the work of **Jack O'Connor,** one of the century's best-known outdoors writers. O'Connor lived in Lewiston and wrote about guns and hunting for the magazine. His travels included African safaris, hunts in India and Iran, and quests for mountain sheep throughout North America. O'Connor died in 1978.

Field and Stream, one of the other "big three" outdoors magazines, relied heavily on the talents of **Ted Trueblood,** a gifted outdoors writer who lived in Nampa. His goal and gift was to write about the simple pleasures of the outdoors, of fishing and hunting, so his readers could be there with him. Trueblood was also one of Idaho's most effective conservationists, guiding the creation of the 2.3-million-acre Frank Church–River of No Return Wilderness in the wild heart of the Idaho he loved. Trueblood died in 1982.

Modern Writers
Idaho's current crop of writers and poets is busy filling bookshelves. Novelists have been among the most noticed of Idaho's pen and paper crowd. Clay Morgan of McCall won notice for his book, *Santiago and the Drinking Party.* Mary Clearman Blew of Lewiston earned raves for *All But the Waltz,* a recollection of girlhood in Montana. Blew teaches on the faculty of Lewis-Clark State College at Lewiston. One of Idaho's most aggressive publishers, James Hepworth of the Confluence Press, also roosts at LCSC. Budding Idaho novelist Gino Sky's books include *Near Postcard Beautiful* and *Appaloosa Rising.* Perched at the tip of the Panhandle is Dennis Johnson of Bonners Ferry whose books include *The Stars at Noon* and *Resurrection of a Hanged Man.* Ridley Pierson of Nampa is famous for his mysteries.

In the nonfiction arena, Cort Conley's Backeddy Press at Cambridge supplies some of the most popular and enthusiastically researched history in Idaho. *Idaho for the Curious* is Conley's most notable achievement. Conley also collaborated with others to write and publish *River of No Return* and *The Middle Fork—A Guide,* about the Salmon River and its middle fork, as well as *Snake River of Hells Canyon,* about that legendary watercourse. This trilogy of river books is required reading of river runners and those who would understand Idaho better.

The poetry scene is also flourishing in Idaho. Robert Wrigley, author of *Moon in a Mason Jar,* is another faculty member at LCSC and one of Idaho's best poets. To the north, another poet of note is Ron McFarland at the University of Idaho. And poet William Studebaker lights up the literary scene in Idaho Falls. Singer Rosalie Sorrels of Boise published *Way Out in Idaho,* a popular book of songs vibrating with her witty and wry view of life.

KAREN WHITE

mountain goat

CATHY CARLSON

OUT AND ABOUT

SIGHTSEEING HIGHLIGHTS

Outdoor Adventure

With almost 70% of the state's 82,751 square miles owned by the public, it's no surprise that the great outdoors provides the bulk of the state's sightseeing highlights. This is big, beautiful land, and no matter if your pleasure runs from backpacking in the wilderness to rafting raging whitewater or skiing virgin powder, you'll have lots of opportunity for adventure in Idaho.

Start with the most famous and photographed mountains in the state, the **Sawtooth Range.** Rising above the spectacularly beautiful Stanley Basin, the Sawtooths have inspired a movement over the years, as yet unsuccessful, to make them a national park. Just south of the Sawtooths is Idaho's famed **Sun Valley** and its Wood River Valley neighbor, **Ketchum.** Sun Valley, the ski area that railroad baron Averell Harriman founded in 1936, still reigns as one of the finest ski resorts in the nation. Other ski areas in Idaho that draw powderhounds include **Schweitzer** and **Silver Mountain** in the Panhandle, **Brundage Mountain** near McCall, **Bogus Basin** outside Boise, **Grand Targhee** on the slopes of the Tetons, and many smaller areas scattered throughout the snowy parts of the state.

Backpackers looking for solitude will be drawn to the largest single wilderness area in the lower 48 states, the **Frank Church–River of No Return Wilderness.** Through this land of steep ridges and deep gorges flows the **Middle Fork of the Salmon River,** which rafters and kayakers know as one of the most popular whitewater runs in the country. Whitewater enthusiasts have plenty more to choose from in the state, however. In addition to the Salmon River, river runners flock to the **Lochsa, Selway, and Payette rivers,** among others, for challenging fun afloat.

Another river, the mighty **Snake River,** defines the geography in the southern portion of the state, irrigating the farms stretching from Wyoming to Oregon across the breadth of the **Snake River Plain.** At its headwaters is one of fly-fishing's hallowed grounds, the **Henry's Fork** of the Snake. Floating downstream from there, the Snake winds its way past the one-time railroad hub of **Pocatello,** over impressive

Shoshone Falls ("the Niagara of the West"), and through Owyhee County past the largest concentration of nesting raptors in the country. Finally, just before it leaves the state on its way to meet the Columbia, it passes through **Hells Canyon National Recreation Area,** where a mile-deep gorge flanks the Seven Devils Mountains, providing a playground for backpackers as well as river rats.

In contrast to the forested lands of much of the state, the lava-strewn landscape near Arco in southeast Idaho is the setting for two more unusual attractions. **Craters of the Moon National Monument** lies in a one-time volcanic hot spot. The eerie landscape here holds such natural wonders as lava tube "caves" and lava "bombs." Due east of Craters of the Moon is a hot spot of a different sort, the **Idaho National Engineering Lab,** birthplace of the nuclear fission reactor. This complex of 52 reactors still supports the economy of Idaho Falls, and makes an interesting place to tour—just don't forget to take your lead-lined underwear!

Civilization, At Last!

Idaho's beautiful backcountry is all well and good, you say. But perhaps your idea of a good time leans more toward the bright lights and the big city. Perhaps you'd rather spend the night in a king-size bed at a luxurious hotel than in a sleeping bag under the starry sky. If so, you'll want to head straight for the state's capital city, **Boise.** A fast-growing, bustling place, Boise has become a land of opportunity for immigrants from all over the country. It has acquired a decidedly cosmopolitan edge—coffeehouse and art lovers will feel right at home there—but as yet has managed to avoid the worst of the usual big-city problems. Time will tell if that trend will continue, but in the meantime, Boise is a supremely livable place. The **Boise River Greenbelt** follows the river right through town, providing a green, tree-filled counterpoint to the modern skyscrapers of the downtown skyline. The city's **Morrison Center for the Performing Arts** draws national touring companies of performing-arts groups to its theater, which has won national recognition for its superior acoustics. And the Bard loves Boise, too; the **Idaho Shakespeare Festival** presents outdoor performances throughout the summer.

In the north, **Lewiston,** at the confluence of the Snake and Clearwater rivers, is a commercial hub thanks to its status as the state's only port. Continuing north, **Moscow** is home to the University of Idaho and combines a lively college-town atmosphere with a spectacular setting on the beautiful Palouse—a rich, green farmland of rolling hills. And still farther north, **Coeur d'Alene** is the gem of the Panhandle with its spectacular setting on the shore of the lake of the same name. Tourists flock here to the first-class shopping and lodging provided by a controversial resort towering over the lakeshore, or go sailing on the lake's pristine waters. Others venture east to the **Silver Valley,** where old mining towns preserve the region's history, or north to **Sandpoint,** an artistic enclave on the state's largest lake, **Lake Pend Oreille.** Far from being one-horse backwaters, each of these cities can provide enough sights and activities to keep even the most confirmed urbanophile happy. Or use them as great base camps to stock up on supplies for your ventures into the state's ubiquitous wilds.

Room To Move

Whatever your pleasure, from the busy city to the untrammeled wilderness, you'll find it in Idaho. And as one of the nation's least densely populated states, there's plenty of room to get around without feeling squeezed. The sights mentioned above are just some of the highlights of a trip to the Gem State. But the state is ideal for those who bring with them a little of Lewis and Clark's pioneering spirit. The two explorers were the first Europeans to come to this land, and they found friendly native inhabitants and a wild and magnificent landscape. Today's explorers, almost 200 years later, will find that things haven't changed all that much. The residents are still friendly, and much of the land is still the same, thanks to modern preservation efforts and a topography unamenable to development. Somewhere in the following pages you'll find your own bit of paradise. Happy exploring!

RECREATION

Famous outdoors writers picked Idaho for a reason. Certainly Jack O'Connor and Ted Trueblood knew a good thing when they saw it. And it's no coincidence that Sun Valley became the nation's first destination ski resort (yes, even before there was a Vail or Aspen). Idaho's grand tradition of excellence in outdoors adventures continues.

Idaho boasts the biggest wilderness area, bar none, in the lower 48 states in the massive and profoundly beautiful Frank Church–River of No Return Wilderness, which sprawls across 2.3 million acres (3,600 square miles) in the wild heart of the state. Flowing within this wilderness is the Middle Fork of the Salmon River. Presidents Carter and Bush, political opposites, both have floated the river here and found common ground enjoying the whitewater exhilaration and whiling away a few hours fly-fishing.

The state's fish and wildlife attract anglers and hunters from throughout the nation, and other countries as well. Among its famous fishes, the steelhead reigns supreme with many anglers. The Clearwater River of north-central Idaho grows some of the biggest steelhead in North America with an average weight of 12-14 pounds. The Henry's Fork of the Snake River is one of the most famous fishing streams in the world because of its heavy and healthy rainbow and cutthroat trout. Upstream, Henry's Lake produces trophy-class trout nearly every day.

Hunters know Idaho for its famous elk herds, and its reputation is growing for trophy white-tailed and mule deer. Strong protection has helped its moose herd grow as well although hunting is limited to residents.

EXPLORING THE BACKCOUNTRY

Idaho's Wilderness Areas

Idaho holds six federally designated wilderness areas, where Congress has decreed that land "untrammeled by the hand of man" shall remain so. No mechanical vehicles may trespass on wilderness trails. That means no motorized trail bikes, three-wheelers, or four-wheelers. That means no mountain bikes. That means no carts. No hang gliders. Those who would see the wilderness will see it afoot or on horseback. Exceptions? But of course. A pilot may land in the wilderness at a designated airstrip. A jet-boat pilot may run his boat up the Salmon or Snake rivers straight into the hearts of either the Church or Hells Canyon wildernesses. The Forest Service could even dispatch bulldozers and crank up the chainsaws to fight fires, if officials chose to light a new fire of political heat. Generally, however, the Forest Service believes that wilderness should be wild. If anything, the agency is a purist in policing the no-mechanical rule.

The **Frank Church–River of No Return Wilderness** encompasses 2,339,000 acres of the heart of Idaho's backcountry. Bigger even than Yellowstone National Park, this wilderness is accessible at Red River, east of Grangeville via Hwy. 14, and at other major access points near McCall, Salmon, Challis, and Stanley. The wilderness features rugged peaks and scenic river canyons, including the canyon of the Middle Fork of the Salmon River, one of the nation's premier whitewater runs. Elevations range from 2,200 feet near Mackay Bar east of Grangeville to more than 10,000 feet in the Big Horn Crags west of Salmon.

The **Selway-Bitterroot Wilderness** north of the Frank Church–River of No Return spans 1,337,681 acres, most of them in Idaho with some overlap into Montana. Another gnarled piece of real estate, the Selway-Bitterroot drops to 1,600 feet along the Selway River and rises to 10,131 feet atop Trapper Peak in Montana. The Selway-Bitterroot was among the first batch of wilderness areas formally protected by Congress with the passage of The Wilderness Act in 1964. For travelers who would see both the Selway-Bitterroot and River of No Return wildernesses, the **Magruder Road** east of Red River Ranger Station winds its way between them, with simultaneous views of both possible in the route's midsection.

Three other wilderness areas are considerably smaller than the first two. The 217,000-acre **Sawtooth Wilderness** is a piece of the 756,000-acre Sawtooth National Recreation Area. This wilderness holds Idaho's best known

WOODS VS. GOODS

If you want to start a debate, maybe even a fight, few words will serve your purpose in Idaho quite like "wilderness."

The nation's preoccupation with wilderness goes back more than a century to the founding of Yellowstone National Park in 1872. We realized then that the frontier was diminished, and while it persisted in some quarters, it couldn't resist the march of settlement forever. In the 1940s, Congress began to concern itself with a national wilderness system. The idea gained footing and volume in the '50s; in the '60s, both the momentum for the idea and the shrillness of the debate escalated.

In 1964, Sen. Frank Church, a Democrat from Idaho, took on the job of floor leader in shepherding the bill through the Senate. The Wilderness Act of 1964 called for the setting aside of lands untrammeled by man. One of the first areas designated was the Selway-Bitterroot Wilderness in north-central Idaho.

For the next two decades, Idahoans and conservationists around the nation fought over what the national forests meant for both state and national interests. Five more wilderness areas in Idaho were proposed, opposed, and finally designated: Hells Canyon, Sawtooth, Gospel Hump, Craters of the Moon, and River of No Return wildernesses.

Idaho and national interests are now locked in a debate about the fate of some nine million roadless acres of national forests in Idaho. Economic interests argue that mining and logging should be allowed to continue on these lands to help the state prosper. Traditional allies such as farmers and ranchers agree. Recreationists who pursue motorized pleasures ranging from trail biking to snowmobiling chime in on development's behalf as well.

A minority of Idahoans counter that Idaho's wild lands offer the state a unique future: protecting Idaho's lands in their natural state means preserving an economic treasure no other state will be able to match. National groups, including the Sierra Club and the Wilderness Society, have added their clout. The outcome of the debate may be decided in the next few months or the next few years. The face of the future may take its final shape during this decade.

and most photographed peaks, the rugged Sawtooth Mountains. The 206,000-acre **Gospel Hump Wilderness** is hunched up between the South Fork of the Clearwater and Salmon river canyons, 65 miles southeast of Grangeville. The **Hells Canyon Wilderness** is smaller still. At 193,840 acres, the wilderness lies like a green mantle across the rims of Hells Canyon. Its most scenic spot is in the Seven Devils Mountains west of Riggins.

Finally, the comparatively tiny 43,243-acre **Craters of the Moon Wilderness** lies wholly within Craters of the Moon National Monument. It was the first wilderness area in the country to be established on National Park Service holdings. Unlike the other wilderness areas, this is not a land of forested mountains and shimmering high-country lakes, but rather a dry, volcanic no-man's-land of supreme desolation.

All six wilderness areas offer extensive trail systems and plenty of solitude for travelers. Travelers should be aware that the philosophy of the Forest Service (or National Park Service, in the case of Craters of the Moon) toward wilderness is that it is a place where "wild" is the watchword; you're on your own and you should be prepared for sudden shifts of weather and medical or logistical problems. That's not to say the outfitters or rangers who work in the backcountry won't help. They will. But with millions of acres of wilderness, visitors should plan on self-reliance.

Camping

Idaho's **state parks** system encompasses some 23 individual parks, give or take a few depending on what definition you're applying. Most of the parks feature developed nature trails suitable for hiking with children. The campgrounds are generally the best in the state, if for no other reason than their real showers, complete with hot water. For information about the parks system write to the **Idaho Parks and Recreation Department,** 5657 Warm Springs Blvd., Boise, ID 83712, or call them at 334-4199. The department still subscribes to the "clean and green" philosophy, meaning the grass gets cut and watered and the litter kept in check. A $2 daily vehicle-entry fee is charged at most of the state parks. Overnight camping fees range from $5 for a tent site in parks without flush toilets or water to $11 for sites with electrical hookups.

IDAHO NATIONAL FOREST OFFICES

Boise: 1750 Front St., Boise, ID 83702, tel. 364-4100

Caribou: Suite 294, Federal Building, 250 S. Fourth Ave., Pocatello, ID 83201, tel. 236-7500

Challis: HC 63, P.O. Box 1611, Challis, ID 83226, tel. 879-2285

Clearwater: 12730 Hwy. 12, Orofino, ID 83544, tel. 476-4541

Idaho Panhandle: 1201 Ironwood Dr., Coeur d'Alene, ID 83814, tel. 765-7223

Nez Perce: Rt. 2, Box 475, Grangeville, ID 83530, tel. 983-1950

Payette: P.O. Box 1026, McCall, ID 83638, tel. 634-0700

Salmon: P.O. Box 729, Salmon, ID 83467, tel. 756-2215

Sawtooth: 2647 Kimberly Rd. E, Twin Falls, ID 83301, tel. 737-3200

Targhee: P.O. Box 208, St. Anthony, ID 83445, tel. 624-3151

Camping is also permitted on federal lands in the state. The **Forest Service** and the **BLM** both operate camping areas. The Forest Service typically charges $4-5 for campsites at developed campgrounds ("developed" meaning potable water, outhouses, and garbage collection). BLM campgrounds may charge similar fees for similar services, but the agency also oversees other camping areas with neither amenities nor fees. Information about BLM camping is available from the Idaho State Office, 3380 Americana Terrace, Boise, ID 83706. For information about camping in any one of the 10 national forests that dominate Idaho's wildlands, contact the national forest headquarters nearest the area you intend to visit (see "Idaho National Forest Offices" chart`).

Idaho is also well equipped with **private campgrounds,** including KOA franchises, among many others.

HIKING, BACKPACKING, AND ROCK CLIMBING

With so much wilderness, both official and unofficial, in the state, it's no great surprise that the state is a backpacker's mecca. Federal wilderness areas, national forests, and state parks all have trails of varying degrees of difficulty. Pick up a map from the supervising entity of your destination area, then get out there and enjoy. Two unique features of Idaho's backcountry might provide a focal point for your explorations. Idaho has a large number of backcountry hot springs that make popular destinations. After a day on the dusty trail under a heavy load, soaking away the aches in a hot spring under a sky full of stars can be a heavenly experience. Another worthwhile backcountry destination might be one of the forest service fire lookouts located on remote peaks and ridgetops in various parts of the state. Here in Idaho, the forest service rents these tower lodgings—made obsolete by modern aerial reconnaissance—to backpackers at reasonable cost. Some of the hot springs and tower lookouts are further described in later chapters of this book. For complete information, write the Supervisor's Office of the national forest nearest your destination (see "Idaho National Forest Offices" chart`).

Rock climbing attracts plenty of rock jocks within the state. The centers for social climbers are the Ketchum, McCall, and Sandpoint areas and the university towns of Moscow, Boise, and Pocatello, where active outdoors programs flourish. One of the most popular climbing areas in the state is the Silent City of Rocks near Almo, southeast of Twin Falls—a veritable Joshua Tree of the north. The area has gotten so popular that stricter quotas and regulations are probably inevitable.

GOLF

Nearly every Idaho community has its golf course, sometimes more than one. Among the state's most famous golf towns are Coeur d'Alene, where a lakeside golf course offers a floating green, and Sun Valley, with acres of manicured greens designed by some of the best course architects in the business. Boise, Twin Falls, Pocatello, Lewiston, and Idaho Falls all have multiple courses. Resort towns like Sandpoint and McCall have courses that capitalize on their scenic surroundings.

BICYCLING

Mountain biking is catching on with fervor in Idaho. Bicycle shops in towns near the state's major ski resorts, mostly Ketchum, Sandpoint, Sun Valley, McCall, Boise, and Driggs, are the best sources of information about suitable trails and trail conditions. One thing to note about mountain biking in Idaho is that all mechanical vehicles, mountain bikes included, are banned from wilderness areas. But the national forests still offer millions of acres of land and thousands of miles of trails that are not designated as wilderness. Backcountry roads, most notably the **Lolo Trail** in the Clearwater National Forest and **Magruder Road** in the Nez Perce National Forest, are gaining a wide following among cyclists. The **Salmon River Valley** near the Sawtooths is also a favorite area.

Bike paths in urban areas offer some local chances for cyclists to enjoy outings without competition from motorists. Idaho Falls has an extensive system of paths along the Snake River, as does Lewiston. Ketchum offers miles of cycling along the Wood River. Boise's Greenbelt paths follow the Boise River.

FISHING

Idaho has thousands of mountain lakes, dozens of reservoirs, and thousands of miles of streams and rivers awaiting the angler. Fishermen can catch sturgeon weighing hundreds of pounds and stretching to 12 feet. And Idaho, 460 miles from the ocean, still supports prized runs of steelhead and chinook salmon. The **Idaho Fish and Game Department,** P.O. Box 25, Boise, ID 83707, tel. 334-3700, maintains a network of license vendors statewide. A season fishing license costs $16 for residents, $51 for nonresidents. Shorter-term licenses are also available for nonresident anglers, including a 10-day for $18, three-day for $11, and one-day for $6. To fish for steelhead or salmon, anglers must buy another $6 permit for each species. Nonresidents can buy a combination three-day license

THE ENDANGERED SOCKEYE

The sockeye salmon returning to the Snake River once fed miners and settlers who fished the streams reaching into the heart of Idaho. Commercial fishing caught the red salmon at Payette Lake near McCall. But unlike other salmon, sockeye need large lakes for their young fish to develop, and the damming of the Payette River at Black Canyon in 1924 blocked access to the lake for the returning fish. As a result, the Payette's sockeye disappeared.

On the Salmon River up near the Sawtooths, the sockeyes surmounted the threat posed by the Sunbeam Dam, which blocked their passage from 1910 to 1934. By 1953, biologists estimated 2,000-3,000 fish had returned to Redfish Lake alone to spawn. But then the slide toward extinction began. In 1985, a fish trap across the Salmon River near Redfish Lake Creek collected 14 sockeyes. In 1986, it collected 29 and in 1987, 16. In 1988, one was spotted and in 1989 another one. In 1990, no sockeye were counted.

The Salmon River sockeye was proposed as an endangered species by the National Marine Fisheries Service in April 1991. The service also recommended that Snake River spring, summer, and fall chinook salmon be protected as threatened species. The move, only the second time the agency had declared an oceangoing salmon run worthy of Endangered Species Act protection, followed on the heels of the 1990 sockeye run.

The Sawtooth lakes, Redfish, and perhaps Alturas, offered the last hope for the sockeye in Idaho. That hope has been dwindling steadily.

BOB RACE

and steelhead permit for $31, which allows the angler to keep two fish. Children younger than 14 don't need to buy steelhead permits for catch and release, although resident children may if they want to keep their own limit of steelhead.

Boats can be hired to take anglers in search of a catch on many of the state's lakes and rivers. Fishing boats most often range 18-26 feet and can haul as many as 10 anglers.

Chinook And Steelhead

The steelhead, a seagoing rainbow trout, is the more numerous of these two game fish. Most years, anywhere between 50,000 and 100,000 steelhead migrate home to Idaho waters to spawn. The big trout are nearly worshipped by those who pursue them for their tenacity, their unpredictability, and their feistiness. In the **Clearwater River,** anglers find some of the largest steelhead anywhere in North America. Trophy fish of 20 pounds and more are caught each year. The average Clearwater steelhead will weigh 12-14 pounds. Steelhead migrating back to the **Snake** and **Salmon** rivers aren't normally as large, averaging about seven pounds. But often the Snake and Salmon rivers will pack in more fish than the Clearwater. Steelhead start returning in good numbers to Idaho waters in September and catch fishermen's fancy until March or so. Idaho's record steelhead was taken on the Clearwater River by Keith Powell of Lewiston on Nov. 23, 1973. The big summer-run fish weighed in at 30 pounds, 2 ounces.

Lower Hanson Lake in the Seven Devils Mountains lures fishermen from afar.

Chinook-salmon fishing is still an iffy prospect in Idaho. Downriver dams, eight of them between Idaho and the sea, have hit the chinook hard and rendered the once-large runs of coho and sockeye salmon almost extinct. But the chinook (or king) salmon brings out crowds when a salmon season is authorized, generally in June. Idaho's chinook usually run 4-25 pounds. The record for sea-run chinook stands at 45 pounds—a big one taken from the Salmon River in September 1964 by Hurbert Staggie of Idaho Falls. An experiment to cull Lake Coeur d'Alene's fecund kokanee is paying big dividends for chinook fans these days. Jane Clifford of Coeur d'Alene pulled a 42-pound chinook from the lake Sept. 13, 1987. It stretched the tape at 41.25 inches.

Trout

Where the water is clean enough for salmon and steelhead, trout can't be far away. Idaho is revered among fly-fishing enthusiasts for the **Henry's Fork** of the Snake River, the **South Fork** of the Snake, and **Silver Creek,** all of which can produce rainbow trout weighing 5-10 pounds. Cutthroat trout also give the state a great reputation among anglers. Northern streams and the Selway, Lochsa, St. Joe, and Coeur d'Alene rivers all attract their share of attention. Idaho's biggest members of the trout family come from the big lakes. Priest Lake produced a massive mackinaw, a 57½-pounder, for Lyle McClure in November 1971. A Kamloops rainbow from Lake Pend Oreille taken by Wes Hamlet in 1947 tipped the scale at 37 pounds.

Sturgeon

Sturgeon fishermen are the elephant hunters of the piscatorial world. An eight-foot sturgeon from the Snake River is a nice fish, no more, no less. Probably 50-70 years old, an eight-

Hunters flock to Idaho's wild country to stalk the mighty elk.

footer may weigh 150 pounds or more. Perhaps most amazing about these primitive giants of the fish world is that they will jump when they feel the hook. Watch a couple of hundred pounds of sturgeon breach the surface like a submarine-fired missile. The biggest sturgeon reportedly taken in Idaho waters was a massive 1,500-pound lunker taken from the Snake River near its confluence with the Weiser River sometime around the turn of the century.

HUNTING

Idaho's hunting for both big game mammals and game birds draws sportsmen from around the nation. The sport's popularity is evidenced in part by the distances hunters travel and by what they pay for the privilege. A resident hunting license, which includes upland and small-game privileges, costs $7. Nonresidents will pay $86 for a season license or $46 for a two-day hunting license that includes upland game and turkeys. The real bill begins with big game. Nonresidents pay $251 for an elk tag, $126 for a deer tag. For the trophy species, mountain goats or bighorn sheep, a nonresident tag will run $512. Residents get off a little easier. Elk tags run $16, deer $10, and bear $7, or residents can save $3 and buy a combination of all three for $30. Many resident sportsmen simply buy the sportsmen's package, which covers fishing (including salmon and steelhead) and hunting (for elk, deer, bear, turkey, and mountain lion), as well as archery and muzzleloading, all for $70. Separately, the big-game tags alone would total $63.

For more information on hunting in Idaho, contact the **Idaho Department of Fish and Game,** P.O. Box 25, Boise, ID 83707; tel. 334-3700.

Elk

Elk is king in Idaho among hunters. Idaho ranks among the top Western states in both the size of its elk herd and the number of elk taken. Idahoans crow most about the large proportion of big bull elk taken each year. The state's rugged mountains and relative scarcity of elk hunters allow the bulls to grow older than in other states. Idaho's elk are concentrated from the boundaries of the Frank Church–River of No Return Wilderness northward to the Canadian border. Nearly all of the state has at least pocket-sized elk herds, however.

Deer

Idaho's other featured attractions for the hunting world are its deer, both mule and white-tailed. Idaho's mule deer (particularly in units open to limited numbers of hunters in the north and in the fertile southeastern Idaho phosphate belt) can make impressive trophies. Idaho's white-tails, largely because they have been virtually unknown, also provide some trophy bucks. For hunters out to put venison on the table, both species of deer have made impressive gains in numbers during the 1980s in particular.

Bighorn Sheep

If the bull elk is king in Idaho, the bighorn sheep ranks somewhere between prince and emperor. Idaho annually awards some 200 sheep permits by lottery. State law allots 90% to Idahoans and 10% to nonresidents. The bighorns are found mostly in the rugged river breaks and canyons of the Selway River country and to a lesser extent in the river canyons of the southern desert. Idaho holds two subspecies of bighorns, the Rocky Mountain and California. A hunter may shoot one of each during his lifetime.

Moose And Other Big Game

Idaho's most sought-after lottery permit, however, is for moose. The state's moose herd has been increasing dramatically in size, and the number of permits awarded by lottery has grown to nearly 400. The odds of drawing a moose permit can be as high as 30 or 40 to one. Moose are so prized by resident hunters that nonresident permits don't exist. Idaho's other main big-game animals include black bear, mountain lion, mountain goats, and antelope.

Game Birds

Game birds include pheasants, chukar and Hungarian partridges, valley quail, and mourning doves. Grouse hunters can pick between blue, ruffed, spruce, sharp-tailed, and sage grouse. Wild turkey flocks are now found throughout the state, and Idaho's hunters are just beginning to learn to hunt them. The wild turkey is one of the bird world's wariest species. Idaho allows only a spring gobbler hunt. In general, waterfowl hunters find the major flocks of ducks and Canada geese either on the big northern lakes or along the Snake River in the south.

WATER SPORTS

Idaho is one of the nation's premier whitewater states. The Middle Fork of the Salmon River, the main Salmon, the Snake River through Hells Canyon, the South Fork of the Snake, and the Selway, Lochsa, and Payette all mean different things to different boaters. Most of Idaho's major rivers are easily accessible and generally plied by float boats, rafts, and kayaks. The state has a major outfitting industry that offers river excursions varying from one to 10 days. Prices can range from $50 for a day float along the Salmon River near Riggins to nearly $1,000 for a major excursion through Idaho's wilderness, either on the Selway or the Middle Fork and Salmon rivers.

The jetboat is another main mode of transportation. Generally big, burly boats to withstand the dramatic forces of the rapids, jetboats are built most often of heavy-gauge aluminum sheets welded together and powered by the biggest gasoline engines available, sometimes employing two or three engines. The jetboat is so named because the engines run powerful pumps that shoot a jet of water behind the boat; speeds of up to 80 miles an hour are no problem for the sleek racers.

Idaho's big lakes—Priest, Pend Oreille, Coeur d'Alene, and Payette—boast extensive powerboat and sailing fleets. Lucky Peak Reservoir near Boise is another popular destination for boaters of both persuasions.

Windsurfers are finding their places on lakes Pend Oreille and Coeur d'Alene in the Panhandle, Payette Lake at McCall, Lucky Peak Reservoir outside Boise, Redfish Lake near Stanley, and along the Snake River at Lewiston and near Idaho Falls.

Scuba diving is also growing in popularity in the state. Coeur d'Alene is one center of the sport with two dive shops. Boise and Lewiston also have diving communities. Although lakes attract most of the attention from divers, rivers attract a few. And many more snorkeling enthusiasts peer beneath the surfaces of rivers and streams, particularly during rafting trips.

GUIDE SERVICES

Sportsmen who appreciate expert advice and direction can hire an outfitter and pursue their activity with a guide. The Idaho Outfitters and Guides Association, tel. 342-1919, offers a free directory of hunting, fishing, rafting, hiking, and other outdoor adventures available through its members; write IOGA, P.O. Box 95, Boise, ID 83701. Another source of information about outfitting is the Idaho Outfitters and Guides Licensing Board, 1365 N. Orchard, Room 372, Boise, ID 83706; tel. 327-7380. The board maintains lists of outfitters permitted to operate in certain areas, such as which outfitters offer steelhead fishing from powerboats on the Snake River.

WINTER SPORTS

Alpine Skiing

With 19 Alpine ski areas, no one should question Idahoans' love of skiing. Northern Idaho has one of the newest major downhill resorts in the nation with **Silver Mountain** at Kellogg, tel. 783-1111. Silver Mountain began operating during the 1990-91 ski season to impressive reviews of both its service and snow. The easily-accessible resort just a quarter mile off I-90 features a gondola that whisks skiers from the base area up 3.1 miles and 3,000 vertical feet to its upper terminal. **Schweitzer Mountain Resort** near Sandpoint, tel. 263-9555, underwent a major face-lift for the same ski season with major realignment of its access road and the construction of a new village at its base. **Brundage Mountain** near McCall, tel. 634-5650, which many downhillers consider their own private Idaho, is planning construction of a mountaintop lodge in the near future. **Bogus Basin,** tel. 336-4500 or (800) 367-4397, serves Idaho's largest city, Boise, and the surrounding valley cities.

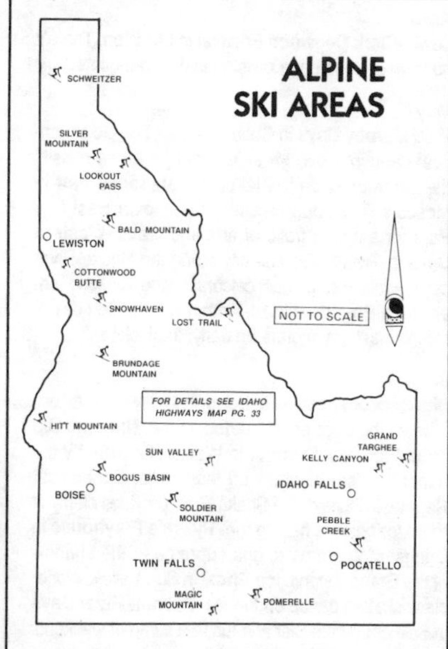

But one can't think skiing in Idaho without thinking **Sun Valley,** tel. 622-4111. Movie stars have come here since the Sun Valley Co. was created in 1936, principally by Averell Harriman of the Union Pacific Railroad. Sun Valley fulfilled Harriman's dream of creating a long-haul destination center that would be both profitable in itself and for the railroad. Sun Valley's glamour helped establish itself as a place to vacation. The skiing proved itself. The 63 downhill runs range from Dollar Mountain's gentle slopes to the challenging Bald Mountain. Sun Valley had the first ski lifts in the nation, and today its lifts can handle 22,000 skiers an hour.

On the eastern front, **Grand Targhee,** tel. (307) 353-2304 or (800) 443-8146, east of Driggs, technically lies in Wyoming on the western slopes of the Tetons. The only access road is from Idaho, though, so the ski area has been all but annexed in the minds of some skiers. Other popular skiing escapes for southeasterners range from **Kelly Canyon,** tel. 538-6261, southeast of Rexburg, to **Pebble Creek,** tel. 775-4451, **Pomerelle,** tel. 638-5599, near Albion, and **Magic Mountain,** tel. 735-2527, south of Twin Falls.

Nordic Skiing

In comparison to downhill skiing, Nordic skiing is just beginning to gain a foothold in Idaho. The major centers for Nordic skiing are **Harriman State Park** and vicinity in southeastern Idaho; **Sun Valley** and the adjacent **Wood River** and **Sawtooth** valleys; **McCall;** and the **Coeur d'Alene** and **Sandpoint** areas. Sun Valley and vicinity offers the most energetic Nordic scene. The **Galena Summit Lodge** north of town was once a premier skinny-skiing haven. Attempts are being made by the community to purchase the Lodge and return it to operation. **Busterback Ranch,** near Stanley, is another resort offering a Nordic scene. The **Idaho State Parks and Recreation Department,** tel. 334-4199 (write 5657 Warm Springs Blvd., Boise, ID 83712) oversees the **Park 'n' Ski Program.** For a $10 permit, Nordic skiers can use 17 groomed trail systems throughout the state.

Snowmobiling

Idaho has an active (some Nordic skiers would grouse a *hyperactive*) snowmobiling community. Snowmobilers maintain thousands of miles of groomed trails throughout the state. The major winter skiing areas also serve as hubs for the snowmobiling crowd. McCall serves as the nerve center for central Idaho snowmobilers. In the Panhandle, Bonners Ferry, Sandpoint, and St. Maries share the honor. Idaho City near Boise draws in the sleds, too, as does Twin Falls and Hailey. In eastern Idaho, Pocatello and Island Park are the major gathering points. Information about snowmobiling is available from the **Idaho Travel Committee,** tel. 334-2470 or (800) 635-7820, or write Statehouse Room 108, Boise, ID 83720. You can also direct inquiries to the **Idaho Parks and Recreation Department,** 5657 Warm Springs Blvd., Boise, ID 83712; tel. 334-4199.

ARTS AND ENTERTAINMENT

VISUAL ARTS

The **Boise Art Museum,** tel. 345-8330, maintains the state's most extensive collection of art. Moscow, home of the University of Idaho, has a vibrant art community. Check out the university's **Prichard Art Gallery,** tel. 882-6000, located downtown at 414 S. Main. It presents the work of university and community artists almost year-round. Lewiston, the home of Lewis and Clark State College, has an art gallery in town and a college-sponsored spring arts festival.

Ketchum and Sun Valley support one of Idaho's most creative and monied arts communities. The Wood River Valley's appeal to the

EVENTS CALENDAR

Every Idaho town has an event or two it calls its own. The communities take pride in these and welcome a chance to share them. Listing them all would be impossible. Those that follow are some of the larger, quirkier, or better known. Check with the local chambers of commerce or the Idaho Department of Commerce for more complete information.

January
Winter Carnival in Sandpoint: Torchlight parade down the slopes and plenty of good food and cheer. **U.S. Pacific Coast Champion Sled Dog Races** in Priest Lake: Mush you Huskies, and enough other breeds of dogs to keep this interesting. **Winter Carnival** midmonth in McCall: Snow sculpting rises to an artform here. Thousands of people drive over snowy roads to get to this one. **Sun Valley Winterfest:** Celebs, good snow, and good times in the shadow of Baldy.

February
Lionel Hampton/Chevron Jazz Festival, University of Idaho, Moscow: The king of the vibraphone swings into town with a host of famous friends.

March
Mardi Gras and Beaux Arts Ball in Moscow: Black-and-white clad revelers rule the streets on a festive night. **Dodge National Circuit Finals Rodeo** in Pocatello: This is a big one where cowboys show their skills.

April
Lewis-Clark Dogwood Festival in Lewiston: There's no town prettier than Lewiston in the springtime.

May
Fred Murphy Days in Coeur d'Alene: The old steamboat captain's love for Lake Coeur d'Alene revisits the community on the lake. **Renaissance Fair** in Moscow: The counterculture takes over East City Park for a spring frolic of arts and crafts. **Western Days** in Twin Falls: The city along the Snake River canyon raises some dust celebrating the frontier. **Fishermen's Breakfast** in St. Anthony: If the first day of fishing can't get anglers up early, flapjacks will.

June
Shakespeare Festival in Boise: The City of Trees celebrates the Bard on an outdoor stage. **National Old Time Fiddlers' Contest** in Weiser: Fiddlers by the hundreds flock to show off their skills. **Speedboat Regatta** in Burley: The Snake River provides plenty of room for boaters having fun. **Pierre's Playhouse** in Driggs: Melodrama reigns supreme in the shadow of the Grand Tetons. **Ice Show** in Sun Valley: World-class skaters dance on the ice. **Salmon River Days** in Salmon: Whitewater and fun fill a summer weekend.

(CONTINUED)

beautiful people brings with it an appreciation for beautiful things. Twin Falls, just a hop and a skip south of Sun Valley, has a spring exhibition of Idaho artists. In the Panhandle, Sandpoint has a long-standing reputation as an art colony.

The closest thing to a central clearinghouse for artistic endeavors in Idaho is the **Idaho Commission on the Arts,** tel. 334-2119, which is based at the Alexander House at 304 W. State St., Boise, ID 83720.

MUSIC

The UI in Moscow is also home to the Lionel Hampton School of Music, tel. 885-6231, which regularly schedules recitals by faculty, staff, and visitors. The school's annual **Lionel Hampton/Chevron Jazz Festival** draws the generous backing of the oil company and jazz greats, bringing in some of the biggest names in the business each February. Thousands of schoolchildren also attend the festival for clinics with the stars.

The Washington-Idaho Symphony Association, tel. 882-6555, is also based in Moscow and schedules performances in fall and spring. The Symphony also performs in Pullman and Lewiston during its season.

THEATER AND DANCE

Performing arts liven up Boise with the **American Festival Ballet Company,** tel. 343-0556, based there; the **Idaho Shakespeare Festival,** tel. 336-9221, held each summer; and the various events staged at Boise State University's **Morrison Center for the Performing Arts,** tel. 385-1609. Rexburg makes its mark on the Idaho arts scene with its **International Dance Festival** on the Ricks College campus in late July and early

July

Days of the Old West in Hailey: Miners and cowboys rise again. **Historic Skills Fair** in Cataldo: Period costumes and pioneer skills reawaken the past. **Sawtooth Mountain Mamas Arts and Crafts Fair** in Stanley: A gathering of talented people display their wares. **Massacre Rocks Rendezvous** in American Falls: Recalling the days of the Overland Migration. **Festival at Sandpoint:** Classical music by classic Lake Pend Oreille. **Snake River Stampede** in Nampa: One of the rodeos to make it to in Idaho. **Idaho International Folk Dance Festival** in Rexburg: Hundreds of dancers from around the world gather to display their traditions. **Sun Valley Music Festival:** Jazz fills the summer air. **St. Ignatius Festival** in Boise: The Basque community convenes to renew friendships and preserve its history. **Budweiser Hot Air Balloon Races** in Driggs: Brightly colored balloons speckle the sky.

August

Northern Rockies Folk Festival in Hailey: Ballads, bluegrass, and the blues, unplugged. **Pierre's Rendezvous Days** in Driggs: A milder-mannered recreation of the rip-roaring rendezvous once held by mountain men here. **Art on the Green** in Coeur d'Alene: The lake city's gathering of artists. **Three Island Crossing** in Glenns Ferry: Wagons cross the mighty Snake in a re-creation of Oregon Trail days. **Caldwell Night Rodeo** in Caldwell: One of Idaho's oldest and wildest events. **Oregon Trail Tour** in American Falls: Walk in the footsteps of the pioneers. **Wagon Days Celebration** in Ketchum: Modern mule skinners recall the past in the community parade.

September

Lewiston Roundup: This rodeo lives up to its motto—She's Wild! Plenty of cowboys and cowgirls ridin' and ropin'. **Lumberjack Days** in Orofino: Loggers show off their skills with traditional tools. **Twin Falls County Fair and Rodeo** in Filer: Rodeo rides and carnival rides keep life lively.

October

Oktoberfest in Sandpoint: A chance to celebrate good food and good friends, with an outdoor beer-garden, superb scenery, and great food.

November

Christmas City U.S.A. Lighting Ceremony in Rupert: It's a big tree and a big event.

December

Festival of Trees in Boise: A cold-weathered but warm-natured celebration downtown in a town where trees have always counted. **First Night/Last Night** in Moscow: Farewell to the old year and ring in the new at Friendship Square.

August. The event brings in dance troupes from around the world for 10 days of performances. The University of Idaho, Moscow's Hartung Theater is home of the Festival of Dance and Performing Arts, tel. 883-3267 for information, 885-6465 or 885-7212 for tickets; and the Idaho Repertory Theater, the summer undertaking of the UI Theatre Arts Department, tel. 885-6465.

SHOPPING

Serious shoppers will find some surprising delights in store in Idaho towns. Sandpoint's Cedar Street Bridge offers shops strung across what was once a covered bridge. Mall mania can hit in Coeur d'Alene where the Silver Lake Mall is growing as fast as the city itself. Moscow's Palouse Empire Mall is the biggest between Spokane and Boise, while Towne Square Mall at Boise is the biggest in the state. All the other major cities have malls too, with the usual array of shops. You'll find the ubiquitous WalMart in Idaho, as well as Costco, the warehouse shopping chain, with outlets at Boise and Twin Falls. For interesting shops, McCall and Ketchum/Sun Valley offer the best variety.

Crafts

Moscow's Renaissance Fair, Lewiston's Dogwood Festival, Coeur d'Alene's Art on the Green, and Stanley's Sawtooth Mountain Mamas Arts and Crafts Fair all provide examples of the state's enthusiasm for home-crafted goods. Other outstanding examples of contemporary crafts can be found throughout the state. Check out Wendt Pottery of Lewiston, which makes an art of making pottery—potters Maggi Fuhriman of Juliaetta and Jeanne Wood have shaped their own distinctive styles with clay. Or Moscow's Frank Werner, who has won an international audience for his decoys by insisting they serve as folk art as well as drawing ducks and geese in to the gun.

ACCOMMODATIONS AND FOOD

Idaho travelers will find accommodations ranging from roadside pullouts where camping is overlooked to the grand rooms in the Sun Valley Inn. At some unique bed-and-breakfast operations you'll find friendly folks who will fill you with a good breakfast before suggesting the best things to see or do in their part of the world. Or perhaps you'd prefer one of the Forest Service cabins or lookout towers deep in the backcountry where lodging means unlocking a door, swinging open the shutters, and making sure the Osborne Firefinder stays ready for use. While Idaho's ranching heritage makes for a meat-and-potatoes majority, vegetarians will find suitable restaurants in the bigger cities. Various ethnic restaurants can also be found throughout the state—from Basque food in Boise to Mexican food in Moscow. The chambers of commerce across the state can provide up-to-the-minute information about dining and lodging options in their areas. For a general list of chambers, contact the **Idaho Travel Council,** tel. 334-2470, at 700 W. State, Boise, ID 83720.

CAMPGROUNDS

Idaho's camping scene varies from wilderness sites 20 miles from the nearest road to the poolside campsites of KOA outposts along the highways. The state publishes a comprehensive booklet listing campgrounds throughout the state. If you have a pack of antsy kids in the back seat, the KOA and a pool may look like heaven. If you have a horse or shank's mare that will bear you, that wilderness campsite can be as close to heaven as you will ever get.

Idaho's campground prices in general vary according to two factors: difficulty in getting there and development. Camping on national forest or other public lands away from developed campsites is free. The Forest Service and BLM generally charge about $5 a night at maintained campgrounds. The Idaho State Parks and Recreation Department charges according to its campground amenities, with fees ranging $5-11. KOA campsites can cost $20 or more a night if you add in utilities. But swimming pools don't come cheap anywhere.

HOSTELS

Idaho has three hostels affiliated with Hostelling International, one at Gooding in southwest Idaho, and two in the Panhandle at Kellogg and Naples. The Kellogg Hostel in the Silver Valley occupies the former headquarters of the Bunker Hill Mine, and is one block from the Silver Mountain Ski Area gondola terminal. The Naples hostel, 35 miles south of the Canadian border, is in a converted old-time dance hall near the Kootenai National Wildlife Refuge. The Gooding Hostel is in the Gooding Hotel.

In addition to these, some individual state parks offer dormitories intended for large groups only. Among these are **Harriman** near Island Park, **Squaw Bay Group Area** at Priest Lake State Park, and the newer, better equipped, and more expensive **Three Meadows Group Camp** at Dworshak State Park. Several resorts, such as **Huckleberry Heaven Lodge** near Elk River or **Busterback Ranch** near Stanley also offer dormitories and will accommodate singles and small groups.

BED AND BREAKFAST INNS

Idaho's network of B&Bs has grown dramatically in the past few years. It seems as though every major town has one, or someone has plans for one. The prices are generally a bit steeper than the average motel room, with rates from $35 to $75, but the little extra money buys you a comfortable, homey atmosphere and an enjoyable breakfast. Two sources of B&B referral information are the **Idaho Innkeepers Association,** at 4930 Umatilla Ave., Boise, ID 83709, and **Idaho Bed and Breakfast,** tel. 342-8066, which operates out of the Idaho Heritage Inn at Boise. Either one can help travelers find a place they'd like to stay.

RECIPES

One of the best cookbooks for quintessentially Idaho cuisine was published by the Idaho Fish and Game Department in 1990. Copies of *Idaho's Wild 100; Recipes from the Idaho Department of Fish and Game* are available for $10 each by writing the department at P.O. Box 25, Boise, ID 83707, Attn: Cookbooks. With the department's permission, here are a few of the recipes the agency's employees and their spouses contributed:

Uncle Jack's Sourdough Starter

2 cups flour
2 Tbs. sugar
1 Tbs. salt
1 Tbs. vinegar

Add enough warm water to make a creamy batter. Leave the batter in a warm place for four days to a week until it begins to sour, or "work." If it is ready, it should have bubbles on top. Pour some in a dish and mix a dash of soda with it; if it is active and ready it will respond.

—Jack Trueblood, information and education specialist, Boise

Sourdough Hotcakes

2 cups sourdough starter
2 Tbs. sugar
4 Tbs. oil
1 egg
1/2 tsp. salt
1 scant tsp. baking soda; full tsp. if starter is real sour

Dump sugar, oil, and egg into the sourdough. Mix well. Dilute soda in 1 Tbs. warm water and add last, when ready for batter to hit the griddle. Fold gently into sourdough. **Do not beat.** Notice deep hollow tone as sourdough fills with bubbles and doubles bulk.

—Dorothy Baker, director's office coordinator, Boise

Trout Cocktail

One 16-inch rainbow, brown, or brook trout, or three eight-inch trout.

Clean, remove head and tail. Cut into pieces three or four inches long. Put into a pan, cover with water. Add:

1 tsp. salt
1/2 tsp. pepper
3 bay leaves
1/2 tsp. Worcestershire sauce
1/2 tsp. thyme

Boil 10 minutes. Remove from heat and cool. Take meat from bones and skin, place in cocktail glasses and chill. Cover with cocktail sauce (recipe below). Serve with lemon slices and crackers. Serves 3-4.

Sauce:
1/2 cup chili sauce
1/2 cup catsup
2-4 Tbs. horseradish
1 1/2 tsp. Worcestershire sauce
Combine and chill.

—Sharon Moore (wife of Bob Moore, Pahsimeroi Hatchery superintendent) Ellis

Conejo Euskad ("Basque Rabbit")

3 lbs. rabbit cut in serving pieces
3 cloves crushed garlic
1 cup white wine
2 Tbs. olive or salad oil

Add garlic and wine to rabbit and let stand overnight. Brown the rabbit in hot oil. Place the rabbit in a casserole dish and prepare sauce:

3 cloves crushed garlic
1 onion chopped
2 Tbs. olive or salad oil
1/3 cup bread crumbs
2 Tbs. tomato puree
1 cup chicken broth or 1 bouillon cube in a cup of water
2 Tbs. white wine

Brown onion and garlic in oil. Add remaining ingredients and cook until the sauce thickens. Pour sauce over rabbit. Place cover on casserole and bake at 275° for 45 minutes. Serves 4-5.

—Maria Anderson (wife of Steve Anderson, shipping and receiving clerk) Boise

Gospel Hump BBQ Elk Roast

1 large elk roast
salt and pepper
1 clove garlic, minced
3 cups water
1/8 cup oil

Season roast with salt and pepper. Brown on all sides with garlic in oil. Drain off oil. Add water and bring to

(CONTINUED)

boil. Cook covered in 325° oven for three hours or until done. Remove from pan and cut into slices.

Sauce:
2 cups barbecue sauce
1 cup catsup
8 oz. tomato sauce
2 medium onions, coarsely chopped
1 cup celery, cut into large pieces
2 green peppers, cut into large pieces
3-4 drops Tabasco

Add remaining ingredients to pan drippings. Mix and cook covered for about an hour or until sauce is thickened in 325° oven. Slice meat and add to sauce; continue cooking for 30 minutes. Serve on slit hard rolls. Serves 4-6.

—Janet and (Director) Jerry Conley, Boise

HOTELS AND MOTELS

Idaho's motels are a utilitarian set for the most part. They offer shelter from the storm, or a relief from long stretches of difficult highway driving. The prices are reasonable; $20-40 will get you a room anywhere in the state. And here and there, motels of distinction appear, oases in an open landscape. Expect to pay more in the major cities or in locales were everyone wants to go. Rooms at the Coeur d'Alene start at $85 and go as high as most of us would like to fantasize. Even Idaho has a high season and a low season. Sun Valley, for example, is filled to overflowing with guests during the peak of the ski season, from mid-November to March and during the summers, from June through August. The lulls between the peaks, from September to mid-November and April through May, offer the cheapest room rates.

FOOD AND COOKING

Idaho cuisine does not necessarily revolve around one immediately obvious ingredient: the potato. The potato plains of southeastern Idaho produce the nation's benchmark for baking potatoes, no doubt. It's ironic that in northern Idaho, finding Idaho bakers can be a challenge in some supermarkets. But in a state where the growing season can stretch as long as 300 days, the farmers' markets in major towns offer not only those famous spuds, but a whole cornucopia of fresh produce through the summer months.

Idaho also prides itself on its livestock industry. Beef is big here, and a safe bet on the menu—whether it's barbecued or baked as prime rib. Look for family-run butcher shops—they still exist, particularly in smaller towns. For many Idahoans, albeit a declining proportion,

The Coeur d'Alene Resort dominates the lake's shoreline.

the best meat is that from the wild. Some children are still raised on elk and deer meat. Idaho's trout farms in the Hagerman Valley produce most of the nation's supply of mild-flavored rainbow trout. Of course, stream-reared trout taste great, too.

Dutch ovens, heavy cast-iron or aluminum pots with fitted covers, are the mainstay of Idaho's outfitting industry, particularly among river rafters. Maybe it's the scenery, maybe it's the invigorating atmosphere that surrounds a dinner in the great outdoors, or maybe it's the Dutch oven's tendency to provide even, moist heat that makes the meals so delicious. But Dutch oven cookery is one cuisine most Idahoans would be proud to call their own.

TRANSPORTATION

Most of Idaho's travelers rely on their own rigs because the alternatives are either limited or nonexistent. Greyhound buses do course through the state but only to major cities. Smaller bus lines have sprung up to provide more frequent scheduling to the medium-sized towns, but even they won't get you to the outlying towns or the most interesting sights. If you are driving, a couple of words of caution. Those highway signs warning of curves ahead carry recommended speeds. Pay them heed; they're almost always accurate and sometimes a bit liberal.

IDAHO BY AIR

You can get virtually anywhere you want to in Idaho by air. Of course you may be flying in a Cessna 185 tail-dragger, and the pilot may have to buzz the local moose to get them off the meadow. But you can get there by air. In some stretches of the Selway-Bitterroot or Frank Church–River of No Return Wilderness, there simply is no other way to get there without a long hike.

Boise International Airport is Idaho's major air hub, serviced by United Airlines (tel. 800-241-6522), Delta Air Lines (tel. 800-221-1212), Horizon Air (tel. 800-547-9308), Alaska Airlines (tel. 800-426-0333), and Empire Airlines (tel. 800-392-9233). Other major airports with at least scheduled commuter service include **Coeur d'Alene, Lewiston, Hailey, Twin Falls, Pocatello,** and **Idaho Falls** with service by either Empire Airlines or Horizon Air. Charter airlines can generally be found to haul passengers into any of the state's smaller airports or airstrips. No major airlines fly into the north state, but they do fly into Spokane, Washington just across the border from Coeur d'Alene. Horizon Air offers connecting flights into Idaho from Spokane, and also from Seattle.

BY CAR

Idaho's highways and byways are scenic to the extreme at times. The state has some white-knuckle stretches on even its major highways. U.S. Hwy. 12 from Kooskia to Lolo Pass on the Montana border literally clings to every curve of the Lochsa River. Splendidly scenic, it's no road to trifle with. Stick to the speed limit and drive it during daylight hours when possible both for safety and the scenery. Most of Idaho's highways, even Hwy. 95, the only complete north-south link, have their stretches of difficult road. Another factor to consider is that there are long stretches of highway with nothing but great country on either side—no houses, no gas stations, no telephones. Try to plan your gas purchases accordingly. Be conscious, too, that many small-town gas stations close by 6 p.m. If you find yourself in a small town after the gas station is closed and you have to have gasoline to reach the next town, one possibility is to check with the local tavern for the whereabouts of the town's policeman. They can often produce a key to the pumps and help you or roust out the gas station's owner. Just make sure your reason for causing the inconvenience holds water. Or better yet, fuel up in major towns or before dark and avoid the hassle altogether.

Rental cars are available at the major airports. In Boise and the larger cities, Ugly Duckling and Rent a Wreck franchises offer beaters that will get you around town in reasonable time, if not in style. Some of the cars may only have a ding or two; others make you wonder. But all will make you smile when you compare the bills. Of course,

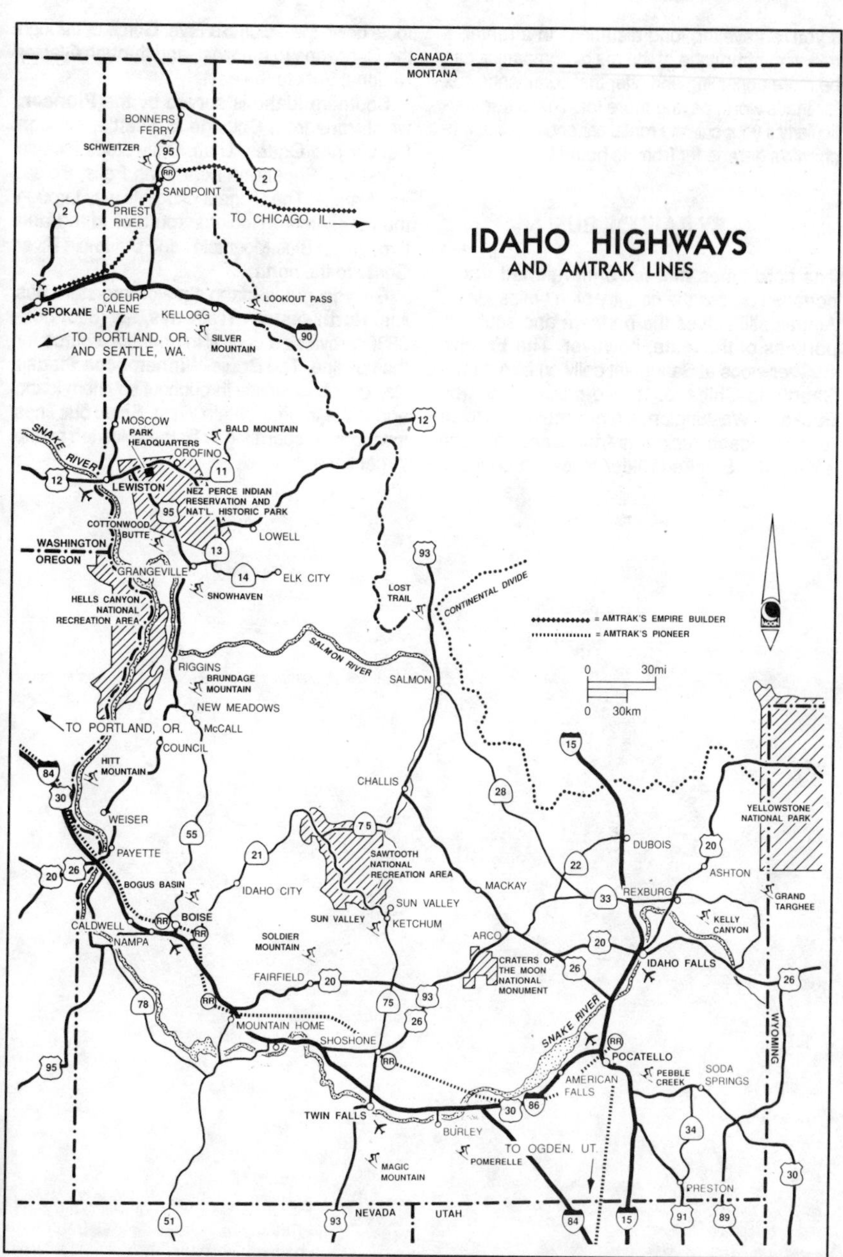
IDAHO HIGHWAYS
AND AMTRAK LINES
= AMTRAK'S EMPIRE BUILDER
= AMTRAK'S PIONEER
0 30mi
0 30km
CANADA
MONTANA
BONNERS FERRY
SCHWEITZER
SANDPOINT
PRIEST RIVER
TO CHICAGO, IL.
SPOKANE
COEUR D'ALENE
KELLOGG
LOOKOUT PASS
SILVER MOUNTAIN
TO PORTLAND, OR. AND SEATTLE, WA.
MOSCOW
PARK HEADQUARTERS
BALD MOUNTAIN
OROFINO
SNAKE RIVER
LEWISTON
NEZ PERCE INDIAN RESERVATION AND NAT'L. HISTORIC PARK
COTTONWOOD BUTTE
LOWELL
WASHINGTON
OREGON
GRANGEVILLE
ELK CITY
HELLS CANYON NATIONAL RECREATION AREA
SNOWHAVEN
LOST TRAIL
CONTINENTAL DIVIDE
SALMON RIVER
RIGGINS
BRUNDAGE MOUNTAIN
SALMON
NEW MEADOWS
TO PORTLAND, OR.
McCALL
COUNCIL
HITT MOUNTAIN
CHALLIS
WEISER
PAYETTE
SAWTOOTH NATIONAL RECREATION AREA
YELLOWSTONE NATIONAL PARK
DUBOIS
ASHTON
BOGUS BASIN
IDAHO CITY
MACKAY
REXBURG
GRAND TARGHEE
SUN VALLEY
KELLY CANYON
BOISE
CALDWELL
NAMPA
SOLDIER MOUNTAIN
KETCHUM
ARCO
IDAHO FALLS
CRATERS OF THE MOON NATIONAL MONUMENT
FAIRFIELD
MOUNTAIN HOME
SHOSHONE
SNAKE RIVER
POCATELLO
AMERICAN FALLS
PEBBLE CREEK
SODA SPRINGS
WYOMING
TWIN FALLS
BURLEY
TO OGDEN, UT.
POMERELLE
MAGIC MOUNTAIN
PRESTON
NEVADA
UTAH
RR

if you're traveling long distances in a rental, a newer car from one of the major companies can be more appealing and offer that confidence factor that's worth paying more for. That's true particularly if your cut-rate rental car ends up in a mechanic's garage far from its home base.

BY RAIL OR BUS

The hard times that have hit railroad transportation across the country didn't miss Idaho. Amtrak still serves the northern and southern portions of the state, however. The **Empire Builder** stops at Sandpoint daily on its run from Seattle to Chicago. It also stops at nearby Spokane, Washington, a more convenient stop for most Idaho residents from Coeur d'Alene south. The Empire Builder follows a beautiful route down the Columbia River Gorge or through the Cascades to the west, and through Glacier National Park to the east.

Southern Idaho is served by the **Pioneer,** which runs from Chicago to Seattle, through Denver and Ogden, Utah. Daily stops include Pocatello, Shoshone near Twin Falls, Boise, and Nampa. The Pioneer chugs its way through the magnificent Rockies south of Idaho and through the Blue Mountains and Columbia River Gorge to the north.

Greyhound is Idaho's major interstate bus line. **Northwestern Trailways,** tel. (800) 366-3830, provides a central information source for the bus line. The **Boise-Winnemucca Stages** also offer bus service throughout southern Idaho and in the intermountain West. Small bus lines have begun operating to fill the voids left by the larger lines.

HEALTH AND SAFETY

ESSENTIALS

Emergency Communication

Idaho phone companies are still converting to 911 emergency service telephone lines in many areas. Alternatives are to call the Idaho State Police, which has statewide jurisdiction, or county sheriff's departments. Of Idaho's cities, perhaps a third have police departments to call their own. The **Idaho State Police,** tel. 334-2900, or **Idaho Transportation Department** can offer reports about road conditions. The Transportation Department's **Highway Condition Reports** telephone number is 336-6600.

Communication can be difficult in Idaho. If you're going to take in the remoteness of Idaho's open spaces, you can leave the cellular phone at home. There is some coverage in population centers like Coeur d'Alene, Lewiston, Boise, Twin Falls, Pocatello, Idaho Falls, and of course Sun Valley. But the existing coverage is generally localized and buzzing down the highway is just about guaranteed to run you out of range. CB radios are preferable in Idaho. In fact, CBs can be downright lifesavers on back roads—logging trucks come equipped with CBs and the channels are normally posted on trees to help loggers and travelers communicate. If it isn't posted, work the dial a bit to see if anyone's talking. Channels 1-18 seem to be the most popular. A CB can also save you in the backcountry if the car breaks down or someone is injured. Channels 9 and 19 are most frequently monitored for emergency messages by police and others.

What To Bring

Bring warm clothing, at least a jacket, no matter what the season. Even in high summer, the desert can cool off dramatically at night. A cold front can turn a week of hot weather into a cold snap overnight. If you're planning on doing much backcountry walking, hiking shoes of some sort are necessary to prevent turned ankles.

Idahoans and wise travelers from out of state take to heart cautions about the state's highways. The long unpopulated stretches also call for some common-sense precautions when traveling both in summer and winter. During the summer, it's a sound idea to keep a jug of water in the car; some cool drinks in a cooler are a good bet. During the winter, driving long distances puts both car and driver out on the road when conditions make mechanical failures most likely. Tossing a good blanket or sleeping bag in the car, hauling along a warm coat even if you don't intend to use it, and packing away some high-energy foods like candy bars can help make a delay more comfortable. Do not forget warm clothes. If your car should quit running for whatever reason, the heat will stop too. Idaho highways in winter can be icy and dangerous. Good snow tires, with chains in the trunk, are considered bare necessities by most.

Keep a road map in the car. In Idaho, a map is essential for navigating and avoiding unnecessary detours that can go on forever. Keeping at least some tools, a couple of screwdrivers, an adjustable wrench, pliers, a bit of wire, gloves, and a flashlight makes a lot of sense. Make sure from time to time that your spare tire still has air in it. Keep basic first-aid supplies in the trunk: plastic bandages, a roll of gauze, disinfectant, insect repellent, and aspirin.

PESTS

Ticks

The common wood tick is prevalent in Idaho. Although the state is part of the Rocky Mountain spotted fever belt, no cases have been reported in recent years. Ticks are abroad during the spring, when the weather is moist, and are most common in areas with livestock, deer, or elk. Removing them once they've sunk their mouths in can be tricky. Use gloves and tweezers to remove ticks from yourself or your animals—never crush the critters with your fingers! The best way to remove ticks is by suffocating them with petroleum jelly first, making it easier to pull them out. Always wash the bitten area and your hands afterward. Disinfect the area and watch for signs of infection. If a pinkish halo develops in the next day or two, see a doctor. Whether ticks that carry

stinging nettle

Lyme disease (smaller deer ticks) are present in Idaho hasn't been clearly established.

On The Wing

Mosquitos and sometimes black flies generally pose the biggest nuisance to visitors to the moister mountain areas. Both can put the bite on campers and hikers any time of the summer, depending on elevation. As lower elevations dry out in spring or summer, high elevation snows still linger, maintaining breeding areas for the biting bugs.

Some of the most bothersome insects in the state belong to the hornet tribe. Yellowjackets, pugnacious members of the wasp family, feel free to invite themselves to picnics or other gatherings. Hot dry weather favors the growth of their colonies. Bald-faced hornets can pose an even worse threat, attacking en masse when their nests are threatened. Unlike honeybees that sacrifice themselves with a sting, wasps can keep on stinging unless killed. Both bee and wasp stings can be treated by cooling the area with ice or a cold wet compress and applying a baking-soda paste, if available. (In the case of a bee sting, first try to find the stinger and pull it out.) Commercial products also exist that can take the sting or itch out of bites.

Spiders And Snakes

Idaho is home to some alarming arachnids, at least for those who think any critter with eight legs can't be viewed with anything but disgust. The black widow spider is actually a quite common member of the state's fauna. Black widows can grow to quarter-size in some hot, dry areas where insects are abundant. Normally reticent, they crawl into cracks in wood or rock or under boards. The black widow spins irregular webs consisting mostly of sticky strands. Another spider of note is the aggressive house spider or hobo spider. Relatively common in north-central Idaho, its bite doesn't look like much but can cause fevers, nausea, and other problems. Some bites can cause severe tissue damage if left untreated.

Rattlesnakes have a bad reputation but pose less of a threat than some of the aforementioned bugs. Herpetologists describe rattlers as dangerously venomous and they are. But your chance of being bitten usually depends on whether you choose to mess with the snake. Telling that to someone who fears reptiles may be a lost cause, but rattlesnakes will crawl the other way if given a chance. Accidents will happen; a hiker can step over a log and onto a snake before either knows what has happened. People also get bit while scrambling over rocks and putting a hand in the wrong place. When in rattlesnake country try to think about both situations. The rattlesnake identifies itself in two ways, by the interlocking horny rattles at the tip of its tail and by the triangular head common to pit vipers. They are generally dusky colored with darker blotches along the back. The tail is there for warning intruders and produces a dry, buzzing sound. Rattlesnakes can be found mostly at lower elevations around the state and mostly near watercourses, where the mice and other prey they feed on are more abundant. Idaho has two subspecies of Western rattlesnake, the Northern Pacific and Great Basin. Adults range 15-62 inches long and can be found at surprisingly high elevations, up to 11,000 feet.

Pesky Plants

In Hells Canyon and elsewhere along the state's waterways in warmer regions, visitors are advised to be wary of poison ivy. A ground-hugging vine, it can be spotted by its glossy-green, three-lobed leaves. In robust patches, stalks of waxy white or yellowish berries also appear. Touching poison ivy can lead to a puffy red rash or watery blisters for those susceptible to the irritating oil found in the plant. If exposed to poison ivy, wash with soap and warm water to help reduce the unpleasant repercussions. Otherwise Calamine or other soothing lotions can help. For major exposures, a visit to the doctor and a shot of cortisone may be the only cure.

The focus on the ivy can lead some to ignore another plant pest, the stinging nettle. The soft green leaves of the nettle seem to obscure the plant's hairy stems. The first sign of trouble for many travelers is a stinging or burning sensation and red skin anywhere the plant has brushed against them. Lotions or even mud can help lessen the stinging.

INFORMATION AND COMMUNICATIONS

Telephone Area Code

All of Idaho shares one area code—**208.**

Tourist Information

Idaho tourism information is available from the **Idaho Division of Travel Promotion,** tel. (800) 635-7820. Individual travel committees are also set up for the state's six regions and offer more detailed information. They include: **North Idaho,** tel. 263-2161; **North-central Idaho,** tel. 882-3581; **Southwestern Idaho,** tel. (800) 635-5240; **South-central Idaho,** tel. (800) 255-8946; **Southeastern Idaho,** tel. (800) 423-8597; and **East-central Idaho,** tel. 523-1010.

Radio And TV

Among the 86 radio stations (at last count) that broadcast from Idaho towns, the one that comes closest to statewide coverage is Boise-based KBOI at 670 AM. Campus radio stations that are affiliated with National Public Radio include Boise State University's KBSU-FM (90.3); KFRA-FM (91.7) at the University of Idaho at Moscow; KISU-FM (89.5) at Idaho State University, Pocatello; and KRIC-FM (100.5) at Ricks College at Rexburg.

Idaho's television menu is limited to 13 stations broadcasting within the state. As with NPR affiliates, the Public Broadcasting System includes affiliates at Boise State University (KAID-TV Channel 4); University of Idaho, Moscow (KUID-TV Channel 12); and Idaho State University, Pocatello (KISU-TV Channel 10). CBS affiliates include KBCI-TV Channel 2 at Boise, KIDK-TV Channel 3 at Idaho Falls, KLEW-TV Channel 3 at Lewiston, and KMVT-TV Channel 11 at Twin Falls. NBC affialiates include KTVB-TV Channel 7 at Boise and KIFI-TV Channel 8 at Idaho Falls. ABC affiliates include KIVI-TV Channel 6 at Nampa, KPVI-TV Channel 6 at Pocatello, and KKVI-TV at Twin Falls. Idaho's lone Fox affiliate is KTRV-TV on Channel 12 at Nampa.

Newspapers

Idaho's daily newspaper scene remains healthy and diverse. At Boise, the *Idaho Statesman,* tel. 377-6200, has the largest circulation of all Idaho newspapers—80,000 on Sundays. It is distributed across southwestern Idaho. At Burley, the *South Idaho Press,* tel. 678-2200, has a Sunday circulation of 6,300. Coeur d'Alene offers the *Coeur d'Alene Press and North Idaho Sunday,* tel. 664-8176, with a Sunday circulation of 30,000. One of the state's better papers is *The Post Register,* tel. 522-1800, in Idaho Falls with a circulation of 28,000 Sundays. Kellogg offers the 4,500-circulation *Shoshone County News-Press,* tel. 783-1107, Tuesdays to Saturdays. The best paper in Idaho—this author is admittedly biased on the subject—is (fanfare, please) the *Lewiston Morning Tribune,* tel. 743-9411, published daily at Lewiston with a circulation of 25,000 Sundays. The

Moscow-Pullman Daily News, tel. 882-5561, at Moscow, has a circulation Mon.-Sat. of about 8,400. The *Idaho Press Tribune,* tel. 467-9251, at Nampa has a circulation of 17,400. Pocatello's *Idaho State Journal,* tel. 232-4161, focuses on the news of southeastern Idaho with a Sunday circulation of 20,000. Sandpoint offers the *Bonner County Daily Bee,* tel. 263-9534, Tues.-Sat. with a circulation of 5,000. Twin Falls supports another strong newspaper with *The Times News,* tel. 733-0931, with a circulation of 22,000 Sundays.

MARK MORRIS

cottontail

CATHY CARLSON

THE PANHANDLE

Blue lakes, thick evergreen forests, and the clean gray of granite mountains make up the bulk of Idaho's Panhandle. Interspersed are a pair of the state's most beautiful cities—Coeur d'Alene and Sandpoint—its oldest building, a defunct naval base turned state park, and a smattering of other attractions compelling enough to make this region Idaho's vacation retreat.

Mining and logging, long the biggest sources of paychecks here, suffered during the 1980s as Idaho weathered a major recession. In efforts to survive, Panhandle interests aggressively courted the tourist, and began to draw Idaho residents and nonresidents alike to the area.

The **Silver Valley,** east of Coeur d'Alene, was once one of the richest mining districts in the world. There the town of Kellogg saw the end of one livelihood and the beginning of another when the old Bunker Hill Co. shut down its smelter and mine. The smelter, which in the course of its operations poisoned children with lead dust, gave way to competing market forces. Its demise led townspeople to gamble on the development of a gondola as the focus of a new economy. The gondola ferries tourists from town to the mountaintop ski area, Silver Mountain Resort. Residents here hope skiers and other tourists will bring back silver to the area, albeit in a different form.

In **Coeur d'Alene,** some critics decry the excesses of a tourist boom. Here newspaper magnate Duane Hagadone set out to create a tourist magnet along the north shore of the lake. His posh, sometimes pretentious "Coeur d'Alene, a Resort on the Lake" towers over the shoreline and represents a road not wanted by many Panhandle devotees. Popular slogans like "Tahoe of the North" do nothing to allay fears that the area will become overdeveloped. Controversy over growth issues continues throughout the Panhandle.

Through all this, the region's residents have remained friendly overall. Don't tell a logger his way of putting bread on the table is wrong and expect a warm reply. But the region has a history as a hospitable place for vacationers, and the locals have developed a well-tempered sense of civility to all but the most direct affronts. Many of the Panhandlers hail from somewhere else and therefore have a good measure of tolerance for outsiders. The biggest reason for the region's mellow nature is its surroundings. Small complaints simply get swallowed up in the midst of all the beauty and opportunities to get out and enjoy the outdoors.

The Panhandle's climate is consistent with its northern latitude. It's cool and breezy in the spring and fall, hot in the summers, and cold and snowy in the winters. Summer days normally arrive sometime in May. Daytime temperatures climb into the 90s by midsummer and drop into the 50s at night. Frost arrives in September and the first heavy storms of winter make an appearance in November. The region receives snow in abundance, bringing out snowmobile enthusiasts and both Nordic and Alpine skiers each winter.

BONNERS FERRY AND VICINITY

HISTORY

Although the area around Bonners Ferry was explored by Canadian geographer and fur-trader David Thompson as early as 1808, the town itself was born in 1863 when a gold rush to Canada's Wildhorse mining district brought hopefuls flooding through in search of fortune. Edwin L. Bonner took advantage of the situation by building a ferry across the Kootenai River here. He later sold out to the Fry brothers, but a short-lived attempt to call the town Fry yielded to Bonner's historical precedent. Formally established in 1893 as Bonners Ferry, the city became the Boundary County seat in 1915 when the county was formed. Interestingly enough, a 1907 act had created Bonner County, named for none other than Edwin. Sandpoint remains its county seat, however.

Long before the white man came along, the area was home to the Kootenai people. The Kootenai in northern Idaho were one of six bands of the Kootenai Nation, whose territory also included northwestern Montana and southeastern British Columbia. They lived by hunting, fishing, and gathering, and they shared a language that set them apart from other Northwest tribes. The Kootenai people were not represented at the 1855 Hellgate Treaty talks and were left without a claim to lands. This was a thorn in their side for generations, and in 1974 they finally took action, declaring war on the U.S.—a legal tactic that attracted international attention and finally forced federal authorities to give ground, 18 acres in fact. The tribe has since turned its attentions to another endeavor, opening the Best Western Kootenai River Inn at Bonners Ferry.

Much of the river valley, today an area of forests and farmlands, was little more than swamp until dikes were completed in the 1920s. Now, however, the valley's rich soils support a cooperative of 17 nurseries, as well as a huge hops farm owned by Anheuser-Busch.

SIGHTS

Boundary County Museum presents displays including a white caribou and remnants of both

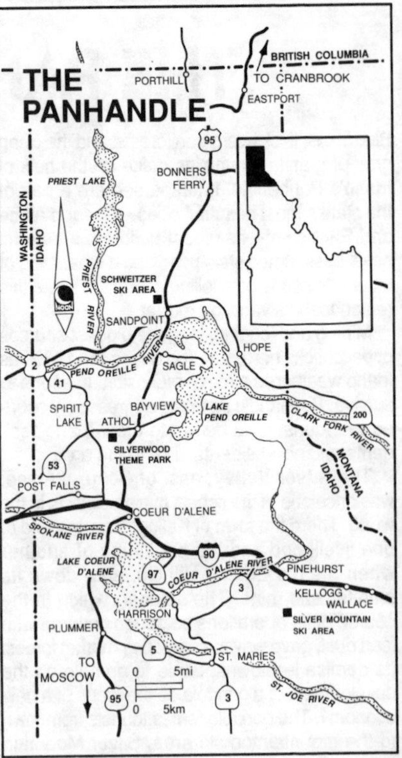

white and Native American history in the region. The museum, tel. 267-7720, is open daily 10:30 a.m.-4:30 p.m., from early May to late September. Admission is free but donations are requested. The museum is at Main Street's north end, across from city hall.

Elk Mountain Farms, owned and operated by Anheuser-Busch, the St. Louis-based brewing conglomerate, is the world's largest farm devoted to Hallertau hops. Elk Mountain covers 875 acres of the valley floor and contains its own processing plant. Hops give beer its aroma and bitter bite. The same fragrance scents the valley during the peak of harvesting in August and September. To arrange a tour, call 267-5840. The **Hops Stop Museum** at the farm presents a free introduction to hops lore; tel. 267-7353.

Kootenai National Wildlife Refuge preserves 2,762 acres of key waterfowl habitat just west of Bonners Ferry. The refuge is only open during daylight hours but offers excellent chances for wildlife-watching, hiking, fishing, and hunting (during the fall, generally from mid-October to December). The refuge office is open Mon.-Fri. 8 a.m.-4:30 p.m., tel. 267-3888.

McArthur Lake Wildlife Management Area, owned by the Idaho Fish and Game Department, covers 1,201 acres 15 miles south of Bonners Ferry along Hwy. 95. It offers another public access point for fishing, birdwatching, and hunting. No camping is allowed here.

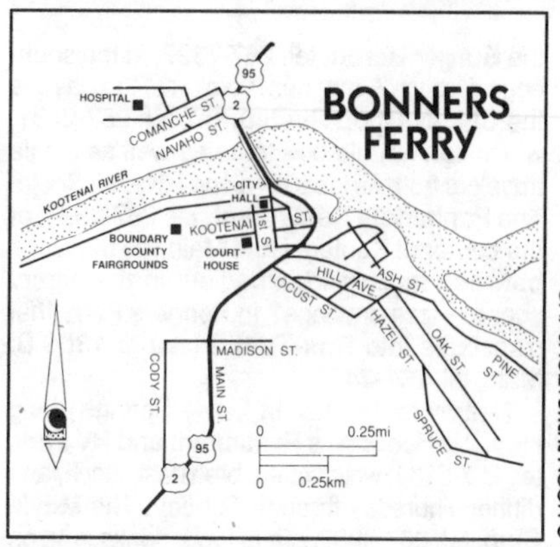

PRACTICALITIES

Accommodations

Just south of Bonners Ferry is the **Valley Motel,** tel. 267-7567, which offers snowmobile and golf specials. The rooms are clean and offer fireplaces, spa access, and cable TV movies. The **Town 'n' Country Motel** lies closer to town and offers kichenettes and a free airport shuttle, tel. 267-7915. The **Deep Creek Inn,** tel. 267-7578, has 12 cabins and a restaurant along the old Hwy. 95 scenic loop. Complete with cafe is the **Lantern Motel,** tel. 267-2422, along the highway south of town.

In Bonners Ferry, the best and most expensive of the motels is the **Kootenai River Inn,** tel. 267-8511 or toll free (800) 528-1234. The Best Western-affiliated inn offers 48 rooms with impressive views of the Kootenai River. The inn's **Springs Restaurant and Lounge** also has a great view, making it a good place for the weary road warrior to unwind. An indoor swimming pool and sauna, jacuzzi, steam room, and fitness room are available for those so inclined. The **Old Rose Inn,** tel. 267-2117, offers three rooms, all with private baths. The King Room is $75, Queen Room, $65, and Twin Room, $50. Prices include a full English breakfast. **Deep Creek Resort,** tel. 267-7587, offers a restaurant, 12 rental cabins along a stream, and a swimming pool. It's located along old Hwy. 95.

Campers have several choices. Five miles north of town, the **Smith Lake Campground,** operated by the Forest Service, has seven campsites and three picnic sites. Just south of town is a **KOA** concession with a hot tub, sauna, and swimming pool. A tent site or RV site without utilities costs $13 a night here; tel. 267-2422. **Blue Lake Camp & RV Park,** tel. 267-2029 or 267-5176, offers license-free fishing for pond-reared rainbow trout and bass. The Good Sam park provides clean showers, swimming, and laundry facilities.

Food

The two fanciest restaurants in town are the **Deep Creek Restaurant and Lounge,** tel. 267-7587, and the **Springs Restaurant and Lounge** at the Kootenai River Inn (see above). Both offer menus leaning to steak and seafood. Cafes and fast-food joints offering alternatives include **R Place** along S. Main, tel. 267-7347, with a basic burger and Mexican menu, and the **Burger Baron,** tel. 267-7397, at the south edge of town. A magnum version of the basic is the **Chic-N-Chop Restaurant,** tel. 267-2431, which can handle bus tours as well as single travelers from its location along Hwy. 95 South. The **Panhandle Restaurant,** tel. 267-2623, at the corner of Kootenai and Main fills the niche between fancy and expedient in the eatery scene. Pizza cravings? In Bonners Ferry that translates into **Rus-Teek Pizza** at 1306 S. Main, tel. 267-3471.

Nearby to the east in Moyie Springs along Hwy. 2 is **Hemlock's Restaurant and RV Park,** tel. 267-5184, which offers breakfast, lunch, and dinner Thursday through Sunday. The **Moyie Club,** tel. 267-9932, offers food, drinks, and on weekends, live music.

Entertainment And Events

The **Rex Theater** at 110 Main provides an opportunity for a cinema break. Theater of a different sort is offered by the **Boundary County Community Theater,** which stages local productions of famous plays in the auditorium of the old high school. Call the chamber of commerce, tel. 267-5922, for the latest on the theater group's activities.

Bonners Ferry folk waste no time in getting the year off to a festive start with January's **Winter Sports Festival** and snowmobile races that bring out the souped-up sleds. June brings the annual **Kootenai Indian Pow Wow,** a chance to share some of the Panhandle's native heritage.

In mid-July, Bonners Ferry celebrates **Kootenai River Days,** with events that have included a rodeo, fiddlers contest, raft races, and dances. The Boundary County Fair in September coincides with the start of another school year.

Recreation

Visitors with mountain bikes will find more terrain than they can cover in the 1,000 miles of dirt roads and trails around the area. **Bushwackin Action** at 1008½ S. Main St., tel. 267-3445, provides a local source of information about the best rides. They can also tell you how to hook up with the Fat Tire Friends club in town.

For those who can't resist the greens, the **Mirror Lake Golf Course** offers nine holes at par 36, with a pro shop, rentals, snack bar, and lounge. The golf course is south of town along Hwy. 95, tel. 267-5314.

River rafting and skiing are two other popular seasonal pastimes in the region. River rafting is popular on the Moyie River to the east of town. Outfitters include **River Odysseys West,** tel. 765-0841, and **Moyie River Outfitters,** tel. 267-2108. To rent cross-country ski equipment, try **Snow and Cycle Specialties,** tel. 267-2973, along Hwy. 95.

Information And Services

The Greater Bonners Ferry Chamber of Commerce operates a well-stocked visitor center at 205 E. Riverside, tel. 267-5922. Their mailing address is P.O. Box 275, Bonners Ferry, ID 83805. At **Bonner's Books,** 303 Main St., tel. 262-2622, the shelves hold volumes of information about the area. The ***Bonners Ferry Herald,*** tel. 267-5521, offers news of the town at 213 Main Street. City **police** and **ambulance** can be summoned by dialing 911. The Boundary County Sheriff's Department is located in the courthouse, tel. 267-3151. Any border crossing questions can be directed to the **U.S. Government Border Patrol** at 267-2734.

The **Boundary County Community Hospital and Nursing Home** offers emergency care and specialty clinics at 551 Kaniksu St., tel. 267-3141.

NORTH TO THE BORDER

Boundary County's 46-mile-long northern border separates Idaho from Canada. The mountainous, thickly forested county shares the rugged beauty of adjacent British Columbia, and bills itself as the last frontier in the lower 48 states and the gateway to Alaska. Forming part of Idaho's eastern border with Montana, Boundary County also claims to be the scenic route to Glacier National Park.

Eastport is the northern terminus of Hwy. 95—Idaho's longest north-south artery—and the site of one of Idaho's two border crossings into Canada. The border checkpoint here is open 24 hours. The other crossing, to the west at Porthill, is open 7 a.m.-11 p.m. Given the close ties between the U.S. and Canada, crossing the border involves minimal hassles. A valid driver's license is all U.S. citizens need for short forays into Canada of a week or two. One caution for those inclined to carry a pistol in the glovebox: don't try to cross the border with it. The Canadians have different ideas about firearms than do their cousins south of the border.

Camping

Even if Canada isn't the goal, visiting Idaho's northern marches has its rewards. The Forest Service maintains two campgrounds within a few miles of the border. Farthest north is the 16-unit **Copper Creek Campground,** two miles south of Eastport off Hwy. 95 along Forest Service Rd. 2517. It offers streamside campsites along the Moyie River and lies within a quarter mile of **Copper Creek Falls.** Seven miles south of Eastport lies the 10-unit **Robinson Lake Campground,** a third of a mile north of Hwy. 95 along Forest Service Rd. 449. The campground reclines along the shore of the 60-acre lake. A boat ramp and two picnic sites attract travelers and boaters as well.

To the southeast in the Purcell Mountains, the Forest Service offers a unique lodging opportunity: the **Deer Ridge Lookout Tower.** The tower, at an elevation of 4,755 feet, is available for rent July 1-Sept. 30 through the **Bonners Ferry Ranger District,** Rt. 4, Box 4860, Bonners Ferry, ID 83805, tel. 267-5561. Contact the ranger station to find out what dates are open and to complete the paperwork.

Long Canyon And Selkirk Crest

Long Canyon to the west is best reached by turning north on Idaho Hwy. 1 at its junction with U.S. Hwy. 95, less than a mile from the intersection at Copeland heading west toward Kerr Lake. Two miles after crossing the Kootenai River, turn north on the West Side Rd. (County Rd. 18). The **Long Canyon Trail** takes off to the southwest just after the road crosses Long Canyon Creek, eight miles from the "T." Long Canyon has long been a battleground between conservation groups and Idaho's timber industry. The last of North Idaho's major glacial valleys without a road, the canyon's forests remain intact. Whether the canyon will be designated as wilderness remains undecided. The canyon's beauty, however, makes it a worthy diversion or a destination in itself.

Long Canyon is one of the most pristine pathways to the Selkirk Crest, an alpine province of high mountain lakes, trout fishing, and spectacular scenery. The crest is home to the last wild herd of woodland caribou left in the lower 48 states. Since the mid-1980s, Canadian, state, and federal wildlife biologists have labored to capture caribou from Canadian herds and have released 60 in the Selkirks. If you should glimpse a caribou during your wanderings, feel fortunate. A majestic animal that once roamed across 11 northern-tier states from Washington to Maine, the caribou now lingers only here and in adjacent northeastern Washington.

Along the same lines, biologists are learning that the grizzly bear still roams the Cabinet Mountains along the Montana border, though no grizzly attacks have been recorded in the region. Prudence calls for following proper camp procedures, mainly keeping a clean camp, as insurance against confrontations.

PRIEST LAKE

Folks who live and work in the beauty permeating the Panhandle's Priest Lake country don't hesitate for a moment to call it Idaho's Crown Jewel. Year-round residents are few here, about 150 at last count, but vacationers are plentiful. Thousands flock here during summer for the clear waters, sandy beaches, and green forests; in winter for cross-country skiing, snowmobiling, snowshoeing, or just plain frolicking in the white stuff.

Priest Lake itself is actually a pair of lakes: lower Priest Lake, where resorts, communities, and roadside recreation prosper, and undeveloped upper Priest Lake, where tourists (we all wear that label here) get a taste of pre-settlement nature at its finest. It's true there are some campgrounds scattered along the shoreline of the upper lake, and one hears motorboats growl at times. But no roads billow with dust here, and going north from lower to upper lake on the riverlike passage between them is like traveling into a different era. Together, the two are 24 miles long and 14 miles across at the widest—the third-largest body of water in the Panhandle after lakes Pend Oreille and Coeur d'Alene.

The lake's name recalls Idaho's earliest recorded history. It was originally named to honor early Jesuit Father John Roothan. But when the Great Northern Railroad came to the area in 1891, the lake was renamed Priest Lake—presumably to make it easier to remember. Diamond Match Co. logged the area actively in the 1940s and '50s, operating a floating camp at the site of present-day **Priest Lake State Park** on the eastern shoreline. Tugs towed rafts of logs across the lake.

The history of Priest Lake has its bit of glitter, too. Nell Shipman, an early star of the silent screen, built a home and studio along the lakeshore, filming several features in the area. Shipman's love of animals led her to establish a private zoo at her home. A couple of years of the rugged life proved enough, however, and she moved away.

SIGHTS

Vinther-Nelson Cabin

Places to see at Priest Lake are wild and woodsy for the most part. One of the exceptions is the Vinther-Nelson Cabin on Eight Mile Island along the eastern shore just south of Indian Creek. Curtis and L. Crenshaw, two prospectors, built the cabin in 1897 to work their Deer Trail Lode mining claim. The diggings proved short-lived for the Crenshaws,

A dock provides entertainment enough for a young visitor to Priest Lake State Park.

who sold them to W.J. Anders on Jan. 1, 1898 for $65, a deal that included the claim, cabin, shop, cellar, smokehouse, and boathouse. The diggings were dry. Anders sold to Samuel Vinther and Nels Nelson, cousins from Spokane, Washington, in the summer of 1900. Their travel to the lake took three days, including stints by rail, horse-drawn buggy, and steamboat. The cabin survived because it was in constant use from 1906 to 1981 as a summer home by the cousins' descendants. The Forest Service now helps operate and maintain the cabin for visitors.

The cabin offers an excellent example of the type of log structures once built in the Priest Lake area. Some 25 by 29 feet, the cabin walls were shaped on the interior with a broadaxe. The corners were joined by mortise and tenon. The cabin and the island are accessible only by boat. A boat ramp and rentals are available at nearby **Indian Creek Marina,** tel. 443-2292.

Hanna Flats Cedar Grove

To view the forest as the Crenshaws could have seen it, the Forest Service offers the Hanna Flats Cedar Grove interpretive trail a mile west of Hwy. 57 from the Priest Lake Ranger Station. The cathedral-like grove of shadowy cedars, named for Jim Hanna and his family who homesteaded on the flats in 1921, survived a major wildfire in 1926 that burned more than 80,000 acres in the area. A detailed trail guide is available at the ranger station or at a register box at the trailhead. Wildflower lovers here will spot queen's cup, wild ginger, twinflower, Oregon fairy bell, and western trillium.

RECREATION

Outdoor pursuits at Priest Lake include golf, powerboating, sailing, windsurfing, fishing, water-skiing, hiking, and camping in the summer; snowmobiling, cross-country skiing, and even dogsled mushing in the winter.

Boating And Swimming

Boaters are the focus at **Bishop's Marina,** tel. 443-2469, which maintains a moorage and store and sells boat gas. Bishop's rents slips in the summer and stores boats for the winter. The marina sells boat licenses and operates a dump station for boats. **Blue Diamond Marina,** tel. 443-2240, operates at 230 E. Shore Rd. at Coolin. **Cavanaugh Bay Marina,** tel. 443-2095, and **Priest Lake Marina,** tel. 443-2405, are other marinas along the lake's southern and western shores. The **Granite Creek Marina,** tel. 443-2325, maintains a boat launch and sells gas. The marina also maintains a campground.

Boaters traveling the "Thorofare" between the upper and lower lakes in powerboats are required to proceed slowly through the no-wake area to protect the fragile shoreline. No water-skiing is permitted on Upper Priest Lake.

Swimmers are allowed along the lakeshore, but the Forest Service recommends against swimming outside marked swimming areas protected by buoys and markers. The recommendation is to help avoid accidents involving boats and water-skiers, in which the swimmer always loses. Marked swimming areas are at **Beaver Creek, Reeder, Ledgewood, Luby,** and **Outlet Bay** recreation areas. No lifeguards are posted. The Forest Service also advises that swimmers taking to the lake before July 1 will find the water uncomfortably cold.

Camping

Two Upper Priest Lake campgrounds, **Plowboy** with its four campsites at the upper lake's southwest end, and **Navigation** with its five campsites at the northwest end, draw campers throughout the summer. Both are accessible by boat or hiking trail only, and both sites have primitive outhouses but lack developed water supplies.

Island campgrounds are a unique feature of lower Priest Lake. **Kalispell Island,** just east of Kalispell Bay along the southwest shore, offers five small campgrounds (North Cove, Rocky Point, Schneider, Silver, and Three Pines camps) ranging in size from four to nine sites each, none with developed water.

The Forest Service also maintains four campgrounds along the lower lake's shoreline. From the south, the campgrounds include **Outlet,** with 28 campsites and a small swimming beach; **Osprey,** 17 campsites; **Luby Bay,** 52 campsites and four picnic sites, program amphitheater, swimming beach, and dump station; and **Reeder Bay,** 24 campsites and a swimming area. The agency also maintains the **Kalispell Bay boat launch** with a ramp, dock, and restrooms, and the **Ledgewood Bay picnic area** a mile north of Reeder Bay with 12 picnic tables, swimming area, and dressing rooms.

Priest Lake State Park offers three camping areas in the Priest Lake area. The first, **Dickensheet,** is along Priest River a mile from where Coolin Rd. branches off Hwy. 57. The campground is open April-October, and offers a raft or canoe launch area and 11 basic campsites with outhouses.

The **Indian Creek Unit,** midway up Priest Lake's eastern shore, is the park's biggest with 92 campsites, 11 offering all utilities, another 11 offering water and electricity. Indian Creek has hot showers, a dump station, boat launch and docks, swimming beach, picnic shelter, and drinking water. The Idaho Parks and Recreation Department accepts reservations at Indian Creek; call 443-2200 for details.

Twelve miles farther north is the **Lionhead Unit,** which holds 47 campsites. Drinking water, a boat ramp, and docks are available. One point of interest at Lionhead is the wreck of the *Tyee II,* which rests along the shoreline near the boat ramp. The vessel was an old tug that once pulled rafts of logs along the lake. Outmoded, her crew started a fire over deep water to scuttle her. She survived long enough to drift to shore where her spirit, if not her figure, survives decades later.

Lionhead has one of the few group camps in the state's park system. Essentially a remodeled lake cabin, the **Squaw Bay Group Camp** once housed Diamond Match Co. executives visiting the lake. The parks department charges a $20 reservation fee and $40-a-night rental with a two-night minimum. **Squaw Bay** also has 12 RV campsites with sewer and electricity, a shower building, group fire pit, beach, boat ramp, and kitchen. The cabin, which sleeps eight, has two bunk rooms. For reservations, call the park staff at Indian Creek, tel. 443-2200.

Fishing

Priest Lake Guide Service, tel. 443-2357, offers trips intended to trap Walter, the legendary lake trout. Priest Lake is known for yielding lakers that average 24 inches long, as well as cutthroat trout, a smaller fish that eagerly attacks artificial flies and lures. Kokanee, the tasty landlocked version of the sockeye salmon, are others' favorite quarry.

Golf

The **Priest Lake Golf Course,** tel. 443-2525, operates nine holes along Luby Bay. The course also offers a pro shop, bar and grill, and lessons.

Hiking

Hiking, picnicking, and camping are summer's other major pursuits along the lake and in the surrounding forests. One of the most popular jump-off points for hikers is the **Beaver Creek Recreation Site,** located at the north end of Forest Service Rd. 2512 at Priest Lake's upper end. Beaver Creek offers a 20-unit family campground and a 30-person group camp. No reservations are taken for the family campground, however the group campground can be reserved—contact the **Priest Lake Ranger District,** Rt. 5, Box 207, Priest River, ID 83856; tel. 443-2512.

Beaver Creek provides the main trailhead for overland access to upper Priest Lake. Canoeists and boaters with small boats that can be carried park here because of the easy access to the Thorofare.

Hikers taking off from Beaver Creek will find the **Navigation Trail, No. 291** starting from the trailhead parking area. The trail winds its way along the Thorofare, reaching the Plowboy Campground after 2.5 miles and the Navigation Campground after 5.5 miles. The trail is rated easy, and covers a total of 10 miles before it intersects Forest Service Rd. 1013. Deer may be spotted at **Armstrong Meadows** a mile north of Beaver Creek.

Other popular hikes in the area include the **Lakeshore Trail, No. 294,** and the **Beach Trail, No. 48,** both of which are rated easy. The Lakeshore Trail parallels the shoreline for 7.6 miles from Beaver Creek south to a trailhead two miles north of Reeder Bay. Users are limited to horseback riders and hikers. The Beach Trail runs nine miles along the shoreline from Kalispell Bay south to Hill's Resort.

Winter Sports

Winter brings different pursuits to the Priest River area. Snowmobilers will find hundreds of miles of groomed trails maintained by the **Ridgerunners Snowmobile Club.** The club's trails link into those maintained by other clubs, creating a network across northeastern Washington and northernmost Idaho. **Priest Lake**

Yamaha, tel. 443-2415, along Hwy. 57 caters to snowmobilers with equipment and repair services. **Hill's Resort,** tel. 443-2551, maintains cross-country skiing trails and rents cross-country skis. **Priest Lake State Park** also offers Nordic ski trails.

PRACTICALITIES

Accommodations

Priest Lake's western fringe is bordered with resorts. **Hill's Resort,** tel. 443-2551, at Luby Bay, the most southerly along the western shore, ranks as one of the most widely acclaimed with its restaurant, tennis court, and boating and swimming areas. Hill's has boat rentals ranging from fishing boats for $65 a day to canoes for $15 a day. Sailboards and Hobie cats are also available. Lodging ranges from one-bedroom housekeeping units that sleep two to three-bedroom cabins that sleep 10. Room rates vary from $49 to $83 a night. The summer season at the resort starts the last Saturday in June and ends the day after Labor Day.

Grandview Resort, tel. 443-2433, at Reeder Bay along the west-central shoreline, offers a swimming pool and dining and dancing. Smaller than Hill's, Grandview offers cabins and suites renting for $395-650 a week during summer. Fishing boats are available for $45 a day. A runabout equipped with a 40-horsepower outboard rents for $80 a day, a canoe for $10. No pets are allowed. Nearby is **Elkins on Priest Lake,** tel. 443-2432, which features a restaurant and log cabins. Rounding out this area's resort scene is the **Kaniksu Resort and Marina,** tel. 443-2609.

At Coolin on the lake's south end is **Outlet Bay Resort,** tel. 443-2444, which features steaks, seafood, and cocktails. Also perched on the southeast shoreline is the **Showboat Lodge,** tel. 443-2161, which offers motel rooms and kitchenettes, along with a restaurant and lounge. Along the lake's east side is the **Indian Creek Resort,** tel. 443-2292.

For campground information, see "Camping," above.

Food

Most of the resorts along the lakeshore have restaurants. But numerous cafes have also sprung up along Priest Lake, mostly at Coolin and Nordman. Coolin's **Blue Pelican,** tel. 443-2387, gives diners a seat on the waterfront and specializes in fresh seafood and steaks. At Luby Bay, **Frizzy O'Leary's Corner,** tel. 443-2203, has prime rib every Saturday night and pizza every day. Mexican cuisine can be found at **Millie's Cocktail Lounge and Mexican Restaurant,** tel. 443-2365. **Marinos Italian Restaurant,** tel. 443-2405, operates at Kalispell Bay.

Events

Priest Lake abandons the old year and christens the new each winter with the **Ridgerunners Snowmobile Poker Run** on Dec. 31. The annual **sled dog races,** which have served as the U.S. Pacific Championship, follow in January. February brings the **snowshoe, softball, and volleyball finals** and the Sportsman's Club **Ice Fishing Derby.** In March, the Ridgerunners return with their annual **Fun Day.**

Memorial Day prompts Priest Lake residents and visitors alike to join in the annual **Spring Festival.** The festival features a flotilla, golf and pool tournaments, canoe races, fun run, and carnival. The Fourth of July holiday sparks the Wooden Boat Club to buff up its mahogany and teak for its annual barbecue, **Midnight Cruise,** and fireworks display. The annual **Firecracker Open Golf Tournament** and **Sportsmen's Club Fishing Derby** keep things hopping in July.

August at Priest Lake brings the **Priest Lake Fire Department Band Concert** on the Elkins Resort lawn, in concert with the **Antique and Classic Boat Show** the same day, the same place. September offers the annual **Wooden Boat Parade,** beginning at the Showboat Lodge, and Priest Lake Yacht Club's **Gin Fizz Barbecue.**

Information And Services

The **Priest Lake Chamber of Commerce,** tel. 443-3191, is located at Steamboat Bay Rd. No. 121, Coolin, ID 83821.

Emergency services at Priest Lake include the **Priest Lake Ambulance,** tel. 263-3136; **Bonner County Sheriff,** tel. 263-3136; **Newport Hospital,** (Washington), tel. (509) 447-2441; **Coolin Medical Center,** tel. 443-2939; and **fire reporting lines,** tel. 443-2551 (Hill's Resort) or 443-2090.

PRIEST RIVER COUNTRY

The first settlers arrived in this verdant valley along the Priest River in 1888, then fled for higher ground after the spring floods threatened to float them away. In 1891 the Great Northern Railroad arrived.

Priest River flourished as a railroad and logging town in its early years. Among the first townsfolk was a thriving community of Italian-born railroad workers who were noted for their neatly tended gardens. Although the economy subsequently grew in other directions, tidy gardens still mark the Pend Oreille River valley.

As the rails' glimmer showed streaks of rust and timber markets drooped, the town's status as the gateway to Priest Lake infused new life. Today, Priest River still has plenty of bustle. With its busy gas stations and grocery stores, it serves as a major provisioning point for vacationers.

Albeni Falls Dam

Located five miles west of town along Hwy. 2, Albeni Falls Dam was built by the U.S. Army Corps of Engineers in the early 1950s to regulate the level of Lake Pend Oreille, 25 miles upstream on the Pend Oreille River. In 1955, the dam began producing kilowatts. The dam's generating gallery is open to the public. Most visitors, however, are attracted to the popular recreation areas upriver.

Camping

Riley Creek Campground, just east of Priest River, has 68 campsites, picnic and swimming areas, a boat ramp, drinking water, playground, children's wading area, dressing house, and trailer dump station.

Springy Point Campground, farther east toward Sandpoint, holds 36 campsites along the Pend Oreille River with amenities similar to Riley Creek. **Priest River Campground** offers 17 campsites, a playground, showers, drinking water, and a changing house. A $3-a-night camping fee is charged at all three campgrounds.

Strong's Island between Priest River and the dam provides 10 campsites, drinking water, and restrooms. It is accessible only by boat.

Golf

Golfers have their chance to enjoy the Priest River area at the **Ranch Club Golf Course,** tel. 448-1731, with nine holes and a pro shop. The course is a mile west of Priest River along Hwy. 2.

Rafting And Canoeing

In May and June, when the winter's snows are charging toward the Pacific Ocean, Priest River is more than most boaters would want to handle—during high water, Binarch and Eight Mile rapids are extremely hazardous. In late summer, however, the river's 44 miles are exciting, yet offer few dangers.

The Forest Service's **Priest Lake Ranger District,** tel. 443-2512, offers a map of popular public-access points and camp spots along the river. For a short family excursion in late summer, one of the most popular outings begins at **Saddler Creek,** three miles north of Priest River near where the U.S. Geological Survey maintains a gauging station. State land there provides an undeveloped access area. It takes an hour and a half to float down to Priest River Park at the town.

Accommodations

Priest River's most interesting getaway is **Mountain Meadows,** tel. 448-2174, along Bear Paw Road. The other choice in town is the **Priest River Motel,** tel. 448-9985, at 1221 Albeni Road. To the east at Laclede is **River Birch Farm,** tel. 263-3705, a bed and breakfast halfway to Sandpoint along the Pend Oreille River. The farm's rates are $50 a day, $225 for five days, and $300 for a week. Guests receive a full breakfast and use of a jacuzzi and dock facilities, including a canoe and rowboat.

Food

For its size, Priest River offers an impressive assortment of cafes and restaurants. **AJ's Country Kitchen,** tel. 448-2609, at 215 High St., and **Aardvark's Pizza,** tel. 448-1931, at 208 Railroad Ave., attract a local clientele. The **Corner Cafe,** tel. 448-1741, boasts a fireplace, homemade pies and soups, and breakfast all day. Another notable is the **River Pigs Inn,** tel. 448-1097, in the Main Street Marketplace at 114 Main, with its bakery and deli. More upscale is the **Wikel House,** tel. 448-1972, along Riverside Rd., which accepts diners only by reservation. The **Riverview Restaurant,** tel. 448-1691,

911 Albeni Rd., just before the junction of highways 2 and 57, offers a menu of prime rib, barbecue, steaks, seafood, and pasta, with an auxiliary offering of pizza for the kids.

Or for another steakhouse, this one with a view, head west along Hwy. 2 to **Cedars Steakhouse,** tel. 437-4046, at Oldtown along the Idaho-Washington border and just across the river from Newport, Washington.

Information And Services

The **Priest River Chamber of Commerce,** tel. 448-2721, maintains both a downtown office and an information booth along the highway for visitors. Finding the police in Priest River means going to city hall at 15 High St. or calling 448-1512. Emergency medical care can be obtained by calling the **Priest River EMT** at 448-1960.

SANDPOINT

Explorer David Thompson noted the sandy point extending into Lake Pend Oreille here. The name Sandpoint stuck in 1880 when Robert Weeks opened a general store and the community grew along the northwest shoreline. This scenic city grew up the way most towns in timbered areas do: it had a long history of sawmills before it reached middle age. The railroads came through, too. At one point, three railroads made tracks through here.

Sandpoint's greatest surge of growth was during the 1970s when the population of surrounding Bonner County jumped by 55% and the village along the lake was discovered. Although still small (some 5,000 residents live here year-round), Sandpoint bustles during both summer and winter with those attracted by its outdoors amenities. The lake, of course, draws most of the attention. But when winter begins dropping snow in the high country, Schweitzer Ski Area 11 miles to the north starts drawing the crowds.

The ski area and the lake reflect what locals enthusiastically call a "four-season climate." That means hot in the summer, cold in the winter, and in between the rest of the time. Sandpoint can get cold in the winters, down below zero when Arctic cold seeps south. Hot in the summer means temperatures in the 90s. The best part about Idaho's climate in general, however, is that even in the summers, the humidity remains low. That makes for pleasant evenings and cool nights.

SIGHTS

Museums

Logging was big in the early days of Sandpoint, and the **Bonner County Historical Museum** at Lakeview Park, 609 S. Ella St., tel. 263-2344, reflects that heritage. Open Tues.-Sat. 10 a.m.-4 p.m., the museum displays a collection of artifacts and maintains a library of books, pamphlets, photographs, and newspapers depicting the county's history. The Bonner County Historical Society operates the museum. Adults pay $1 and students 50 cents for admission.

The Vintage Wheels Museum, tel. 263-7173, occupies a storefront at Third and Cedar streets downtown. Open daily 9:30 a.m.-5:30 p.m., it contains an extensive collection of antique cars ranging from the venerable Model T to the Stanley Steamer. The museum also houses an extensive collection of refurbished horse-drawn buggies. The **Company Store** art gallery and gift shop is part of the building. It sells Christmas specialties and Idaho goods ranging from souvenirs to local pottery, artwork, and foods.

City Beach

Sandpoint makes the most of its waterfront location by protecting a quarter mile of white-sand beach along its eastern quarter. The beach is a popular hangout for locals and visitors alike during the warm summers. You'll find boating, swimming, water-skiing, volleyball, tennis, horseshoes, picnic tables, playgrounds, a kiddie pool, and public boat launch here. For more information call 263-3158.

Round Lake State Park

Round Lake is a compact park of 142 acres that offers hiking, fishing, and camping. The main feature of the park is Round Lake itself, where anglers happily pursue a variety of fishes ranging from trout to bass. Round Lake is open year-round, and during the summer it offers nature programs. The **Swamp Tromp,** a self-guided nature trail, offers a diversion for camping

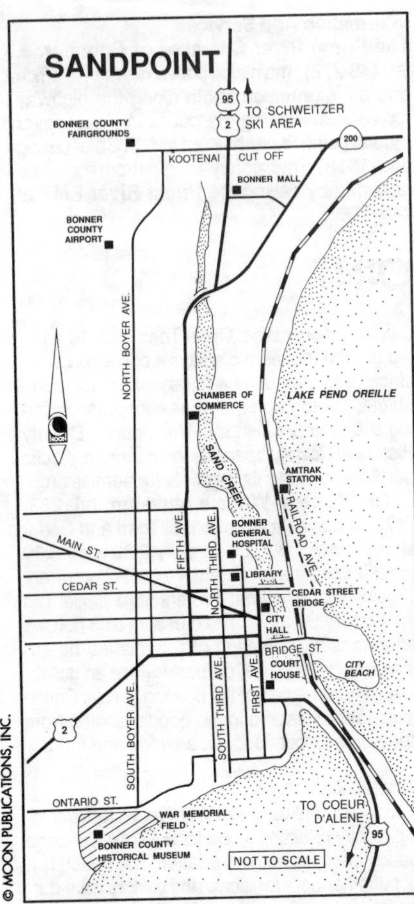

kids with nothing to do. The **Trappers Trail** provides kids and parents with a longer diversion as it makes a two-mile circuit around the lake. The park, tel. 263-3489, is 12 miles southwest of Sandpoint. Take Hwy. 95 10 miles south, then turn west along Dufort Rd. and continue two miles to the park.

RECREATION

Skiing

Water in one form or another makes Sandpoint what it is for outdoor sports. As snow, it attracts thousands of skiers to **Schweitzer Mountain Resort,** tel. 263-9555 or (800) 831-8810, each winter. Powder's the name of the game here—the management will happily tell you it's the Northwest's driest snow. The resort has set out to become one of the region's premier ski destinations. Their slopes include 2,400 vertical feet of ski terrain, 48 named runs, and 20 powder chutes. The mountain offers a good variety of terrain, rated 20% beginner, 50% intermediate, 25% advanced, and 5% expert. Schweitzer's longest run is the Great Divide at 2.7 miles.

During good snow years, more than 300 inches cloak Schweitzer's runs. To handle the crowds, Schweitzer offers one high-speed quad lift and five double chairlifts. Presenting a breathtaking view of Lake Pend Oreille in clear weather, the resort guarantees skiers a satisfactory outing. "If skiing or snow conditions do not meet your expectations, simply return your lift ticket within one hour of purchase, pick up a snow check, and ski free on us the next time," the area's skier guarantee states. Schweitzer also offers night skiing Thursday through Saturday.

Full-day lift tickets at Schweitzer are $32 for adults 18 and older, $25 for juniors age 7-17, and $23 for seniors 65 and older. Schweitzer has modified its previous frequent-skier program with a Great Escapes offering. Adults who buy the $100 membership can ski 15 times during the season for $15 a day. Junior and senior skiers pay $75 to ski 15 times during the season for $12 a day. Children six and younger ski free. Child care is available for $15-20 a day. Children's ski lessons range $20-30 a day. Ski and snowboard rentals are available at **The Alpine Shop.** An adult downhill-ski package rents for $20 a day; snowboards are $15.

For those devoted to skinny skis, Schweitzer also offers eight km of groomed trails. Cross-country packages rent for $6-9 a day for children and adults respectively.

Other rental agencies include **Alpine Boat and Ski Shop,** tel. 263-5157, at 213 Church, and **5th Ave. Board and Ski,** tel. 263-5821, which rents downhill and cross-country equipment as well as snowboards. **The Outdoor Experience,** tel. 263-6028, at 314 N. First Ave. also rents cross-country skiing equipment.

Schweitzer accommodations on the hill include two hotels, **Green Gables Lodge** and

SCHWEITZER MOUNTAIN RESORT PHOTO BY R.J. O'NEILL

A skier negotiates Schweitzer's powder.

Overnighter Lodge, and six condominium complexes with lodgings for parties of four to eight. The resort offers lodging-and-lift ticket packages of three and five days at prices ranging $109-360 a day per person.

Sleigh Rides

What would winter be without a sleigh ride? **Hidden Valley Ranch,** tel. 263-3538, is south of Sandpoint at 3665 Dufort Rd. (just past Round Lake State Park). The ranch offers sleigh rides for $8 a person, $50 minimum. During the summer, the ranch offers covered-wagon rides for the same prices.

Hiking And Biking

A walking and bicycling trail starts at the Bonner County Courthouse at the east end of Lake Street. The trail parallels Hwy. 95 south of the city and crosses two miles of open water via the old highway bridge across the Pend Oreille River. The bicycle path also includes Lignite Road.

The **Mineral Point Trail,** a hiking trail maintained by the Forest Service's Sandpoint Ranger District, tel. 263-5111, provides a self-guided introduction to the northern Idaho forest along the western shore of Lake Pend Oreille. The trail is 10 miles east from the Sagle Rd. junction with Hwy. 95, which is five miles south of Sandpoint.

At **Schweitzer Mountain Resort,** summers begin officially in mid-June and end in early September. Adults ride the chairlifts for $6; children and senior citizens ride for $4. Mountain-bike trails pitch and yaw through the 2,400 acres managed by the resort. Rental bikes, complete with helmets, are available for $10 for a half day and $15 for a full day.

Mountain-bike rentals are also available in downtown Sandpoint from **The Outdoor Experience,** tel. 263-6028, at 314 N. First Avenue. The shop is open daily. **5th Ave. Bikes,** tel. 263-5821, is also open daily at 219 N. 5th Avenue.

Boating

Windbag Marina, tel. 263-7811, at Sandpoint's City Beach does a swell job of trying to cover all of today's numerous watersports options. Windbag offers sailboats, sailboards, canoes, paddleboats, and accessories for sale or rent. Its staff also conducts lessons for landlubbers who want to learn.

Elsewhere in Sandpoint, **The Boatworks,** tel. 263-1808, at 8235 Sunnyside Rd., and **Bottle Bay Resort and Marina,** tel. 263-5916, at 1360 Bottle Bay Rd., cater to the nautical crowd. **Sandpoint Marina,** tel. 263-1493, at East Lake offers sailors its services, too. **Mountain Sail,** tel. 263-7475, boasts that their *Flying Scot* is the best 19-foot family sailboat around and offers demonstrations and lessons.

Golf

Sandpoint offers enthusiasts two golf courses. **Hidden Lakes Golf Course,** tel. 263-1642, has 18 holes with an abundance of water hazards and sand bunkers. Hidden Lakes is eight miles east of Sandpoint along Hwy. 200 at 8840 Lower Pack River Road. Closer to town is the **Elks Golf Course,** tel. 263-4321, 1.25 miles east of town along Hwy. 200.

Fishing

Based to the east of Sandpoint at Kootenai along Hwy. 2, **Seagull Charters,** tel. 263-2770, runs fishing charters for up to 10 anglers at a time on Lake Pend Oreille, which is noted for its giant kamloops rainbow trout. A 37-pound kamloops from the lake holds the record as Idaho's biggest rainbow trout catch. Seagull operates a 34-foot boat with a 12-foot beam, a substantial boat for a substantial lake that can generate some big waves. The boat is also wheelchair accessible. **Trophy Trout Charters,** tel. 683-2960, is based at Sandpoint. Anglers can write to P.O. Box 1812, Sandpoint, ID 83864, for more information. **Mehler Fishing Charters,** tel. 263-1012, also chases kamloops. Brochures can be requested from P.O. Box 1465, Sandpoint, ID 83864. For private boaters, the guides can be a source of information about fishing along the lake, and folks at the marinas generally are tuned into what's happening on the water.

Horseback Riding

Caribou Creek Morgan Horse Ranch, tel. 263-4500, provides trail riding in the Selkirk Mountains along Upper Pack River and Caribou Creek aboard America's horse, the Morgan.

ACCOMMODATIONS AND FOOD

Motels

Sandpoint's status as a resort community is most responsible for its wide selection of lodgings. Visitors come here to enjoy themselves, and the motels try to keep that in mind. **Lakeside Inn,** tel. (800) 543-8126 or 263-3717, at 106 Bridge St. ties for the largest motel with 60 rooms with rates from $39-89. The Lakeside is next to the city park and has boat docks. The motel has both inside and outside spas and saunas. Private balconies have water views. **Super 8 Motel,** tel. (800) 843-1991 or 263-2210, also offers 60 rooms. Located a mile north of Sandpoint along Hwy. 95, its prices ($30-38) and amenities (cable television and phones in the rooms) rank below the Lakeside's.

Quality Inn Sandpoint, tel. (800) 635-2534 or 263-2111, at 807 N. Fifth Ave., boasts the city's only indoor pool, as well as the **Fifth Avenue Restaurant** and **Mitzy's** lounge. Its 57 rooms range $32-58. **The Edgewater Resort Motor Inn,** tel. (800) 635-2534 or 263-3194, perches along the lakeshore with its 55 rooms. It includes the **Beach House Restaurant,** a lounge, conference rooms, a jacuzzi, saunas, and tanning booths. Rates range $42-90.

Connie's Motor Inn, tel. 263-9581, is part of the Best Western chain. Located at 323 Cedar St., it's an easy walk to downtown shops. The 54-room motel with rates of $45-85 offers guests a conference room, lounge, dining room, coffee shop, whirlpool bath, and outdoor heated swimming pool. **The Monarch,** tel. (800) 543-8193 or 263-1222, rounds out the big motels in town with its 49 units. Located next to the Bonner Mall, the Monarch, with rates of $23-32, is along Hwy. 95 north of town.

Other Sandpoint digs include the **K2 Motel,** tel. 263-2441, at 501 N. Fourth, with rates of $25-38 and kitchenettes, and the **Best Spa Motel,** tel. 263-3532, downtown at 521 N. Third Ave., with rates ranging $20-50, offering paddle boat and bike rentals. The **Lucky Inn,** tel. 263-3333, is 14 miles from Schweitzer and offers a hot tub and in-room microwaves and refrigerators. It also offers a play area for children, and a picnic area. Rooms run $20-32.

Outside of town is the **S&W Motel,** tel. 263-5979, at 3480 Hwy. 200 east of Sandpoint, with kitchenettes and rates ranging $22-30. North of Sandpoint are the condos offered by **Schweitzer Mountain Resort,** tel. 263-9555 or (800) 831-8810, with units, some with hot tubs, ranging $65-200; and the **Overnighter Lodge,** tel. 263-9564, with rates of $35-65.

Bed And Breakfast Inns

Sandpoint offers a couple of bed and breakfast establishments. **Osprey Cove Bed & Breakfast** on Lake Pend Oreille, tel. 265-4200, is at 8680 Sunnyside. The **Angel of the Lake Bed and Breakfast,** tel. 263-0816, is at 410 Railroad Avenue. All of its rooms come with private baths for $75 a night, which includes a full breakfast. Guests should check in advance about bringing children.

Campgrounds And Picnic Areas

In addition to Round Lake State Park (see "Sights," above), several other campgrounds can be found in the area.

The **Sandpoint KOA,** tel. 263-4824, is five miles south of Sandpoint along Sagle Road. The KOA offers shaded pull-through campsites, hot showers, a picturesque laundry room, and outdoor swimming pool.

Garfield Bay Recreation Area is eight miles east of Hwy. 95 along Sagle Road. It has 27 campsites, nine picnic sites, drinking water, boat ramp, and toilets. Two miles to the east of Garfield Bay along Forest Service Rd. 532 is **Green Bay Campground.** Green Bay offers three tent pads, six picnic tables, and outhouses. Across Lake Pend Oreille and 10 miles south of Garfield Bay is **Whiskey Rock Bay Campground,** which offers nine campsites, four picnic sites, a dock, beach, and outhouses. The campground can also be reached by taking Forest Service Rd. 278 southwest 30 miles from Clark Fork.

In addition to those campgrounds, there are a couple of maintained picnic areas where no camping is allowed, but you can spread out the blanket, open the picnic basket, and invite the ants to join you. The Sandpoint Ranger District, tel. 263-5111, offers the **Evans Landing Picnic Ground,** which is eight miles south of Garfield Bay along Lake Pend Oreille's western shore. The picnic area has two picnic tables, an outhouse, and a beach. Six miles south along the lakeshore from Garfield Bay is the **Maiden Rock Picnic Ground,** which can be reached only by boat. Maiden Rock offers four picnic sites, outhouses, and a beach.

Food

Restaurants in Sandpoint include **Arthur's Chick-N-Fish Delivers,** tel. 263-3474, at Fifth and Cedar, a takeout joint, and **Bottle Bay Resort and Marina,** tel. 263-5916, at 1360 Bottle Bay Rd., which features open-air dining on the lake and a pleasant lunch and dinner menu. Old Southern pit barbecue can be found just south of town across the Hwy. 95 bridge at the **Long Horn Barbecue,** tel. 263-5064. **Big Joe's,** tel. 263-5732, advertises "tasty home cookin'" and sticks to a basic menu of chicken, soups, steaks, and sandwiches at 202 N. Second Avenue. For a good cup of coffee, the **Coffee Mill,** 504 Oak, tel. 263-0846, draws fans on the strength of its espresso. For fast food, **The Cupboard,** tel. 263-9012, offers a homegrown alternative at 116 N. Second Avenue. Breakfast and lunch are the specialties at the **East West Cattle Co. Cafe,** tel. 263-5083. The **Fabulous Fifties Fountain,** tel. 263-0853, sells ice cream, burgers, fries, sandwiches, and yogurt at 109 Cedar.

Among Sandpoint's distinctive restaurants is the **Hydra,** tel. 263-7123, at 115 Lake, which features prime rib, steaks, and seafood at prices ranging $5-16. The Hydra lets kids eat at half-price and is open Mon.-Sat. 5-10:30 p.m. **Ivano's Restaurante Italiano,** tel. 263-0211, offers an impressive Italian menu ranging from veal to tortellini at 124 S. Second. **Jose Stromboli's,** tel. 263-2852, has pizza, Mexican food, and Italian pasta available to eat there, at 710 Pine, or for takeout. **Garden Restaurant,** tel. 263-5187, at 15 E. Lake, overlooks the Sandpoint Marina and features international cuisine. The Garden's wine list is among the most impressive in the Panhandle. Pizza means **Papandrea's Pizzeria,** tel. 263-9321, at 215 S. Second, or **Riccardo's Pizza,** tel. 263-6764, at 223 Cedar for many Sandpointers and visitors. **Savory's,** tel. 263-8588, in the Cedar Street Bridge Public Market offers soups, gyros, espresso, and seafood. The **Whistle Stop Donut and Coffee Co.,** tel. 263-7474, at 312 N. First offers a cozy stop mornings and for lunch.

For those with revelry on their minds, **Bugatti's,** tel. 263-4796, at 105 S. First Ave. labels itself "A Pub of Distinction" and boasts the best selection of beer in northern Idaho.

For budding herbalists, Sandpoint offers the **Peaceable Kingdom Herb Farm,** 8375 Rapid Lightning Rd., tel. 263-8038, where one can visit an herb shop, buy herbs, explore herb gardens, and take part in workshops. The farm is open summers only, Fri.-Sun. 10 a.m.-5 p.m.

OTHER PRACTICALITIES

Entertainment And Events

The **Cinema 4 West,** tel. 263-5811, is at 401 Oak Street. Stage productions can be seen at the **Panida Theatre,** tel. 263-9191, where the Unicorn Theatre Players present summer dramas in July and August. The **Pend Oreille Arts Council,** tel. 263-3169, also presents events at the venerable Panida. In addition, the council sponsors free classical-music concerts and an arts-and-crafts fair in mid-August.

Sandpoint's economy relies heavily on tourism, so the town offers plenty in the way of festivals. January here kicks off the season with the **Winter Carnival** the third and fourth weekends of the month. **Schweitzer Ski Area,** north of town, celebrates the Winter Festival with enthusiasm and a cross-country ski race, face painting, fireworks, and a torchlight parade. Ice sculptures turn the area into a fantasy land—as if all the festivities at midwinter weren't unreal enough for those who question the wisdom of winter at all.

February brings the **Mardi Gras,** during which the weather usually conspires to drive the revelers indoors.

April's offering is the **K&K Fishing Derby,** when anglers set out to probe the lake's depths for kokanee—the landlocked sockeye salmon that sometimes stretch a foot in length—and kamloops, the monster rainbows that need no introduction.

Sweet May, when the world seems sure it's ready for spring, brings out the boaters and **Waterfest,** with its Sand Creek Challenge Run and Fifties celebrations.

Summer means music at Sandpoint, first in July with the **Bluegrass Festival,** typically held the last weekend in concert with the opening of the three-week **Festival at Sandpoint.** The festival features classical-music workshops, recitals, and evening concerts along the waterfront. Also during August is the **Sandpoint Arts and Crafts Festival,** which encourages artists in the region to display their works at 20 locations around town.

Oktoberfest brings out the crowds in October for a Bavarian-style celebration of fall. The **International Draft Horse Show** shows off various breeds of draft horses—the blockbusters of the equine world weighing 1,500-2,400 pounds at maturity.

December means Christmas, specifically **Hometown Christmas,** at Sandpoint. Schweitzer Mountain celebrates the season with a torchlight parade on the slopes.

Shopping

If you can't ski, you shop, right? Sandpoint has plenty of shops to browse in while off the boat or the slopes. At First Ave. and Cedar in the heart of downtown is **The Cedar Street Bridge,** tel. 263-0502, which is open daily 10 a.m.-5 p.m. and features 14 specialty shops ranging from restaurants to an art gallery in its 350-foot span across Sand Creek. **Foster's Crossing,** tel. 263-5911, at 509 Oak St. comprises nine shops selling antiques, jewelry, books, and balloons. For the mall set, **Bonner Mall,** tel. 263-4272, occupying the triangle between Hwy. 95 and Hwy. 200 north of town, is open daily with climate-controlled shopping and 35 stores. A roller rink gives shoppers something to do that doesn't involve charge cards.

Transportation

Sandpoint is easier to get to than any other Idaho town north of Boise, in one respect at least. Amtrak calls here. The station serves as a whistle stop for the **Empire Builder** as it shuttles between Seattle and Chicago. The depot is located on Railroad Avenue. For reservations or scheduling, call (800) 872-7245.

More basic for those trying to reach other Idaho cities is bus service provided by **Empire Bus Lines,** tel. 263-7721, at 402 Fifth Avenue. Innercity transportation is provided by **Sandpoint Area Transit,** tel. 263-7287, and by **Bonner Cab Co.,** tel. 263-7626, and **City Taxi,** tel. 263-9330.

Air travel to Sandpoint is still restricted to charter flights, although major improvements to the **Sandpoint General Aviation Airport,** tel. 263-9102, may herald the arrival of a commuter airline. **Sandpoint Aviation,** tel. 263-9102, at the airport offers airplane rentals and scenic flights.

For motorists, Hwy. 95 is fast becoming a congested thoroughfare where getting there can't equal the fun of being there. It's 50 miles south on Hwy. 95 from Sandpoint to Coeur d'Alene and the junction with I-90.

Information And Services

The **Greater Sandpoint Chamber of Commerce,** tel. 263-2161, offers information at its headquarters along Hwy. 95 north of town or by mail at P.O. Box 928, Sandpoint, ID 83864.

Bonner General Hospital, tel. 263-1441 for general business and 265-4733 for the emergency room, is located at 520 N. Third Ave. and is a full-service hospital.

The Bonner County Courthouse at the east end of Lake St. houses the **Sheriff's Office,** tel. 263-3136. **Sandpoint Police and Fire Department,** located at Main and N. Second Ave. may be summoned by dialing 911. For non-emergency business, call the police or fire department at 263-3158.

HOPE AND BEYOND

Hope could be considered the "birthplace of Idaho"—it was the site of the first building constructed by explorers in the territory. David Thompson, a Northwest Fur Co. partner, came down from Canada in 1808 while exploring the Kootenai River country. Thompson was talented as both a geographer and a surveyor. He explored and mapped the Northwest's interior for the company, communicating the region's extensive resources. Thompson began fur trading at Lake Pend Oreille on Sept. 8, 1809, wheeling and dealing with the local Pend d'Oreille tribe, named for their pendulous earlobes. His party built a fur-trading outpost, **Kullyspell House,** along the shoreline near the main channel of the Clark Fork River and Memaloose Island. The log building has long since crumbled, but its significance as the first white fur-trading outpost in the Pacific Northwest remains.

Thompson later abandoned Kullyspell House in favor of Spokane House, in what would later be Washington state. His presence in the area is commemorated with a monument at Hope and the David Thompson Game Preserve on the peninsula jutting into the lake between Ellisport Bay and Denton Slough.

Two settlements sprang up along the lake's northeast shoreline in the general vicinity, Hope and Clark Fork. Both are reached via Hwy. 200 and have capitalized on their scenic settings. Hope, along Lake Pend Oreille, offers one of the densest concentrations of lakeside resorts in Idaho. Clark Fork is most notable as the home of the University of Idaho's Clark Fork Field Station, a beacon for budding naturalists or those who want to learn more about the region's ornithology, geology, mycology, or botany in a relaxed setting.

A roadside historical sign along Hwy. 200 notes that this valley was formed by glaciers. In the Pleistocene epoch, about 15,000 years ago, the ridges of ice were as high as mountains, and backed up waters 800-1,000 feet at Missoula, Montana. Glacial Lake Missoula, as the inland sea was known, finally breached its ice dam, but Lake Pend Oreille persists as a memory of the sea that once was.

SIGHTS

The **Cabinet Gorge Dam** east of Clark Fork along Hwy. 200 impounds a reservoir 200 feet deep and 24 miles long. A Washington Water Power Co. hydroelectric plant, the dam is less than a half mile from the Montana border.

To compensate for the loss of fish to Lake Pend Oreille, a consortium of entities built the **Cabinet Gorge Fish Hatchery** across the river from the main highway just west of the dam. Turn south less than a mile from Clark Fork and cross the river to reach the hatchery, which is open for public viewing. The **Spring Creek Fish Hatchery** north of Clark Fork raises trout for release in the lake. The hatchery is near the **Whitedelf Mines,** which yielded lead and silver and gave Clark Fork its start early this century.

The **Clark Fork Wildlife Management Area** at the delta of the Clark Fork River offers boating access to the south channel and the lake. Primitive camping is permitted here by the Idaho Fish and Game Department, which owns the Johnson Creek access point.

A mile and a half north of the Chevron station in Clark Fork is the University of Idaho **Clark Fork Field Campus,** tel. 266-1452. A small museum in the administration building of this former Forest Service experiment station maintains a collection of animal, plant, and geological specimens from the area. Programs at the field campus range from a weekend program about animal tracks and winter ecology in January to courses about rocks and minerals or fly-tying. The Boston-based Elderhostel program has held sessions about backcountry botanizing here. To obtain a schedule of programs, write Clark Fork Series, College of Forestry, Wildlife and Range Science, University of Idaho, Moscow, ID 83843.

PRACTICALITIES

Accommodations

When Panhandle residents want to take a break, Hope is where they're apt to end up. Resorts here are plentiful. **Blue Spruce Lodge,** tel. 264-5512, which has seven rooms for $37.50-50; and **Driftwood Resort,** tel. 264-5214, with rooms for $30-40, are popular choices. **Pend Oreille Shores Resort,** tel. 264-5211, offers a time-share option, in addition to as-available rentals of its 50 units starting at $119-159 a night. Off-season specials are available. **Rainbow Resort,** tel. 264-5412, has kitchenettes for $80-100, and **Red Fir Resort,** tel. 264-5287, offers a dozen cabins for $55-100 a night.

Clark Fork offers a twist on the resort scene with the **Diamond T Working Guest Ranch,** tel. 266-1186, which rents six cabins for $25-70.

Camping

All the campgrounds here offer variations on a theme, the main melody featuring water, relaxation, boats, and RVs. **Beyond Hope Resort,** tel. 264-5251, ranks as one of the classics with its 90 campsites priced at $12-14 a night. **Island View Resort,** tel. 264-5509, is located at 300 Island View and is two miles south along Samowen Road. It offers 64 spaces at $15-20. **Jeb and Margaret's Trailer Haven,** tel. 264-5406, has 125 camping spaces for $14.

Elsewhere, the **River Delta Resort,** tel. 266-1335, has 55 campsites for $12.50 a night. The **River Lake Trailer Resort,** tel. 266-1115, offers 31 campsites for $11 a night.

Campers flock to the **Samowen Campground** south of Hope along the shoreline. It's operated by the **Sandpoint Ranger District,** tel. 263-5111. The campground offers fishing, swimming, and boating in Lake Pend Oreille from its 56 campsites. The area has eight group picnic sites and 18 family picnic units. A covered picnic shelter is also available.

Food

Some of the region's better restaurants, many with great views, help bolster Hope's popularity. **Thompson's North Bay Landing,** tel. 264-5514, offers lunch and dinner. The menu focuses mainly on steaks and seafood. Home cooking is the focus of the **Edelhaus Restaurant, Deli and Sausage Kitchen,** tel. 264-5531, which prides itself, not surprisingly, on its homemade sausages. At last count it offered 27 varieties. Its selection of beers also wins raves from diners. One of Hope's favorites, it's open daily 6 a.m.-9 p.m. **Pend Oreille Shores,** tel. 264-5311, presents the upscale alternative with the lake's only floating restaurant. Scenic dinner cruises on the water feature a menu running the gamut from steaks to seafood.

Clark Fork offers the **Cedars Cafe,** tel. 266-1229, along Hwy. 200.

Recreation

Hope's watery orientation includes two marinas offering slips and gas. **Holiday Shores Marina** is in East Hope, tel. 264-5515. **Pend Oreille Shores,** tel. 264-5311, also maintains a marina.

For fishing, **Diamond Jim,** tel. 264-5746, operates in the summers out of Hope and offers fishing charters and excursions aboard a 28-foot, twin-engine cruiser. Full- or half-day fishing charters are available.

Information And Services

Hope, East Hope, and Clark Fork all rely on the **Bonner County Sheriff's Department** at Sandpoint for police protection. Call 263-3136 for help.

The communities of Hope, Clark Fork, and Trestle Creek offer information for travelers through P.O. Box 304, Hope, ID 83836.

SOUTH TO COEUR D'ALENE

The glacial valley known as the **Purcell Trench** between Sandpoint and Coeur d'Alene holds some of northern Idaho's most famous lakes and pinewoods and is experiencing a new boom. Drawn by the region's beauty, thousands of new settlers are immigrating. Most of the wave consists of those in love with the land, many of them skilled professionals who can work anywhere. A few are bad apples, the kind found in any barrel.

During the late 1980s, North Idaho became known in some circles, mostly the media, for its hate-mongers, those who choose to hate based on one's color of skin or religious beliefs. Called the Aryan Nations, this beautiful land's blight exists in a remote compound outside Hayden Lake, walled in by its own misanthropy. The misbegotten few in that church of hate, however, have inadvertently offered proof that the divine will can work in mysterious ways. Once the Aryan Nations became known in the region for what it was, a countermovement of goodwill rose like a wave washing over a rock of ignorance. A little help from law enforcement hasn't hurt either. The group's vehemence seems to be winding down as the '90s hit their stride. While some stain remains, most people in the region seem intent on erasing it with goodwill toward new neighbors and travelers. Unless, of course, we're talking about the new waves of immigrants from surrounding states, particularly California. While most of the complaints about the region's popularity remain rooted in good humor, there is a streak of anti-newcomer sentiment that sometimes surfaces.

A man prepares his jumbo jet at Farragut State Park.

The major lakes in this sliver of the Idaho Panhandle cannot compare in size with lakes Pend Oreille and Coeur d'Alene, their neighbors north and south. Beauty has little to do with size, however, and Spirit, Twin, Hauser, and Hayden lakes need apologize to none on that account. They attract admirers enough to prove that fact.

SIGHTS

Farragut State Park

Farragut State Park along the southwest shoreline of Lake Pend Oreille packs a fair share of history important to the nation. After the American decision to enter WW II, the U.S. Navy chose this site for a Naval Training Center, in part because of massive Lake Pend Oreille which is more than 1,200 feet deep. The lake's landlocked status made it ideal for training submariners.

By the end of 1941, the Navy had bought a large share of the land near Lake Pend Oreille's Buttonhook and Scenic bays. Condemnation of remaining properties allowed the War Department to consolidate its holdings. Construction on the Farragut Naval Training Center began April 10, 1942, and continued at a feverish pace—at its peak, 22,000 workers were putting in 10-hour days, 13 out of every 14 days in order to finish the base as quickly as possible. Less than two weeks before the first camp opened, President Franklin D. Roosevelt personally inspected the new base's progress.

The first unit, Camp Bennion, opened Sept. 15, 1942. Five more camps were opened within six months. Each camp could train, house, and feed 5,000 sailors. The camp buildings, laid out in an oval, surrounded a drill field. A huge drill hall capable of holding six basketball courts stood along one side. Two-story barracks (22 in all), a mess hall, two dispensaries, a recreation and ship's stores building, an indoor rifle range, and regimental headquarters rounded out the recruits' world.

In just 15 months, nearly 300,000 sailors were given basic training at Farragut. The nation funneled $100 million into the facility, making it the second-largest naval training base in the world behind the Great Lakes Naval Training Center. The base was named for Adm. David Glasgow Farragut, who during the Civil War won the Battle of Mobile Bay aboard the U.S.S. *Hartford* by defeating the C.S.S. *Tennessee* on Aug. 5, 1864. It was Farragut who exclaimed, "Damn the torpedos, full speed ahead!"

The need for the Farragut Naval Training Center vanished as quickly as it arose, and the base was decommissioned in 1946. After being decommissioned, Farragut served for a time as Farragut College and Technical Institute, which occupied part of the base from 1946 to 1949. Servicemen returned to school there to take advantage of their educational benefits. A massive water tower and crumbling asphalt roads are now all that remain.

Farragut became one of the Idaho Parks Department's initial parks when the department was created in 1965. Encompassing 4,000 acres, Farragut is one of the state's largest. It ranks fourth behind Harriman, Heyburn, and Bruneau Dunes state parks. The visitor center has one of the state's most extensive museum displays of both its own history and that of the natural world. It also displays photographs of class after class of bright young U.S. Navy sailors who learned their duties in Idaho.

For camping information at Farragut, see "Practicalities," following.

Pend Oreille City

Two miles south of the park's headquarters, Pend Oreille City sprang up in 1866 to cater to a booming gold rush trade. Steamboats docked at the city on Buttonhook Bay. The paddlewheelers hauled miners along their route to Montana gold fields and British Columbia's Wildhorse mines. At its peak, Pend Oreille City had two grocery stores, a billiard saloon, a hotel, and a stable. Buttonhook Bay was also a vital station for Pony Express riders carrying the mail from Missoula, Montana to Walla Walla, Washington.

Bayview

This hamlet, a modern successor to Pend Oreille City, offers one of the most picturesque views of Lake Pend Oreille. Bayview's early history revolved around limestone deposits nearby. Steamboats made regular calls at Bayview to ferry lime across the lake to a Northern Pacific Railway dock at Hope beginning in 1887. And lime kilns operated here from 1904 to 1932, producing lime for nearby mines and Spokane buildings.

These days tiny Bayview has a bigger mission: national defense. That role is a continuation of the area's participation in Naval operations during WW II and explains the presence of the **David Taylor Research Center** and **Navy Ship Research & Development Center.** Much of the developmental work for the *Seawolf* submarine has taken place here. A 90-foot scale model of the real thing has been tested in the inky depths of Idaho's waters. Naval researchers also test their equipment's acoustics in these waters, far from the ears of unwanted listeners.

The national symbol, the bald eagle, has visited here in increasing numbers in recent years. The majestic birds with their snowy heads and tails come here in the winter from Canadian nesting areas to shelter from the Arctic cold and to fish.

Silverwood

South from Athol along Hwy. 95 lies Silverwood theme park, tel. 772-0513, which is open June 13th through Labor Day, daily 11 a.m.-8 p.m. Billed as "A Step Back in Time," this re-creation of an early frontier town offers biplane rides, an aircraft museum, steam locomotives, and theme restaurants.

Silverwood began life as the Henley Aerodrome, a private airport and restaurant popular with the private pilot set. Building on its airstrip's popularity, the owners set about to create a sort of Knott's Berry Farm in the forest 15 minutes north of Coeur d'Alene. (In fact, Silverwood recently acquired **The Corkscrew,** a vin-

riding the Corkscrew at Silverwood theme park

tage roller coaster that once thrilled the crowds at Knott's.) Then Silverwood's owner decided the park needed more pep still for young visitors so he added a Ferris wheel, octopus, paratrooper, scrambler, tilt-a-whirl, and other rides to create a permanent midway.

New attractions include Thunder Canyon—a wet and wild ride through a concrete canyon, the last of it through a dark tunnel spritzed with special effects—and a watery firing range where gunners with a naval flair can engage in mock battle, firing tennis balls at fellow combatants on land and "at sea."

A train ride along three miles of track carries visitors out into the piney woods where Indians live the village life and desperadoes wait for the right time to lift the payroll. There's a mock gunfight in the observation cars' aisles most trips.

Another of Silverwood's unique attractions is its **biplane tours,** offered for a relatively modest fee. Just watching the barnstorming planes of old take off, circle, and land at Silverwood is an attraction in itself. Aerial shows are also part of the schedule summer afternoons.

If all that excitement makes you hungry, try the park's **Victorian Cafe,** which dispenses coffee and rolls in an elegant setting, or the **High Moon Cafe,** which gets plenty rowdy at times. Knickknack shops along the wooden sidewalk sell the usual mementos to take home. The admission price to Silverwood ($17.99) gives visitors access to the vintage aircraft and car museum as well as the rides. Silverwood still has some customer service wrinkles to iron out. The lines can be long. The best strategy for visitors is to plan on coming on a weekday.

Spirit, Twin, And Hauser Lakes

These lakes in the forest along Hwy. 41 north of Post Falls are known mostly for their fishing and boating. And count on golfing at the **Twin Lakes Village Golf Course,** tel. 687-1311, with 18 holes, a pro shop and **Mulligan's Restaurant and Lounge.** The area around these lakes is known for the opportunity it provides to relax and escape the mean streets of the cities.

PRACTICALITIES

Camping

Camping at Farragut State Park is plentiful and various, everything from group loops to secluded campsites tucked away in the bushes. Farragut is also one of the few state parks in Idaho's system where campers can make advance reservations by calling park headquarters, tel. 683-2425. The park offers 138 campsites, 45 with full hookups, and 30 that are pull-through. Campsite rates are $11 a night with utilities and $8 a night without. A nonrefundable $5 reservation fee is charged. In addition to camping, the park has boat ramps, swimming beaches, fishing, a nature trail, bicycle route, cross-country skiing in winter, and even a shooting range for organized groups. Bridle trails weave their way through Farragut's forests (but you'll have to bring your own horse) and **Buttonhook Bay Beach** is a must if it's summer and there are children along. You might also spot locals flying model airplanes at the field just across from park headquarters.

The **Coeur d'Alene North KOA** campground is 10 miles north of Coeur d'Alene along E. Garwood Rd., tel. 772-4557. It provides full utilities, a shaded tent-camping area, playground, recreation room, and small store. Campsites cost $10-12 a night. Television reception here is excellent because of the location on a flat.

Alpine Country Store and R-V Park, tel. 772-6883, is nine miles north of Coeur d'Alene at the intersection of Hwy. 53 West. It offers 25 campsites for $12-13 a night, with facilities including a convenience store and gasoline station (both open 24 hours a day), video rentals, barbecue pits, and a playground.

At Hayden Lake, six miles north of Coeur d'Alene along Hwy. 95, you'll find the Forest Service's **Mokins Bay Campground** on the lake's eastern shoreline. Campers reach the area by turning east off the highway onto Sportsman Access road, then following the road 11 miles around the lake. The campground offers 16 campsites near the lake.

Resorts And Motels

Hayden Lake offers visitors the **F. Lewis Clark Mansion,** 3.6 miles off Hwy. 95 along the lake's southern shore. The 15,000-square-foot mansion was built at the turn of the century and is on the National Register of Historic Places. It contains dozens of rooms, nine fireplaces, and seven bathrooms. Rooms here range $100-165 including a three-course breakfast. The mansion overlooks Hayden Lake.

Bayview's focus is Lake Pend Oreille. Accommodations here include **MacDonald's Hudson Bay Resort,** tel. 683-2211, with rooms for $55-140 and campsites for $10-15; and **Scenic Bay Marina,** tel. 683-2243, with campsites and rooms for $11-75. Both offer marina and resort services. **Scenic Motel,** tel. 683-2215, has rooms on the lakefront at rates ranging $35-40 daily. Weekly and monthly rates are also available. **Bayview Resort,** tel. 683-2224, and **Boileau's Resort,** tel. 683-2213, offer standard resort amenities.

West of Bayview, on the northern end of Hwy. 41, the town of Blanchard offers **Stoneridge Resort,** tel. 437-2451, with its condominiums and golf course. Daily rentals are available for $40-115. Spirit Lake offers the **Fireside Lodge,** tel. 623-2871; **Lake Haven Resort and Marina,** tel. 623-2791; and **Silver Beach Resort,** tel. 623-4842. Near Athol are the **Kelso Lake Resort,** tel. 683-2297, with campsites and cabins for $8-25; and **Silverwood RV Park,** tel. 772-0515. Near Rathdrum is **Twin Echo Resort,** tel. 687-1045, with campsites and rooms for $12-50. **Twin Lakes Mobil Park,** tel. 687-1360, is five miles north of Rathdrum along Hwy. 41 and has 10 campsites for $6-8 a night. Hauser Lake offers the **Westside Resort,** tel. 773-4968, with campsites for $7 a night.

Aside from resorts, motels are relatively limited in the area, largely because of the wealth of lodging to the south. Athol has **Athol Motel,** tel. 683-3476, with rooms ranging $20-45; **Kelso Lake Resort,** tel. 683-2297, with camping spaces and three cabins $10-35; and **Silverwood,** tel. 772-0515, with 127 camping spaces. The **Affordable Inn,** tel. 772-4414, at 9986 N. Government Way at Hayden, offers 21 rooms at $25-100 a night, some with kitchenettes. It's very quiet and located close to two golf courses and a couple of restaurants.

Food

Athol offers a limited menu of eateries, mostly cafes, such as **Bettie's Country Inn,** tel. 683-9914, and **Schoony's Restaurant,** tel. 683-2006, both north along Hwy. 95, and the **Grey Goose,** tel. 683-2480, along Hwy. 54 West.

Restaurants at Bayview include the **Buttonhook Inn,** tel. 683-2424, and **Vista Bay Resort Restaurant,** tel. 683-2214, which focuses on roadhouse food like the others but with specials ranging from chicken enchiladas to fresh salmon. Entrees range $6-10.

Along Hwy. 41, Spirit Lake weighs in with **Maggie's Missouri Mule Cafe,** tel. 623-4215, at 314 Maine Street. **Campus Pizza,** tel. 687-1137, at 1550 S. Hwy. 41, at Rathdrum offers breakfast and video rentals in addition to basic pizza. The **Carriage Inn,** tel. 687-2639, is at Twin Lake Village in Rathdrum, as is **Mulligans Restaurant,** tel. 687-1311. Also at Rathdrum are **Granny's Pantry,** tel. 687-0881, at 819 S. Hwy. 53; and **Karen's Steak House and**

Lounge, tel. 687-1359, both offering more of the basics. Another steak house, the **Westwood Inn,** tel. 687-1303, rounds out Rathdrum's offerings. **Chef in the Forest,** tel. 773-3654, offers a more eclectic menu with entrees from the new cuisine along the Hauser Lake Road. Reservations are suggested here.

Hayden Lake is the social hub north of Coeur d'Alene and functions mostly as a suburb because of its proximity. Restaurants here include **The Steak Corral and Mama's Grotto,** tel. 772-5291, which specializes in steaks, of course, but also Italian cuisine. Chinese fans will find the **Dim Sum Inn,** tel. 762-2381, between Hayden Lake and Coeur d'Alene at the Silverlake Mall. Hayden Lake is urban enough to have pizza delivered free from **King Pizza,** tel. 765-5000, which also operates parlors in Coeur d'Alene and Post Falls. **Lomcevak Restaurant and Lounge,** tel. 772-4906, is near the airport. **The Sandtrap,** tel. 772-7991, recognizes the town's attraction for golfers. **Trader on the Lake,** tel. 772-6156, offers another option for diners.

Events

Bayview, Athol, and Farragut State Park join forces to sponsor **Celebrate Summer Weekend** in June. Bayview celebrates the Fourth of July with traditional fireworks over the lake and continues the summer fun with its annual **Bayview Fun Run and Rowing Regatta,** sponsored by the Bayview Chamber of Commerce early each August.

Sports And Recreation

Golf and boating dominate the recreation scene north of Coeur d'Alene. Hayden Lake is home to both the private **Hayden Lake Country Club,** tel. 772-3211, and public **Avondale Golf and Tennis Club,** tel. 772-5963. Blanchard offers the **Stoneridge Golf Course,** tel. 437-4682. Rathdrum is home to the par-three **Twin Lakes Mobile Park Golf,** tel. 687-1360, and **Twin Lakes Village Golf Course,** tel. 687-1311.

Boating makes Bayview what it is; the town seems to be mostly marinas to the visitor. Bayview is home to the **Bitter End Marina,** tel. 683-2534. **Scenic Bay,** tel. 683-2243, has 180 slips for power and sailboats, plus gas, groceries and supplies, a lounge, and sailboat rentals. Travelers with little more than a day's good time in mind may find **Bayview Fun Rentals,** tel. 683-3467, enticing. Located at J.D.'s North Dock and at Farragut State Park's swimming area, the business offers hourly and daily rates for two- and four-person boats. Canopies are optional; life jackets are provided.

At Hayden Lake, **The Tobler Marina,** tel. 772-3255, sells trailers and boats along the lakes south shore. **Northwest Adventures,** tel. 772-7531, is based at Hayden Lake but promises to help arrange adventures ranging from glider flying to seaplane rides nearly anywhere in the region.

Information And Services

Chambers of commerce are found throughout the area. Contact: **Hayden Lake Chamber of Commerce,** tel. 772-6883, P.O. Box 122, Hayden Lake, ID 83835; **Athol Chamber of Commerce,** tel. 683-2056, P.O. Box 130, Athol, ID 83801; **Bayview Chamber of Commerce,** tel. 683-2243, P.O. Box 121, Bayview, ID 83803; and **Spirit Lake Chamber of Commerce** P.O. Box 68, Spirit Lake, ID 83869.

Police services north of Coeur d'Alene are provided by the **Kootenai County Sheriff's Department,** tel. 664-1515, with the exception of Blanchard, which is served by the **Bonner County Sheriff's Department,** tel. 263-3136.

POST FALLS

In 1871, Frederick Post engineered the first commercial development of the Spokane River along its course from Lake Coeur d'Alene toward Washington. In a deal negotiated with Seltice, a Coeur d'Alene Indian chief, Post obtained the right to 200 acres at the upper falls of the Spokane River, on which he built a mill. The deed literally was written in stone—the inscription remains on **Treaty Rock** in Post Falls. Post's mill has long since vanished but the falls have been harnessed for hydroelectric power by the Washington Water Power Company.

Post Falls today still relies on the river for much of its popularity. But the city, which also recalls Chief Seltice in the name of one of its main streets, has grown to include other tourist draws as well, including Coeur d'Alene Greyhound Park and the Post Falls Factory Outlet Mall near the dog track.

Sights

The **Coeur d'Alene Greyhound Park,** tel. 773-0545 or (800) 828-4800, is Idaho's only dog track. Those who play the ponies will find the same sort of excitement here, where trifectas are just one of the exotic betting games available. The track offers eight performances a week Tues.-Sunday. Each performance includes 12 races. General admission is $1, clubhouse seating is $3, general parking is $1, and buses park free, Greyhound or not.

Accommodations

Templin's Resort Hotel and Conference Center, tel. 773-1611, has rooms for $35-85 and is affiliated with the Best Western chain. It advertises casual elegance with a view. Located at Post Falls' southern fringe along the Spokane River, Templin's has a swimming pool, jacuzzi, and sauna. Nearby is **Seltice Beach** along the river for strolls or barbecues. Jogging or walking trails also trace the river's edge. Templin's marina offers slips for motel or Mallards Restaurant guests. **Kamp's Motel,** tel. 773-4215, is at 201 W. Seltice with eight rooms for $21-29. **Nendels at Riverbend,** tel. 773-3583, offers 70 rooms for $38-80 along Riverbend Ave. near the greyhound track. **Suntree Inn** at W. 3705 5th Ave., tel. 773-4541, rounds out Post Falls' lodging with 54 rooms for $37-42.

For campers, the **Quarterhorse RV Park,** tel. 773-9982, at N. 390 Spokane Rd., provides 100 campsites, a clubhouse, and a pool.

Food

Carnegie's Restaurant, tel. 773-0066, is located at the Highland's Golf and Country Club. Live music accompanies diners who come to enjoy the view and the interesting atmosphere, which includes an embossed copper ceiling. **Mallards Restaurant,** tel. 773-1611, is part of Templin's Resort, serving breakfast, lunch, and dinner along the shoreline of the Spokane River. **Andy's Restaurant,** tel. 773-2722, at 615 N. Spokane; **Bobby's Cafe,** tel. 773-9912, at 604 Seltice Way; **Coeur d'Alene Greyhound Park,** tel. 773-0545; **Pizza Hut,** tel. 773-3538, at 920 E. Poulston; **Pizza-to-Go,** tel. 773-1269; **Robs Seafoods and Burgers,** tel. 773-5214, at Seltice and Spokane; **Silver Diner** at 2788 E. Seltice; and finally the **Southern Style Ribs and Delicatessen,** tel. 773-1479, at 309 E. Seltice complete the offerings at Post Falls.

Information And Services

The **Post Falls Chamber of Commerce and Visitor's Bureau,** tel. 773-5016, is located at 510 E. 6th Avenue. You can also obtain information from **Post Falls Tourism,** P.O. Box 908, Post Falls, ID 83854, tel. 773-4080 or (800) 292-2553. The **Post Falls Public Library** is at 821 N. Spokane, tel. 773-1506. Post Falls maintains a **City Police Department** at 101 E. 4th, tel. 911 or 773-3517. The **Kootenai County Sheriff,** tel. 664-1515, also provides emergency services.

COEUR D'ALENE

HISTORY

Coeur d'Alene is the Panhandle's hub. The region's largest city with 27,000 residents, Coeur d'Alene takes its name from the Indian tribe that first inhabited this contrasting land of pine-covered mountains and deep blue lakes. Early fur traders found the native peoples—who called themselves the Shee Chu Umsh—at least their match, sometimes more. In their frustration, the French traders named the people the Coeur d'Alenes, referring to their shrewd bargaining powers that the traders attributed to hearts as small and as sharp as an awl.

In 1877, Gen. William Sherman passed through the area looking for potential military fort sites. The broad glacial flat that occupied Lake Coeur d'Alene's northwest shoulder caught his eye. He asked Congress to set aside lands for a fort here, and Congress complied with 1,000 acres. In 1878, the city was founded and a post office established, and in 1879 the fort was commissioned.

Coeur d'Alene grew not so much as a military outpost but as a lumber and trading center, as well as a provisioning center for the rich mining district of the Silver Valley to the east. Its history as a tourist enclave goes back to its earliest days, well bolstered even then by its status as a port for paddlewheel steamers ferrying goods and vacationers south on the massive lake. Its beauty, resplendent in blues and greens bright enough to please a peacock, drew visitors, too.

Coeur d'Alene has all but left behind its basic industries. The sawmill that once dominated the lakeshore on the town's southeast flank has yielded to a golf course. Beaches have yielded to a major resort and other development.

SIGHTS

The Coeur D'Alene, A Resort On The Lake

This sight dominates the horizon along the city's shoreline, for better or worse. So massive is the Coeur d'Alene and so unusual is its architecture of lake-facing balconies and peaked copper-clad roofs, that this one development has offered the lake city a new identity. The resort has been the focus of photographs in publications ranging from *Travel and Leisure* to *USA Today* and the *Los Angeles Times.* The resort claims the world's longest floating boardwalk at nearly two-thirds of a mile. As the most extensive (and expensive) resort north of Sun Valley, the Coeur d'Alene draws visitors both nationally and from surrounding towns as folks find themselves enthralled by this behemoth on the lakeshore. The resort lies between two city parks, making it an ideal stop for a summer afternoon drink or lunch, whether you're staying the night or not.

Historic Buildings

St. Thomas Catholic Church, at 919 Indiana, is listed on the National Register of Historic Places. The impressive brick church, finished in 1911, was built at a cost of $46,000. Several buildings from **Fort Sherman** still survive, including the chapel at 332 Hubbard and the officers quarters at 917 W. Garden on the town's southwest flank.

Museum Of North Idaho

The Museum of North Idaho, tel. 664-3448, occupies two prime locations in southwest Coeur d'Alene on the point between the lake and Spokane River. The **Park Branch** at 115 Northwest Blvd. operates April 1-Oct. 31, Tues.-Sat. 11 a.m.-5 p.m. The **Fort Sherman Branch** is on the North Idaho College campus, open May 1-Sept. 30, Tues.-Sat. 1-4:45 p.m. Each branch requests a $1 donation.

The campus branch features Fort Sherman history and is located in the fort's powder magazine. A nearby enclosure contains the **Big Hank Cabin,** a firefighter's cabin built in 1924. The Park Branch of the museum focuses on the area's development and the local native peoples.

North Idaho College

Just west of the City Park is the neighborhood once dominated by Fort Sherman and now home to North Idaho College, tel. 769-3300. In

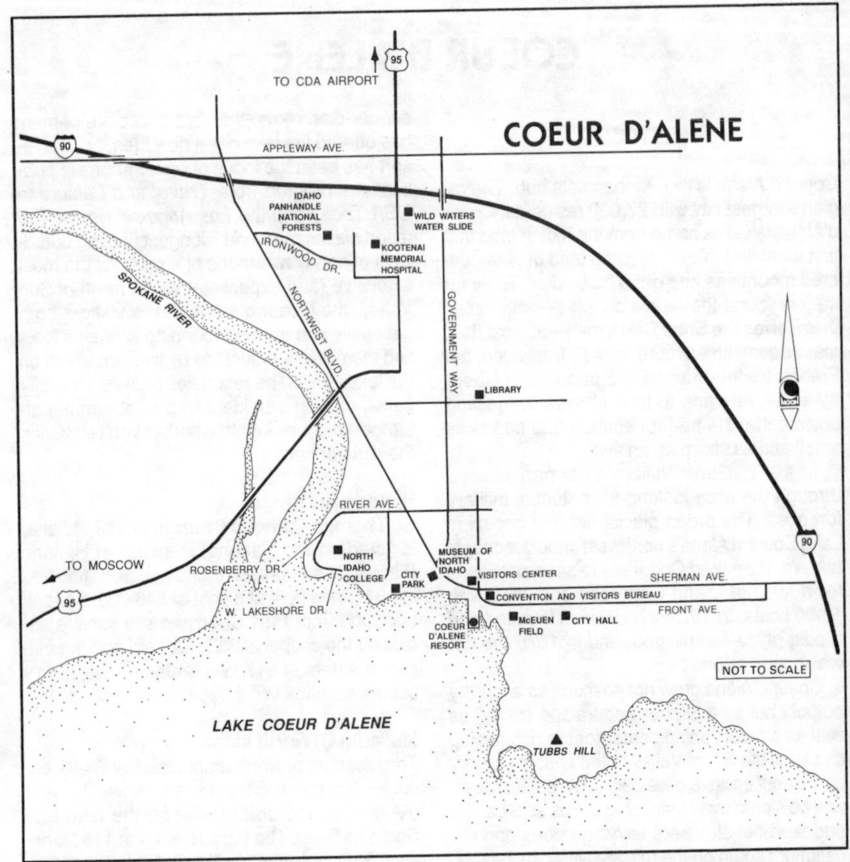

addition to Fort Sherman's historic buildings, the campus is also home to a repertory theater.

Parks

City Park, maintained by the City Parks Department, tel. 667-9533, is a good example of what makes Coeur d'Alene work for visitors and inhabitants. The city beach is here. So is a wide walk known as the promenade, where strollers and bike riders can be found in large numbers on fine evenings. The park, along Northwest Blvd. just west of the Coeur d'Alene Resort, is a playground that fills the summer with fun ranging from pickup basketball games to splashing in the water. **Independence Point** contains giant concrete steps that reach down to the water's edge like bleachers. A tiny fountainlike stream runs through their midst across a bed of native stone. Just off the point is a dock where seaplanes and party boats dock for cruises over and upon these blue waters.

Tubbs Hill

Tony A. Tubbs, a German immigrant, moved to Coeur d'Alene in 1882 and filed a claim that staked out much of what is now Tubbs Hill. In 1884, he platted the western portion of the site to become part of the city.

In his memory, the **Tubbs Hill Nature Trail,** mainly a two-mile loop, follows the outer edge of 135 acres comprising the undeveloped hill. The trailhead is located at the south end of the parking lot between McEuen Park and the Coeur d'Alene Resort. The trail, which includes some steep pitches, requires a couple of hours and comfortable shoes to navigate. Along it, walkers encounter examples of the area's natural history, mainly ponderosa pines and other characteristic plants. Human history is represented along the trail by concrete footings from the D.C. Corbin House and a grandstand built in 1914 to view festivities on the lake. An excellent brochure about the trail is available from the City Parks Department.

Mullan Tree Historic Site

Just east of Lookout Pass, 13 miles east of Coeur d'Alene along I-90, the Mullan Tree Historic Site preserves a portion of the 1861 military wagon road to Fort Walla Walla. The area also contains a remnant of the historic Mullan Tree.

Tours

Coeur d'Alene's status as a tourist center has prompted the development of two homegrown tour companies. **P.A.T. Tours,** tel. 667-9494, at 1844 Government Way, provides tours of mining districts and lakes Coeur d'Alene or Pend Oreille for $22-25, with plenty of walking or driving. **Flamingo Town and Country Tours,** tel. 664-2159, at 718 Sherman Ave., leads day-long driving tours of area mines and museums, lakes, rivers, and the outback. The company also offers a two-hour scuba dive and snorkeling tour.

In summer, **Lake Coeur d'Alene Cruises,** tel. 765-4000, gives daily scenic cruises around the lake, an extended St. Joe River cruise twice a week and sunset dinner cruises catered by chefs from the Coeur d'Alene Resort. Prices range $6.50-18.50 for adults and $4.50-12.50 for children younger than 10. Cruises last 1½-6½ hours and depart from City Park's Independence Point at 1:30 and 5 p.m.

Aerial vantages of the lake are presented by **Lake Helicopters,** which also offers heli-skiing excursions, tel. 664-4158. **Brooks Seaplane Service,** tel. 664-2842, takes off on tours from the dock at Independence Point near the Coeur d'Alene Resort.

RECREATION

Coeur d'Alene delights with a deluge of things to do. And owing to its lakeside location, many of them involve water.

Wild Waters

The water-slicked slides here draw kids from more than 100 miles around. Adults pay $12 and children $9 to play all day. Afternoon discounts go into effect at 5 p.m., dropping the cost to $7 for adults and $5 for kids. For more information call 667-6491.

Boating

Houseboat rentals are available on Lake Coeur d'Alene through **Northwest Travel and Recre-**

party boats carry sightseers around the scenic shore of Lake Coeur d'Alene

ation, P.O. Box 2586, Spokane, WA 99220, tel. (509) 535-6422. Rates vary from $550 for a four-day midweek package to $1,390 for a full week on the biggest boats during the peak of summer. Smaller watercraft ranging from canoes to open kayaks are available for rent at **North Shore Rentals,** tel. 664-1175, which operates May 1-Sept. 30 at the city dock at Independence Point.

Boats are also available for rent from **Coeur d'Alene Marine,** tel. 667-9483, at E. 1100 Lakeshore Dr., for rates varying from $125 a day for a ski boat to $150 for a pontoon boat. Fishing boats fetch $50 a day, a canoe $25, and small sailboats $100. Rental rates do not include gas. A day rental runs 9 a.m.-5:30 p.m.

Crescendo Charters, tel. 765-2238 or (800) 826-2390, ext. 7129, offers 37-foot sailboats for rent. A skipper will be provided and hands-on sailing or instruction is optional.

Diving

Scuba divers will find a chance to explore old steamboat wrecks on the lake's bottom with **Divers West,** tel. 664-0751, at 1675 W. Appleway. Divers West offers a variety of dive trips starting with a shallow dive for $25. For those not yet introduced to the underwater world, they offer scuba certification classes for $175.

Cycling, Riding, Skating

Bicycles are available from **Coeur d'Alene Bike Rentals,** tel. 667-2663, at 323 Front Ave., by the hour, half day, or full day for both adults and children.

For those who agree with the saying "The outside of a horse is good for the inside of a man," **Rider Ranch,** tel. 667-3373 or 667-6573, has the cure. Located east of Coeur d'Alene off I-90, Exit 22, Rider offers various options ranging from short pleasure rides to an adventure ride or evening dinner ride. Hayrides and sleigh rides are also available in season. The options cost $5-35 a person, with minimums ranging $35-150. **Coeur d'Alene Outfitters,** tel. 667-0168, also offers hayrides by appointment. Roller skating is available at the **Skate Plaza Roller Rink,** tel. 772-9803, at N. 5685 Pioneer Drive.

Happy Trails

Hiking trails are at a premium in the Coeur d'Alene area. The two-mile **Tubbs Hill Nature Trail** starts just southeast of the Coeur d'Alene Resort (see "Sights," above). The **Fernan Ranger District,** tel. 765-7381, at 2502 E. Sherman Ave., offers the best information on nearby trails in the Idaho Panhandle National Forests. Two major trail systems within the ranger district are the **Independence Creek Trail System,** which is a National Recreation Trail, and the **Caribou Ridge Trail.** The Independence Trails offer 32 miles of paths, most of them of moderate difficulty, for those who want to get away from the crowds. Locating the trail system will require a Coeur d'Alene National Forest map, available at the district office. The Forest Service brochure about the trail system will also be helpful in making choices. The Caribou Ridge Trail along the eastern shore of Lake Coeur d'Alene provides a good day's walk for most hikers. The four-mile trail links the Beauty Creek Campground and Mt. Coeur d'Alene Viewpoint and Picnic Area. It is rated as moderately difficult, traversing nearly 2,000 feet of elevation from Beauty Creek (2,200 feet) to the picnic area (4,000 feet).

Bald eagles call Beauty and neighboring Wolf Lodge bays home during the winter months. The BLM's **Coeur d'Alene District,** tel. 765-1511, maintains a three-mile hiking trail across Mineral Ridge, which separates the two bays along Lake Coeur d'Alene's northeastern shoreline just south of I-90. The eagles begin to congregate here in November when Canada's winter pushes them south; they come to feed on the spawning kokanee salmon in their liveries of green and red. The eagles, more than 70 at times, remain until mid-March most years.

Skiing And Snowmobiling

Ski and snowmobile rentals are available from **Specialty Sales,** tel. 667-3571, at 115 E. Harrison; **The Great Escape,** tel. 667-1342, at 317 Sherman Ave.; **Mountain Outfitters,** tel. 765-6386, at 509 Sherman Ave.; **Ski Shack,** tel. 772-3112, at 9437 Government Way at Hayden Lake; and **Sun Rental,** tel. 664-0457, at 6640 Government Way.

Golf

Golf, anyone? Three courses occupy the city's outskirts but one occupies the center of attention. The **Coeur d'Alene Resort** course paints a swath of green along the lakeshore east of Tubbs Hill. The course completed in 1991 is best known for its 14th hole, which is set in a floating green anchored along the lakeshore. A ferry carries golfers out and back. A boom contains the floating golf balls issued to players. The green is a moveable target and can be anchored from 75 to 175 yards offshore. If you're not staying at the resort, it will cost you $135 to play a round here. Guests of the hotel can get packages that allow entry for a fraction of that. One recent package offered a night's lodging plus greens fees for two for $195. Guests can play additional rounds at discounted rates. For information on the course, call the resort's reservation line, tel. (800) 688-5253. The course is open from April to October.

Coeur d'Alene Public Golf Club, tel. 765-0218, is located at 2201 S. Fairway Dr.; **Ponderosa Springs Par 3 Golf Course,** tel. 664-1101, is located at 2814 Galena; and **Pumpkin Patch Golf and Restaurant,** tel. 772-4533, is at 1130 W. Prairie Avenue.

ACCOMMODATIONS AND FOOD

Coeur d'Alene has few equals in Idaho for providing lodging in both quantity and variety. Choices range from the Coeur d'Alene Resort with its 338 rooms and penthouse suites to cozy bed and breakfasts and a wide range of clean motels at moderate cost.

The Coeur D'Alene, A Resort On The Lake

This is the most famous, and most controversial, lodging in Coeur d'Alene. Is it a stunning magnet that draws tourist dollars to the area with its first-class resort facilities? Or an unfortunate eyesore, spoiling the pristine beauty of one of the most beautiful shorelines in the Northwest? You decide. The resort offers 338 rooms for $110-220, 13 condos, a four-star rating, two restaurants, three bars, and two pools. Off-season rates from Nov. 1 to March 31 can mean substantial savings as prices fall to $85-155. For reservations and information, call 765-4000 or (800) 688-5253.

Bed And Breakfast Inns

The Blackwell House, tel. 664-0656, at 820 Sherman Ave., offers rooms in a home built in 1904. Rooms with shared or private baths are available at rates ranging $75-119, including a continental breakfast. Guests must book for two nights on holiday weekends. The Blackwell House is inappropriate for children younger than 12 or pets. **Cricket on the Hearth,** tel. 664-6926, at 1521 Lakeside Ave., features a large enclosed deck, a front porch with wicker chairs and a swing, and bicycles for guest use, including one built for two. Rooms for two rent for $45-75, singles are $10 less. **Katie's Wild Rose Inn,** tel. 765-9474, occupies a house built around 1906. Its rooms range in price $65-85 depending on the room and the number of guests. The Inn is inappropriate for children younger than 12 and pets.

Greenbriar Inn, tel. 667-9660, is at 315 Wallace. The 1908 home is on the National Register of Historic Places and features mahogany staircases and high ceilings, also gourmet four-course breakfasts and dining by reservation Friday and Saturday nights. A hot tub and private-bath suites are available. Its rates are $55-85 a night. **Gregory's McFarland House,** tel. 667-1232, at 601 Foster Ave., dates from about 1905. It offers four guest rooms for rates ranging $65-95, including a gourmet breakfast. All rooms have shared baths.

Named for its resting wagon wheels, **Sleeping Place of the Wheels,** tel. 765-3435, at 3308 Lodgepole Pine Rd., offers rooms for $25-40 a night. Children are welcome here for $10 extra apiece. Rooms are also available at the family rate of $40 a night. Children will find an up-in-the-air playhouse with a fireman's slide that drops into a sandbox. **Someday House Bed & Breakfast,** 790 Kidd Island Rd., tel. 664-6666, is five miles south of Coeur d'Alene off Hwy. 95. It offers three rooms for $55-75 a night. The **Warwick Inn,** 303 Military Dr., tel. 765-6565, has three rooms at rates from $75 to $105.

Motels

Motel lodging in Coeur d'Alene includes **Bates Motel,** tel. 667-1411, 2018 Sherman Ave., with 11 rooms for $30-65, and **Bennett Bay Inn,** tel. 664-6168, along Lake Coeur d'Alene at E. 5144 I-90, with rooms for $30-150, a lake view, unique suites, free canoe and paddleboat use; **Boulevard Motel and RV Park,** tel. 664-4978, at 2400 Seltice Way catering to campers as well with rooms and campsites for $15-60; **Cedar Motel and RV Park,** tel. 664-2278, at 319 S. 24th St., where rooms are $25-85 and campsites are $11-15.

Comfort Inn, tel. 765-5500 or (800) 228-5150, at 280 W. Riverside, offers a pool, spa, kitchens, and laundry. Rooms go for $49-185. **Days Inn,** tel. 667-8668 or (800) 325-2525, at 2200 Northwest Blvd., is near downtown and has rooms for $50-110. **El Rancho Motel,** tel. 664-8794, is one of the vintage digs around town at 1915 E. Sherman Ave. with rooms for $27-70. **Flamingo Motel,** tel. 664-2159, has rooms for $66-140 and offers tours and a close-to-downtown location at 718 Sherman Avenue. **Garden Motel,** tel. 667-2743, at 1808 Northwest Blvd., is AAA rated as an excellent value with rooms for $45-110. **Holiday Inn,** tel. 765-3200 or (800) HOLIDAY, offers a full-service restaurant and pool at 414 W. Appleway near the Interstate. Rates range $62-120.

Holiday Motel, tel. 765-6760, is at 219 S. 24th St., and advertises clean rooms at affordable prices, $25-75. **Lake City Inn,** tel. 765-3011, at 330 W. Appleway, has rooms for $29-70 and offers senior rates. **Monte Vista Motel and RV Park,** tel. 664-8201, at 320 S. 24th St., offers campsites and rooms for $10-60. **Motel 6,** tel. 664-6600, at 416 Appleway, provides a known quantity with rooms for $25-43 and an outdoor heated pool. **Pines Resort Motel,** tel. 664-8244, at 1422 Northwest Blvd., has rooms for $26-77. It's close to downtown and offers old-style lodging, updated with an indoor-outdoor pool, jacuzzi, and restaurant.

Portal Motel, tel. 667-9505, at 1519 Sherman has 25 units with in-room movies and cable television. **Sandman Motel,** tel. 664-9119, provides clean and affordable rooms at 1620 Sherman. **Siesta Motel,** tel. 664-5412, is close to shopping at 2115 Sherman Ave. and has rooms for $19-45. **Star Motel,** tel. 664-5035, offers rooms for $29-45 and more of the basics at 1516 Sherman Avenue. **State Motel,** tel. 664-8239, at 1314 Sherman Ave., offers 13 rooms for rates ranging $24-38. **Super 8 Motel,** tel. 765-8880 or (800) 843-1991, has 95 rooms for $34-52 near the Interstate at 505 Appleway.

Campgrounds

Bambi RV Park, tel. 664-6527, offers 20 campsites and cable television for its customers at 3113 Government Way. It's open year-round and offers sites for $13 a day or $70 a week. **Robin Hood RV Park and Campground,** tel. 665-2306, at 703 Lincoln Way, has 45 campsites for $12.50 a night that are close to the downtown, City Park, and North Idaho College. **Lake Coeur d'Alene RV Resort,** tel. 664-4471, offers campsites for $11-15 a night and occupies the southern shore of Wolf Lodge Bay seven miles east of the city off I-90 at Exit 22. The resort offers horseshoe pits, a store, laundry, swimming pool, hot tub, mini golf, boat rentals, and a playground. **Shady Acres,** tel. 664-3087, has trees and 30 spaces for $12-14 at N. 3630 Government Way.

Squaw Bay Resort, tel. 664-6782, is along the eastern shore of the lake off Exit 22, 15 minutes past Beauty Bay. The resort offers cabin, chalet, apartment, trailer, or campsite rentals. Cabin and room rentals range $65-85 per night. Campsites are $15. Boat moorage is also available. **Tamarack RV Park and Campground,** tel. 667-1124, offers 10 spaces for adults for $8-12 in pine trees and shade at N. 3640 Government Way. **Wolf Lodge Campground,** tel. 664-2812, is east of the city at 12425 I-90 and features 100 campsites for $9.50-13.50, a putting green, and campfire circles.

Food

Restaurants, including some very good finds, abound here. Clearly top of the heap, in elevation at least, is **Beverly's,** tel. 765-4000, the Coeur d'Alene Resort's seventh-floor restaurant that is open for lunch and dinner, specializing in seafood and prime beef. It's pricey but the experience measures up. Also in the resort is **Dockside,** tel. 765-4000, the family restaurant located at the water's edge with a pleasing view of the marina's comings and goings. Dockside boasts the region's finest Sunday brunch and "gooey" desserts.

In addition to elegant or even opulent, Coeur d'Alene has a wealth of fun restaurants. Count among them: **Cricket's Restaurant and Oyster Bar,** tel. 765-1990, at 424 Sherman Ave., where there's good beer and an energetic interior design that keeps kids occupied; **Frontier Pies Restaurant,** tel. 667-9459, at 501 Sherman, with reliable basics and great pies; **T.W. Fisher's Brewpub,** tel. 664-BREW, at 204 N. 2nd St., with beers brewed on the premises and good food; and **Jimmy D's Cafe,** tel. 664-9774, at 320 Sherman Ave., with a surprisingly continental menu. **Henry's,** tel. 664-0718, specializes in fresh seafood, prime rib, and steaks at 1001 Sherman Avenue. A well-heeled favorite of the supper club set has long been **The Cedars Floating Restaurant,** tel. 664-2922, at the south end of the Hwy. 95 bridge over the Spokane River, which has drawn diners out for a good time from 100 miles away for its excellent seafood and beef. **Spats,** tel. 765-3200, at 414 W. Appleway in the Holiday Inn, offers a Sunday brunch and chicken and rib buffet.

Ethnic restaurants are widely varied here, ranging from the entertaining Mexican joint, the **3rd Street Cantina,** tel. 664-0581, at 201 N. 3rd St., featuring a wide variety of dishes at surprisingly inexpensive prices, to **Leonardus Ristorante,** tel. 664-0595, at 117 N. 2nd, which specializes in authentic Italian food. **Chinese Gardens,** tel. 667-6014, offers Szechuan and Mandarin cuisine to eat in or take out. **China Gate,** tel. 664-8506, offers Cantonese, Mandarin, and Shanghai cuisines at 1210 Sherman Avenue. **Papino's Italian Cuisine,** tel. 765-2348, is a taste treat tucked away at 315 Walnut. **Eduardo's Mexican Restaurant,** tel. 664-6236, serves up its specialties at 300 S. 24th.

The **Iron Horse,** tel. 667-7314, at 407 Sherman Ave., is a Coeur d'Alene tradition with a seafood buffet Fridays. **Rustler's Roost,** tel. 664-5513, at 819 Sherman Ave., offers a country breakfast that's long on authenticity. Distinctive inside and out is the **Log Cabin Restaurant,** tel. 664-9814, at 213 Appleway. **Catcher in the Rye,** tel. 667-7966, at 414 Mullan, offers great sandwiches, good coffee, and dinners, too. **Mountain Brew Coffee,** tel. 765-4818, at 307 Sherman Ave., brews a wicked cup of espresso or cappuccino. So does **Roger's Ice Cream,** tel. 667-0010, at 324 Sherman Avenue.

Fast food is thoroughly represented in Coeur d'Alene with "the strip" north of the Interstate along Appleway. **The Atrium,** at 757 *West* Appleway, and **Kentucky Fried Chicken,** at 218 *East* Appleway bracket an abundance of establishments including **Arby's, Burger King, Domino's Pizza, McDonald's, Ritz Cafe,** and **Rax.** A cruise down the strip will soon lead you to what you're looking for.

OTHER PRACTICALITIES

Entertainment And Events

First-run movies make stops at Coeur d'Alene. The major movie theaters in town are **Coeur d'Alene Cinemas,** tel. 667-3559, at 3555 N. Government Way, and **Showboat III Tri-Cinema,** tel. 772-5695, at 5725 N. Pioneer Drive.

The Coeur d'Alene Community Theater, tel. 667-1323, at 1320 E. Garden Ave., and **Summer Theater,** tel. 667-0254, stage live performances during the year. Summer shows are presented at North Idaho College's Boswell Hall.

Area events begin in January with the **Polar Bear Plunge,** guaranteed to raise goosebumps on participants and spectators alike. The month's **Winter Festival** and **Hangover Handicap Fun Run** provide (slightly) saner approaches to winter's dark days. February offers the **Mid-town Mardi Gras.**

Come April, the weather has started to sweeten and grass is ready to green up and start growing again. Major events of the month include **Fort Sherman Day, Home and Garden Show,** and the **Kamloops and Kokanee Derby.**

May means the **Coeur d'Alene Marathon** as part of **Fred Murphy Days** in the Lake City, as well as **Lake City Days.** Memorial Day brings out the best of the city's chefs to strut their best snacks, lunches, and desserts in **A Taste of the Coeur d'Alenes.**

June brings events ranging from the **Coeur d'Alene Volkssport** to the **Coeur d'Alene to Spokane Canoe Marathon** and **Old-Time Fiddlers Contest.**

July means a bevy of celebrations of our past including the **Old Timers Picnic, Wooden Boat Show, Sailboat Race,** and **American Heroes Fourth of July Parade.**

Art on the Green, a city-wide celebration of art and artists, inaugurates August. The **Floating Art Auction** takes the general theme to the water. Art of a different sort surfaces during the **Coeur d'Alene Resort on the Lake Regatta** and the **Idaho State Chili Cookoff.** The **Coeur d'Alene Triathlon, Jazzfest,** and **"Big One" Chinook Salmon Derby** keep August hopping.

Fall brings the **North Idaho Fair** to the Kootenai County Fairgrounds in September. **Oktoberfest** celebrates autumn and the year departs with December's **Christmas in Coeur d'Alene.**

Shopping

Coeur d'Alene is the hub of Idaho's antique trade. Antique malls flourish here like nowhere else in Idaho. Looking for a musket? Or an out-of-the-ordinary butter churn? Chances are good one of the several antique malls or stores will have what you're seeking.

Major malls dealing only in antiques include **Coeur d'Alene Antique Mall,** tel. 667-0246, which counts 75 individual dealers among its fold at 3650 Government Way; the **Wigget Antique Mall,** tel. 664-1524, at 119 N. 4th St., which offers 27,000 square feet in the old three-story Montgomery Ward and Co. store; and **Lake City Antique Mall,** tel. 664-6883, at 401 N. 2nd.

Individual antique dealers include **A Precious Past,** tel. 667-6882, at 802 N. 4th; **Antique Gun Shoppe and Collectibles,** tel. 773-1320, at 2640 E. Ponderosa Blvd. at Post Falls; **Basil's Used Furniture and Antiques,** tel. 664-1625; **Collector's Antiques,** tel. 667-5810, at 808 N. 4th; and **Country Store Antiques,** tel. 667-1422, at 810 N. 4th.

A bright new shopping mall with all the best stores is Coeur d'Alene businessman Duane Hagadone's latest effort to enhance the city and his Coeur d'Alene Resort. The downtown mall is just across the street from the resort, and a covered pedestrian bridge links the two. Stores include Alpine Silver, Bennetton, Mirabella, and the Phoenix Gallery. Antiques have been the biggest shopping game in town for Coeur d'Alene visitors.

Other malls of the general, contemporary sort also sprout at the northern outskirts of town. **Coeur d'Alene Mall** is located at 101 Best Ave. near Appleway and 4th and is anchored by such stores as Kinney's, Lamont's, Montgomery Ward's, Radio Shack, and Sprouse-Reitz. Newer is the **Silver Lake Mall** at Hwy. 95 North and Hanley Ave. two miles north of the city.

Coeur d'Alene's downtown, bisected by Sherman Ave., is still vital, recently benefiting from a major face-lift. Among the many engaging downtown stores are two exceptional offerings (in the opinion of children and others who love toy stores, at least): **The Purple Dragon Toy Store,** tel. 667-4646, at 513 Sherman Ave., and **Kamalot,** tel. 667-0466, at 302 N. 4th.

Transportation

Coeur d'Alene Airport northeast of town off Hwy. 95 offers commuter service to Boise, Lewiston, and Seattle via **Empire Airlines,** tel. 772-7502, based at Hayden Lake. **Stene Aviation,** tel. 772-9558, offers charter service with Turbo Commanders capable of carrying six or seven passengers.

Bus service is offered by **Greyhound Bus Lines,** and **Roadrunner Bus Lines,** both at 1923 1/2 N. 4th, tel. 664-3343. **Panhandle Area Transit,** tel. 334-9769, is located at 137 Spruce Avenue.

Taxi services include **Taxi by Hall,** tel. 664-2424; **Sunset Taxi,** tel. 664-8000; and **Call-A-Cab,** tel. 765-3315.

Information And Services

The **Coeur d'Alene Convention and Visitors Bureau,** tel. 664-3194 or (800) 232-4968, is located at 140 S. 2nd, Coeur d'Alene, ID 83814.

Coeur d'Alene Police may be summoned by dialing 911 within the city or 667-9526 elsewhere. **Kootenai Medical Center,** tel. 667-6441, is located at 2003 Lincoln Way.

The **Coeur d'Alene Public Library,** tel. 667-4676, is at 201 Harrison. The **Coeur d'Alene Post Office,** tel. 664-8126, is at 111 N. 7th.

THE SILVER VALLEY

HISTORY

The Silver Valley drew its name from the rich veins of silver, lead, zinc, and gold ores that marble its mountains. Although the first discoveries of lead and silver ore in the Coeur d'Alene Mountains occurred in 1884, Noah Kellogg hit the biggest find in 1885. The outcropping he, or his jackass if the story is right, stumbled onto along Milo Creek eventually became the Bunker Hill and Sullivan Mine—one of the richest sources of lead, silver, and zinc in the world.

Other mines dotted the Silver Valley, too, pulling a wealth of minerals from an area 23 miles long by nine wide. The arrival of a narrow-gauge railroad at the doorstep of the Bunker Hill in March 1887 helped foster the mining boom, and soon the valley became the nation's richest source of silver, at one time producing eight percent of the world's supply. Less than a century after discovery, the Coeur d'Alene mines had produced more than $3 billion in booty.

Miners were, and still are, a tough lot, able to endure considerable physical hardship. In quest of the ore, they pushed tunnels as deep as 6,000 feet below the surface. The Bunker Hill Mine, now largely abandoned, contains 125 miles of tunnels and other underground workings, all excavated since 1886.

For all their physical fortitude, the miners had little tolerance for political or management strains. In 1892, miners signaled displeasure at their working situation by dynamiting the Gem Mill at Burke. In 1899 the mines of the Coeur d'Alene district were unionized by the Western Federation of Miners. After resistance from Bunker Hill and Sullivan Mine officials, the miners commandeered a train, stuffed the firm's ore concentrator with dynamite, and touched it off. Governor Frank Steunenberg called in the Army and declared a state of martial law. Miners who were pro-union were kept in a stockade. Six years later Steunenberg was assassinated at his Caldwell home by a dynamite bomb that detonated when he opened his front gate. Harry Orchard was arrested for Steunenberg's murder, found guilty, and imprisoned for life—his efforts to implicate union officials failed.

A New Era

The mining boom lasted nearly a century before environmental concerns and sagging silver and base-metal markets cut the heart out of the valley's economy. Foreign competition deflated world silver, lead, and zinc prices to near or below the northern Idaho mines' costs of production. As mining faltered, the valley began to

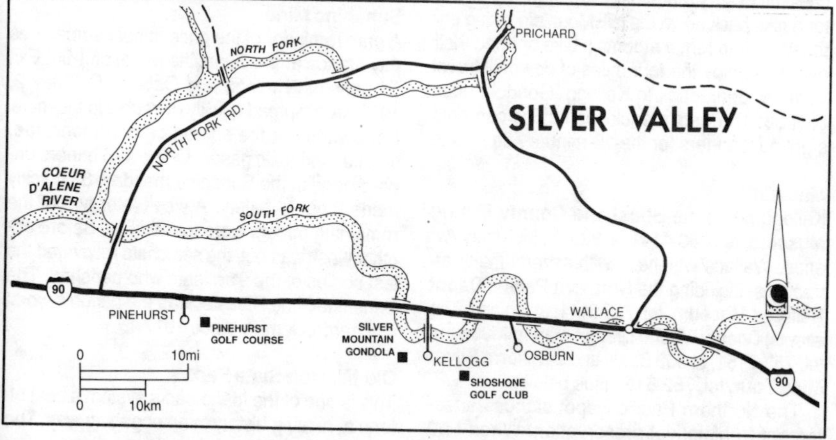

refocus its smarts and its energy on catching the next wave of prosperity. The mining heritage perseveres but the Silver Valley, like much of Idaho, plans to develop other industries, chief among them tourism.

From silver gleaming beneath the earth, businesspeople have turned their attention to the silvery sheen of snow on the surrounding mountains. Kellogg is now a base for the world's longest gondola, which reaches more than three miles north of town to a newly refitted ski area, **Silver Mountain.** Kellogg has remodeled itself into the image of a Bavarian village. Neighboring Wallace, long the holdout as the last stoplight along I-90, updated its looks, too, with the **Northern Pacific Depot Railroad Museum** (see below).

SIGHTS

Silver Mountain Resort

Silver Mountain, off I-90, Exit 49 at Kellogg, tel. 783-1111, promises to be the central attraction of the Silver Valley in the foreseeable future. Its gondola rises 3,400 vertical feet in three miles from the base at Kellogg to the Mountain Haus terminal.

The resort has been planned as both a summer and winter escape. Summers mean barbecues, picnics, and sunset dinners on the Mountain Haus deck for casual visitors. Those with a wish for something more aerobic will find chairlifts to ferry them to the top of Kellogg Peak for a hike back down the hill. Mountain-biking enthusiasts can rent a mountain bike or bring their own and enjoy the four miles of downhill travel from the peak back to Kellogg. Gondola rides cost $8. The tram's enclosed cabins can hold eight passengers for the 16-minute ride.

Museums

Kellogg offers the **Shoshone County Mining Museum,** tel. 786-4141, at 820 W. McKinley Avenue. Wallace weighs in with several major attractions, including the **Northern Pacific Depot Railroad Museum,** tel. 752-0111, at 6th and Pine streets; **Coeur d'Alene District Mining Museum,** tel. 753-7151, at 509 Bank; and the **Sierra Silver Mine Tour,** tel. 752-5151 (see below).

The Northern Pacific Depot stands as testament to historical preservation. When I-90 was finally diverted around the town, some proposed simply knocking down the old depot that stood in its way. Backers refused and the depot survives with its elegant chateau styling, imported brick, and concrete made from mine tailings. The museum, which captures the flavor of railroading in 1910, is open daily, summers 9 a.m.-7 p.m., spring and fall 9-5. Winter hours are Tues.-Sat. 10 a.m.-3 p.m. The depot also serves as home base for horse-drawn carriage tours which run every 20 minutes from 10 a.m. till dusk when the weather permits. Fares are $4 for adults and $2 for children. More information is available from **Pony Creek Carriage,** tel. 682-4597.

Sierra Silver Mine Tour

Tours of the Sierra Silver Mine, tel. 752-5151, begin at the Coeur d'Alene District Mining Museum in Wallace, then take visitors on a one-hour exploration of a worked-out silver mine. Tourists are taken to the mine by a Jeep and 16-passenger trailer and issued hard hats at the door. Going underground, the travelers walk about 1,000 feet of mining tunnel where they see mining equipment and methods ranging from hand-drilling to mechanized means used to remove the silver ore. Tours leave every 20 minutes 9 a.m.-4 p.m. daily during the summer. Adult tickets are $6.50 and children's (four to 14) are $5.50. No children younger than four are allowed to go. To receive a brochure, write to P.O. Box 712, Wallace, ID 83873.

Sunshine Mine

A grim reminder of the price miners sometimes pay stands at the Sunshine Mine, off I-90, Exit 54 between Kellogg and Osburn. On May 2, 1972, word spread quickly of trouble in the mine. Deep within, a fire spread carbon monoxide, smoke, and toxic gases. Of the 176 miners underground in the Sunshine that day, 83 quickly made it out to safety. A week later two of the remaining miners were found alive. Before another week was out, the searchers recovered the last bodies of the 91 miners who perished. The Sunshine Mine Disaster was the nation's worst in a hardrock mine since 1917.

Old Mission State Park

This is one of the Idaho parks system's best efforts at relating history in an engaging way. The

Old Mission State Park draws thousands of visitors each year.

exhibits and program in the modern visitor center capture one's attention. Well-planned brochures weave together the mission's past and present significance. Located 39 miles east of Coeur d'Alene and a mile east of Cataldo off I-90, Exit 39, tel. 682-3814, its 18 acres include a restored parish house, picnic tables, and the visitor center. Guided tours or self-guided historical and nature trails are available. The park is open daily 8 a.m.-6 p.m. A $2 motor vehicle entry fee is charged.

The Mission of the Sacred Heart here goes back to the beginnings of the inland Northwest's recorded history. The grand and imposing mission with its six columns of hand-hewn tree trunks ranks as Idaho's oldest standing building. A relic now, the mission illustrates the trends leading to Idaho's settlement.

Roman Catholic Jesuits moved into Idaho only three decades after the Lewis and Clark Expedition brought the first white men into the interior. By the 1830s the Jesuits were offering spiritual succor to Montana's Blackfeet Indians. The neighboring Coeur d'Alene Indians let it be known they wanted Black Robes of their own. The Jesuits arrived and raised their first mission along the St. Joe River, until flooding convinced them to abandon it in 1846. A knoll along the Coeur d'Alene River offered the best prospects for a new mission. Father Anthony Ravalli designed the new mission, and the Coeur d'Alenes and Jesuits joined hands to build again with a penknife, broadaxe, and auger.

The mission, started in 1848, first had walls of willow branches and grass daubed with mud. Wood boards were later added for siding outside and panelling inside. Father Joseph Cataldo arrived in 1865 and became the guiding light of Idaho Catholicism, expanding the church's influence and even serving as a peacemaker in the Nez Perce War of 1877.

Through the decades since, the mission and neighboring parish house built in 1887 fell into disrepair. Restoration efforts date back to 1930. The most recent effort to preserve the mission came in 1974, a year before the dedication of Old Mission State Park. The parish house and the Church of the Sacred Heart now stand repaired and restored, ready for their second century.

RECREATION

Skiing

Skiers have two choices. **Silver Mountain,** tel. 783-1111, or (800) 678-8633 for a snow report, is the newly refurbished ski resort that has updated and replaced the venerable Silverhorn Ski Area. The resort offers 2,200 vertical feet of skiing and plenty of snow-making equipment to extend the season. Daily lift rates range from $26 for adults to $10 for junior, senior, or college night-skiing passes. Season passes are available. The resort is open daily 9-4 with night skiing Wed.-Sat. until 9 p.m. **Lookout Pass Ski Area,** tel. 744-1301, is up the valley near Mullan. Lookout offers 850 vertical feet of skiing, a cafeteria in the day lodge, and rentals.

Hiking Trails

The South Fork of the Coeur d'Alene River runs through the towns of the Silver Valley. Hiking trails are scribed across the surrounding hills like a delicate filigree. **Wallace Ranger**

District, tel. 752-1221, at Silverton offers a brochure of trails in the area. Trails range from the easy one-mile outing to Lost Lake to the moderately difficult **St. Joe Divide Trail** that spans 22 miles.

River Floats

Unlike the Coeur d'Alene's south fork, the main river north of the Silver Valley presents an escape from civilization. Its 55 miles between Senator Creek on the north and Cataldo on the south present a range of options. Rafters come here when the runoff from surrounding mountains peaks in late spring. Summer dries up the rushing rapids but boaters find that rafts and canoes can still navigate the Coeur d'Alene until late July most years. Even then, inner tubes or just plain swimming make the river a popular haunt. **Wallace Ranger District,** tel. 752-1221, offers detailed information about the river.

Golf

Golfers will find two courses, **Kellogg Golf Course,** tel. 682-2013, at Pinehurst, and **Shoshone Golf Course,** tel. 784-0161, off I-90, Exit 54 at Kellogg.

PRACTICALITIES

Bed And Breakfast Inns

Hillcrest House, tel. 682-3911, offers a loghouse retreat in the forest at 210 Hillcrest in Pinehurst with two rooms for $45 a night. Nearby are hiking trails, golf courses, fishing, and skiing. In Wallace is the **Jameson,** tel. 556-1554, at 3045 6th St., with six rooms from $59 a night. The old hotel offers a dining room complete with chandeliers and oriental carpets. A saloon on its ground floor has the mirrored back bar and polished brass of a different era. The third floor has been refurbished as a bed and breakfast. In recent years, the Jameson has operated only during the summer season, from May through September. **Patrick's Inn and Steakhouse,** tel. 786-2311, has nine rooms for $22-28 at 305 S. Division in Kellogg. The inn operates during the summer but the restaurant is open only during the ski season. **The McKinley Inn,** tel. 786-7771, offers eight rooms for $40-75 a night, and breakfast.

Motels

Kellogg offers **McCreary's Motel,** tel. 786-0591, at 900 W. Cameron Ave., with kitchenettes for $20; **Motel 51,** tel. 786-9441, at 206 E. Cameron Ave., with rooms for $22-34; **Silverhorn Motor Inn and Restaurant,** tel. 783-1151, at 699 W. Cameron Ave., with rooms for $45-63; **The Sunshine Inn,** tel. 784-1186, at 301 W. Cameron Ave., with rooms for $24-42; and **Trail Motel,** tel. 784-1161, at 206 W. Cameron Ave., with rooms for $25-35. **The Ward's Sunshine House,** tel. 783-0371 or (800) 800-6181, is billed as an executive retreat with five double bedrooms and a nightly rate of $300. It's located at 1 Golf Course Rd., four miles east of Kellogg.

Wallace offers a similar variety of lodging, ranging from **Molly B'Damm Motel,** tel. 556-4391, along Hwy. 10, with kitchenettes and rooms for $21-38, to **Ryan Hotel,** tel. 753-6001, at 608 Cedar Ave., with rooms for $20-35; **Silver Leaf Motel,** tel. 752-0222, along Hwy. 10, with rooms and kitchenettes for $20-23; and the **Stardust Motel,** tel. 752-1213, at 410 Pine with rates of $30-60. The **Wallace Inn,** tel. 752-1252 or (800) 528-1234, is a Best Western and has rooms for $50-200.

Hostel

Kellogg International Hostel, tel. 783-4171, offers 44 beds for $10-12 a night, at 834 W. McKinley. The hostel occupies the building that once served as the headquarters for the Bunker Hill Company.

Campgrounds

Kampgrounds of America at Pinehurst, tel. 682-3612, is at 801 Division Ave., and offers cabins, swimming pool, shade trees, and a trout stream. Campsites range $14-16.50. Kamping Kabins range $15-30 a night. The campground knocks off a couple of dollars a night during the off-season, which begins in November and ends in April. **Coeur d'Alene River Campground,** tel. 682-4171, has campsites for $8-10 off I-90, Exit 40.

The Forest Service maintains four campgrounds, **Big Hank, Berlin Flat, Devils Elbow,** and **Kit Price,** along the Coeur d'Alene River north of the Silver Valley. They're located along Forest Service roads 208 and 412. The Wallace Ranger District, tel. 752-1221, also maintains three picnic areas in the vicinity; **Shoshone Rest Stop, Avery Creek, and Shoshone Park.**

Food

Food in the Silver Valley leans toward the hearty, with steaks the main option. **The Enaville Resort,** tel. 682-3453, off I-90 at Exit 43 and 1.5 miles up the Coeur d'Alene River, pretty much captures the spirit of the place. Among other notables are **Albi's Steak House,** tel. 753-3071, at 220 6th in Wallace; **Third Generation,** tel. 681-2810, at Cataldo; and the **Tall Pines Drive Inn,** tel. 682-4294, at 203 N. Division Ave. in Pinehurst. **Danadabru,** tel. 682-4792, is open for lunch and dinner at 9 Country Club Lane in Pinehurst.

At Kellogg is the **Gondola Cafe** at the tram's base and the **Mountain Haus,** tel. 783-1111, the latter offering barbecue fare and sandwiches atop the mountain. Also in town is the **Humdinger,** tel. 786-7395, at 205 Hill St.; and the **Broken Wheel,** tel. 784-0601, at 102 E. Cameron Avenue.

JG's, tel. 752-1252, is at 100 Front St. at Wallace; also here are **Allen's Quick Lunch,** tel. 753-8801, at 519 Cedar, and the **Jameson,** tel. 556-1554, at 304 6th Street.

Elsewhere in the area you'll find the **Silver Valley Cafe,** tel. 784-4211, at 314 Main St. in Smelterville; **Italian Barrel,** tel. 752-6111, at 1341 Mullan Ave. at Osburn; and the **Country Chef,** tel. 682-4298, at I-90's Rose Lake Exit near Cataldo.

Entertainment And Events

Sixth Street Melodrama, tel. 752-8871, or 753-4773 during the off season, occupies the historic Lux Building at 212 6th St. in Wallace. During the season, from late June through late August, $8 for adults and $6 for seniors and students gets you a ticket to an "emotion-packed performance of heart-rending, soul-searching melodrama to the joyful, toe-tapping fun of an old-time revue." Ahem. Movie theaters in the area include the **Rena Theatre,** tel. 784-7101, at 310 N. Division at Kellogg, and the **Valley Center Flick,** tel. 786-4311, at Smelterville.

Events kick off in February with **Kellogg's Winter Games** and the **Prichard Logging Days Festival.** April brings the **Wallace Basketball Classic** and **Silver Valley Arts and Crafts Fair. Wallace Depot Days** marks May, and things bust loose with the **Gyro Lead Creek Derby** at Wallace in June. **Pinehurst Days** and **Frontier Days** at Smelterville round out June's events. July offers **Old Mission State Park's Historical Skills Fair.**

August means the **Coeur d'Alene District Mining Contest, Silver Valley Horseshoe Classic at Kellogg,** and the annual Coeur d'Alene Indian pilgrimage to Old Mission State Park for the **Feast of the Assumption.** Also in August, Wallace offers its **Huckleberry Festival.** In September, Kellogg gets the jump on neighboring communities with Bavarian ties by hosting **Septemberfest.**

Shopping

Silver Capital Arts and Wine Cellar, tel. 556-7081, at 524 Bank St. in Wallace, displays an extensive mineral collection rivaling a museum and offers a credible selection of wine as well. **Unique Antiques,** tel. 786-3911, is at 201 Main St. in Smelterville. **Elk Creek Store,** tel. 786-8791, stands between Kellogg and Osburn and offers fishing and hunting supplies. A specialty here is rod-and-reel repair. **Excelsior Cycle and Sport Shop,** tel. 786-3751, at 10 W. Portland Ave. in Kellogg, maintains a good selection of goods. So does **Loulou's of North Idaho,** tel. 783-1123, a clothing store at 610 Bunker Ave. in Kellogg.

Information And Services

Information for visitors is available from the **Kellogg Chamber of Commerce,** tel. 784-0821, at 712 W. Cameron Ave., Kellogg, ID 83837 and the **Wallace Chamber of Commerce,** tel. 753-7151, at 509 Bank St., Wallace, ID 83873.

Medical care is available at **Henry L. Day Medical Center,** tel. 752-1248, at Silverton and **Shoshone Medical Center,** tel. 784-1221, at Jacobs Gulch Road near Kellogg.

Police services are provided through the **Shoshone County Sheriff's Office,** tel. 556-1114. **Wallace City Police,** tel. 911 or 753-3000, are at 415 6th Street.

The **Wallace Public Library,** tel. 752-4571, is along River Street. The **Kellogg Public Library,** tel. 786-7231, is at 16 W. Market Avenue.

SAINT MARIES AND VICINITY

St. Maries rose along the lower reaches of the St. Joe River, east of where the river empties into Lake Coeur d'Alene. It grew up as a river town and the hub of a busy logging industry. Logs are smaller now, and harder to come by, too. The river traffic that flooded the town with prosperity early this century has also diminished. But what has not diminished is this town's spirited pride.

Located close to the southeastern end of Lake Coeur d'Alene, St. Maries draws some lake-bound traffic but more of its visitors are bound for the shadowy **St. Joe River,** the highest navigable river in the world. Rafters and canoeists converge on the St. Joe to test themselves on its whitewater rapids. The **St. Maries River** south of the city along Hwy. 3 can also provide more challenge and thrills than some can handle, despite its placid appearance in town.

Nearby **Harrison** is at the delta of the Coeur d'Alene River along Lake Coeur d'Alene's eastern shore. Two marinas here make this the east shore's boating center. The Coeur d'Alene River's broad floor east of Harrison holds a string of 15 lakes popular with fisherfolk and birdwatchers. **Killarney Lake** is judged the most scenic and offers a boat ramp.

Plummer along Hwy. 95, is a hub for the lake's western shore.

SIGHTS

State Parks

Harrison is a popular departure point for **Mowry State Park,** due west across Lake Coeur d'Alene and along the southwest shoreline near Windy Bay. The lakeside park is split into two parcels, Gasser Point and Mowry Point. **Gasser Point** is developed with docks, a picnic shelter, several free campsites, and outhouses. It offers a rustic retreat for a picnic or weekend campout along the lakeshore. Heyburn State Park serves as Mowry's headquarters.

Heyburn State Park, tel. 686-1308, is the granddaddy of Idaho's park system, dating back to 1908 when Sen. Weldon Heyburn pushed the legislation through Congress, reserving 7,825 acres at the lake's southern tip. The park was a popular excursion for vacationers from Coeur d'Alene when steamboats still plied the lake. What Senator Heyburn wanted was a national park. His colleagues, while unconvinced, did allow the lands to be set aside for purchase by the state. Heyburn fumed.

Mowry State Park is available only to boaters.

(Top) The Finger of Fate scratches the skyline above Hell Roaring Lake in the Sawtooth National Recreation Area. (Bottom left) A successful steelhead fisherman, Paul Emerson, holds up an 18-pounder on the Clearwater River near Lewiston. (Bottom right) A hiking trail in Dworshak State Park near Orofino offers hikers a cool escape during the warm summers. (PHOTOS BILL LOFTUS)

(Top) Bruneau Dunes prove the colors of sunrise yield their own rewards. (Bottom) Boaters enjoy the Snake River south of Lewiston in the Hells Canyon National Recreation Area. (PHOTOS BILL LOFTUS)

Indian Cliffs ranks as a popular trail at Heyburn State Park.

State parks, he groused, were always a source of embarrassment.

He wasn't too far wrong. Heyburn suffered years of neglect for decades. The Idaho Parks and Recreation Department has renewed its commitment to the park in recent years with the refurbishing of **Hawley's Landing Campground,** where campsites are $8-11, and other projects. The **Indian Cliffs Nature Trail** provides a pleasing escape. The park's **Chatcolet** and **Rocky Point** picnic areas also are pleasant spots to while away an afternoon. Civilian Conservation Corps crews operating during the Great Depression built shelters here that still retain their grace.

Emerald Creek Garnet Area

Clarkia, south of St. Maries along Hwy. 3, provides the jumping off point for the Emerald Creek Garnet Area, where visitors can get down and dirty in pursuit of six-rayed star garnets, found in only two parts of the world, here and in India. The gems are found near bedrock and that means mucking out pits along the stream. The **St. Maries Ranger District,** tel. 245-2531, operates the garnet digging area from Memorial Day to Labor Day. Prospectors must buy a $5 permit, which entitles the bearer to five pounds of the purple gems in the rough.

For those who would just as soon avoid the mud, **Emerald Creek Garnet,** tel. 245-2096 or 245-2797, will allow visitors, for a modest fee, to sift through their mining spoils. The company mines for garnets to sell as abrasives and is not allowed to keep large, gem-quality stones.

Hobo Creek Cedar Grove

From Clarkia, travelers with sturdy vehicles can take a backcountry tour along Forest Service Rd. 321 north across the Marble Creek Divide. At the top of the divide and 10 miles from Clarkia is the turnoff to Hobo Creek Cedar Grove. The grove is two miles east of the main route along Forest Service Rd. 3357. The 240-acre grove is sheltered by a dense roof of lacy western red cedar boughs and carpeted by lady ferns. A half-mile trail loops through the grove and a brochure and signposts tell visitors about the area.

Back Roads And Trails

The **Grandmother Mountain** area nearby is one of the Moscow-area's best loved escapes. A major land trade helped consolidate national forest land in the area, opening up previously untapped recreation potential.

On the other side of the divide from Hobo Creek is the rugged **Marble Creek drainage,** which is laced with hiking trails. The trail system reaches the creek just a mile upstream from its junction with the St. Joe River. An alternate route is to take Forest Service Rd. 301 just outside Clarkia and follow it to **Marks Butte** where Trail No. 275 branches off to Grandmother and Grandfather mountains. The **St. Maries Ranger District,** tel. 245-2531, maintains the trail system in the area.

From Marble Creek, **St. Joe River Rd.** offers a scenic route back to St. Maries again or a gateway to even wilder scenery to the east. The St. Joe is included in the nation's Wild and

Scenic River System for 60 miles upstream from **Avery,** which is east of Marble Creek. Avery is home to a community museum and historical ranger station. This one-time transportation hub also served as the switching point between steam engines and electric trains.

PRACTICALITIES

Bed And Breakfast Inns

The Owl Chalet, tel. 686-1597, with rooms for $40-45, is at Rt. 1, Box 96A, Plummer, ID 83851 and perches three miles from the southern end of Lake Coeur d'Alene above Heyburn State Park. There's a cozy sunroom with a jacuzzi, sauna, 15-foot heated swimming pool, and garden.

The Knoll Hus, tel. 245-4137, at P.O. Box 572, St. Maries, ID 83861, offers a view of Round Lake and the St. Joe River with room rates from $85. Garden paths and songbirds are a couple of the amenities here, as are a bicycle built for two and a canoe. **Peg's Bed 'n' Breakfast Place,** tel. 689-3525, has three rooms for $50-95 near Harrison. More information is available by writing P.O. Box 144, Harrison, ID 83833..

Motels

Hiway Motel and Sports Shop, tel. 686-1310, offers rooms for $23-34 at the junction of highways 95 and 5 at Plummer. **Lakeview Lodge,** tel. 689-3318, offers rooms at Harrison for $60-110 a night. St. Maries weighs in with the **Pines Motel,** tel. 245-2545, at 1117 Main Ave., with rooms for $30-55. It offers cable television and a restaurant, and is close to the public pool and tennis court and a mile from the St. Maries Golf Course.

Resorts

Seven miles west along Hwy. 5 toward Plummer is the **Benewah Resort,** tel. 245-3288, offering cabins, a lodge, and boat rentals along the shore of Benewah Lake. Cabin rates range $28-32 a night. Campers can check into the Carlin Bay Camp-a-Rina, HCR2, Box 45, Harrison, ID 83833. Call ahead at 689-3200. The campground has 12 spaces for $5-12 a night and is located 10 miles north of Harrison. **Cave Lake Resort,** tel. 689-3230, offers a restaurant and bar near Harrison. **Ed's R&R Shady River RV Park,** tel. 245-3549, is located at 1211 Lincoln in St. Maries, and offers 14 campsites for $7-9 a night. Up the St. Joe River, **Misty Meadows RV Park & Camping,** tel. 245-2639, offers 35 campsites from $5 a night. It's located three miles east of town along the Calder-Avery Road. **St. Joe Lodge and Resort,** tel. 245-3462, takes care of travelers venturing east of St. Maries with rooms from $30 a night, $40 with kitchens.

Food

Restaurants in this part of the world mean mostly cafes, with some exceptions. **Granny's Pantry,** tel. 245-4301, promises home cooking at 1117 Main St. in St. Maries. It generally lives up to its menu claims. **Benewah Resort,** tel. 245-3288, maintains a dining room overlooking Benewah Lake. **The Big Eddy,** tel. 245-2107, offers steaks, seafood, and prime rib along the St. Joe River Rd. east of St. Maries. **Gateway Cafe,** tel. 686-1314, serves cinnamon rolls, pies, and cafe meals to Hwy. 95 travelers and locals at Plummer. **The Windmill,** tel. 686-1810, offers a cure for highway hypnosis at Plummer, too, and gets consistently good reviews from its customers. **Parker's Log Cabin Inn,** tel. 245-5495, ranks as the most remote at its base in Avery.

Marinas

Two marinas draw boaters to Harrison, where **Carlin Bay Resort,** tel. 689-3200, and **Gateway Resort and Marina,** tel. 689-3951, offer slips and gas. **Pike Alley,** tel. 689-3746, east along the Coeur d'Alene River from Harrison, also offers marina services and boat rentals.

Events

The two biggest events of the year at St. Maries are the **Benewah County Fair** during the last week of August and **Paul Bunyan Days,** a celebration of logging skills and heritage, held each Labor Day weekend.

Information And Services

St. Maries Chamber of Commerce, tel. 245-3563, at 538 Main Ave., offers comprehensive information about the area. Police services in the area are provided by the **Benewah County Sheriff's Department,** tel. 245-2555, at the Benewah County Courthouse in St. Maries.

NORTH~CENTRAL IDAHO

MOSCOW

Moscow rises from a sea of wheat inundating the prairie and camas swales of the region early settlers called "Hog Heaven." The nickname reflected the delight that the early settlers' pigs must have felt upon finding long meadows filled with camas bulbs south of town along the fledgling Palouse River. The Nez Perce Indians in the area had harvested the starchy bulbs for centuries before white settlement.

Moscow served as a busy crossroads for settlers—everyone from Volga Germans to displaced gold rushers—who flocked to the fertile hills where the soil measured 100 feet deep or more. Latah County, with Moscow as its seat, was created by Congress in 1888, two years before Idaho achieved statehood. Named after sister towns in Pennsylvania and Iowa, Moscow flourished primarily because of the founding of the University of Idaho in 1889. This land-grant school was located there largely to quiet agitators seeking to annex northern Idaho to Washington.

The university still accounts for most of the town's culture and population; half of Moscow moves out when summer begins. The shops and restaurants are typical of college towns, from a downtown art gallery maintained by the university community to the friendly bars staffed by both students and faculty. Sit back and order dinner and a drink at nearly any establishment along Main Street, and the sense that good cheer flows easily here will follow.

EXPLORING THE TOWN

Walking Tours

William J. ("Poker Bill") McConnell was an early-day Moscow merchant whose background included a spell as a vigilante trying to curb the excesses of rustlers. He was elected as a U.S. Senator representing Idaho and later served two terms as the state's governor. His family's home at 110 S. Adams now houses the **Latah County Historical Society,** tel. 882-1004, which offers engaging museum displays and two excellent walking-tour pamphlets to help Moscow

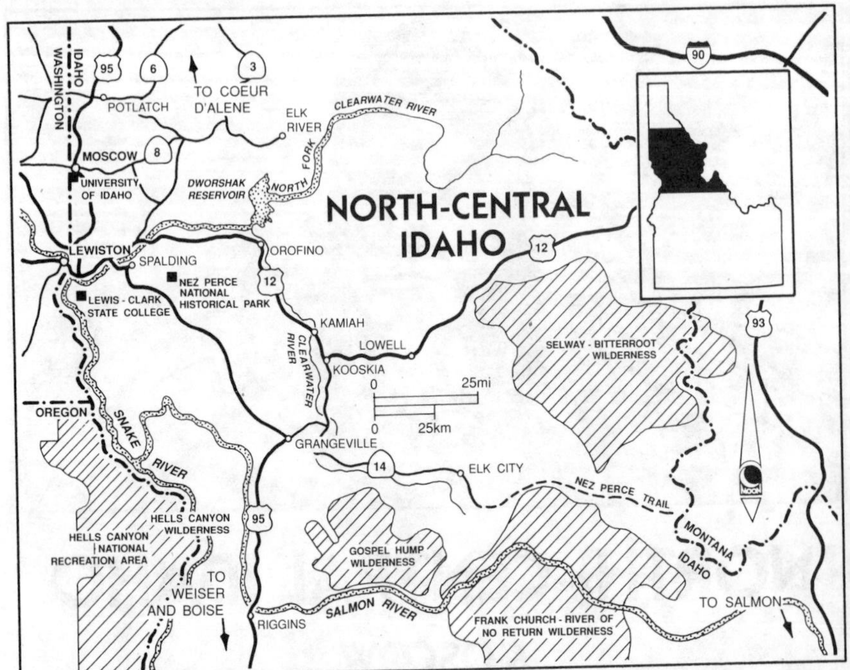

visitors get the true sense of the town.

The first, **"A Walking Tour of Residential Moscow,"** leads visitors on a guided tour of Moscow's most compelling neighborhoods beginning with the McConnell Mansion, the society's stately headquarters. The pamphlet gives a bit of history about each of the homes. Of particular note is 124 N. Polk St., a Queen Anne cottage once occupied by Alex Ryrie and family. Although Alex Ryrie once served as Moscow's mayor after arriving in 1880, the family name lives on mostly through the accomplishments of his daughter, author Carol Ryrie Brink, the author of *Buffalo Coat.* At 430 E. A St. is the 1904 home of Jerome J. Day, Moscow's first millionaire. Still in immaculate condition, the Day home is one of Moscow's neighborhood tour favorites.

The society's **"A Walking Tour of Downtown Moscow"** is just as interesting, tracing the history of Moscow's commercial buildings. The Henry Building at 520 S. Main, built by Andrew Henry, a hardware and machinery dealer, was the first brick building on Main Street. Not long after, the Moscow Hotel at 313 S. Main rose in 1891 to replace the Barton House, which a fire destroyed in 1890. The hotel began operations in 1892. Although it has shed its hotel functions, the building still serves as a gathering point for travelers who congregate for food and drink in the restaurants and bars on its ground floor. The **Carnegie Library** that now serves the Moscow-Latah County Library System earned its place on the National Register of Historic Places with its elegant architecture. The library at 110 S. Jefferson, tel. 882-3925, offers a pleasant refuge to readers and strollers. A new addition has expanded the library's shelf space.

Appaloosa Horse Club Museum

While you're tripping through the past, check out the Appaloosa Horse Club Museum, tel. 882-5578, on Moscow's western edge where Hwy. 8 crosses the state line into Washington. Its exhibits engage the imagination about the Nez Perce Indians and the origins of the spotted horse. The museum has a fenced pasture to keep the real thing on hand.

UNIVERSITY OF IDAHO

One must-stop for the knowledge-hungry is the University of Idaho campus, tel. 885-6111 for general information. The University's academic strengths lie in agriculture, architecture, engineering, forestry and wildlife, mining and metallurgy, and law.

Campus Highlights

Several **museums** find niches in campus buildings; one of the most unusual features a legion of large animal skeletons. The old bones, gathered by the late professor and author Earl J. Larrison are on the top floor of the Life Sciences Building at the campus's core along University Avenue. In a nearby room is the **Jack O'Connor Gallery,** a collection of mounted big-game trophies amassed by the late outdoor writer from nearby Lewiston. To make arrangements to see either collection call 885-6329.

The **Idaho Union** toward the east regularly shows films and occasionally schedules adventure programs. A student union in all the best senses, this heart of campus bustles with life at all hours. It also serves as home to the ***Argonaut***—the UI student newspaper distributed free on campus and in town—and student radio station KUOI-FM (89.3).

the administration building at the University of Idaho, Moscow

The **Shattuck Arboretum** behind the Administration Building offers a pleasant retreat from life in town. The hardwoods planted here are unusual in a state dominated by evergreens and sagebrush. The arboretum was the first established west of the Mississippi River.

The 15-story **ASUI/Kibbie Dome,** once the tallest building in Idaho, dominates the campus's western quadrant, providing a forum for sports events year-round.

Also on campus is the **University library,** the state's best with 1.6 million volumes of books, periodicals, and U.S. government publications. A new addition completed in 1993 dramatically increased its space. The library's reading room offers a good selection of state, regional, and national newspapers for browsing. The government documents section is well run and offers an impressive collection of Congressional hearing records and similar holdings. The section also contains some 140,000 maps, including an excellent collection of topographic maps from the U.S. Geological Survey and U.S. Defense Mapping Agency. The **Idaho Geological Survey** office, in nearby Morrill Hall, has a complete line of USGS Idaho maps.

Research Centers

Research centers on campus explore all realms of human endeavor. The **Boyd and Grace Martin Institute of Human Behavior** focuses on the causes of violence, terrorism, and war. The **Bureau of Public Affairs Research** tackles government needs.

The University of Idaho is best known within the state and nationally, however, for its natural resources expertise. Several campus research institutes reflect that emphasis. Among the most prominent are the Forest, Wildlife, and Range Experiment Station; Glaciological and Arctic Sciences Institute; Idaho Agricultural Experiment Station; Idaho Cooperative Fish and Wildlife Research Unit; Idaho Wilderness Research Instititute; and Idaho Mining and Minerals Resources Research Institute. The Wildlife Research Institute, which is not affiliated with the university except by proximity and cooperation, is also located on campus. The institute is directed by Maurice Hornocker, a widely recognized expert on the mountain lion.

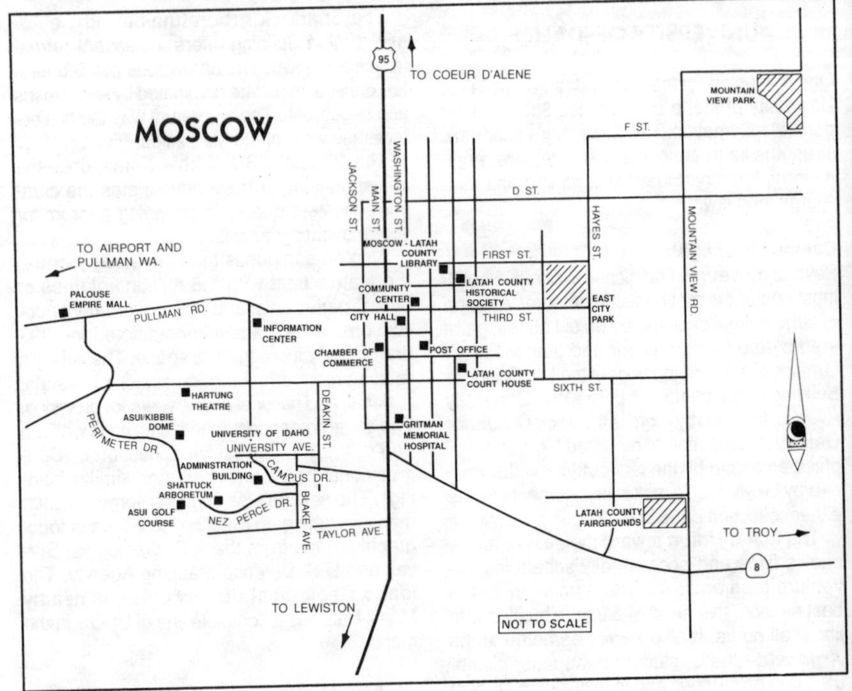

Continuing Education

The university offers an extensive menu of continuing education opportunities including nontraditional and correspondence courses. The **Conferences and Enrichment Program** offers noncredit classes and conferences, workshops, and short courses on specific subjects. It is also beginning to offer outdoors activities, such as rock-climbing and kayaking classes. For more information, write CEP Office, University of Idaho, Moscow, ID 83843, or call 885-6487.

Elderhostel programs are also offered on the Moscow campus and at UI field stations at Clark Fork and McCall. The programs are open to those 60 and older at a cost of about $225 a week, which includes classes, room, board, field trips, and entertainment. For a general catalog of Elderhostel programs, write: Elderhostel, 80 Boylston St., Suite 400, Boston, MA 02116, or call the UI CEP office (above).

RECREATION

Outfitters

With millions of acres of wilderness, both official and otherwise, within four hours' drive from Moscow, outdoor recreation is a prime pastime in the area. The town has several sources for outdoor gear. The Idaho Union on Deakin Ave. houses the **Associated Students University of Idaho Outdoor Program,** tel. 885-6170. The program rents an amazing variety of outdoor gear for personal adventures in the surrounding forests and rivers—everything from a sleeping pad (50 cents for two days) to a fully outfitted 18-foot raft ($120 for two days). **Northwest River Supplies,** tel. 882-2383, 2009 S. Main, can supply anything from rafts to information.

Northwestern Mountain Sports, at the Palouse Empire Mall, tel. 882-0133, and **Gart Brothers,** tel. 882-9547, at 121 E. 5th, offer outdoor equipment and information for outdoors enthusiasts. **Follett's Mountain Sports,** tel. 882-6735, at 428 W. 3rd, offers a comprehensive bicycle and ski selection. **Paradise Creek Bicycles,** tel. 882-0703, carries a strong inventory of bicycles and gear as well at 511 S. Main. For fishers and hunters, **Husky Sports Shop,** tel. 882-0205, 1006 W. Pullman Rd., will have what you need and offers some of the best information available about what's current in the outdoors scene.

Golf, Swimming

The university's student government offers an 18-hole public golf course that drapes across the Palouse hills like a comfortable sweater. The **UI Golf Course** and driving range, tel. 885-6171, is located at 1215 Nez Perce Drive. Another public links is the **Moscow Elks Golf Course,** tel. 882-3015.

Swimming in Moscow means a visit to the University Inn or Mark IV motels (the Mark IV offers a swim-only deal), Gormley City Park pool (summer only), or the University of Idaho Swim Center (year-round). The UI Swim Center is located at 204 Memorial Gym behind the magnificent old gym building south of the library. For a tape-recorded listing of hours, call 885-6180. For more information, the office number is 885-6381. Recreational swimming is generally offered weekday evenings (except Wednesday) and weekend afternoons and evenings. The fee is $1 a day for adults not affiliated with the university, 75 cents for seniors and children.

ENTERTAINMENT

Books, Art, Movies, Theater

Across Deakin from the Student Union Building is the **UI Bookstore,** a popular source of souvenirs from what to some is an obscure university (to others, such as the author, an alma mater that helped form a life's course) and one of the two best book sources in town. The other bookstore of note is **Book People** downtown, 512 S. Main, tel. 882-7957, which would attract fans in any college town. A block north of Book People is the university's **Prichard Art Gallery,** tel. 882-6000, which brings an eclectic selection of artwork to Main Street.

Moscow has movies, a sometimes rare treat in a rural state like Idaho. To find out films and times for the bulk of the theaters, call 882-9600. The two downtown theaters, the **Kenworthy** and **Nuart** are along the 500 block of Main. The **University Four,** tel. 882-9600, is at the west edge of town at 120 Farm Rd. behind the University Inn and across from the Palouse Empire Mall. All three are operated by Carmike Theaters. The idiosyncratic **Micro Moviehouse,** tel. 882-2499, is located at 230 W. 3rd. It shows second-run movies and generally pulls together an entertaining list each month. Together the seven screens give this town a surprisingly good choice of movies.

While you're on campus, check out the offerings of the **Idaho Repertory Theatre** at Hartung Theater (on the west edge of campus); call 885-7212 for tickets. The university's theater department stages plays during the regular semesters and summers.

Events

Either the premier or the penultimate event of the season is **First Night, Last Night,** a community parade and dance held New Year's Eve and on into the wee hours at Friendship Square, Fourth and Main, and elsewhere. The **Lionel Hampton Jazz Festival** in February at the University draws a distinguished crowd of musicians. In early May, the town migrates to East City Park at 6th and Hayes for the **Renaissance Fair.** In early September, schools let out for the annual staging of the **Latah County Fair** at the fairgrounds on the southeast corner of town.

ACCOMMODATIONS AND FOOD

Motels

On Moscow's western edge, the **University Inn Best Western,** 1516 W. Pullman Rd., tel. 882-0550, is Moscow's biggest motel, and has a lounge, indoor pool, coffee shop, restaurant, and meeting rooms. Rates are $54-94. **Motel 6,** 101 Baker, tel. 882-5511, offers the basics; $22 s, $29 d. The **Super 8 Motel** at 175 Peterson, tel. 883-1503, has rooms ranging $24-42. The **Royal Motor Inn,** 120 W. 6th, tel. 882-2581, occupies the heart of downtown and has rooms for $24-52. The **Mark IV Motor Inn,** 414 N. Main, tel. 882-7557, has an indoor pool, restaurant/lounge, and rooms for $29-85. **The Hillcrest,** 706 N. Main, tel. 882-7579, $28-60, is one of Moscow's older motels but remains clean and comfortable.

Bed And Breakfast Inns

The Cottage, tel. 882-0778, offers a one-room cottage for the night for $85. The mini-B&B is located at 318 N. Hayes. **Peacock Hill,** tel. 882-1423, is located at 1245 Joyce Rd. on Moscow's northeastern outskirts, and has a commanding view of town and country. It also offers a hot tub, and a meeting room accommodating 30. Its three rooms with private baths range $65-85. **The VanBuren House,** tel. 882-8531, at 220 N. Van Buren, is in one of Moscow's finer neighborhoods. Its three rooms range $45-75 a night.

Twin Peaks Inn, 2455 W. Twin Rd., tel. 882-3898, offers three guest rooms located in a separate log cottage with a hot tub nearby. Weeknight rates run $35-45, weekends $45-55 d, depending on the room; single rates run $5 less. **Empty Nest,** 811 N. Grant, tel. 882-7344, has two main guest rooms sharing a bathroom, with an overflow room for parties; $55 for couples, $45 for singles. **Beau's Butte,** 702 Public Ave., tel. 882-4061, offers a tranquil setting for $40-45 a night, additional person $10. Children over 12 welcome; no pets.

Food

Moscow's best places to eat cluster along Main Street between 6th and 2nd streets. **Mikey's Greek Gyros,** tel. 882-0780, is at 527 S. Main. The **Old Peking,** tel. 883-0716, at 505 S. Main, offers its authentic selection of Chinese cuisines at moderate prices. The hot and sour soup here is some of the best around. Moscow's other Chinese restaurants include the **Chang Sing,** tel. 882-1154, at 512 S. Washington; **New Hong Kong,** tel. 882-4598, at 214 S. Main; and **Chinese Village,** tel. 882-2931, at the south end of town along Hwy. 95. **Nobby Inn,** tel. 882-2032, at 501 S. Main, features the traditional American menu at moderate prices. The bar in the back of the Nobby is one of Moscow's best watering holes. On its first floor, the Moscow Hotel offers the engaging **Main Street Deli,** tel. 882-0743, which converts from a lounge to a dining room to an adventuresome and pricey restaurant on weekends. The hotel's old dining room is resurrected in the Fourth Street Cafe on weekends. The food is comparable with the best anywhere else in town.

Across 3rd St. and still on Main, **Cafe Spudnik,** tel. 882-9257, operates as Moscow's newwave deli and espresso bar. Its pizza is repeatedly rated the best in town. Another popular Moscow eatery with an Italian flair is **Gambino's Italian Restaurant,** tel. 882-4545, at 308 W. 6th. There's sometimes a line waiting for a table at lunch, but service is fast and can accommodate the crowd quickly. Gambino's has a unique (for Moscow, anyway) dining court covered with a glass roof that can be rolled aside on warm days. The food here is as friendly to the palate as the proprietors to the customers. **Johnnie's Las Hadas,** tel. 883-1182, offers a wooden deck for summer dining and one of the most authentic Mexican menus available in north-central Idaho. It's located a few doors down from Gambino's at 226 W. 6th.

The rest of Moscow's eating scene revolves mostly around fast food. Most of the range is represented along Pullman Rd. from **Bonanza Family Restaurant** at 1710 Pullman to **Skipper's Seafood 'n' Chowder House,** 828 W. Pullman Rd. at its eastern boundary. **McDonald's, Karl Marks Pizza, Arby's,** and **Bonanza** occupy the same strip. **Taco Time** borders the east entrance to campus along 6th St., and the University of Idaho's **Idaho Union** offers several dining areas, ranging from similar fast food to a faculty cafe. **Pizza Hut,** tel. 882-0444, occupies Moscow's eastern flank at 1429 S. Blaine.

Libations

Camas Winery, tel. 882-0214, 110 S. Main, sells its own made-in-Idaho wine (notably Hog Heaven Red) and offers tastings and tours Thurs.-Mon. noon-6 and by appointment. The **Wine Co. of Moscow,** tel. 882-6502, at 113 E. 3rd, offers an expert selection of good wines at good prices. Stop by on Saturdays when a bottle has generally been uncorked for a tasting. The Wine Co. also offers Moscow's best selection of beers from around the world, again at reasonable prices.

Treaty Grounds Brew Pub, tel. 882-3807, occupies a former pizza place at 2124 W. Pullman Rd., and is a satellite to the Palouse Empire Mall, situated out on the edge of the mall's galactic parking lot. The beer is good and the food is pub fare.

Grocery stores with respectable wine and beer selections include **Safeway** on the east edge of town along Hwy. 8 in the Moscow Mall, **Tidyman's** just across the highway from the mall, and **Rosauers** at 411 N. Main.

The **Idaho State Liquor Dispensary,** tel. 882-1538, is located at 904 W. Pullman Road. It's open Mon.-Sat. 10 a.m.-7 p.m.

OTHER PRACTICALITIES

Shopping

Moscow is home to the largest mall between Coeur d'Alene and Boise: the **Palouse Empire Mall** bordering Pullman Rd. on the west edge of town. Shoppers can find K mart, Lamonts, The Bon, JCPenney, and Pay 'N Save here. The mall also includes the usual miscellany of small shops. The **Moscow Mall,** east along Hwy. 8, is the town's first mall and is the smaller of the two. In recent years it has evolved toward providing meeting rooms rather than retail businesses. A mall of a different sort, the **Moscow Antique Mall,** tel. 882-4575, occupies a 7,000-square-foot building at 805 N. Main. The mall is open Mon.-Saturday. **Gem State Crystals,** tel. 883-0939, at 404 S. Main, offers an eclectic array of gem and semiprecious stones and geological specimens. This is a popular stop for kids, who especially key in on the rattlesnake in a glass case that holds some of the more intriguing merchandise.

Transportation

By car, Moscow is one hour and 45 minutes south of Coeur d'Alene along U.S. Hwy. 95 or 45 minutes north of Lewiston on Hwy. 95. **Northwestern Greyhound Bus Lines,** tel. 882-5521, 120 W. 6th, uses the Royal Motor Inn as its base in Moscow. **Wheatland Express,** tel. 334-2200, operates smaller buses between Moscow and Pullman. Around town travelers can call **Richard's Taxi,** tel. 882-1881. The nearest major airline service is at Spokane, Washington. **Campus Link,** tel. 882-1223, offers a ground shuttle to Spokane airport.

The **Pullman-Moscow Regional Airport,** five miles west of town off Pullman Rd., offers commuter and connecting flights aboard **Horizon Air,** tel. (509) 334-1877 or (800) 547-9308.

Services And Information

The **Moscow Chamber of Commerce,** 411 S. Main, Moscow, ID 83843, tel. 882-3581, offers maps and activity information. The **University of Idaho Visitor Center** on Line St. has current information about campus activities. The UI general information number is 885-6111.

Gritman Memorial Hospital, 715 S. Washington, tel. 882-4511, has 24-hour emergency care. Dial 911 for emergency service or 882-5551 for **Moscow Police** or 882-2216 for the **Latah County Sheriff's Department.**

VICINITY OF MOSCOW

East Of Town

Idler's Rest Nature Preserve, six miles northeast of Moscow, is owned by the Nature Conservancy. A great place for a hike, fern-leafed red cedars and a corkscrew ponderosa pine more than 10 stories tall are the major attractions here. The directions can be confusing. Call the University of Idaho **Wildlands Recreation Management Department,** tel. 885-7911, for details.

The main road heading east from Moscow is Idaho Hwy. 8. Along this road, **Troy** is an old farming town that still maintains a grocery store, gas station, and convenience store.

Spring Valley Reservoir, five miles east of Troy off Hwy. 8, is a 50-acre lake owned and managed by the Idaho Fish and Game Department. This little reservoir is a popular fishing hole and overnight camping spot for the university and local crowd.

Helmer is the turnoff point for **Little Boulder Campground** with its eight campsites and three picnic tables two miles to the south. The overnight camping fee is $5. The campground, with its brook stocked with rainbow trout, is a popular retreat for campers and anglers.

Moose Creek Reservoir, reached by a turnoff a half mile west of Bovill, is another recreational haven managed by the Idaho Fish and Game Department. Trout fishing is the main activity here both winter and summer, but camping in roadside pullouts along the reservoir is popular during the summer.

Bovill, named for the Englishman Hugh Bovill, provides the next stop along Hwy. 8. University of Idaho lore includes the infamous Bovill Run, a drinking tour named because of this town's status as the route's eastern terminus. Tougher laws and a realization of the dangers of drinking and driving have all but ended the practice.

Heading east from Bovill along Hwy. 8, you'll come to **Elk River,** literally the end of the highway. Before you reach that point, however, find the sign two miles west of town marking the route south to **Elk Creek Falls.** The graceful trio of waterfalls, the tallest of which plunges 70 feet, is a popular attraction lately imperiled by plans for a hydropower project. Easy hiking and Nordic skiing trails wend their way to the falls a half mile from the parking lot.

Elk River proper is the home of **Huckleberry Heaven Lodge and General Store,** tel. 826-3405. Huckleberries, wild cousins of the blueberry, muster a loyal following in Idaho for their robust flavor. Here you can get a diverse supply of commodities ranging from huckleberry ice cream cones to chocolates with centers tinted purple by the berry. The lodge offers dormitory-style sleeping quarters, hot tubs, and private rooms. Rates vary. In addition to the lodge, several taverns and motels in town also offer food and lodging, albeit none with quite the style.

Elk Creek Reservoir is another popular stop in Elk River. The Elk Creek Recreation District has developed two dozen campsites along the reservoir's shoreline. A rough boat ramp and several docks offer alternate ways to enjoy the water. Past the reservoir, the gravel road winds along Elk Creek to several undeveloped camping spots. Eventually, the road leads into the heart of the Clearwater River's North Fork country.

One of the best uses of the federal budget in recent years greets visitors to the north of Elk River in the Elk Creek Basin. A giant western red cedar there ranks as the biggest of its species east of the Cascade Mountains. With several thousand visitors a year trekking to see the big tree, Forest Service officials decided they needed to do something to protect the tree's roots from trampling and provide better access. The result is a paved trail that winds down a gentle slope to the giant tree and majestic grove surrounding it. A boardwalk around the tree protects the roots and offers a marvelous chance to get up close and personal with a tree that is hundreds of years old. The new trail system also offers disabled visitors a chance to do the same. For information about the tree or the Clearwater National Forest's extensive holdings in the area, contact the **Palouse Ranger District** at its ranger station at Potlatch, tel. 875-1175, or the agency's information office at Moscow, tel. 882-1152. Visitors can also tap the **North Fork Ranger District** at Orofino, tel. 476-3775, for information on lands to the east.

North Of Town

Potlatch lies 17 miles north of Moscow, just off Hwy. 95. It was founded as a company town in 1905 to support what was billed as the world's largest white pine sawmill. Like most of the tall forests that fed it, the sawmill is gone now. Only concrete foundations suggest lumber once boomed here. A well-preserved steam engine is worth a stop for passersby. A grocery store—**Floyd's Excell Foods,** tel. 875-0616—and **Brown Hut Restaurant,** tel. 875-0040, serve those seeking provisions or a break from the road.

Follow Hwy. 95 north another dozen miles to reach the Benewah County line. A gravel road, **Skyline Dr.,** heads west at the summit of the divide between Latah and Benewah counties and leads to one of Idaho's least developed state parks. **Mary Minerva McCroskey State Park** was founded by her son Virgil, a Colfax druggist. He donated 4,500 acres to the state in 1955. Since then the original character of the park, which McCroskey envisioned as a sort of Blue Ridge Parkway, has been maintained. The turn at the top of the divide is risky, either for those turning off the highway to the gravel road or those entering the highway from it. The steep slopes on either side block a clear view of traffic. The Parks Department recommends a safer way to reach the park: north of the divide within sight of the old DeSmet school, a gravel road branches west and signs show the route to the park.

From Potlatch, Hwy. 6 heads east, first to **Princeton,** then **Harvard,** both towns named during the development of the Washington-Idaho-Montana Railroad. The **Bennett Lumber Products** mill at Princeton, tel. 875-1121, stands as an example of a modern, high-tech lumber mill. Tours may be arranged by calling in advance.

Five miles north of Harvard, watch for the turnoff to the Clearwater National Forest's **Laird Park Recreation Area.** Call the Palouse Ranger District, tel. 875-1131, for information. The campground has 25 campsites and seven picnic sites. The **Palouse River** here offers a pebbly beach where children can splash and swim. Two miles north of the turnoff, a thin strip of the mighty trees that once cloaked these slopes rise along the highway as **White Pine Scenic Drive.** These trees are still impressive. The **Giant White Pine Campground** is 1.5 miles north of the beginning of the six-mile scenic drive. Here you'll find 13 campsites and the trailhead for hiking trails in the area. A particularly big white pine dominates the forest here.

More trails branch off the Palouse Divide Rd. that runs along the ridgeline. During the summers, the **North South Ski Bowl,** tel. 245-4222, to the east offers mountain biking. In winter it offers Alpine skiing and serves as the trailhead to the Palouse Divide Nordic ski trails.

LEWISTON AND VICINITY

Lewiston was born of the rush that followed the discovery of gold in 1860 in the Clearwater River country to the northeast. The town was plotted in 1861 at the confluence of the Snake and Clearwater rivers as a supply point for prospectors making the final leg of their trek to the goldfields. It started out as a rip-roaring tent camp; even the venerable Luna House hotel began life as a tent. A visiting dignitary first objected to the piles of sandbags surrounding his bed. He demurred when the proprietor told him the bags were sure to stop any stray bullets that might pierce his room's canvas sides.

The town was originally designated as the territorial capital, but in 1864, a thief stole away with the official territorial seal, and the capital was subsequently transferred to Boise. Because of its location, Lewiston flourished nonetheless as a supply depot for settlers and as a transportation hub. As the state's only port—some 460 miles inland at the terminus of the Snake River arm of the Columbia River waterway system—steamboats, including the *Lewiston,* frequented its shores. Stagecoach lines threaded their way across the countryside. In 1903, the railroad made it to town on a bright steel bridge across the Clearwater River and put its horse-drawn or paddlewheel precursors mostly out of business.

The area was also touted as one of the best agricultural settings in the region. The vast Lewiston Orchards grew on the steppes above the young city. Eventually, the city grew and annexed those, too.

The Snake River flows out of Idaho into Washington just downstream from town at an elevation of 738 feet, the lowest point in Idaho. The Clearwater River was the first leg of the water route west from the Bitterroot Mountains to the Pacific Ocean taken by the Lewis and Clark Expedition in 1805. The city is named for Meriwether Lewis. Neighboring Clarkston, Washington, was named for the Corps of Discovery's coleader William Clark.

Economy

Lewiston ranks as Idaho's fifth-largest city behind Boise, Pocatello, Idaho Falls, and Nampa. Its prosperity results from the rich agricultural lands surrounding it. A frozen-pea-processing plant gives downtown the odor of a vegetarian kitchen during spring evenings when the harvest trucks roll in day and night. The sprawling wheat farms of the Nez Perce Prairie to the south and Palouse to the north stock the grain elevators lining the Clearwater's bank in Lewiston. And above all, lumber is king.

Potlatch Corporation built a sawmill and pulp mill during the early part of the century along the Clearwater on Lewiston's eastern flank. The mill's payroll still dominates the town's economy—much of the town's workforce reports to work at the mill or supplies those who do. Less dominant these days is the unmistakable smell of digesting pulp. The company invested more than a half-billion dollars to modernize its pulp mill, and these days the plumes from the mill are almost entirely steam. Only on windless days does the mill's smell recall days gone by.

Lewiston's tourism trade is growing as the Northwest and the nation learn more about the Clearwater and Snake rivers' mighty steelhead runs and the thrilling whitewater rapids of the Salmon River or Hells Canyon along the Snake. Outfitting businesses in Lewiston are becoming more numerous to service this growing segment of the economy. Finally, the payrolls of Lewis-Clark State College and St. Joseph Regional Medical Center round out the city's economy.

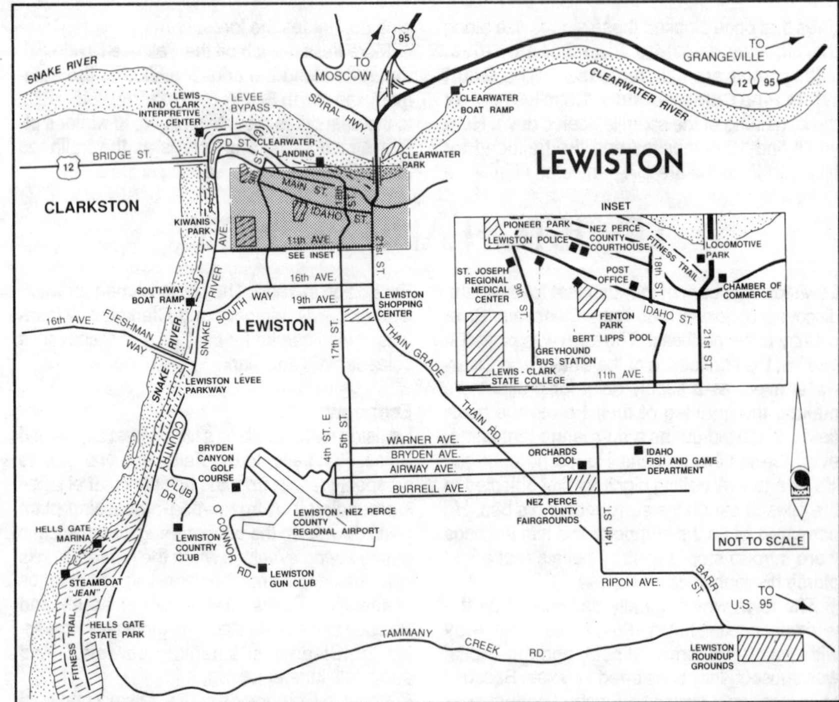

In The Vicinity

Two major sights are found some distance from Lewiston and are covered separately at the end of this section, after Lewiston proper. Hells Canyon, once thought to be America's deepest gorge, is now preserved as the Hells Canyon National Recreation Area. Although the canyon is south of the city along the Snake, Lewiston is the major outfitting center and base of operations for river runners through the canyon. East of Lewiston at Spalding is the headquarters of Nez Perce National Historic Park, a wide-spread conglomeration of sites having historical importance to the most famous of Idaho's indigenous peoples.

SIGHTS

Scenic Highway

One of the best sights to see near Lewiston is the city itself from the top of 2,000-foot-high Lewiston Hill. And getting there is half the fun. The **Spiral Highway,** which branches off from Hwy. 95 eight miles north of town or at the rose garden just north of the Clearwater Memorial Bridge, was the main road out of town when it was built in 1913. Now it's more of a scenic attraction than a busy travel route. The eight-mile adventure of twisting curves and steep dropoffs winds down 2,000 feet from the rim of the prairie to the bank of the Clearwater. Motorists in a hurry use the modern four-lane highway that follows a straighter, steeper route down the hill.

Luna House Museum

The Luna House Museum at 3rd and C streets, housed in an early Lewiston hotel, is now operated by the **Nez Perce County Historical Society,** tel. 743-2535, and is open Tues.-Sat. 9-5.

Parks

If savoring scenic beauty is the object of your sojourn in Idaho, there's no place more beautiful than Lewiston in the springtime, along about late April or early May. The valley of the Clearwater and Snake rivers is verdant then, green as grass can be. Lewistonians have planted dogwoods by the hundreds and the climate agrees with them. Some dogwoods have become trees, as big as oaks it seems. The whole city takes on a parklike setting then and revels in it during the annual Lewis Clark Dogwood Festival (see "Events," following).

The **Lewiston Levee Parkway** parallels the path of Hwy. 12 through the city. The asphalt pathways draw flocks of birdwatchers, joggers, bicyclists, and strollers throughout the year. The best time to walk the pathways is in April when extensive plantings of flowering shrubs and trees are at their floral peaks. The parkway was designated a National Recreation Trail in 1988.

The levee trails stretch some 21 miles along the Clearwater and Snake. Along the Snake's Washington shoreline, the trail system also includes the Clarkston Greenbelt. On the Idaho side of the Snake, two visitor centers offer displays about the rivers' history. The **Clearwater Landing,** which is opposite the Port of Lewiston along the Clearwater River, tells of early and present navigation along the river. The second visitor point, the **Lewis and Clark Interpretive Center,** also along the levee parkway, is at the confluence of the Snake and Clearwater less than a mile downstream. The Lewis and Clark Expedition, which passed down the Clearwater toward the Pacific on October 10, 1805, was the first party of voyagers to record their passage. Parking is available where D St. intersects the Hwy. 12 bypass along the levee. A pedestrian bridge allows walkers to safely cross the busy bypass and gain access to the asphalt trails.

Hells Gate State Park, four miles from Lewiston's downtown, is the southern terminus of the levee trail system. The park has a marina with moorage and a store offering minimal supplies. The marina also serves as a departure point for tour boats bound for Hells Canyon upriver on the Snake. The ***Steamboat Jean,*** a paddlewheeler, is berthed next to the marina in the park. The park's day-use area and beach are popular destinations during the warm months April through October. Hells Gate also offers a horseback concession, tel. 743-3142, for those wishing to ride its trails. The trails are also open to mountain bikers and hikers.

RECREATION

Boating

With its prime riverfront location, it's no surprise that boating is very popular in the area. The **Clearwater Jet Boat Rally** draws racers from throughout the continent each June. The race, and another along the Salmon River near White Bird in May, serves as part of the U.S. championship most years. But most boaters are content to cruise **Lower Granite Reservoir** along the Snake or to head upriver to try some whitewater. Lewiston is gaining a reputation as the jet boat

A rider explores the uplands above Hells Gate State Park.

manufacturing capital of the Northwest. The boats are so named because their powerful engines drive pumps that shoot out a jet of water. The jet pushes the boat and eliminates the need for propellers, which normally have short lives in the rocky rapids of the Snake, Clearwater, and Salmon rivers.

Lewiston's large number of boat dealers and boat service companies underscores the valley's status as a boating center. Establishments include **Clearwater Marine,** 206 22nd N at the north approach to the Clearwater Memorial Bridge, tel. 746-7919; **Valley Boat and Motor,** 419 Snake River Ave., tel. 743-2528; and **Riverview Marina,** 711 Snake River Ave., tel. 746-1412. All three are landlocked. The only place to moor boats on the Idaho side of the Snake is at **Hells Gate Marina,** tel. 743-8833, at the state park at 3620-S Snake River Avenue. If no one answers at the marina, call the park at 743-2363. The marina offers minimal facilities but does maintain a gas dock. Boat ramps are spread along the Snake and Clearwater rivers' shorelines. Popular ramps with docks are located at the park and near the foot of Southway Ave. along the Snake River and opposite the Potlatch mill along the Clearwater in North Lewiston.

Golf

Lewiston has two 18-hole golf courses: **Bryden Canyon,** tel. 746-0863, a public course at 445 O'Connor Rd. to the west of the Lewiston-Nez Perce County Airport, and the **Lewiston Golf and Country Club,** tel. 743-3549, a private course at 3985 Country Club Drive. Two other courses are across the Snake River in Clarkston. **Clarkston Golf and Country Club,** tel. (509) 758-2546, is at 1676 Elm along Hwy. 12 and the Snake River at the town's western edge. **Quail Hollow Golf Course,** tel. (509) 758-8501, is at 3600 Swallows Nest Dr. off Hwy. 129 heading for Asotin and Critchfield Road.

Rodeo

The **Lewiston Roundup** in early September (see "Events," following) is the most well-known event to the non-cowboy crowd. But a spring buckout and other events throughout the year at the **Lewiston Roundup Grounds** south of town, tel. 746-6324, keep things hopping nearly year-round.

Other Sports

Baseball is probably the most popular team sport in town, due largely to the dynastic Lewis-Clark State College Warriors. They've won the National Association for Intercollegiate Athletics crown so often that the organization located the championships at Lewiston for several years. For the masses, city-league softball and American Legion hardball keep the field lights shining during summer evenings.

While less organized, **log-rolling,** at Clearwater Park at the northeast corner of the Clearwater Memorial Bridge, helps keep the city's championship log birlers on their toes with a pond and practice logs.

ACCOMMODATIONS AND FOOD

Bed And Breakfast Inns

Carriage House Bed and Breakfast, tel. 746-4506, 611 5th St., has two rooms. Rates are $65 and $85. The Carriage House is located a couple of blocks from the **Lewis-Clark State College** campus. Lewiston also offers **Shiloh Rose Bed and Breakfast,** tel. 743-2482, at 3414 Selway Dr., in one of the city's prettier neighborhoods along the Snake River.

Motels

The **Ramada Inn** at 621 21st St., tel. 799-1000, is likely to be your first view of Lewiston while crossing the Clearwater Memorial Bridge heading west on Hwy. 12. With 102 rooms ranging $54-145, a restaurant, bar, and convention center, the Ramada is Lewiston's most complete lodging.

A couple less expensive favorites are **Pony Soldier Motor Inn,** 1716 Main, tel. 743-9526, with rooms for $44-64; and the **Sacajawea Motor Inn,** 1824 Main, tel. 746-1393, with rates of $33-48.

Other motels include **El Ranch Motel,** tel. 743-8517, at 2240 3rd Ave., with rooms for $22-30; **Hillary Motel,** tel. 743-8514, at 2030 North and South Hwy., with rooms for $19-45; **Ho Hum Motel,** tel. 743-2978, with rooms for $18-32; **Sundance Motor Inn,** tel. 743-4501, at 1021 Main St., with rooms for $25-40; **Super 8 Motel,** tel. 743-8808 or (800) 848-8888, along Hwy. 12 at Lewiston's eastern fringe, with rooms for $34-42; and **Tapadera Motor Inn,** tel. 746-3311, at 1325 Main St., with rooms for $31-38.

Food

Lewiston has an extensive strip of fast-food joints ranging from taquerias to the Big Five: **Hardees, Burger King, McDonald's, Arby's,** and **Wendy's.** All but Hardees crouch along the shoulders of 21st St.; the lone stray is at the intersection of 20th St. near the base of 21st.

The strip also offers some more eclectic choices. Starting at the bottom of the hill and heading upward and southward, these include the **Mighty Potato,** 826 21st, tel. 746-7783, classic American cuisine from chops to burgers; **Mandarin Pine,** 833 21st, tel. 746-4919, good authentic Chinese food; and **Zany Graze,** 2004 19th Ave., tel. 746-8131, one of the most fun places to eat in Lewiston, with a great barbecue selection and inspired sandwiches.

For classic dining, avoid 21st and head downtown to **Jonathan's,** tel. 746-3438, in the Bollinger Plaza at D and 3rd streets. The menu—from Cajun-style prime rib sandwiches to rich fettucine, steaks, seafood, and gigantic salads—is on the pricey side, with entrees to $18. But with a comfortable bar and interesting, even plush, basement dining, this place dictates Lewiston-Clarkston Valley style.

Also downtown is the **It Shop,** 631 Main, tel. 746-3054, where no one counts calories or cholesterol because of the juicy burgers. The It Shop recalls life before McDonald's. **Pioneer Pies,** 1407 Main, tel. 746-0010, and **Waffles N'More,** 1421 Main, tel. 743-5189, anchor the breakfast scene. The former also serves lunch and dinner. **The Helm,** 1826 Main, tel. 746-6991, sticks to the traditional with its menu of seafood, steaks, and burgers.

Across the Clearwater Memorial Bridge, **Italian Gardens Cafe,** 1st Ave. and W. 22nd N, tel. 743-7632, offers steaks and seafood in addition to its ethnic specialties, such as chicken parmigiana. Farther east along Hwy. 12 is **Spencer's,** 3041 North and South Hwy., tel. 743-3736, the best steak house in the valley.

OTHER PRACTICALITIES

Shopping

Morgan's Alley downtown at 3rd and Main represents a major effort to preserve one of Lewiston's historic buildings. The building houses antique shops, tobacco shops, a tavern, and a restaurant.

Lewiston's plethora of chain stores makes it a regional shopping mecca. The **Lewiston Center** between 21st and 20th streets along 19th Ave. houses JCPenney, The Bon, Lamonts, Sears, and PayLess Drugstore. Across 21st St. to the east is **K mart.** To the south and up 21st is **Shopko,** a major discount retailer in the valley. **WalMart** is just a little farther up the hill from Shopko. **Best,** another discount retailer, rounds out the selection at 1521 6th Ave. N, across the Clearwater River.

A dozen or more boat-building companies line the shores of the Clearwater and Snake rivers in the valley. They churn out 500-600 boats a year. Customers can have a boat designed for their needs or order standard models. Jet boats, named because they are propelled by a jet of water, are pricey, though. A 22-footer, about average, routinely commands $25,000 or more.

Events

The **Lewiston Roundup,** traditionally held the first full weekend of September, has been the main event in Lewiston for years. Held at the Roundup Grounds south of town behind the Tammany School, the rodeo attracts some of the top Professional Rodeo Cowboys Association competitors each year. A parade, barbecue, bucking horse sale, and other events round out the schedule.

Coming on strong in recent years to rival the Roundup is the **Dogwood Festival,** several weeks' worth of events ranging from the Seaport River Run to the Confluence Wine Faire. Held in late April and early May, the festival coincides with the peak season for the valley's spectacular dogwoods and other shrubs and trees, from rhododendrons to flowering crabapples.

Transportation

Lewiston is 270 miles north of Boise along Hwy. 95, a scenic highway often derided as a goat path by politicians eager for progress. Northwestern Greyhound Bus Lines maintains a terminal at 1002 Idaho St., tel. 746-8108.

The **Lewiston-Nez Perce County Airport** could handle large jets, if it only attracted the customers. **Empire Airlines,** tel. 746-8866, and **Horizon Airlines,** tel. 743-9293, fly small commuter aircraft to Lewiston. Rental cars are available at the airport from **Budget Rent-a-Car,** tel. 746-0488; **Hertz,** tel. 746-0411; and **National Car Rental,** tel. 743-0176.

Information And Services

St. Joseph Regional Medical Center, tel. 743-2511, at 4th Ave. and 6th St., offers a 24-hour emergency room. **Police** and **fire** departments are reached by dialing 911.

The **Lewiston Chamber of Commerce,** tel. 743-3531, is located at 2207 E. Main, Lewiston, ID 83501, and offers information about local and regional events.

The ***Lewiston Morning Tribune,*** tel. 743-9411, is the region's largest newspaper with a circulation of 25,000 weekdays and Sundays. It celebrated its centennial in 1992. The newspaper's editorial writers, Bill Hall and Jim Fisher, tend to be the talk of the town with liberal editorials in a town that tends toward conservative views. Lewiston is also served by CBS affiliate KLEW-TV on channel 3. Radio stations include country station **KRLC,** at 1350 AM, and rock stations **KATW,** 101.5 FM, **KMOK,** at 106.9 FM, and **KOZE,** at 950 AM and 96.5 FM.

HELLS CANYON NATIONAL RECREATION AREA

In 1975, Congress acted to settle years of political turmoil in Idaho by creating the 652,488-acre Hells Canyon National Recreation Area in Idaho and Oregon. The Hells Canyon debate flared in the 1960s when developers wanted to build hydroelectric dams along the Snake. The river's frothy, tumbling rapids in Hells Canyon, including such notables as Granite Creek, Wild Sheep, and Rush Creek, signal one notable feature: a rapidly sloping riverbed. It was that steep gradient that drew the interests of dam builders. To build a major hydroelectric project, engineers need a large river, as well as canyon-like terrain where the concrete plug can be placed. Hells Canyon fit both criteria.

But Hells Canyon also had fans of its wild state, who knew the dams would flood the rapids and tame the river. Early on, they watched the U.S. Army Corps of Engineers take its rock samples and knew what was up. They launched an ambitious lobbying campaign and hauled federal, state, and other influential powerbrokers through Hells Canyon, arguing that those wild rapids—some of the continent's most challenging whitewater—and that sometimes whisper, sometimes roar of a free-flowing river deserved Congressional protection. After a few refreshing baptisms in Granite Creek Rapid's "Green Room," a whitewater hole the size of a house, enough of the undecided agreed to protect the river from dam building and other development.

The Hells Canyon law protected 67.5 miles of the Snake River. A 31.5-mile section of the Snake, from Pittsburg Landing upstream to Hells Canyon Dam, is now classed as a wild river, and another 36 miles downstream from Pittsburg to the NRA boundary near the Oregon-Washington border is classed as a scenic river.

The NRA also features nearly 1,000 miles of foot and horseback trails. Access by roads is limited. On the Idaho side, the main access to the area is at **Pittsburg Landing** near White Bird; **Windy Saddle** and **Heavens Gate** near the Seven Devils Mountains west of Riggins; and at **Black Lake** north of Cambridge. Sedans can travel all three roads leading to the areas during dry summer weather. However, the Black Lake Rd. requires a vehicle with high clearance. The roads are rough and open for only a few months each year, most years July to September.

One part of the NRA is the 215,000-acre Hells Canyon Wilderness which surrounds the **Seven Devils Mountains** on the Idaho side. Here visitors may ride horseback or hike only. No mechanical vehicles, bicycles, or motorized vehicles may enter.

Camping

Camping is allowed at the road's end at Pittsburg Landing, so named because paddlewheelers used to tie up there. A campground has recently taken shape there and still seems somewhat out of place with its sun shelters on the broad grassy flat. The landing is one of the most popular places to see the interior of the canyon, and until the newly planted trees can provide some shade, the shelters will see plenty of use during the heat of summer. The road to Pittsburg is a gravel road much improved from the past, but it will still strike most neophyte mountain travelers as a white-knuckle adventure. If anyone in the party suffers vertigo, it may be time for blinders or a good book to divert

Rugged walls define Hells Canyon along the Snake River.

the attention. The road demands caution and slow speeds but is used by thousands of vehicles a year. Campgrounds (none with potable water) are also available at Black Lake and Windy Saddle near Heavens Gate, and at nearby Seven Devils Campground. Watch the close-by granite cliffs for mountain goats here. For information about road conditions, call the Forest Service office at Clarkston, Washington, tel. (509) 758-0616; or the Hells Canyon NRA office at Riggins, tel. 628-3916.

Whitewater Rafting

Hells Canyon is a major destination for whitewater rafting enthusiasts. For many people, rafting down the Snake River is a thrill comparable to viewing the Grand Canyon. Private outfitters for rafting trips are scattered throughout the region; expeditions range from overnighters to multiday trips. Names of commercial outfitters operating in the canyon can be obtained from the Forest Service's Clarkston office. Among the companies offering float trips down the Snake through the Canyon are **Idaho Afloat,** tel. 983-2414, at 404 S. College, Grangeville, ID 83530; **Holiday River Expeditions,** tel. 983-1518, at P.O. Box 86, Grangeville; and **Northwest Voyageurs,** tel. (800) 727-9977, at P.O. Box 373G, Lucile, ID 83542. **Northwest Dories,** tel. (800) 877-3679, offers trips through the canyon in graceful, whitewater-worthy wooden dories.

Private parties also may float the Snake in the NRA, but must obtain a Forest Service permit to launch during the summer months, from late May through early September. The number of rafting permits is limited. Each winter the Forest Service conducts a computerized lottery to determine who will get popular launch dates. Permits remaining after the lottery are given out first-come, first-served by telephone.

Jet Boats And Fishing

Equally thrilling for many visitors are jet-boat tours of the canyon. These tours are a popular industry in the region and generally require less time and money than rafting trips. A jet boat survives the river by trying to cow it with a mighty roar of its own and by bullying its way up through the rapids. The best captains learn that finesse has its rewards but otherwise power will do. The biggest jet boats come equipped with two, even three, big gasoline engines ranging from the 454-cubic-inch Ford to the 460 Chevy.

Fishing outfitters also use these water-jet powered boats to seek the best spots in the canyon to catch trout, bass, and white sturgeon. There's nothing modest about the fish here. The biggest sturgeon caught in the canyon in recent years stretched the tape to 12 feet and could have weighed more than 500 pounds. To preserve the mighty fish, however, all sturgeon caught must be released unharmed.

The Forest Service maintains a complete list of fishing and jet-boat tour operators. Some are listed following. **Beamer's Landing,** at the western edge of Clarkston, Washington along Hwy. 12, tel. 743-4800, is the largest and best-

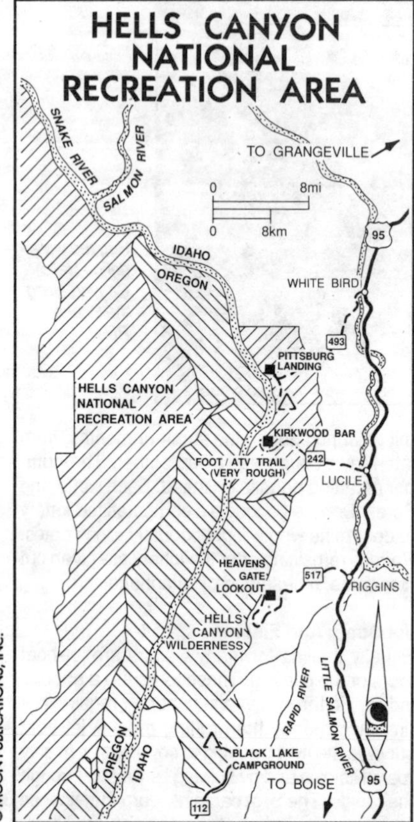

known Hells Canyon tour outfit. Beamer's offers one-day sightseeing tours for $85 and overnight excursions from $185 with lodging at **Copper Creek,** the outfit's resort in the canyon. **Snake River Adventures,** tel. 746-6276, offers day trips for $75, $85, or $120, depending on the length of the trip. An overnight trip includes a stay at the historic **Sheep Creek Ranch** for $160 per person and $45 for additional days. **Cougar Country Lodge,** P.O. Box 448, Asotin, WA 99402, tel. (509) 758-1441, specializes in the sinful pleasures of fishing, particularly for big sturgeon. Day trips range in cost from $70 to $105. Overnight steelhead fishing trips are $250 per person.

Private-party boaters must fill out a self-issue permit from the Forest Service before launching. Unlike its policy for rafters, the Forest Service has set no limit on permits for power-boaters.

NEZ PERCE NATIONAL HISTORICAL PARK

"From where the sun now stands, I will fight no more forever," said Chief Joseph on an October day in 1877 as he stood along Snake Creek in central Montana. Did he really utter this or did a magazine embellish the wise chief's words? The answer to some is elusive but Chief Joseph's plight was indisputable. He and his struggling band of non-treaty Nez Perce tribe members had been forced to surrender their dream of escaping to Canada, just 42 miles to the north. Their defeat meant they would be forced to live on a reservation, far from their homeland.

The 1877 Nez Perce War earned Joseph fame as a wise and compassionate leader both in war and in peace. Except for that brief convulsion of frustration lasting from June 13 to October 5, 1877, the Nez Perce have been known as a peaceable people. They also are known for developing America's most unique breed of horse, the Appaloosa. Although the Appaloosa Horse Club's headquarters is in Moscow, the heart of the breed's history is still in the Lapwai area, the core of the reservation 13 miles east of Lewiston.

The Nez Perce National Historical Park, headquartered at Spalding, 11 miles east of Lewiston along Hwy. 95 (P.O. Box 93, Spalding, ID 83551; tel. 843-2261), recalls the tribe's past and explains its present. The park, created in 1965, is unified conceptually but not geographically. It is comprised of 24 different sites scattered across some 12,000 square miles of the Nez Perce's homeland. Congress has fielded a proposal to add sites in Montana, Oregon, and Washington as well. A 400-mile circuit is required to see all of the sites.

The sites cover diverse terrain, ranging from river canyons to mountain peaks. The Spalding headquarters, open 8 a.m.-4:30 p.m. in winter and 8 a.m.-6 p.m. in summer, offers exhibits and information about the tribe's past and white settlement in the area. The headquarters theater shows a film about the Nez Perce culture, both past and present. A favorite picnic area, open

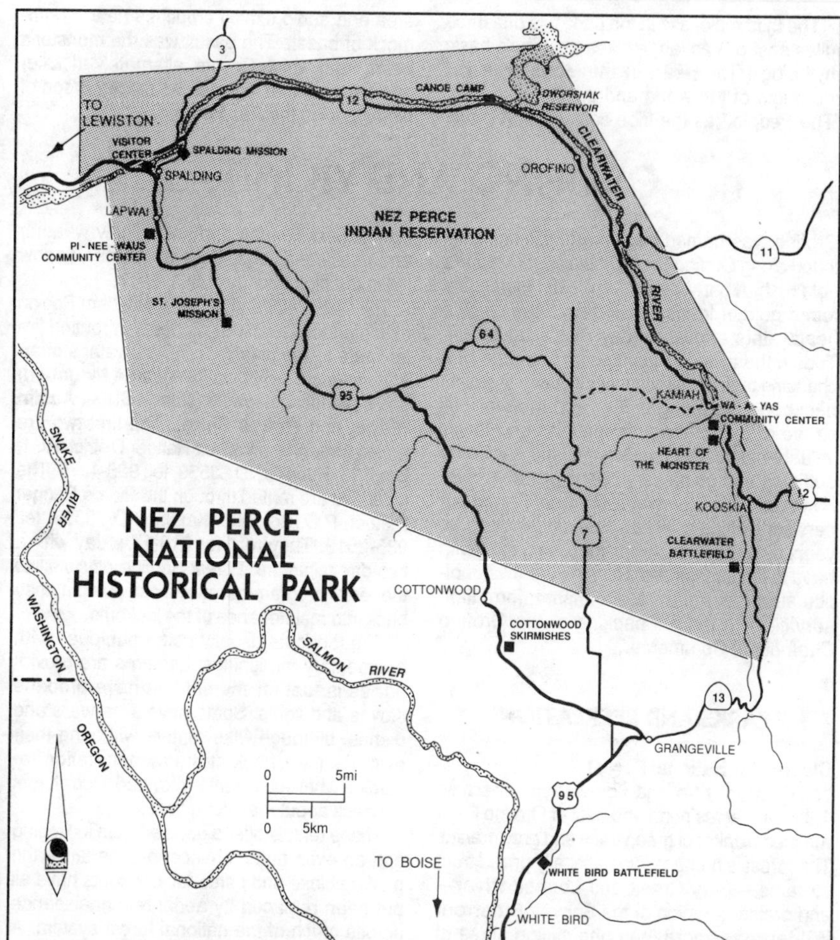

only during daylight hours, now lies on the flat once occupied by pioneer missionaries Henry and Elizabeth Spalding. A nearby cemetery is the burial ground for missionaries and Nez Perce; it dates back to the 1880s.

The three most impressive outlying sites are St. Joseph's Mission, the White Bird Battlefield, and the Heart of the Monster or East Kamiah sites. Father Joseph Cataldo dedicated **St. Joseph's Mission** on Sept. 8, 1874; it was the first Roman Catholic mission to the Nez Perces. The mission, 6.3 miles south of Spalding off Hwy. 95 (3.8 miles south of Jacques Spur along Mission Rd.), is open in summer Thurs.-Mon. 10 a.m.-4:30 p.m.

The **White Bird Battlefield** is 64 miles farther south along Hwy. 95. In the days after the initial attacks on settlers, the Nez Perce prepared for retaliation by the U.S. Cavalry. On June 17, the first battle of the war occurred at White Bird. A small band of warriors defeated a larger force, killing 34 soldiers and losing none themselves. An exhibit helps bring the battle to life. An excellent map for auto tours is also displayed.

The third major site in the park, this one three miles east of Kamiah, evokes the tribe's basic mythology. The **Heart of the Monster** marks the origin of the world and the Ne-Mee-Poo, "The People," as the tribe calls itself. A picnic area and audio exhibit crouches near a hummock of basalt. The basalt was the monster's heart, from which Coyote, alternately trickster and hero in tribal legends, squeezed drops of blood to form the Nez Perce.

OROFINO AND VICINITY

Orofino was named because of the fine gold found along Orofino Creek at the start of Idaho's gold rush. A party led by Capt. E.D. Pierce first found gold in Idaho in 1860 near the creek's headwaters at present-day Pierce upstream. Today, the town is balanced on the edge of a changing tableaux. The timber industry that is its backbone is getting leaner and meaner because of toughening competition and fewer valuable logs. The tourism industry, including outfitting and guide services, is growing here, however. The Clearwater National Forest supervisor's office here has been under siege for years by environmentalists for paying too much heed to timber interests. Now the Clearwater office supports a first-rate tourism information service with the full backing of the Orofino Chamber of Commerce.

PARKS AND RECREATION

Clearwater National Forest

The Clearwater National Forest stretches across 1.8 million acres north and east of Orofino like a rumpled blanket of green trees and gray granite. The forest is home to two nationally prized trout streams—**Kelly Creek** and **Lochsa River**—and drains a portion of the **Selway-Bitterroot Wilderness,** more than one million acres of pristine streams, steep mountains, and scenic valleys. North of Orofino, the **Mallard Larkins Pioneer Area** offers gemlike high-mountain lakes in spectacular settings.

The Clearwater is user-friendly; 21 campsites and picnic areas are scattered throughout the national forest. A $4-5 nightly fee is charged at most of the campsites to help pay for water systems and garbage collection. For more information about reservations and campground fees, contact the supervisor's office (see "Information and Services," following). If you're heading out into the backcountry, be sure you have a Forest Service map and know likely weather and road conditions. Several inches of snow fell in the high country July 4, 1987.

The Clearwater and the other Northern Region national forests rank as pioneers in renting fire lookouts to the public. The Clearwater's offerings include a lookout cabin (**Walde Mountain**) and three lookout towers (**Castle Butte, Austin Ridge,** and **Weitas Butte**). The first two are rented through the Lochsa Ranger District, Rt. 1, Box 398, Kooskia, ID 83539, tel. 926-4275. The latter two are rented through the Pierce Ranger District, P.O. Box 308, Kamiah, ID 83536, tel. 935-2513. They rent for $15-17 a day with a two-day minimum. Forest Service officials like the rental program because it can pump money back into maintenance of the lookouts.

The lookouts usually come equipped with rudimentary furnishings. Lanterns are provided, as is fuel for them. Most have propane stoves and lights. Some have silverware and dishes, although wise renters will bring their own. Double-check at the ranger station regarding what equipment is provided. Don't forget to check about road conditions.

These rentals offer a good bargain in lodging and an even better chance to experience the past up close and personal. Lookouts have all but been replaced by aerial reconnaissance across much of the national forest system. A few fire lookouts are still operational, but they're the exceptions.

Dworshak State Park

Dworshak State Park, tel. 476-5994, five miles up the reservoir from Dworshak dam, is one of Idaho's newest state parks and one of the most modern. The Army Corps of Engineers built this park to compensate for recreation losses caused by the dam. Boat ramps, a swimming beach, picnic shelter, playground, 92 family campsites, and three group camping areas were intended to help atone for the losses. The **Three Meadow**

BUREAU OF OUTDOOR RECREATION, DEPARTMENT OF THE INTERIOR

The rugged Clearwater Mountains stop a hiker in his tracks along the Lolo Trail.

Group Camp, the best equipped in the state parks system, can house and feed up to 100.

While the park is accessible by boat, a narrow road winding some 24 miles through Cavendish and down the steep slopes of Freeman Creek is the most used access. Getting to the reservoir from Orofino means going through **Ahsahka,** along Hwy. 7, an old Indian town routinely invaded by fishermen after steelhead trout, and climbing up the twisting road to reach a small prairie above the Clearwater River and Dworshak Dam.

Big Eddy Marina

The marina, which at the time of this writing consisted of little more than a boat ramp, is a convenient starting point to reach some six dozen mini-camps the corps has sprinkled along the reservoir's shoreline. The mini-camps' secluded settings offer an alternative to the state park, which is open for camping upstream along the reservoir. One caution: check the reservoir level before heading out to camp. Slogging up 50 vertical feet of muddy slope makes having fun at a mini-camp more of a challenge than some appreciate. Those who don't mind a little hike are doubly rewarded because the reservoir offers even more peace and quiet at such times.

OTHER SIGHTS

Dworshak Dam And Reservoir

The Army Corps of Engineers offers tours of this, the highest straight-axis concrete dam in the West. The dam was completed in 1973. Don't worry about the sounds of splashing water here; all dams leak a little, the corps says. **Dworshak Excursions,** tel. 476-4742, was created because its founder believed the 53-mile long Dworshak Reservoir had the potential to be a mini-Lake Mead. Pontoon boats and an inventive "RV Afloat" contraption, which carries a camping trailer, offer a different way to reach mini-camps along the shoreline.

Dworshak National Fish Hatchery

The steelhead run to the Clearwater's north fork here is supported by Dworshak National Fish Hatchery, tel. 476-4591, just across the river from Ahsahka and three miles from Orofino. Dworshak is one of the world's biggest steelhead and salmon hatcheries, producing some five million smolts for release each year. Smolts are young fish ranging in size from a few inches to nearly a foot that turn silvery bright as they begin the physical changes needed to migrate to and enter the sea. The young fish are carried down the Clearwater, Snake, and Columbia rivers 500 miles to the rich pastures of the Pacific Ocean. The fish grow big there; the Clearwater steelhead, a seagoing rainbow trout, reaches 12-14 pounds on average.

Federal money built a new hatchery the size of Dworshak Hatchery just across the Clearwater's north fork. Like Dworshak, the **Clearwater Anadromous Fish Hatchery** is intended to replace the millions of fish killed each year by Dworshak Dam and eight other dams along the Snake and Columbia rivers downstream. Together, the hatcheries have the capacity to release nearly 10 million chinook salmon and steelhead smolts.

Clearwater County Historical Museum

Care to see the tools of the trade from the olden days when lumberjacks ruled the woods? The Clearwater County Historical Museum at 315 College is open Thurs.-Sat. 1:30-4:30 p.m. Displays also include Lewis and Clark Expedition artifacts, Nez Perce beadwork and cornhusk bags, and old guns.

PRACTICALITIES

Accommodations

Motels are limited in the Orofino area, particularly during the peaks of the steelhead season (November and March) when anglers create a frenzy on the water and fill up the rooms. The **Riverside Motel,** tel. 476-5711, is at 10560 Hwy. 12 and offers 12 rooms at $20-39. The **Konkolville Motel,** tel. 476-4312, which also offers a good restaurant, is three miles north of Orofino. Rates are $26-42. **Helgeson Place Motel,** tel. 476-5729, is downtown at the corner of Michigan and Johnson avenues. Its rooms range $32-40. **White Pine Motel,** tel. 476-7093, has rooms for $32-48 at 222 Brown Street. **Vacation Land Motel and R.V. Park,** tel. 476-4012, offers 13 rooms and 33 campsites for $11-70 and 40 campsites for $9. Vacation Land has a hot tub. **Hidden Village,** tel. 476-3416, at 14615 Hwy. 12, has 26 campsites for $7.50-9.

Food

The Lewis & Clark Trail Cafe, tel. 476-7548, at 10290 Hwy. 12 in Orofino has coffee by the gallon and honest hamburgers, including those ground from buffalo. **Copper Hood Pizza,** tel. 476-7770, is another favorite of Orofino residents. It's located at 115 College Ave. and offers homemade soup, pasta, and sandwiches, in addition to pizza. At Big Eddy Marina just above the dam on the west side, **Medley's on the Lake,** tel. 476-5331, has a view that could outshine its food. The restaurant earned a good reputation until recent wrangling with the Army Corps of Engineers high command disrupted its operations. **Michael's Restaurant,** tel. 476-5761, at 246 Johnson Ave., is a popular spot with pizza on its menu as well as steak, seafood, and chicken. The homemade pies will top off any meal or offer a great excuse to stop by for a break from the highway. Other favorites include **Konkol's Steakhouse Tavern and Lounge,** tel. 476-4312, at 2009 Konkolville Rd. east of Orofino; and **Ponderosa Restaurant and Brass Rail Lounge,** tel. 476-4818, at 220 Michigan Avenue.

Information And Services

The Clearwater National Forest supervisor's office is at 12730 Hwy. 12 in Orofino, tel. 476-4541. Stop at the **Riverside Sport Shop,** tel. 476-5418, to find out how fishing is in the river or on Dworshak Reservoir, where the Clearwater's north fork lies submerged. **West's Sporting Goods,** tel. 476-5314, just across the bridge in Orofino proper, is a good bet, too.

In the Orofino area, the **Clearwater County Sheriff's Department,** tel. 476-4521, enforces the law and oversees emergency services. **Clearwater Valley Hospital,** 301 Cedar, tel. 476-4555, maintains a trauma center. The **Orofino Chamber of Commerce,** tel. 476-4335, is at 217 First Street.

EAST ON HIGHWAY 12

Back On The Highway

Heading east on Hwy. 12 takes you first to Greer and then Hwy. 11. After crossing the Greer Bridge, an eight-mile white-knuckle climb up Hwy. 11 and the canyon wall brings you to the Weippe Prairie. The sight of this rolling open country convinced the Corps of Discovery it might survive. Captain Clark and his advance party of six hunters flushed three startled Indian boys from their hiding places in the tall grass that day, Sept. 20, 1805, and eventually caught up to two. Giving them bits of silk ribbon, he sent them ahead to the village to foretell the expedition's peaceful intentions. The Nez Perce village provided a horse-load of roots and three salmon to send back to the main party.

Pierce And Weippe

Pierce, where a party led by Capt. Elias D. Pierce made Idaho's first gold discovery in 1860, and Weippe (pronounce it "we-IPE") are both timber towns at heart. Both are learning to live with tourists, though one could argue xenophobia strikes deep in the roots here. On Sept. 18, 1885, some locals threw a necktie party near here for some unfortunate Chinese residents, hanging five. The Chinese had been charged with hacking to bits a prominent local merchant. A posse had just set out on a 240-mile trip to the county seat to take them to trial, but a force of masked and armed vigilantes took the prisoners from the posse and hanged 'em high.

Things are friendlier along the main streets of both towns these days. Pierce and Weippe offer mostly a place to grab a bite and get final provisions before heading off into the backcountry. **Weippe Pizza** offers a familiar reentry to civilization with pitchers of draft beer and more-than-passable pizza as its main attractions. At Pierce, the **Flame Bar** offers beer, burgers, and pool, while **Ruark's Sporting Goods,** tel. 464-2858, is the provisioning point for hunters and fishermen and a reliable source of information about what's happening in the backcountry.

Pierce is also notable for the historic **Shoshone County Courthouse,** one of Idaho's oldest standing buildings. This was the seat of government in 1864 when the Pierce country boomed. Shoshone County's seat of government shifted north to **Murray** the following year and later to its present county seat of **Wallace** as richer veins of ore were discovered. Clearwater County, which now surrounds Pierce, later split from Shoshone, and Orofino became the seat of its government.

Backroad Adventure

The **Lolo Motorway,** Forest Service Rd. 500, can be reached from Weippe through a maze of logging roads decipherable with a Clearwater National Forest map. If your sedan has good shocks and the road is dry, you can make it. Drive slowly and savor the scenery. You won't forget it. The Forest Service has recently installed excellent signs recounting the Corps of Discovery's exploits as it struggled across these ridges.

East of Weippe along the route are some memorable recreational adventures, namely the Forest Service rent-a-lookouts. Clearwater National Forest has four lookout towers for rent along or near the motorway. **Weitas Butte** and **Austin Ridge** lookouts perch atop high steel towers. Renting for $34 for two nights, both are favorites of ham radio operators, who appreciate the ready-made broadcasting towers. Just remember to sit on the wooden stools with glass insulators on the bottom during lightning storms. For reservations and more information about these two lookouts, contact the Kamiah Ranger Station, tel. 935-2513. Another lookout, at **Castle Butte,** also rents for $34 for two nights. It is more suitable for families with children because a plain set of a dozen wooden steps leads up to its perch. Still, keep an eye on the kids and make sure they know what's safe and what isn't. For more information about Castle Butte, contact the Kooskia Ranger Station, tel. 926-4275.

Kamiah

Highway 12 wriggles southeast without more than an occasional turn lane to indicate anything else exists but the road and the river. **Kamiah** is the next reminder that something does. The home of one of the Nez Perce tribe's main bands, Kamiah has the **Wa-A-Yas Community Center** where tribal officials and members gather. Kamiah also has a bakery and the normal roadside restaurant fare. The **Kamiah Cafe,** tel. 935-2563, at 714 3rd, fronting the highway, dishes up a piece of pie that's worth stopping for.

The **Kamiah Inn Motel,** tel. 935-0040, 216 3rd, is Kamiah's newest lodging, built in 1993. Rooms here rent for $24-28. **Snooky's Carriage Inn,** along Hwy. 12, tel. 935-2531 or 935-0622, has rooms for $21-35. **Sundown Motel,** tel. 935-2568, is nearby with rooms for $24-26. A modern campground tempts tourists to pull over and smell the roses to the east of town. The **Lewis Clark Resort,** tel. 935-2556, offers 270 spaces. Kamiah is also the base of operations for **Whitewater Ranch,** tel. 935-0631, in the Frank Church–River of No Return Wilderness, 40 miles south of Elk City. The ranch has four rooms for $65 a night.

The **Kamiah Ranger Station** here, tel. 935-2513, offers information about the Clearwater National Forest's Pierce Ranger District. You can find out more about the Weitas Butte and Austin Ridge lookout rental program here too.

In mid-June, things bust loose in Kamiah with the running of the Clearwater Jetboat Rally. Riverside Park is the race's terminus, and barbecue pits, kegs, and other trappings of a good time welcome racers, visitors, and anyone else interested in the show.

South of Kamiah, just off Hwy. 62 along Lawyers Creek, is the **Flying B Ranch,** an exclusive hunting preserve. The Flying B offers 5,000 acres of protected canyon where sunflowers, milo, Sudan grass, and sorghum are planted and irrigated to produce the best conditions for the hunted. Three-day hunts for upland birds at the Flying B start at $1750. Cheaper hunts may be available to hunters in the area, however, to fill the schedule between bookings. To find out, call 935-0755.

Kooskia

Heading southeast from Kamiah along Hwy. 12 leads you over the Clearwater and on to Kooskia. **Kooskia National Fish Hatchery** is the second half of the U.S. Fish and Wildlife Service's Dworshak Hatchery complex, built to raise salmon and steelhead for the Clearwater. Kooskia is home to the **Lochsa Ranger District,** tel. 926-4275, which offers information about Lochsa River rafting and campgrounds. The district office also offers the Castle Butte and Walde Mountain **lookout rentals** here. Caution: the last 22 mile stretch to the Castle Butte Lookout up the Saddle Camp Rd. and along the Lolo Motorway from Hwy. 12 is steep, narrow, and slippery if it's raining or snowing. The road is unsuitable for travel trailers. All that aside, the view from 6,659-foot Castle Butte is spectacular.

Keep on trucking along Hwy. 12, but beware of massive grain trucks doing the same. Be alert for the extremely rare renegade driver, and more importantly, drive slowly enough to stay on your side of the double yellow line. That's all the truckers ask.

Along The Middle Fork

Along the Clearwater's middle fork here, between Kooskia and Syringa, is **Bear Hollow Bed 'n' Breakfast,** tel. 926-7146 or (800) 831-3731. Bear Hollow is about eight miles east of Kooksia and offers a convenient place to stay to reach hundreds of miles of foot trails in the surrounding mountains. It also displays art and handicrafts by local artists and artisans. It offers three rooms ranging $55-85, two with private baths (Mama Bear's and Papa Bear's suites). Rates are based on double occupancy and additional guests are $10 apiece. Bear Hollow maintains kennels for pets. Just down the road is the **Looking Glass Guest Ranch,** tel. 926-0855. The ranch, 10 miles east of Kooskia, offers guests access to nearby horseback riding and hiking. Breakfast is available by reservation; rooms are $50 s, $60 d.

Farther along, the Forest Service maintains the **Three Devils Picnic Area.** It's a serene place to stretch, fix a sandwich, or drink a soda—19 miles east of Kooskia along Hwy. 12. **Wild Goose Campground,** a mile more upriver, provides six campsites and two picnic tables. It is the first of a string of campgrounds stretching up both the Lochsa and Selway rivers before they meet at Lowell to form the Clearwater's middle fork.

In Lowell is **Three Rivers Resort,** tel. 926-4430, with a general store, bar, and cafe. They offer motel rooms and cabins, either log or A-frame, spread about the Lochsa's shoreline. You might find a governor in the cafe, his name hand-tooled on his belt, or other escapees from the real world. But mostly you're apt to find locals who know a good deal when they see it. Campsites, rooms, and cabins range $10-95 a night. Swimming pool and hot tubs are available. **Ryan's Wilderness Inn,** tel. 926-4706, across the Lochsa and along the highway also offers motel rooms for $30-35, camping spaces for $5-6, and a cafe. It's less distinctive than Three Rivers but clean and comfortable.

Up The Selway

At Lowell, travelers face the choice of taking a detour up the Selway River or continuing up Hwy. 12 along the Lochsa. Worthy stops along the Selway include **O'Hara Campground,** where the Forest Service will reserve you a campsite through a national toll-free number, (800) 283-2267. You can even use Visa or MasterCard. The **Fenn Ranger Station,** tel. 926-4259, is home of the Selway Ranger District, which maintains the campground and offers the best information about conditions and recreation opportunities in the area. There's just more of the same up the Selway: peace, serenity, solitude, and scenery. Several more campgrounds occupy level spots along the river. Find a sandy beach here, drag the cooler out of the trunk, and have a picnic. For the hearty, 23 miles of winding, mostly gravel road leads to **Selway Falls,** an impressive cataract where steelhead and chinook salmon sometimes can be seen in spring and summer leaping to reach their spawning grounds. Against the far bank is another way the fish can climb the falls, a fishway. The submerged tunnel allows the fish to slip past the most challenging torrents.

A sign on the plank bridge just upstream warns rafters and kayakers that the falls are unrunnable. For one of the best stops anywhere, take the clackety wooden bridge across the river and drive just over a mile to **Slims Camp.** A wonderfully level National Recreation Trail leads three miles through cedar groves along Meadow Creek before climbing and getting serious about heading into the backcountry. You can go as far as you want, but the lower trail is a gem. Motorcycle and bicycle riders should be aware, however, that the trail is closed to them once it climbs the bluffs. Mechanical vehicles are banned because they could spook horses and mules into a suicidal decision along this stretch of trail. The Meadow Creek Trail also leads to another Forest Service rental offering. The **Meadow Creek Cabin,** 16 miles by trail from the campground, rents for $30 for the first night and $25 for additional nights. It can accommodate six and is available April 15-Sept. 15 for a maximum stay of seven days. The cabin retains the atmosphere of an early Forest Service outpost more so than others because of its remoteness.

The **Selway Ranger District,** tel. 926-4258, is based at **Fenn Ranger Station,** five miles south of Lowell along the Selway Road. The Fenn Ranger Station celebrated its 50th anniversary in 1990. Crafted of native stone by Civilian Conservation Corps workers in the 1940s, the station is listed on the National Register of Historic Places. The district staff oversees the Meadow Creek Cabin rentals. The district also offers the **Lookout Butte** lookout tower for rent June 15-Sept. 30. The tower rents for $15 per night.

Along The Lochsa

For 77 miles east of Lowell, Hwy. 12 twists and turns along the Lochsa River without passing a single commercial establishment. But campgrounds and camping spots occupy favorable spots along the bank, bringing yearly pilgrims.

One of the don't-misses along this stretch is the **Lochsa Historical Ranger Station,** 25 miles east of Lowell. Forest Service retirees are on hand here from Memorial Day to Labor Day to watch over the extensive collection of agency memorabilia and talk about old times. The retirees also offer a living link to the Forest

A fly fisherman tests his skill in the gin-clear water pf the Lochsa River.

Service's past. Many were employed by the agency when the development of this area was still new. The road didn't reach the old ranger station here until the late 1950s and Hwy. 12 wasn't formally dedicated as a new route to Montana until 1962. The collection of log cabins survived the great fires of 1934 when employees fought as long as they could, then dumped their tools in the Lochsa and jumped in themselves to escape the flames.

Wilderness Gateway Campground, a mile upstream, is a well-laid-out place to lay over. The campground offers 50 campsites for $5 a night and is a major portal for the Selway-Bitterroot Wilderness just over the ridge.

The Lochsa Ranger District is serious about recreation here. The **Lochsa River Trail** runs 16 miles along the highway from Sherman Creek at Wilderness Gateway to the Split Creek pack bridge upstream. Other access points for the trail can be found at Lochsa Historic Ranger Station, Fish Creek Bridge, and Sherman Flat. The trail climbs up along the hillside but it's not too steep or too far for some pleasurable day hikes. The stretch from the ranger station to Fish Creek stretches a couple of miles and can be hiked readily by families. If the weather is warm, it would be wise to go during the mornings. Bring water because there are few places to stock up along the way and *Giardia,* the intestinal parasite, is an ever-present risk, even in streams as beautiful as these.

Colgate Licks, 15 miles upstream from Wilderness Gateway, offers a chance to hike a short nature trail through a natural salt lick. Things can get exciting here. A newspaper photographer stopped to ski one winter, heard a battle in nearby trees, and watched a mountain lion drag down a 500-pound cow elk. He didn't even consider using the camera around his neck.

For a more civilized stopover, **Powell** is tucked 10 miles inside the Idaho-Montana border and just under the final climb to Lolo Pass. The **Lochsa Lodge,** tel. 942-3405, is even better in some respects than Three Rivers Resort (see "Along the Middle Fork," above). Cabins here start at $20 a night. The bar has a pool table and a woodstove. Its low ceiling makes for a warm, close, and instantly welcoming atmosphere on cold winter nights. Move into the dining room and move back in time. It's not hard to imagine that Andrew Erickson, who built the lodge in 1929, would still recognize the place. Some of the stuffed critters lining the walls and the mantlepiece may reflect his past exploits. Interesting bits of natural history, rocks and such, lie scattered comfortably about by the bookshelves flanking the fireplace. If you want to see Idaho's past, here's part of it.

Powell is also home to the **Powell Ranger Station,** tel. 942-3113, where Forest Service workers try to balance logging and recreation interests. The Ranger District's **Lolo Pass Visitor Information Center,** at the top of Lolo Pass along the Montana border, runs nearly year-round, shutting down briefly as snows melt in spring and before they pile deep enough for fun each fall. (Spring and fall are the two times of the year when the number of visitors is lowest.) Lolo Pass has an extensive system of cross-country skiing and snowmobiling trails. The meadows are also good for summer strolls.

SOUTH TO CAMAS PRAIRIE

Highway 95 heads south from Lewiston, crossing the Clearwater River and leaving the river's valley south of Culdesac. There it begins the climb onto northern Idaho's Camas Prairie (there's another near Fairfield northeast of Boise). Immediately after topping out, the highway passes by **Winchester,** a logging town named for the rifle. The lumber mill that once helped the town prosper is long since gone but the reservoir created to hold its logs remains. **Winchester Lake State Park,** tel. 924-7563, has 74 campsites and many scenic hiking trails around the old lake. The park recently received a face-lift from the state and now has showers and campsites with utility hookups.

COTTONWOOD

A little town on the prairie, Cottonwood, 22 miles south of Winchester, got its start as a stage stop in 1862. During the Nez Perce War of 1877, a skirmish took place nearby. Today, Cottonwood is visited mostly by those on their way to see the museum at **St. Gertrude's Convent of the Benedictine Sisters.** The museum, tel. 962-3224, is open daily 1-5 p.m., although visitors may have to visit the convent to arrange to have the museum unlocked. The museum houses an extensive collection of Idaho County artifacts as well as religious books dating back to the 1800s. It also shelters some of the earthly goods of Polly Bemis, the Chinese woman sold for 1,000 pieces of gold before finding her niche in a Salmon River mining camp.

The **BLM** office at Cottonwood, tel. 962-3245, manages the Lower Salmon River. Check here about finding an outfitter for a trip down the river's scenic rapids. Just outside Cottonwood along Hwy. 95 is a memorial marking the site of the Cottonwood skirmishes. On July 3, 1877, 2nd Lt. Sevier Rains and 10 men were killed after being dispatched to investigate reports of hostile Indians. Two days later Army and civilian patrols skirmished with Nez Perce. The toll included three white casualties and the first Nez Perce killed in the war. While the skirmishes were keeping the Camas Prairie residents occupied, the main group of Nez Perce were heading into the Middle Fork of the Clearwater River country.

Weis Rock Shelter

Also near Cottonwood is the Weis Rock Shelter, south of Hwy. 95 off Graves Creek Road. Archaeological evidence shows this natural shelter was first occupied more than 8,000 years ago. The natural overhang was home for humans until about 2,000 years ago, when it was apparently abandoned in favor of nearby Rocky Canyon. Artifacts found here have included needles, arrowheads, spear points, and tools.

Cottonwood Butte Ski Area

This community ski hill has waxed and waned through the years, and is currently up and running. The terrain here is made for fun, not breathtaking adventure. The area's proximity to town and its prices ($10 for a lift ticket at last check) draw local skiers back to the butte each year to ski with their friends and neighbors. The ski area offers a T-bar and rope tow, four runs, and a vertical drop of 845 feet. A day lodge, snack bar, and rental shop are available at the base; call 962-3624 for more information.

GRANGEVILLE AND VICINITY

Located near the base of the early mining districts in the Gospel Mountains and Buffalo Hump, Grangeville became a supply center for the mines. Started in 1874 with the building of a Grange Hall, the growing town got a newspaper in 1886 and 16 years later wrested the status as county seat for Idaho County away from nearby Mount Idaho. The railroad arrived six years after that.

The **Bicentennial Historical Museum,** tel. 983-2104 or 983-1722, is located at 305 N. College, and presents a collection of early mining, farming, and wilderness artifacts. The museum is open during the summer Wednesday and Friday afternoons 1-5. Winter tours can be arranged.

Grangeville now is an interesting mix of occupations and personalities. Fishing guides and river-runners use the town for a base, mainly to reach the Salmon River to the south. With more than three million acres of wilderness areas within a four hours' drive, Grangeville is also a base for horseback outfitters and hikers who revere nature at its wildest. The Forest Service maintains a sizable workforce here, including a summertime stable of smoke jumpers (the agency's airborne firefighting troops) at the Grangeville Airport. During hot, dry weather, DC-3s scramble off the runway to drop fire retardant on remote blazes. The supervisor's office for the 2.2 million acre **Nez Perce National Forest** occupies a modern building at the east end of Main St., tel. 983-1950. Grangeville is also home to the modern IdaPine Mills, where timber is converted to lumber, and sentiment favoring loggers runs deep.

RECREATION

Ah, Wilderness

Grangeville offers a departure point for travelers to four of Idaho's six wilderness areas: the Selway-Bitterroot, Gospel Hump, Frank Church–River of No Return, and Hells Canyon. (The other two are the Sawtooth Wilderness south of Stanley, and the Craters of the Moon Wilderness in southeast Idaho.) Within a few hours' drive of Grangeville are more than 3.7 million acres that remain pretty much as they were in 1492 when Columbus sailed the ocean blue. The **Nez Perce National Forest supervisor's office,** tel. 983-1950, can provide information on access points to all four of the region's wildernesses because all four occupy some of its lands.

One off-highway adventure possible near here is a drive across **Magruder Rd.,** east of

The Magruder Road carries travelers between the greatest expanses of wilderness in the lower 48 states.

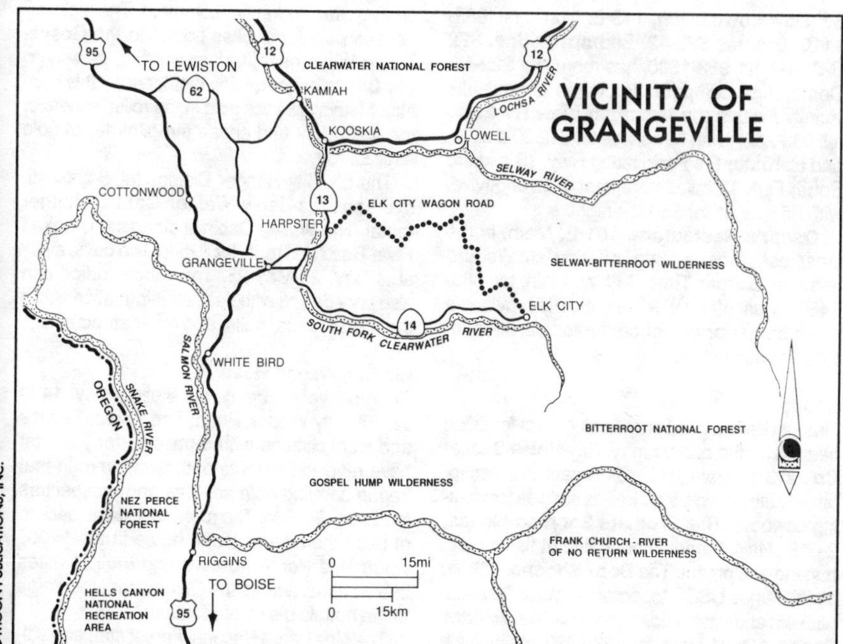

Red River Ranger Station. The road winds its way between the Selway-Bitterroot and River of No Return wildernesses, providing great views into both from around the halfway point.

Camping

On the tamer side, a campground and recreation area at **Fish Creek,** eight miles south of the supervisor's office, is maintained by the Nez Perce National Forest's Clearwater Ranger District, tel. 983-1963. Popular as a Nordic skiing area when the snow flies, the trail system welcomes hikers and mountain bikers during the rest of the year. The campground is one of more than two dozen scattered across the national forest. Some of the most popular are along the Clearwater River's south fork on the way to Elk City (see "East to the Backcountry," following).

Rafting, Fishing

Holiday River Expeditions, tel. 983-1518, offers rafting trips on the lower Salmon River and the Snake River in Hells Canyon. **Idaho Fishing Charters,** tel. 983-2803, guides fishermen on the Salmon River in quest of trout, smallmouth bass, sturgeon, and steelhead. **Idaho Afloat,** tel. 983-2414, offers rafting adventures on the Salmon River and Snake River in Hells Canyon, varying its menu with trips designed to cater to different groups.

Skiing

Another community ski hill like Cottonwood Butte, **Snowhaven Ski Area,** tel. 983-2851, is seven miles south of Grangeville. It offers a snack bar, ski shop, day lodge, and rental. The hill has a 400-foot vertical drop with three runs. Getting uphill means riding a T-bar or rope tow.

PRACTICALITIES

Accommodations And Food

Monty's Motel, tel. 983-2500, boasts a heated swimming pool. River rafters rendezvous here for adventures on the lower Salmon River. Rooms are $29-43. **Crossroads Motel,** tel. 983-1420, is at 620 W. Main and has rooms for $35-

60. **Downtowner Inn,** 113 E. North, tel. 983-1110, charges $28-42. **Elkhorn Lodge,** 822 S.W. 1st, tel. 983-1500, has rooms for $29-45. Commercial campgrounds in the Grangeville vicinity include the **Mountain View RV Park,** tel. 983-2328, with 52 spaces for $12.50 a night, and **Harpster RV Park,** along Hwy. 13 and the South Fork 12 miles northeast of Grangeville, with 25 spaces for $8-10 a night.

Oscar's Restaurant, 101 E. Main, is the classiest place in town, offering steaks and seafood. **Burger Time,** 711 W. Main, tel. 983-2480, is just off Hwy. 95 and mostly provides a quick burger or cup of coffee for travelers intent on making time.

Shopping

Grangeville is a good provisioning point for those headed for the backcountry. **Ray Holes Saddle Co.,** 213 W. Main., still makes pack saddles for backcountry travelers as well as saddles for working cowboys. **Rae Brothers Sporting Goods,** 247 E. Main, carries a good line of fishing and hunting equipment. The **Book Shoppe,** 227 W. Main, carries USGS topographic maps for backpackers and other wilderness travelers. **Holiday Sports,** 126 W. Main, tel. 983-2299, maintains a full skiing, mountain biking, and hiking shop. The shop offers ski rentals and current information about Snowhaven, the city-operated ski hill.

Information And Services

The **Nez Perce National Forest** supervisor's office on the east end of Main St. can be reached at 983-1950. **Syringa General Hospital,** tel. 983-1700, along W. Main, maintains an emergency room. Grangeville is also the base for the **Idaho County Sheriff's Office,** tel. 983-1100, at the courthouse along Main.

The **Grangeville Chamber of Commerce,** 201 E. Main, tel. 983-0460, maintains an extensive information collection about recreation and outfitters in the area.

EAST TO THE BACKCOUNTRY

Heading east through Mount Idaho leads you down an exciting grade to the Clearwater River's south fork and a string of campgrounds along Hwy. 14 there. The stream, a turbulent froth of whitewater, becomes a popular fishing spot and playing area during the summers. The highway passes popular access points to the Gospel Hump Wilderness, before winding its way to **Elk City,** a major mining district early this century. Miners still seek gold in the roiled waters of the south fork and chase the glimmer of gold near Elk City.

The Elk City Ranger District, tel. 842-2245, oversees the **Jerry Walker Cabin,** another rental. The Walker Cabin is along the Crooked River Road and rents for $25 for two days, available Nov. 25-May 25. The ranger office can also provide you with detailed information about the area's roads, trails, and other attractions.

Elk City Wagon Road

Roughly, very roughly, paralleling Hwy. 14 is the Elk City Wagon Road. The Forest Service and local citizens with a passion for the past have revived the route of the wagon road that began carrying gold seekers and prospectors to Elk City in 1894. The route itself dates back to at least the advent of the horse in the 1700s when Nez Perce hunters and their families blazed a trail across the Clearwater Mountains to the buffalo plains of Montana.

The Nez Perce National Forest staff and volunteers have pieced together and marked the network of rugged roads from Harpster to Elk City. Perhaps more importantly for those who would travel the 53-mile route today, an excellent brochure is available at the national forest's offices at Grangeville and Elk City. It's a good idea to check in to find out about road conditions before you attempt the route. The **Clearwater Ranger District,** tel. 983-2363, is based just behind the forest supervisor's office at the eastern edge of Grangeville. The **Elk City Ranger District,** tel. 842-2245, is in Elk City. The Forest Service recommends against taking large recreational vehicles or rigs with large trailers in tow across the wagon road. Some steep, rocky grades and tight switchbacks make travel difficult-to-hazardous, depending on conditions and the driver's skill.

The wagon road starts at Harpster and climbs up to the divide between the main Clearwater and its south fork. Although the road is 53 miles long, the Forest Service recommends averaging 10-15 miles an hour to pass the road safely. Expect the trip to take six hours. Pack a picnic lunch; the scenery is worth savoring, too. The

Fire lookouts dot the high ridges in the backcountry; most can be rented by backpackers.

brochure notes that today's trip across the wagon road is quick compared to the past. After the road was completed, the trip from Stites, near Kooskia, took two days by stage. The fare was $6 in 1910.

East Of Elk City

Beyond the picturesque Red River Ranger Station, the Forest Service oversees a wild and remote adventureland. A graveled road heads south to **Dixie,** where the **Lodgepole Pine Inn** offers a basic burger-based menu and serves as a mecca for snowmobilers and horsemen, each in season.

East of the ranger station, Magruder Rd. stretches more than 100 miles east to the Montana border, threading its way between the Selway-Bitterroot and Frank Church–River of No Return Wildernesses. The only buildings along the ridgetop road, which travels at elevations of 8,000 feet and more in spots, are fire-lookout towers. The one exception is the **Horse Heaven Cabin,** which the Bitterroot National Forest's West Fork Ranger District (West Fork Route, Darby, MT 59829; tel. 406-821-3269) offers for rent. The cabin is about 50 miles east of Red River. It can house four and rents for $20 a night year-round.

Before taking off on this adventure, check in with the Forest Service to find out about road conditions.

RIGGINS

Riggins was named for pioneer stage driver and postmaster R.L. Riggins. It must have seemed a friendlier name than its earlier moniker, Gouge-Eye. Mostly a ranching community in the early years, Riggins also attracted a lumber company. In the late 1970s, the lumber mill burned down. The loss left residents wondering who would be the last ones out of town and whether they would remember to turn out the lights.

Economic succor came in the form of a burgeoning interest in recreation on the Salmon River. The river is now packed with rafters, kayakers, and floaters each summer. Main St. in Riggins, which doubles as Hwy. 95, is crammed with businesses offering float trips.

Sights

Idaho Power Co. built the Circle C or **Rapid River Salmon Hatchery** along Rapid River just south of Riggins to compensate Idahoans for the chinook salmon losses that resulted from building dams in Hells Canyon along the Snake River. The hatchery attracts big sea-run chinook from early May until July each year. Small salmon reared from eggs taken at the hatchery fill its ponds until April when they're released to migrate to the Pacific and complete the circle again.

Bed And Breakfast

The Lodge Bed & Breakfast, tel. 628-3863, has four rooms for rent at rates ranging $24-50. The lodge offers a hot tub to soak away the cares of the highway or the exertions of the river.

Motels

The **Salmon River Motel,** tel. 628-3231, offers a clean roadside stop for travelers who want to linger in the Salmon River Canyon or want more rest before facing any more of Hwy. 95. Rates range $24-60. Other Riggins lodgings include **Bruce Motel,** tel. 628-3031, with rooms for $28; **Halfway Inn,** tel. 628-3259, south along Hwy. 95 with rooms for $18-35; **Riggins Motel,** tel. 628-3001, with rooms for $26-75; and **Taylor Motel,** tel. 628-3914, with rooms for $20-45.

Commercial campgrounds include the **Sleepy Hollow RV Park,** tel. 628-3402, with campsites for $12; and **Riverside RV Park,** tel. 628-3390, with spaces for $5-10. The **River Front Gardens RV Park,** tel. 628-3777, is 15 miles north of Riggins along Hwy. 95 and offers 32 campsites for $10-12 a night.

A resort that could hold up its head in any crowd of the West's best would be **The Lodge at Riggins Hot Spring,** tel. 628-3785. Its seven units rent for $150 a night for singles and $250 for doubles. The rates include all meals, refreshments, and use of facilities. A two-night minimum is required on weekends. Just in case the beautiful hot springs spa, hot tubs, or swimming pool won't occupy your time here, there's also a trout pond to divert you and 155 acres to wander around on.

Food

Summerville's Cafe offers the best dining selection in Riggins, leaning heavily to beef. The pies are worth the stop. Roadside cafes and taverns, including the venerable **Seven Devils,** cater to travelers as well.

Recreation

River outfitting is Riggins's major business these days. **Salmon River Challenge,** tel. 628-3264, offers one-day rafting trips on the Salmon River for less than $50 and provides lunch as well. **Wapiti River Guides,** tel. (800) 488-9872, offers drift-boat trips of the lower Salmon. Other Riggins area river outfitters include **Exodus,** tel. 628-3484, (800) 992-3484, which offers both jet boat and rafting excursions on the Salmon; **Discovery River Expeditions,** tel. 628-3319, offering two- to four-day trips on the Salmon; **River Adventures LTD,** tel. 628-3952 or (800) 524-9710, offering jet boat tours of the Salmon and Hells Canyon and combination jet boat, rafting, horseback trips; and **Northwest Voyageurs,** tel. (800) 727-9977 at nearby Lucile, offering a complete range of rafting trips on the Salmon and Snake rivers.

Lewiston-based outfitters include **Barker River Trips,** tel. 743-7459, specializing in rafting trips in the summer and steelhead fishing in the fall on the Salmon, Snake, and Clearwater rivers; and **Northwest Dories,** tel. (800) 877-DORY (or 3679), which runs the Salmon and Snake. Moscow-based **Salmon River Experience,** tel. 882-2385, offers Salmon River rafting, and mountain-biking tours along the river.

Information And Services

The **Salmon River Chamber of Commerce,** tel. 628-3778, maintains an up-to-date list of river guides and outfitters. The **Idaho County Sheriff's Office,** tel. 983-1100, maintains a deputy here. For travelers interested in reaching the Hells Canyon National Recreation Area to the west, the **Forest Service** maintains an office just south of town, tel. 628-3916.

(Top left) Burnt Knob Lookout is a popular stopping point along the Magruder Road east of Elk City. (Top right) September snow dusts the bear grass in the Frank Church-River of No Return Wilderness. (Bottom) The City of Rocks National Historic Reserve near Almo was a landmark along the Oregon Trail. (PHOTOS BILL LOFTUS)

(Top) A floating dock provides a focus for fun at Round Lake State Park south of Sandpoint. (Bottom) Water traffic on Lake Coeur d'Alene, with its namesake resort in the background. (PHOTOS BILL LOFTUS)

BOISE

INTRODUCTION

Boise is Idaho's capital and the state's biggest city by far. With over 135,000 residents at last count, it's over twice as big as runner-up Pocatello. Here the Idaho legislature fills the marble-clad halls of the statehouse, making laws and keeping order—such as it is in a state that relishes its independence. And here more than any other town in the state, you'll find the trappings and hustle of city life: arts and entertainment galore, Idaho's biggest shopping malls, great dining, and yes, traffic.

But woven right through this urban core you'll also find easily accessible places to escape the rat race. The comfortable little Boise River flows right through town, with a greenbelt of parks along its shore perfect for jogging, bicycling, or even fishing. Many other parks lace the city as well, almost all of them full of the trees that gave the city its name. Some say trappers called the stop along the river's cottonwood-clad banks Boissie; others say Les Bois ("The Woods"). Either way, the trees were the main attraction then. Skim across the sagebrush-dominated Snake River Plain from any angle and it's easy to see why. The city remains a green respite from the silvery sage—lush and gentle against the backdrop of rumpled hills known as the Boise Front.

Boise's climate is hot in the summer, cold in the winter. Winter days here can be icy as warm air flows over the valley, causing inversions below. That's when skiing at nearby Bogus Basin seems sweetest; many days the ski area's runs are bathed in sunlight while Boise looks out on a chilling fog.

HISTORY

As early as 1811, five years after the Lewis and Clark Expedition headed homeward from the Pacific coast, American fur trappers began to visit the Western interior. The tributaries to the Snake River offered lucrative opportunities for the mountain men, who made up a culture where adventure was as important as commerce. In 1824, it was Peter Skeen Ogden who noted that his trappers had called the area along a major Snake River tributary "Boissie."

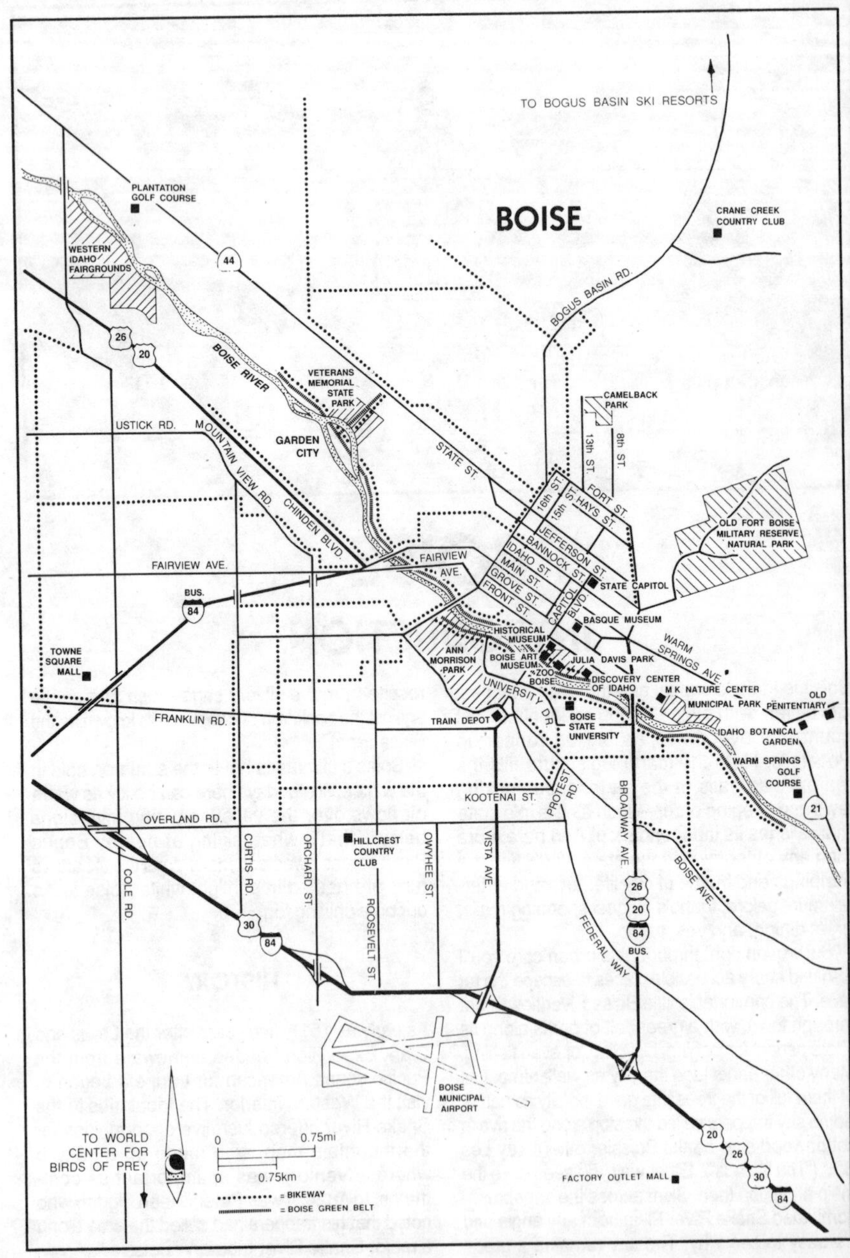
BOISE
TO BOGUS BASIN SKI RESORTS
CRANE CREEK COUNTRY CLUB
PLANTATION GOLF COURSE
WESTERN IDAHO FAIRGROUNDS
BOGUS BASIN RD.
44
26
20
BOISE RIVER
VETERANS MEMORIAL STATE PARK
CAMELBACK PARK
13th ST.
8th ST.
GARDEN CITY
USTICK RD.
MOUNTAIN VIEW RD.
CHINDEN BLVD.
STATE ST.
16th ST.
15th ST.
FORT ST.
HAYS ST.
JEFFERSON ST.
BANNOCK ST.
IDAHO ST.
MAIN ST.
GROVE ST.
FRONT ST.
CAPITOL BLVD.
OLD FORT BOISE MILITARY RESERVE NATURAL PARK
FAIRVIEW AVE.
STATE CAPITOL
BUS.
84
BASQUE MUSEUM
HISTORICAL MUSEUM
WARM SPRINGS AVE.
TOWNE SQUARE MALL
ANN MORRISON PARK
BOISE ART MUSEUM
ZOO BOISE
JULIA DAVIS PARK
DISCOVERY CENTER OF IDAHO
M K NATURE CENTER
MUNICIPAL PARK
OLD PENITENTIARY
UNIVERSITY DR.
FRANKLIN RD.
TRAIN DEPOT
BOISE STATE UNIVERSITY
IDAHO BOTANICAL GARDEN
WARM SPRINGS GOLF COURSE
KOOTENAI ST.
PROTEST RD.
BROADWAY AVE.
21
OVERLAND RD.
HILLCREST COUNTRY CLUB
CURTIS RD.
ORCHARD ST.
OWYHEE ST.
VISTA AVE.
BOISE AVE.
COLE RD.
ROOSEVELT ST.
30
FEDERAL WAY
BOISE MUNICIPAL AIRPORT
TO WORLD CENTER FOR BIRDS OF PREY
0
0.75mi
0.75km
= BIKEWAY
= BOISE GREEN BELT
FACTORY OUTLET MALL

Boise itself was little more than a river crossing until the Overland Migration of Oregon-bound emigrants boosted the number of travelers passing through the area. Confrontations with Native Americans then became more frequent, the most notable being the Ward Massacre of 1854, during which all but two of a party of 20 Overlanders were killed. The site of the massacre is near Caldwell to the west of Boise. The Otter-Van Orman wagon train also met its fate east of Boise on Sept. 9, 1860, when a band of Indians attacked. Eighteen members of the train were killed in the fighting. After a standoff of several days, the survivors abandoned the circled wagons to the Indians and broke for the desert. Of a straggling band of 16, four more died during a month of deprivation before help could reach them. Three young Van Orman girls disappeared and were presumed killed. The boy of the family, Reuben, was recovered from Shoshone and Bannock Indians two years later.

The actual route taken by the Overlanders through the present city followed the ridge to the south above the main river valley, about where the Union Pacific Depot stands. The route dipped to follow the river just upstream from where Fairview Avenue crosses the river today.

In 1863, cavalry and infantry troops were dispatched to build an outpost along the Boise River. A site near where the Oregon Trail and a road between the Boise and Owyhee mining districts crossed won out and the city's formation followed.

Boise attained its status as the territorial (and later, state) capital in a strong-arm maneuver by Territorial Secretary C. Dewitt Smith, who enlisted the help of the U.S. Army to gain possession of the state's seal, treasury, and records. Without the trappings of power, the original capital of Lewiston could no longer claim that status. And Boise, with the coveted goods firmly in the possession of new resident Smith, took its place.

FAMOUS FOLKS

Like a magnet, Boise attracted or produced some of the most famous leaders in Idaho's history. Moses Alexander left Missouri to find Alaska's goldfields. He paused in Idaho, first in Pocatello, then Boise, where he settled in 1891. His talent for campaigning and speaking won him the job as Boise's mayor. The same talents, after two attempts, led him to the governor's office in 1914. He is credited with the honor of being the nation's first Jewish governor.

The same year Alexander came to Idaho, 1891, attorney William E. Borah migrated west, landing in Boise with $15.75 in his pocket. The young lawyer chose to settle in the town after watching a drunken colleague try a case. Borah decided then and there that if a drunk could succeed, he could prosper. He did. His biggest case was the prosecution of mining labor leader Big Bill Haywood, who stood accused of murdering Governor Frank Steunenberg. Borah won national fame opposing Clarence Darrow but lost the case.

Borah, a Republican, won election to the U.S. Senate in 1907, in what turned out to be a lifetime lock on the office. He served as chairman of the powerful Senate Foreign Relations Committee from 1921 to 1940, the year of his death.

Another Boisean, this one native-born, also gained national fame in the U.S. Senate. Democrat Frank Church won election in 1956 at the age of 35, becoming the youngest senator in Washington at the time. In 1960, Church gave the keynote address at the Democratic National Convention, which nominated John F. Kennedy for president. Church championed passage of the 1964 Wilderness Act and served as an active proponent of the nation's wildlands. He also served as chairman of the Senate Foreign Relations Committee for two years before his election defeat by Steve Symms in 1980. The nation's largest wilderness, 2.3 million acres of rugged mountains, dramatic canyons, and pristine rivers at Idaho's heart, was rechristened the Frank Church–River of No Return Wilderness as Church lay dying of cancer in 1984. The addition of Church's name was made at the urging of Republican Sen. James McClure, who often opposed his colleague ideologically during their eight years together in the Senate.

Boise has produced more than politicians. One name Baby Boomers in particular will tumble to is Revere Dick. Huh? He was better known as the dandily dressed Paul Revere, who, with his band The Raiders, counter attacked the British rock 'n' roll invasion. While in his teens, he worked as a barber. In 1963, he, Mark Lindsay, and Roger Hart rented a Portland, Oregon, recording studio for $57. They re-recorded "Louie Louie" and adopted the name Paul Revere and the Raiders. The Raiders hit the big time from there, becoming regulars on Dick Clark's "American Bandstand," the nation's top rock 'n' roll television show. Paul Revere and the Raiders still rekindle the memories and play Boise occasionally.

EXPLORING BOISE

The **state capitol** makes a nice, easy landmark to start your tour of Boise. Drop in on Idaho's lawmakers as they debate and direct the state's future. From the capitol, some of the city's best sights are just to the southwest along Capitol Boulevard. In the vicinity of Sixth and Main, you'll find the **Old Boise Historic District,** where the town was born; lots of history here in the beautifully preserved buildings. Farther down Capitol Blvd. toward the river you'll come to a mother lode of sights—**Julia Davis Park** with its cluster of state and city museums just north of the Boise River. If you could talk to the animals, you wouldn't want to miss **Zoo Boise** here.

Across the river, you'll find the campus of **Boise State University,** and, for historical architecture buffs, the **Union Pacific Railroad Depot,** one of the city's prettiest buildings. Southeast from the capitol, Warm Springs Blvd. leads to the **Pioneer Cemetery** and the **Old Idaho Penitentiary,** where Idaho's desperadoes once met their just rewards.

Dozens more attractions are spread across the city and its surrounding area. Everything from parks to museums to nature centers await the urban explorer. Many of them are listed below.

THE CAPITOL

One of Boise's main attractions is the statehouse at the end of Capitol Blvd., which delineates Boise's midsection. The sandstone building houses the Idaho Senate and House of Representatives. Office suites house Idaho's governor, lieutenant governor, secretary of state, and attorney general as well. The current Idaho capitol replaced a five-floor brick building—erected in 1885 by the territorial legislature—that served Idaho officials through the first few years of statehood. The original building had no indoor plumbing, a lack that no doubt helped convince officials a new capitol was needed.

Architect J.E. Tourtellotte patterned the new statehouse after the nation's Capitol, in the standard neoclassical style, and construction of the central building and dome began in 1905. Sandstone from a nearby quarry sheaths the iron frame of the central section's dome. Convicts from the nearby state penitentiary quarried the sandstone from Table Rock east of town and hauled it to the capitol. Some of the blocks weighed 10 tons. With the central building and dome completed in 1912, state officials next contracted with architects Tourtellotte and Hummel to design east and west wings. Construction began on the additions in 1919 and finished the next year, bringing the capitol's total cost to $2.3 million. The state has estimated replacement cost in 1991 at $60 to $75 million.

The Legislature

There's very little heavy lifting taking place in the statehouse these days. Legislators and the governor wrestle with the weighty issues of state that sometimes seem to become as light as a feather, shifting with the slightest political breeze.

The Idaho legislature with its 42 senators and 84 representatives convenes here Jan.-March each year. During particularly difficult sessions, Idaho's farmer legislators may not make it home until spring planting season is well advanced in April. As the legislative season lengthens, tempers shorten. Galleries for the public to observe the proceedings perch on the fourth floor above the chambers. The Senate occupies the west wing and the House occupies the east wing.

In all, some 400 people call the capitol the office. The marbled halls tend to amplify whispers and turn shouts into explosions of sound. The hallways provide interesting displays to examine as visitors browse their ways through the building.

Capitol Tidbits

•This is the only statehouse in the nation heated by a geothermal well.

•The eagle perched on the dome is solid copper and is bronze plated. Including its sandstone perch, it stands five feet, seven inches tall and weighs 250 pounds.
•The foundation extends 15 feet below ground and holds granite shipped in from Vermont.
•Inside, marble covers 50,646 square feet. The red marble is from Georgia, the black from Italy, green from Vermont, and gray from Alaska. The pillars are ascagliola veneer—a mixture of gypsum, glue, marble dust, and granite dyed to look like marble.
•The capitol contains 201,720 square feet of floor space and occupies a 4.69-acre plot.
•The rotunda dome holds 43 stars set against a sky-blue field, commemorating Idaho's status as the 43rd state. The 13 largest stars represent the original colonies.
•The second-floor statue of George Washington on horseback was carved by Austrian immigrant Charles Ostner. He spent five years carving it from a single ponderosa pine log, using a postage stamp as a model.
•The replica of the Winged Victory of Samothrace is one of 48 sent by France in 1949 to state capitals as a thank you for U.S. help in WW II. The original is in the Louvre in Paris.

Capitol Grounds
The grounds of the capitol provide a home for several trees planted by U.S. presidents to commemorate their visits to Boise. Benjamin Harrison planted a water oak on May 8, 1891, a year after he signed the proclamation granting Idaho statehood. Theodore Roosevelt planted a rock maple on May 18, 1903; and William Howard Taft planted an Ohio buckeye on Oct. 9, 1911. The rather ordinary Douglas fir near the eastern entrance traveled to the moon as a seedling on Apollo 11. Outside the western entrance, the Tree of Quernica is a transplant from the Basque region of northern Spain and commemorates the roots of Idaho's Basque community.

Monuments flank the statehouse. The **Pioneer Monument** was placed by Boise schoolchildren on May 8, 1905, to honor the emigrants of the Oregon Trail. On the west lawn is a 1935 monument to the Grand Army of the Republic. The cannon at the left of the capitol's front is a cast-iron cannon used during the Civil War by the Confederacy to defend its seacoast. Across Jefferson St. from the capitol stands a statue of Gov. Frank Steunenberg, who was assassinated in 1905, four years after he had retired from office.

The capitol (along with other parts of Boise) is unique for its geothermal heating system. Although homes along Warm Springs Ave. on the city's eastern flank have been heated with natural hot water since early this century, the capitol and other government buildings switched only in 1982. The 1,000-gallons-a-minute of 165° F groundwater can heat 750,000 square feet of buildings on all but the coldest winter days.

OLD BOISE HISTORIC DISTRICT

At the east end of Boise's downtown district, Old Boise's brick-and-mortar buildings harken back to Americans' first efforts to tame this vale of trees in 1863. The district's historic charms have been preserved and added to the National Register of Historic Places.

Cyrus Jacob's brick home at Grove and Sixth served as the nucleus (see "Basque Museum and Cultural Center," following). The Good Templar Hall, built in 1865, served as the setting for minstral shows, theater productions, lodge meetings, and firemen's balls. In addition, the territorial legislature met for its first two sessions here. The hall, unfortunately, was razed to make way for the **Pioneer Tent Building,** which still stands at the northeast corner of Sixth and Main.

Most of Old Boise's buildings share similar architectural traits: two stories, brick and stone trim. A few vintage buildings from the 1870s to 1890s—the 1879 **Perrault Building,** 1892 **Masonic Hall** at 615 Main, and **Spiegle Grocery** (now Pengilly's Saloon) at 513 and 515 Main—were a bit more daringly designed. Gas street lamps lit Old Boise until they were replaced by ornate electrically lit glass globes on cast-iron poles. A few of the cast-iron lights still remain.

Basque Museum And Cultural Center
A museum that's also a notable Boise historical attraction is the Basque Museum and Cultural Center, tel. 343-2671, at 611 Grove St. in the heart of the Boise Historic District. The Cyrus Jacobs-Uberuaga House, which houses the museum, is Boise's oldest brick home, built by pioneer merchant Cyrus Jacobs in 1864. Jacobs rose through the political ranks and was

eventually elected Boise's mayor. The brick house functioned as a home to hundreds of young Basque sheepherders passing through Boise. The museum recaptures the building's life as a Basque boardinghouse and social center for men who excelled at a lonely job, yet knew how to enjoy themselves around people. The museum is open May 1-Sept. 30, Tues.-Sat. 10 a.m.-5 p.m.; the rest of the year, Thurs.-Sat. 11 a.m.-3 p.m. A donation is requested.

Boise City Canal

The Boise City Canal Co. developed the Boise City Canal in 1866. The canal still runs along the north side of Grove Street, although the waterwheels, formerly every 50-100 feet along the Grove Street Ditch, as it was called, are long gone. Grove Street ranked as the city's most prestigious residential address in Boise's early days, anchoring such homes as the **DeLamar Mansion** and the **Lafayette Cartee** house. Natural hot water, similar to that which heated homes along Warm Springs Ave., heated the Grove Street homes and was supplied by the Artesian Hot and Cold Water Company, beginning in 1891.

Main Street

Main Street grew substantially in importance in 1891 when the Boise City Rapid Transit opened a streetcar line. For a nickel, riders could venture out Warm Springs Ave. to the Natatorium. Six years later, Main was paved. Crawford W. Moore, who built the DeLamar Mansion, gave the city two lots for a children's park in 1916. In 1982, the lots at Fifth and Grove were developed into a pleasant play area as Moore had intended.

Live theater and music brought throngs to the **Turner Theater** at the southeast corner of Sixth and Main. The 1906 building now houses Jake's Restaurant. The Empire Theater occupied the building now housing Idaho Blueprint. The opulent **Ada-Egyptian Theater** of 1927 still brings in moviegoers.

JULIA DAVIS PARK

This 90-acre park along the river offers the most popular escape for Boiseans, providing a home for Zoo Boise, the state's historical museum, and Boise Art Museum. The park also offers the Boise **Memorial Rose Garden,** along with picnic grounds, playgrounds, tennis courts, horseshoe pits, boat rentals, and a band shell. The main access is from Capitol Boulevard.

Zoo Boise

Zoo Boise, tel. 384-4260 or 384-4230, draws crowds to see the largest exhibit of birds of prey in the Northwest—including condors, eagles, and hawks—as well as a raven who likes visitors to lavish it with special attention. On display are 273 animals representing 95 species, including Idaho's big-game animals and more exotic species like Bengal tigers, zebras, elands, camels, and monkeys. The river otter display is a favorite. There's also a petting zoo of more approachable critters for the up-close-and-cuddly set. The zoo is open daily 10-5 and Thursday nights until 9 p.m.; closed Christmas and New Year's Day. Admission rates vary from free for those three and younger, to $2 for those ages 12-61; half-price admission on Thursdays. The Idaho Zoological Society, 1104 Royal Blvd., Boise, ID 83706, organizes events to benefit the zoo. For more information about events, call 384-4486.

Boise Art Museum

The Boise Art Museum, tel. 345-8330, stands out along Capitol Blvd. just before the bridge, and holds Idaho's best public collection of artwork. The museum, open Tues.-Fri. 10 a.m.-5 p.m., weekends noon-5, exhibits both its own permanent collection and traveling exhibitions. It offers about 20 exhibitions a year and docent-guided tours to help visitors put the artwork in perspective. The museum sponsors educational programs, lectures, films, art classes, and community events throughout the year. Admission is $2 for adults, $1 for college students and seniors. Children 17 and younger enter free.

Idaho Historical Museum

Across Julia Davis Dr. from the art museum is the Idaho Historical Museum, tel. 334-2120, which includes exhibits portraying a Wild West saloon, kitchen, Chinese apothecary shop, and blacksmith shop. The museum also houses an excellent collection of cowboy and Indian artifacts, ranging from weapons to basic trappings. Basque history is also preserved and examined here. The historical museum is open Mon.-Sat. 9-5 and Sunday 1-5 p.m. Admission is free.

Pioneer Village
The Idaho State Historical Society has assembled some of Idaho's historic buildings in a pioneer village near the Idaho Historical Museum. Two of these are historic homes that span the dozen decades since Boise's founding: the Pearce log cabin and early mayor Thomas Logan's old adobe home. They were originally built near Cyrus Jacob's home. The Pearce cabin was built in 1863, the year of Boise's founding. Logan's house is one of the few remnants from the city's early reliance on mud bricks. It survived in part because red oil paint coated its exterior and extended the life of the adobe. Also in the pioneer village are the Richard C. Adelmann frame house and the Colson Homestead Shack. Adelman was a saloon keeper, and his simple home typified Boise homes from 1870 to 1890. The Colson shack was built in 1909 and represents the board-and-batten buildings that typically sheltered homesteaders across the sagebrush claims of southern Idaho.

Tour Train
Boise's Tour Train departs from Julia Davis Park several times daily June 1-Labor Day (weekends only in May, Sept., and Oct.) for one-hour narrated tours. Call 342-4796 for details. The train features open-air coaches pulled by a simulated 1890 steam engine.

ACROSS THE RIVER

Boise State University
Crossing the Boise River heading southwest on Capitol Blvd. brings you to the western edge of Boise State University, the focal point for much of Boise's fun and culture. The university is home to Morrison Center, BSU Pavilion, Hemingway Western Studies Center, Simplot/Micron Technology Center, and Bronco Stadium, where Boiseans hoot and whistle on autumn weekends for their football heroes. Cultural events on campus include film festivals, concerts, art exhibits, student theater, lectures, and other trappings of student life—open to visitors as well. The school's general information number is 385-1011.

The Union Pacific Railroad station at the south end of Capitol Boulevard commands attention.

Boise State enrolls 12,000 students and specializes in business, nursing, and high technology. Founded by the Episcopal Church in 1932, the institution evolved to Boise Junior College and was promoted to a university in 1974. The campus of 50 buildings covers 110 acres along the river. The **Student Union Building** at the corner of University Dr. and Lincoln Ave. serves as the heart of the campus. The **Visitor Center,** tel. 385-2065, is located along Chrisway Dr. just south of University Drive. For those with a hunger to learn more about politics, Boise State's **library** also houses the papers of the late Sen. Frank Church. Church served as chairman of the Senate Foreign Relations Committee and distinguished himself as an ardent conservationist before losing his Senate seat in 1980 after four terms. The **Hemingway Western Studies Center,** tel. 385-1819, probes the consciousness of the West from its base on campus.

Union Pacific Railroad Depot
Anchoring the southern end of Capitol Blvd. is the Union Pacific Railroad Depot, a classic

Spanish-style station that rivals the statehouse as Boise's most beautiful historic building. The beautiful **Platt Gardens** surround the depot, which serves as the Amtrak station.

ALONG WARM SPRINGS AVENUE

Heading southeast from the capitol brings you to Warm Springs Avenue, lined by the stateliest homes in Boise. Many of the homes, like the state buildings, are still heated geothermally.

Pioneer Cemetery

You won't spot Idaho's pioneers strolling down the street these days, but their final resting spots are only 10 blocks east of the capitol where Avenue C meets Warm Springs Avenue. You can find the grave of Cyrus Jacobs here, as well as those of Thomas E. Logan and Isaac Newton Coston, the early day movers-and-shakers whose homes still stand. Thomas Jefferson Davis lies here as well. Davis was a founder of Boise, one of eight men who met July 7, 1863, in a cabin he and William Ritchie owned. The men plotted the townsite for the city that would become known as Boise. Thomas Jefferson Davis is best known today for his loving memorial to his wife, Julia (nee McCrumb) Davis. He donated the land for Julia Davis Park, now housing the pioneer village and historical museum. Two governors also lie in the cemetery: George L. Shoup, who served first as territorial governor, then as state governor when Idaho made the transition on July 3, 1890; and Frank W. Hunt, Idaho's fifth governor.

The Old Idaho Penitentiary

The Old Penitentiary was built in 1870 and served the state until 1973, housing more than 13,000 prisoners. Then a series of riots convinced officials a new prison was needed. The old prison was listed on the National Register of Historic Places in 1974, and now offers an engaging tour for visitors, with some tales of desperate folks thrown in for spice. Tour guides tell of women jailed for stealing food for their families, and of the outlaw who swung from the gallows. Exhibits in the penitentiary museum preserve captured contraband weapons, balls and chains, Oregon boots, and other mementos of a mean past, and recount tales of famous convicts and lawmen, escapes, and prison life there. The tour includes the maximum-security building, where Death Row held those waiting for the slate to be wiped clean, and where the state's gallows were used, only once—in 1957.

The old prison shirt factory now houses the **Idaho Transportation Museum,** which portrays Idaho's travel history. The **History of Electricity in Idaho Museum** occupies the false-front buildings, which once served as commissary, library, hospital, and barber shop.

Admission to the Old Penitentiary, tel. 334-2844, is $3 for adults, $2 for seniors and children age 6-13, and free for those six and younger. The prison is open noon-5 p.m. summers and noon-4 p.m. winters.

Bishop's House

The Bishop's House outside the penitentiary walls was moved from downtown to make way for construction there in 1975. The house may be rented for receptions by calling 342-3279.

Idaho Botanical Gardens

Before leaving the prison area, summer visitors will want to spend at least a few minutes admiring the Idaho Botanical Gardens, tel. 343-8649, open from late April through mid-October. The seven gardens feature collections of herbs, heirloom roses, historical irises, and others. Attractive meditation, children's, and butterfly-hummingbird gardens provide some surprises along the way. The gardens are open April 29-Oct. 14, Tues.-Fri. 10 a.m.-3 p.m., Sat.-Sun. 10 a.m.-5 p.m. Admission costs $2 for adults, $1 for seniors and students ages 6-18.

SCIENCE AND INDUSTRY

Discovery Center

Boise's status as a high-technology center gains by the year. One of the cities most popular attractions for children and adults alike can only help build that reputation by showing young minds and old that science can be fun. Located at 131 W. Myrtle, The **Discovery Center of Idaho,** tel. 343-9895, presents a chance to participate hands-on in science and technology. The exhibits encourage both kids and their elders to learn through doing. The Discovery Center was developed by a group of professional and amateur scientists, engineers, architects, and others ranging from business executives to students. They shared a desire to make this place a synthesis of science and industry. Their work paid off.

Kids need a couple of hours to find their way through the several rooms that offer experimental setups primarily exploring various aspects of the physical sciences. Even those who never quite got physics in high school or college can have fun with this gear. A personal favorite here is the bubble curtain.

General admission to the Discovery Center is $3 for adults, $2 for seniors and students ages 5-18, and free to children younger than five. The center is open Thurs.-Fri. 9-5, Sat.-Sun. noon-4.

Boise Interagency Fire Center

When summers warm up and forests dry out, the crew at the Boise Interagency Fire Center readies for action. This is the command center for the thousands of firefighters that go afield each year to try to control nature's fiery temper. The center, tel. 387-5512, handles the logistics for all wildfire fighting in the United States. Tours are given but must be arranged in advance (and are not usually offered during summer's peak fire season). The tours take visitors through a technological wonderland of gadgets and gizmos that the modern firefighter just can't live without. Literally!

The center boasts a remote lightning-detection system, infrared-mapping system, radio-communication shops that rival the military's, remote solar weather stations, and similar high technology. Acres of shovels, pulaskis, fire-retardant clothing, sleeping bags, and similar material are ready to supply an army of firefighters.

To get to the facility, take the Vista exit off I-84 and head south toward the airport. The center is at 3833 S. Development Avenue.

Industry Headquarters

For those intrigued, even enthralled, by American industry, Boise offers corporate headquarters worth a drive-by, maybe even a stop. Among Boise-based corporations, **Boise-Cascade Corporation** ranks at the top. Its five-story office building at 954 Jefferson spans a block and is worth a visit during business hours just to ogle the forest growing within its atrium. Boise-Cascade grew from Idaho and Washington logging companies early this century to become one of the nation's largest lumber and paper-milling companies.

Morrison Knudsen branched out across the world as the construction company that could do almost any job right. MK built the DEW line (the old Defense Early Warning radar system that spanned the northern marches, watching for incoming Intercontinental Ballistic Missiles) and nearly 100 dams across the globe, locks on the St. Lawrence Seaway, the Manned Spacecraft Center, and ships. It dammed Hells Canyon. It grew into one of the largest construction companies in the United States. Its headquarters stands proud along Myrtle St. between Walnut and Broadway.

Also based in Boise are **Idaho Power Co.,** 1120 W. Idaho; the grocery chain **Albertsons,** 250 E. Park Center Blvd.; and the **J.R. Simplot Co.,** 999 Main. It's no exaggeration to say much of Idaho's economy finds itself passing through these corridors.

Wineries

An industry that some would find considerably more fun is also growing up around Boise. Three wineries—Petros, Ste. Chapelle, and Hells Canyon—maintain tasting rooms in Boise. **Petros,** tel. 322-4739, is located at 264 N. Maple Grove Rd. in Boise but offers tastings at its shop at Boise Towne Square Mall. **Ste. Chapelle,** tel. 344-9074, is based to the west near Marsing, but maintains a tasting room at Boise's The Grove downtown, tel. 344-9074. **Hells Canyon** offers tastings by appointment at Mussel's Fish Market, tel. 336-2277, at 3107 Overland Road.

BIRDS OF PREY

World Center For Birds Of Prey

Dramatically updated with a new visitor center in 1993, this facility is a laboratory and conservatory for some of the world's most endangered species of hawks, falcons, and eagles. It's also one of the best places in the nation to learn about endangered species and the dedicated people working to ensure their survival.

The center is operated by the Peregrine Fund, which was founded in 1970 to prevent the extinction of the peregrine falcon, the world's fastest bird. The peregrine can reach

PROTECTING PREDATORS

In 1980, Congress created the Snake River Birds of Prey Area—483,000 acres along 81 rugged miles of the Snake River Canyon south of Kuna. The area is refuge to the greatest concentration of nesting raptors on the continent.

Biologists estimate 700 pairs of birds of prey live there, ranging from prairie falcons and golden eagles to great horned owls, turkey vultures, and Swainson's, red-tailed, and ferruginous hawks. The birds nest on the lava cliffs that reach up 600 feet from the river. They feed on ground squirrels, jackrabbits, and mice. The area protects more than just birds of prey. Badgers go after the same ground squirrels that attract the keen-eyed stares of eagles. Lizards abound along the canyon as well.

The idea of protecting chicken hawks didn't sit well with some when a birds of prey sanctuary was first proposed. The area has since proved popular enough that Congress considered another effort to expand it in 1991.

KAREN WHITE

prairie falcon

speeds faster than 200 miles an hour during its aerial pursuit of other birds. Thanks to the Peregrine Fund's efforts, the falcons have been returned to most of the states where they once soared. Now the fund's work continues with other species, and the center functions as both a clearinghouse for information and a national intensive care unit for birds of prey (biologists use the term "raptors"). In 1993, a dozen California condors were transferred here from southern California to establish a third breeding population of the continent's biggest birds. Eventually they will be released back into the wild in hopes of starting a self-sustaining wild population.

The new Velma Morrison Education Center here offers a wealth of displays about the biology of raptors. At the back of the building is a darkened hallway where visitors can view a variety of the birds from around the world. Large windows open onto the center's incubator and brooder laboratories where young birds are hatched and given a start on life before being shipped off to release sites. Tours of the center are offered throughout the year by appointment only. Groups are limited to 30.

The center is located south of Boise off Cole Rd., tel. 362-3716, in an area chosen for its proximity to the Snake River Birds of Prey Area just south along the Snake River. It's open Tues.-Sun. 10 a.m.-4 p.m. A donation of $4 for adults, $3 for seniors, and $2 for children is requested.

Snake River Birds Of Prey Area

The Snake River Birds of Prey Area encompasses 81 miles of the Snake River's rugged canyon south of Boise and some 483,000 adjoining acres. Golden eagles, hawks, falcons, and other species of predatory birds nest along here during the spring. The area is managed by the BLM's Boise District office, tel. 384-3300, at 3948 Development Ave., and is best reached by turning south on Hwy. 69 at the Meridian/Kuna exit off I-84, 10 miles west of Boise. Follow the highway south through Kuna then follow a good gravel road to the canyon. Head east for a mile and southeasterly for five. **The Idaho Outfitters and Guides Association** in Boise, tel. 376-5680, can also provide information about which outfitters are offering birdwatching raft trips down the Snake.

The cliffs here stand 600 feet or more above the Snake River, and the nesting raptors can be tough to spot. Remember to bring your binoculars. But hundreds of pairs nest along the river, nearly 10 pairs a mile, the densest concentration of nesting raptors in the nation. Biologists recommend that you schedule your trip beween mid-March and late June to catch the peak of the nesting season.

More than a dozen kinds of birds of prey breed here, including prairie falcons, golden eagles, American kestrels, red-tailed hawks, northern harriers or marsh hawks, ferruginous hawks, Swainson's hawks, and turkey vultures. Owls breeding in the area include the barn owl, northern saw-whet, burrowing, short-eared, long-eared, great horned, and western screech. During the late spring evenings, the cacophony of the owls' hoots and screeches can range from comical to downright eerie.

And where raptors are found at the top of the food chain, other small animals must be around to play the role of food. They're here. Some 250 kinds of mammals, birds, reptiles, and fish are found in the area, each of which might end up feeding the falcons, eagles, and hawks at some point.

PARKS AND RECREATION

CITY PARKS

Boise's park system is the best developed in Idaho. Downtown, **The Grove** functions as the city's public plaza. It serves as the site for many community activities, including Boise's **Alive After Five** weekly music-and-entertainment series during spring and summer. **Julia Davis Park** (see its own listing under "Exploring Boise," above) is one of the two most popular parks in the city—Zoo Boise, the Boise Art Museum, and the Idaho Historical Museum are among its attractions. Other city parks are described below.

The Greenbelt

The Boise River Greenbelt stretches 9.5 miles along the river from the Willow Lane athletic complex on the west to Eckert Rd. and Barber Park on the east. **Barber Park,** which is operated by Ada County, also serves as the launching point for some 250,000 tubers who ply the Boise each summer. The greenbelt idea was approved by the Boise City Council in 1968; the council passed an ordinance creating the greenbelt zone in 1971. Development is prohibited within the zone.

Officials estimate that the Greenbelt itself covers only about 86 acres, but it links more than 850 acres of other parkland along the river. The city oversees most of the Greenbelt pathways, about nine miles of which are paved. Some of the city's most popular parks provide access to the Greenbelt. Two of them—Julia Davis Park (see its own listing under "Exploring Boise," above) and Ann Morrison Memorial Park—occupy positions of popular acclaim like queens among the throng.

Ann Morrison Memorial Park

Southwest of downtown, Ann Morrison Memorial Park, with entrances off Americana and Royal boulevards, is less developed than Davis Park and occupies three-quarters of a mile of Boise River shoreline. The park's 153 acres hold picnic groves with fireplaces, an extensive playground, an illuminated fountain, tennis courts, soccer fields, lighted softball fields, an archery range, and horseshoe pits. The park also serves as the end point for much of the river's tubing flotilla. The **River Runner** tuber transport hauls the weary back upriver from the park to retrieve their vehicles.

Other City Parks

Just across Americana Blvd. from Morrison Park lies **Kathryn Albertson Park,** with 41 acres of picnic pavilions and nature and walking paths winding through trees and lagoons. This park is the city system's best spot to get away from the madding crowd. Two other parks in the city system, 15-acre **Municipal Park** and 15-acre **ParkCenter Park,** serve as large-scale escapes. Municipal Park on the 500 block of Walnut offers a popular picnic shelter; the city recommends making reservations for its use. Municipal also provides picnic grills, a playground, and greenbelt access. ParkCenter Park, located along Parkcenter Blvd., fronts a lagoon and a physical fitness course. A windsurfing concession offers a chance to test the breeze. **C.W. Moore Park** at Fifth and Grove offers bits of Boise's past architecture and a working waterwheel.

Nature Reserves

In addition to its greenbelt and host of parks, Boise's **nature reserves** shelter some suprisingly wild places close to the city's heart. The biggest (466 acres) is **Military Reserve Park** at Reserve St. and Mountain Cove Road. Foot trails follow a stream, then break out across the high-desert sage. Other reserve parks include **Flying Hawk Reserve,** the 290-acre home to the **World Center for Birds of Prey** (see "Birds of Prey," above); **Camelback Park,** 60 acres at 13th and Heron; and **Foothills East Reserve,** 23 acres at Pierce St. and Shenandoah Drive.

Recreation Centers, Athletic Fields

Boise's park system, tel. 384-4256, also includes three **recreation centers** which can host sports, dances, and art activities, or simply be places to gather. The **Activity Center** at 801 Aurora in Boise Park sponsors gymnastics instruction and adult fitness and aquatic programs. The **Fort Boise Community Center** is in Fort Boise Park at Fort St. and Reserve. Indoor basketball and volleyball courts, exercise equipment, saunas and showers, and recreation activity classes take place here. Fort Boise Park is also home to the **Art Center** where art classes, a darkroom, potter's wheels, and kilns provide the focus for activities.

The park system also maintains **athletic fields** at Fort Boise Park and at Willow Lane west of State Street. Fort Boise has softball fields, a baseball field, football fields, and tennis courts, all lighted. There's a physical fitness course here, too. Willow Lane is the most extensive with its soccer fields, softball fields, baseball fields, football fields, a children's playground, and a fitness course.

City Park Information

The **Boise Park System** administrative office, tel. 384-4240, is located at 1104 Royal Blvd. at Ann Morrison Park's fringe. The office serves as the clearinghouse for baseball-diamond reservations and provides general information about the parks and events in them.

STATE PARKS

Veterans Memorial State Park

Veterans Memorial State Park, maintained by the Idaho Parks and Recreation Department, is the only truly urban state park in the system. The cottonwood trees lining the lake and riverbank here are a reminder of how the city got its name: In the earliest days of white exploration, French-Canadian trappers first reached the area and its plentiful trees after their travels across dusty miles of sagebrush plains. ("Bois" is the French word for "woods.") The Boise Valley is still a haven of trees in the sagebrush desert, and this park captures the best of the allure of running water and cool shade.

The park's 86 acres feature a number of nice touches. Kids will enjoy a modern playground and open areas to run and play. The park also offers a picnicking area with tables (although there are no grills). More than three miles of paved and unpaved trails attract plenty of visitors wanting to stretch their legs, and serve as an important link to the Greenbelt trail system. A summer's evening on these paths proves their popularity beyond a doubt. Couples, children riding bicycles, joggers, youths, and families meander along them. A small pond near the park's entrance features a wooden boardwalk where one can reflect on this little corner's serenity.

In addition to the paths, visitors to Veterans Memorial State Park flock to Boise Cascade Lake for fishing, swimming, floating, and fun. Docks at the water's edge give anglers and swimmers convenient access points. A mile of shoreline around the lake gives fishermen plenty of room to spread out in hopes of reeling in a tenacious little bluegill sunfish or a largemouth bass. On a sunny day, folks ply the lake's quiet surface in craft ranging from canoes to inflatable rafts and even inflatable mattresses. The adjacent Boise River also attracts its share of anglers and paddlers.

Waterfowl flock to the park as well. Mallards, American coots, and mergansers are the most common visitors. Belted kingfishers and great blue herons can be found at the water's edge. Winter months may bring bald eagles, though rarely. More common are red-tailed and rough-legged hawks. Summer may bring occasional ospreys to the capital city's big-hearted river.

The park began as a 12-acre gift in May 1972. The quest for more green space over the years helped it grow to its present size. In 1976 it was dedicated as Veterans Memorial State Park to honor Idaho's servicemen. The park has no campgrounds and closes at dark. To find out about Veterans or other state parks in the Boise area, call the department's state headquarters at 327-7444.

Morrison Knudsen Nature Center

This facility offers a glimpse of life in the river as well as along it. Special underwater observation windows have been set up here so you won't need your diving mask to enjoy the scenery. The observatory is adjacent to the Idaho Fish and Game Department's state headquarters at 600 S. Walnut. "Where else can you watch fish develop from quarter-inch eggs to 16-inch trout?" asks the Idaho Fish and Game Department, the patron agency for the observatory. The wildlife area includes 4.5 acres of stream, wetland, woodland, and semiarid habitat, and a pond. Although the underwater windows are the show-stopper, decks elsewhere allow visitors to remain aloof and undetected from wildlife. A nature center will help supply explanations for what's happening out there.

Pathways steer visitors past displays depicting the life cycles of fish. The stream holds mountain whitefish, kokanee salmon, suckers, and several species of trout, including rainbow, cutthroat, brook, and bull.

The wildlife area is also home to songbirds and waterfowl, including valley quail, mallard ducks, and Canada geese. Look for the hanging nests of northern orioles slung in the cottonwoods. The nature center was established to teach visitors about nature and also to demonstrate how wildlife can find a home even in the city, with a little help. Since its construction, a building has been added to accommodate displays that extend the educational value of the area. Tours are available through special arrangement by calling the Fish and Game Department, tel. 334-3700.

Lucky Peak State Park

Lucky Peak State Park lies along Hwy. 21 just east of Boise. Its three sub-units glimmer jewel-like along the Boise River, and on warm afternoons its bright sands lure city residents by the thousands.

Most of the beach-going activity concentrates at the 17-acre **Sandy Point Unit** at the base of Lucky Peak Dam, 10 miles southeast of Boise along Hwy. 21. A large, modernist stainless steel sculpture sprays water out in the middle of a warm lagoon fronting the main swimming beach off the Boise River. The fountain functions like a magnet, drawing children out into the warm waters aboard tiny rubber rafts, inner tubes, and all sorts of other watercraft. Sandy Point was developed with picnickers in mind, too. Shade trees on a grassy lawn cast inviting plumes of shade for dozens of picnic tables. No pets are allowed at the Sandy Point Unit. A snack bar dishes out a steady supply of soft drinks and vacation foods during the long summer afternoons.

The park's **Discovery Unit** is designed more for picnickers. Three picnic shelters are available for groups or family reunions. Discovery occupies the river's shore just nine miles east of Boise below the dam and offers an inviting place to cast a line for rainbow and brown trout, channel catfish, and smallmouth bass. Strong currents here—lurking beneath the surface and ready to sweep unwitting anglers away—demand caution.

Finally, the **Spring Shores Unit** is like a hybrid of the other two, offering fishing access, two boat ramps, and an extensive picnic area. Spring Shores is 16 miles southeast of Boise along Hwy. 21, then east a mile after the Mores Creek Bridge. Spring Shores also boasts the largest marina in the state parks system. With 285 boat slips, it is a popular launch point for Boise sailors. And fishermen flock to this unit of Lucky Peak State Park because it offers access to the reservoir and its kokanee salmon, trout, and bass fishing.

This park was one of the first created in the state's fledgling parks system. The state reached an agreement with the Army Corps of Engineers in 1956 that paved the way for the park's development. Wildlife along the river here includes muskrat and mink, beaver, and the occasional river otter. Birdlife includes migrant waterfowl, ranging from teal to Canada geese. Look for riverside birds here during the summers. Northern orioles hang their pendulous nests from the upper tree branches, and belted kingfishers chatter their way up and down the riverbank.

Eagle Island State Park

The little town of Eagle, just west of Boise, is one of the close-in havens for those who work in the big city but don't want to live there. Little may not apply much longer, though; new subdivisions are creeping steadily westward along Hwy. 44. Eagle is still a valued escape, however, and is likely to remain that way for a long time to come. It's also the home of Eagle Island State Park, tel. 939-0696, one of Idaho's most popular parks. Weekends are a constant blur of motion here during the hot summers.

Most park visitors focus their attention on the sandy beach stretching 1,000 feet along the 11-acre manmade lake or on a nearby hillside dominated by a water slide. A neat picnic area, snack bar, and a covered picnic shelter also rank high among the park's attractions.

Those features alone are enough to satisfy most visitors, who might be surprised to learn the park proper includes a much larger area. Eagle Island encompasses 546 acres between the northern and southern channels of the Boise River. The undeveloped portion of the park is meant to remain that way. Parks officials tend to avoid publicizing the park's shaggy side to keep it a sanctuary for wildlife. Both mule and white-tailed deer may wander through these areas. Birdlife includes valley quail and pheasants among the weeds. Birds of prey include bald eagles, red-tailed hawks, rough-legged hawks, and kestrels. American crows pass through during the summer. Great blue herons stalk the river's shorelines.

Eagle Island State Park's hydro tube supplies plenty of chances to unwind.

The flat, irrigated farmland once served as the Idaho Corrections Department's Prison Honor Farm, a role it was purchased to fill in 1929. The construction of the new prison south of Boise led the state to abandon the prison farm in 1974. After much wrangling, the Idaho Land Board voted in 1978 to transfer the farm to the Parks and Recreation Department. But the park wasn't funded until April 1980, and didn't open until June 1983.

The park is open Memorial Day-Labor Day, 10:30 a.m. till evening. No pets allowed. The water slide is open for business at noon to cool visitors during the heat of the afternoon. There is a modest charge for using the slide.

Getting to Eagle Island State Park can be an adventure in itself. Highways 44 or 20 and 26 head west from Boise. Find their intersection off Linder Road. The park lies between the highways, along the river. Once you cross either branch of the river look for Hatchery Rd. and turn east.

RECREATION

Les Bois Park

The Western Idaho Fairgrounds is also the home of Les Bois Park, tel. 376-3985, at 5610 Glenwood Road. The three-quarter-mile oval track is one of the major tracks in the nation for American quarter horse racing. For those who like the long and lean, thoroughbreds also race here. Post times are 5 p.m. Wednesdays and Saturdays and 2 p.m. Sundays and holidays during the 50-day racing season stretching from May to August. Playing the ponies here means a $2 minimum bet, with singles, multiples, quinielas, trifectas, exactas, and daily doubles available each day.

Swimming

The biggest water attraction in Boise, with the exception of the Boise River of course, is **Wild Waters,** tel. 322-1844, a water slide theme park. Wild Waters is fun for both adults and kids. Sliding down the fiberglass flumes with names like Twister, Bonzai, or Drop-off can be an exhilarating break from the driving routine. Located at 1850 Century Way just off I-84 at its intersection with Overland Rd., Wild Waters is open 11 a.m.-7 p.m. daily between Memorial Day and Labor Day. The park also has a diving platform, Tarzan swing, volleyball courts, even swimming lessons. A large grass lawn is equipped with picnic benches and shady umbrellas. There's an ice cream concession and an arcade room to keep the kids occupied if their parents aren't quite ready to leave.

The Boise Parks System also offers the **Natatorium and Hydrotube,** tel. 384-4240, at 1811 Warm Springs Ave. near the Old Idaho Penitentiary. The pool uses the same warm waters that give the avenue its name and that heat many of the fine residences and government buildings in this part of town. The Natatorium was once covered with an elaborate wood and glass shell. A shrieking windstorm in 1934, however, so badly damaged the structure that it had to be torn down, leaving a perfectly enjoyable outdoor pool behind that still entertains children during summer vacations. The parks system also operates the following municipal pools: **Borah Park Pool,** at 801 Aurora just west of Borah High School; **South Pool,** 921 Shoshone St. at South Junior High School and Bowden Park; **Fairmont Park Pool,** at 7929 Northview west of Fairmont Junior High School; and **Lowell Pool,** 1601 N. 28th St., at Lowell School. Call 384-4486 for more information about the pools.

Skiing

Bogus Basin Ski Area, tel. 343-1891, offers powder skiing and groomed trails during the winter months. Only 16 miles north of town off Harrison Blvd., Bogus Basin's 2,000 acres are a favorite escape for Boiseans who ski. The basin was named for a deceiving discovery of pyrite, or fool's gold. The deep snows that blanket the basin in winter proved to be the true wealth. Bogus also offers night skiing. The **Pioneer Inn Condominiums,** 2405 Bogus Basin Rd., tel. 336-4500, offer convenient lodging there for those who'd rather spend their time on the slopes than in their car driving back and forth to Boise. Rooms are $52-200.

Boise remains the focus of the ski rental and sales domain. Among the major ski shops in town are **McU Sports,** which offers two shops in town and two at Bogus Basin. In-town stores are at 822 W. Jefferson, tel. 342-7734, and 8045 Fairview at its intersection with Milwaukee, tel. 378-9504. The Bogus rental shop phone number is 342-2521, and the Bogus sales shop, at 2314 Bogus Basin Rd., can be reached at 336-2300. The full-service company sells and rents both Alpine and Nordic equipment and also makes repairs.

High Country Sports, at Fifth and Idaho, tel. 344-3822, specializes in Nordic gear and offers clothing as well. **Idaho Mountain Touring,** 912 W. Jefferson, tel. 336-3854, offers specialized gear for rent, such as metal-edge skis designed for backcountry touring and Telemarking. **Benchmark,** tel. 323-1700, is another Nordic specialist, at 5321 Emerald just north of the I-84 Orchard Ave. exit.

Bob Greenwood's Ski Haus has offered both Alpine and Nordic gear since 1957. The Ski Haus at 2400 Bogus Basin Rd. both sells and rents equipment. For sales call 342-6808 and for rentals call 336-4445. The shop also offers an extensive demonstrator collection of skis and boots.

Sports Exchange, 1029 Broadway Ave., tel. 385-0440, has new and used sports equipment, including skis, for sale or trade. **The Skiers Edge,** 1521 N. 13th, mounts, repairs, and tunes skis. Ski and ski-rack rental specialist **Brown Rental** operates two shops, one at 2905 Overland Rd., tel. 344-6581, and one at 8520 Fairway Ave., tel. 376-5155. **Herman's World of Sporting Goods** operates two branch stores at Boise that sell and rent skis. Herman's stores are at 5805 Fairview, tel. 376-1100, and 219 Main, tel. 336-5096.

Boating

The Boise River is beautiful but the city's status as a major boating center may leave some people shaking their heads. There's very little room in the river for a fiberglass runabout, and the farmland and sagebrush seems to stretch forever from the edges of the capital's city limits. Boiseans know best on this subject. Trust them. The Snake River offers **C.J. Strike Reservoir** pretty close to town, lurking south of Mountain Home along the Snake River. At **Lucky Peak Reservoir,** east of the city along Hwy. 21, running about is what it's all about for some visitors. Then there's **Owyhee Reservoir** not too far away in southeastern Oregon. And to the north you'll find **Brownlee Reservoir** along Hwy. 95 and **Payette Lake** and **Cascade Reservoir** along Hwy. 55.

Various forms of watercraft are available for rent in the area. Those who like a lot of contact with the wet stuff during their boating excursions will head for **S&L Jet Ski Rental,** tel. 338-1718. They rent the floating motorcycles that rip around the big reservoirs. Operated with some sense of manners, they're as fun for others to watch as they are to operate. Raft and tube rentals are available at **Barber Park Raft and Tube Rental,** tel. 336-8823, at Barber Park east of Boise along Hwy. 21, and **Boise Army-Navy Surplus,** tel. 322-0660, at 4924 Chinden Blvd., open daily.

Fishing

The Boise River offers some of southwestern Idaho's most popular fishing. For anglers, that can be both good and bad. The series of lakes along the Greenbelt give many young anglers their first taste of fishing at the water's edge and, subsequently, at the dinner table. For others, the Boise's rainbow and brown trout prove fitting adversaries for even the most accomplished angler. It's not uncommon to walk the greenbelt paths and see children frolicking at the water's edge on one side of the river and an angler patiently casting flies to promising pockets along the other.

During years of good steelhead runs in the Snake and Clearwater rivers to the north, the big sea-run rainbow trout are also released into the Boise for anglers to pursue. The Clearwater steelhead average 12-14 pounds, big fish by anyone's book.

Nearby Lucky Peak Reservoir offers another spot where anglers can troll for kokanee salmon, the landlocked version of the toothsome sockeye or red salmon. Trout fishing is good here too.

Major fishing tackle shops in Boise include **Flat King-Rocky Mountain Anglers** tel. 336-5464, at 1002 Vista Ave., **Jolley's State Street Beverage and Sporting Goods,** tel. 342-6419, which sells tackle and licenses at 3412 W. State; **Rocky Mountain Anglers,** tel. 336-3336, at 1002 Vista Ave.; and **Streamside Adventures,** tel. 375-6008, at 6907 Overland Rd., selling a range of tackle. **Vista Sporting Goods,** tel. 384-9202, at 620 Vista Ave., is another shop with an extensive collection of tackle. Information about fishing seasons and locations is available from the **Idaho Fish and Game Department** tel. 334-3700, at 600 S. Walnut.

Bicycling

Bicycling is big in Boise. The bike paths designated by the city include those separate from

A 12-pound steelhead makes just about any fisherman happy.

streets as well as streets with a designated bike lane. The Greenbelt along the Boise River has most of the non-street paths. Streets designated for bicycles or with separate lanes include Kootenai in the city's southern precincts; Milwaukee on the west; Northview from Milwaukee toward the center of town; 16th and 15th streets from the center of town northward; and Ellis Ave. to the northeast.

Mountain biking has caught on like a wildfire in Boise. Military Reserve Park offers some trails. More extensive trails for mountain biking are available in the Boise National Forest; for more information call 364-4100, or stop by the forest supervisor's office at 1750 Front Street. The BLM's Boise District office, 3948 Development Ave., tel. 334-1582, also offers maps and information.

Boise is also full of bicycle shops that can equip riders for competition on road or trails. **Bob's Bicycles,** tel. 322-8042, at 6112 Fairview Ave., sells and repairs bicycles. The shop offers to arrange financing for mountain, racing, family, and BMX bikes. **Boise Cyclery,** tel. 322-6777, at 5125 Glenwood in the Glenwood Center, sells and services a full array of bicycles as well. **George's Lightweight Cycles,** tel. 343-3782, at 119 Broadway Ave., claims the Boise Valley's largest selection of mountain bikes. **Spoke N'Wheel,** tel. 377-2091, sells, trades, repairs, and rents mountain bikes. **Wheels R Fun,** tel. 343-8228, at 831 S. 13th, also rents bicycles. **Capitol Schwinn Cyclery,** tel. 336-2453, at 1214 Front, sells and repairs bicycles. **Idaho Mountain Touring,** tel. 336-3854, at 912 W. Jefferson, specializes in mountain and touring bikes and equipment. **The Cycle Works,** tel. 343-4184, at 602 N. Orchard; **Jim's Bicycle Shop,** tel. 336-5229, at 1517½ N. 13th St.; **Ken's Bicycle Warehouse,** tel. 376-9240, at 10400 Overland Rd.; and **Pedal Pusher Bikes,** tel. 342-9721, at 1015 Vista Ave., round out Boise's cycling scene.

Golf

Green fairways against the desert sage are one contradiction that capital city golfers savor. **Indian Lake Golf Course,** tel. 362-5771, at 4700 S. Umatilla Ave., is open from dawn to dusk and offers a driving range, pro shop, restaurant, and lounge. A public swimming pool and tennis courts there offer nongolfers an alternative. Lessons are available. **Quail Hollow Golf Club,** tel. 344-7807, is at 4520 N. 36th. **Shadow Valley,** tel. 939-6699, is five miles north of town along Hwy. 55. Shadow Valley is set at the edge of the Boise Front. It offers a lounge, golf shop, driving range, practice green, and cart rental. **Warm Springs Golf Club,** tel. 343-5661, at 2495 Warm Springs Ave., fronts the Boise River. It has a driving range, putting green, and pro shop. Cart rentals are available, as are group or private lessons.

Crane Creek Country Club is a private course at 500 W. Curling Dr., tel. 344-6529. **Hillcrest Country Club** is at 4610 Hillcrest Dr., tel. 343-5425. **Plantation Golf Club,** tel. 853-4440, is at 6515 W. State Street. **Quail Hollow Golf Club,** tel. 344-7807, is at 4520 N. 36th.

Golf USA, tel. 375-4653, offers club repair, equipment, and instructioh. **Nevada Bob's** is open daily during the peak golf and tennis season. Located at 5825 Franklin Rd., tel. 343-4996, the store caters to golf and tennis players. **Bartlett's Golf Service,** tel. 322-5827, offers custom-built clubs and club repair. The shop has a computerized swing analyzer and instructional aids. **Boise Golf Service,** tel. 336-9985, is located at 2319 N. 28th Street. **Hole-In-One Shop,** tel. 336-1028, offers club repairs and refitting at 1218 E. Franklin.

ENTERTAINMENT AND EVENTS

Boise is Idaho's entertainment, as well as political, capital. The stage of choice for most performance groups is the **Morrison Center for the Performing Arts,** tel. 385-1609, at 1910 University Drive. The center offers a 10-story stage house and six-story performance hall, and is home to most of the performers who pass through Boise. The 2,030-seat main hall has earned a Triple A rating, the highest available, for its acoustics.

On the BSU campus is the **Multi-Purpose Pavilion,** which can seat 12,000, whether they're screaming Broncos fans enjoying a little B-ball, or Willie Nelson devotees cheering on their favorite cowboy.

TWO TICKETS, PLEASE!

Dance

The **American Festival Ballet,** tel. 343-0556, hangs its toe shoes at 217 N. 10th when it's not on the road. The company maintains a ballet school, too. The **Oinkari Basque Dancers,** a very colorful and active group, reflect the capital's heritage as a cultural center for generations of Basque sheepherders. The troupe stages several performances each year and is based at 2418 Pendleton, tel. 336-8219.

Music

Boise Master Chorale, tel. 336-6767, at 6925 Copper Dr., tunes up three times annually for the public's pleasure, twice with the Boise Philharmonic Orchestra and once alone. Boise's peak cultural achievement for some is the **Boise Opera Co.,** tel. 345-3531, at 910 Main St., which attracts both local and national performers. The **Boise Philharmonic,** tel. 344-7849, at 205 N. 10th St., serves as musical accompaniment for most of the performances. The orchestra schedules six performances of its own each year, in addition to youth concerts.

Drama

The question remains, can Puccini better the Bard on any stage? **Idaho Shakespeare Festival** brings to life Shylock, Falstaff, and other ageless characters. The theater, tel. 336-9221, is located at 412 S. Ninth St., and the office is open Mon.-Fri. 10 a.m.-5 p.m. The troupe's performances are held outdoors at ParkCenter Park near the Boise River. The audience may bring picnics and enjoy the summer evenings and Shakespeare simultaneously. Wine, beer, soft drinks, and desserts are available at the theater. Performances are held weekends from mid-June to mid-August and a varying schedule of weekdays during the summer season. Tickets are $11 for adults and $7 for students and seniors; tickets to preview performances are $6.

The **Boise Little Theater,** tel. 342-5104, at 100 E. Fort, stages regular comedy and drama performances, a children's Christmas play among them. The group also offers a summer musical in its annual repertoire. The **Boise State University drama students** present a regular schedule of plays each year. To find out about campus plays, call 385-3957.

Cinema

Movie theaters are well seeded throughout Boise. The biggest concentration of screens is at the **Cineplex Odeon Towne Square Cinemas,** tel. 323-0430, at 130 N. Milwaukee Road. Opulence survives at the **Egyptian Theater,** tel. 342-1441, at 700 Main, which recalls the gilded age of silent films. **Eighth Street Market Place Theatre,** tel. 342-0299, at Eighth and Front streets, is close to downtown. **Fairvu Cinema,** tel. 375-6600, is at Fairview St. and Maple Grove Rd., next to the **Fairvu Drive-In,** tel. 375-3600, one of the few outdoor theaters still surviving. **Flicks Movie Theater,** tel. 342-4222, at 646 Fulton, offers art films and Sunday brunch. **Frontier Cinemas,** tel. 362-1344, at 10495 Lake Hazel Rd., is part of a southwestern Idaho chain. Another complex of screens is at **Overland Park Cinemas 1-2-3,** tel. 377-3072, at Cole and Overland roads. **Plaza Twin Theatres,** tel. 344-2212, at 5220 Overland Rd., wraps up the Boise movie scene.

EVENTS

The best of the big city expresses itself when it comes time to find something to do in Boise.

Small enough for residents and visitors to explore freely, Boise is big enough to have something going on almost all of the time.

Boiseans may seem to hibernate from January to March, but in reality they're just out of town, skiing. March, however, begins to roll with events, including the **Boise Roadster Show** at the Western Idaho Fairgrounds early in the month. Call 344-0411 for more information. Midmonth brings the **Festival of Wheels** at Ann Morrison Park, geared for nonmotorized wheels enthusiasts of all ages. For information on events in Boise parks, call 384-4240.

Spring Fling

April is windy in Idaho, more so than March—or maybe it just seems that way because the days are warmer and more of us are outside. The first weekend of April draws people out for the **Kite Festival** in Ann Morrison Park. An **Easter egg hunt** is held in Ann Morrison Park each year, too. The **drag racing** season gets off to a roaring start in early April at the Western Idaho Fairgrounds, tel. 344-0411. Julia Davis Park draws crowds of its own late each April with **Music in the Park** at the bandshell. The afternoon of music is free.

Boise delights in its colorful spring each May with the **Festival of Gardens and Flowers,** tel. 343-9520, at the ParkCenter Mall the first weekend in May. A **Children's Fishing Derby** is held at the ParkCenter Pond in early May for anglers age 13 and younger. Zoo Boise gets into the festival scene in mid-May with **Zoo Day,** with reduced admission for visitors. Call 384-4260 for details. The Idaho Botanical Gardens, tel. 343-8649, lures in visitors in mid-May with its **Spring Garden Tour.** The **Birds of Prey Festival,** tel. 362-3716, is held each May at the World Center for Birds of Prey south of town and includes fun runs and art exhibits geared toward educating people about the world's predatory birds.

Summer Events

Alive After Five is Boise's weekly gathering held Wednesday from late May to the end of August at The Grove, the plaza at the city's heart. The evenings bring city residents, local musicians, and entertainers there. A nearby farmer's market runs at the same time, with vendors selling fresh fruit, vegetables, and flowers.

Run for the Greenbelt kicks off the summer season in Boise in early June with a six-mile run or one-mile run or walk along the Greenbelt. Call 384-4240 for information. The **Children's Art Festival** occupies the Grove during June's second weekend. Call 336-2631 for details.

Ongi Etorri Jaunak! Held each July, the **St. Ignatius Festival** celebrates Basque culture with music, sporting events (such as wood chopping and weight lifting), and educational programs—dancing and food, too, of course. Performers come from the Basque communities of the Intermountain West and from Euskadi, the Basque homeland in the Pyrenees Mountains of Europe. Registration is handled through the Basque Museum and Cultural Center at 611 Grove St., tel. 343-2671.

A Boise event that quickly became tremendously popular is the **Boise River Festival,** scheduled the third week of June. A nighttime river parade has been part of the attraction in past years. Hot-air balloons ride air currents, an air show generates more than a few sound waves, and other entertainment leaves plenty of excitement in its wake. Late June also marks the start of the **Ore-Ida Women's Challenge Bicycle Race.** The last of the month brings Julia Davis Park's **Sundae in the Park,** an ice cream social, as such events were once known.

July offers **Streets for People,** tel. 336-2631, a street fair held downtown. Food stalls are everywhere, and local performing-arts and sports talent performs. ParkCenter Pond becomes the focus for the **Cardboard Boat Races** held late in the month each year. Then there's the **Western Idaho Fair,** tel. 376-3247, where the county fair takes on a regional, even statewide, flavor. The fair is held every August at the city's western edge at the intersection of Chinden Blvd. and Glenwood.

Falling Into Winter

Boise, like the rest of the world, begins returning to real life as September rolls in. **Art in the Park** after Labor Day offers one last glimpse of fantasy each year in Julia Davis Park near the Boise Art Museum. The event displays the finest works of Boise-area artists. Exhibits include photographs, paintings, sculpture, and similar media. A children's art festival is also featured. Entertainment and food round out the offerings during the event. Late September brings **Zoo Zoom** at

Zoo Boise. Boise's Towne Square Mall gets into the art scene late in the month by sponsoring an annual **art show.** The mall also promotes performances of classical music each September.

A series of parades held from mid-November on get the city ready for winter. Included on the list are the **Holiday Parade, Festival of Trees, Festival of the Night Skies,** and **Candle Lantern Parade.** The Boise Convention and Visitors Bureau, tel. 344-7777, can help you track when and where the parades will be held. Thanksgiving weekend is when old is in at Boise, when the **Boise's Best Antique Show and Sale,** which includes some 50 dealers from Idaho and seven surrounding states, returns to the fairgrounds.

MARK MORRIS

greater sandhill crane

ACCOMMODATIONS AND FOOD

LODGING

In keeping with Boise's wealth of sights and corporate clout, motels and hotels offer a rich trove of places in which to put up for the night. Rooms for rent range from the Kamping Kabins at the KOA outpost close by I-84 to the stately Idanha downtown or the elegant Red Lion Inn Riverside.

Bed And Breakfast Inns

Idaho Heritage Inn, 109 W. Idaho, tel. 342-8066, offers four rooms renting for $59-79 a night. If you find politics fascinating, this may be your place to stay in Boise. Once the governor's mansion, the inn's period furniture contributes to the, well, stately surroundings. A free limo from the airport will have you feeling important, too. The Governor's Suite offers a private bath and enclosed sun porch. The Judge's Chambers and Senator's Room carry their own authority. For the budget-minded, the Mayor's Study offers a semiprivate bath for $59.

Bed and Breakfast at Victoria's White House, 10325 W. Victory, tel. 362-0507, was built in 1980 yet captures some fine points of the past: pewter chandeliers, oak floors, and a 1906-vintage solid quartersawn oak staircase. The modern plantation-style house is two miles from the I-84 exits to Overland and Orchard. The bill for its two rooms will range from $35 to $85. Similar accommodations are available at **Sunrise Inn,** 2730 Sunrise Rim Rd., tel. 344-0805, which also features a sweeping view of the city. Sunrise offers two rooms for $30-40, one with a bath and two double beds and the other with a queen bed and shared bath.

Hotels And Motels

Boise's more than 3,000 motel rooms range from the elegant to the utilitarian. Most of the rooms are within a mile of downtown. Two of the best stays in Boise are at Red Lion Motor Inns: the **Downtowner,** tel. 344-7691, at 1800 Fairview, and the **Riverside,** tel. 343-1871, at 29th and Chinden. The Downtowner's 182 rooms are within a few blocks of downtown. The lounge, coffee shop, and dining room are competently staffed. Its rooms range $72-300. The Riverside, with rooms for $82-395, may appeal more to those who like the idea of sleeping alongside a river, even if it is in clean linen on a queen-sized mattress. A little farther from downtown, this Red Lion hardly ever sleeps; its **Misty's Restaurant** is well populated by Boiseans as well as hotel guests, and Misty's Lounge hops. A more intimate retreat is available in the Quiet Bar. The Red Lion toll-free reservation line is (800) 547-8010.

The **Owyhee Plaza,** at 11th and Main streets, made its mark by serving business travelers in Boise. Ten minutes, or seven blocks anyway, from the capitol, the Owyhee is near Boise-Cascade, J.R. Simplot Co. and the big banks of downtown. The motel, recently remodeled, began operations in 1910, making it one of the oldest lodgings in Boise still operating. Single rooms run $48-74. The toll-free reservation lines are (800) 821-7500 in Idaho or (800) 233-4611 out of state.

The word "venerable" in Boise belongs to just one hotel, however. The **Idanha,** at 928 Main St., tel. 342-3611, could trademark the word and hardly anyone would object. After all, it was founded in 1901. Noted for its corner towers, the Idanha has undergone major renovations in the last two decades. It's still funky in some ways. Still, if you have one night to stay in Boise and want it to be memorable, here's the spot. Weekend packages shave some off the moderate price and throw in amenities such as continental breakfast, champagne, and, during the summer, free passes to Les Bois Park, the local horse-race track. Rooms range $45-62.

Quality Inn Airport Suites, tel. 343-7505, at 2717 Vista Ave., has rooms with kitchenettes for $45-65 a night. Business travelers will appreciate the well-equipped rooms, each with sofas, desk, work area, and two telephones; fax machines available too. Just across Vista is the **Holiday Inn,** tel. 344-8365 or (800) 465-4329, 3300 Vista Ave., with 265 guest rooms and three suites, just across I-84 from the Boise Airport. Rooms range $49-65. The Holidome, an enclosed swimming pool and recreation center with saunas and a whirlpool, makes the hotel a favorite for families with children eager to be out of a car and into the water. A bar by the pool, the Tiki Lanai, offers the travel-weary a little liquid relaxation.

Best Western offers two franchise motels adjacent to each other near the airport, the **Vista Inn,** tel. 336-8100, at 2645 Airport Way, and the **Airport Inn,** tel. 384-5000, at 2660. Both are reached from Exit 53 along I-84. The difference is the Airport pitches its economy with rooms at $44-56 while the Vista is a bit more plush with rooms for $54-69. The **Safari Inn,** tel. 344-6556 or (800) 541-6556, is the other Best Western in Boise, offering rooms downtown for $39-60.

Doubletree Club Motel, tel. 345-2002, at 475 Parkcenter Blvd., has been gaining ground on its longer-established competitors. The Doubletree's 158 rooms range $49-111. The motel is close to the Boise State University campus and the ParkCenter Racquet Club. For those who like their shopping close by, the **Plaza Suite Hotel,** tel. 375-7666 or (800) 443-7666 in Idaho or (800) 833-7666 outside, lies within easy striking distance of the Boise Towne Square Mall. It offers private whirlpools in the Anniversary or Heritage suites and a heated pool year-round. Rooms range $48-99.

The Statehouse Inn, at 981 Grove St., tel. 342-4622 or (800) 243-4622, has 85 rooms within a block of downtown and four blocks from the capitol. The Statehouse has free parking in the adjacent parking garage. Rooms go for $50-125.

Boise Center Travelodge, tel. 342-9351, at 1314 Grove, has 49 rooms and is near the downtown convention center. Pets are allowed here. Room rates range $32-55. **Boulevard Motel,** tel. 342-4629, at 1121 S. Capitol, and **Cabana Inn,** tel. 343-6000, at 1600 Main, both fall into the under-$30 set and both allow pets. **Grandview Motel,** tel. 342-8676, at 1315 Federal Way, offers a playground and 18 rooms in the $20 range. **Flying J Motel,** tel. 322-4404, is a newer motel at 8002 Overland. Its 87 rooms run $35-50.

Marriott Residence Inn, tel. 344-1200, at 1401 Lusk, is on the pricey end of the scale, with rooms ranging $75-120. But few other motels offer complimentary buffet breakfasts and evening snacks. A spa and jacuzzi complement the outdoor pool. The staff will even pick up groceries for you if you ask.

Back to the inexpensive option? **Motel 6,** tel. 344-3506, is in Boise at 2323 Airport Way, with its cookie-cutter rooms and rates that bring budget-minded travelers back again. Rooms start at $30. The **National 9 Inn Capri Motel,** tel. 344-8617, offers 44 rooms comparable to Motel 6's for $24-45. The inn has a restaurant, however, and a sauna. **Nendel's,** tel. 344-4030, at 2155 N. Garden, has 52 rooms for $31-49.

Boise River Inn, tel. 344-9988, offers Western hospitality. Located at Beacon St. and Colorado Ave., it fronts the Boise River Greenbelt. Offering 88 fully furnished studio apartments beginning at $50 a night, the inn has a mix of overnight guests and those seeking temporary housing. The heated swimming pool overlooks the river.

The Boisean, tel. 343-3645, occupies the corner of Capitol Blvd. and University Drive. It's close by campus, and a short skip to Julia Davis Park and the museum cluster there. The Boisean staff keeps itself occupied trying to find vacancies among its 130 rooms. Rooms range $30-80 a night. Across the street is the **University Inn,** tel. 345-7170, at 2360 University Drive. The University allows pets and has in-room movies. Its rooms fall into the moderate ($42-64) price range. Nearby is the **Ramada Inn,** tel. 344-7971, at 1025 S. Capitol Blvd., with 127 rooms. It offers a restaurant and lounge, sauna, and jacuzzi. Guests have free use of the Boise Valley Athletic Club. Rooms range $45-150. A bed and breakfast option begins at $49 a night for a single.

Just off the freeway is the **Rodeway Inn,** tel. 376-2700, at the intersection of N. Curtis Rd. and Business 84, with 100 rooms for $55-65. The toll-free reservations line is (800) 228-2000.

CAMPING

Boise, this city by the mountains, this city of the plain, has a definite deficiency: camping. There's a serviceable **Kampgrounds of America** outpost here at 7300 Federal Way (off I-84, Exit 57), tel. 342-9714. But the trees are small and it lacks the grace of most state park campgrounds. It makes up for the parking lot feeling with plenty of amenities, such as a swimming pool, laundry room, playground, and grocery store. Its campsites begin at $20 a night. It also offers Kamping Kabins.

Another commercial campground option is **Fiesta Park,** tel. 375-8207, at 11101 Fairview. The park offers 80 pull-through spaces, a swimming pool, game room, laundry room, showers, horseshoe pits, and propane for sale. Campsites range $14.50-18.50 a night. **Atlasta RV Park,** tel. 342-2235, offers a similar refuge for the travel weary at 3605 Federal Way. **Americana Kampground,** tel. 344-5733, has 107 campsites for $11-15 a night at 3600 Americana Terrace.

FOOD

Boise masquerades as a meat and potatoes town, but actually has a surprisingly diverse cuisine for those who care, and sometimes dare, to look beneath its cowboy veneer.

Asian Cuisine

A pleasing menu of Chinese-food restaurants is available in Boise. **Wok-In Noodle** offers three branches for lunch, dinner, and carry-out. The three branches are at 4912 Emerald, tel. 343-7262; 624 W. Emerald, tel. 336-0018; and 10534 W. Ustick, tel. 377-0818. **Yen Ching Restaurant** offers two branches: downtown, at 305 N. Ninth, tel. 384-0384; and ParkCenter Mall, tel. 336-3113. This is Szechuan cuisine—don't bite those little red peppers if you want to taste anything else for the rest of the meal. **Golden Star,** at 1142 N. Orchard, tel. 336-0191, tries for authenticity and economical lunch specials; takeout orders available. **Mandarin Palace,** tel. 345-6682, is at 5020 Franklin Rd. and offers similar virtues. **Twin Dragon,** tel. 344-2141, at 2200 Fairview Ave., is just across 22nd Ave. from the Red Lion Downtowner. Hot and spicy dishes are its pride, although more sedate Chinese cuisine is also on the menu.

Vietnamese Kitchen, tel. 377-0818, at 10534 Ustick near the intersection with Five Mile Rd., rolls Thai, Chinese, and Vietnamese cuisines into an adventuresome menu. It's open for lunch Mon.-Fri. and dinner Mon.-Saturday. **Nha Trang Restaurant,** tel. 336-1770, at 4898 Emerald, is open daily 11 a.m.-10 p.m. It offers Vietnamese and Chinese dishes.

Tsuru, tel. 323-8822, at 303 N. Orchard, offers a sushi bar and Japanese favorites like tempura and sukiyaki, teriyaki, and even bento boxes. Tsuru is open Tues.-Fri. for lunch and dinner, and weekends for dinner only.

American Fare

Isn't Elmer's everyplace? **Elmer's Pancake and Steak House,** at 6767 Fairview, ought to be. With traditional upholstered booths and wholesome food for breakfast, lunch, and dinner, this is the archetypal American cuisine. **Marie Callender's,** tel. 375-7744, at 8574 Fairview Ave., offers breakfast, lunch, and dinner too; takeout available. **Parkplace Cafe,** tel. 336-1661, one-ups Elmer's and Marie's: this place delivers. Chicago-style hot dogs, soups, salads, English bangers for breakfast, Belgian waffles, cereal, and burgers make up the menu at this cafe at 401 W. Parkcenter Boulevard.

The Plaza Grill is located in the Owyhee Plaza Hotel at 1109 Main. It's a cut above for breakfast, lunch, and dinner. You can also get a drink here. **Red Robin Burger and Spirits Emporium,** tel. 344-7471, at 211 E. Parkcenter Blvd., is one of those upscale burger joints. It's a good place to take the kids when the family begins to make the Golden Arches too much of a habit. This place can even make burgers seem fun again. There's an outdoor patio and a children's menu here at the end of Beacon St. off Broadway. Burgers aren't cheap, ranging to $5, but consider the atmosphere as an amenity worth the price.

Lest we forget one of the most offbeat dining experiences Boise has to offer, the **Blue Note Cafe,** tel. 345-9831, is at 1805 W. State Street. Lunches, dinners, and Sunday brunch here break from tradition. If you want something different and aren't quite sure what that might be, this is the place. In fact, this is the counterpoint to Elmer's. It's new American cuisine: Cajun, mesquite grilling, gooey desserts. Live jazz livens up summer evenings as diners sit beneath a hundred-year-old English walnut tree.

Peter Schott's Restaurant and Lounge seems vaguely out of place in the venerable Idanha at 10th and Main streets. The seafood, beef, lamb, veal, and pasta (fresh, of course) are all prepared according to the new American cuisine. Lunch is served Mon.-Fri.; dinner is served Mon.-Saturday. Call 336-9100 for reservations. **The Statehouse Inn,** tel. 342-4622, at 981 Grove St., offers small, private dining rooms for those confidential conversations. Breakfast, lunch, and dinner are served and a nearby bar dispenses refreshments. It's open Sunday and it takes credit cards.

Give **Peg-Leg Annie's** one credit: it couldn't have come up with a more frontier-sounding name. The place advertises "Food at its best, Idaho style," and its prime rib, baby-back ribs, seafood, and choice beef make this lunch and dinner restaurant a spot to hit when you're doing the town or just out for a hearty meal. It's at 3019 N. Cole Rd., tel. 374-3050.

The **Piper Pub and Grill,** tel. 343-2444, serves breakfast, lunch, and dinner, with distinction. Located at Eighth and Main in Capitol Terrace, the Piper offers pub sandwiches from 11 a.m. until 1 a.m. **Angell's** tel. 342-4900, at 999 Main St., has an excellent selection of Idaho wines to go with its seafood menu. **The Chart House,** tel. 336-9370, at 2288 N. Garden St., specializes in dinner, specifically steak, prime rib, and seafood. There is a kids' menu here, too.

Flicks, tel. 342-4222, at Sixth and Myrtle, offers the sensible alternative for those planning a night out with dinner and a show. Two auditoriums offer an eclectic selection of independent, foreign, and art films. And the adjacent cafe boasts an intimate dining room or patio tables for dinner. There's also a champagne Sunday brunch for those who find Sunday at the cinema irresistible.

One of Boise's best-loved restaurants, evidenced by its long life, is **The Sandpiper,** tel. 344-8911, at 11th and Jefferson. The prime rib here is famous. The seafood is good and there are steaks and chicken to keep the rest of the customers happy. The bar is quiet enough for a nightcap and there's live entertainment nightly, too.

Basque

This may be Boise's best or at least most basic cuisine. Located at 3544 Chinden, **Onati,** tel. 343-6464, wins a recommendation from Basques and fans of their cooking style. Onati is open Mon.-Sat. 11:30 a.m.-2 p.m. for lunch and 5:30-10 p.m. for dinner.

Bavarian?

It's true. **Bavarian Food and Delicatessen,** tel. 342-8129, at 1307 S. Orchard, offers German lunches with soups, sandwiches, and sausages. This place claims the best Reuben in town, and features German cold cuts and a variety of German sausages, rye breads, and other bakery goods. Open Tues.-Sat. 10-6.

Bistros

Three small and enjoyable eateries in Boise make great alternatives for a casual lunch. **Le Poulet Rouge,** at 106 N. Sixth, tel. 343-8180, excels in soups and seasonal specialties. Breakfast is served here, too. Hours are Mon.-Sat. 9 a.m.-4 p.m. The **Heartbreak Cafe,** at 607 Main, tel. 345-5544, features patio dining, gourmet salads and desserts, fresh fish, and Angus beef. **Everett Co.,** at 215 N. Fifth, tel. 336-2005, is open for lunch weekdays 11 a.m.-6 p.m., Sat. 11-4.

Brick Oven Beanery fans may suffer some disorientation when they pull up to the old location at Fifth and Main and find it gone. Gone but not departed, simply moved. The Beanery is now down at The Grove, opposite the intersection of Main and Eighth, tel. 342-3456. A local favorite, try it once and you'll return whenever the chance strikes, even if you don't live in Boise. Slow-roasted meats, crusty bread, and beans of some sort, of course, dominate the modestly priced menu. Most meals under $6; open for lunch and dinner daily.

A light lunch is also available at **Swiss Village Cheese** at the corner of Garrity and Star roads off I-84, Exit 38 to the west. Cheese? They make it here and will show you the process. Then you can eat it on one of their deli sandwiches.

Coffee And More

Boise's coffee scene exploded in recent years with all the vigor of an espresso maker gone wrong—but with better results. In a 1993 survey, the Boise Weekly rated the **Soho Caffe** at the Northgate Shopping Mall as Boise's best. Runners-up were **Giuseppi's** along Eighth St., the **Flying M,** and **Coffee News-Coffee News** at Eighth and Main on the Grove (which also offers Idaho's widest selection of newspapers).

Coffee fans will also like the **Koffee Klatsch** at 409 S. Eighth St., offering breakfast and lunch. Soups, daily lunch specials, and live acoustic music make up the main attractions. This place carries 50 varieties of coffee and special teas. **Moxie Java** has six locations in Boise: 570 Main St.; 1525 S. Five Mile; 199 E. 52nd St.; Parkcenter Blvd. at Apple St.; Albertson's Market Place at 1750 W. State St.; and 441 Milwaukee St. in the WestPark Towne Plaza. It's hard to miss with its mirrored neon and spectacular glass. Coffee from exotic lands and honest espressos give caffeine lovers what they came for. Pastries and desserts, soup, and other basic lunch fare embellish the menu just a bit.

Cristina's at Fifth and Main downtown offers espresso and pastries, cakes, and tortes to go with it. The shop's good bread helped win it a popular poll award as Boise's best bakery. The **Old Style European Bakery and Cafe** is at 301 Myrtle, tel. 345-5417. It offers Turkish coffee and fresh pastries and breads for breakfast and lunch.

Need more? Other shops in no particular order include **The Coffee Critic,** at 3000 Lakeharbor in State Street's Lake Harbor Development; **Milano Espresso,** located in Albertson's State Street store parking lot; **David's Espresso,** at Eighth and Main; **Neville and Neville** in Old Boise; **Espresson Italia,** offering succor for espresso fans at Boise Towne Square Mall near Mervyn's; and **Lucky 13,** at 1602 N. 13th in historic Hyde Park, serving giant bran muffins and good coffees beginning at 9 a.m., as well as pizza and a variety of domestic and imported beers and wines in the evenings.

Fine And Fancy

Those with a bit more sophisticated palate can try the **Gamekeeper Restaurant** in the Owyhee Plaza Hotel at 1109 Main Street. Reservations are suggested here; call 343-4611. **Misty's,** tel. 343-1871, offers four-star dining at the Red Lion Riverside. Dinners range $12-20.

Healthy

The unabashedly nonconformist **Mrs. Beesley's Healthy Foods,** tel. 376-8484, at 10370 Overland Rd., specializes in vegetarian offerings, mainly soups and sandwiches. The **Boise Co-op,** tel. 342-6652, offers an eclectic selection of good breads and organic and bulk foods. Located at 1674 Hill Rd., the co-op also offers a serviceable deli and boasts the most comprehensive selection of wines and beers in Boise.

Italian Food

Italian-food aficionados will appreciate **Amore,** tel. 343-6435, at 921 W. Jefferson. Diners will find antipasto, authentic entrees that taste right, and some unusual fare, too. The name reflects the restaurant's dedication—make that devotion—to good food. **Renaissance,** tel. 344-6776, at Fifth and Main, offers classic northern Italian dishes and fresh seafood. It's open for lunch and dinner. With a name like **Giovanni's Ristorante,** what else could it be but Italian? Pasta, chicken, and veal entrees are the specialties. Open Mon.-Sat. 11 a.m.-10 p.m., Giovanni's is located at 5900 Fairview Ave. (at Curtis). Call 323-1769 for reservations. **La Mia Cucina,** tel. 322-0535, at 5602 Fairview, offers take-out Italian ranging from tortellini and soups to oven-ready casseroles and sauces. It's open Mon.-Sat. 8 a.m.-6 p.m.

Mall Food

The **Eighth Street Marketplace** offers a bevy of eateries at Capitol Blvd. and Front Street. **Cafe Olé,** tel. 344-3222, occupies the lower level of the Marketplace with a fun atmosphere that recalls happy times south of the border. Mexican entrees here range $6-10. The **8th Street Deli,** tel. 336-9177, offers "killer pizza," beer, and gourmet sandwiches. **Milford's Fish House** rounds out the marketplace's offerings with the largest and freshest selection of seafood flown into Idaho. An oyster bar, microbrewery beers, and Northwest wines contribute to a fine dining experience. Reservations are suggested; tel. 342-8382.

Boise Towne Square Mall at Franklin and Cole roads maintains the most diverse eating opportunities in the smallest space and with the highest volume in Boise. Don't take that as a lukewarm review; it's not. This may be the only place where a party of four with radically different tastes can eat together without compromise. Fast-food shops ringing the central eating area range from **Orange Julius** and **Taco Time** to the **Gyro Shop, Pic-a-Pocket, Wayne's Wok, Broiler Works, Sandwich Loft, Mr. Bee's,** and **Marie Callender's.** Fish? **Skippers** is also here.

Mexican Food

Garcia's, along Beacon at ParkCenter near the lake, makes its fare from scratch daily. With 30 years experience, Garcia's is a tradition. Lunch, dinner, or a nightcap draw customers here. Call 336-3363 for reservations. **Acapulco,** tel. 375-4896, boasts authentic south-of-the-border dishes from throughout Mexico. It's located at 5181 Glenwood across from the Western Idaho Fairgrounds and Les Bois Park on the western edge of town. **La Fiesta,** tel. 343-4334, at 1221 W. Boise Ave., advertises authentic Mexican food. **A La Fajita,** at 3447 Chinden Blvd. in adjacent Garden City, tel. 385-0288, carries 11 varieties of Mexican beer and specializes in home-style tamales and rib-eye fajitas. It's open daily 10-10.

OTHER PRACTICALITIES

SHOPPING

Malls

Two major malls make Boise an Idaho shopper's paradise of sorts. **Boise Towne Square** enjoys its role as the city's biggest shopping mall. Located at Milwaukee and Franklin just west of the I-84 Business loop to downtown, the mall holds more than 140 specialty shops, restaurants, and large retail stores. The big stores include **The Bon, Mervyn's, JCPenney,** and **Sears.** One store that would find a home in no other state is **Made In Idaho,** tel. 378-1188, which features everything from huckleberry jam to postcards. Souvenirs are also the specialty at **Three Cs Gift Gallery,** tel. 376-1945. **Eye Masters,** tel. 322-2933, promises to produce prescription glasses in about an hour, handy if you're on the move.

Among other Towne Square stores **Victoria's Secret** offers some decidedly impractical evening wear for those who need lingerie while touring. **Waldenbooks,** tel. 375-6211, belongs to a chain but the Towne Square version offers a credible selection of interesting Idaho books. **Kay-Bee Toys,** tel. 377-1720, in the mall is good for a bribe to keep young ones silent just a little bit longer. The mall's central eating area, the **Courtyard,** is a bustling spot to grab a bite. Just be quick to grab a chair.

ParkCenter Mall is just east of the Boise State campus off Beacon Dr. at 415 Parkcenter Boulevard. ParkCenter offers **Bittner's Confection and Fine Edibles,** tel. 342-8652, which sells imported confections and gourmet foods. **D.K. Browns,** tel. 344-6764, has party gifts, cards, and similar items. **Coyote and Mr. Twain,** tel. 345-4912, is a bookstore featuring an eclectic selection ranging from best-sellers to new-age music. **Dragonfly,** tel. 342-6861, and **Alexis,** tel. 386-9632, are two stores catering to the career woman. **Idaho at Heart,** tel. 343-2485, is ParkCenter's specialist in Idahoniana. For those who need to wear their allegiances on their sleeves, **Jersey Room,** tel. 338-9562, offers sports fan's T-shirts, sweatshirts, caps, and other wear licensed by NFL, NBA, NHL, NCAA, and Major League Baseball teams. ParkCenter also has a short-order optical shop in **Optic One,** tel. 343-2020, which promises prescription glasses in a day or less.

Vista Village is Boise's vintage shopping mall, laid out long and lean along Vista. Stores of note here include **Idaho Camera,** tel. 343-8075, still one of Boise's best camera shops. **Joker's Wild,** tel. 343-4889, has the tricks and gadgets that can liven up any trip. **Vista Book Gallery,** tel. 336-3011, caters to readers.

Downtown Stores

The **Old Boise Shopping District** lies downtown along Main St. between Capitol Blvd. and Fourth Street. A pleasing mix of well-cared-for old buildings, eateries, and exciting shops, the downtown shopping area remains a pleasant excursion. **Gem State Crystals,** tel. 385-0652, at 598 Main, is a rock hound's candy store. Fascinating fossils and colorful crystals lurk within. **Idaho Watch Co.,** tel. 342-0002, at 560 Main, has its own unique options on timekeeping. **Old Boise Music,** tel. 344-7600, at 515 Main, sells instruments, books, records, and accessories. For that perfect plant, there's **Greens & Things,** tel. 343-1787, at 108 N. Sixth.

The **Eighth Street Marketplace** at Capitol Blvd. and Front St. offers the **Top Shoppe,** tel. 344-9814, with its Idaho souvenirs and novelties. **Camile Beckman of Rose Cottage** sells body and bath products made in Idaho. It also has a branch of **Jersey Room,** the place with all the sports shirts.

Five Mile Plaza at Five Mile and Overland roads has 35 stores ranging from grocers to clothing shops. **Harper House Mall** at 36th and State St. offers 10,000 square feet of antiques and collectibles.

Bookstores

Just outside the formal Old Boise district is **The Book Shop,** tel. 342-2659, at 908 Main, specializing in Western Americana and Idaho books. It's regarded by local book-lovers as the bookstore to check out when in the capital. For those who like their vacation reading a little lighter, **King's Komix Kastle,** tel. 343-7142, at 1706 N. 18th, or tel. 343-7055, at 2460 Leadville Ave., boasts of too many comics to count and claims one of the Northwest's largest collections. **New Mythology,** tel. 344-6744, specializes in comics and science fiction at 1725 Broadway Avenue. **Parnassus Books,** tel. 344-7560, at 218 N. Ninth offers rare, scarce, or out-of-print books as well as current books in most fields. **The Book Shelf,** tel. 377-5294, at 10390 Overland, bills itself as Idaho's largest bookstore, offering a broad selection including books on cassette and a rental library.

TRANSPORTATION

Airlines

Boise's airport is a stop for **United Airlines,** tel. (800) 241-6522; **Delta Air Lines,** tel. (800) 221-1212; **Horizon Air,** tel. (800) 547-9308; **Alaska Airlines,** tel. (800) 426-0333; and **Empire Airlines,** tel. (800) 392-9233. The airport serves as a hub for several charter aircraft companies, including **Harrah's Middle Fork Charter,** tel. 342-7888, at 3815 Rickenbacker, a backcountry specialist; and **Mountain Air-Mackay Bar,** tel. 344-1881, at 3190 Airport Way, offering backcountry charters. Helicopter charter services include **Idaho Helicopters,** tel. 344-4361, at 2471 Commerce Ave.; and **Crew Concepts,** tel. 344-4691, at 3815 Rickenbacker.

Buses

Boise Urban Stages, a.k.a. The Bus, tel. 336-1010, operates municipal transit throughout the city. Fares are 50 cents for adults (45 cents with tokens sold in packs of 10) and 25 cents for senior or handicapped riders. Saturday fares are a quarter, children younger than six ride free. Bus tokens are available at city hall, Boise State's Student Union building, First Interstate banks, Albertson's, and several other grocery stores.

Greyhound Bus Lines, tel. 343-3681, is based at 1212 W. Bannock. **Boise-Winnemucca Stages** offers charters from its base at 1105 La Pointe, tel. 336-3300. **Northwestern Stage Lines** shares the same offices. Another charter line, **Sun Valley Stages,** operates a base at the airport, tel. 383-3085, and at 815 Ann Morrison Park Dr., tel. 336-4038.

Train

Amtrak serves Boise from the Union Pacific Depot, tel. 336-5992 or (800) 872-7245, at the south end of Capitol Boulevard. The Pioneer starts in Chicago and finishes its westward journey at Portland before heading north to Seattle. It arrives at Boise at 6:56 a.m. daily heading west, and at 10:11 p.m. heading east.

Taxis

Taxis in Boise range from the basics to the **VIP Limo Service,** tel. 866-0646, with its four-door Cadillac sedans, cellular phones, and sunroofs. **Kwik Taxi Cabs** operates a station at the airport, tel. 342-1300, and downtown, tel. 384-9197. **Orange Cab Co.,** tel. 345-3535, and **Yellow Cab Co.,** tel. 345-5555, also shuttle Boise visitors.

Car Rentals

Sun Valley's steady stream of visitors has led Boise to evolve into a car-rental capital of sorts. **U-Save Auto Rental,** tel. 322-2751, offers special rates for those heading for the state's most famous ski complex. **Budget,** tel. 383-3090 or (800) 527-0700; **Sears,** tel. 343-2600 or (800) 527-0770; **Alamo,** tel. 336-1904 or (800) 327-9633; **Avis,** tel. 383-3350 or (800) 331-1212; **Dollar,** tel. 345-9727 or (800) 421-6878; **Hertz,** tel. 383-3100 or (800) 654-3131; and **National,** tel. 383-3210 or (800) 227-7368, are all here, too.

Payless Car Rental, tel. 342-7780 or (800) 237-2804, joins the franchise options along with **Thrifty Car Rental,** tel. 342-7726 or (800) 367-2277. Two rental companies for the cheap at heart are also here in the form of **Ugly Duckling Rent-A-Car,** tel. 344-3732 or (800) 843-3825; and **Rent A Wreck,** tel. 342-2468 or (800) 535-1391.

SERVICES AND INFORMATION

Emergency Telephone Numbers

Boise uses the **911** number for emergency services such as police or fire department calls. For nonemergencies when a Boise police officer is needed, call 377-6790; for other information from the police, call 384-4041. The Boise Police are based at 7200 Barrister Drive. The **Ada**

County Sheriff's Department, tel. 377-6500 for information, 377-6790 to request a deputy, is also based at 7200 Barrister.

Boise has an extensive medical community. **St. Alphonsus Regional Medical Center,** tel. 378-2121, at 1055 N. Curtis Rd., dispatches Life Flight medical helicopters and maintains an information center for poisoning victims at 378-2707 in Boise or (800) 632-8000 outside. The hospital's emergency number is 378-3221. **St. Luke's Regional Medical Center,** tel. 386-2222, at 190 E. Bannock, maintains an emergency department as well at 386-2344.

Tourist Services, Post Offices

The Boise Chamber of Commerce, tel. 344-5515 is located at 300 N. Sixth, Boise, ID 83702. The **Boise Convention and Visitors Bureau** is located at 100 N. Ninth, tel. 344-7777. Information about events at the city's heart is also available from the **Downtown Boise Association,** tel. 336-2631. Boise's main **post office,** tel. 383-4211, is at 770 S. 13th. Substations are at Eighth and Bannock, 3485 N. Cole Rd., 4650 W. State, and 2424 Bank Drive.

Radio Stations And Newspapers

Radio stations in the area include **KBOI** (AM 670) and its companion station, **KQFC** (FM 98). KBOI can be picked up across most of southern Idaho and some of the mountainous north at night. On the ground, both are at 1419 W. Bannock in Boise, tel. 336-3670. The local affiliate of the National Public Radio network is **KBSU** (FM 90.3), tel. 385-3663.

Boise's, and Idaho's, biggest newspaper is ***The Idaho Statesman,*** tel. 377-6200, at 1200 N. Curtis Road. The *Statesman* is a member of the Gannett chain. The newest newspaper on the block is the ***Boise Weekly,*** a free publication widely distributed around town. The *Weekly* may end up giving Boise the flash and pizzazz that many devoted newspaper fans have complained bitterly of missing.

Government Offices

As Idaho's capital, local and state government are intertwined here with little clear distinction between where one starts and the other stops. Government offices are spread throughout the city. Most state agencies—ranging from the **Idaho State Library,** tel. 334-5124, at 325 W. State, which houses the state archives and historical and genealogical libraries, to the **Supreme Court,** which houses the **Idaho Law Library,** tel. 334-3316, at 451 W. State—cluster around the capitol mall. The mall stretches from Third to Ninth streets and Idaho to Franklin. The **Idaho Commission on the Arts,** tel. 334-2119, is located in the Moses Alexander House at 304 W. State.

The **Old U.S. Assay Office** at 210 Main St. now houses the **Idaho Historical Society,** tel. 334-3356. Other offices outside the mall include the **Idaho Parks and Recreation Department** office at 2177 Warm Springs Ave., tel. 334-2154; **Idaho Fish and Game Department,** tel. 334-3700, at 600 S. Walnut; **Idaho Agriculture Department,** tel. 334-3240, at 2270 Old Penitentiary Rd.; and **Idaho Department of Law Enforcement,** tel. 334-2521, at 3311 W. State. **Idaho's Outfitters and Guides Board,** tel. 327-7380, has its offices at 1365 N. Orchard.

Federal offices in Boise include the **Boise National Forest,** tel. 364-4100, at 1750 Front St. and the **Boise Ranger District,** tel. 343-2527, at 5493 Warm Springs Avenue. The state office of the **BLM,** tel. 334-1414, is at 3380 Americana Terrace. The BLM oversees most of the rest of Idaho's federal lands which lie outside the national forests. The office of the **BLM's Boise District,** tel. 334-1582, is at 3948 Development Avenue. The bureau's **Birds of Prey Research Center,** tel. 334-9296, is based at the Boise District office.

Other federal offices of note include the **U.S. Environmental Protection Agency,** tel. 334-1450, at 422 W. Washington; and **U.S. Fish and Wildlife Service,** tel. 334-1931, at 4696 Overland Road. Another major Interior Department agency, the **Bureau of Reclamation,** tel. 334-1906, is based at 550 W. Fort. **Immigration and Naturalization Service** offices, tel. 334-1821, are located at 4620 Overland Road.

SOUTHWEST IDAHO

Southwestern Idaho's diverse terrain includes sere hills and deep blue alpine lakes, sagebrush expanses of desert, and long valleys with lush meadows. Farmers and ranchers settled this land, although they never quite tamed it—fierce droughts and plagues of grasshoppers are not uncommon here. Still, every patch of dirt level enough and near enough water shimmers green in the summer. Alfalfa, bright green against the gray sage, blankets the desert, surviving by the network of irrigation lines. Drive near Parma, and the smell of onion fields works its way into even an air-conditioned car. Toward Nampa, the spicy redolence of mint rests heavy on the summer air. Cattle graze here where the irrigation cannot reach. The traditional mahogany-and-white Herefords and their crossbred cousins wander among the sage looking for patches of grass and vegetation worth eating.

The region's historical importance lies etched in the wagon tracks that marked the route of the Oregon Trail. Waves of immigrants looking for a new start "out west" passed through here some 150 years ago on their way to the promised land of Oregon. Fading reminders of the era remain in Old Fort Boise—an important trail outpost—and the ghost towns that dot the region. Silver City was once the queen of the Owyhee Mountains. The Boise Basin mining center of Idaho City has become a town living on its charm, long after the paydirt played out.

Like Idaho City, southwest Idaho today draws most of its visitors for a reason the area's early settlers recognized but enjoyed all too little: recreation. Idaho Power dammed the Snake River to squeeze energy from it as it tumbled toward the sea, and the reservoirs behind the dams draw thousands of boaters and anglers on summer days. Where the river still runs free, rafters take to it for some wild rides. And the mountain snows that once pushed ranchers and their herds to lower elevations now invite crowds of skiers and snowmobilers. This modern leisure rush has helped crown McCall the capital of southwestern Idaho. When Idahoans head for a resort to find snow, many choose McCall for its relaxed atmosphere and homeyness.

Most winters here are on the mild side, with perhaps a short spell of subzero cold that lasts just long enough for residents to appreciate the temperance of the rest of winter. The summers are hot but with short streaks of days that stretch the thermometer's red line above 100°.

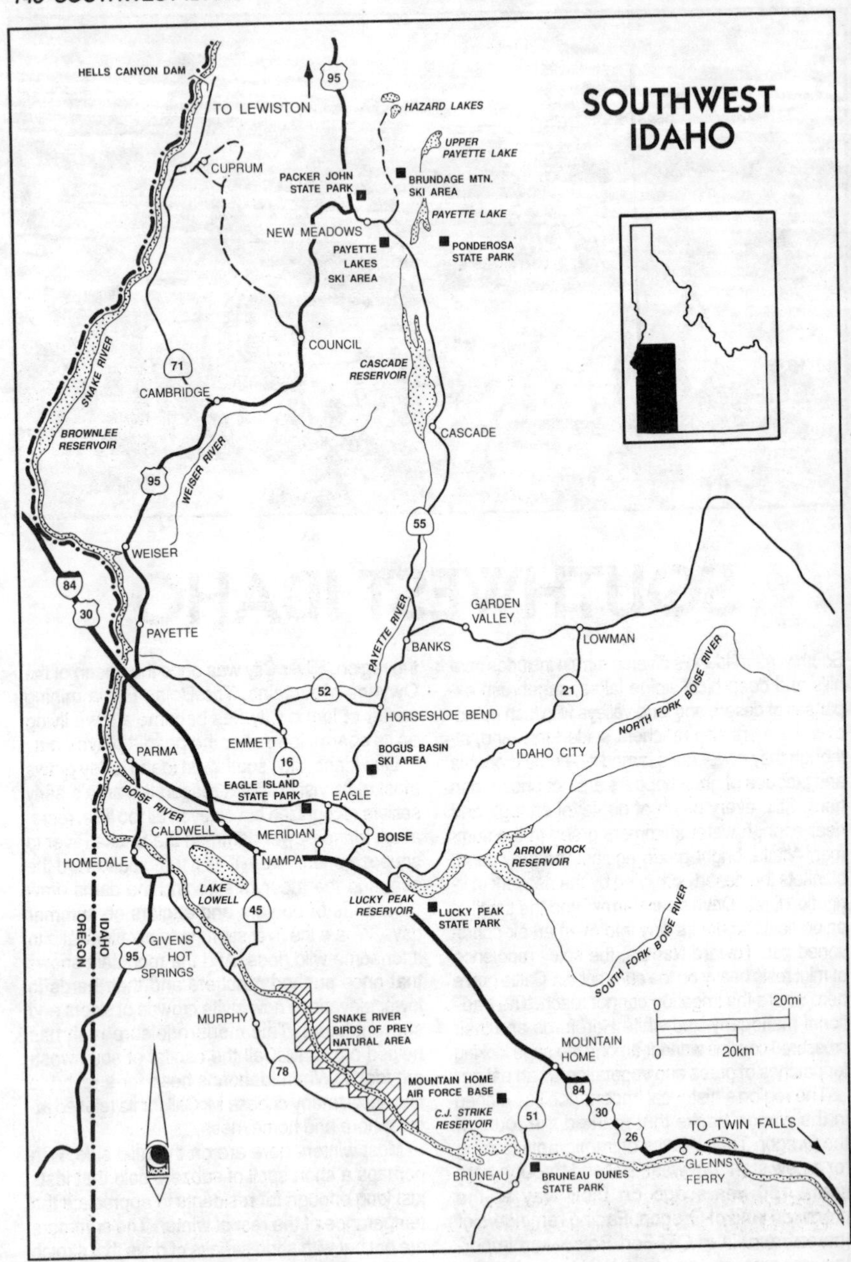
SOUTHWEST IDAHO
HELLS CANYON DAM
95
TO LEWISTON
HAZARD LAKES
UPPER PAYETTE LAKE
CUPRUM
PACKER JOHN STATE PARK
BRUNDAGE MTN. SKI AREA
PAYETTE LAKE
NEW MEADOWS
PAYETTE LAKES SKI AREA
PONDEROSA STATE PARK
COUNCIL
71
CASCADE RESERVOIR
SNAKE RIVER
CAMBRIDGE
BROWNLEE RESERVOIR
CASCADE
WEISER RIVER
95
55
WEISER
84
30
GARDEN VALLEY
PAYETTE RIVER
PAYETTE
BANKS
LOWMAN
NORTH FORK BOISE RIVER
52
21
HORSESHOE BEND
EMMETT
PARMA
16
BOGUS BASIN SKI AREA
IDAHO CITY
EAGLE ISLAND STATE PARK
EAGLE
BOISE RIVER
CALDWELL
MERIDIAN
BOISE
ARROW ROCK RESERVOIR
HOMEDALE
NAMPA
LAKE LOWELL
45
LUCKY PEAK RESERVOIR
LUCKY PEAK STATE PARK
OREGON
IDAHO
95
GIVENS HOT SPRINGS
SOUTH FORK BOISE RIVER
0
20mi
0
20km
MURPHY
SNAKE RIVER BIRDS OF PREY NATURAL AREA
MOUNTAIN HOME
78
MOUNTAIN HOME AIR FORCE BASE
84
30
C.J. STRIKE RESERVOIR
51
26
TO TWIN FALLS
MOON
BRUNEAU
BRUNEAU DUNES STATE PARK
GLENNS FERRY

NEW MEADOWS

New Meadows is one of those towns that seldom draws more attention from passersby than a quick stop at the gas station—or a lunge into the Crossroads Cafe at the intersection of highways 95 and 55 for a cup of coffee to go. For those heading south from Lewiston, New Meadows sets their course: the left fork, Idaho Hwy. 55, bounces down to Boise, while the right fork, U.S. Hwy. 95, winds its way to Weiser. There are a few, of course, who make New Meadows and the adjacent town of Meadows their destination. The towns have long served as stopping places.

SIGHTS

Packer John Park

Tiny Packer John Park offers a replica of the cabin where Idaho's first territorial Republican and Democratic conventions were held, in 1863 and '64, respectively. Formerly a state park, the area is now owned by Adams County, which is still trying to decide what to do with it. Until they do, the New Meadows Chamber of Commerce, tel. 347-2406, will try to answer your questions.

Packer John, whose Christian name was John Welch, packed supplies south from Lewiston for miners who flocked to the Boise Basin in 1862. The founding host of Idaho politics, he nevertheless failed to make a lasting impression on the state's political system. Surviving reports indicate that his politics were allied with the Fenian movement, a secret Irish and Irish-American group dedicated to ending British control of Ireland.

The park's campground offers the weary a quick spot to park a camper. Pine trees dominate the campground and a modest little stream provides relief from the noise of the nearby highway. But for all its history, the park is better in a pinch as a highway pulloff than as a spot to base a vacation.

Ceilann Hot Spring

Ceilann Hot Spring is just a few miles east of the park on Goose Creek Rd. where Little Goose Creek joins Goose Creek. A trail leads to this undeveloped springs, made famous by a National Geographic photograph. This spa-in-the-rough is three-quarters of a mile from the road.

Lava Ridge National Recreation Trail

The Lava Ridge National Recreation Trail wends its way across part of the New Meadows Ranger District between New Meadows and McCall off Goose Creek Road. The trail is a high-elevation mixture of volcanic buttes and the more common cirques with alpine lakes imbedded at their bases. The trail system begins just north of **Hazard Lake Campground,** which has 13 campsites and is open from July to September. **Big Dave Creek Trailhead** is about four miles north of the campground on Payette National Forest Rd. 50257, then east on Rd. 50308 about a quarter mile. After seven miles of trail, hikers arrive at Hershey Point Lookout, located for its expansive view. Information about trail conditions is available from the New Meadows Ranger Station, tel. 347-2141.

PRACTICALITIES

Resorts

Once public but now private, **MeadowCreek Golf and Field Club** (formerly Kimberland Meadows), tel. 347-2162, flanks Hwy. 95 north of New Meadows and has a golf course, tennis courts, and groomed cross-country skiing trails. The public can still have access to the recreational facilities, but only if sponsored by a member.

Just down the road from MeadowCreek is **Zim's Hot Springs,** tel. 347-2686, where campsites attract summer campers and a large covered pool filled by the springs attracts crowds throughout the year. Zim's is open daily in summer 9 a.m.-10 p.m. and winter 10 a.m.-9 p.m. Pool admission costs $4 for swimmers 12 and older and $3 for seniors and kids three to 11. Children three years or younger enter free. Snacks are available. Campsites at Zim's cost $5 for bicyclists; $7 for car-campers with tents or for RV's, no hookups; and $10 for RV sites with hookups. An RV dump station is available.

Motels And B&B's

Hartland Inn and Motel, tel. 347-2114, in New Meadows offers an elegant and unique place to stay in a beautiful valley. Its three B&B rooms rent for $75 a night, including a full breakfast. The cost for the motel units ranges from $30 for a single room for one person to $52 for a three-room unit sleeping 4-5.

Meadow's Motel, along Hwy. 95, tel. 347-2175, is a tidy little motel that offers double rooms for $38 and a kitchenette for $48. As this book went to press, ownership was about to change, and prices may then change also.

Food

High Meadows Cafe and Pizza, on Hwy. 95 on the south side of town, tel. 347-2513, has a full menu of three meals a day in addition to pizza. Try owner Hal Cusick's special "High Meadows Supreme" pizza with 10 toppings. Delicioso! Breakfasts include a full range of omelettes and other egg dishes. Open seven days a week.

Also in town is the aptly-named **Crossroads Cafe,** at the junction of Highways 95 and 55; tel. 347-2643. You can get breakfast, lunch, or dinner here. (The beef supreme sandwich is a house recommendation.)

For those traveling Hwy. 95 south of New Meadows, seven miles from town is **Pineridge,** tel. 347-2234, featuring prime rib, seafood, and steaks.

Information And Services

New Meadows Chamber of Commerce offers information about recreation in the area at P.O. Box 170, New Meadows, ID 83654. **Police** protection at New Meadows is provided by the **Adäms County Sheriff's Department,** tel. 253-4227, at Council, about ten miles south on Hwy. 95. The same number can be used to report a **fire** or summon an **ambulance.**

(Top) A fisherman, Lenny Frasure, plucks a smallmouth bass from the Snake River near Lewiston.
(Bottom) Hell Roaring Lake's brilliant blue waters mirror the sky above the
Sawtooth National Recreation Area. (PHOTOS BILL LOFTUS)

(Top) Remote cabins are available for rent from the U.S. Forest Service. (Bottom) Castle Butte Lookout along the Lochsa River offers a rental room with a view. (PHOTOS BILL LOFTUS)

McCALL

McCall got its start when a wagon train camped beside Payette Lake in 1899. Members of the wagon train, Tom McCall and his family, decided to stay. He bought the eastern part of what is now McCall from Sam Devers and the town was laid out in 1901. The Union Pacific Railroad arrived and bestowed the name of Lakeport on the new town. It didn't stick, obviously.

McCall's greatest charms are sapphire blue Payette Lake and the mountains surrounding it. During the summer, the lake provides a watersports playground, and in winter, the snow-covered mountains draw skiers to the slopes. Brundage Mountain Resort has ranked as one of Idaho's best ski areas almost since it was built in 1961. And the Little Ski Hill, another local ski area, began attracting its following in 1937! The reason Idahoans make this town their retreat summer or winter, though, is because it embodies the best of Idaho: friendliness, beauty, and plenty of room to play.

SIGHTS

Ponderosa State Park

Ponderosa pines form the columns of Nature's temple on this peninsula that juts out into Payette Lake northeast of McCall proper. The trees of Ponderosa State Park, some of them centuries old, glow orange in the afternoon sunlight. Glaciers shaped this peninsula and ground out the soils that nurture the roots of these magnificent pines. The park's fields are glacial tilth, its ridges the remnants of mountains the glaciers couldn't erase.

The park's origins stretch back to the early 1900s. A gathering of Idaho's press association in McCall in 1906 was impressed by what they had seen there. They started a clamor in the media for the creation of a state park near Payette Lake. A 1907 resolution called for the state to hold onto, rather than sell, all state lands within two miles of Payette and Upper Payette lakes. The state lands, legislators argued, would soon be valuable for pleasure resort and park purposes. The House approved the resolution but the Senate did not. However, the Legislature as a whole did vote to set aside some area lands for parks, including specified parcels on Payette Lake's southern shore.

Modern times prove those early backers of this scenic peninsula absolutely correct. Ponderosa State Park is a popular escape both as a destination and a stop along the road for travelers. The park's main unit encompasses 840 acres and hugs the shoreline, preserving a variety of landscapes ranging from a high ridge with a gorgeous lake view to sandy beaches along the lake itself. The park's **visitor center,** tel. 634-2164, offers plenty of information about the wildflowers and wildlife.

The campsites at this park are some of the best laid out of any in Idaho's park system, offering an unusual degree of privacy. Of course, starting with a wondrous stand of ponderosa pines didn't hurt the cause. The campground seems far less crowded than its 170 campsites allow. Two-thirds of the campsites offer water and electrical hookups. An ongoing restoration project will improve the campsites over the next few years.

Ponderosa also preserves another stretch of shoreline along the Payette River at its North Beach Unit, which bids summer farewell with a blaze of glory each fall when the aspens turn their characteristic gold. North Beach is open only for picnickers, hikers, and swimmers. No camping is allowed. The North Beach Unit is currently being improved to include restrooms and a boardwalk.

Swimming, boating, and fishing are popular summertime pursuits at Ponderosa. But the fun doesn't stop when the snow blankets the ground; the park is one of the state's best developed for cross-country skiing. The roads and trails that attract mountain bikers and hikers in the summer beckon those on skinny skis during the winter. The park offers 7.3 miles of hiking trails and seven miles of cross-country trails. A gravel road loops across the peninsula's highest point. A popular hiking trail strikes off near the beginning of the loop where adventuresome cross-country skiers can find some of the best skiing in the park. The park's road system also wanders past a popular picnic area with a shelter and sandy

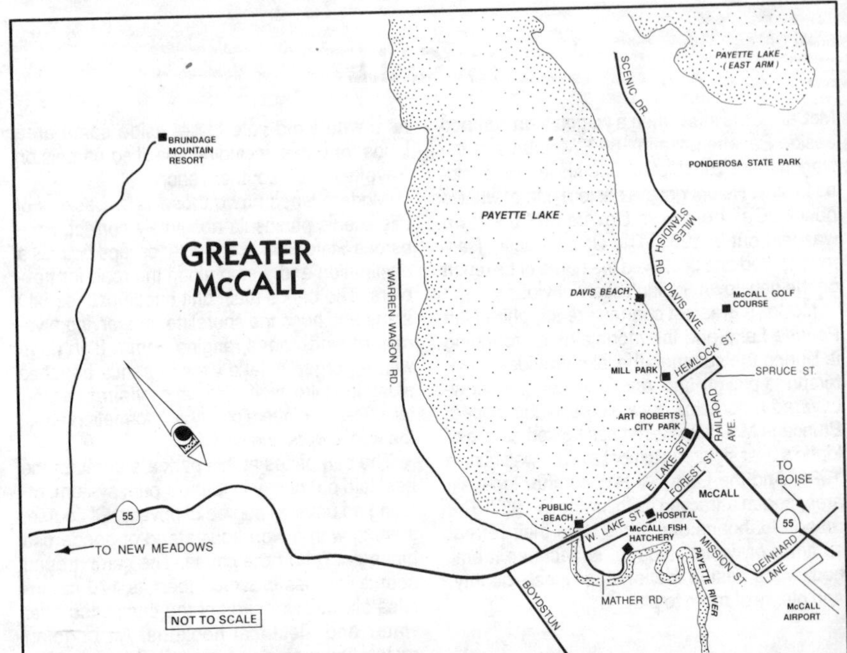

beaches where boaters can pull up for a break. A deep-draft boat ramp along the way gives boaters access to the beautiful seven-mile-long Payette Lake.

Spring and summer are the best seasons for wildlife watchers. Sharp-eyed visitors may catch a glimpse of the red fox here. Elk, moose, and white-tailed deer show up in the park from time to time, too. Snowshoe hares, with their changing wardrobes—brown for summer, white for winter—hop through the thickets. Aquatic wildlife ranges from beavers and muskrats in the park's marshes to the rarely seen otters and mink that may be found either in the marshes or along the lakeshore.

According to the park's bird list, 139 species have been sighted here. Some 112 are included on the list. Waterfowl include trumpeter and tundra swans during migratory stops; common loons; snow geese; and mallard, wood, and ring-necked ducks.

A mile-long nature trail that takes off near **Lilly Lake** is one of the best approaches for watching wildlife. In early summer, the bugs here can be ferocious, so include insect repellent in your travel gear.

University Field Campus

The University of Idaho's McCall Field Campus, P.O. Box 1025, McCall, ID 83638, tel. 634-3918 in summer and 885-7302 winter, once received most of its students as conscripts. Forestry students were required to attend for a summer, botanizing and generally behaving as foresters-in-the-making here along the scenic shore of Payette Lake. That's changed. The camp still trains foresters but the public at large now has a chance to enjoy the same opportunities.

Past classes open to the public have included single-day and month-long sessions ranging from wildland ecology to landscape watercolor painting. Fees for food and lodging are about $25 a day; registration fees for classes are separate and begin at $25. The 11-acre campus includes 600 feet of beach. A volleyball court and horseshoe pits are also available. Nearby Ponderosa State Park has hiking trails and evening programs.

Llama Ranch

High Llama Ranch, tel. 634-4151, invites visitors for Saturday morning tours by appointment. The working llama ranch near Jughandle Mountain had about 50 of the Andes natives at last count. Visitors are asked to make a donation to the River of No Return Foundation. You can write for more information about the ranch through the McCall Chamber of Commerce, P.O. Box D, McCall, ID 83638.

Smoke-Jumper Complex

The Payette National Forest maintains a base for smoke jumpers—aerial firefighters—at 605 S. Mission. Guided tours are available by reservation through the office, tel. 634-8151, extensions 187 or 178. Smoke jumpers are the paratroopers of modern firefighting. They're generally the first to arrive on a fire and are the most highly trained and best equipped of Forest Service firefighters. The complex at McCall has operated since 1943, first as a base for ground forces, later for jumpers.

McCall Fish Hatchery

The Idaho Fish and Game Department operates the McCall Fish Hatchery at 300 Mather Rd. off Hwy. 55. The hatchery was built as part of an effort to restore chinook salmon in Idaho's rivers. The young chinook reared at the hatchery are released in the South Fork of the Salmon and other streams to help rebuild the runs. The grounds of the hatchery are open daily 8 a.m.-5 p.m.

Parks And Beaches

Public Beach along Payette Lake's southern shoreline just east of the Payette River's outlet is a popular hangout during the summer months. Another popular access point for the lake is **Davis Beach** at the end of Diamond St., off Davis Ave. along the lake's southeastern shore. **Art Roberts City Park** lies at the end of 2nd St. downtown and gets as much attention in the winter as it does during the summer—during Winter Carnival, the third week of January, the park is the setting for the carnival's giant ice sculptures. **Mill Park** at the end of E. Lake St. includes another stretch of public lakefront.

RECREATION

McCall has plenty of places to find good food, drink, and entertainment in town. But the real reason people come here is to find their fun in the great outdoors. McCall is the base for Brundage Mountain Ski Resort and the Little Ski Hill, both north of town. A well-maintained system of trails for snowmobiles draws enthusiasts throughout the winter, too. Anglers come to the Long Valley for ice fishing during the winter. Come summer, McCall transforms itself into a boating, fishing, camping, mountain-biking, and hiking center. **Payette Lake** attracts most of the action but the Payette National Forest holds hundreds of miles of streams and hiking trails that lace the backcountry.

McCall Public Beach

Skiing

Brundage Mountain Resort, tel. 634-4151, is where Olympians and Idahoans choose to ski. Brundage cofounder Cory Engen of McCall competed in seven of 10 Olympic Winter Games from 1948 to 1988. The main lodge phone number is 634-7462 or (800) 888-7544. Snow information is available at tel. 634-5650.

Like Idaho's other ski resorts, Brundage recently entered into a major expansion phase. Quality remains the watchword here, though. The snow is famous for cooperating with that goal; Brundage won its fans by providing some of the state's best powder skiing. The spectacular view from the top offers a vista that stretches from the Seven Devils Mountains in the northwest to Oregon's Wallowa Mountains, the Payette lakes, and the rugged mountains beyond.

Brundage boasts a vertical rise of 1,800 feet and its three chairlifts access some 1,300 acres. The lifts operate daily 10 a.m.-4 p.m. weekdays and 9 a.m.-4 p.m. weekends and holidays. The ski area's 36 runs stretch as long as three miles. Brundage offers a nearly balanced package for skiers of varying abilities. Twenty percent of its runs are suitable for beginners, 55% are rated suitable for intermediates, and 20% are for advanced skiers, including five percent rated for experts only.

The elevation at the top of its runs is 7,640 feet, which means the ski season normally starts in late November and continues until April. Brundage is also famous for keeping lift ticket prices down. A full-day ticket for an adult in the '93-'94 season was $23.

The day lodge offers a restaurant serving breakfast and lunch, wine, and beer. The Bunny Hutch provides day care for infants six weeks and older and for children to age eight ($20-25 a day, half-day and family rates available). The lodge also offers a full line of equipment rentals with package prices ranging from $10.50 a day for children to $30 for performance gear.

A ski school using a staff certified by the Professional Ski Instructors of America is part of Brundage's offerings. Information about the ski program is available by calling the lodge or (800) 888-7544 (-SKII). Multiday lesson packages reduce the cost per lesson.

The **Little Ski Hill,** tel. 634-5691, is operated by the Payette Lakes Ski Club, a nonprofit group. Located three miles south of McCall, the ski hill first opened in 1937. The area has a T-bar to give skiers a lift up its 405 vertical feet and serves both Alpine skiers and Nordic skiers who want to Telemark. The area also has 30 miles of groomed skating lanes and touring trails. It's open Tues-Fri. 3-5 p.m., Sat.-Sun. 10 a.m-5 p.m., and Friday and Saturday nights 6-10 p.m. The ski area is one of five sanctioned biathlon ranges in the nation. McCall has helped staff the U.S. biathlon team during recent Winter Games.

Little Ski Hill offers a lodge and snack bar and the Nordic Skiing Center with a warming shelter at the cross-country skiing track. Locker rentals are available. Lift tickets are about half the price of Brundage and cross-country skiing passes are $5 a day.

Cross-country Ski Trails

Ponderosa State Park offers eight miles of groomed cross-country skiing trails, with stretches suitable for nearly all levels of ability. The park also holds ungroomed routes for those who want to break trail themselves. Skiers may purchase a $10 Park 'n' Ski sticker from the park or pay a $2 daily admission fee.

Ski Rentals

Home Town Sports, tel. 634-2302, rents ski equipment at 402 W. Lake Street. **Brundage Mountain,** tel. 634-7462 or (800) 888-7544, and **Gravity Sports,** tel. 634-8530, at 503 Pine St., also offer skiing equipment for rent. **Alpine Sciences,** tel. 634-4707, offers ski tuning, and sells snowboards and ski equipment.

Snowmobiling

Snowmobiling—high-speed skimming across the white tableau of winter—is big in the McCall area. From McCall, a network of trails heads into the rugged backcountry in all directions. A favorite adventure for snowmobilers in the McCall area is to take off from the **Warren Wagon Road** on a 40-mile jaunt to Warren or a 28-mile excursion to **Secesh.** Another favorite is a 26-mile loop that begins across from the Little Ski Hill three miles north of McCall and takes riders to **Bear Basin,** Brundage Mountain Resort, and back again. Information about trail conditions is available from the McCall Area Snowmobilers Club, which cooperates with other clubs to groom the trails for riding.

Snowmobiles for sale or rent and information about trails are available at **Big Boy Toys,** tel. 634-4759, at 190 Industrial Loop; and **Harry's Dry Dock and Winter Sports,** tel. 634-8605, at 315 N. 3rd. Snowmobiles rent for about $90 a day or $50 a half-day. Machines suitable for two riders rent for about $100 a day. **Medley Sports,** tel. 634-2216, is also a good source of information and outdoor gear. **Baum Shelter,** at 13876 Hwy. 55, tel. 634-7178, sells snowmobiles and accessories.

Bicycling

McCall's quiet streets and nearby state park offer excellent bicycling opportunities. **Gravity Sports** and **Home Town Sports** (see "Ski Rentals," above) both sell and rent bicycles.

Boating

Payette Lake is well served by boat ramps at Ponderosa State Park's main unit and at North Beach across the lake, and at the **Sports Marina,** tel. 634-8361, at 1300 E. Lake. Ramps are also available at Upper Payette and Little Payette lakes.

Boats in Valley County must be equipped with efficient exhaust mufflers or other devices to keep noise below 92 decibels. However, noise isn't a problem for much of the Payette Lake fleet. Sailboats and sailboards offer a bit of colorful spice to the deep blue of lake and sky and the green backdrop of mountains.

Boats are available for rent at **Harry's Dry Dock and Winter Sports,** tel. 634-8605, at 315 N. 3rd, and **Sports Marina,** tel. 634-8361, at 1300 E. Lake. Sports Marina also rents Jet Skis. Other boat dealers include **Baum Shelter,** tel. 634-7178; **Gravity Sports,** tel. 634-8530, which specializes in paddleboats; and **Medley Sports,** at 809 N. 3rd., with its line of personal watercraft.

Lake Excursions

Western Tours, tel. 634-3560, is located at 317 E. Lake and offers boat rides on Payette Lake and guided fishing trips.

Fishing

Stream fishermen can find their fill of bright waters east of McCall along the **South Fork of the Salmon River,** a stream loved for its beauty by those who know it. Lake fishermen, however, will find the McCall area particularly well endowed. Upper, Little, and main Payette lakes offer about 1,500 acres of water to fish. **Payette Lake** proper has 1,000 acres of water that holds rainbow and lake trout, whitefish, and kokanee salmon. There's even a sea monster here dubbed Sharlie by locals that offers a ready-made story for the one that got away. **Upper Payette Lake** is 17 miles north of McCall along the road to Burgdorf. Campsites are on the west side of the 200-acre lake. Rainbow trout are the main quarry here, as they are at **Little Payette Lake,** just south of the main lake, and at **Brundage Reservoir,** 12 miles northwest of town. Little Payette in particular is becoming a new mecca for trout fishermen because of its big, feisty rainbows.

Golf

McCall Golf Course, tel. 634-7200, offers 18 holes at the corner of Davis Ave. and Lick Creek Rd. along the lake's southeast shore.

Flightseeing

Each summer, McCall's airport serves as a staging point for smoke jumpers heading out into the backcountry to subdue forest fires. It also supports several flying services that cater year-round to visitors including hunters, anglers, and hikers.

Pioneer Aviation, tel. 634-7127, offers backcountry charter flights to all of Idaho's airstrips, including those within the Frank Church–River of No Return Wilderness to the east. The company will also help book hunting, fishing, rafting, or other trips with outfitters.

McCall And Wilderness Air, tel. 634-7137, also offers backcountry flying, including winter flights in ski-fitted planes to remote airstrips.

ACCOMMODATIONS AND FOOD

Special Lodgings

The most venerable lodging in town is the **Hotel McCall,** tel. 634-8105, along the lakeshore. Rooms on the lower level with queen or twin beds and a shared bath rent for $55 a night. Two suites are available for $99-115 a night. Rates include a homemade breakfast featuring a variety of delectable items such as sourdough english muffins and fresh fruits in summer, or piping hot bowls of oatmeal in winter. Group rates are available, as are occasional seasonal specials. Arrangements can be made for dinners at the hotel. The hotel welcomes children 12 years and older.

Northwest Passage, tel. 634-5349, at 201 Rio Vista Blvd., offers a homey atmosphere for those traveling alone or with children. A huge fireplace dominates the front room that doubles as a parlor for guests. A full breakfast is included in the rates, which start at $60 and range up to $125.

Other B&B choices include **1920 House Bed and Breakfast,** tel. 634-4661, with three rooms for $65-70; and **The Chateau Bed and Breakfast,** tel. 634-4196, located at 1300 Warren Wagon Rd., with four rooms for $55-75.

Motels

McCall's newest motel, the **McCall Best Western,** is at 415 N. 3rd St., tel. 634-6300. Its 51 rooms range in price from $40 to $125 depending on size and season. The motel features an indoor pool and hot tub, and a microwave and refrigerator in every room. A restaurant is located across the street.

McCall's most famous lodging is the **Shore Lodge,** tel. 634-2244, along Hwy. 55 at the east edge of town. Rooms for a family of four range from $68 for streetside to $149 for lakeside. The lodge has docks on the lake and a dining room and coffee shop with gorgeous lake views.

One of McCall's most whimsical places to stay is the **Brundage Bungalows,** tel. 634-5150, with its eight cabins right along the highway at the north end of town along the lakeshore. Other accommodations include the **Riverside Motel,** tel. 634-5610, at 400 W. Lake St. ($40-50; kitchenettes available); **Village Inn Motel,** tel. 634-2344, at 1005 W. Lake St. ($36-75); **The Woodsman Motel,** tel. 634-7671, at 402 N. 3rd ($32-55; custom designed beds); and the **Scandia Inn Motel,** tel. 634-7394, at 400 N. 3rd ($40-55). The **Waterhole,** tel. 634-7758, offers five rooms for $18-30 a night, five miles south of McCall toward Lakefork.

Condominiums

During the winter at least, Brundage Mountain offers the main attraction for McCall visitors. The company's **Mill Park Condos,** tel. 634-4151 or (800) 888-7544, are for rent throughout the year. Each unit overlooks the lake and contains three bedrooms, two baths, a living room with fireplace, and a dining room. Each unit has a private deck. The condos also have a jacuzzi tub. Rates range $150-175 per night and all units sleep 6-10 depending on configuration. All units have a two-night minimum.

Aspen Village, tel. 634-7041, offers timeshare condominiums at 1607 Davis Avenue. Other companies listing condos for rent include **Clark/Kangas Property Rental,** tel. 634-7766; **Daveco Enterprises,** tel. 634-7321; **Engen Real Estate,** tel. 634-2114; **Fircrest Condominiums,** tel. 634-4528; **J. Staup Management,** tel. 634-4366; **Johnson and Co. Real Estate,** tel. 634-7134; **McCall Vacations,** tel. 634-7056; **Mountain Lakes Realty,** tel. 634-2728; **Riverside Motel,** tel. 634-5610; **Tamarack Bay Condo Association,** tel. 634-2185; and **Timberlake Timeshares,** tel. 634-8764.

Campgrounds

McCall serves as home base for the 2.3-million-acre **Payette National Forest,** tel. 634-0408, which surrounds the town like a blanket of green. The Forest Service maintains 24 campgrounds in the area, including **Buckhorn Bar,** 46 miles northeast of McCall; **Lake Fork,** nine miles east of McCall; **Upper Payette,** 18 miles north of McCall; and **Ponderosa,** 31 miles northeast of McCall. The campgrounds are generally available June to November and fees are $5 a night.

Private campgrounds include **Lakeview Village RV Park,** tel. 634-5280, along Pearl St., with campsites for $12 a night, and **McCall Campground,** tel. 634-5165, a mile and a half south of town, with sites for $12-15. **Payette Lakes Trailer Park,** tel. 634-3747, at 1401 Davis Ave., offers RV camping. **Bethel Park Campground,** tel. 634-7678, and **Pilgrim Cove Camp,** tel. 634-5555, round out the options.

Food

Bev's Cottage Cafe, tel. 634-3737, at 801 N. 3rd, is an espresso and muffin shop to get you started in the morning. **The Yacht Club Restaurant,** tel. 634-3433, at 203 E. Lake, on the lower level of the Yacht Club offers excellent Italian dishes. Like all good ski towns, Mexican cuisine has found a place in McCall. **Si Bueno,** tel. 634-2128, features bueno margaritas and a wide range of dishes, including flan for dessert, across from the McCall Airport at the south edge of town. **Maria's,** tel. 634-7436, at 319 N. 3rd, boasts grand margaritas in addition to traditional home-style Mexican food.

The McCall experience would hardly be complete for many without a visit to a couple of the longer-lived burger emporiums. One of them, **Bryan's Burger Den,** tel. 634-7964, pins down the southern flank of town along N. 3rd. **Toll Station Pizza,** tel. 634-7818, at 409 Railroad Ave., offers the other major food group ruled essential by most vacationers.

Dining options with a lake view include **Hot Off the Grill,** tel. 634-2688, at 317 E. Lake, featuring steaks, seafood, and prime rib. Across from the Shore Lodge at 406 W. Lake is the **Lake Street Cafe,** tel. 634-8551. And just down the block are two McCall favorites: **Player's Pizza,** tel. 634-7185, combines pizza with miniature golf at 504 W. Lake; and **Lardo Grill and Saloon,** tel. 634-8191, guards the northern marches at 600 W. Lake.

At 402 N. 3rd, **The Huckleberry,** tel. 634-8477, offers fresh pasta, omelettes, seafood, and homemade soups at the Woodsman Motel. Breakfast and lunch are the specialties of **The Pancake House,** tel. 634-5849, which is open 6 a.m.-2 p.m. daily at 209 N. 3rd.

McCall's Winter Carnival unfreezes the imaginations of local ice artists.

OTHER PRACTICALITIES

Entertainment And Events

McCall may have the only combination movie theater and building-supply store in the state, the nation, the world. Unique it may be, but provide entertainment it does. **Evergreen Theater,** tel. 634-4133, shares a driveway with the Payette Lakes Lumber Co. along Hwy. 55 south of town across from the airport.

McCall's annual **Winter Carnival,** which harkens back to the great winter of 1964, has attracted national attention to this scenic mountain town. The carnival normally begins on the third weekend of January and concludes before February gets too good of a grip on the year. The hallmark of the carnival is its imaginative snow sculptures that have ranged through the years from St. George and the Dragon to the sphinx to Sharlie, Payette Lake's own sea monster, a sculpture that also included an imaginative slide for children. The first Friday of the carnival is marked by a torchlight parade downtown and a bonfire. The grand parade is reserved for the following noon. Snowmobile races are also planned during the week.

McCall's other season, summer, peaks in July with fireworks on the fourth and the mid-July **Summer Music Festival** that began back in 1978. August brings the **Mountain Triathlon** at Rotary Park and the **McCall Road and Rock Challenge** for mountain bikers around Payette Lake. September's first weekend offers the annual **Lake Run.**

Nordic skiers take control in December with the **Citizen's Special** and other races. In January there's **Cross Country Idaho,** a run to Ponderosa State Park, which takes place about midmonth, and the **Payette Lakes Ski Marathon.**

Shopping

A mountain town ought to have a good bookshop to keep visitors happy. McCall does in the form of the **Blue Grouse Book Shop,** tel. 634-2434, at 1001 N. 2nd in the McCall Drug Store. **Dreams Alive,** tel. 634-5583, offers new and used books, comics, and sports cards at 114 N. 3rd. Most souvenir seekers end up at **K&L Jewelry and Gifts** at 312 Lake Street. **Calico Gifts and Collectables** at 1101 E. Lake and **Country Closet** at 204 Leonora offer McCall souvenirs as well. Need something to do? **Country Craft Tole Supplies,** tel. 634-7177, at 212 N. 3rd, might be able to help. More eclectic in their selections are **Crystal Visions,** tel. 634-7633, at 1100 E. Lake and **Mountain Monkey Business,** tel. 634-2027, at 501 W. Lake. The **Heartline Gallery** at 317 E. Lake and **Woven Wishes,** tel. 634-4001, at 5280 Mile High Dr., offer hand-built mementos.

Transportation

Northwestern Stage Lines, a Greyhound affiliate, serves McCall with a stop at **Bill's Gas and Grocery,** tel. 634-2340, at 147 N. 3rd.

Charter flights are available from Boise or other cities through **McCall And Wilderness Air,** tel. 634-7137, and **Pioneer Aviation,** tel. 634-7127. Both are located at the McCall Airport on the south edge of town. Pioneer also operates a Payless car-rental franchise at its facility, tel. 634-5445.

Information And Services

The **McCall Chamber of Commerce,** tel. 634-7631, is headquartered at 1001 State Street. **City Hall,** tel. 634-7142, is at 216 E. Park Street. The city **Recreation Department** is housed at the Depot.

You'll find the **McCall Police** in the back of city hall at 216 E. Park, tel. 634-7144 for routine business and 911 for emergencies. Outside city limits, police protection is provided by the **Valley County Sheriff's Department,** tel. 382-4202. **McCall Memorial District Hospital,** tel. 634-2221, offers 24-hour emergency service at 1000 State Street.

CASCADE AND VICINITY

It must seem at times to residents of Cascade that their town gets no respect compared with neighboring McCall. Their fair city, named for a once-spectacular falls now dammed for hydropower, cozies up next to Cascade Reservoir, one of Idaho's bona fide fishing hot spots. But all folks can ever do apparently is talk about skiing at Brundage, or boating on Payette Lake. Then again, fishermen are not always anxious to share the wealth, so maybe Cascade relishes its relative lack of limelight.

SIGHTS

Long Valley Museum

Between McCall and Cascade, the Long Valley Museum—located at **Roseberry,** a mile and a half east of Hwy. 55—is open Saturdays and Sundays 1-5 p.m. and preserves logging, ranching, and farming artifacts from the valley's history. The museum is housed in Roseberry's Methodist Church. A turn-of-the-century schoolhouse has also been moved from McCall to Roseberry.

Sleigh Rides

Near Roseberry along the Goldfork River, modern ranchers offer a new twist on winter work. Although draft horses and sleds have been used for decades to haul hay to cattle in the Long Valley, visitors can now join a hayride to feed elk. The **Hap and Florence Points Memorial Sleigh Rides** have become an institution in the Donnelly area. The rides cost $8 for adults and $5 for children. For reservations and more information, call 325-8876.

South On Highway 55

Heading south on Hwy. 55 from McCall, the blue reflection of **Cascade Reservoir** soon catches the traveler's attention. Although 30,000-acre Cascade Reservoir is a U.S. Bureau of Reclamation project, Idaho Power Co. operates the powerhouse that squeezes energy from the water at Cascade's north edge. Tours of the generating station are available weekdays 1-3 p.m. Special arrangements for large tour groups can also be made by calling 382-3372.

Although it formally begins at New Meadows and ends where Hwy. 55 intersects Hwy. 44 west of Boise, the **Payette River Scenic Route** really comes into its own near Smith's Ferry. One of Idaho's most famous sights is the graceful arch of the narrow bridge that carries the highway across the Payette's north fork. During the spring, the Payette here resembles a washing machine with all its turbulence and froth. No word short of "amazing" describes the feeling of standing at one of the highway turnouts and watching, feeling the force of the water crashing down. More amazing still, however, is seeing the bright blues, magentas, yellows, and greens of kayakers immersed in all this power. Some are grim, others jubilant as they bob along downriver.

At Horseshoe Bend, the **Boise Cascade Sawmill,** tel. 382-4241, offers tours Mon.-Thurs. 8 a.m.-4 p.m. by prior arrangement. The mill is

A graceful arch spans the Payette River along HIghway 55.

an example of high technology in the timber industry. Logs from nearby forests come in and finished lumber goes out. The process in between is exciting, which visitors will see for themselves.

Area Hot Springs

Valley and neighboring Adams counties are hotbeds for hot springs. **White Licks Hot Spring** is wedged about halfway between Donnelly and Council along Payette National Forest Rd. 186. Two small bathhouses enclose pools with natural hot and warm running water. Campsites and picnic tables are available. Fee campsites are $5.

Trail Creek Hot Springs lies east of Cascade along Boise National Forest Rd. 22. **Molly's Hot Spring** is south along National Forest Rd. 474, about two miles toward Stolle Meadows. **Vulcan Hot Springs** is also south of Stolle Meadows along Rd. 474 about seven miles. All are undeveloped hot springs. Information is available at the **Cascade Ranger Station,** tel. 382-4271.

RECREATION

Cascade Reservoir Boating And Camping

Cascade is the main access point for Cascade Reservoir, so it should surprise no one that fishing and boating are two preoccupations here. The lake is one of the best places to catch fat and scrappy rainbow trout year-round. Yellow perch, one of the best-tasting fish around, grow as large here as anywhere. Kokanee salmon also call Cascade Reservoir home.

The reservoir is ringed with boat launches and campgrounds. Cascade itself has a good boat ramp with a 140-space parking lot. Occupying the lake's southern shore near the town is **Crown Point** with 36 campsites. **Carbarton** campground has a good boat ramp and 12 campsites. Along the southwestern shore, **Campbell Creek** and **French Creek** both have boat ramps. French Creek has 38 campsites as well, making it the largest campground along the lake. Other boat ramps and campgrounds along the western shore are **Poison Creek** with 20 campsites and **Rainbow Point** with 12. Access areas between Donnelly and Cascade include the **Donnelly Boat Docks** with 25 campsites, and the **Sugar Loaf** boat ramp. Information about the boat ramps and campgrounds is available from the **U.S. Bureau of Reclamation,** tel. 382-4258.

Nearby Boating And Camping

Horsethief Reservoir, nine miles east of Cascade on the Warm Lake Highway, encompasses 275 acres when full. The reservoir offers fishing for rainbow trout. Out the same road toward Landmark is a large concentration of Boise National Forest campgrounds stretching from **Yellow Pine** in the north to **Deadwood Reservoir** and **Lowman** in the south. Yellow Pine, home of Zane Gray's Thunder Mountain, offers a cluster of four campgrounds. Another cluster surrounds **Warm Lake** about 20 miles east of Cascade. Current information about the campgrounds and road conditions is available from the **Cascade Ranger District,** tel. 382-4271.

The Payette River is why Banks, south of Cascade, and Garden Valley, east of Banks, are bases for rafting companies. **Cascade Raft Co.,** tel. 462-3639, is based at Garden Valley.

Winter Sports

In winter, ice fishing isn't the only thing happening in Cascade. Nordic skiers get their due near Cascade with the **Crawford Park 'n' Ski Area,** four miles east of town along the Warm Lake Highway. The seven miles of trails here are most suitable for intermediate skiers. Four miles farther along the road to Warm Lake lies the **Scott Valley Park 'n' Ski Area,** which features an additional seven miles of trails for both beginner and intermediate skiers.

The **West Mountain Snowmobilers** take an active interest in grooming trails which branch off from the county road on the reservoir's western shore and head up and over scenic West Mountain. Snowmobilists can also hook into the extensive trail system linking Cascade Reservoir and West Mountain with points north. The trail starts at the intersection of Anderson Creek Rd. and the county road that follows the reservoir's southwestern shoreline just across from Cascade.

Wellington Snow Park, south of Cascade at Smith's Ferry along Hwy. 55, is one of the largest snowmobile developments in the state. Wellington offers a 250-car parking lot, warming shelter, and heated restrooms, a luxury in snow country. The park is the locus for 400 miles of trails, 250 miles of them groomed for better riding conditions. The trails thread their way through rolling hills and large clearcut areas where a sledder can play as long as the snow's deep enough.

Golf

Cascade Golf Course, tel. 382-4835, is a nine-hole course open from 8 a.m. to dusk daily during the summer. The clubhouse has a pro shop, cart and club rentals, and a pro available for lessons.

PRACTICALITIES

Motels

Motels in Cascade range from the **Aurora Motel RV Park and Storage,** tel. 382-4948, at 900 S. Hwy. 55 ($26-35), to the **Breeze Motel,** tel. 382-4370. Others include the **High Country Inn,** tel. 382-3315, at 112 Main ($27-49), and **Mountain View Motel,** tel. 382-4238, a half mile south of town ($29-49).

Resorts And RV Parks

Warm Lake Lodge, tel. 257-2221 or 734-2387, includes a restaurant and campground at a scenic lake far in the backcountry. **North Shore Lodge,** tel. 634-5012, also offers campsites, a restaurant, and meeting room.

At Garden Valley, southeast of Smith's Ferry, **Terrace Lakes Resort,** tel. 462-3250, has a private 18-hole golf course, a naturally heated pool, tennis courts, and a cafe. The resort includes a 50-space RV park.

Arrowhead Mountain Village on the River, 955 S. Hwy. 55, tel. 382-4534, is a 100-site RV park with all the usual amenities. Sites with full hookups including cable TV cost $14.50 per night.

Campgrounds

In addition to the Bureau of Reclamation campgrounds along the reservoir, campers will find four Payette National Forest campgrounds nearby. They include **French Creek** west of Cascade; **South Fork of the Salmon River,** 24 miles northeast; **Shoreline,** 25 miles northeast; and **Warm Lake,** 26 miles northeast. All are along the Warm Lake Highway. For more information, contact the Cascade Ranger District, tel. 382-4271.

Restaurants

Cascade Chef's Hut, tel. 382-4486, at 806 Hwy. 55, offers a quick pit stop for travelers or diners who have a quick meal in mind. **Clear Creek Inn,** tel. 382-4616, along the southern edge of town; **Cascade Pub and Grill,** tel. 382-3602, at 401 N. Main; and **Grandma's Homestead Family Restaurant,** tel. 382-4602, at 224 N. Main; invite diners to linger a bit longer.

The view from the **Lakefront Restaurant and Lounge,** tel. 382-4682, at 119 Lakeshore Dr. promotes many leisurely meals. **Tortilla Mountain Mexican Food and Cantina,** tel. 382-4708, offers a change of pace in Cascade at 112 Main Street.

Donnelly-area eateries include **The Donnelly Club,** tel. 325-8770, which offers a menu heavy on steaks and seafood for dinner. It also serves breakfast and lunch. For a more intimate meal, **Dave and Kathy's Place,** tel. 325-8244, shoulders up next to the highway.

Alongside the highway at Smith's Ferry is one of the state's great roadhouses, the **Cougar Mountain Lodge,** tel. 382-4464. A two-story log inn, the lodge offers basic road food, a limited selection of groceries, and atmosphere in abundance.

Road food pretty much describes the offerings south of Smith's Ferry, too. Garden Valley's **Longhorn Restaurant,** tel. 462-3108, is one option for the hungry traveler. Banks is most notable for **The Ponderosa,** tel. 793-2700, a restaurant that always has a crowded parking lot. The daily steak special has a lot to do with that, as does the restaurant's location on the bank of the Payette River.

Closest to Boise along Hwy. 55 is the town of Horseshoe Bend, where the **Long Branch Saloon,** tel. 793-2266, offers the same sort of hospitality that made thirsty cowpokes happy.

Events

Cascade's biggest event of the year is **Thunder Mountain Days,** held early each July. The event features a rodeo, parades, a dawn buckaroo breakfast, and an evening barbecue. For more information call the Cascade Chamber of Commerce.

Information And Services

The **Cascade Chamber of Commerce** offers information at P.O. Box 571, Cascade, ID 83611, or tel. 382-3833. Cascade is the county seat for Valley County. The **Valley County Sheriff's Department,** tel. 382-4202, is based there. Cascade also has a **police department,** tel. 382-4202, the same number as the sheriff's. The **Valley County Hospital,** 402 Old State Highway, tel. 382-4242, offers 24-hour emergency services.

CAMBRIDGE, COUNCIL, AND VICINITY

Hwy. 95 heads west, then angles southwest from New Meadows. Rather than the pine forests that surround McCall and the Long Valley along Hwy. 55, travelers on this route get the green out of the way relatively quickly before heading south into a patchwork of irrigated farmland and gray sagebrush hills.

This area's main claims to fame lie west of Hwy. 95. Council serves not only as the Adams County seat but also as the jumping-off point for the Seven Devils Mountains and the Hells Canyon NRA. Council occupies a scenic valley that was named because of the native peoples—Umatilla, Nez Perce, Shoshone, and others—that once mingled here.

Farther south, Cambridge serves as the main access for Idaho Power Company's popular recreation areas that are part of its Snake River Dam complex: Brownlee, Oxbow, and Hells Canyon. One of Cambridge's distinctive features is its newspaper. The *Upper Country News-Reporter* has covered the community's news since March 1889.

SIGHTS

Seven Devils Mountains

The southern Seven Devils are reached from Council by heading northwest and following the signs. **Black Lake** is 54 miles northwest of Council along Payette National Forest Rd. 112. It offers a popular trailhead for horseback riders and campers heading into the wilderness. Mountain bikers will need to remember that the Wilderness Act of 1964 bans all mechanical conveyances, not just the motorized ones. **Black Lake Campground** at 7,200 feet in elevation offers four campsites and is available from July to September. **Huckleberry Campground** to the south is at 4,800 feet and has eight campsites. It is open from June to October.

The southern fringe of the Seven Devils shows the greatest evidence of the region's early mining endeavors. Copper ore discovered here prompted the construction of several mines. A sign in Council's City Park commemorates ambitious turn-of-the-century plans to build a railroad to the Seven Devils. Remnants of an old mining smelter at Landore can still be seen, as can the beginning of a railroad grade near Kinney Point. Also northwest of Council is **Cuprum,** from the Latin for copper. The truly intrepid can descend into Hells Canyon on Kleinschmidt Grade, an adventure that makes the most sense when the winding road is snow-free and dry.

Snake River Dams And Parks

The three-dam hydropower complex operated by Idaho Power Co. can be reached from either Council or Cambridge, although Cambridge offers the speedier route by far along Hwy. 71. The reservoirs behind Hells Canyon, Oxbow, and Brownlee dams draw boaters and campers from spring to fall.

Three of the company's four parks occupy the Idaho shoreline, beginning with **Woodhead Park,** just south of Brownlee Dam off Hwy. 71. Woodhead offers 40 tent sites and 40 RV sites. Two boat ramps are also available. **McCormick Park,** between Brownlee and Oxbow dams, has 10 tent sites and 36 RV sites, and a boat ramp. **Hells Canyon Park** is also on the Idaho side between Oxbow and Hells Canyon dams and offers 30 tent and 30 RV sites with one boat ramp. All three parks provide picnic areas. The company's campgrounds are a bargain: tenters pay $1 and RVers $3 a night. The company maintains a toll-free recreation information line, tel. (800) 422-3143 for Idaho callers and (800) 521-9102 in Oregon and Washington.

While driving along Hwy. 71, here's something to consider: The Hitt Mountain Ski Area may be revived if it already hasn't. One of numerous small ski hills that suffered from its relative remoteness

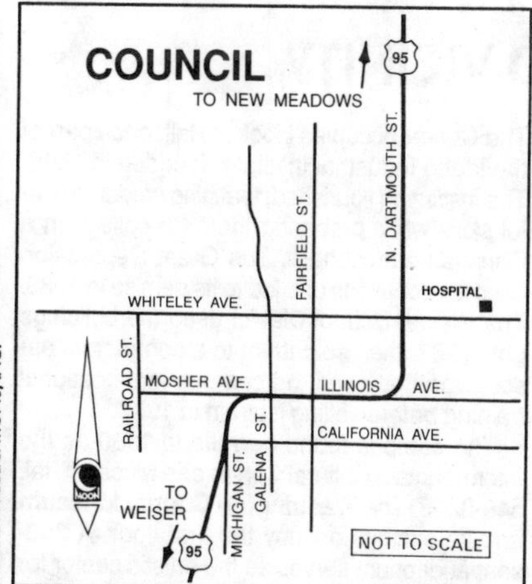

and the droughts that visited Idaho during the 1980s, Hitt Mountain attracted new interest in 1993 as Idaho's winter tourism industry showed new signs of life.

PRACTICALITIES

Accommodations

At Cambridge, the **Frontier Motel and RV Park,** tel. 257-3851, offers nine campsites from $12, and 17 rooms ranging $28-52. **Hunter's Inn,** tel. 257-3325, has four units renting for about $20. **Bucky's Motel,** tel. 257-3330, has three rooms ($23-39) and a cafe.

Council offers **The Old Heartland Inn,** tel. 253-6423, a bed and breakfast with three rooms in the $40 range. **Starlite Motel,** tel. 253-4868, has 12 rooms for $25-40.

Food

Council offers **The Grub Steak,** tel. 253-6002, at 103 Illinois Ave. focusing on steaks and other basic fare. Cambridge restaurants include **Bucky's Cafe,** tel. 257-3330, at the intersection of Highways 95 and 71; **Gateway,** tel. 257-3531 (open 7-7); **Kay's,** tel. 257-3561 (open 6 a.m.-10 p.m.); and the **Pioneer Express,** tel. 257-3360, at 125 Superior (open noon-10).

Sports And Events

Council Mountain Golf Course, tel. 253-6908, lies along Hwy. 95 near town. If you're not golfing on Independence Day, check out the town's annual extravaganza, its **Fourth of July Celebration and Porcupine Races.** Cambridge celebrates **Hells Canyon Days** the first week of June.

Information And Services

The **Council Visitor Center,** tel. 253-0161, on Hwy. 95 by the Forest Service office on the north end of town, and **Cambridge City Hall,** tel. 257-3318, dispense visitor information. Police services are provided at Council by the city police, who can be reached through the **Adams County Sheriff's Department,** tel. 253-4227 (emergencies) or 253-4258 (business). **Council Community Hospital,** tel. 253-4242, is located at 205 N. Berkeley. The **Council Valley Free Library,** tel. 253-6004, is located at 104 California Avenue.

Police service for Cambridge is provided by the **Washington County Sheriff,** tel. 549-2121 (911 in emergencies), at Weiser. The **Cambridge Community Library,** tel. 257-3434, is downtown at 80 Superior Street.

SOUTH TO WEISER

South of Cambridge, Hwy. 95 descends into the grassy valleys that are home to citizens who seem intent on keeping Idaho's seats in the U.S. Senate occupied. Sen. Larry Craig grew up on a cattle ranch near Midvale. His predecessor, James McClure, hailed from Payette.

Midvale lies eight miles south of Cambridge, and just south of town are the remnants of one of Idaho's oldest industries. Archaeologists estimate the age of a quarry at the top of Midvale Hill at about 3,000-5,000 years. The quarry furnished fine-grained basalt that artisans turned into spear points, knives, and scrapers. The people who fashioned the weapons were hunter-gatherers, living on deer, the salmon that migrated upstream, and fruits and roots. Ten miles south of Midvale on Hwy. 95 is Weiser.

WEISER AND VICINITY

SIGHTS

Weiser is a handsome town with its elegant brick homes and a Knights of Pythias castle downtown at 30 E. Idaho Street. Idaho and Third streets present a charming display of mostly Queen Anne style homes. Weiser also stands out as the former home of baseball great Walter "Big Train" Johnson, who lived at the corner of W. Park and W. First streets from 1906 to 1907, before heading for Washington, D.C. and the big leagues. Johnson is a charter member of the Baseball Hall of Fame.

Weiser's biggest claim to fame is the **National Oldtime Fiddlers' Contest,** held here annually the third full week in June at Weiser High School and other locales around town. Fiddling contests have been held in Weiser for over 100 years, and these days the contest draws the very best fiddlers from around the country. The **Fiddlers Hall of Fame** is located in the city community center downtown.

Intermountain Cultural Center And Museum

Weiser is home to the Intermountain Cultural Center and Museum, located at 2295 Paddock Ave. just north of the high school, tel. 549-0205.

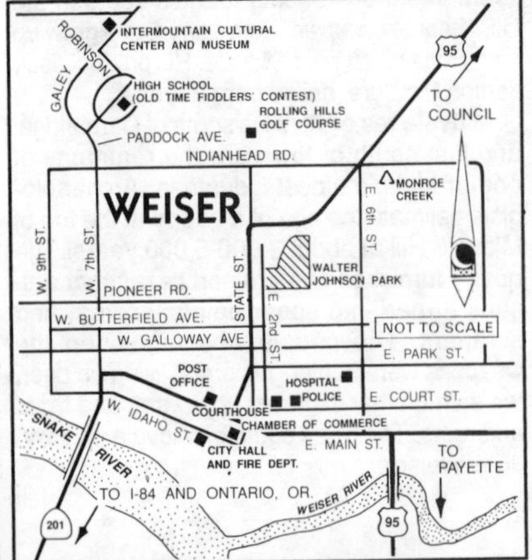

The Center occupies Hooker Hall, once part of the Idaho Industrial Institute, founded in 1899. The institution flourished, teaching students useful skills while preparing them for college in a Christian atmosphere. The Great Depression dried up donations and led to its demise in 1933. The Weiser School District used the buildings until 1967, then sold them to a contractors association that used the campus for vocational training before selling it again in 1977.

The campus found new life in 1980 as the Intermountain Cultural Center and Museum, tel. 549-0205. The **Washington County Museum** and its exhibits occupy the first floor. A 300-seat auditorium serves as the artistic center for Weiser.

Indian Hot Springs

Indian Hot Springs, tel. 549-0070, is a developed hot springs located 10 miles north of Weiser on the Weiser Flats. It's closed in winter.

PRACTICALITIES

Accommodations

Motels in Weiser include the **Colonial Motel,** tel. 549-0150, at 251 E. Main, with 24 rooms ranging $30-60. **State Street Motel,** tel. 549-1390, 1279 State St., has 13 rooms ranging $25-45. **Monroe Creek Campground,** tel. 549-2026, is a mile and a half north of town and has 60 spaces for $6-10. It's open May 1-Oct. 31. Payette offers the **Montclair Motel,** tel. 642-2693, with 10 rooms ranging $25-40.

Food

Weiser eateries include **Beehive Family Restaurant,** tel. 549-3544, at 611 Hwy 95; **The Golden Horse** (Chinese and American food), tel. 549-2500, at 1 Main Place; the **Fireside Cafe** along Hwy. 95 N; and **Keystone Pizza,** tel. 549-0203, with decent pizza and Italian fare. Payette offers another **Keystone Pizza,** tel. 642-9333, at 17 S. 8th; as well as the **Mandarin Restaurant,** tel. 642-3567, at 107 N. Main; **Tips Restaurant,** tel. 642-4109, at 126 S. Main; and **Polly's,** tel. 642-4157, also on Main.

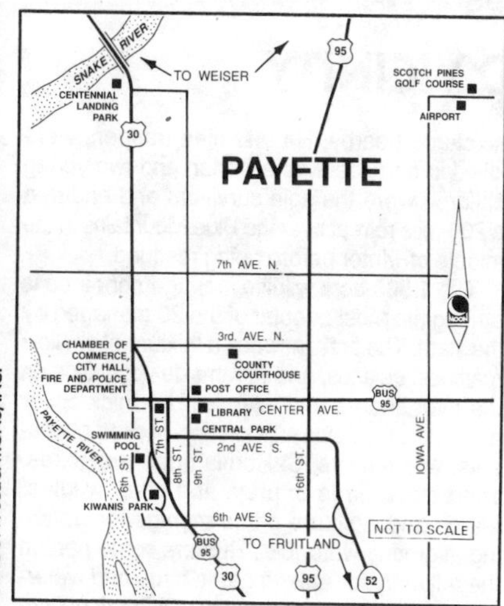

Festivals

Weiser is known throughout the West as the focal point for old-time fiddling. During the third week of June each year, the Weiser High School auditorium attracts thousands of fans for the **National Old Time Fiddlers' Contest.** The music is right from the hearts of fiddlers both old and young. Payette's major event comes in the first week of May. The **Apple Blossom Festival** acknowledges both the arrival of spring and the region's heritage of productive orchards.

Golf

Weiser golfers hit the links at the nine-hole **Rolling Hills Golf Course,** tel. 549-0456, at the intersection of State St. and Indianhead Drive. Payette offers the **Scotch Pines Golf Course,** tel. 642-4866, with its 18 holes.

Information And Services

The **Weiser Chamber of Commerce,** tel. 549-0452, is located at 8 E. Idaho, Weiser, ID 83672. The **Washington County Sheriff,** tel. 549-2121, is based at the Weiser courthouse at E. Court and 2nd. **Weiser Police,** tel. 549-2244 (911 for emergencies), is next door to the courthouse. **Memorial Hospital,** tel. 549-0370, is located at 645 E. 5th. **The Weiser Public Library** is located at 628 E. 1st.

The **Payette Chamber of Commerce** is located at Payette City Hall at 700 Center Ave., Payette, ID 83661. **Payette Police,** tel. 642-6026, are also in city hall, and open weekdays only. The **Payette County Sheriff** can be summoned by dialing 911, or calling 642-6006. The **Payette Public Library** can be reached at 642-6029.

PAYETTE

Payette, some 10 miles south of Weiser, is named for the good-hearted manager of the Hudson's Bay Company's Old Fort Boise just upriver along the Snake (see "Emmett And Vicinity"). François Payette was a generous friend to the Oregon-bound emigrants who trod the dusty Western trail in the 1840s. The town holds a couple of notable landmarks. One is the 90-foot geodesic dome that began life as a radar dome in Oregon and now shelters the Payette High School gymnasium. The **Payette County Historical Society Museum** is housed in the former Methodist Episcopal Church at First Ave. and S. Ninth Street.

EMMETT AND VICINITY

Emmett lies in a rich valley along the Payette River. Like its sister communities of Middleton, Parma, and Wilder to the south and west, agriculture rules the roost here.

Emmett is a lot friendlier place today than it was in the late 1880s. That's when Pickett's Corral in the foothills east of town sheltered a band of road agents and horse thieves who were harassing travelers and preying on settlers. Vigilantes, including none other than William J. McConnell (see "Exploring the Town" under "Moscow" in the North-central chapter), eventually cleaned out the robber's roost.

Parma, in contrast, has always been known as a hospitable and safe haven. The Hudson's Bay Co. maintained a trading post at the Boise River's confluence with the Snake River five miles west of town. François Payette, the post's manager, set a fine table for Overlanders stopping at the fort on their way west.

SIGHTS

Gem County Museum

The Gem County Museum, tel. 365-9530 (summers), provides Emmett's major attraction for many visitors. Housed in the old Emmett Library at 1st and Hawthorne, the museum features memorabilia of the pioneer days in the Emmett Valley, including a complete early ranching display, and a re-created blacksmith shop, Victorian house, and schoolhouse. It's open June-Sept., Sat.-Sun. 2-5 p.m., the rest of the year by appointment (call 365-2990 or 365-2350 for an appointment).

Old Fort Boise Wildlife Management Area

In Parma, a replica of Old Fort Boise is of interest to travelers. The site of the Hudson's Bay Co. outpost is now part of the Old Fort Boise Wildlife Management Area, tel. 722-5888, overseen by the Idaho Fish and Game Department. The name commemorates the old fort, the most lasting trade undertaking in the area. Although Hudson's Bay Co. ran a trading post here from 1834 to 1855, trappers and traders had focused on the spot since 1814 when John Reid built a stockade nearby. He and nine trappers were killed in a fracas. Marie Dorian and two young children were the sole survivors and endured a 200-mile retreat over the Blue Mountains in the middle of winter before being rescued.

The 1,500-acre wildlife management area is among the most popular of the 20 managed by the state. The area includes a mixture of shallow marshes, uplands, and streamside vegetation on the river shores and islands. The thick cover and cultivated fields support ring-necked pheasants, wild turkeys, California quail, songbirds, shorebirds, birds of prey, and other wildlife. March and April are prime months for watching migrating waterfowl. Hunters come here in the fall to try for upland game birds and waterfowl. The area is also popular with anglers fishing for channel catfish, black crappie, largemouth bass, and smallmouth bass. The area is open April-Sept. 5 a.m.-10 p.m. From Oct. to March, its hours are 6 a.m.-8 p.m.

PRACTICALITIES

Accommodations

Emmett offers the **Holiday Motel,** tel. 365-4479, at 1111 S. Washington with 14 rooms for $26-37; and **Capital Mobile Court,** tel. 365-3889, with 10 RV spaces for rent at $11 per night.

In Parma travelers can hole up at the **Court Motel and Beverage Store,** tel. 722-5579, with 11 rooms ranging $20-35. Campers can also stay at the **Old Fort Boise Wildlife Management Area,** tel. 722-5888, five miles west of town.

Food

Diners in Emmett will find **Geriken's,** tel. 365-6573, at 2001 Washington, worth checking out with its all-American menu at breakfast, lunch, and dinner. Other purveyors of the basic food groups include **Keystone Pizza,** tel. 365-5011, at 1200 S. Washington Ave.; and **Rose Ann Drive-In,** tel. 365-9926, at 929 S. Washington Avenue. At **Cocoa Beach Tanning and Espresso Bar,** tel. 365-6703, 819 S. Washington, you can drink French roast while you roast yourself.

In Parma, dining selections include **Big Ben's Golden Wheel Drive-In,** tel. 722-5284, at 203 N. 9th Ave.; **Fort Boise Cafe and Lounge,** tel. 722-6014, at 303 Main; **Fort Boise Pizza Emporium,** tel. 722-6048, at 206 N. 1st St.; and the **J Bar K Drive-In,** tel. 722-5463, at 911 E. Grove Avenue.

Festivals

June brings out the best in Emmett's orchards, so it's no coincidence that one of the year's biggest events is the annual **Cherry Festival** held the second week of that month. The nearby Payette River also draws throngs of jetboaters and fans during the annual mid-May running of the **Black Canyon Jet Boat Races.** The Payette River race attracts racers from throughout the state, and some from as far away as New Zealand. Parma's biggest party of the year is **Old Fort Boise Days** held in mid-May.

Recreation

The **Gem County Golf Course,** tel. 365-2675, offers nine holes to enthusiasts. **High Valley Snow Park** is 25 miles north of Emmett near High Valley. The parking area provides access to 200 miles of groomed trails plus 150 miles of roads and trails through rolling timber, meadows, and clearcuts. Information about trail conditions is available from the **Emmett Ranger District,** tel. 365-7000, at 1805 Hwy. 16, Room 5.

Information And Services

The **Gem County Chamber of Commerce,** tel. 365-3485, supplies information about the Emmett area from its location at 231 S. Washington Ave. in Emmett. Its counterpart is the **Parma Chamber of Commerce,** tel. 722-5634. The **Gem County Sheriff** is based at the county courthouse in Emmett at 415 E. Main. **Emmett Police** are based at 233 S. Washington Avenue. Both can be reached by calling 365-3521. Police protection in Parma includes the **Canyon County Sheriff's Office,** tel. 454-7531. The **Emmett Public Library,** tel. 365-6057, is located at 275 S. Hayes.

NAMPA AND CALDWELL

These two cities, though both rank among Idaho's top 10 by size, live in the shadow of nearby Boise for better or worse. Both are clearly pleasant enough places to visit on their own. Nampa, once known as New Jerusalem, was later rechristened for the Shoshone chief Nampuh, a giant whose name, according to popular legend, referred to his big feet.

Legends don't always reflect reality, of course. The big-feet legend lives on from a 1919 publicity stunt to draw attention to the Nampa Harvest Festival. It was concocted, historians say, by Fred Wilson, that year's secretary. The historically correct version notes that the town's name is drawn from the Shoshone word "namb" which does mean footprints. But contrary to the fanciful reports of a renegade chief named Nampa, the word applied to the area because visitors often found large moccasin prints in the area after cold weather. The reason for the large prints was that the Shoshones would stuff their moccasins with sagebrush leaves during cold weather, giving their mocassins an outsized imprint. Alert reader Brent Burnett of Nampa helped clarify the origins for the name, drawing the author's attention to an engaging history of the city, "My Home Town," by Annie Laurie Bird.

Caldwell drew its name from a U.S. Senator from Kansas, C.A. Caldwell, who was president of the Idaho and Oregon Land Improvement Co. and who owned and platted the townsite in 1883. The name no doubt handily beat the alternatives, particularly Bugtown, another early name.

SIGHTS

Albertson College Of Idaho

Nampa and Caldwell both have college campuses to add to their appeal. The Albertson College of Idaho, tel. 459-5011, a liberal arts college with an excellent reputation, is based at Caldwell. It was founded by southern Idaho Presbyterians and opened in 1891, making it the state's oldest indepedent college. The college enrolls about 1,100 students each fall. The C of I Coyotes are noted for the first-rate liberal arts education they receive as much as for their prowess in National

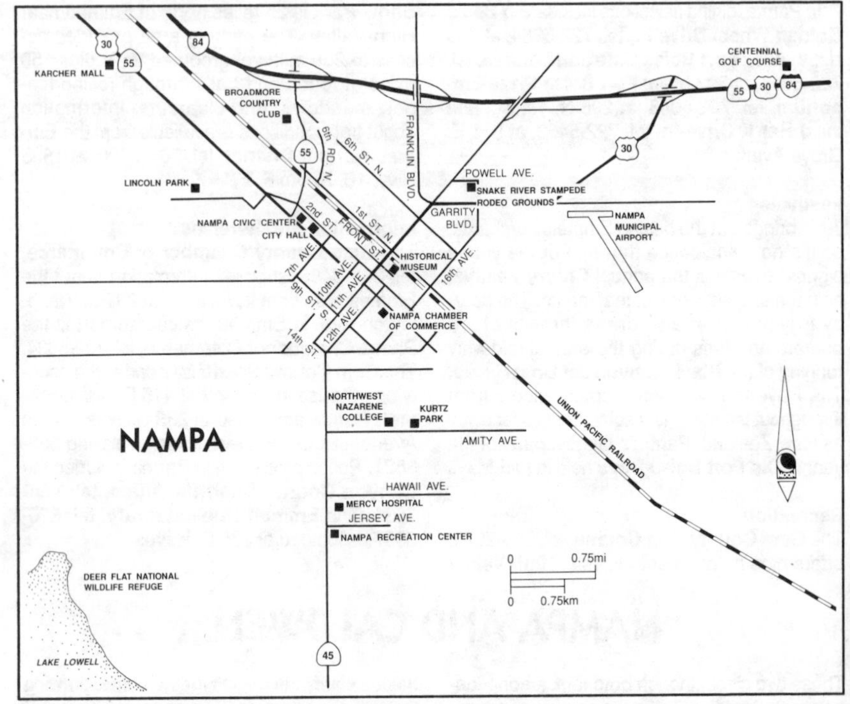

Association for Intercollegiate Athletics basketball or National College Skiing Association ski teams. C of I alumni include a Rhodes scholar, governors of two states, a Pulitzer Prize winner, and industry magnates including the founders of Albertson's supermarkets and Patagonia Clothing. On campus, its **Museum of Natural History** is the main draw. Also on campus in the science building is the **Evans Gem and Mineral Collection,** which showcases colorful and carefully polished rocks. Caldwell also offers visitors the **Van Slyke Agricultural Display** at Memorial Park at S. Kimball and Grant streets. The park is home to two log houses dating back to 1864.

Nampa Sights

Nearby Nampa is home to **Northwest Nazarene College** at 12th Ave. and E. Dewey Avenue. The college was founded by the church in 1937. Its principal attraction is the campus museum. Like its neighbor, Northwest Nazarene has been ranked by *U.S. News and World Report* as one of the top liberal arts colleges in the region. The college has produced Rhodes scholars and an astronaut.

Nampa also serves as home to the **Canyon County Historical Museum.** On the city's northwest fringe is the **Amalgamated Sugar Co.** refinery that processes sugar beets. The imposing brick sugar factory was built in 1942 and ranks as the largest sugar refinery in the country. The factory has developed a unique attraction in recent years—a pair of peregrine falcons has nested on its heights and successfully reared young.

Wineries

South of Caldwell lies the Sunnyslope area. Idaho's most famous and successful winery, **Ste. Chapelle Winery,** tel. 459-7222, operates here. The tasting room at the winery is open Mon.-Sat. 10-5, Sunday noon-5. The winery is located 14 miles southwest of Nampa along Hwy. 55. The surrounding gentle slopes are covered with fruit trees and vineyards.

Also southwest of Nampa is **Pintler Cellars,** tel. 467-1200, which offers tastings Fri.-Sun. noon-5 and weekdays by appointment. **Indian Creek Winery,** tel. 922-4791, is open noon-5 for tastings and lies southeast of Nampa off McDermott Rd. toward Kuna. **Mussel's Fish Market,** tel. 336-2277, at 3107 Overland Road in Boise, offers scheduled tastings of selections from the area's dozen-plus wineries approximately every two weeks. But they will be happy to pop a cork or two for informal tastings from their vast selection any other time as well.

Deer Flat National Wildlife Refuge

Deer Flat National Wildlife Refuge, tel. 467-9278, which is administered by the U.S. Fish and Wildlife Service, protects 86 islands in the Snake River. Much of the refuge is closed to the public Oct. 1-April 14 to protect Pacific Flyway waterfowl—as many as 10,000 geese and 100,000 ducks have been counted here in this important wintering area. Boating is allowed during daylight hours April 15-Sept. 30. Water-skiing docks and marked swimming areas provided by Canyon County are located at the upper and lower dams. Refuge headquarters is located in Nampa along Lake Avenue. Regular hours are 7:30 a.m.-4 p.m. weekdays.

The 11,600-acre refuge proper is headquartered at the intersection of Lake and Lake Lowell avenues south of Nampa along Hwy. 55. A one-mile nature trail is laid out for refuge visitors there, and a picnic area and prime panfish and bass fishing draw the crowds during the summer. Established by President Teddy Roosevelt in 1909, Lake Lowell was formed to store irrigation water. The New York Canal diverts Boise River water into the 9,500-acre-lake. The lake provides a popular place for swimming and boating with three boat ramps for access.

Beginning south of Lake Lowell and extending northward to near the headwaters of Brownlee Reservoir and west of Weiser is the Snake River Islands sector. Fishing from shore here is banned during the Canada goose nesting season Feb. 1-May 31 each year. The river portion includes 107 islands that stretch 113 miles from the Canyon and Ada County line to Farewell Bend, Oregon.

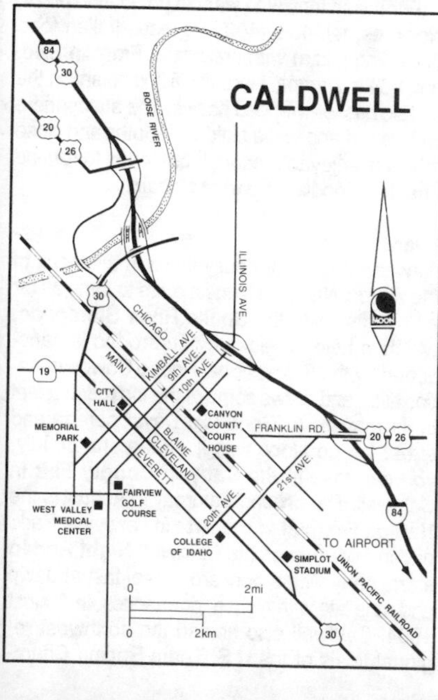

PRACTICALITIES

Accommodations

Caldwell's lodging ranges from **Manning House Bed and Breakfast Inn,** tel. 459-7899, at 1803 S. 10th Ave., which has two rooms for $45 and $50, to **Comfort Inn,** 901 Specht Ave., tel. 454-2222, with 65 rooms ranging $54-64. Other lodgings include the **Holiday Motel,** tel. 454-3888, at 512 Frontage Rd., with 24 rooms ranging $29-48, and the **Sundowner,** tel. 459-1585, at 102 Arthur St., with 68 rooms ranging $39-42. Campgrounds include **Aspen Village,** tel. 454-0553, with 15 campsites off I-84, Exit 26, and **Camp Caldwell Campground,** tel. 454-0279, off the same exit with 100 campsites ranging in price from $11 (for tents) to $18 (for full hookups).

Nampa's offering for the B&B trade is the Marshall House, tel. 466-8884. Located on the Northwest Nazarene College campus, the Marshall House offers rates ranging $31-45 for rooms with one or two beds. Children ages 6-12 may stay for an additional $5 apiece.

Nampa's motels reflect its larger size, with medium-to-large establishments making up the choices. **Shilo Inn,** tel. 466-8993, ranks as the largest with 61 rooms ranging $49-71 at 617

Nampa Boulevard. **Shilo Inn Nampa Suites,** tel. 465-3250, is located at 1401 Shilo Dr. and has a restaurant on site. The suites offer rooms from $59 to $65 for singles with additional people $6 a night. Facilities include steam and sauna rooms, an indoor pool, and a fitness center. Rooms with kitchenettes are available. **The Five Crowns Inn,** tel. 466-3594, has 43 rooms ranging $28-39 at 908 3rd St. South. The **Desert Inn,** at 115 9th Ave. S, tel. 467-1161, offers 40 rooms ranging $32-46. The **Alpine Villa Motel,** tel. 466-7819, at 124 3rd St. has 11 rooms for $30-40. **Starlite Motel,** tel. 466-9244, has 16 rooms at 320 11th Ave. N ranging $21-40.

Food

Nampa and Caldwell offer the full range of dining options from sandwich shops and pizza parlors to ethnic eateries and elegant restaurants.

For sandwiches, **Blimpies** at the Karcher Mall at Nampa, **Subway Sandwiches and Salads** at 1104 Caldwell Blvd., and **Ye Olde Deli Shoppe** at 122 12th Ave. S make between them just about every sandwich known to man. **Brick Oven Beanery,** at 16 12th Ave. S provides a welcoming atmosphere for families. **The Mall Cafe,** tel. 466-0822, at Nampa's Karcher Mall is another family favorite with its old-fashioned fountain. The **Red Sage Grill and Pub** is at 512 12th Ave. Rd. in Nampa, tel. 466-9233.

Fast-food restaurants are also well represented. **Kentucky Fried Chicken** is at 1003 E. Cleveland Blvd. in Caldwell, and at 177 Caldwell Blvd. at Nampa. **McDonald's** is at 2923 E. Cleveland Blvd. in Caldwell, and at 148 Caldwell Blvd. in Nampa. **Wendy's Old Fashioned Hamburgers** is at 600 N. 10th Ave. in Caldwell, and at 1028 Caldwell Blvd. in Nampa. **Taco Time** restaurants can be found at 2605 Blaine in Caldwell and 1015 3rd St. S in Nampa.

Pizza parlors offer as much or more variety at fast-food prices. **Keystone Pizza** is at 9th and Arthur in Caldwell, tel. 454-3044. **Mancino's Pizza** offers shops in both Caldwell and Nampa. In Caldwell, they're located at 2404 E. Cleveland Blvd., tel. 459-7556, and in Nampa at 220 1/2 Holly, tel. 466-2129. **Pizza Hut** parlors are here too at 140 Caldwell Blvd., tel. 467-4252, in Nampa, and 710 N. 10th Ave., tel. 454-1341, in Caldwell. **Round Table Pizza** is at 4816 E. Cleveland Blvd., tel. 454-3000, in Caldwell and at 12th and Iowa, tel. 467-1900 in Nampa.

Steak houses in the area cater to the serious meat-eater. **Sizzler** serves up steaks at 501 Caldwell Blvd. in Nampa, tel. 466-8570, and **Cattlemen's Livestock Cafe,** tel. 454-1785, grills 'em at 1900 E. Chicago in Caldwell.

Fine-dining restaurants include **Key Largo,** tel. 466-8181, at 623 Caldwell Blvd. in Nampa with its menu of steaks, prime rib, and seafood; and **Black Canyon Restaurant,** tel. 454-8448, just off the freeway at 5240 Black Canyon Exit.

Ethnic cuisine abounds in Nampa and Caldwell with Mexican fare ranking first. **Acapulco,** tel. 465-0073, is at Longbranch Station in Nampa. Homegrown versions that offer a wider variety of individual styles include **El Charro,** tel. 467-5804, at 1701 1st St. N in Nampa; and **El Rinconcito,** tel. 466-6963, at 824 1st St. South. **Art's Casa,** tel. 467-6811, is located at 1125 Caldwell Blvd. in Nampa.

Chinese cuisine fans will find the **Jade Garden Restaurant,** tel. 467-6611, at 1514 Caldwell Blvd. (across from the Karcher Mall) in Nampa; **Shanghai Restaurant,** tel. 466-2921, at 332 Caldwell Blvd; and the **Asia Restaurant,** tel. 459-4303, at 703 Main in Caldwell, which also includes Japanese dishes on its menu.

For Italian fans who want to go beyond pizza, **Noodles,** tel. 466-4400, promises Italian food (including pizza) with pizzazz at Franklin Blvd. and I-84 in Nampa. Here you'll find chianti in the classic basket-wrapped bottles. The atmosphere with its red-and-white plaid tablecloths and close tables is enjoyable enough but tends to remind one that Noodles is part of a chain.

Events

July and August are busy times in this neck of the woods. Nampa's biggest claim to fame as far as events go is the **Snake River Stampede,** which is held in mid-July. The rodeo is sanctioned by the Professional Rodeo Cowboys Association and draws some of the top rodeo talent in the nation. A "Good Old Days" parade and street fair go along with it. At the end of July, you can take in the **Canyon County Fair** in Caldwell. The second Saturday in August is the **Nampa Festival of the Arts** in Lakeview Park, and in mid-August, the **Caldwell Night Rodeo** starts early with a buckaroo breakfast at dawn and runs late with night performances. In August 1994, Caldwell also hosted the northwest regional finals of the U.S. Team Roping Championships. For more information about these events, contact the Caldwell Chamber of Commerce at 300 Frontage Rd., tel. 459-7493.

Golf

Golfers have the nine-hole **Fairview Golf Course,** tel. 455-3090, and 18-hole **Purple Sage Golf Course,** tel. 459-2223, to keep them occupied while visiting Caldwell. **Nampa Centennial Golf Course,** tel. 467-3011, offers 18 holes open to the public. **Broadmore Country Club,** tel. 466-1114, is a private course with nine holes.

Information And Services

Write the **Caldwell Chamber of Commerce** at P.O. Box 819, Caldwell, ID 83606, or call 459-7493. The **Nampa Chamber of Commerce,** tel. 466-4641, is at 1305 3rd St. S, Nampa, ID 83653. The **Canyon County Sheriff's Office,** tel. 454-7531, is located at 1115 E. Albany at Caldwell. **Caldwell Police,** tel. 455-3123, are located at 605 Main. **Nampa Police,** tel. 465-2257, are at 211 12th Ave. South. (In both Caldwell and Nampa, call 911 in emergencies.) Nampa is served by **Mercy Medical Center,** tel. 467-1171, at 1512 12th Ave. Road. **West Valley Medical Center,** tel. 459-4641, is at 10th and Logan in Caldwell. **Caldwell Library,** tel. 459-3242, is located at 1010 Dearborn. **Nampa Public Library,** tel. 465-2263, is located at 101 11th Ave. South.

OWYHEE COUNTY

The Owyhee Mountains, Owyhee Desert, Owyhee County, and Owyhee River in the extreme southwestern corner of the state all harken back to the earliest days of settlement. "Owyhee" is an archaic form of Hawaii; the region was dubbed this because fur-trading companies that stopped here en route to the mouth of the Columbia River and the wide Pacific often had Hawaiian crewmen. In 1818 Donald MacKenzie sent a brigade of Hawaiians south to trap along the Snake River. They were lost on the journey and **Kanaka Rapids** marks their passage. The high northern desert here is still a lonely place. That's just fine with folks eager to flee the bustle of Boise or the expanding Nampa-Caldwell community.

Owyhee County is the state's second largest, encompassing 4.9 million acres. Its population is one of the smallest, with only about 8,500 souls at any given time. Most of them live in the towns of **Homedale** and **Marsing** along the Snake River or **Murphy,** the county seat, not far away from the river. The wagon ruts of the Overlander's covered wagons persist in perhaps more places here than anywhere else in Idaho, because much of the land remains untouched. Like the emigrants, most of the miners and others who accompanied them in their frantic rushes to find easy gold before someone else did were just passing through. The county's gold rush towns of Silver City, Del Lamar, Ruby City, and Flint collectively once held more population than the entire county does today. The county's past at times seems more vibrant and alive than its present.

SIGHTS

Island Park

Marsing's Island Park recalls with a historical marker what was once the town's main claim to fame. George Froman's ferry operated here from 1888 to 1921, when it was superseded by a steel bridge. The ferry used ropes attached to a pulley that slid along a cable spanning the river. The current would swing the ferry back and forth, depending on which direction its nose was pointed by the ferryman.

Marsing To Murphy

Southeast of Marsing along Hwy. 78 is **Givens Hot Springs,** a campground and hot springs that was used by Oregon Trail travelers as early as 1842. The remains of pit houses discovered here show native peoples used the springs between 4,300 and 1,200 years ago as well. Givens Hot Springs has the distinction of being one of the oldest commercial hot springs in Idaho, with operations dating back to 1881. Although the Oregon Trail has been erased by highway building and farming along the Snake, ruts are still visible just a little more than two miles from where Hwy. 78 takes a sharp jog south heading for Murphy. There, the ruts run within 100 yards of the highway's eastern shoulder for more than a mile. Murphy's main attraction is the **Owyhee County Historical Complex.** The ranching town is better known, perhaps, for the lingering image of its lone parking meter in front of the county courthouse.

Silver City

Five miles south of Murphy along Hwy. 78 is the junction of the Silver City Road, which leads up into the Owyhee Mountains and straight back into the past. Silver City is the queen of Idaho's ghost towns. Founded in 1863, it succeeded Ruby City, which in turn had succeeded Boonville. Silver City prospered as some of the West's richest veins of gold were opened there. The Poorman and War Eagle mines were among the richest; War Eagle yielded $30 million in ore during its first decade.

The Poorman's discovery prompted an armed showdown when owners of a nearby mine contended, rightly, that the golden ledge angled in the direction of the claim they were already working. The dispute was eventually settled without shots being fired.

Shots *were* fired and two men died during an underground war in March 1868 between workers of the Golden Chariot and Idaho Elmore mines. The Idaho Elmore's owner, J. Marion More, for whom More's Creek is named, was shot in the head during the dispute. Governor D.W. Ballard dispatched a deputy marshal to calm things down. When that failed, Ballard followed up by ordering 95 cavalry men from Fort Boise to ride to Silver City and take control.

The violence didn't stop the town from growing larger after Silas Skinner completed a toll road in 1866 to supply the mines. The *Owyhee Avalanche,* the territory's first (and once widely regarded as the best) newspaper, chronicled the town's rise. By 1867, it had two schools, one meeting in the assay office. Silver City's Catholic Church, its first house of worship, was built in 1868. The church still stands on its hilltop rise.

Mining is a business of booms and busts. Silver City's rich veins proved to run shallow. After the town began to fail, it was a steady slide downhill from there. By the 1930s all but the dreams had died. Murphy became the Owyhee County seat in 1934; Silver City's school closed its doors in 1938. In 1943, the U.S. Postal Service closed up the post office. In the 1940s, Silver City gained notoriety again, this time as a one-man town with Will Hawes as its last resident.

For modern visitors, Silver City is a way to experience history—to contemplate the past in the solitude of the present. The Idaho Hotel now serves as the town's social center and the source of information and limited supplies. In mingling with the past, visitors these days must preserve what they can for the future by doing no damage. Self-preservation should also be a conscious effort. Avoid entering hazardous buildings or exploring around old mineshafts.

PRACTICALITIES

Accommodations

Visitors can experience Silver City's history firsthand by staying at **The Idaho Hotel,** tel. 495-2520. The hotel oversees 12 campsites that are free and offers 20 rooms which are rented on a donation basis. This is definitely an opportunity to step back in time. The services are minimal, water by the pitcher, the restroom is just a short hop to the back. The furnishings, like the amenities, are sometimes direct reflections of what visitors would have found in the 19th century. Staying here with an oil lamp for light and moonlight dappling the room through waving curtains is like a night spent in history. **Silver City Cabins,** tel. 583-2868, offers three cabins for rent ranging $20-40.

Near Marsing, **Givens Hot Springs,** tel. 495-2000, has 17 RV sites with hookups (water and electricity) for $8.50 a night, and lots of space for tent camping at $5 a night (which includes water and shower privileges).

Food

Homedale, northwest of Marsing on Hwy. 95, offers the most selections among Owyhee County restaurants, beginning with **Ferdinand's Pizza** at 6 N. Main. Cafes include **Freddy's,** at 19 W. Idaho; **Frosty Palace,** at 32 E. Idaho; and the **Homedale Drive-In,** at 305 E. Idaho, which features broasted chicken. Other Homedale eateries include **Jane and Jerry's Restaurant** at 120 W. Idaho; **Owyhee Lanes and Restaurant** at 18 N. 1st W; and **Tango Lounge and Cafe** at 2 W. Idaho, which features live music.

The **Sandbar River House Restaurant** in Marsing, tel. 896-4124, is one of the region's finer restaurants, with a good selection of state and regional wines. **Rubble's Roadhouse** along Main St. promises home cooking seven days a week.

Owyhee County Fair And Rodeo
Homedale's main event is the Owyhee County Fair and Rodeo which is held in early August.

Information And Services
Visitor information is available at **Marsing City Hall,** tel. 896-4122, P.O. Box 125, Marsing, ID 83639. Police services are handled through the **Owyhee County Sheriff,** tel. 495-1154 (emergencies and business), in Murphy.

MOUNTAIN HOME AND VICINITY

Mountain Home started civic life as Rattlesnake Station along the old Overland Stage Line, which ran for 20 years beginning in 1864. When the Union Pacific Railroad arrived in 1883 to replace the stage lines, Mountain Home was moved down Rattlesnake Creek to its present location. The city is now best known for the Mountain Home Air Force Base, home to F-111A tactical fighter-bombers. To the south of Mountain Home on Hwy. 51 is Bruneau and the nearby Bruneau River Canyon and Bruneau Dunes State Park.

SIGHTS

Mountain Home Air Force Base
For tours of the base, which lies 10 miles southeast of Mountain Home, call the public affairs office, tel. 828-6800. Mountain Home is Idaho's only active military base, employing 4,000 civilian and military workers, and is home to the 366th Tactical Fighter Wing. Defense Department spending priorities have been shifting in recent years, posing varying scenarios for the base's future. Plans range from a growth phase, during which other fighter wings would be relocated here, to eventual shutdown. The military gave Mountain Home a vote of confidence during the belt tightening of the early 1990s by transferring a composite wing of fighters and bombers to Mountain Home.

The base's future ignited a controversy as Gov. Cecil Andrus pitched a proposal to expand the size of the base's desert training range. Idaho's conservationists in general and sportsmen in particular, with the help of the Idaho Fish and Game Commission, rebelled. The commission, which oversees the protection of the state's wildlife, voted to oppose the governor's plan for a split training range. The range's northern area, wildlife advocates said, threatened the fawning area for a major pronghorn antelope herd. They also complained there was minimal assurance that Air Force planes would not damage the California bighorn sheep herd that is thriving in the canyons of the Bruneau and Jarbidge rivers.

The base's past is much more clear. The Elmore County site for the base was chosen over another candidate near Jerome because land was cheaper: the government bought up private holdings in the area for $1-2 an acre. The base was approved Nov. 30, 1942, and by Aug. 7 of the following year, the main runways, both 10,000 feet long, were available for operations. By the end of August 1943, the job was nearly done after $13 million had been spent on construction. The base was formally christened in mid-October 1944.

The base encompasses 10,000 acres and oversees the Saylor Creek Bombing and Electronic Combat Range 20 miles to the southeast. The F-111A fighter-bomber crews use the range for their main training. Recently, the Air Force found Idahoans weren't willing to give up much more land, even in the Owyhee Desert, for a new bombing range. They launched a major expansion proposal in 1989 only to find it drew heavy flak from an angry public before it was abandoned.

Mountain Home also has the **Elmore County Historical Museum,** which preserves artifacts of emigrants, miners, and ranchers who populated the county's past.

Bruneau Dunes State Park
Bruneau Dunes State Park, tel. 366-7919, about 12 miles south of Mountain Home off Hwy. 51, draws a surprisingly loyal contingent of fans to what some call Idaho's Sahara. At 470 feet high, the principal sand dune here dominates the setting with its impressive bulk and ranks as the largest in the Northwest. It and other ridges of sand cover more than 600 acres.

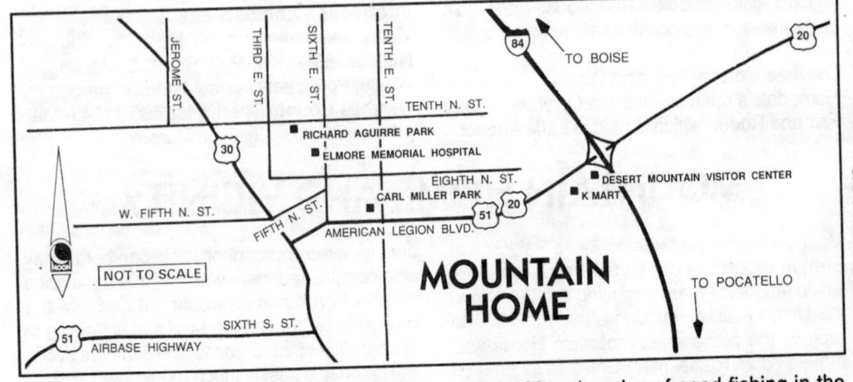

First-time visitors to Bruneau Dunes generally waste little time before exploring, running down through the sugary gray sand, or just walking along the dune crests. Children love the dunes, breaking away from their parents to dig holes, roll down the sandy slopes, or pursue any one of a thousand sandbox fantasies.

Visitors can be more inventive, too. Old skis, those worn and battered warriors that have seen their best days on snow, end up here in one of the stranger athletic activities, sand-skiing.

The dunes themselves are thought to have resulted from the Bonneville Flood some 30,000 years ago. The flood eroded sand from Eagle Cove, the semicircle carved in the surrounding mesa by the ancient Snake River, and began piling it up here. Arid winds off southern Idaho's high desert have continually added more sand to the dunes. The sheltered nature of the cove and some unusual wind patterns help keep the sand piles intact. NASA found the dunes so intriguing, particularly the circular pit where the two main dunes meet, that it paid for a study. According to records from the nearby Mountain Home Air Force Base, the wind blows southeasterly 28% of the time and northwesterly 32% of the time. What one wind pushes away, the other pushes back, apparently.

Bruneau Dunes are less arid now than they were when Oregon Trail travelers first ventured by more than 100 years ago. The reason is a rising water table brought on by irrigating the fertile Snake River Plain. The higher water table has created two large ponds at the base of the dunes. The ponds now boast sizable numbers of bluegill sunfish in particular, and some channel catfish. After decades of good fishing in the park, anglers became concerned in the mid-1980s when changing irrigation practices led to dropping water levels. The Idaho Fish and Game Department responded to the loss by installing a pipeline to the Snake River to refill the ponds. The ponds have also become important as a new home for endangered trumpeter swans, which were transplanted here from the Henry's Fork of the Snake River to relieve overcrowding there.

Early spring (March and April) also sees campers here by the score. The park is normally green then, unlike the rest of the year when its basic color is the brown of dried grasses. The number of campers visiting the park wilts with the summer heat. Those who do camp here are generally out and around at sunrise or sunset, or are simply passing through.

The park's air-conditioned **visitor center** becomes a hit when the mercury climbs above 100 degrees. Inside are all kinds of quirky and interesting specimens, including a barbed wire collection, some fascinating fossils ranging from laminated mammoth molars to a sabertooth-tiger skull with both canines broken off, and a display case holding scorpions. While scorpions do live here at Bruneau Dunes, they are seldom if ever seen.

For those who don't find the stinger-tailed scorpion creepy enough, the black widow spider loves Bruneau Dunes, too. The visitor center at times keeps a shiny black widow in a jar on the counter. It's a great chance to see the red hourglass that identifies her, if your phobia doesn't happen to involve *Arachnida*. If there isn't a black widow on the counter, just cast a careful eye around. You'll probably find evidence of them somewhere close by in the form of delicate little patches of web.

The rest of the park's wildlife tends to be a little more inviting. Lizards include horned toads, which really are lizards, that favor the sandy soil around ant hills. Leopard and collared lizards are also present but can be difficult to find. The most likely reptile that visitors will spot is the side-blotched or sagebrush lizard.

In addition to the swans, waterfowl by the hundreds stop by the ponds during the migratory season. During the nesting season, cinnamon teal, American coots, mergansers, and mallards are likely candidates for the bird list. Mule deer, coyotes, badgers, and ground squirrels are the most numerous mammals in the park.

Bruneau Scenic Canyon

The Bruneau River joins the Snake River northwest of Bruneau. Its mild-mannered confluence with the Snake gives barely a clue about the geologic violence it has endured. The Bruneau tears its way through one of the starkest and most abrupt river canyons in the state. To reach the canyon, travelers turn southeast at Bruneau and take what begins as a paved road south past Indian Bathtub or **Bruneau Hot Springs.** After 16 miles of what can become a very rough road, a spur road heads west. After three miles the spur yields an impressive view of a very steep-walled canyon at **Bruneau Overlook.** The canyon here is 800 feet deep and only 1,300 feet wide.

C.J. Strike Reservoir

Idaho Power Company's C.J. Strike Reservoir also is close to Mountain Home. Motorists traveling south on Hwy. 51 cross over the reservoir before reaching Bruneau. The best way to reach the dam and campground nearby, however, is via Hwy. 67, which travels southwest from Mountain View to Grand View. The reservoir offers some of Idaho's best bass and crappie fishing. Rainbow trout fishing can also produce some tasty catches. Another important contingent that uses the reservoir is the boating crowd, both those with sailboats and those with high-speed ski boats. Two boat ramps are available at C.J. Strike Dam, one above and one below.

Snake River Birds Of Prey Natural Area

The Snake River Birds of Prey Area draws a large number of rafters to the base of C.J. Strike Dam to launch spring floats down the Snake, the only way to see the greatest concentration of nesting birds of prey in the United States. No roads reach into the Snake River Canyon from here to **Swan Falls Dam** south of Kuna. Outfitters offer guided float trips down the Snake. The **Idaho Outfitters and Guides Association,** tel. 342-1919, maintains a list of outfitters licensed for float trips on this portion of the Snake. (See also "Birds of Prey," under "Exploring Boise," in that city's chapter.)

PRACTICALITIES

Accommodations

Mountain Home is the base of operations both for the Air Force and for travelers in this part of Idaho. Lodging here includes the **Best Western Foothills Motor Inn,** tel. 587-8477, at 1080 Hwy. 20, with a swimming pool and 76 rooms for $32-45. **Hi Lander Motel and Steak House,** tel. 587-3311, is at 614 S. 3rd W with 34 rooms for $26-49 and a swimming pool. **Motel Thunderbird,** tel. 587-7927, has 27 rooms ranging $20-32 at 910 Sunset Strip. **Towne Center Motel,** tel. 587-3373, has 32 rooms ranging $24-30 at 410 N. 2nd East.

Camping

Campers will find the **Mountain Home KOA,** tel. 587-5111, with 50 spaces renting for $10 and up at 22 E. 10th North. **Bruneau Dunes State Park,** tel. 366-7919, is 18 miles south of Mountain Home and has 48 campsites. North of Mountain Home, off Hwy. 20 in the Pine-Featherville area, is **Deer Creek Lodge,** tel. 653-2454, which has 12 rooms for $29 and 26 camping sites for $10 with hookups, $4.50 without.

The **Mountain Home Ranger District,** tel. 587-7961, at 2180 American Legion Blvd. maintains a string of campgrounds to the north of Mountain Home and Hwy. 20 toward Pine, Featherville, and Atlanta. Rangers suggest that those camping in the district pick up their free travel map to the area. A fire in 1992 blackened parts of the area and logging of the burnt areas continues, mandating road closures in some places. The map indicates the closed areas.

Food

Mountain Home may not shout the worldwide nature of its citizens through its restaurants but Joe's Cafe earns praise as a source of excellent international meals. Mexican dominates the ethnic cuisines, as might be expected. **Carlos' Mexican Style Family Dining,** tel. 587-2966, is at 1525 American Legion Boulevard. **Cavazos Mexican Food,** tel. 587-9900, is located at 2150 Sunset Strip. The **Top Hat Restaurant,** tel. 587-9223, at 170 N. Main specializes in brisket, ribs, and catfish. Scrubby's Smokehouse Restaurant, tel. 832-7074, delivers and specializes in pizza and Texas pit-style barbecue. They're one mile north of the airbase on Airbase Road. Other pizza places include **Pizza Place,** tel. 587-8432, at 210 E. 5th N; and **Pizza Hut,** tel. 587-4405, at 605 Airbase Road.

Other eating choices include **El Rancho** at the corner of Main and Jackson, tel. 587-2088; and **Maple Cove Restaurant,** tel. 587-9781, at 720 E. Hwy. 30. **Stoney's Desert Inn** near I-84 along Hwy. 30 bills itself as the place where truckers stop.

Festivals

Mountain Home's biggest event is **Air Force Appreciation Day,** which is held the first Saturday following the Labor Day holiday each September. **Ag Day** is held by Mountain Home residents in late July to celebrate the industry that forms the economic backbone of the area.

Golf

Mountain Home offers golfers two nine-hole courses; one, **Desert Canyon Golf Course,** tel. 587-3293, is open to the public and will soon be expanded to 18 holes. The other, **Silver Sage Golf Course,** is for the military.

Information And Services

The **Mountain Home Chamber of Commerce,** tel. 587-4334, is located at 165 E. 2nd N, P.O. Box 3, Mountain Home, ID 83647. The **Mountain Home Police Department,** tel. 587-2100, is located at 125 S. 5th East. The **Elmore County Sheriff,** tel. 587- 2100 or 911, is at the same address. **Elmore Medical Center,** tel. 587-8401, is located at 895 N. 6th East.

IDAHO CITY AND VICINITY

Silver City to the southwest may have been Queen of the Owyhees, but history has been kinder to Idaho City, the Boise County seat and center of the Boise Basin. Close enough to Boise to benefit from a portion of its economy, Idaho City persists in part because some are willing to commute here despite the 40-mile trek from the capital. If there's a reason for their endurance, it must be the beauty of the surroundings during the drive.

Idaho City was founded by a party of miners led by J. Marion More on Oct. 7, 1862. More's Creek is named in his honor. More, the man who helped jostle Idaho toward its eventual statehood as much as anyone of the period, died at Silver City, the victim of a squabble over gold there. In 1863, it should be noted, Idaho City's 6,275 residents made it the most populous city in the Pacific Northwest.

In 1864 Idaho City was still riding high but when it coveted the territorial capital, then at Lewiston, it lost out to rival Boise City down in the valley. The Boise Basin surrounding Idaho City was a place of ambition and greed. More's and Elk creeks bore witness to the ravages that gold fever could bring: long sinuous tailing piles and huge barren gravel bars created by hydraulic giants. Miners thought little about washing away entire hillsides to get down to the gold-bearing gravel beneath.

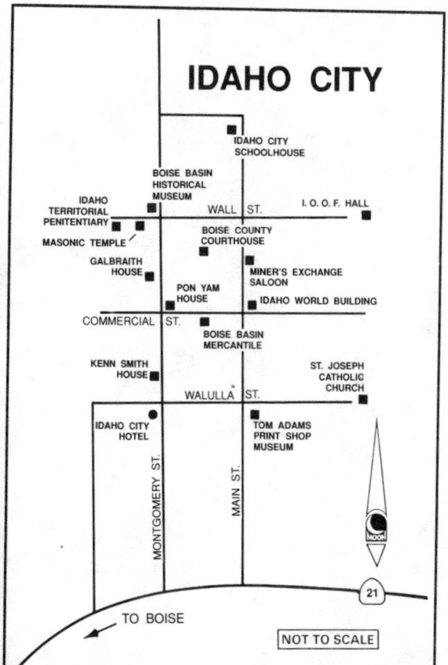

With its background, it's not surprising that Idaho City is also the main route into other Idaho gold rush communities, including Placerville to the northwest toward Garden Valley and Pioneerville along Grimes Creek.

In addition to Idaho City's historic buildings, the **Boise Basin Historical Museum,** tel. 392-4550, at Wall and Montgomery offers a closer view of what the old placer miners did and what their lives were like. **Boot Hill Cemetery** near town reveals another aspect of the miners life through some colorful epitaphs.

PRACTICALITIES

Accommodations

Camping has been part of the Boise Basin's heritage since the great gold rushes. The Boise National Forest's **Idaho City Ranger District,** tel. 392-6681, maintains a couple of cabins and a bevy of campgrounds east of the city. Most of the national forest campgrounds are east of Hwy. 21 and Idaho City, and most offer a respite from city congestion along rushing streams and slopes carpeted by ponderosa pines. For RVers with self-contained units, the Idaho City Community Center and city shop provides a free dump station to empty the tank. In the private sector, **Steamboat Gulch Recreation,** tel. 342-0750, has 17 campsites a mile and a half southeast of Idaho City along Hwy. 21.

Prospector Motel, tel. 392-4290, offers seven rooms ranging $31-47. **Idaho City Hotel** at the same phone number has five rooms in the same price range.

Food

Gold Pan Cafe, Chalet Drive-In along Hwy. 21, **Clear Creek Lodge** along Clear Creek, and **Diamond Lil's** at 401 Main provide the alternatives for Idaho City diners.

Recreation

From Idaho City, Nordic skiers flock north some 15 miles to the **Whoop-Um-Up Creek Park 'n' Ski Area** with four miles of trails (some of which require advanced abilities), plowed parking lot, and restroom. Two miles beyond is **Gold Fork Park 'n' Ski Area,** which offers eight miles of marked trails that are groomed periodically. **Banner Ridge Park 'n' Ski Area** is 20 miles north of Idaho City and offers 16 miles of trails that are suitable for intermediate to expert skiers.

Granite Peak Snow Park, three miles east of Idaho City, draws the snowmobiling crowd with access to 50 miles of groomed snowmobile trails and 150 miles of snow-covered Forest Service roads.

Information And Services

The **Idaho City Chamber of Commerce** can be reached at 392-4372. Police services are performed by the **Boise County Sheriff,** tel. 392-4411, at 415 Main Street.

CATHY CARLSON

SOUTH~CENTRAL IDAHO

Boise ranks as Idaho's most visible city, but south-central Idaho is a strong contender for the state's most representative area. Sun Valley, good snow, glitter, and a wide-open beauty are here. The area also includes the Sawtooths, fields of potatoes on the rich Snake River Plain, great big patches of the sagebrush desert, and Silver Creek, one of the holy waters of trout fishing in America.

Craters of the Moon National Monument is here, as is the Snake River Canyon, where daredevil Evel Knievel made his unsuccessful flying leap on a rocket-powered motorcycle. By contrast, the emigrants made a habit of successfully reaching the other side of the Snake River here, at Glenns Ferry where three islands break the flow into manageable sections.

The area's rich farm fields exist because of the dams that block the Snake's flow. The same dams from Twin Falls northwest to Bliss provide some exciting reservoirs to water-ski, fish, and otherwise escape the desertlike surroundings of the sagebrush plain.

WEST OF TWIN FALLS

The Snake River played a dominant role in the development of southern Idaho, and nowhere is this more obvious than in the stretch from Glenns Ferry through the Hagerman Valley toward Twin Falls. The two state parks along this stretch of the Snake are both river-oriented and are also easily reached from I-84.

THREE ISLAND CROSSING STATE PARK

Three Island Crossing State Park, P.O. Box 609, Glenns Ferry, ID 83623, tel. 366-2394, was purchased by the state's expanding parks

WESTERN BAPTISM

The Snake River Plain terrified Overlanders on their way to the Oregon country. Water was scarce on the high plain and the crossing of the river itself treacherous. Three Island Crossing was one of the Snake's two major fords. Most emigrants preferred it because the islands divided the river's force. In late summer, the stream was shallow enough most years to provide a safe crossing for heavy wagons and the oxen or horses that pulled them.

An excellent publication by the Idaho Historical Society preserves passages from pioneer diaries regarding the crossing here. Missionaries Marcus and Narcissa Whitman, who helped blaze the Oregon Trail, had seen the cart and pair of mules they were crossing with turned upside down by the current. "The mules would have been drowned but for a desperate struggle to get them ashore," notes Narcissa, in a diary entry dated Aug. 13, 1836. On Aug. 21, 1851, Elizabeth Wood forded the Snake "which runs so swift that the drivers (four to a team) had to hold on to the ox yokes to keep from being swept down by the current."

Not all was dangerously dramatic about the crossing, however. "On the 10th of September, we crossed the Snake River by fording without difficulty, and in crossing we killed a salmon weighing twenty-three pounds, one of our wagons running over it as it lay on the bottom of the pebbly stream," noted Peter H. Burnett on that date in 1843.

Most of the Overlanders crossed the river from 1841 to 1848. By the mid-1860s the tides of emigration had largely passed the crossing by. Today, it is easy to contemplate the Overlanders' troubles: a Conestoga wagon replica occupies a shelter near the Oregon Trail's route through the park. Pause at the wagon and consider the limited room inside. Where would all the supplies fit? At the visitor center, note the iron shoes. Long on endurance, these shoes must have extracted a price from their wearer in other ways.

A beaten path and wooden markers show the route of the old trail through the sagebrush. Whether the path was etched by Overlanders or has been blazed by modern visitors is difficult to say. But across the river on the facing bluff, experienced trail-watchers can spot where the pioneers made their way down to the river. Walking along the present trail, real or not, gives children an excellent chance to imagine what it must have been like to walk hundreds of miles across the West, fearful of Indian attacks much of the way.

department in 1968 to preserve the point where the Oregon Trail crossed the Snake.

Three Island is one of those comfortable parks where a first-time visitor wonders why he hasn't stopped to spend a night before. The prime camping spots here are on the bluff overlooking the Snake as it floods the valley floor with silver. The **visitor center** offers some excellent displays of Oregon Trail history. And the stars that dominate the night sky here are worth a visit in themselves. Glenns Ferry is a small town and doesn't cast too big a glow into the night sky. As a result, every two-bit shooting star and every satellite remains visible.

In August, **Glenns Ferry** enthusiastically supports a dramatic re-creation of the Overlanders' crossing here. In some ways, paying homage to the difficult ford is the least the town can do. After all, Gus Glenn, the town's namesake, put the old ford out of business in 1869 when he built a ferry about two miles upstream.

Wildlife

Wildlife in the park includes a herd of longhorns, the progenitors of which were a gift from the state of Oklahoma. The longhorns now appear as a park curiosity, but in the late 1800s, southern Idaho cattle ranchers believed the breed was their future because of its hardiness. The winter of 1888 proved even the longhorn was not immune to weather extremes. Deep snow and bitter cold that winter devastated the herds.

The park also was once home to a herd of buffalo brought from the National Bison Range at Moiese, Montana. Unfortunately, the difficult-to-manage buffalo became too much of a headache and liability for the state and were shipped out to other locations.

Other interesting wildlife can still be found here, though. Badgers roam through the park. So do coyotes. Both come for a chance to find a jackrabbit, although the badgers probably prefer ground squirrels if the choice is available.

Among the park's birdlife, some of the most dramatic and watchable species include meadowlarks, which love to perch in the tops of sagebrush and sing the strains of spring; and bold white pelicans, which cruise the Snake River's placid surface during the summer, looking for their next meal. In winter, the pelicans migrate south to more familiar habitat, the Great Salt Lake.

MALAD GORGE STATE PARK

The Big Wood River is one of Idaho's best-loved trout streams. Malad Gorge State Park, tel. 837-4505, offers one of the most spectacular settings along the entire river, yet few anglers come here. The park's name offers one obvious clue. For visitors, a quick glance tells it all. The river ends at the crest of the falls that adorn the Devil's Washbowl, where the Malad River begins. The 60-foot falls and churning pool at their base create one of the most dramatic sights in the entire parks system. While the Malad River also holds trout, access to this 2.5-mile river involves too much of a climb down for most anglers starting at the park.

Geology

The park proper runs more than a mile along the canyon, offering several points where visitors can stop to contemplate the geologic forces that created this place. The best known vista point at Devil's Washbowl is within a few yards of I-84. Few speeding by along the interstate know the beauty of this canyon.

The Malad River here has dug itself quite a hole. One school of geologic thought believes the canyon was formed about a million years ago as the torrent from an ancient glacier cascaded over the Snake River's canyon rim. Bit by bit, the waterfall created the canyon, zigzagging its way along the weakest zones in the rock. Some of the minor channels followed by the impressive flow still appear along the hiking trail.

Some geologists believe the Big Wood and Malad occupy a canyon carved by the great Bonneville Flood, which occurred when Lake Bonneville escaped Utah via the Snake River Canyon through Red Rock Pass near Pocatello. Weeks of roaring waters, almost unbelievable in their scope and power, overflowed the Snake River's normal channel, ripping and plucking any loose rocks in their path. These rocks, called melon gravel because of their giant size, still litter some of the flat ledges along the Malad Gorge. Look for the melon gravel—when you can tear your eyes off the majesty of this gorge, of course. The canyon walls are 250 feet deep and, at Devil's Washbowl, only 140 feet wide.

Natural Springs

The canyon is also lined with springs, thought to originate from the Lost River some 100 miles to the northeast. The Big and Little Lost rivers disappear dramatically in swirling sinks. They reappear just as dramatically here and elsewhere along the Snake in the famous **Thousand**

Rafters accept the Snake River's challenge near Hagerman.

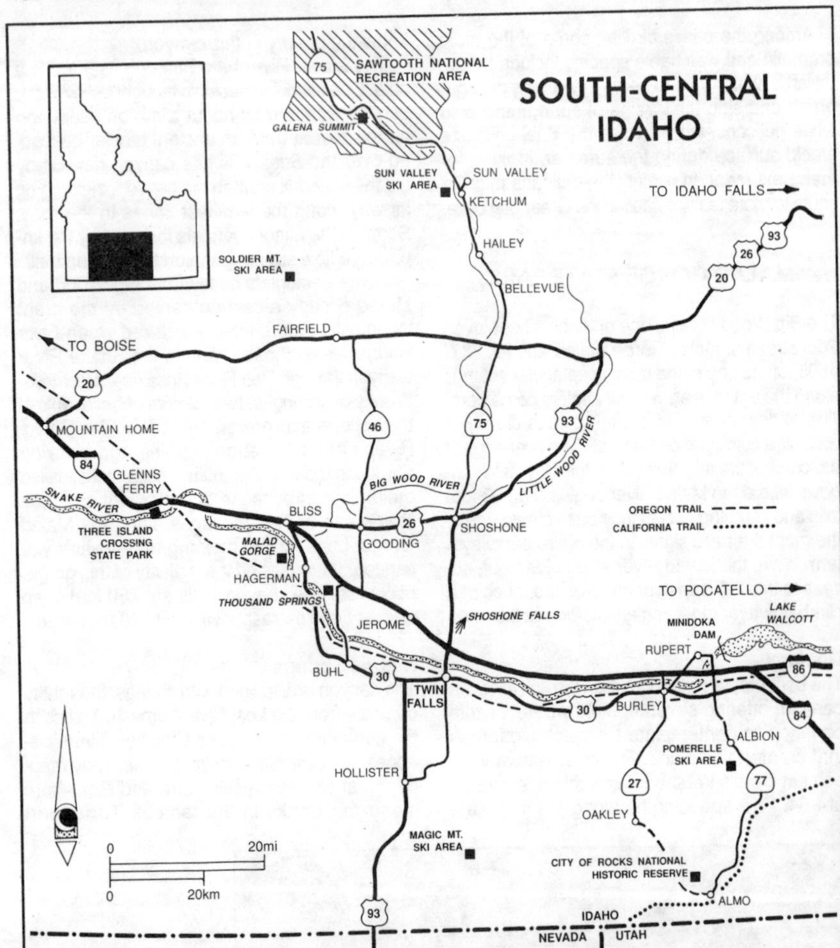

Springs area, about 10 miles southeast of Malad Gorge. The park's two other units, **Niagara Springs** and **Crystal Springs,** are much more accessible than the springs lining the bottom of the gorge.

Malad's springs offer unique chances to fish and enjoy some of the least developed springs still available to the public. Niagara Springs ought to be a stop in any steelhead fisherman's pilgrimage. The **Hagerman National Fish Hatchery,** tel. 837-4892, near the park unit is one of the most reliable producers of young seagoing rainbow trout. The spring's pure waters and consistent temperatures make them ideal for hatcheries, and one of the world's most extensive aquaculture industries devoted to trout has grown up around them. The fish from Niagara sometimes can be found in the Snake, Salmon, and Clearwater rivers.

History

During the last 15,000 years, plenty of people have undoubtedly stopped to visit the gorge, whether in wonder or consternation at the ob-

(Top) An old log cabin near Stanley bears witness to the rugged nature of the Sawtooths.
(Bottom) Shoshone Falls near Twin Falls sparkles along the Snake River. (PHOTOS BILL LOFTUS)

Black Lead Mountain reigns over the upper reaches of Kelly Creek in north-central Idaho. (PHOTO BILL LOFTU

stacle it presented. Sometime around the great Bonneville Flood, nomadic hunters first crossed into southern Idaho. On a point along the canyon a primitive blind, little more than a pile of rocks, still shows where some ancient hunter once lay in wait for passing antelope. Or was the quarry some more exotic beast? Some 7,000 years ago, permanent villages of the western Shoshone culture began to appear. The villagers were fed by the rivers' wealth of salmon, a wealth now mostly squandered in Idaho.

Malade, Riviere Malades, and Sickly River were all names for the stream beneath the park. Researchers who have exhaustively traced Idaho's place names indicate a trapping party led by Donald Mackenzie originated the name first in 1819. Several parties of trappers, however, apparently ate beaver from the lower river and soon wished they hadn't.

Near Devil's Washbowl, faint traces exist of a more recent chapter in the area's history. The scattered rocks still forming the remains of walls mark the location of one of some two dozen stops along the Kelton Road. Mule skinners and freight wagons were the main travelers along the route, which fell from favor in 1879. The park's modern history may be said to begin with the purchase of lands to complete the department's 652 acres surrounding the gorge. But the park itself was not opened until 1979.

Park Highlights

A picnic shelter and the lawn near the gorge offer a good chance to stop along the highway during the summer travel season. Scenic overlooks along the canyon rim route offer more interpretations of the lay of the land and its history. At one such overlook on an April day, the discerning eye can pick out a golden eagle protectively shielding its nest on a cove-like cliff. Mule deer often bounce along through the sagebrush lining the canyon walls. There is even a herd of elk that occasionally passes through. Have mercy on the marmots: these little yellow-bellied rockchucks barrel across the road along the canyon rim with abandon.

A footbridge across the gorge provides some excitement for the adventurous. The more landlubberly and cautious types might feel just a teensy bit concerned as the new bridge shivers and shakes beneath one's feet, personal research reveals. But kids love it, jumping happily up and down. Be sure to stay close to temper their exuberance.

A hiking trail follows the canyon rim along the far side of the bridge. It's a walk that is worthwhile, although it may not be for the faint-of-heart or foolish. There isn't much of a second chance for those who find themselves over the edge. It is also worth remembering that not all of the edge is exactly rock solid. Some shelves along the canyon rim have peeled off just in the decade that park workers have been maintaining them.

OTHER SIGHTS

Hagerman Fossil Beds National Landmark

Hagerman Fossil Beds National Landmark near Hagerman offers the best fossil site for ancient horses in the nation. The Hagerman horse roamed the grasslands along the Snake River some three million years ago. A new **interpretive center** is planned by the National Park Service across the Snake from the fossil beds proper and off the highway some five miles north of Hagerman. For now, a modest visitor center is located at 221 N. State St. in Hagerman and is as close as the agency gets to sharing the fascinating story of the fossil beds. Park Service employees offer occasional tours of the fossil bed as well. To find out about their schedule, call 837-4793.

The fossils helped outline the evolutionary history of the horse, which originated in North America. The national landmark was created in 1975 to protect "the world's richest known deposit of upper Pliocene Age terrestrial fos-

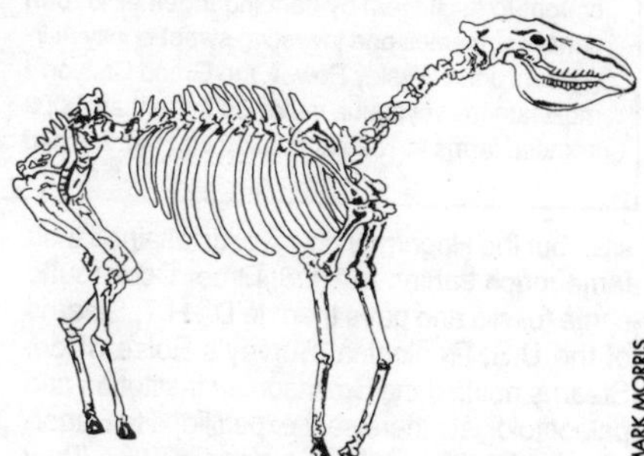

MARK MORRIS

The Hagerman horse fossil dates back to the Pliocene age.

IDAHO'S THIRSTY FARMLANDS

Idaho's preoccupation with water permeates its very soul. One state publication calls it Idaho's no. 1 natural resource. In an arid state, that is no exaggeration. Idaho has always had a surplus of farmland, but nearly all of the richest farmlands receive less than 12 inches of rain a year. Much of the rest receives 24 inches or less. The supply of water in mountain snows maintains Idaho. When the snows are too skimpy, farmers don't have enough water for their crops. The state's reservoirs shrink as the river flows dwindle; electricity costs rise as power is imported to make up for shortages from hydroelectric dams. River-runners have to live with shorter rafting seasons. As a result, it's easy to see why occasional threats by Los Angeles County to look to the Northwest for water are taken seriously here, mobilizing Idaho's political hierarchy into a frenzy of arm-waving and shouting.

Ever since settlers first began to till Idaho's rich volcanic soils, water has been a primary consideration. In 1837, missionary Henry Spalding diverted water from Lapwai Creek for his garden. In 1855, a party of Mormons ventured north into the Lemhi River Valley. One of their first acts was to build Fort Lemhi to protect themselves. Their next was to dig irrigation ditches, some of which persist even now. The Boise River Valley underwent extensive irrigation in the 1860s and farmers overclaimed the river's waters by several times, so eager were they for the prosperity water could bring.

The migration to the West in the 1890s doubled Idaho's population in a decade. Many who arrived on the Snake River Plain had fled the Great Plains and the soddies and droughts there. The sodbusters had little money but many dreams. They sought to fulfill them by banding together to form canal companies and investing sweat equity in irrigation. John Wesley Powell, the Grand Canyon's most famous voyageur, surveyed more than 4,000 irrigated farms in 1890 and found that farmers had invested less than $5 an acre to bring water to their lands.

The Mormon emphasis on communal efforts helped spread irrigation throughout southern Idaho, whether the church was involved or its methods copied by nonmembers. However the greatest spark for irrigating the desert lands was the passage by Congress of the Carey Act in 1894. Idaho, like nine other arid-land states and territories, was given one million acres of federal land. Free-enterprise interests were then to build canal systems and sell the land and water to farmers. Projects near American Falls and Marysville failed. Free enterprise fizzled for the most part.

In 1902, the Reclamation Act called on the Department of the Interior to dam rivers to help irrigators. The Reclamation Service first took aim on the Minidoka area along the Snake River and the Payette and Boise rivers. The Carey Act was revived by Peter Kimberly and Frank Buhl, who successfully irrigated 200,000 acres in the Twin Falls South Side project; by 1910, the desert had been made to bloom.

Other Carey Act projects remained bogged down in shady financing schemes or ineptitude. Federal efforts led to the damming of the Payette River at Black Canyon in 1924, its tributary the Deadwood River in 1931, and at Cascade in 1948. The Boise was turned into storage reservoirs with the construction of Anderson Ranch Dam in 1950 and Lucky Peak Dam in 1952, the latter a flood control dam built by the Army Corps of Engineers that incidentally supplied more irrigation water. When dams declined in popularity or failed, figuratively for the most part and literally with the Teton Dam's collapse in 1976, pumping from underground water supplies allowed more desert to green. The combination of federal and state projects, free enterprise, and cooperative projects ultimately supplied enough water to irrigate 3.8 million acres.

sils," but the Hagerman fossil beds attained their fame much earlier. In 1928, Elmer Cook found some fossils and gave them to Dr. H.T. Stearns of the U.S. Geological Survey's Boise office. Stearns notified the Smithsonian Institution and paleontologists there sent expeditions to Hagerman from 1929 to 1931 and again in 1934. They collected thousands of fossils, including nearly two dozen complete skeletons of the Hagerman horse, which most closely resembles the modern African zebra.

Historic House

Just north of the fossil bed along a side road that follows the Snake River is Idaho's only building designed by Frank Lloyd Wright, the master architect. The house was built for Archie Teater, who won international attention for his landscapes of the scenic West, particularly mountain views.

Teater loved the Hagerman Valley near Bliss. His dream was a studio-home designed by Frank Lloyd Wright, and with that in mind, he wrote to the architect in October 1951. At the time, Wright was designing the Solomon Guggenheim Museum in New York City, one of his masterworks. Wright replied to the letter quickly, however, because much of his career had been built on providing affordable housing for clients he found interesting. Teater had begun to attract national interest and had been noted in *Look* and *Saturday Evening Post* articles. Whether Wright read them or not, the Teaters apparently fit his criteria.

The home would be built on a bluff overlooking the Snake River (now known as Teater's Knoll). Wright designed the home to make use of native stone and estimated its cost at $10,000. The Teaters began collecting stones for their home and hauling them back to the bluff. The following May, Teater solicited financing for the building. Local bankers were taken aback by the lack of right angles and the presence of only one small bedroom. After studying the plans, one banker reportedly advised Archie to "throw them away and get a good local architect."

The cost of the house rose to $15,000, then $22,000. Some bids came in as high as $44,000. In 1953 work started. The house rose fitfully due to disputes with Wright apprentices and builders, and problems getting materials. The house was finally finished in 1957 and the Teaters moved in. They lived there at least part of the year until the 1970s when they set up a studio in Carmel, California.

Teater died July 19, 1978, at Rochester, Minnesota. The house fell into disrepair for a time but was restored in the early 1980s and has since been added to the National Register of Historic Places. It is now privately owned and is not open to the public, nor is it easy to see.

Balanced Rock

Southwest of Buhl and west of Castleford stands the 40-foot balanced rock. The large pedestal of rock seems poised to crash from its narrow base with the slightest breeze. So far it hasn't. Nearby is **Balanced Rock Park,** a favorite place for families to go tubing in the stream that runs through it. Castleford drew its name from the rocky spires that loom over the Salmon Falls Creek ford.

BOB RACE

Balanced Rock

Museums

The **Glenns Ferry Historical Museum** in Glenns Ferry provides some fascinating artifacts from both the Oregon Trail days and more modern ranching. In Hagerman, the **Hagerman Valley Historical Museum,** tel. 837-6288, is located at 100 S. State St. and provides an interesting diversion. Casts of Hagerman horse skeletons dominate a diorama inside. Displays about local Indians and geology, as well as the area's history, make the museum one of the more fascinating in Idaho. The museum is open Wed.-Sun. 1-4 p.m.

Rose Creek Winery

On a hot summer day, Hagerman seems to shimmer in the heat waves. That would be reason enough to visit the Rose Creek Winery, tel. 837-4413, which is located in the basement of the Idaho State Bank. The old lava-block building was built during the last century, but its basement has been converted to a modern winery. The age of the sturdy building is its chief asset for both visitors and vintners because the thick walls mean the cellar stays a cool and constant temperature. Rose Creek gets most of its grapes from the Hagerman Valley and produces some very drinkable wines, from rosés to cabernets.

Thousand Springs Scenic Route

Highway 30 from Bliss to Twin Falls is called the Thousand Springs Scenic Route. Though diminished now, the springs that flow from the bluffs along the north shoreline of the Snake River remain impressive. The major water sources for the Thousand Springs, which begin near Hagerman, are the Big and Little Lost rivers. When irrigation doesn't consume their flow, the swirling and sucking waters vanish into cracks in the lava fields near Howe, some 120 miles to the northeast. Water from the Snake River Plain follows old river courses now hundreds of feet below the lava, gushing from the hillsides near Hagerman and farther east. The **Nature Conservancy,** tel. 536-6797, has been a leader in helping protect the springs. The conservancy's **Thousand Springs Preserve** shelters several miles of spring creeks and the last undeveloped canyon-wall springs. The preserve includes Snake River frontage with canyon walls soaring 400 feet above. A heron rookery in the preserve offers a modern glimpse into a prehistoric scene. Visitors should be careful not to disturb the rookery. A raucous cascade of whitewater bursts forth from the canyon wall at the northern end of the preserve, and 400-foot **Sand Springs Falls** emerges at the preserve's southern end. Tours can be arranged by calling the conservancy office.

The Idaho Fish and Game and Parks and Recreation departments have joined forces to preserve the **Niagara Springs** area, now a national natural landmark. The park is a popular picnic area and the springs and nearby Snake River hold a wealth of birdlife, summer or winter. As many as 5,000 waterfowl winter in the area.

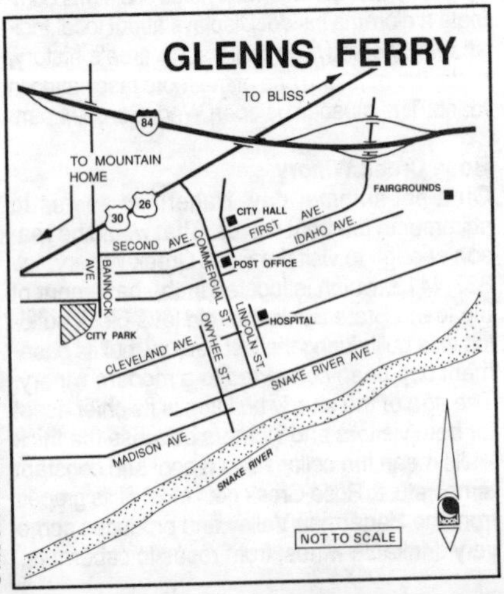

Banbury Hot Springs

Highway 30 also offers some of Idaho's best hot springs developments. Banbury Hot Springs, tel. 543-4098, is a favorite playground for resident tourists. The Olympic-sized swimming pool is almost unbelievably clean. Open 10 a.m.-10 p.m. during the summers, the outdoor pool is a great place to while away a day or two. The water from the pool is drained out each night, the walls of the pool are scrubbed down, and the pool refilled for the next day's recreation. The resort also has hot tubs in individual rooms for those who want more privacy.

Sligar's Thousand Springs Resort, tel. 837-4987, is open year-round because its hot springs pool is indoors. The pool has a view of the spectacular **Thousand Springs** cascade just across the Snake River. Near Buhl is **Miracle Hot Springs,** tel. 543-6002, which is also open year-round. The modest admission fee includes use of the private dressing area and pool.

Dams

The Idaho Power Co. maintains picnic areas at its dams between Bliss and where Hwy. 30 crosses the Snake River south of Hagerman, including **Bliss Dam, Lower Salmon Dam,** and **Upper Salmon Dam.** A park is also located at the **Upper Malad Plant,** which is just upstream on the Malad River. The company also provides parks along the Snake at its Thousand Springs and Clear Lake plants.

Fish Hatcheries

The Hagerman Valley, with its abundant supply of springs, is the center of the nation's commercial trout-farming industry. Each year thousands of pounds of fresh trout are shipped to market from here. The biggest of the commercial fish farms is the **Clear Springs Trout Co.,** tel. 536-2595. The valley's 58° waters also attracted federal and state fish hatcheries. The U.S. Fish and Wildlife Service operates the **Hagerman National Fish Hatchery,** tel. 837-4892, while the Idaho Fish and Game Department operates the **Niagara Springs Fish Hatchery,** tel. 536-2283. The two hatcheries supply young steelhead trout for release in the Snake and Salmon rivers and tons of more mundane and popular rainbow trout for release in public waters for anglers.

RECREATION

Fishing

The Hagerman Valley is as good for trout fishermen as it is for trout. The **Snake River** is a hotspot for trout anglers; an even bigger magnet is the **Malad River** in the short two-mile stretch from the Devil's Washbasin downriver to the Snake River. Fly fishermen in particular love to fish its waters. **Billingsley Creek** is a spring creek revered by fishermen for its big, selective trout. Regulations reserve the stream for fly fishers.

Idaho Fish and Game maintains a wildlife management area two miles northeast of Hagerman along Hwy. 30, as well as the **Hagerman Wildlife Management Area** along the Snake River shoreline three miles southeast of Hagerman, where anglers will also find trout waiting for them. The **Oster Lakes** near the Niagara Springs hatchery provide some of Idaho's most dependable fishing, starting March 1 each year. **Riley Creek** here offers anglers stream fishing that is as good as anywhere in the state, if not better. **Anderson** and **West** ponds open for fishing a little later, July 1, but yield good numbers of trout, bluegills, and bass.

For those who want as close to a sure thing as possible when fishing, the Buhl Country Club offers their **Clear Lakes** to anglers for a fee. There are some monster trout in these waters and the old saw, "the bigger they are the harder they fall," applies. The smaller fish are easier to catch.

For current information about fishing regulations or just fishing, anglers can check in with the Fish and Game Department's Magic Valley Region office at 868 E. Main St. in Jerome, tel. 324-4350.

Hunting

The Hagerman Valley and the Snake River running through it offer some of Idaho's best waterfowl hunting. Hunters and Idaho Fish and Game Department officials were understandably upset when the National Park Service sought to restrict traditional hunting areas near the fossil beds, a move that was preempted by Congress. Fish and Game's Billingsley Creek Wildlife Management Area provides upland bird hunting and waterfowl hunting.

Golf

The **Clear Lake Country Club,** tel. 543-4849, offers a nine-hole course to golfers in the Hagerman Valley.

PRACTICALITIES

Motels

Glenns Ferry provides travelers with the **Redford Motel,** tel. 366-2421, where rooms range $18.50-50. Hagerman offers the **Rock Lodge and Creekside RV Park,** tel. 837-4822, along Billingsley Creek near town with rooms to $39 a night and campsites for $12 a night. **Sportsmen's River Resort,** tel. 837-6202, has rooms for $25-38, tent sites for $10, and RV sites including hookups for $12. In Buhl itself are the **Oregon Trail Motel,** tel. 543-8814, with rates ranging $28-42, and the **Siesta Motel,** tel. 543-6427, with rooms for $20-34.

Campgrounds

Campers will find shady, although fairly primitive, campgrounds at **Banbury Hot Springs,** tel. 543-4098, along Hwy. 30 between Buhl and Hagerman. The swimming pool with its natural hot water is the star attraction here. The 30 campsites, which line the banks of the Snake River, range $7-10 a night. **Miracle Hot Springs,** tel. 543-6002, also offers camping with 14 spaces for $10 a night, and hot springs, of course. **Sligar's 1000 Springs,** tel. 837-4987, offers 50 campsites for $5-10 a night. Campers with self-contained RVs will find a public dump station at the Hagerman rest area south of town along Hwy. 30. Two other public, and free, dump stations are located at the Bliss rest areas along both eastbound and westbound I-84. Another free disposal station is located at Smith's Quick Stop off I-84, Exit 141 along Hwy. 30 near Gooding.

Food

Dining in Hagerman boils down to two choices. **Frog's Lilypad,** tel. 837-6227, at State St. and Hagerman Ave. may be the choice matchbook collectors won't want to miss. The other option is the **State Street Diner,** tel. 837-6536, on State Street. In Buhl, the choices include **Mr. B's Fine Food,** tel. 543-4397, at 631 Broadway Ave. S; and the **Countryside,** tel. 543-6272, at 1000 Burley Avenue.

Events

Glenns Ferry's major event is the **Elmore County Fair,** which is held in late July. Hagerman's main event is the **Hagerman Horse State Fossil Day** in May. Buhl weighs in with the annual **Sagebrush Days** the first week of July.

Transportation

The closest public transportation to the Hagerman Valley is in Bliss or Buhl. In Bliss, **Greyhound Bus Lines,** tel. 733-3002 (Twin Falls), stops at the Royal Cafe. In Buhl, Greyhound stops at Buhl Glass and Paint, while **Trans IV Buses,** tel. 736-2133 (Twin Falls) or (800) 531-2133, stops at both R&B Market and Circle K.

Information And Services

Visitors can obtain information about the Thousand Springs area from the **Hagerman Valley Chamber of Commerce,** tel. 837-4822, at P.O. Box 599, Hagerman, ID 83332. The **Buhl Chamber of Commerce,** tel. 543-6682, is located at 104 S. Broadway.

Police services at Glenns Ferry are provided by the **Elmore County Sheriff's Department,** tel. 587-2121. The **Hagerman City Police Department,** tel. 837-6636, is located at 218 W. Main. The **Buhl Police Department,** tel. 543-4200, is located at 201 Broadway Ave. North.

The **Hagerman Public Library** is located at 290 S. State. Buhl's library is located at 215 Broadway Ave. North.

TWIN FALLS AND VICINITY

Twin Falls is one of Idaho's major cities and one of the most dramatic because of the Snake River Canyon that borders it. It's a farm town first and foremost, but it also serves as home to the 6,000-student College of Southern Idaho, and as a jumping-off point for many tourists heading for Sun Valley to the north along Hwy. 93.

SIGHTS

Shoshone Falls

Shoshone Falls is higher than Niagara Falls (212 feet versus 167 feet) and carries a volume roughly equivalent during the heaviest spring runoff. The waterfall has been besmirched somewhat for power production and irrigation diversions, but its beauty still shines no matter what the season. For the most impressive view, try to see the falls in March or April, before irrigation diversions put the Snake's water to work. To reach the falls, take Falls Ave. seven miles east of Blue Lakes Boulevard.

Shoshone Falls has been a popular tourist attraction since early this century when an electric railroad was built to carry visitors the five miles to the falls. The city of Twin Falls now operates and maintains a 337-acre park at the southern edge of the falls. Shoshone Falls was also significant in the evolutionary scene, once marking the upstream end of fish migration from the ocean. The falls separated the wide-ranging salmon and steelhead of the Columbia Basin from the cutthroat trout of the interior West.

Sadly, **Twin Falls,** the cataracts for which the town was named, are deemed barely worth a visit anymore because of projects to tap them for power production. The overlook for the falls is two miles east of Shoshone Falls on Falls Avenue.

College Of Southern Idaho

Twin Falls is home to the College of Southern Idaho, tel. 733-9554, which educates 6,000 full- and part-time students on its campus at the northern edge of town. A junior college, CSI was created in 1964 by Twin Falls County voters; Jerome County pitched in shortly afterward. The campus was completed in 1968, forming a cultural nucleus for Twin Falls.

Like most junior colleges, the school focuses on academic, vocational, and continuing-education programs. The campus also recognizes the importance of commercial fish farming in the region. Their fish farm in nearby Rock Creek Canyon has grown trout to 18 pounds, bigger than some toddlers. The Herrett Museum, Fine Arts Center, an art gallery, and the Expo Center are the focal points for most activities on campus.

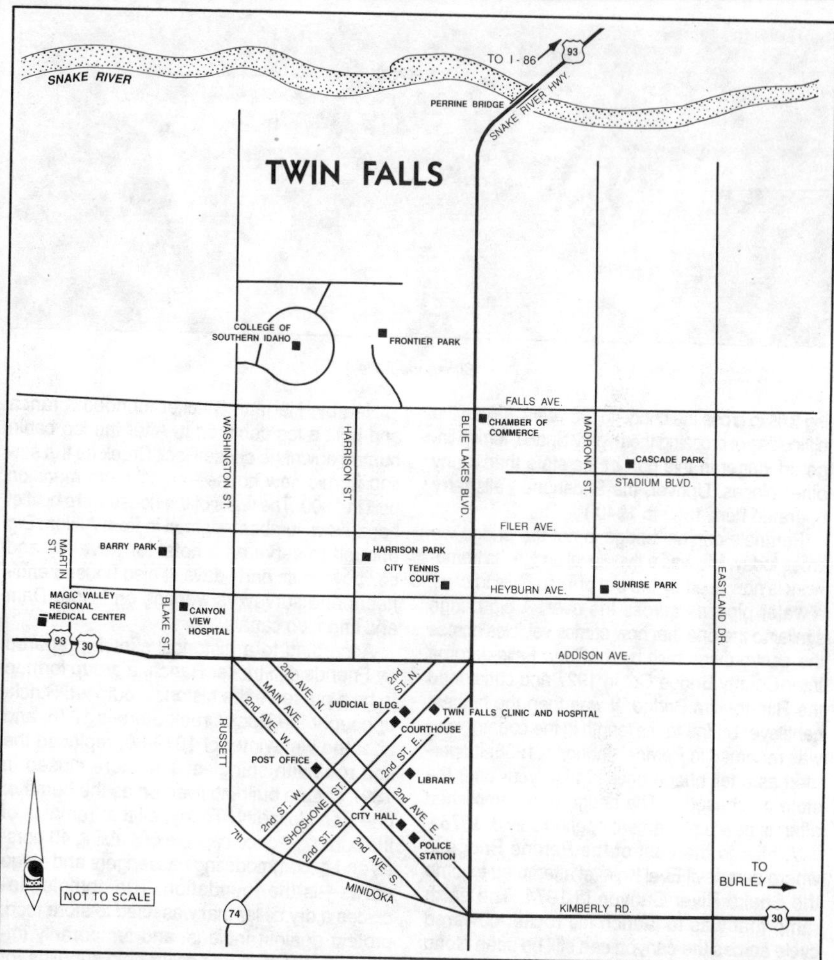

The **Herrett Museum** houses a major collection of Central and North American Indian artifacts. The museum is open Tuesday 9:30 a.m.-8 p.m., Wed.-Fri. 9:30 a.m.-4:30 p.m., Saturday 1-4:30 p.m. On the second floor of the Taylor Administration Building is the **Sunspot Photography Gallery,** which features photographs by regional artists and students. The gallery is open Mon.-Sat. 8 a.m.-8 p.m.

The **Fine Arts Center** is the venue for the CSI Drama Department, as well as a stage band, concert band, chamber and jazz choirs, and other performers. The Magic Valley Chorale and Magic Valley Symphony both perform here.

Perrine Bridge

The Perrine Bridge on Hwy. 93 ranks as one of Idaho's most scenic, soaring over the Snake River to carry traffic north toward Shoshone and Sun Valley. The 1,500-foot-long bridge stands 486 feet above the canyon floor. Historian Virginia Ricketts noted that I.B. Perrine's construction of the bridge in 1911 put his own Blue Lakes ferry out of business, but he made up the loss by charg-

BOB RACE

Shoshone Falls

ing tolls to cross the bridge for 10 years. (Given the difficulties of crossing the mighty Snake, ferries lingered longer in this part of the state than many other places. Upriver, the Shoshone Falls ferry operated from 1883 to 1940.)

Perrine's original bridge is not the bridge we cross today. His was a river-level bridge. Its framework is now used by the city of Twin Falls to carry a water pipeline across the river. A big bridge similar to the one that now carries vehicles across the canyon was built by the Twin Falls-Jerome Inter-County Bridge Co. in 1927 and christened the Rim-to-Rim Bridge. It was then the highest cantilever bridge for its length in the country, and was renamed in Perrine's honor in 1936. It operated as a toll bridge until 1940, a year after the state purchased it. The bridge was demolished after its new replacement opened July 3, 1976.

A mile to the east of the Perrine Bridge is where daredevil Evel Knievel attempted to jump the Snake River Canyon in 1974. The earth ramp that was to launch his rocket-powered cycle across the canyon can still be seen along the southern rim. Knievel's jump failed because a chute opened prematurely, just as he was taking off from the ramp. He landed not so softly on the rocks below, suffering more hurt to his reputation, however, than to himself.

Rock Creek Store And Stricker Ranch

Southeast of Twin Falls and five miles south of Hansen on the way to Magic Mountain Ski Area is the Rock Creek Store, which was established in 1864 as an Overland Stage stop and a year later became a store operated by James Bascom.

Nearby, Herman Stricker founded a ranch and built a log cabin on it. After the log cabin burned down, he chose Rock Creek as the setting for his new house—an 11-room mansion built in 1900. The walls of the house were built of hand-sawn lumber freighted in from Albion. Big enough to serve as a hotel for travelers and cowboys in its early days, it also housed engineers and surveyors working on Milner Dam and irrigation canals.

According to a historical sketch prepared by Friends of Stricker Ranch, a group formed to help preserve the historical outpost, Stricker bought the Rock Creek Store in 1876, and after the wet winter of 1879-80, replaced the sod roof with shingles. The store closed in 1897 but the building lived on as the home of one Ben Holladay. Today, all that remains of the building—once capable of stabling 40 horses and accommodating passengers and stage crews—is the foundation. The complex includes a dry cellar that was used to store food, protect against Indians, and temporarily imprison outlaws. A wet cellar held supplies for the saloon. The buildings remain as tangible links to Idaho's past.

Minidoka War Relocation Center

To the northeast of Twin Falls, a different sort of history was made during WW II. Near Eden, the Minidoka War Relocation Center, which was called **Hunt** by the U.S. Post Office, housed 9,400 Japanese-Americans from the West Coast. The internees were kept in tar-paper barracks from 1942 to 1945 and warned to keep their distance from the fences surrounding the camps or they would be shot. They were good Americans, though; their efforts helped save the region's sugar beets when other farm labor had been siphoned off by the war effort. In 1945, the U.S. Supreme Court ruled that U.S. citizens, no matter what their heritage, could no longer be so detained. Hunt became the state's most recent ghost town. All that remains these days is a faint whiff of bigoted hysteria.

RECREATION

Fishing

Ignoring for the moment the Snake River that runs almost through it, Twin Falls is a staging area for anglers. With Magic Reservoir to the north and Salmon Falls Creek Reservoir to the south, Twin Falls is bracketed by some exceptional fishing.

The impoundment along Salmon Falls Creek is notable in several ways. The reservoir is one of the few in southern Idaho to offer fishing for kokanee—the diminutive but tasty landlocked version of sockeye or red salmon—as well as walleye, which is just as tasty as the kokanee and quite a bit bigger. The walleye, a giant member of the perch family, was first stocked in the reservoir in 1974. Most of Salmon Falls Creek's walleyes weigh in at several pounds apiece with 6-10 pounders typical. Idaho's record "walley" was caught here in 1987. It weighed 15 pounds, 9 ounces, and stretched 32¾ inches.

To get to Salmon Falls Creek Reservoir from Twin Falls, head west out of town on Hwy. 93/30 for six miles, turn south at the junction with Hwy. 93 and continue 24 miles to Rogerson. From there it's about six miles west to the dam.

Magic Reservoir was built for $3 million in 1910, an investment fishermen appreciate today. The lake is a favorite spot for anglers because the rainbow trout here grow big. Magic's rainbows draw most of the attention to the reservoir, although tasty yellow perch attract a devoted following of their own. During drought years, which outnumbered normal or wet years combined during the past decade, boat access can be impossible. Fishermen on foot or toting inner tubes can follow the receding water level more easily.

The reservoir also holds enough water to irrigate 89,000 acres of farms stretching from Shoshone to Richfield, and is popular with waterskiers and windsurfers as well as fishermen. To get there, take Hwy. 75 north of Twin Falls about 50 miles to just before its intersection with Hwy. 20. The reservoir is just west of the highway. Approaching by gravel road, the manmade lake in the rolling sagebrush seems to fill the horizon like magic.

Rafting

The Murtaugh Reach of the Snake River east of town and the Hagerman Reach to the west bracket Twin Falls with some exciting whitewater for rafters. The Murtaugh Reach is known for its exciting whitewater from Star Falls or Caldron Linn to Shoshone Falls (which all boaters definitely want to avoid). Just upstream from the Murtaugh Reach is the Milner Reach of the Snake which can, but doesn't always, offer exciting whitewater. Its flow is tightly controlled by Milner Dam nine miles west of Burley. The Idaho Power Co., which operates the dam, issues periodic updates during the rafting season about how much water boaters can expect to find in the river during the spring runoff. The company provides a toll-free recreation hot line, tel. (800) 422-3143. The stretch of river below Milner Falls is known for its Class V and V-plus rapids when the flow is more than 4,000 cubic feet of water per second. Such rapids are capable of injuring boaters and should not be attempted without expert-level skills and equipment.

The proximity of the Snake as well as other famous Idaho rivers has made Twin Falls a hub for commercial outfitters specializing in river trips. The town is home to **High Adventure River Tours,** tel. 733-0123; **Idaho Outfitter Guide Services,** tel. 734-8872; and **Middle Fork Rapid Transit,** tel. 734-7890. Expect to pay about $50 a person for one-day trips on the Snake. River tours on the Middle Fork of the Salmon cost hundreds more and typically last four to five days.

Golf

Twin Falls stands out for golfers with its canyon-bounded golf courses, including the private **Blue Lakes Country Club,** tel. 733-2337; the public **Canyon Springs Golf Club,** tel. 734-7609; and **Twin Falls Municipal,** tel. 733-3326. Blue Lakes offers its 18 holes over 5,751 yards with par at 72. Golfers are advised to bring plenty of balls because some unique holes await. Canyon

The Perrine Bridge arches across the Snake River Canyon along U.S. 93 north of Twin Falls.

Springs west of Perrine Bridge offers a par 72 challenge with 18 holes over 6,205 yards. It is equipped with a pro shop, driving range, lounge, and restaurant. The shortest of the three, Twin Falls offers 18 holes over 5,234 yards and par of 68. It's noted for its small and quick greens. The course offers a pro shop and snack bar and the shade of mature trees.

The courses' sheltered locations along the floor of the Snake River Canyon mean golfers can keep at their sport year-round through mild winters. (Harsher winters can be a different story, although they generally don't last as long down along the river.) The municipal course is an exception. It closes from about mid-November to March 1 to protect its greens. The greens fees for the city course run $7 for nine holes, $9 for 18 holes weekdays and $12 for 18 holes weekends.

Skiing

With Sun Valley only 81 miles to the north, Twin Falls would seem blessed enough to most skiers. But there's an even closer alternative. In the opposite direction is **Magic Mountain Ski Area,** tel. 423-6221, 28 miles south of Hansen. The ski hill has a day lodge, cafeteria/lounge, and ski rentals. Magic Mountain operates 20 runs served by two chairlifts, a poma, and a rope tow. The vertical drop is a modest 800 feet.

Snowmobiling

Snowmobilers also get their kicks south of the city in the region's beloved South Hills. The **Diamondfield Jack Snowplay Area** is located 35 miles southeast of Twin Falls and contains more than 200 miles of marked and groomed snowmobile trails. A warming shelter is maintained by the **Magic Valley Snowmobile Club.** More information about the area and conditions is available from the Sawtooth National Forest's **Twin Falls Ranger District,** tel. 737-3200.

Hiking

Hikers will find hundreds of square miles of federal lands awaiting their explorations in the South Hills and elsewhere around Twin Falls. The city is the home of the **Sawtooth National Forest** office, tel. 737-3200, at 2647 Kimberly Rd. East. The **BLM,** tel. 734-5121, maintains an office at 634 Addison Ave. West. The **Snake River Rim Recreation Area** lies along the Snake River Canyon's northern rim to the east, across the Perrine Bridge. The area offers trails for walking, jogging, horseback riding, and other activities.

Bicycling

Just as hikers will find dozens of trails to tempt them, the back roads and trails surrounding Twin Falls are a magnet for bicyclists. Plenty of bicycle shops can help with information or repairs. Among the shops are **Blue Lakes Cyclery,** tel. 733-9305, at 1240 Blue Lakes Blvd. N; **Haffner's Key and Bike Shop,** tel. 733-0016, at 336 4th Ave. W; **Pedersen's,** tel. 733-2519, at 259 Main Ave. E; **Spoke and Wheel,** tel. 733-6033, at 148 Addison Ave.; and **Valley Schwinn Cyclery,** tel. 733-0671, at 1841 Addison Ave. East.

Gambling

Gambling, with the exception of the state lottery, bingo, and horse racing of course, is illegal in Idaho. That's why Twin Falls operates as the major funnel for casino-crazed travelers. Just 47 miles south of the city limits along Hwy. 93 lies the Nevada border and Jackpot. This little city tries hard to keep the northerners interested. Its growth and bustle is testament to Idahoans' fascination with games of chance. Although lacking the volume of Reno or Las Vegas, several noisy slot shops keep the bells ringing and the lights flashing.

PRACTICALITIES

Motels

Newest in town is **Comfort Inn,** tel. 734-7494, 1893 Canyon Springs Rd. (across from Magic Valley Mall). Their 52 rooms go for $40-82 a night. Features include an indoor pool and hot tub, complimentary continental breakfast, and cable TV. **Amber Inn,** tel. 825-5200, near Eden, has 25 rooms ranging $27-38 a night. Pricier rooms are available at **Apollo Motor Inn,** tel. 733-2010, at 296 Addison Ave. with rooms for $40-58, and **Canyon Springs Inn,** tel. 734-5000, 1357 Blue Lakes Blvd. N, with rooms for $54-62. Both are Best Westerns. Two Westons, the **Weston Inn,** tel. 733-6095, at 906 Blue Lakes Blvd., with rooms for $36-50, and **Weston Plaza Hotel,** tel. (800) 333-7829, at 1350 Blue Lakes Blvd., with rooms for $45-56, shelter Twin Falls travelers. **Econo Lodge,** tel. 733-8770, rents rooms for $30-47 a night at 320 Main Ave. South.

Other alternatives include **Capri Motel,** tel. 733-6452, at 1341 Kimberly Rd.; **Holiday Motel,** tel. 733-4330, at 615 Addison Ave. W; **Motel 6,** tel. 734-3993, at 1472 Blue Lakes Blvd. N; **Super 8,** tel. 734-5801, at 1260 Blue Lakes Blvd. N; **Motel 3,** tel. 733-5630, at 248 2nd Ave. W; and **Twin Falls Motel,** tel. 733-8620, at 2152 Kimberly Road.

Campgrounds

The Twin Falls area's major campground is **Anderson's Best Holiday Trav-l Park,** tel. 733-2010, with 150 campsites to the northeast near Eden, off I-84, Exit 182, then east on Tipperary Road. Campsites cost $11.50 a night. **The Twin Falls/Jerome KOA,** tel. 324-4169, is open year-round except January and is located a mile north of I-84, Exit 173, along Hwy. 93. The 116 sites start at $16. West of Twin Falls is the **Curry Trailer Park,** tel. 733-3961, with 19 campsites for $9 a night. **Blue Lakes Mobile Court,** tel. 734-5782, is located at 1122 N. Blue Lakes Blvd. and has 14 sites starting at $11.50.

To the southeast of Hollister along Hwy. 93 is **Nat-Soo-Pah Hot Springs and RV Park,** tel. 655-4337, with 75 campsites ranging $6-8. Nat-Soo-Pah is a fun place for the family to spend the day. Both Shoshone Indians and early settlers used the natural hot spring for bathing. In 1926, the first pool was built. Bathhouses for men and women followed. Its large pool, 125-by-50 feet, has a slide and hydrotube. A large and hot soaking tub is located just off the main pool. The dressing rooms at poolside are clean and tidy, as is the campground. Shade is at a premium in the camping area, so plan to spend some time in the water during a hot summer's day. The picnic grove's shade offers another respite from the sun. Nat-Soo-Pah offers video games and snacks. The resort is open May 1 to Labor Day. The daily swim fee is $1.75 for children ages one to five and $3.75 for those six and older. The camping fee is $10 for two persons, and $1 for each additional person.

Food

Twin Falls has a lively dining scene. One of the most elegant places in town is **The Sandpiper,** tel. 734-7000, at 1309 Blue Lakes Blvd. N, where the appetizer menu has included Pernod escargot and Cajun calamari. Steaks from filets to sirloin teriyaki, fresh Idaho trout, chicken Oscar, and fresh tuna steaks are a few selections on the menu. Prices reflect the quality with entrees topping $20. **Rock Creek Restaurant,** tel. 734-4154, at 200 Addison Ave. W, carries a menu to rival the Sandpiper. Less rarefied fare can be found at the **Depot Grill,** tel. 733-0710, open 24 hours a day at 545 Shoshone St. S. It features an all-day breakfast menu, sandwiches, and an extensive dinner menu with entrees to $13. The Depot also offers inexpensive smorgasbords throughout the week ranging from $3.75 at lunch to $6.45 for a Friday-night fish fry. **North's Chuck Wagon,** tel. 734-1223, at 1839 Kimberly Rd., also offers buffets daily. The **Buffalo Cafe,** tel. 734-0271, specializes in omelettes and is open for breakfast and lunch daily at 218 4th Ave. West.

Mexican-food enthusiasts will find **La Casita,** tel. 734-7974, waiting at 111 S. Park Avenue. The house specialty is the chimichanga. **Cafe Ole,** tel. 734-0685, is also in Twin Falls at 1288 Blue Lakes Blvd., and its food maintains the same quality as the chain's other Idaho restaurants.

Elsewhere on the ethnic front, **A'Roma Italian Cuisine,** tel. 733-0167, does Italian, obviously, at 147 Shoshone St. N; **The Gyros Shop,** tel. 733-3100, at 113 Shoshone N, represents Greek cuisine, and several restaurants prepare Chinese dishes: **Wok 'n Grill,** tel. 734-6898, at 1188 Blue Lakes Blvd. N; **Mandarin House,** tel. 734-6578, at 705 Blue Lakes Blvd. N; and **George K's Fine Foods,** tel. 734-3100, at 1719 Kimberly Road. The **Wok 'n Grill** ranks as a personal favorite. Its hot and sour soup is nicely spicy. Broccoli beef and curry chicken are likewise well seasoned. For dinner parties divided, the Wok 'n Grill also offers a generous selection of meat entrees and sandwiches.

Events

Western Days, held in late May and early June each year, commemorate the heritage of Twin Falls with a barbecue, dances, a chili cook-off, and reenactments of shoot-outs. **Art in the Park** is held during July each year. The **Twin Falls County Fair** is held in early September at the fairgrounds at Filer, south of Twin Falls on Hwy. 93. The fair includes a rodeo sanctioned by the Professional Rodeo Cowboys Association. **Oktoberfest** follows, and a month later Twin Falls celebrates the **Harvest Festival.**

Information And Services

Information about the Twin Falls area is available from the **Twin Falls Chamber of Commerce,** tel. 733-3974, 858 Blue Lakes Blvd. North. Police services are provided by the **Twin Falls Police Department,** tel. 736-2200 or 911 for emergencies, at 356 3rd Ave. East. The **Twin Falls County Sheriff,** tel. 736-4040, is located at the courthouse at Shoshone St. and 4th Avenue.

Twin Falls hospitals include **Magic Valley Regional Medical Center,** tel. 737-2000, at 650 Addison Ave. W, **Twin Falls Clinic and Hospital,** tel. 733-3700, at 666 Shoshone E, and Canyon View Hospital, tel. 734-6760, at 228 Shoup Avenue.

BURLEY AND VICINITY

SIGHTS

Minidoka National Wildlife Refuge

The Minidoka National Wildlife Refuge, tel. 436-3589, lies 12 miles northeast of Rupert along I-86. The heart of the refuge is the 11,000-acre **Lake Walcott.** Impounded by Minidoka Dam, the narrow reservoir attracts as many as 100,000 ducks and 10,000 geese during the spring and fall migrations. The roads on the refuge can be difficult; hiking is an option but a strenuous one. Boating is restricted to the lake's western end in deference to the flocks. Some of the more spectacular or unusual birds here include snowy egrets, double-crested cormorants, white pelicans, American avocets, white-faced ibises, long-billed curlews, and tundra swans. Minidoka's main strength is its ducks. Ruddy ducks, redheads, canvasbacks, hooded mergansers, and northern shovelers are a few of the many. For teal lovers, it doesn't get any better, with green-winged, blue-winged, and cinnamon teal all represented.

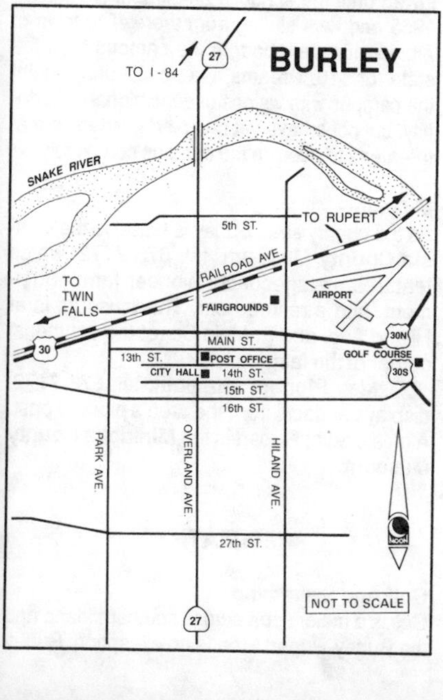

At the west end of the lake is Walcott Park, where you'll find a Bureau of Reclamation picnic area and campground. The campground is open Memorial Day through Labor Day. Sites cost $6 per night. For more information call the Bureau at 436-4187.

Silent City of Rocks

During the great Overland Migration from the 1840s to 1860s, a remote corner of the route through what is now southern Idaho generated a frenzy of fantasy among the emigrants that was matched by no other stretch; spires and domes of ancient rock pierce the desert floor, reminding some of great buildings of stone.

The Silent City of Rocks was named by those in the wagon trains heading for Oregon or California. "A most wild and romantic scenery presents to the eye rocks upon rocks, naked and piled high in the most fantastic shapes," witnessed one passerby. Some emigrants called the valley of weathered granite Steeple Rocks or Castle City. As is true elsewhere along the pioneer trails, the emigrants left evidence of their passing. Using the ubiquitous axle grease that came with every wagon, the pioneers focused on **Register Rock** to smear their names on the bright granite. Here and there throughout the city, other greasy graffiti remains.

Some 14,000 acres of juniper-covered desert stretching between Oakley, south of Burley on Hwy. 27, and Almo to the southeast have been protected by the National Park Service. Plans call for turning the area over to the Idaho Parks and Recreation Department. At present, the City of Rocks offers the barest of creature comforts. Water was only developed at the area in 1989, the year Congress gave formal recognition to the area as a National Historic Reserve.

A popular camping spot, the area has also been receiving increasing notice from rock climbers who value the granite faces, which can rise as high as 700 feet. The names given the rocks reflect the city's long history of fantasy, including Andy Gump, Dragon Head, Devils Bedstead, Flaming Rock, Giant Toadstool, and

City of Rocks National Historic Reserve offers a peaceful landscape.

Elephant Rock. The area has become so popular that the National Park Service is weighing in with a quota system.

To reach the city, follow Hwy. 27 to Oakley and head southeast from there, or follow Hwy. 77 through Albion to Almo and then turn west. The drive is a fascinating dip into the geological province of the Great Basin with the looming presence of 10,339-foot **Cache Peak** close at hand. For more information about the area, contact the park service office at 963 Blue Lakes Blvd., No. 1, Twin Falls, ID 83301, tel. 733-8398, or call the reserve at 824-5519.

Albion And Oakley

For period buildings dating back to Idaho's early history, Oakley and Albion both have their share. Oakley is said to have the greatest concentration of old buildings in the state, with most of them lining Main and Center streets. Among the stars are the Opera House, Worthington Hotel, and Judge Howell's home. The city park preserves the jail cell that once housed Diamond Field Jack Davis, who was imprisoned for killing two sheepherders during the region's cattle and sheep wars. Diamond Field Jack served six years and narrowly escaped hanging twice before the Idaho Board of Pardons decided in 1902 that he wasn't guilty. Two other cattlemen confessed to the killing.

Albion holds the now-abandoned campus of the Albion State Normal School, created by a vote of Cassia County residents in 1892. Although the school trained 3,000 teachers between its founding and its demise in 1951, Southern Idaho College of Education, as it grew to be known, could not survive a cut in funding by the state legislature in that year. Legislators decided the school offered the same training available at Idaho State University to the east at Pocatello. The Church of Christ leased the campus beginning in 1957 and reopened the school as the Magic Christian College. A brief prosperity followed until the school's enrollment crashed in 1965 and kept sliding from there. The town of Albion ultimately bought the campus from the state for $10. Dreams rise up still and repaint the campus with visions of educational opportunity, but none have yet reversed the decline that threatens to overrun the campus completely.

Museums

As the county seat, Burley is home to the **Cassia County Museum,** tel. 678-7172, which features a stagecoach, pioneer farm equipment, and a railroad car. The museum is at Hiland Ave. and E. Main St. (at the southeast corner of the fairgrounds).

Oakley Pioneer Museum, tel. 678-7172, displays artifacts from the area's pioneer past. A mile east of Rupert is the **Minidoka County Museum.**

RECREATION

Golf And Swimming

Golf is a major sport across southern Idaho and the Burley-Rupert area is no exception. Burley offers two courses, the 18-hole **City of Burley Golf Course,** tel. 678-9807, east of the town and **Ponderosa Golf Course,** tel. 678-5730, to the north. **Rupert Golf Club,** tel. 436-9168, serves the Rupert golf crowd. Rupert has a public swimming pool, tel. 436-6413.

Skiing

Calling yourself a skier here could mean two different things, depending on the season. Summer means water-skiing. Maybe the desert surroundings account for water-skiing's fantastic popularity along the Snake River reservoirs that hang like a chain of watery beads across the width of southern Idaho. Burley counts itself blessed by its location along some 20 miles of the most accessible shoreline along the Snake. Ramps are located at the north side of the Burley Bridge off I-84, Exit 208. The Burley Golf Course off I-84, Exit 211, is also a popular access point. **Walcott Lake** near Rupert has boat docks and floating docks available. Its picnic area and restrooms are popular with water-skiers.

Say skiing when the snow is flying and **Pomerelle,** tel. 638-5599, will come to mind. Located south of the Albion Exit off I-84, and a short distance off Hwy. 7, Pomerelle has a vertical drop of 1,000 feet, 22 ski runs, two chairlifts, and a rope tow. Astride the timbered slopes of Mt. Harrison, Pomerelle offers trails for beginner to advanced skiers. A lift ticket in the '93-94 season cost a modest $18.

Cross-country skiers can head for the Conner Flat trail system, which offers 3.5 miles of groomed tracks for beginners and seven miles of marked trails. It's located near Pomerelle on the slopes of Mt. Harrison.

Snowmobiling

The **Howell Canyon Recreation Area** is 25 miles southeast of Burley and southwest of Albion. The area is maintained by the Mt. Harrison Snowmobile Club, and information is available from the Sawtooth National Forest's **Burley Ranger District,** tel. 678-0430.

PRACTICALITIES

Motels

Burley's major motel is the **Best Western Burley Inn,** tel. 678-3501 or (800) 632-3569 within Idaho and (800) 635-4952 outside, with 127 rooms for $46-62 at 800 N. Overland. **Budget Motel,** tel. 678-2200 or (800) 824-5317 inside Idaho, at 900 N. Overland, has 140 rooms for $35-56. Other choices in Burley include the **Greenwell Motel,** tel. 678-5576, at 904 E. Main St. ($28-52); **Lampliter Motel,** tel. 678-0031, at 304 E. Main ($22-46); **Parish Motel** tel. 678-5505, at 721 E. Main ($20-33); **Powers Motel,** tel. 678-5521, at 703 E. Main ($22-35); and **Starlite Motel,** tel. 678-7766, at 500 Overland ($24).

In Rupert, the **Flamingo Lodge Motel,** tel. 436-4321, at the east edge of town has rooms for $22-41.

Campgrounds

Burley-area campgrounds include **Greenwood RV Park,** tel. 829-5735, at 1015 Ridgeway Rd. S in Hazelton, with spaces for $13. **Snake River Campground,** tel. 654-2133, is near Declo off I-84, Exit 216, and offers campsites for $10.

Food

Burley and Rupert are the major restaurant centers for the area. In Burley, Overland Ave. holds a generous selection of fast food and other restaurants ranging from McDonald's to Pizza Hut and Dairy Queen.

In Burley, for diners who like to eat at a more leisurely pace and consume food that was made the same way, **Price's Cafe,** tel. 678-5149, at 2444 Overland Ave., offers steak and lobster, and homemade pie for dessert. The **Burley Inn,** tel. 678-3501, at the Best Western at 800 N. Overland, is another option. **Nelson's Cafe and Pilot's Club,** tel. 678-7171, is downtown at 125 W. Main and offers steaks, seafood, and spirits.

Chinese cuisine fans will find **George K's East Restaurant and Lounge,** tel. 678-9173, at 325 E. 3rd N, and **China First Restaurant,** tel. 678-7937, at 1242 Overland Ave., which also includes Vietnamese dishes on its menu. Mexican food is offered at **Tio Joe's,** tel. 678-9844, at 262 Overland Avenue.

Rupert diners can choose between the **Pancake House,** tel. 436-3660, at 5th and Scott; **Smitty's Restaurant,** tel. 436-4801, at 325 Oneida; and **Wayside Inn,** tel. 436-4800, at the junction of Hwy. 24 and I-84.

Information And Services

The **Burley Chamber of Commerce,** tel. 678-2730, is located at 1401 Overland, Burley, ID

83318. The **Rupert Chamber of Commerce,** tel. 436-4793, is located at 324 Scott, Rupert, ID 83350.

Greyhound Bus Lines serves Burley at 1214 Oakley Ave., tel. 678-0477, and Rupert at Rupert Gas & Oil on 8th St., tel. 436-4373.

Police in the Burley area and surrounding Cassia County can be reached at the county courthouse by dialing 678-2251. The Rupert police station is at 8th and H streets, tel. 436-9651.

Medical care is available at **Cassia Memorial Hospital and Medical Center,** tel. 678-4444 at 2303 Park Ave. in Burley, and **Minidoka Memorial Hospital,** tel. 436-0481, at 1224 8th St. in Rupert.

NORTH OF TWIN FALLS

The road to Sun Valley, Hwy. 93 and then Hwy. 75, heads north from Twin Falls with the tautness of a bow string. The asphalt runs like a fault, parting the sides of the sagebrush desert and cleaving rugged lava flows. The gleam of rails intersects at **Shoshone,** a pioneer town once known for almost constant hullabaloos but which has since mellowed considerably. Shoshone sprouted in 1870 as settlers began to drift in. The rich strikes of mostly silver and lead in the Wood River mines to the north in 1879 increased the town's tempo. The pace stepped up dramatically with the arrival of the railroad in 1882. **Gooding,** west on Hwy. 26, got its start with the arrival of the railroad in 1883. **Jerome,** south of Shoshone on Hwy. 93—platted while the sagebrush still ruled the desert—commemorates the arrival of irrigation water.

SIGHTS

Gooding City Of Rocks

Thirteen miles northwest of Gooding is the Gooding City of Rocks, a collection of spires and pillars, some say gargoyles, set amongst the sagebrush. This city, eroded from volcanic ash hardened into tuff, lacks the stature of the City of Rocks between Oakley and Almo but can be a must-stop for kids who like to exercise their imaginations.

Caves

Lava tubes form when a shell hardens around a still-flowing stream of lava. As the lava advances, the shell is left behind, forming a tube or cave. **Mammoth Cave,** seven miles north of Shoshone along Hwy. 75, then a mile and a half west, has been developed as a tourist attraction and is open year-round. Admission to the cave is $3.50 for adults and $2 for children 12 and younger; babes-in-arms are admitted free. The cave was first found in 1902 by a group of explorers who wrote their names in charcoal. In 1954 it was rediscovered by its present owner, Richard Olsen, who developed it as a tourist attraction. A zoo (which includes buffalo, emus, and pygmy goats), a gift shop, pioneer cabins, and a museum with bear skeletons and Indian artifacts have been added as well. **Shoshone Ice Cave,** about 12 miles north of Shoshone, is another lava tube. Its floor and back are covered with ice, however, a testament to the often vertical, rather than horizontal, air flow common to such caves. In the past, blasting altered the air flow and the ice melted. A door now seals the entrance, and the old excavation has been sealed off in the back of the cave. The cave is open May 1-Oct. 1 for guided tours; tel. 886-7123. A gift shop and display of pioneer wagons is also at the cave.

Jerome County Historical Museum

The Jerome County Historical Museum, tel. 324-5641, maintains a collection of Jerome County memorabilia focusing on the area's farming history. Among its notable displays are those recalling the history of the Hunt Relocation Center. The museum, which is located at 22 N. Lincoln, also contains a Northside Canal District display about irrigation development in the area and offers a research room with old history books, letters, maps, journals, and other items. The museum is located at 220 N. Lincoln, behind the library, and is open Tues.-Sat. 1-5 p.m.

Gooding County Historical Museum, tel. 934-4624, is open March-Sept., Fri.- Sat. 11 a.m.-4 p.m. The museum is located at 210 Main St. North.

PRACTICALITIES

Bed And Breakfast Inn
In Shoshone, the **Governor's Mansion,** tel. 886-2858, offers a full breakfast with a night's stay. Its four rooms range in price from $30 to $65. The inn is located at 315 S. Greenwood.

Motels
Jerome lodgings include **Big Trees Mobile Park,** tel. 324-8265, at 300 1st Ave. W, where spaces rent for $9 a night; **Holiday Motel,** tel. 324-2361, at 401 W. Main with rooms for $26-50; **Towle's Motel,** tel. 324-3267, at 261 E. Main; and **Crest Motel,** tel. 324-2670, at 2983 S. Lincoln, with rooms for $26-40.

Gooding offers the **Motel Evergreen,** tel. 934-9987, at 1331 S. Main St., with rooms ranging $22-35, and the **Gooding Hotel,** tel. 934-4374, which was built in 1906 and is now on the National Register of Historic Buildings. It offers 17 rooms for rent at $33 for singles or $38 for doubles. The rates include a full breakfast. The hotel is also an affiliate of American Youth Hostels and offers nonsmoking rooms. It welcomes children and has a community kitchen and lounge area. The **Lincoln Inn,** tel. 934-4423, at 413 Main St., has 10 rooms ranging $27-35, and offers a restaurant, and two bars featuring live county-western and rock music on the weekends.

Food
Jerome offers a surprising variety of restaurants for a town of 7,500 or so. Eateries range from **China Village,** tel. 324-8777, at 123 S. Alder to the **El Sombrero Restaurant,** tel. 324-7238, at 153 W. Main. Other choices include **The Wrangler,** tel. 324-4642, at 400 Main; **Wood's Family Restaurant,** tel. 324-4911, at 120 W. Main; and **Cindy's Restaurant,** tel. 324-4991, at 3201 S. Lincoln.

In Gooding, dining choices include the **Lincoln Inn,** tel. 934-4423, at 413 Main; **Wood River Inn,** tel. 934-4059, at 530 Main; and **Wyant's Family Cookhouse,** tel. 934-9903, at 222 4th Ave. East. Shoshone dining boils down to the **Manhattan Cafe,** tel. 886-2142, at 133 S. Rail St. W, and several drive-ins.

Events
Jerome offers two major events each year, **Jerome County History Fair** in late February and **Live History Days** in early August. Gooding holds its **Summerfest** the third week in July, which coincides with its annual **Basque Picnic.**

Recreation
Golfers have two courses to play in the area. The **Jerome Country Club,** tel. 324-5081, is a private 18-hole course located at 649 Golf Course Road. Par 72, it covers 6,245 yards and offers a pro shop, snack bar, and what players will find to be two different faces. **Gooding Country Club,** tel. 934-9977, at 1951 U.S. Hwy. 26, has nine holes with 5,956 yards and is rated a par 71. It is a private course and features a pro shop, lounge, and driving range. For **hunting and fishing information,** contact the Idaho Fish and Game Department's Magic Valley regional office, tel. 324-4350, at 868 E. Main St., Jerome, ID 83338.

Transportation
Amtrak stops at Shoshone's Union Pacific Railroad Depot at 304 N. Rail St. W, tel. 886-2496.

Information And Services
The **Jerome Chamber of Commerce,** tel. 324-2711, is located at 220 N. Lincoln. The **Gooding Chamber of Commerce** is located at 618 Idaho St., tel. 934-4402.

Police services in Jerome and Shoshone are available by dialing 911. In Gooding, the city police are reached by dialing 934-8435. The **Gooding County Sheriff,** tel. 934-4421, is at Gooding. **Gooding County Hospital,** tel. 934-4463, is at 1120 Montana. **St. Benedict's Family Medical Center,** tel. 324-4301, serves Jerome at 709 N. Lincoln.

SUN VALLEY AND VICINITY

The Wood River Valley can be summed up for most people in two words: Sun Valley. Idaho's premier destination resort, Sun Valley enjoys a national and international following. Sun Valley is where you're most likely to meet an astronaut, glimpse Clint Eastwood, or witness any one of a host of other two-legged signals that this place is on the map. Of course, many Idahoans view the crowds of skiers or summer visitors as a mixed blessing. Some even as an intrusion. Two things natives and nonnatives agree on without dissension are that Sun Valley offers some marvelous skiing and the Wood River Valley is beautiful.

The Big and Little Wood rivers offer some of Idaho's best fishing. Silver Creek is on a higher plane altogether, where fishing becomes more an art than an avocation, where the poetry of a fly well cast and taken exceeds the size of the fish for most anglers. For the rest, there are some monster trout here, and the buggers are tough to catch.

History

The Wood River Valley began to attract attention more than a century ago when rich strikes of lead and silver ore were discovered there. Mining attracted a railroad, and the wealth that was generated led **Hailey** to become the first Idaho city with telephone service in 1883 and **Ketchum** to pioneer the use of electric lighting. Hailey at one time had three daily newspapers.

The echoes of those days still linger in the area's hills with the remnants of miners' cabins and the mines themselves. But the bustle that once focused on the riches under the mountains now depends on the snows that cover the hills each winter and the beautiful scenes they present throughout the year.

Sun Valley Lodge was developed in 1936 after W. Averell Harriman dispatched an expert skier to survey the West for the most likely place to develop a destination ski resort that could help boost railroad traffic. Count Felix Schaffgotsch, an Austrian, was sure that Sun Valley was the spot. Harriman followed up the January 1936 report with a two-week visit and directed the purchase of a 4,000-acre ranch. The first chairlifts, improvised from banana transports, were developed by Union Pacific Railroad engineers and erected on Dollar and Proctor mountains, where the first ski runs were laid out. The ski lifts quickly became popular and were soon marching up the slopes at other ski areas. One 1936-style chairlift remains along Trail Creek Road.

Harriman's vision for Sun Valley included a major resort. A 220-room lodge with two V-shaped wings on either side was built. The construction technique was simple: concrete was poured in forms of rough-sawn lumber. The wood-grained concrete was then treated with acid to turn it brown, furthering the imitation. The lodge was opened in December 1936 and immediately began to gain a name. The railroad used its influence to attract stars, who attracted other stars plus a pool of admirers and others who wanted to enjoy a stay at an exotic location.

SIGHTS

Museums

The Wood River Valley's history as a mining center is preserved at the **Ore Wagon Museum** at Ketchum and **Wood River Historical Society Museum** along Main Street in Hailey. The **Blaine County Museum** is particularly interesting with its photographs of the area, artifacts, and an extensive collection of political buttons. The museum is open Tues.-Sun. 10 a.m.-5 p.m., from Memorial Day to Labor Day.

Hailey

Hailey is well worth a stop. River Street here was once Chinatown's red-light district—the focus for Hailey's houses of ill repute that operated under such colorful names as Mabel's, Lizzie's, Gloria's, and Anita's. In this neighborhood, in January 1886, residents voiced their anti-Chinese sentiments when they issued a May 1 deadline for the Chinese to get out of the valley. And on the night of Sept. 21, 1911, Dot Allen's at Riverside and Bullion St. gained more attention than it wanted when its piano player was shot dead during an attempted rob-

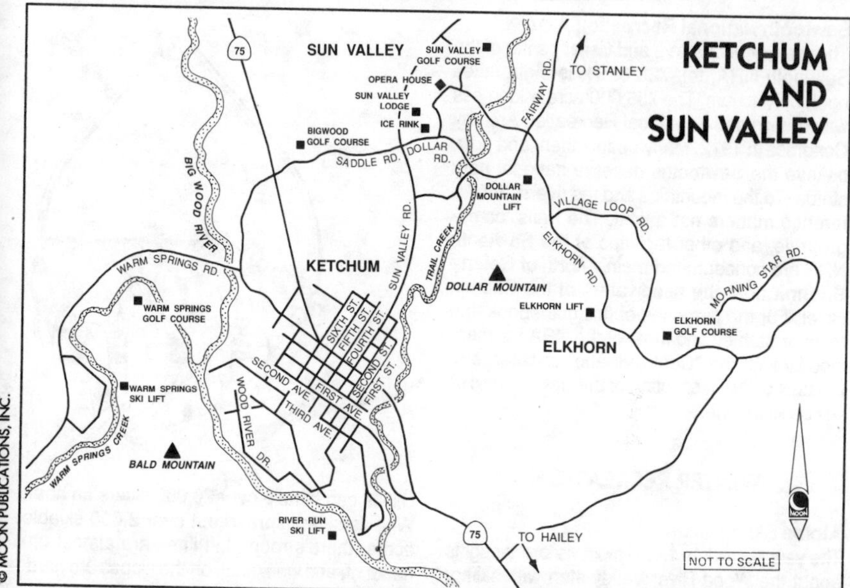

bery. The investigation into the killing exposed many of the town's prominent citizens.

The **birthplace of Ezra Pound** is near the corner of Pine St. and 2nd Avenue. Pound was born Oct. 30, 1885. His father was U.S. Land Office registrar until his parents fled the valley's cold and snow in 1887, behind the railroad's first rotary snowplow. Pound's role in literature is a source of local pride, but offsetting it is revulsion for his outspoken support for Benito Mussolini, and his flagrant anti-Semitism.

The **Blaine County Courthouse** is one of the most historically grand government buildings in Idaho. The building rose in 1883, originally housing the sheriff and jail as well as offices. Now the county's government offices alone are enough to fill it.

Hemingway Memorial

Along Trail Creek within sight of Sun Valley, a bust of Ernest Hemingway tops a memorial in a grove of trees.

"Best of all he loved the fall. The leaves yellow on the cottonwoods—leaves floating on the trout streams and above the hills. The high blue windless skies . . . now he will be part of them forever," reads the plaque on the simple memorial.

Hemingway never forgot Sun Valley or his love of fishing the Big Wood River and hunting waterfowl and upland birds nearby. The Pulitzer and Nobel Prize winner moved to Ketchum from Cuba in 1960. Plagued by failing health and alcoholism, Hemingway shot himself July 2, 1961. The grave of one of America's greatest writers is in the Ketchum Cemetery. Hemingway's family still calls Ketchum and the area home for at least some of the year.

Hot Springs

Some visitors to the Wood River Valley fairly bubble with excitement about hopping in the area's abundant hot springs. To the north of Ketchum some 18 miles is **Russian John Hot Springs,** located near the Russian John Guard Station along Hwy. 93. **Warfield Hot Springs** is southeast of Ketchum along Warm Springs Creek, about three miles beyond Cottonwood Campground. **Worsewick Hot Springs** is an undeveloped set of hot springs that lie 20 miles northwest of Hailey near Carrietown. Other commercial hot springs near Ketchum include **Easley Hot Springs,** tel. 726-5007, 14 miles north of Ketchum; day-use fee is $3 kids, $4 adults.

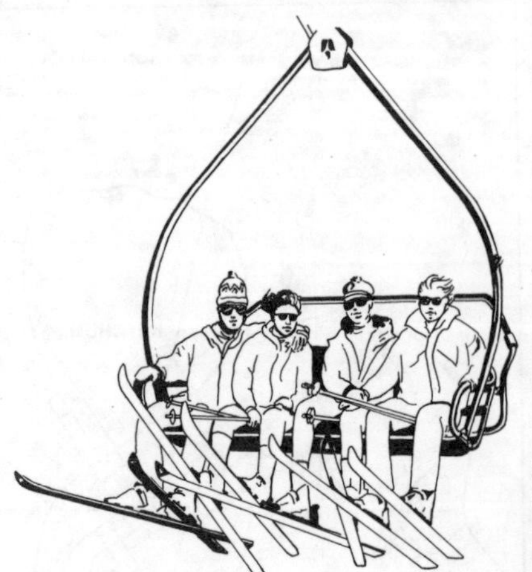

KAREN WHITE

Sawtooth National Recreation Area

The main headquarters and visitor center of the Sawtooth NRA, tel. 726-8291, is eight miles north of Ketchum. The 756,000-acre wilderness was designated a National Recreation Area by Congress in 1972. Many people then, and now, believe the Sawtooths deserve national park status. To the mountains and the rivers, the difference matters not a whit. The trails, campgrounds, and other facilities of the Sawtooth NRA are concentrated mainly north of **Galena Summit** near the headwaters of the Salmon River. For the purposes of this guidebook, the town of Stanley and most of the NRA fits more closely with the "Central Idaho" chapter, and the bulk of the description of the Sawtooth NRA will be found there.

WINTER RECREATION

Alpine Skiing

The year starts Jan. 1, and most visitors' thoughts about the Wood River Valley start with skiing. While all skiers would agree that Sun Valley is one of America's best-known ski resorts, here in Sun Valley and in the rest of Idaho, it is *the* American ski resort. Sun Valley pioneered the rise of destination ski resorts. Would Vail exist without Sun Valley? Would Aspen? Yes, in some form or another, undoubtedly, but at least Sun Valley fans can claim their favorite was first.

The 1994 Winter Olympics in Norway didn't hurt Sun Valley's or Idaho's reputation as a skiing kind of place. Idaho native Picabo Street's silver medal performance in the downhill competition won her a place in Sun Valley history, and the honor of having a street at the base of Bald Mountain named for her.

Sun Valley, tel. (800) 632-4104 within Idaho or (800) 635-8261 elsewhere, shines with a glow of self confidence that no other Idaho ski area can match. Its international reputation and status as the chosen place for so many discriminating skiers would bolster any ski area's confidence. This bit of swagger is easily defended, too. Sun Valley can point to a massive 3,200-foot vertical drop, 16 lifts, among them six detatchable quads, and more than 70 runs. The runs are divided into 38% easy, 45% intermediate, and 17% advanced. In all, the **Bald Mountain** and **Dollar Mountain** runs and facilities can handle over 26,000 skiers an hour. With its skiers spread out over 2,000 skiable acres, there's room. Lift lines are almost unheard of, and weekends on the slopes are hardly ever crowded.

The price of greatness? One-day adult lift tickets run $45. Skiers can and do substantially cut the price of their pleasures at Sun Valley by purchasing ticket packages. A three-day pass brings the daily average down to $43. A five-day pass cuts the daily cost to $40. Children 11 and under ski for $25 a day, multiday packages also available.

For skiers who want to learn more and hone their skills, the **Sun Valley Ski School** has been at it for 53 years and employs more than 160 teachers. Adult lessons are available for $41 a day for three hours or $109 for a three-day package. Children can join four-hour skiing classes for $55 a day or $147 for three days.

Rotarun Ski Area, tel. 788-6204, at 234 Croy Creek Rd. at Hailey, is where the locals go for both cross-country and Alpine skiing. This area is close, comfortable, and cheap compared to the world-class skiing on Baldy to the north.

Soldier Mountain, tel. 764-2300, is another local ski hill with 1,400 feet of vertical to ski. It's located 60 miles southwest of Sun Valley and 12 miles north of Fairfield along Hwy. 20. Soldier Mountain has 36 runs and two double chairlifts. The ski area has a day lodge with beer and wine, pizza, and snacks.

For skiers who want to start at the top, **Sun Valley Helicopter Ski Guides,** tel. 622-3108, is based at 260 1st Ave. W in Ketchum. They offer a day of heli-skiing for $400, or a special "three amigos rate" of $375 per person for groups of three. They also offer guided or unguided trips to a backcountry yurt, for overnight adventure.

Nordic Skiing

Sun Valley Nordic Center, tel. 622-2250, (800) 632-4104 in Idaho, or (800) 635-8261 elsewhere, offers 25 miles of marked and groomed trails leading from the Sun Valley Lodge. Cross-country skiers will find the amenities of a large destination resort and first-class Nordic skiing along with opportunities for Telemarking, skating, or simple relaxation along scenic trails. The **Nordic ski school** at the center is one of the first and best developed of its kind. Trail fees range from $11 per day and $9 per half-day for adults to $6 per day and $5.50 per half-day for children ages 6-12. Ski packages rent for $13 for adults and $8 for children. Guided lunch and dinner tours are also available. The Nordic Center pays attention to kids, too, setting special tracks for children three years and older. A children's terrain garden helps keep it interesting. Children's tracks and adult tracks also run parallel to each other. The center offers ski rentals and refreshments daily 9 a.m.-5 p.m. during the winter season.

One of the most popular destinations for Nordic skiers is the **Trail Creek Cabin,** 1.75 miles from the Nordic Center. The cabin is a warming shelter; a cheery fire is kept stoked. The trail to the cabin passes by the Hemingway Memorial along Trail Creek. The cabin has been a favorite New Year's Eve hideaway for stars in years past.

Galena Lodge, located 24 miles north of Ketchum along Hwy. 75, once ranked as the Wood River Valley's other major Nordic skiing center, but has been closed for the past couple of years. Ownership has been in limbo but is scheduled to shift to the community as a result of a large individual donation and a major fund-raising campaign. Organizers hope to have the resort operational by the winter of '94-95, and hope to make it a year-round enterprise with summer activities as well as winter skiing.

Radisson Elkhorn Resort, tel. 622-4511, also offers a Nordic skiing trail system and charges a trail-use fee. Like Sun Valley and Galena, Elkhorn maintains a ski shop and offers lessons and rentals. **Warm Springs Ranch,** tel. 726-3322, at 1801 Warm Springs Rd., also operates a Nordic center and trail system.

For a unique dining experience, **Sun Valley Trekking Co.,** tel. 788-9585, at Sun Valley offers dinner tours suitable for beginning skiers to the Boulder Yurt for $45, which includes the dinner and guide service. Menus range from Indian to Mongolian and European. The first party to make reservations gets to select the evening's menu.

Noncommercial cross-country trail systems in the Sun Valley area include the **Prairie Creek** and **North Fork** systems, both of which are groomed periodically. Information about both areas is available from the Sawtooth National Recreation Area, tel. 726-7672. Others include the **Lake Creek Trails,** which are maintained by the Sun Valley Ski Education Foundation, tel. 726-4129, near Hulen Meadows, and the **Wood River Trails,** which stretch from Hulen Meadows south to Bellevue. Information about the Wood River trails may be obtained by calling the Blaine County Recreation District, tel. 788-2117. Skiers are asked to donate $2 a day toward trail maintenance.

General information about cross-country skiing in the area is available from **Sun Valley Cross Country Skiing Association,** tel. 726-3423 or (800) 634-3347, at P.O. Box 1806, Ketchum, ID 83340.

Shops offering cross-country equipment for sale or rent include **Backwoods Mountain Sports,** tel. 726-8818, at 711 N. Main in Ketchum; and **Elephant's Perch,** tel. 726-3497, at 220 East Ave. N in Ketchum.

For the latest information about **avalanche conditions** and **weather forecasts** in the backcountry, call the Forest Service weather line, tel. 622-8027.

Snowmobiling

Mulligan Snowmobile Tours, tel. 726-9137, at Sun Valley, outfits and guides snowmobile tours of the trails in the area. Tours are available seven days a week during the winter season. The company furnishes snowmobiles, guides, snowsuits, and boots. Lunches and a video of the trip are optional. Clients must furnish warm headgear, gloves, and a sense of adventure.

For snowmobiling, Hailey offers the **Wood River Recreation Area,** with its 200 square miles of open sagebrush hills, valleys, and mountains. Marked and groomed snowmobiling trails are provided by the Sawtooth Snowmobile Club. The trailhead three miles west of Hailey offers a warming shelter and parking lot.

Sleigh Rides

Sleigh rides have always been part of Sun Valley's allure. When Clark Gable, Gary Cooper, and Ava Gardner, not to mention Ernest Hemingway, used to hang out here, sleighs carried them to the Trail Creek Cabin for lunches and dinners. The sleighs still leave the Sun Valley Inn at noon for lunch, and hourly 6-9 p.m. for dinner. Cost varies from $6 for lunch to $10 for dinner (for adults).

Sawtooth Sleighs, tel. 622-5019, offers dinner sleigh rides to a heated wall tent in the Sawtooth NRA. The menu includes steak and lobster dinners for $48 a person.

SUMMER RECREATION

The Wood River Valley and Ketchum in particular seems almost as busy during the summer as during the winter. The same mountains that give rise to skiers' hopes yield a treasure of places to get out and away from it all. One of the best sources of information about hiking trails close to Ketchum is the Sawtooth National Forest's **Ketchum Ranger Station,** tel. 622-5371, which is located along Sun Valley Rd. to the east of town.

Walking Trails

Lewiston has its Levee Parkway, Boise its Greenbelt. But neither town's walking-trail system can quite compare with the 20-mile **Wood River Trail System** maintained by the Blaine County Recreation District, tel. 788-2177. Trails run 20 miles from Lake Creek through Bellevue. Most of the route follows the Union Pacific Railroad right-of-way that was abandoned, then purchased by the state in 1987.

A tunnel under Hwy. 75 links the Wood River Trail with 10 miles of Sun Valley trails. An excellent trail brochure detailing the area's historic sites is available through the recreation district office. The brochure mentions such notable locations as Quigley Gulch east of Hailey, where George Pierson was hanged Aug. 1, 1884, in a feud over a woman; Knock Wu Choi swung a month later for killing a Chinese doctor in Altanta. Just down the trail at Bellevue is the site of the railroad depot completed in 1883, marking the arrival of civilization to the valley.

Big Wood National Recreation Trail

One of the closest trail systems, and one scenic and challenging enough to whet most visitors' appetites for more, is the **Big Wood National Recreation Trail,** which was established in 1978. The trail system includes several connected loops that can be taken on separately or combined. In early spring, the trails here become passable to hikers long before those in the higher mountains to the north. The main gateway to the trail system is the **Lake Creek Trailhead,** located three miles north of Ketchum along Hwy. 75. A highway sign marks its location.

From the trailhead, where you'll find parking, a restroom, and a footbridge across the Big Wood River, walkers can wander 2.5 miles along the river trail. Picnic tables and a bench are available along the route, which is popular for fishing and picnicking.

The **Fox Creek** loop offers a more ambitious destination. The six-mile loop ascends the western slopes of the valley. For those planning on one of the more strenuous hikes, a supply of water, a snack, a jacket, and matches are essential. The Forest Service warns against drinking water from the streams. Most carry cysts of *Giardia,* which can cause severe intestinal distress. Another caution: do not underestimate the weather. In the mountains, the weather can change in a hurry. If you plan to take one of the more ambitious loops, carry a day pack and stuff a jacket in it, even if the weather is sunny when you leave.

Remember, a six-mile hike along Fox Creek means gaining 900 feet of elevation, a three-hour jaunt more or less. The time will depend on the hiker's fitness and how long he or she takes to enjoy the route. For the fit, the confident, and the ambitious, the Big Wood trail system also offers loops to **Adams Gulch, Upper Fox Creek,** and **Oregon Creek.**

Overnight camping is allowed along the backcountry loops. Campfires may be allowed depending on the season and the fire danger. Most backpackers prefer to carry gasoline or butane stoves to cook with and have relegated campfires to the realm of an option. Keep your camp away from the trail and away from the stream if possible. This will provide you with more privacy and avoid interference with other hikers' enjoyment of the trip.

Norton Lakes Trail
For those who want to try casting for trout in a high mountain lake, Norton Lakes Trail offers what they're seeking. Hikers can reach the trail by taking Baker Creek Rd. south from Hwy. 75. Norton Creek Rd. is 6.4 miles from the highway, and the trailhead is another mile along the primitive single-lane road. The trail starts in a deep gully and hikers must ford the stream to find the trail. The trail itself stretches 2.6 miles to **Upper Norton Lake,** which is a fifth of a mile beyond the lower lake. The route is mostly through open trees and grassland; hikers ascend 1,460 feet in elevation to reach the upper lake at 9,100 feet.

If camping at **Lower Norton Lake,** the Forest Service asks that camps be kept well away from the lakeshore to cut down on the damage that scars too many mountain lakes. No motorized vehicles are allowed on the trail, which is popular with both horse riders and hikers.

Pioneer Cabin Trail
To experience outdoor life before Sun Valley, hike the Pioneer Cabin Trail to the cabin. It was built by Union Pacific Railroad crews in 1937 at the 9,400-foot level to shelter spring skiers who would hike up the trail on skis outfitted with climbing skins. The skiers would find the bowls and valleys of the Pioneer Mountains the reward for their exertions.

Today the cabin remains as it was then. The Forest Service maintains the cabin and provides firewood. Hikers and backpackers are fond of stopping to picnic on the cabin's steps. The rewards also include a panoramic view of majestic mountains—on the left is 12,009-foot Hyndman Peak, along with Old Hyndman and Handwerk peaks; on the right is Cobb Peak.

To reach the trailhead, take Trail Creek Rd. from Ketchum 5.5 miles to Corral Creek Rd., then take the dirt road for four miles to a parking area near a meadow. A footbridge across the creek leads to the trail and the registration box. An old logging road and series of switchbacks winds along the mountain's shoulder. Another mile of open slope gradually climbs to another series of switchbacks. Survive the switchbacks and the cabin is just over the rise. The trail gains 2,500 feet of elevation in 3.8 miles, a climb that would be considered steep anywhere but in Sawtooth country. Carrying water is a necessity because there is none along the trail; packing a lunch should be considered a necessity too. Expect to spend four to five hours to reach the cabin and return. Leave yourself more time if you like to gawk.

For those who would rather do more, **Long Gulch Trail** is 4.2 miles back to the Corral Creek Trailhead, stretching the roundtrip from 7.6 miles to eight miles. The Long Gulch Trail offers a route that is steep in places but gives hikers a new area to explore.

North Fork Of Hyndman Creek Trail
Another option is the North Fork of Hyndman Creek Trail, which was completed by the Forest Service in 1986. The 8.5-mile loop starts along Hyndman Creek's north fork, climbs up a series of switchbacks to the cabin, then takes the high road back to the south and branches off, heading south from the Corral Creek Trail before dropping back down to the **Johnstone Creek Trailhead.** To reach the trailhead, drive south of Ketchum along Hwy. 75 and turn east at East Fork Road. Keep going through **Triumph,** an old mining town, take Hyndman Creek Rd. to the left, and park at the new bridge.

Guided Hikes
Sun Valley offers a relatively rare commodity in Idaho's outdoor world: hiking guides. **Sun Valley Trekking Co.,** tel. 788-9585, offers full- and half-day hikes. Fees range from $20 a person for outings lasting three to five hours with groups of 5-10. Individuals may hire private guides for $95 a person or $45 apiece for two for a half-day outing. Fees for all-day hikes range $40-185, depending on group size. Catered lunches that will be almost as memorable as the country (jerky, baklava, and lemon-lime mousse with biscotti) are available for $5.50-9.50 a person.

Fishing Silver Creek
The Big and Little Wood rivers, the Salmon River to the north (with its trout and the rainbow's cousin, the oceangoing steelhead), and

Silver Creek make Hailey-Ketchum-Sun Valley one of Idaho's principal sites for fly fishermen on pilgrimages.

Silver Creek is a spring creek that emerges west of **Gannett,** heads east for **Picabo** (as in now you see me, now you don't, or in acknowledgment of Idaho's most recent Olympic medalist, Picabo Street), and then drops south to the Little Wood River. Its course and physical parameters have been charted by fly fishermen for decades, ever since the introduction of rainbow trout and the later invasion by brown trout.

Silver Creek bewitches anglers with a simple formula. It is home to a lot of trout, a lot of *big* trout, and few of them will bite, at least not on just anything. The anglers who come here worry about water levels and temperatures, taking them as formulas for auguring when the aquatic mayflies will emerge that will put trout on the feed. Maybe then tiny flies, some only an eighth of an inch long, tied to a gossamer strand of clear fishing line that would barely lift a pound without parting, will catch a six- or seven-pounder. Then again, maybe they won't.

That temptation brings thousands of anglers to Silver Creek. The rules along the best stretches of the stream are tough. Anglers must use fly-fishing gear on most of the stream and they must release the fish they catch. The **Nature Conservancy of Idaho,** tel. 726-3007, based at 400 E. Canyon Run Blvd., serves as river-keeper and guardian of Silver Creek. The conservancy owns 2,500 acres surrounding Silver Creek and 14 miles of the stream. More than 8,000 anglers have registered at the conservancy's headquarters at the **Silver Creek Preserve,** which is due south of Gannett, Hwy. 20, and the stream itself.

Silver Creek's fishing can pose hefty challenges for anglers. So can the fishing regulations. The Idaho Fish and Game Department allows anglers to keep trout they catch from the stream's mouth up to the Point of Rocks on the Fish and Game access area three miles northeast of Picabo along Hwy. 20. From there upriver, the department requires catch-and-release fishing. From Kilpatrick Bridge upstream to the confluence of Grover and Stalker creeks, the department's regulations allow only fly-fishing tackle. Silver Creek, like most Idaho streams, is open to fishing from the last week of May normally to the end of November.

Fishing The Big And Little Wood Rivers

The Big Wood and Little Wood rivers are also beloved by fly fishers. The Big Wood in particular, with its proximity to Ketchum and Hailey and its lush growth of cottonwoods, draws anglers.

Proximity aside, the Big and Little Wood both offer outstanding trout fishing, about 40 miles' worth apiece. The Big Wood's most popular access points are between Bellevue and Hailey at bridges along Lower Bradford Road. Anglers also wade in at Ketchum and Hailey. Hulen Meadows Bridge provides another access point for a favored stretch upriver to the north fork, near the Sawtooth NRA visitor center. The Big Wood is catch-and-release fishing from the first bridge north of Hailey on upriver. The best fishing occurs about the height of the summer season in early August.

To offer visitors a chance to catch a trout for the pan, Idaho Fish and Game releases nearly 20,000 fish a year in the Big Wood. The two Woods present a smorgasbord of opportunities for anglers. The Big Wood, in various reaches, offers rainbow, cutthroat, brook, and brown trout. The Little Wood offers mostly rainbows and browns.

The Little Wood River starts in the Pioneer Mountains to the east then flows southwest to its meeting with the Big Wood. Only a 2.5-mile stretch in the **Taylor Williams State Recreation Area,** along the Little Wood 8.5 miles northeast of Richfield, is limited to catch-and-release fishing. The Little Wood's passage through the lava and sagebrush of the great southern desert can fool newcomers.

Lake Fishing

High mountain lakes sprinkle Idaho's landscape with glints of sapphire among the green and gray tapestry of pines and granite. Ketchum-area visitors have a rare opportunity to drive right up to a string of such gems at the **Lake Creek Lakes.** To reach the lakes, turn right off Hwy. 75 at the Lake Creek Rd. sign and continue four miles.

Fishing Guides

Fishing guides have found their places in the Wood River Valley helping anglers make their dreams a reality. Rates range from $150 for a half day to $200 for a full day for one or two anglers. Guide fees go up as more anglers join the party. **Sun Valley Outfitters,** tel. 622-3400, specializes in trips on the Big Wood, Warm Springs Creek, and Big Lost rivers in addition to Silver Creek. **Lost River Outfitters,** tel. 726-1706, offers fly-casting and fly-tying clinics, in addition to fishing expeditions along famous trout streams. The company also leases lakes on local ranches in the Big Lost River drainage for hard-to-top trout fishing. The Lost River Outfitters store is located at 620 N. Main in Ketchum. Other major fly-fishing shops you can go to for supplies or to track down guides include **Silver Creek Outfitters,** tel. 726-5282, at 507 N. Main, and **Snug Co.,** which maintains shops at Elkhorn Village, Sun Valley Mall, and 680 Sun Valley Rd. in Ketchum.

Mountain Biking

Steep mountains and valleys mean one thing to summer bicyclists: a challenge. The rise of mountain biking as a sport indicates thousands of cyclists are eager to face that challenge. The Sawtooth National Forest and NRA staffs have recognized the boom and geared up to meet it. For information about routes, contact the **Ketchum Ranger District,** tel. 622-5371, which is located along the Sun Valley Rd. east of Ketchum. The **Sawtooth NRA office,** tel. 726-8291, is 18 miles north of Ketchum along Hwy. 75.

Some of the routes recommended by the Ketchum Ranger District include: **Ketchum to Corral Creek,** a route that follows Trail Creek Rd. and then Corral Creek Rd. for a total of eight miles, one-way; and **Ketchum to Warm Springs Rd.,** covering 16 miles of fairly easy riding until the road steepens as it climbs toward Dollarhide Summit. Off Warm Springs Rd. is the **Red Warrior Creek Trail,** past Warfield Hot Springs. Taking the trail three miles to the Lodgepole Gulch Trail, then downhill to the Greenhorn Gulch Rd. and back to Ketchum, makes for an outing labeled strenuous. A good spot to explore from Ketchum is the **Adams Gulch Rd.,** north of town along Hwy. 75 about a mile and a half.

When spring makes for muddy conditions at higher elevations, generally those north of Ketchum, the Forest Service suggests looking south for options. One favorite is **East Fork Rd.,** which stretches 16 miles from Hwy. 75 past the Mascot Mine. Off East Fork Rd., riders can connect with Cove Rd., and from it with Quigley Creek Rd., which passes through the gulch of justice where Hailey residents once hanged outlaws. Another good ride traces **Elkhorn Gulch Rd.** until it forks at the pavement's end. Go left on Parker Gulch Rd., then take the Bear Gulch Trail to Hyndman Creek Rd.; turn east from there on East Fork Rd. until you pass Triumph. Turn right on Peters Gulch Rd. at the power lines, then back up the gulch to Elkhorn Rd. again.

A good ride near Hailey is **Quigley Creek Rd. to Slaughterhouse Creek Road.** On Quigley Creek head out eight miles to the fork, take the right one, and ride toward the top of Quigley. A mile from the summit and just past a cabin, turn right at another fork and ride back down. Indian Creek climbs steeply for about a mile. After 8.5 miles, turn right and ride down Quigley Creek Road.

Galena Summit Lodge may be reopened by the time you read this. It was once a haven for mountain bikers. (See "Nordic Skiing," under "Winter Recreation," above, for more information.)

Mountain bikes are available for rent for about $15 a day and $10 a half day in Ketchum at **The Elephant's Perch,** tel. 726-3497, along Sun Valley Rd.; **Formula Sports,** tel. 726-3194, along Main St. two blocks north of the stoplight; **Sturtevants,** tel. 726-4502, at 314 N. Main St.; and **Backwoods Mountain Sports,** tel. 726-8826, at the intersection of Main St. and Warm Springs Road. **Pete Lanes** in Sun Valley, tel. 622-2279, rents 10-speed, tandem, and mountain bikes. Mountain bikes are $10 an hour and $20 a day.

Camping And Picnicking

The Wood River Valley may be known internationally for its world-class resort and its world-class skiing, but in Idaho and much of the West it's also known for the quality of both its scenery and camping.

The Sawtooth National Forest maintains a string of campgrounds and picnic areas to the south and west of the magnificent **Sawtooth National Recreation Area,** with its 29 campgrounds in some of the most magnificent scenery in Idaho. In Sun Valley, the **Boundary Picnic Area** is popular with its four tables that are available June-October. In the nearby Pioneer Mountains east of Hailey and Bellevue are the small **Sawmill, Federal Gulch,** and **Copper**

Creek campgrounds, which are open May-October. Sawmill has five campsites, Federal Gulch six, and Copper Creek seven. To the west of Hailey is the **Deer Creek Picnic Area** with three picnic tables. North of Fairfield is the **Pioneer Campground** with nine sites.

Between Fairfield and Featherville are 11 campgrounds. **Baumgartner** ranks as the largest with 28 campsites along the Boise River's south fork. Others include **Pioneer,** which has a group picnic area and nine campsites; **Abbott,** along the south fork with eight sites; **Chaparral** with two campsites; **Bird Creek** with five; **Skeleton Creek** with four; and **Big Smokey Creek** with a dozen campsites.

Two privately owned campgrounds also operate in the Wood River Valley. **Red Top Meadows,** tel. 726-5445 or 726-5656, has 45 campsites starting at $17 a night. **Riverside Campground,** tel. 788-2020, is located along Bradford Rd. at Bellevue with 31 campsites for $14.50-15.50. **Sun Valley RV Resort,** tel. 726-3429, offers 79 spaces for $16-18.

For those who would rather rent gear than haul it, **The Elephant's Perch,** tel. 726-3497, along Sun Valley Rd., rents camping equipment, everything from backpacks to sleeping bags, foam pads, and tents. **Backwoods Mountain Sports** in Ketchum, tel. 726-8826, also rents camping equipment ranging from tents to stoves.

Horseback Riding

The Sun Valley Company's **Horsemen's Center,** tel. 622-2387, offers scenic horseback tours into the surrounding mountains in summer, and sleigh rides in winter. Call for current prices. Another stable is **Hoof Beats,** tel. 788-4247, at 809 Canyon Rd. near Hailey.

Tennis

Sun Valley Lodge is the focus of the tennis scene with 18 courts where guests pay $6 a person for singles and $3 per person for doubles, and nonguests pay $8 and $4 respectively. A ball machine can be rented for $10 per half-hour. But the resort's not the only game in town, nor does it claim to be. Some 85 tennis courts are scattered throughout the valley. Along Warm Springs Ave. a mile from Ketchum, **Warm Springs Tennis Club,** tel. 726-4040, arranges games and lessons. Public courts are available at **Prospector Tennis and Swim Club,** tel. 726-9404, at 319 Skiway Dr. at Ketchum. Tennis racket rentals are available from **Sturtevants,** tel. 726-4502, at 314 N. Main Street.

Shooting

Sun Valley offers an archery range at the **Sun Valley Gun Club,** tel. 622-2311, open daily 11 a.m.-6 p.m. Equipment can be rented for an hourly fee. Information about trap and skeet shooting is available by calling 622-2310. A round of either can be shot Tues.-Sun. 11 a.m.-6 p.m. for $6.50. Ammunition and rental guns are also available.

Ice-skating

Name the biggest names in modern U.S. figure skating circles and they've taken a turn or two on Sun Valley's splendid outdoor ice rink. Sun Valley offers lessons and skate rentals. Admission to its indoor and outdoor rinks is $5. Information is available by calling 622-2194. Sun Valley Lodge is also famous for its June-Sept. lunch and dinner skating shows.

Golf

Sun Valley Golf Course, tel. 622-2251, was designed by Robert Trent Jones, Jr. and labeled by *Golf Digest* as "one of the best 100 golf courses in the United States." The 18-hole, par-72 course spans 6,565 yards and brackets Trail Creek, crossing it seven times on the front nine. Greens fees for 18 holes are $40 for guests, $50 for nonguests. Electric carts, required to play the course, are available for $18 for nine holes, and $22 for 18. Clubs may be rented for $20 a day. The other Robert Trent Jones, Jr. course is the **Elkhorn Golf Club,** tel. 622-4511, at neighboring Elkhorn Village. Other golf courses include **Bigwood Golf Course,** tel. 726-4024, along Saddle Rd. near Ketchum, and **Warm Springs Golf Course,** tel. 726-3715, along Warm Springs Rd. west of Ketchum, both of which offer nine holes.

Soaring

Sun Valley Soaring, tel. 788-3054, is based at the Hailey airport and takes clients on sailplane rides over the surrounding mountains winter and summer. Flights vary from winter rides over Baldy during the peak of the ski season to morning rides over the mountain in summer—smooth trips good for children and the faint-of-heart, according to the company. The opposite experience, an extended mountain excursion in the often turbulent, always exciting, atmosphere above Idaho's mountains in summer, is also available.

ACCOMMODATIONS

Prices for lodging in the Wood River Valley area fluctuate widely depending on the season. Peak winter season rates are highest, followed by peak summer season. Cheapest rates are available during the "slack" times, generally mid-April through May, and October to mid-December. During these periods, rates can be as low as half the peak winter rates.

Bed And Breakfast Inns

Idaho Country Inn, 134 Latigo Ln. in Ketchum, tel. 726-1019, has 10 rooms at rates ranging $115-155 a night, which includes a full breakfast. Several rooms can be connected to form suites. **The River Street Inn Bed and Breakfast,** 100 Rivers St. W in Ketchum, tel. 726-3611, has nine rooms for $115-165.

Bellevue And Hailey Accommodations

Taking the valley's towns in alphabetical order would put Bellevue first with the **High Country Motel,** tel. 788-2050, at 626 S. Main, and the **Southern Gentleman,** at 110 N. Main. Hailey's next on the list as well as next along Hwy. 75 heading north for Ketchum and Sun Valley. The **Hailey Hotel,** tel. 788-3140, at 201 S. Main, has six rooms for $25-35 a night. Also at Hailey is the **Hitchrack Motel,** tel. 788-2409, at 619 S. Main, with rooms for $42-55. The **Airport Inn,** tel. 788-2477, at 820 S. Fourth Ave., is near guess where and has rooms for $50-65.

Ketchum/Sun Valley Property Management Services

Ketchum is the capital of independent lodging in the Wood River Valley. Several property management companies operate as clearinghouses for local accommodations. **Base Mountain Properties,** tel. 726-5601, works with a number of property managers in the area. They can arrange accommodations in condos, townhomes, or houses, ranging in price from $65 to $1500 a night. **Bitterroot-Alpine Property Management/Sun Valley Vacations,** tel. 726-5394 or (800) 251-3037, at 380 Washington Ave. N, handles over 200 condominiums ranging $50-1500 a night. **Mountain Resorts,** tel. 726-9344 or (800) 635-4444 outside Idaho, has 50 condos ranging $55-1000 a night. **Sun Valley Area Reservations,** tel. 726-3660 or (800) 635-1076, handles registrations for accommodations ranging $65-1000 a night. **Sun Valley Company,** tel. 622-4111 or (800) 632-4104 in Idaho, (800) 635-8261 outside Idaho, in addition to running the Sun Valley Lodge and Sun Valley Inn, also handles reservations for a number of other accommodations in the valley ranging $69-700 a night. **Sun Valley Resort Reservations,** tel. 726-3374 or (800) 635-8242, has condos for $65-1500. **Warm Springs Resort at Sun Valley,** tel. 726-8274 or (800) 635-4404, has condos for $60-975. **White Cloud Property Management,** tel. 726-0110 or (800) 245-6443, has condos in the usual wide range of prices, depending on size and season.

Ketchum/Sun Valley Accommodations

If condo rentals aren't your bag, conventional hotel and motel rooms are also abundant in the area. Sun Valley Ski Resort's two primary lodging facilities include the venerable **Sun Valley Lodge** and the more casual **Sun Valley Inn,** a few blocks away. The Lodge has 125 rooms, two restaurants, a pool, and lots of history. This is the place you're most likely to see the Hollywood celebs up playing in the snow. Depending on the season, a standard room here costs $64-125. Or you can splurge on the Parlor Suite, which has its own sitting room and fireplace for $155-299 a night, depending on the season.

A standard room at the Inn goes for $64-99 a night, depending on the season.

Reservations for both the Inn and the Lodge are taken by the Sun Valley Company's central reservations office, tel. 622-4111 or (800) 632-4104 inside Idaho, (800) 635-8261 outside Idaho.

Bald Mountain Lodge, tel. 726-9963, has rooms ranging $45-105 at 151 S. Main. **Best Western Christiana Lodge,** tel. 726-3351, at 651 Sun Valley Rd., has rooms ranging $55-82. **Best Western Tyrolean Lodge,** tel. 726-5336, is at the base of Mount Baldy near the River Run Lift. Its rooms range $50-150. The lodge has two-story suites with spa tubs, plus two common indoor spas and saunas. The **Clarion,** tel. 726-5900, is at 6th and Main with units ranging $60-250.

The **Radisson Elkhorn Resort,** tel. 622-4511 in Idaho or (800) 635-9356 outside, has rooms and condos ranging $94-402. **Heidelberg Inn,** tel. 726-5361, is along Warm Springs Rd. and has rooms ranging $60-104. **Ketchum Korral Motor Lodge,** tel. 726-3510, has rooms ranging $50-115. **Lift Tower Lodge,** tel. 726-5163, has rooms for $49-79.

River Run Lodge, tel. 726-9086, has rooms for $60-190. **Ski View Lodge,** tel. 726-3441, has rooms for $35-65 at 409 S. Main. **Tamarack Lodge,** tel. 726-3344 or (800) 521-5379, has rooms for $64-154.

FOOD

American And Continental

The epitome of Sun Valley dining is **The Lodge Dining Room,** tel. 622-4111 (the same phone number for all Sun Valley Co. restaurants). In the Dining Room the menu ranges from fresh Idaho trout to filet mignon and rack of lamb; entrees range from $18 up to $48 (for a chateaubriand). Other lodge restaurants include **Gretchen's,** which specializes in lighter meals; **The Ram,** with its roasted meats and baked trout; and the **Ore House** and **Konditorei** where a more informal atmosphere prevails. The Sun Valley Co. also operates five mountaintop restaurants.

Also in Sun Valley, at the Radisson Elkhorn Resort, tel. 622-4511, **Tequila Joe's,** has prawns and some refreshing twists, such as skirt steaks; **Jesse's** has steak and seafood; **Papa Dino's** offers pizza and pasta; and the **Clubhouse** serves up breakfast and lunch for the linksters. **The Ore House,** tel. 622-4363, is in Sun Valley Mall. Its menu ranges from smoked pork back ribs to teriyaki chicken.

In Ketchum, **Evergreen Bistro,** tel. 726-3888, has ambience and good food and wine. It has been voted the valley's best restaurant and won a *Wine Spectator* excellence award. Reservations are required. **Chez Michel,** tel. 726-3032, which recently moved into the spot vacated by the Christiania, offers nouvelle cuisine in a country-French atmosphere. **Desperados,** tel. 726-3068, at 406 Washington Ave. N, offers a traditional American menu.

The **Ketchum Grill,** tel. 726-4660, at 502 E. Ave. N, serves up rustic country-American fare with international influence. Most entrees are under $14.50. **A Matter of Taste,** tel. 726-8468, at Trail Creek Village along S. Main, offers an extensive salad and appetizer menu, with selections ranging from Chinese beluga caviar to empanadas. Meals include venison tenderloin in morel sauce, beef Wellington, or whatever the chef's whims may lead to. **The Pioneer Saloon,** tel. 726-3139, along Main St., has a menu that stretches to include hamburgers, prime rib, and seafood. Entrees range about $8-22.

Something Special, tel. 726-7247, at 406 N. Washington, features prime rib, garlic lemon chicken, and hollandaise artichoke chicken. Specializing in catering, the restaurant offers complete meals for carry-out and will arrange delivery by cab. The delivery is free with orders meeting the minimum. **The Sawtooth Club,** tel. 726-5233, at 231 N. Main St., serves steaks and seafood, pastas, and a wide range of appetizers. They also offer an extensive wine list. Entrees run about $8-19. **Warm Springs Ranch Restaurant,** tel. 726-2609, features entrees like fresh trout and roast pork loin for about $7-17.

In Hailey, **The Hailey Ritz,** tel. 788-3140, at the Hailey Hotel, goes with the country's basic strengths: 16-ounce T-bones, sirloin, lamb chops, and snake-bite chili. Entrees range $7-20.

Ethnic Restaurants

Ketchum is the place to go for international cuisine. **China Pepper,** tel. 726-0959, at the corner of Sixth and Washington, offers some familiar favorites, such as hot and sour soup, and some more exotic entrees, such as Thai shrimp with coconut-peanut sauce. Prices range $12-17. **Panda Chinese Restaurant,** tel. 726-3591, is at 515 N. East Ave., and features Mandarin, Szechuan, and Hunan dishes.

Piccolo, tel. 726-9251, along East Ave. between First and Second streets, offers authentic Italian cuisine for lunch and dinner. **Peter's Restaurant,** tel. 726-9515, features Northern Italian as well as Austrian dishes at 180 Sixth Street. **Salvatore's,** tel. 726-3111, at 111 Washington Ave. N, has patio dining in the summer and a roaring fireplace to dine beside in winter. The fine-dining Italian restaurant offers eclectic pasta recipes ranging $10-15, and meat entrees in the $16-22 range. The **Baldy Base**

Club, or "BBC's" as it's known locally, serves fresh pasta and other Italian specialties at the Warm Springs Village, tel. 726-3838.

Mama Inez, tel. 726-4213, is at Seventh and Warm Springs Rd. and offers tortillas made within driving distance and the best ingredients available elsewhere.

Breakfast, Lunch, And Lighter Fare

Ketchum's breakfast and lunch specialists include **The Kneadery,** tel. 726-9462, at 260 Leadville Ave., with its menu of omelettes, soups, and salads; and **The Kitchen,** tel. 726-3856, along Main St., with omelettes, pancakes, baked goods, and soups (no smoking). **Buffalo Cafe,** tel. 726-9795, is open for breakfast and lunch at 320 East Ave. North. **Perry's,** tel. 726-7703, at 141 W. Fourth St., offers espresso, continental breakfasts, and deli lunches.

Apples Bar & Grill, tel. 726-7067, at 215 Lloyd Dr., is at the base of Baldy in the Alpine Greyhawk Building, and focuses on burgers and other charbroiled sandwiches. **Lefty's,** tel. 726-2744, at the corner of Sixth and Main, features sandwiches and grilled items and a good selection of imported beers. **Mutley's,** tel. 726-8143, at 721 Sun Valley Rd., boasts the best doggone barbecued ribs in the valley with dinners about $4-9, and barbecued beef, pork, or chicken sandwiches for $3.50.

X's Trough and Brew Pub, tel. 726-2267, along Main St., offers a wide selection of microbrewery draft beers with their lunch and dinner, while **Rico's Pizza,** tel. 726-3200, at 209 N. Main, has a dining room and offers takeout.

Elsewhere in the area, **Treat Haus,** tel. 622-4089, at Elkhorn Village, has burgers and sandwiches with sweet-tooth specials ranging from fine chocolates to cookies and espresso. **Beaner's,** tel. 726-2962, is located at 271 Sun Valley Rd. in Hailey and offers an enticing selection of desserts and espresso. And joining the brewpub scene is **Sun Valley Brewing Co.,** at 201 N. Main in Bellevue, tel. 788-5777.

ENTERTAINMENT AND EVENTS

The **Sun Valley Ice Show,** tel. 622-2231, is held every Saturday night at the Sun Valley Lodge rink and attracts the greatest figure skaters in the world. Olympic gold medalists are standard fare here most summers—a tradition that stretches back to the resort's founding. The show runs from mid-June to mid-September. Tickets are $20 for children 12 and younger and $24 for adults. Reserved seating is available on the Sun Room Terrace for $34. A buffet is served Saturday nights on the terrace—$63 for adults and $44 for children.

Movies are shown at the **Sun Valley Opera House,** tel. 622-2244, with first-run movies showing at 7 and 9 most evenings. The classic tale of the valley, *Sun Valley Serenade,* with Sonja Henie, John Payne, and Glenn Miller and his Orchestra, shows year-round at 5 p.m., sometimes alternating daily with a seasonal film such as one of Warren Miller's ski extravaganzas.

Events

Something is happening nearly every night and every weekend in Sun Valley and the Wood River Valley. For more information on the events listed, contact the Sun Valley/Ketchum Chamber of Commerce, tel. 726- 3423 or (800) 634-3347, or write them at P.O. Box 2420, Sun Valley, ID 83353. Winter events include a **Christmas Parade** of 100 ski instructors bearing torches down Dollar Mountain on Christmas Eve to begin an evening of fireworks, carolers, and the arrival of Santa Claus. **New Year's Eve** is marked by a bonfire-lit food festival and a dance with a big band. **January Theme Weeks** (such as singles week or ski-clubs week) draws in fun crowds.

The event schedule heats up dramatically with spring's arrival and the emergence of fly fishermen, golfers, bicyclists, tennis players, and others. **Hailey Springfest,** with its arts and crafts, music, and other attractions during the Memorial Day Weekend, generally coincides with the opening of fishing season. The end of May is given over to the annual **Sun Valley Pro Am Golf Tournament.**

In June, the major events begin early with **Sun Valley Gallery Association Openings** (the first Friday of *every* month), and in mid-month, the Governor's Cup Golf Tournament takes place at Sun Valley Resort. The **Groshong Memorial Polo Tournament** is held in late June each year at Bellevue.

The Independence Day holiday brings out the crowds for the **Hailey Days of the Old West,** with its parade, rodeo, barbecue, and shoot-out. The **Wood River Valley Arts and**

Crafts Festival is held in Ketchum during July's second week and coincides with the opening of the **Sun Valley Music Festival.**

August brings the **Sun Valley Wine Auction** and some of the leading vintners and their fans to Idaho. The **Sun Valley Symphony** normally tunes up the first week of August and keeps playing through most of the month. In mid-August, the annual **Sun Valley Center Arts and Crafts Fair** rolls around. The **Blaine County Fair** is held at Carey at midmonth, while Sun Valley hosts the White Knob Challenge, a 20-mile mountain-bike race, also midmonth. The **Northern Rockies Folk Festival** occupies Hailey during the third weekend of August. The month's end brings the **Danny Thompson Memorial Golf Tournament** to Sun Valley.

The Labor Day holiday continues the fun with Ketchum's **Wagon Days Arts and Crafts Festival,** which includes a big hitch parade, pancake breakfasts, and Western music. **Swing 'n' Dixie Jazz Jamboree,** held at Sun Valley in mid-October, provides one of the liveliest events of the season, drawing master jazz musicians and groups from throughout the West.

SHOPPING

In terms of quantity and variety, Ketchum and Sun Valley shopping follows the lead of area lodging and food, with plenty of choices for all tastes.

Art Galleries

Sun Valley and Ketchum boast a greater concentration of art galleries than any other part of Idaho, a combined 15 galleries for the two towns. **Sun Valley Center for the Arts and Humanities,** tel. 726-9491, is a nonprofit group that maintains a gallery at 191 E. Fifth St. in Ketchum. **Valley Artists' Gallery,** tel. 726-0955, exhibits works by local artists and functions as a cooperative at Ketchum Town Square at Fourth and Main streets. Other Ketchum galleries include the **Toneri Art Gallery,** tel. 726-5639, at 320 Leadville Ave. N, specializing in watercolors, prints, and posters of fish and wildlife, flowers, and landscapes by Idaho artist Lynn Toneri; **Anne Reed Gallery,** tel. 726- 3036, at 620 Sun Valley Rd.; **Bruschofsky Galleries,** tel. 726-4950, at Sixth and Leadville; **CODA Galleries,** tel. 726-4484, at 380 Leadville Ave.; **Donna Rose Galleries,** tel. 726-4133, at 201 N. Main St.; **Gail Severen Gallery,** tel. 726-5079, at 620 Sun Valley Rd.; **River Run Gallery,** tel. 726-8878, at 291 First. Ave. N; and **Stonington Galleries,** tel. 726-4826, at Trail Creek Village along S. Main, and at Baldy Base Camp Building in Warm Springs Village, tel. 726-2146. **The Friesen Gallery of Fine Art,** tel. 726-4174, at 391 First Ave. N; and **Steve Snyder Gallery,** tel. 726-8100, at 131 W. Fourth St. and First Ave., round out the Ketchum art scene.

More Shopping

Legacy Antiques and Imports, at N. Main and 10th St., offers selections from Europe, the Orient, and Mexico. It specializes in country furniture and silk floral wreaths and arrangements. **Country Cousin Store,** at 411 Sun Valley Rd., has antiques, collectibles, and handicrafts.

Boutiques include **Apropos of Sun Valley,** at 711 N. Main, and **Benetton-Forza 12,** at 471 Leadville. **Comme Les Filles,** in lower Giacobbi Square, specializes in French imports, and **La Bottega,** in the Colonnade Mall along Sun Valley Rd., offers sportswear from New York, Europe, and London. Other boutiques include **Maggies of Sun Valley,** in the Galleria, and **Souleiado,** at Trail Creek Village.

For clothing from the fashionable or functional to the just plain comfortable, **Ketchum Corner,** at 191 N. Main, stocks Levis by the hundreds; **Pete Lane's,** in the Sun Valley Mall, specializes in sportswear; and **T. Kay's Fashions** focuses on stylish and comfortable fashions. **Timberland/Mercantile of Sun Valley,** at Main St. and Sun Valley Rd., is fun to shop. **Snug,** at 680 Sun Valley Rd., stocks the familiar names: Reebok, Ralph Lauren, Royal Robbins, and other designers. T-shirt companies have also found their places in the valley with **Local Daze,** at 240 Main St.; and **Mountain Tops,** at Giacobbi Square at Fourth and Leadville. Children's ski outfits and clothing are available at **Duck Soup,** in the Walnut Avenue Mall along Sun Valley Rd.; and **Kidfitters of Sun Valley,** at 711 N. Main.

Jewelers abound in the valley. **Barry Peterson Jewelers,** at 400 E. Sun Valley Rd., features unusual gemstones, while **Expressions in Gold,** at 260 N. Main, has Idaho garnets and opals. **Impostors Copy Jewels** specializes in such faithful copies of jewels that all but the owners would have trouble telling the difference. The owners could tell by the price, $25-95. **The Silver Company,** at Giacobbi Square, displays Idaho silver, crystals, gemstones, and silverware. **Towne & Park Fine Jewelry,** at Sun Valley Mall, is the oldest jewelry shop in the valley. **Davies-Reid Tribal Arts,** at 312 East Ave., features handmade silver jewelry, lapis lazuli, handloomed scarves, and antique furniture, in addition to Oriental rugs.

Bookstores are another specialty in the valley with the sheer number of shops unmatched elsewhere in Idaho. **Book Cellar,** at 400 Sun Valley Rd., is open daily and offers a coffee corner to peruse the merchandise and "The Castle" to keep the kids occupied. **Chapter One,** at 190 N. Main, has a good selection of magazines, newspapers, and books. **Ex Libris,** in the Sun Valley Mall, is a fine bookstore featuring frequent visits from authors. The bookstore has an impressive collection of books about Idaho and the West, and about and by Ernest Hemingway. Phone and mail orders are taken at 622-8174 or P.O. Box 225, Sun Valley, ID 83353.

Food stores range from gourmet to basic. **Good Taste,** at 131 First Ave. N, specializes in the good food grown in Idaho, everything from smoked trout from the Hagerman Valley to wild rice from St. Maries; also gourmet legumes. **Atkinsons,** at Giacobbi Square at Fourth and Leadville, provides delivery service if you call 726-5668 in Ketchum or 788-2294 in Hailey.

OTHER PRACTICALITIES

Child Care

Parents who need a haven for kids will find several in Ketchum and Sun Valley. **Sun Valley Play School,** tel. 622-2288, in Sun Valley Lodge, offers care for infants and children from six months to five or six years old. Rates range from $6 an hour or $39 a day (for the older kids) to $9 an hour or $58 a day (for infants).

Other child-care centers include **Early Start Day Care and Kindergarten** tel. 788-3295, at 511 N. Main in Hailey; **A Child's Place,** tel. 726-3240, at 706 Washington Ave. N in Ketchum; and **Hemingway Learning Institute,** tel. 726-3113, at 1201 Campus Way, also in Ketchum.

Ketchum's **The Great Escape,** tel. 726-8666, at 1514 Warm Springs Rd., offers babysitting service at your hotel or condo.

Transportation

Hailey's **Friedman Memorial Airport,** tel. 788-4956, is 12 miles from Sun Valley and provides the major air link. **Horizon Air,** tel. (800) 547-9308, and **Delta Air Lines,** tel. (800) 221-1212, offer scheduled airline service to Hailey. Horizon schedules 37-passenger Dash-8 aircraft. Air charter services include **Augustus Airlines,** tel. 726-9422, at Ketchum, and **Barken International,** tel. (800) 845-5572, in Hailey.

Bus service from Sun Valley to the Boise Airport is provided by **Sun Valley Stages,** tel. 622-4200. One-way fares are $35 for adults and $20 for children 10 and younger; roundtrip fares are $60 for adults, $30 for children. The trip takes three hours each way. Within the Wood River Valley, free bus service is provided by **Ketchum Area Rapid Transit (KART),** tel. 726-7140.

Taxis are available from **A-1 Taxicab,** tel. 726-9351; **Idaho Limousine Services,** tel. 726-LIMO; or for service to Twin Falls, Shoshone, Boise, or Stanley, **Town and Country Tours,** tel. 788-2012, in Hailey.

Car-rental companies in the valley include **Ram Motors,** tel. 788-3501; **U-Save Auto Rental,** tel. 622-9312 (Sun Valley), 788-9707 (Hailey), (800) 995-9707 (valley locations) or (800) 999-9404 (outside the valley); **Avis,** tel. (800) 331-1212 or 788-2382; **Budget,** tel. (800) 527-0700 or 788-3660; and **Hertz,** tel. (800) 654-3131 or 788-4548.

Information And Services

The **Sun Valley/Ketchum Chamber of Commerce,** tel. 726-3243 or (800) 634-3347, at 410 N. Main or P.O. Box 2420, Sun Valley, ID 83353, provides information about the area. The **Hailey Chamber of Commerce,** tel. 788-2700, is at P.O. Box 100, Hailey, ID 83333.

Police services at Bellevue and Hailey are provided by the **Blaine County Sheriff,** tel. 788-5555 or 911 in emergencies, next door to the courthouse at 220 First Ave. S in Hailey. In Ketchum, **city hall,** tel. 726-3841, is located at 480 East Ave. North. **Ketchum Police,** tel. 726-9333 for routine business and 911 for emergencies, are also located at city hall.

Hailey City Hall, tel. 788-4221, is located at 12 W. Carbonate. **Hailey Public Library** recently moved into new digs at 7 Croy St., tel. 788-2036. **Ketchum Community Library,** tel. 726-3493, is located at 415 Spruce Avenue.

CATHY CARLSON

SOUTHEAST IDAHO

Southeast Idaho is the center of some of the state's most colorful history. Just a few years after Lewis and Clark became the first white men to traipse into Idaho in 1805, the mountain men arrived here. Although their lifestyle was rigorous, they had some rollicking good times—at least when they all got together at the regular rendezvous, many of which were held in Pierre's Hole on the west side of the Tetons near what is now Ashton. The Snake River country was rich in furs, and the mountain men played a significant role here. Fort Hall was built in 1834 to guard a hefty cache of trade goods that had been taken to the rendezvous but had failed to sell. Nathaniel Wyeth built the fort and sold it two years later to the Hudson's Bay Company. For the next 20 years, the fort became an important trading post and a place of succor for emigrants on the great Overland Migration to the Oregon country.

The laws that shaped southeastern Idaho included the Homestead Act of 1862, which allotted each head of a family 160 acres if he would live on it and farm it for five years. The Desert Land Act of 1877 promised 640 acres per family if they could bring water to it. In 1894, the Carey Act speeded the development of irrigation.

Religion played a large part in the greening of southeastern Idaho as well. The Church of Jesus Christ of Latter-day Saints started irrigating Idaho lands along Pattee Creek, near the present city of Salmon in 1855, but an Indian attack sent them packing southward to Utah. The Mormons returned in 1860 to found Franklin and construct another irrigation system. The communal effort that the church instilled in its followers was the doctrine that tamed this dry land.

Now the heartland of Idaho's famous potatoes, the eastern margin of the Snake River Plain still awaits the completion of an irrigation system to water all its fertile lands. The dam to accomplish much of that was once in place. East of Sugar City, the Teton Dam stood 305 feet high on Nov. 26, 1975, a month after the reservoir behind it began to fill. By the following spring, the reservoir had grown dramatically. On June 5, 1976, the dam's lava abutments developed a major leak and about noon of the same day, Teton Dam collapsed. In Sugar City, homes and businesses were wiped out by the flood. In Rexburg even farther downstream,

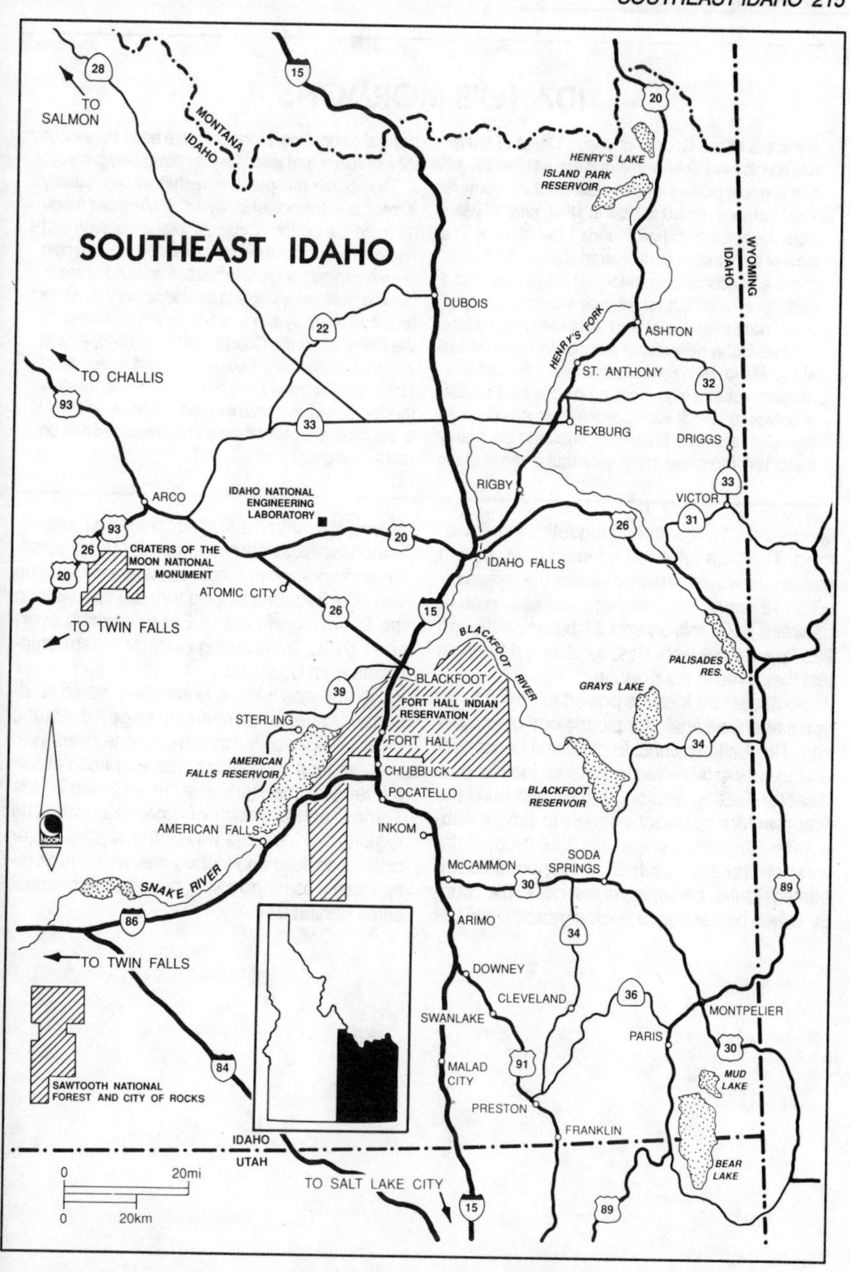

SOUTHEAST IDAHO
TO SALMON
MONTANA
IDAHO
WYOMING
IDAHO
HENRY'S LAKE
ISLAND PARK RESERVOIR
HENRY'S FORK
DUBOIS
ASHTON
ST. ANTHONY
TO CHALLIS
REXBURG
DRIGGS
RIGBY
VICTOR
ARCO
IDAHO NATIONAL ENGINEERING LABORATORY
CRATERS OF THE MOON NATIONAL MONUMENT
IDAHO FALLS
ATOMIC CITY
TO TWIN FALLS
BLACKFOOT RIVER
PALISADES RES.
BLACKFOOT
GRAYS LAKE
FORT HALL INDIAN RESERVATION
STERLING
FORT HALL
AMERICAN FALLS RESERVOIR
CHUBBUCK
BLACKFOOT RESERVOIR
POCATELLO
INKOM
AMERICAN FALLS
MOON
McCAMMON
SODA SPRINGS
SNAKE RIVER
ARIMO
TO TWIN FALLS
DOWNEY
CLEVELAND
SWANLAKE
MONTPELIER
PARIS
MALAD CITY
MUD LAKE
SAWTOOTH NATIONAL FOREST AND CITY OF ROCKS
PRESTON
FRANKLIN
IDAHO
UTAH
BEAR LAKE
0
20mi
0
20km
TO SALT LAKE CITY
28
15
20
22
32
93
33
33
31
26
26
93
20
20
26
15
39
34
30
89
34
86
36
30
91
84
15
89

IDAHO'S MORMONS

Members of the Church of Jesus Christ of Latter-day Saints have been some of the most significant—and controversial—players in Idaho's development. The Mormons moved to Utah in 1847, only 17 years after Joseph Smith had founded the church. The trials of the western frontier strengthened the Saints' social and economic ties, forging the religion into a dominant force. But for all their industry, the Mormons were tolerated at best, despised more often.

Most Idaho newspaper editors, including those at the *Idaho Tri-Weekly Statesmen*, attacked Mormonism vehemently, focusing on the sect's belief in polygamy. Block voting by the Mormons drew ire too. Until an 1890 manifesto declared polygamy dead, anti-Mormonism played a major role in Idaho political campaigns. Mormons were often stripped of their property and jailed for practicing polygamy.

The church prospered nonetheless with steady increases in membership. By 1876, Mormons made up more than a fifth of Idaho's total population and nearly two-thirds of those who claimed membership in an organized religion. In 1920, the church's members began to play a role in statewide politics, a role foreshadowed by the election of Alfred Budge to the Idaho Supreme Court in 1914. In 1945, Arnold Williams of Rexburg became the first governor of Idaho who belonged to the church. Since 1950, a third or more of the state's legislators have belonged to the church, a political force to be reckoned with on moral matters.

floodwaters 12 feet deep inundated the downtown. The dam released a torrent of 80 million gallons of water, which drained the reservoir within 12 hours. In all, damage was estimated at between $500 million and $1 billion. Although 925 farm homes were destroyed, only 11 people lost their lives in the disaster.

Southeastern Idaho is poised to gain the nation's attention again for technology of another sort. The Idaho National Engineering Laboratory (INEL) was established in 1949 as the National Reactor Testing Station, and helped build the first reactors compact enough to power submarines and other ships. In 1955, Arco, to the west of "the site," as INEL is known in southeastern Idaho, became the first city in the country lit with power from a nuclear reactor. INEL is among the nation's nuclear weapons and research facilities now coming under closer scrutiny. Before leaving office early in 1995, Idaho Gov. Cecil Andrus helped turn the spotlight on the U.S. Department of Energy, which oversees INEL, by refusing nuclear waste shipments from Colorado.

Southeastern Idaho presents a varied landscape: quiet expanses of sage, dramatic mountains, fresh vulcanism, serene rivers with trout as long as your leg, the edge of Yellowstone National Park, the "other" side of the Tetons, and a wealth of other features. The region also includes two of the state's major cities, Pocatello and Idaho Falls, which rank respectively as Idaho's second- and third-largest cities behind Boise.

AMERICAN FALLS AND VICINITY

SIGHTS

Massacre Rocks State Park

Just west of American Falls is Massacre Rocks State Park, tel. 548-2672, which marks the general location of an Indian attack on emigrants. Today, the peaceful setting of the Snake River shoreline, the majestic white pelicans floating upon it, and the sigh of the wind in the junipers present little of the sinister atmosphere that once prevailed here. The Overlanders gave this stretch of the Oregon Trail the name Devil's Gate or Gate of Death because of the rocks that rimmed the river and forced them into a narrow passage.

Emigrant John C. Hillman wrote to Mrs. Bronson of St. Louis about the events that occurred east of the present park. "I little thot when I wrote you on the 8th that an occurance was to take place next day and the day following, and which will long impress itself upon my mind, and that we were in the midst of great danger and seemed to be almost unconscious of it," he wrote to his friend in a letter dated Aug. 11, 1862.

A horseman's hasty approach yielded news of a wagon train that was under attack by Indians. Hillman's party made haste itself to catch up. "I found quite a quantity of blood, and fragments of such things as immigrants carry with them, and it was evident that the Indians had done their hellish deeds in a hasty manner and left," he wrote.

The next day Hillman's party caught up to the ox train that had sustained the casualties. The initial Indian attack had killed three men and left several wounded, including a woman who suffered mortal wounds. The emigrants decided to even the score and a band of 30 set out after their attackers. In the fight that followed, the whites broke rank and ran while the Indians pursued them some three miles back toward the wagons, killing three more emigrants and wounding five before giving up the pursuit. The skirmishes of Aug. 9 and 10 resulted in the deaths of 10 emigrants.

Register Rock

Downstream along the Snake from the main park is Register Rock, a massive basalt boulder that bears the scratches of travelers eager to leave their mark. The pavilion near Register Rock is the focal point for a lush picnic area.

The park is also a good spot to consider the geologic history of the area. The Snake River Valley here was once covered by Neeley Lake. Later volcanic eruptions tossed thick clouds of ash into the air, which settled as layers of tuff

Massacre Rocks State Park's lovely scenery belies its violent past.

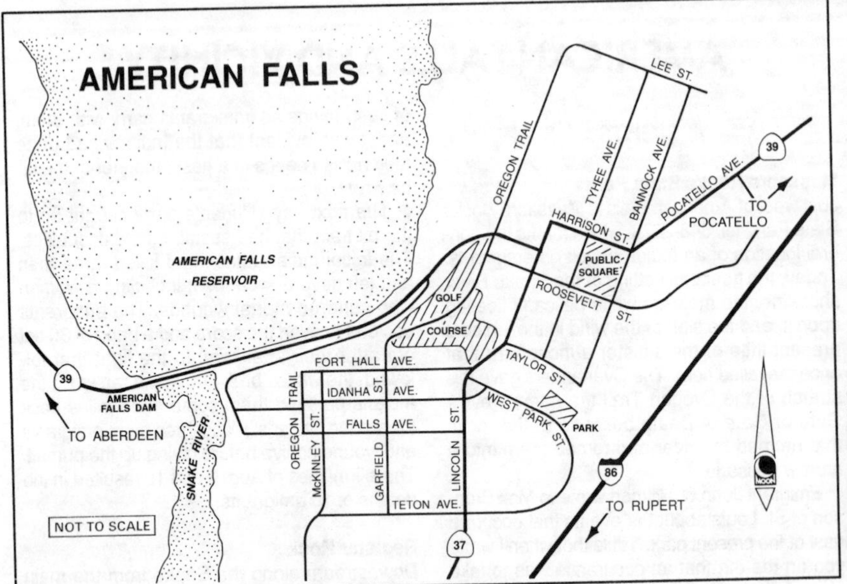

15-50 feet thick. In some areas the lake sediments and tuff form striking bands. Other areas reveal thick layers of pyroclastic debris that once flowed with incandescent fury from the volcanic vents. Massacre Rocks marks the location of one such vent. About 72,000 years ago, geologists figure, the Cedar Butte eruption threw an arm of basalt across the Snake River, forming the first incarnation of American Falls Lake. But 15,000 years ago, Lake Bonneville went bust, roaring down through Red Rock Pass at Pocatello to the east. That gigantic flood ripped through the old lava dam and created the present scene. One minor volcanic feature continues to attract visitors' attention. The miniature **Devils Garden** marks the location of a former steam vent.

The park offers a three-quarter-mile hiking trail—the **Yahandeka Trail**—and another shorter self-guided hike that stretches a third of a mile from the visitor center. The **visitor center** offers some interesting displays about the area's history and natural setting. The 900-acre park contains 51 campsites with electricity and water. A boat ramp is available to launch excursions on the adjoining Snake River.

American Falls Dam

American Falls Dam impounds the second-largest reservoir in Idaho, stretching 36 miles eastward along the Snake River. The reservoir is noted for its trout fishing. **Idaho Power Co.** offers tours of the powerhouse near the dam. Call 226-2434 to make arrangements. The company also developed its first public recreation area at American Falls in 1933. Taking the road west of American Falls to the present dam reveals a view of the powerhouses that came before the present dam and powerhouse. The company provides boat ramps above and below the dam. The terraced picnic grounds of **Trenner Park** are popular with visitors. **American Falls Fish Hatchery,** tel. 226-2015, raises trout for release in the reservoir and surrounding areas. The hatchery is operated by the Idaho Fish and Game Department. Tours are available.

Great Rift Natural Landmark

To the northwest of American Falls is the Great Rift Natural Landmark, a network of fresh-looking lava flows and deep rifts that extend at least 800 feet into the earth. The best way to reach the area is to take Hwy. 39 north toward Aberdeen, then head west at the sign.

The landmark was established in 1968 and represents the longest rift system in the United States, as well as the world's deepest. Geologists call it a world-class geological spectacular. The Kings Bowl and Wapi Lava fields look as though they are so fresh that volcanic heat should still keep visitors at bay. But the lava here is cool; in fact, efforts to date the lava using bits of sagebrush charcoal from beneath the flows indicate the events happened about 2,000 years ago. For information about the Great Rift area, check with the **BLM** Idaho Falls District office, tel. 529-1020, at 940 Lincoln Rd., or the East Idaho Visitor Center, tel. 523-1012, at 505 Lindsey Blvd. in Idaho Falls.

Potato Research

One of several University of Idaho research outposts across the state, the **Aberdeen Branch Experiment Station,** tel. 397-4181, is the home of efforts to produce better potatoes in a state already renowned for its bakers. Aberdeen is also a jumping off point for those heading off into the wilds of the Great Rift country.

PRACTICALITIES

Accommodations

The **Indian Springs Campground** offers 105 campsites for $7-14 with the natatorium as the featured attraction. The campground is located a mile east of I-86, off Exit 36.

Motels in American Falls include **Hillview Motel,** tel. 226-5151, at 2799 Lakeview Rd., with rooms for $25-50, and **Ronnez Motel,** tel. 226-9658, at 411 Lincoln, with rooms for $26-45.

Food

Restaurants in American Falls include the **Lakeview Cafe,** tel. 226-2194; **Melody Lanes,** at 152 Harrison; **Mr. G's Golden Fried Chicken,** at 616 Fort Hall Ave.; and **Poppa John's,** at 202 Idaho. Familiar chain outlets include **A&W Restaurant,** at 105 Idaho; **Pizza Hut,** at 2840 Pocatello Ave.; and **Taco Time,** at 2854 Pocatello Avenue.

Events

The first weekend of June brings modern mountain men to American Falls for the **Black Powder Rendezvous.** The annual **Father's Day Fish Derby** follows. In July, American Falls celebrates the fourth with fireworks, followed by **Rowland's Regatta.** August brings the **Power County Rodeo** and accompanying **American Falls Day** during the third week.

Recreation

Golfers will find two courses in the American Falls area. The **American Falls Golf Course,** tel. 226-9631, at 610 Oregon Trail, offers nine holes. In Aberdeen to the north, the nine-hole **Hazard Creek Golf Course,** tel. 397-5308, is located at 411 E. Bingham Avenue. Both are open to the public. Swimmers will find the **Indian Springs Natatorium,** tel. 226-2174, at 3247 Indian Springs Rd., a mile east of I-86 along Hwy. 37.

Near Aberdeen to the north along Hwy. 39, travelers will find the **Sterling Wildlife Management Area** maintained by the Idaho Fish and Game Department. The 3,304-acre area is used mostly for both waterfowl and upland game-bird hunting. To the north near Springfield along Hwy. 39 is the department's **Springfield Lake** sportsmen's access, which offers camping, restrooms, a boat ramp, and fishing.

Information And Services

The **American Falls Chamber of Commerce,** tel. 226-7214, is located at 258 Idaho. **Police** services are provided by the city police, 239 Idaho St., tel. 226-2622, or outside the city by the **Power County Sheriff,** 550 Gifford St., tel. 226-2311. Both have offices at the courthouse.

POCATELLO AND VICINITY

Pocatello ranks as Idaho's second-largest city with 45,000 residents. By 1890, the town had grown dramatically as the administrative center for the Union Pacific Railroad. Eventually it became well known as the largest rail hub west of the Mississippi River. Even Judy Garland sang a song of tribute to Pocatello, "The Gate City."

SIGHTS

Architectural Highlights

Pocatello's bustling heritage is reflected in the architectural refinements in many buildings from that era. Among the landmarks are the **Oregon Shortline Depot,** a three-story station at the end of Bonneville St., just off Main St.; and the historic **Yellowstone Hotel,** located just across the street from the old depot. **Amtrak** and the Union Pacific Railroad share the old depot at 300 S. Harrison Avenue. Pocatello's most famous old building is the **Stanrod Mansion,** tel. 234-6184, at 648 N. Garfield. The house was completed by Drew Stanrod in 1901 from stone quarried at McCammon, south on Hwy. 91. The house is now owned by the city and open for tours.

Idaho State University

Pocatello is home to Idaho State University, tel. 236-0211, which is headquartered at 741 S. 7th Avenue. Idaho State's curriculum includes a pharmacy school, extensive science program, and the **Idaho Museum of Natural History,** tel. 236-3317. The museum contains working seismographs, an interesting depiction of the desert food web, an extensive collection of skeletons (including a giant ice-age bison, sabertooth cat, and giant ground sloth), and Indian artifacts, and a spectacular collection of rocks. It's open Mon.-Sat. 9 a.m.-5 p.m. except holidays, and is located in the Museum Building near the Earl Pond Student Union Building between S. 5th and 8th avenues along E. Dillon Street. Admission is free, although a donation is requested to help the museum pay for new exhibits and projects.

The Idaho State campus is also home to **Holt Arena,** tel. 236-2831, the nation's first enclosed college football stadium. Better known as the Minidome, the arena hosts Big Sky Conference basketball, plus football games and track meets where the Idaho State Bengals normally prevail. Located on the edge of campus, the Minidome is also home to concerts, major shows, campus exhibits, and frequent rodeo competitions, including the **Dodge National Circuit Finals** for professional rodeo cowboys.

The **Idaho State University Outdoor Program,** tel. 236-3912, offers information about outdoor recreation in the area and maintains an outdoor-equipment rental program. The **University Bookstore,** tel. 236-3237, offers one of the best book selections in Pocatello.

Bannock County Historical Museum

In addition to the campus natural history museum, Pocatello is home to the Bannock County Historical Museum, tel. 233-0434, which occupies a modern glass and concrete building

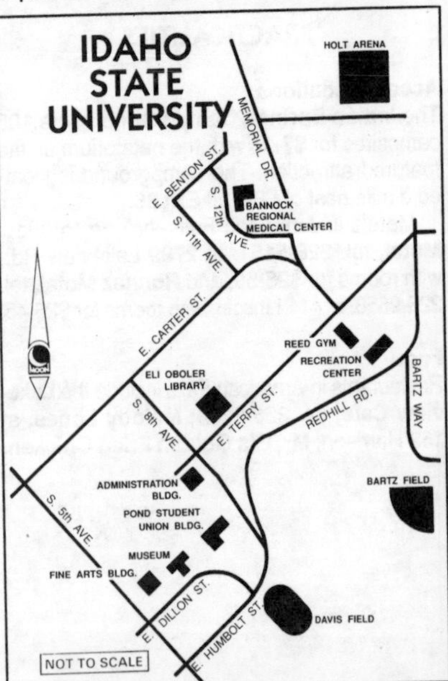

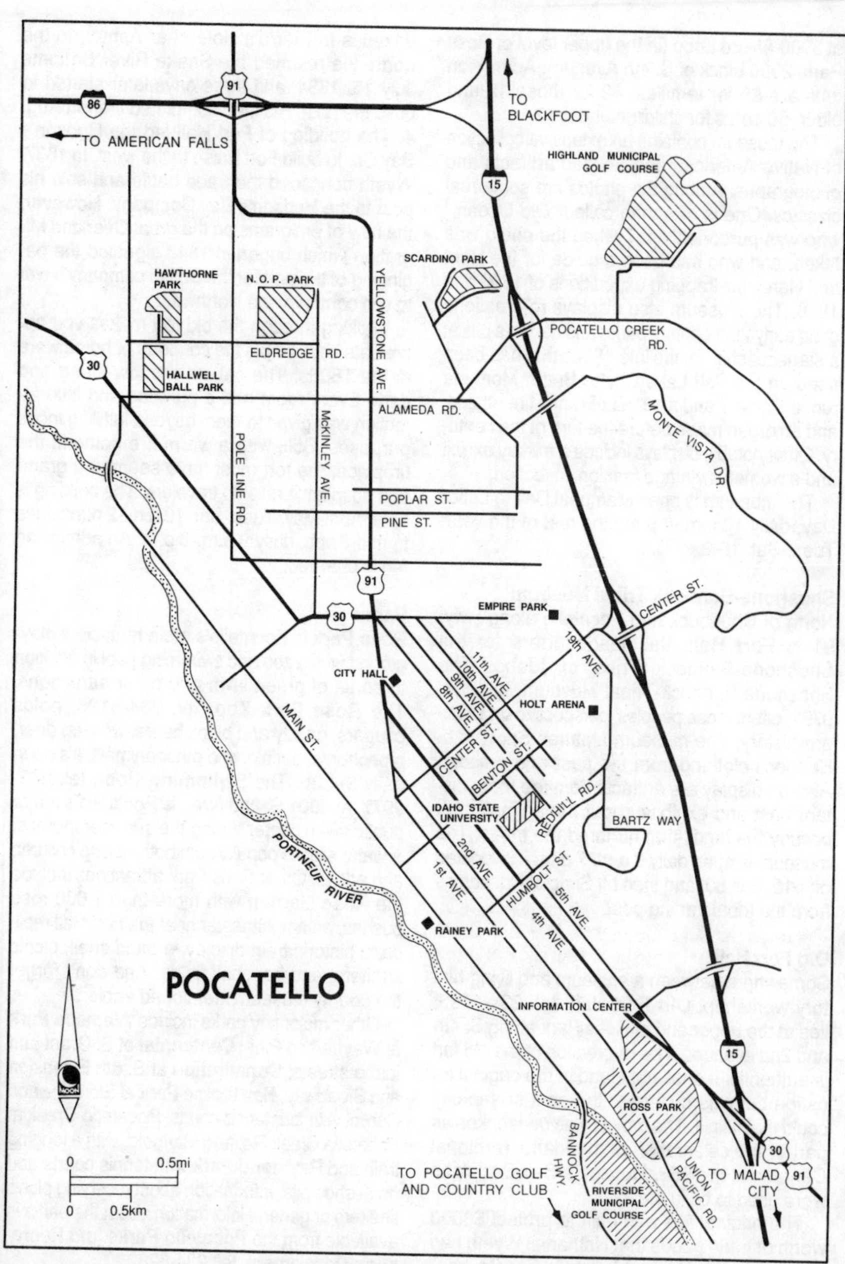
TO AMERICAN FALLS
86
91
TO BLACKFOOT
HIGHLAND MUNICIPAL GOLF COURSE
15
SCARDINO PARK
HAWTHORNE PARK
N. O. P. PARK
YELLOWSTONE AVE.
POCATELLO CREEK RD.
30
ELDREDGE RD.
HALLWELL BALL PARK
ALAMEDA RD.
MONTE VISTA DR.
McKINLEY AVE.
POLE LINE RD.
POPLAR ST.
PINE ST.
91
CENTER ST.
EMPIRE PARK
30
19th AVE.
11th AVE.
10th AVE.
9th AVE.
8th AVE.
CITY HALL
HOLT ARENA
MAIN ST.
CENTER ST.
BENTON ST.
REDHILL RD.
IDAHO STATE UNIVERSITY
BARTZ WAY
2nd AVE.
1st AVE.
HUMBOLT ST.
5th AVE.
4th AVE.
PORTNEUF RIVER
RAINEY PARK
POCATELLO
INFORMATION CENTER
15
ROSS PARK
BANNOCK HWY.
UNION PACIFIC RD
30
91
TO POCATELLO GOLF AND COUNTRY CLUB
RIVERSIDE MUNICIPAL GOLF COURSE
TO MALAD CITY
0
0.5mi
0
0.5km
MOON

at 3000 Alvord Loop (in the upper level of Ross Park, 2900 block of S. 4th Avenue). Admission fees are $5 for families, $2 for those 12 and older, 50 cents for children under 12.

The museum contains an extensive collection of Native American and railroad artifacts and photographs. Among the photos are some real classics. One is of a man called "Old Ocean," who was purportedly 117 when the photo was taken, and who had been a guide for the Hunt and Henry fur-trapping expeditions of 1809 and 1810. The museum also displays re-creations of an early 20th-century parlor and dentist's office; a stagecoach from the late 1800s that had been used on the Salt Lake City to Butte, Montana run; a Model T and a 1915 LaFrance fire engine; and an organ made before the turn of the century. Other notable displays include a military exhibit and a women's vintage fashion collection.

The museum is open Memorial Day to Labor Day, daily 10 a.m.-6 p.m.; the rest of the year, Tues.-Sat. 10-2.

Shoshone-Bannock Tribal Museum

North of Chubbuck and Pocatello along Hwy. 91 is **Fort Hall,** the headquarters for the Shoshone-Bannock Tribe of Idaho. The Shoshone-Bannock Tribal Museum, tel. 237-9791, offers these peoples' perspective on Western history. The museum features Shoshone-Bannock clothing from the past and present. Also on display are artifacts from the more distant past and exhibits about the animals that occupy the lands that nurtured the tribes. The museum is open daily 9 a.m.-7 p.m. It is located off I-15, Exit 80, and then off Simplot Rd. across from the tribal trading post.

Old Fort Hall

Somewhere between a museum and living-history workshop, **Old Fort Hall,** tel. 234-1795, lies at the upper end of Ross Park along S. 4th and 2nd avenues. The re-creation of the old fort is authentic. It does not stand in the original location but was built near the park so the city could maintain it. The project was undertaken as part of the celebration of the Idaho Territorial Centennial in 1963. Hudson's Bay Co. plans were used to build the fort.

The original fort was built to protect $3000 worth of trade goods that Nathaniel Wyeth had brought to the Rocky Mountain Fur Co. rendezvous in Pierre's Hole near Ashton to the north. He reached the Snake River Bottoms July 15, 1834, and three days later started to build the post. His men completed the fort Aug. 4. The building of Fort Hall led the Hudson's Bay Co. to build Fort Boise to the west. In 1837, Wyeth conceded the trade battle and sold his post to the Hudson's Bay Company. However, the flow of emigrants on the great Overland Migration which began in 1843 signaled the beginning of the end for the British company's war to win control of the Northwest.

Walking through the old fort makes you appreciate how simple the comforts of home were in the 1800s. The cabins are low-slung and dark. Every room had a purpose and little attention was given to them beyond fulfilling those purposes. Still, with a warm fire going in the fireplace, the fort must have seemed a grand and hospitable relief to travelers. The building is open April-May, Tues.-Sat. 10 a.m.-2 p.m.; June to mid-Sept., daily 9 a.m.-8 p.m. An admission fee is charged.

Parks

Ross Park is Pocatello's main municipal playground with a zoo and swimming pool in addition to acres of green lawn and other attractions. The **Ross Park Zoo,** tel. 234-6196, holds cougars, grizzly and black bears, wolves, deer, pronghorns, buffalo, and other animals. It's open daily 9-4:30. The **Swimming Pool,** tel. 232-9977, at 2901 S. 2nd Ave., is Pocatello's major public swim center during the summer months. A water slide is popular with both visiting children and adults. Other Ross Park attractions include the **Rose Garden** with more than 1,000 rose bushes, an amphitheater near the Fort Hall replica, a historic train display, a band shell, picnic shelters, and baseball fields. And don't forget the county museum mentioned earlier.

Other major city parks include **Alameda Park** at Wayne and Pine; **Centennial** at S. Grant and Idaho streets; **Constitution** at S. 5th Extension and Broadway; **Hawthorne Park** at Eldredge and Conlin, with four tennis courts; **Pocatello Creek** at Pocatello Creek Rd. and Marigold, with a jogging trail; and **Raymond Park** with tennis courts and horseshoe pits. Information about reserving picnic shelters or general information about the parks is available from the **Pocatello Parks and Recreation Department,** tel. 234-6232.

RECREATION

Skiing

Alpine skiers will find 2,000 feet of vertical awaiting them at **Pebble Creek,** tel. 775-4451, 15 miles south of Pocatello near Inkom. The ski area features four chairlifts and 24 runs. It's open from December to mid-April, 9:30 a.m.-4:30 p.m., and offers a day lodge, cafeteria, lounge, ski rental, and lessons. Rental skis run $15 for adults and $10 for children. Child care is available for $12 a day.

Nordic skiers can generally find good skiing at the **Mink Creek Park 'n' Ski** area south of Pocatello off Hwy. 30 toward the Bannock Guard Station. The area provides five ski trails totaling about 15 miles. North of Pocatello, **Highland Golf Course** has also been designated a Park 'n' Ski area, and trails are groomed when there is sufficient snow. Trail systems designated by the state require skiers to purchase $15 season passes, unless they possess similar passes from Washington or Oregon. The permit revenues help pay for trail grooming and maintenance. For updates on **ski conditions,** check in with the **Idaho State University Outdoor Program,** tel. 236-3912.

Ski equipment is available for rent from **Scott's Ski and Sports,** tel. 232-1449, at 218 N. Main, or **Gateway Performance Outfitters,** tel. 232-3711, at 404 S. Arthur Avenue.

Snowmobiling

Inman Canyon Parking is located four miles northeast of Inkom and provides access to 200 square miles open to snowmobiling, plus miles of groomed trails. Funds for keeping the parking lot plowed and trails groomed come from snowmobile registrations, available through the Bannock County Snowmobilers.

Fishing and Hunting

Southeastern Idaho's Portneuf River is one of the state's popular trout fishing streams. The Idaho Fish and Game Department stocks trout for anglers in Mink Creek and the Portneuf. (In Pocatello, the Portneuf is closed to fishing from the Center St. bridge upstream to the E. Main St. bridge.) Nearby, the Snake River and American Falls Reservoir are also popular escapes for anglers.

Hunting is also extremely popular in the Pocatello area. Waterfowl hunting is a prime pursuit along the Snake River and in surrounding national wildlife refuges. The U.S. Fish and Wildlife Service's **Southeast Idaho National Wildlife Refuge Complex,** tel. 237-6616, is based at 1246 Yellowstone Ave., A-4, in Pocatello. The office oversees the Bear Lake, Camas, Grays Lake, and Minidoka refuges and the Oxford Slough Waterfowl Production Area.

The Shoshone-Bannock tribal government, tel. 785-2080, oversees some of the best fishing and hunting opportunities in the area. The tribal Fish and Wildlife Department sells hunting and fishing licenses to non-Indians. For information, write to the tribes at Fort Hall, ID 83203. The Idaho Fish and Game Department's Southeastern Region office, tel. 232-4703, can help steer anglers and hunters in the right direction.

Golf

Pocatello has three 18-hole golf courses. The par-71, 6,098-yard **Juniper Hills Country Club,** tel. 233-0241, is headquartered at 6600 Bannock Highway. The two public courses are the par-72, 6,372-yard **Highland,** tel. 237-9922, north of Pocatello; and the par-71, 6,097-yard **Riverside,** tel. 232-9515, to the south.

Horse Racing

The **Bannock County Fairgrounds,** tel. 237-1340, features pari-mutuel horse racing during the summer. The fairgrounds are located off I-15, Exit 71.

PRACTICALITIES

Accommodations

Motels are plentiful in Pocatello. Best Western has two motels in town, the **Cotton Tree Inn,** tel. 237-7650, at 1415 Bench Rd., with rooms for $54-150, and the **Weston Inn,** tel. 233-5530, at 745 S. 5th Ave., with rooms for $36-66. **Howard Johnson's,** tel. 237-1400, at Exit 71 off I-15, is the biggest motel in town with 197 rooms ranging $42-57.

The **Imperial 400 Motel,** tel. 233-5120, has rooms for $27-60 at 1055 S. 5th Ave.; **Laab's Motel,** tel. 232-3360, at 1119 N. Main, offers rooms for around $20-30; and **Days Inn,** tel. 237-0020, has rooms for $40-80 at 133 W. Burnside. Other motels include **Motel 6,** tel. 237-7880, at 291 W. Burnside, with rooms for $20-33; **Nendel's,** tel. 237-3100, with rooms for $30-35; and **Pocatello Super 8 Motel,** tel. 234-0888, at 1330 Bench Rd., with rooms for $35-55. **Quality Inn and Convention Center,** tel. 233-2200, has rooms for $42-75, at 1555 Pocatello Creek Road. **Thunderbird Motel,** tel. 232-6330, at 1415 S. 5th, has rooms for $25-37.

Camping

Pocatello is headquarters for **Caribou National Forest,** tel. 236-7500, in Suite 282 of the Federal Building at 250 S. 4th Avenue. Just downstairs is the BLM's **Pocatello Resource Area** office. Together these two agencies control a significant portion of the land in this corner of the state.

Scout Mountain Campground, in Caribou National Forest southwest of Pocatello, is popular. The 32 campsites here recently received a touch-up with some new picnic tables and grills.

Privately operated campgrounds in the vicinity include **Littletree Inn,** tel. 237-0020, at 133 W. Burnside, with 10 RV spaces with hookups for $10 a night; **Pocatello KOA Campground,** tel. 233-6851, off I-15, Exit 71, with 95 campsites ranging $17 and up; and **Parkway Motor Court,** tel. 237-7110, at 4613 Yellowstone Avenue.

Food

Pocatello has 50 restaurants, give or take. The restaurant menu ranges from a bevy of fast-food restaurants—to keep ISU students and others happy—to more elegant options.

Frontier Pies, tel. 237-7650, serves breakfast, lunch, and dinner, and offers nightly entertainment. It's at the Cotton Tree Inn at 1415 Bench Rd., off I-15, Exit 71. The **Quality Inn,** tel. 233-2200, at 1555 Pocatello Creek Rd., offers prime rib and seafood. **The Cattle Baron,** tel. 233-8830, specializes in beef at the Pocatello Municipal Airport. **The Sandpiper,** tel. 233-1000, offers great steaks and prime rib at 1400 Bench Road. **Puffer Belly's,** tel. 237-1400, is at the Howard Johnson's at Exit 71 off I-15. **Remo's,** tel. 233-1710, offers Angus beef, fresh pasta, and outside dining during the summer.

Chinese restaurants in Pocatello almost outnumber all the other categories. The list includes **Chee Gong Restaurant,** tel. 237-8768, at 4010 Yellowstone Ave. in nearby Chubbock; **Chop Stick Cafe,** tel. 232-5782, at 228 S. Main; **Mandarin House,** tel. 233-6088, at 990 Yellowstone Ave.; and the **Hong Kong Cuisine,** tel. 232-3500, at 495 Yellowstone Avenue.

Fast-food restaurants are clustered mostly along Yellowstone Avenue. Offerings include **Arby's** at 791 Yellowstone; **Blimpies** at 1021 Yellowstone or 905 S. 5th Ave.; **Burger King** at 905 Yellowstone; **Kentucky Fried Chicken** at 66 Yellowstone; **McDonald's** at 831 Yellowstone or 1011 S. 5th Ave.; and **Mr. Steak** at 621 Yellowstone. **Prime Cut** is at 1200 Yellowstone and **Red Steer** seems to be on every street *but* Yellowstone, with restaurants at 1513 S. 5th, 1156 N. Main, and 978 Hiline Road. **Sea Galley Restaurant** is at Pine Ridge Mall at 4105 Yellowstone and **Skipper's Seafood 'N Chowder House** is at 303 E. Alameda.

For a final flurry of fast-food eateries, consider **Taco Bandido** at 4250 Yellowstone; **Taco Bell** at 941 Yellowstone; **Taco John's** at 249 Yellowstone; **Taco Time** at 546 S. 5th Ave. or 1060 Yellowstone; and **Wendy's** at 939 Yellowstone.

Family-style restaurants also abound, including **Butterburrs,** tel. 232-3296, at 917 Yellowstone; **Buddy's,** tel. 233-1172, with its fresh pasta at 626 E. Lewis; **Denny's,** tel. 238-1223, at 4310 Yellowstone in Chubbuck; and **Elmer's Pancake and Steak House,** tel. 232-9114, at 851 S. 5th Avenue.

Pocatello pizza parlors include **Domino's Pizza,** tel. 232-4332, at 250 N. 5th Ave.; **Father Guido's Original Take and Bake Pizza,** tel. 233-1271, at 858 N. 7th Ave.; **Mario's Pizza,** tel. 233-9210, at 905 S. 5th Ave.; **Pizza Express,** tel. 232-1040, at 690 Yellowstone Ave.; **Pizza Hut,** tel. 237-5211 (1151 Yellowstone), tel. 237-1371 (113 W. Burnside Ave. in nearby Chubbuck), or 234-0449 (945 S. 5th Ave.); and **Shakey's Pizza Parlor & Ye Public House,** tel. 233-6066, at 285 E. Alameda Road.

Events

In mid-February, Pocatello plays host to the **World Cutter and Chariot Races,** which involve hitching up fast horses to chariots and trying to keep control of the situation. The **Dodge National Circuit Finals Rodeo** follows in mid-March. The finals rank as the second-largest points-qualifying rodeo in the nation. For color and pageantry, however, the best bet of summer is the **Shoshone-Bannock Indian Festival** at Fort Hall, usually in early August. A powwow of the first rank, the events include traditional and war dances, team dances, and an all-Indian rodeo. August is a busy month in Pocatello—also on tap are the **Days of Old Fort Hall and Frontier Festival** bringing back the mountain men and pioneers for a few days early in the month; and the **Fly Pocatello Air Fair** the first weekend.

Transportation

Pocatello Municipal Airport, tel. 234-6154, is served by Horizon Air, tel. 233-1731 or (800) 547-9308, and Skywest Airlines, tel. 234-1664 or (800) 453-9417, which is affiliated with Delta Air Lines.

Amtrak provides regular rail service to Pocatello via its Pioneer which runs from Chicago to Seattle. The Pioneer stops daily in Pocatello at the Union Pacific Railroad Station, 300 S. Harrison.

Local bus service is provided by **Pocatello Urban Transit,** tel. 234-2287. **Greyhound Bus Lines,** tel. 232-5365, is based at 215 W. Bonneville. **Sunshine Taxi Service,** tel. 232-1115, provides cab service in Pocatello.

Pocatello is a hotbed for rental cars, including **U-Save Auto Rental,** tel. 237-9010 or (800) 426-5299, at 1407 Yellowstone Ave; **Avis,** tel. 232-3244 or (800) 331-1212, at the municipal airport; **Budget,** tel. 233-0600 or (800) 527-0700, also at the airport; **Dollar** at Glens Chevrolet, tel. 232-2511, at 2400 Garrett Way; **Courtesy Ford,** tel. 232-2661, at Yellowstone Ave. and Cedar; **Hertz,** tel. 233-2970 or (800) 654-3131, at the airport; **National,** tel. 233-6042 or (800) 328-4567, at the airport; and **Park Price Motor Co.,** tel. 232-1062, at 300 N. 5th Avenue.

Information And Services

Pocatello Chamber of Commerce, tel. 233-1525, at 427 N. Main, provides information about the area. Police services in Pocatello are provided by **Pocatello Police,** 911 N. 7th Ave., tel. 234-6100 for business or 911 for emergencies. Outside the city, the **Bannock County Sheriff,** 141 N. 6th Ave., tel. 236-7114 for routine calls or 911 for emergencies, is in charge of police services.

Hospitals in Pocatello include **Pocatello Regional Medical Center,** tel. 234-0777, at 777 Hospital Way, and **Bannock Regional Medical Center,** tel. 232-6150, along Memorial Drive.

EAST OF POCATELLO

LAVA HOT SPRINGS

Lava Hot Springs has an attraction that stretches back into prehistory, namely the springs themselves that bubble forth along the Portneuf River here. Most of them warm, many of them hot, the springs were visited for their curative powers by the native inhabitants and the settlers who came after, and have been enjoyed by residents and passersby ever since.

Baths And Pool

The town has undertaken an ambitious program of self-improvement in recent years, building an Olympic-sized pool with diving platforms as a complement to its developed hot baths. Both facilities are operated by the **Lava Hot Springs Foundation,** tel. 776-5221 or (800) 423-8597.

The water in the four hot baths (two of which are equipped with jacuzzi pumps) at Lava Hot Springs ranges 104-112° F. The large swimming pool is set at the other end of town and conforms to American Athletic Union standards. It features 50-meter racing lanes and a 10-meter diving platform. Water temperature in the pool is kept at 86°. Much of the appeal at Lava Hot Springs is the quality of the water. The flow of water through the pools is estimated at 3.33 million gallons a day.

The swimming pool is open from Memorial Day to Labor Day, weekends 10 a.m.-8 p.m, weekdays from 11 a.m. The hot baths are open year-round except for Thanksgiving and Christmas, summers 8 a.m.-11 p.m., winters 9 a.m.-10 p.m.

Admission fees for the four hot baths or the swimming pool are $4 for adults and $3.50 for children. A daily combination pass good for both costs $7 a day for all ages. A card good for 11 admissions to the hot baths is available for $35, and a special $10 family pass is available Mon.-

Stay cool in the pool at Lava Hot Springs.

Thursday. Swimsuit rentals are available for $1 a day with a $3 deposit; towel rentals are 50 cents.

Portneuf River Tubing

Also a major source of fun at Lava Hot Springs is the Portneuf River. Although it's almost narrow enough to jump across, the stream flows with a volume of water sufficient to carry happy hordes of inner-tubers. The short tube-ride here lasts little more than a mile, and keeps both children and adults entertained.

Sidewalk vendors offer fancy vinyl tubes for rent on downtown street corners during the season (generally from when the weather warms in May until September). Tube rentals are also available from **River Rat Tube Rental,** tel. 776-9917, operating near the Lava Spa Motel. The rates are by the hour, in the $3 range. The giant tubes are equipped with handles, a detail that becomes important during the ride. The best attire is a swimsuit and an old pair of tennis shoes to protect your feet when climbing out of the water or hurrying back up the path for another run.

Young children in the 12 and younger range would be wise to be sure an adult goes along for the ride. Parents can judge best the age at which young children can solo in their own tube. A couple of riffles require a strong grip to hang on.

Fine Family Fishin'

For families who want to be sure their kids catch fish or who are more interested in landing a fish for the fry pan, **Smith's Trout Haven,** tel. 887-5348, offers two ponds. The ponds are split between a children's pond, where pan-sized fish prevail, to a trophy pond, where lunkers can range up to 20 pounds. The prices vary accordingly. Anglers pay 20 cents an inch for trout to two pounds, generally a 16- to 18-inch fish. The going rate for fish weighing two pounds or more is $2 a pound. Anglers do not need a state fishing license here. Tackle is also available for rent for a modest fee. The ponds open May 15 and the "season" lasts until the snow starts to stick, generally in late October or November. The fishing ponds are at 9589 E. Maughan Rd., a mile west of Lava Hot Springs.

Museums

South Bannock County Historical Center, tel. 776-5254, at 110 E. Main, houses a collection of photographs that recalls the earliest days of this hot springs resort community. The museum is open noon-5 p.m. or by special arrangement; admission is free but donations help keep the door open. The museum gift shop has a good selection of books about the history of the area and curios. Its library is also available to visitors. Some of the most intriguing displays in the museum preserve the history of the Lava

City Hospital and date from the 1920s. The museum also has a collection of historical clothing, from women's dresses to swimsuits.

Accommodations

Royal Hotel, tel. 776-5216, at 11 E. Main, has rooms ranging $39-59, including a continental breakfast. **Home Hotel and Motel,** tel. 776-5507, at 305 Emerson, has rooms for $21-31. **Hot Springs Village Condominiums,** tel. 776-5445, along Hwy. 30, has 28 units ranging $45-79. **Lava Spa Motel,** tel. 776-5589, at 318 E. Main, has rooms for $30-55. **Dempsey Creek Townhouses,** tel. 776-5000, at 196 E. Main, has rooms for $30-45. One of the state's undiscovered secrets with its old-time charm is **Riverside Inn,** tel. 776-9906, with rooms for $35-65 at 212 Portneuf Avenue.

Camping

Cottonwood Family Campground, tel. 776-5295, has 115 campsites for rent for $15-20 for two people, $3 each additional person. **Smith's Trout Haven,** tel. 776-5348, offers campsites for $5.50 a night from late May to October most years. The campground also offers two trout ponds where anglers pay for their catches. The campground is located a mile west of Lava Hot Springs at 9589 E. Maughan Road.

Food

The **Lazy A Ranch,** tel. 776-5035, is a quarter mile west of Lava Hot Springs along Hwy. 30. It offers authentic chuck-wagon meals with campfire songs of the Old West for about $10, Mon.-Saturday. Live melodramas can be seen weekdays by reservation. Restaurants include **Royal Hotel,** tel. 776-5216, Lava's pizza specialists; **Chuckwagon Cafe,** tel. 776-5626; **Blue Moon Steak and Stein,** tel. 776-5607; and **Silver Grill Cafe,** tel. 776-5562.

Recreation And Events

Thunder Canyon Golf Club, tel. 776-5048, serves the Lava linksters. Lava Hot Springs's biggest event of the season is the **Mountain Man Rendezvous and Pioneer Days,** held each year the third week of July. Further information on that or other events can be obtained from the **Lava Hot Springs Foundation,** tel. 776-5221, at 405 E. Main.

SODA SPRINGS AND VICINITY

Along the Oregon Trail, Soda Springs to the east along Hwy. 30 is one of the state's oldest towns. The first settlers here established a community in 1863. But the town didn't really take hold until after 1870, when Brigham Young built a cabin in the valley nearby and a dozen families followed his lead. The history of Soda Springs was a bloody one for Oregon Trail travelers. Records show 55 Overlanders died along seven miles of trail from the springs to Alexander Point to the west. The city cemetery's first occupants were a family of seven killed by Indians and buried in their wagon box.

The Springs

Soda Springs has a more effervescent reputation these days. It has a **geyser.** The eruptions are exciting, even if they are controlled by man. The spring that produces the eruptions is artificial to the core, having been created by drillers looking for a source of warm water for a swimming pool for the town. The drillers hit a pocket of carbonated water that sent a four-inch stream of water 135 feet into the air. The pipe was capped and is now controlled by a valve. Hey, it's still a gusher.

The other springs in the area are also carbonated. A bottling plant at one time operated to nationally market the waters of 80 Percent Spring near Stampede Park. Now mineral-water lovers will have to gather their own. The springs in the city park are still a popular source of refreshment for visitors.

A mile north from town is **Hooper Spring,** a popular picnic area, where a spring prized for its drinking qualities still bubbles. Other springs in the area include **Champagne Springs,** and **Mammoth Soda Spring,** which is almost the same size as Mammoth Hot Springs in Yellowstone National Park. Unfortunately, many other springs were inundated by the **Soda Point Reservoir** southwest of town. One of the most famous of these was Steamboat Springs, which shot a jet of water up three feet and rumbled with the authority of a steamboat boiler. On calm days its plume can still be seen bubbling at the surface of the reservoir from beneath 40 feet of water.

Museums

The **Daughters of the Utah Pioneers** built a museum in town to display antiques, photographs, and books illuminating the pioneers' migration west through the area. The museum, at 60 Center St., is open June-Oct., Fri.-Sat. 1-4 p.m. or by special arrangement (call 547-3814). Admission is free but donations are appreciated.

Formation Springs Preserve

Two miles north of Soda Springs along Hwy. 34 north of town, then off Trail Canyon Rd., is the Nature Conservancy's Formation Springs Preserve. The springs deposit layers of travertine, giving the stream in the area a unique appearance. Formation Cave is 20 feet tall at the entrance and 1,000 feet long. The conservancy sometimes offers tours to explain the natural history of the area. For more information about the preserve, contact the conservancy at their office in Ketchum, tel. 726-3007.

Grays Lake National Wildlife Refuge

Grays Lake National Wildlife Refuge, 30 miles north of Soda Springs along Hwy. 34 near **Henry,** was named for John Gray, an Iroquois trapper who accompanied Hudson's Bay Co. trappers west. Grays Lake is part of the U.S. Fish and Wildlife Service's Southeast Refuge Complex headquartered at Wayan, tel. 574-2755. It's one of Idaho's largest lakes, if surface area of its wetlands is taken into account. But the lake is shallow at best and bulrushes and cattails occupy most of the area, some 33,000 acres. Most of the wetland is part of the refuge. It supports some 5,000 ducks and 2,000 geese during the breeding season.

The refuge is home to Idaho's largest nesting flock of sandhill cranes, which number some 200 pairs. During the fall, the refuge becomes a staging area where cranes—some years numbering more than 3,000—gather before migrating south to New Mexico, Arizona, and Mexico. The sandhills propelled Grays Lake to national prominence, indirectly. American scientists from the University of Idaho and Canadian biologists focused on Grays Lake in a noble attempt to protect the whooping cranes from extinction. The idea was to create a second free-living flock of whoopers as insurance in case the only other wild flock, which nests in Wood Buffalo National Park in Canada, met with trouble. The scientists gathered whooping crane eggs from the Canadian park each spring, then airlifted them to Grays Lake, where they were slipped into sandhill nests.

The sandhills successfully raised some of the foster chicks each year. But drought years kept the flock small and losses during the winter migration to New Mexico and back trimmed their numbers still further. The lack of females also hindered hopes that the whoopers would find each other and mate, the one measure of success that eluded the effort. The U.S. Fish and Wildlife Service finally threw in the towel in 1991, opting to try to establish a resident flock of whoopers elsewhere. The majestic whoopers may be missing from the refuge 27 miles north of Soda Springs but the spring mating dances of Sandhills will still inspire awe.

Blackfoot Reservoir

Blackfoot Reservoir is 20 miles north of Soda Springs via Hwy. 34. Both the Blackfoot River and its reservoir are famed for their big cutthroat and rainbow trout, some of which can top 10 pounds.

Parks

Soda Springs offers several interesting parks. **Thomas Corrigan Park,** alongside Hwy. 30 downtown, holds a pair of antique locomotives. The Galloping Goose provided transportation for phosphate miners and others to Conda from 1922 to 1936. The Dinky Engine in the park hauled supplies to build Soda Point Dam. Trapped by rising waters when the dam was completed in 1924, the engine spent the next 52 years underwater before it was recovered when the reservoir was drained for repairs. **Kelly Park,** off 2nd St. N at the east edge of town by Rabbit Mountain, offers a kids' fishing pond and three miles of trails. **Hooper Springs,** two miles north of town off 3rd St. E, is the park where visitors can fill jugs with sparkling soda water for free.

Two other areas, both along Hwy. 30 east of the city, offer quieter surroundings. **Oregon Trail Park** is along the shoreline of Soda Point Reservoir and was built as a cooperative venture between Utah Power and Light and the Idaho Fish and Game Department. The park features a covered picnic area, picnic tables, and a boat ramp. Toward town along the shoreline is a wild-looking stretch that is in fact just that. The state-owned parcel is protected as a natural area because of its unusual vegetation. The easily twisted pines here are limber pines, trees that normally occupy higher terrain. The trees' presence confirms the cold and windy microclimate here.

Practicalities

Soda Springs motels include **Caribou Lodge and Motel,** tel. 547-3377, at 110 W. 2nd St., with rooms for $25-41; **J-R Inn,** tel. 547-3366, at 179 W. 2nd St., with rooms for $30-42; and **Lakeview Motel,** tel. 547-4351, along Hwy. 30, with rooms for $22-50.

Soda Springs Golf Course, tel. 547-2204, gives golfers a chance to relax in the nearby springs. The ruts of a branch of the Oregon Trail form an interesting hazard along the 9-hole course here. The course is located east of the city along Hwy. 30. The **Soda Springs Ranger District,** tel. 547-4356, provides information about hiking, camping, and other opportunities to enjoy the outdoors in the area. The ranger station is located at 421 W. 2nd South.

The **Soda Springs Chamber of Commerce,** tel. 547-3706, gets its mail at P.O. Box 697, Soda Springs, ID 83726. They can tell you about all the goings-on in the area, including the **Caribou County Arts and Crafts Fair** in November.

EXPLORING THE VICINITY

Chesterfield

Between Lava Hot Springs and Soda Springs along Hwy. 30 is **Lund.** North of Lund is **Bancroft,** and north of Bancroft is the ghost town of Chesterfield. The town was named for Chesterfield, England, birthplace of Chester Call who was dispatched from Utah to found a new Mormon town. Chester Call convinced a dozen other families to settle on the windswept knoll that promised good grazing. The town finally succumbed to its isolation. What Chesterfield retained, however, was a loyal following. The town is still remarkably well-kept. Its fans have tried to breathe new life into it, most recently by seeking to have it designated as a new state park. The town's historical worth is recognized by its inclusion on the National Register of Historic Places. Standing among its dozen brick buildings, its general store, church, and school give visitors a chance to take a different view of the past, one in which the future has ended.

One More Hot Springs

South of McCammon off I-15, the Downey exit (at Malad Summit) will lead travelers to **Downata Hot Springs,** tel. 897-5736, at 25900 S. Downata Road.

KAREN WHITE

mule's ear flowers

BEAR LAKE COUNTRY

MONTPELIER AND VICINITY

Montpelier stands as the first Idaho settlement along the Oregon Trail—the post office here has been in operation since 1873. Mormons were the first settlers here, and history tells us Brigham Young himself named the town for the capital of Vermont, his home state. Bear Lake country was among the first areas settled by members of the Church of Jesus Christ of Latter-day Saints. Young and the church had a "feed them, don't fight them" philosophy with the Shoshone and Bannock Indians who had traditionally used the valley. After the area had been scouted and found suitable for farming, elders of the church met with Bannock Chief Tighi and Shoshone Chief Washakie to arrange the pact that would allow both groups to live peaceably.

In 1863, the first settlers chose a spot along Paris Creek for their home. The Indians were to have the south end of Bear Lake and the settlers agreed to share their crops with them. The **Sleight Cabin,** one of the first settler cabins, was built by Thomas Sleight and Charles Atkins in 1863 and housed both men and their wives for the winter. The cabin still stands in a park at Paris, southwest of Montpelier, near the Paris Stake Tabernacle.

Paris Stake Tabernacle

This beautiful tabernacle celebrated its centennial in 1989. Listed on the National Registry of Historic Places, the tabernacle served as ecclesiastical headquarters for the Bear Lake settlements. The building was constructed of red sandstone hauled 18 miles from Indian Creek along Bear Lake's eastern shore by Swiss stonemasons.

The church's interior shows the same craftsmanship as the exterior stonework. The ceiling is wood, the handiwork of a former shipbuilder. The interior wood is all nailed together with handmade square nails. Guided tours of the church are held daily from Memorial Day to Labor Day.

Bear Lake National Wildlife Refuge

Bear Lake National Wildlife Refuge, tel. 847-1757, is based at Montpelier. The refuge proper is seven miles southwest of town and protects an important migratory stop and nesting area for waterfowl and other birds. It was established in 1968, originally to protect Canada geese. Management of redheaded and can-

The Wild Bunch (l-r): Harry Longabaugh (Sundance Kid), Bill Carver, Ben Kilpatrick, Harvey Logan (Kid Curry), and George Parker (Butch Cassidy)

BUFFALO BILL HISTORICAL CENTER

BUTCH CASSIDY VISITS IDAHO

Montpelier was visited with infamy on the afternoon of Aug. 13, 1896, when its bank was robbed of more than $7,000 by three armed men. A member of the trio, one Bob Weeks, was caught. Never caught were Butch Cassidy and fellow outlaw Elza Lay. Weeks said they held up the bank to raise the money to hire a lawyer for another member of the Wild Bunch, Matt Warner, who faced a murder charge in Utah.

The robbers worked dressed as cowboys. The town's policeman couldn't find the transportation he wanted and ended up grabbing a bicycle. Cassidy escaped, and the robbers made their way back to Browns Hole in northwestern Wyoming.

The bank robbed by Butch and the boys is long since gone but the building it occupied still remains as part of the Montgomery Ward store along Washington Street.

vasback ducks, and white-faced ibis is now the focus because their numbers have been falling. In 1988, U.S. Fish and Wildlife Service biologists estimated the refuge was home to as many as 5,000 adult ibises, one of the country's largest nesting colonies. Bear Lake refuge is particularly important for the ibises and 10 other species of colony nesting birds that occupy the bulrushes. The colonies range from 10 pairs of Caspian terns to an estimated 6,400 pairs of Franklin gulls, according to the service. Whooping cranes have also been sighted here, most migrating with flocks of sandhill cranes.

The refuge, a popular waterfowl hunting area in season, encompasses 18,000 acres of mostly bulrush-cattail marsh with some flooded meadows. Most of the marsh is at about 6,000 feet elevation, which means snow and ice begin to take control in mid-November and linger until mid-April. Nonmotorized boats, mainly canoes, are allowed on the refuge July 1-Jan. 15. Motorized boats may be used Sept. 25-Jan. 15. Visitors may hike through areas of the refuge from July 1 through February, or cross-country ski until the closing date, assuming there's sufficient snow.

Minnetonka Cave

Just off Hwy. 89 near St. Charles is a canyon of the same name. A dozen miles up the canyon is Minnetonka Cave, which is operated by the Forest Service's Montpelier Ranger District, tel. 847-0375. The caves contain nine chambers and a wonderland of various formations. The stalactites, stalagmites, soda straws, banded travertine, and helicites have names like Ballerina, Caramel Corn Point, Treasure Room, and Bride and Groom. (The cave was first named Porcupine Cave around 1906 when a live porcupine was found there.) Developed in 1938 by the Works Progress Administration, in 1964 the Forest Service took over control and operation of the cave and installed an electric lighting system. Hour-long tours of the cave are offered daily between June 15 and Labor Day. The tours range 1,800 feet into the cave and include 448 stair steps, so good walking shoes are recommended. The cave's temperature is 48° F; bring a jacket.

Bear Lake State Park

Blue enough to be a misplaced patch of sky, Bear Lake lies like a jewel in a landscape of green and brown. One of Idaho's most-popular and least-developed recreation areas, Bear Lake State Park, occupies the lake's northern shoreline. The park has two divisions, the North and East Beach units. The North Beach runs 1.8 miles along the shoreline and offers soft sand and a gentle slope, perfect for family swimming outings. A boat ramp draws plenty of traffic here. Many boaters launch their boats, play around awhile, then pull up to the beach. They set up a sun canopy there and just enjoy the day, picnicking or swimming. A picnic shelter and outhouses are the only amenities at the North Beach unit. At the East Beach unit, drinking water is available and camping is permitted, though facilities are limited. A $2 vehicle entry fee is charged.

Bear Lake is also a popular fishing hole. In the early days, commercial fishermen caught trout and suckers, salting them and hauling them to Evanston, Wyoming. The lake is also home to the Bear Lake cisco, a smeltlike member of the whitefish family prized by anglers.

Bear Lake's deepest point (210 feet) is along the eastern shore. The presence of beaches 33 feet above current water lines appears to

Fine woodwork adorns the interior of the Paris LDS temple.

evidence a wetter climate during the last ice age. Just what color is Bear Lake's water? It depends on the mood and whim of the weather, although the most consistent descriptions call it robin's-egg blue, greenish blue, or morning-glory blue. Whatever name fits, it's beautiful. Some believe the tint results from the high concentrations of carbonates in the water; others pin it on the white-sand bottom.

Museums

Montpelier is home to two museums, the **Daughters of Utah Pioneers Museum,** and **Swiss Settlers Museum.** Call 847-1427 for an appointment.

PRACTICALITIES

Accommodations

Motels in Montpelier include the **Best Western Crest Motel,** tel. 847-1782, at 243 N. 4th St., with rooms ranging $48-55; **Budget Motel,** tel. 847-1273, at 240 N. 4th St., with rooms for $29-43; **Michelle Motel,** tel. 847-1772, at 401 Boise St., with rooms from $22; **Park Motel,** tel. 847-1911, with rooms for $26-37; and **Sunset Motel and Cafe,** tel. 847-2802.

Camping

Camping in the area includes **Montpelier KOA,** tel. 847-0863, east of Montpelier along Hwy. 89, with spaces for $10-14. In St. Charles, along the eastern shoreline of Bear Lake, is **Bear Lake Hot Springs,** with its hot springs pool and hot tubs.

The Forest Service maintains several campgrounds in the Montpelier and St. Charles areas. East of Montpelier are **Montpelier Canyon** and **Home Canyon.** Both are open from about May to October, depending on the year. West of St. Charles are **Clover Leaf, Porcupine, St. Charles,** and **Beaver Creek** campgrounds. Clover Leaf is a popular camping spot for those visiting Minnetonka Cave.

Food

Butch Cassidy's Restaurant and Saloon, tel. 847-3501, at 230 N. 4th in Montpelier, offers steak and seafood for dinner and live music in the saloon most weekends. Cafes and roadside stands are also available in Montpelier and St. Charles.

Events And Information

Peg Leg Smith Oregon Trail Rendezvous is held the closest Friday to July 24 and includes reenactments of historic and legendary events. Hatchet-throwing contests and Dutch-oven cookoffs are among the activities presented. The first Thursday and Friday in August you can attend the **Bear Lake Raspberry Parade,** just south of the border in Lakeview, Utah.

The **Greater Bear Lake County Chamber of Commerce,** tel. 847-3717, is at P.O. Box 265, Montpelier, ID 83254.

FRANKLIN AND PRESTON

Franklin, just north of the Utah border on Hwy. 91, was the first permanent settlement in Idaho. The members of the Church of Jesus Christ of Latter-day Saints didn't intend it that way. They were simply another outpost in Utah's Cache Valley until a subsequent survey in 1868 showed they were north of the 42nd parallel, the border with Idaho. The settlers arrived in April and by summer had plowed fields in the area for their first crops.

Franklin is still home to some beautiful old brick buildings. The **Franklin City Hall** and jail recalls the past accomplishments of the Mormon pioneers. Within the city is also the **Mathias Crowley Home,** which was the residence of an early Mormon apostle.

Franklin's **Relic Hall Museum** preserves pioneer tools and other artifacts in a stone store built in 1895 and an adjacent log building. A block north is the stately **Hatch House,** finely crafted of stone and brick and standing as the finest example of Greek revival architecture in Idaho. Lorenzo Hatch, who built the house, served four terms in the Utah Legislature, then was elected to the Idaho Territorial Legislature.

To the north of Franklin along Hwy. 91 is **Preston,** which was originally called Worm Creek when it was settled in 1888. Preston, too, has its beautiful historic homes. **Oneida Stake Academy** is on the campus of the Preston Senior High School along E. 2nd Street. The academy was built as a reaction to Idaho's anti-Mormon Idaho Test Oath, which prevented Saints from serving in government, including school boards. One of the students of the academy was Ezra Taft Benson, who served as Secretary of Agriculture to President Dwight Eisenhower and later was elected president of the Church of Jesus Christ of Latter-day Saints.

SIGHTS

Bear River Battleground

The nation's greatest Indian massacre occured 2.5 miles north of Preston, and was known as the Battle of Bear River. Witnesses to the horror reported that 300-400 warriors, women, and children were killed along the Bear River in 1863 by the Third California Infantry under the command of Col. Patrick Connor.

Connor sallied north of his station at Salt Lake City after a party of miners was attacked by Indians along Bear River. In January, the troops—an infantry of 60 soldiers and a cavalry unit of as many as 250 men—marched on to find the Indian camp at the mouth of Battle Creek. Seeing the cavalry massed across the Bear River, Indians began to taunt them. The cavalry charged across the river, and the Indians, firing from cover, killed 14. The cavalry reached the far shore, however, and then helped the infantry across. The soldiers burned 70 Indian tepees, leaving women and children to survive on their own.

Red Rock Pass

Nearly 20 miles north of Preston, Hwy. 91 crosses Red Rock Pass, the breach that drained Lake Bonneville. About 30,000 years ago a lava flow sent the Bear River south to flow into prehistoric Lake Bonneville. The lake found its outlet at Red Rock Pass, where a sill of rock once stood 300 feet higher. Once the water topped the soft rock, it began to quickly erode it. The more it eroded, the quicker the water flowed and the more quickly still the rock failed. Ultimately millions of cubic feet of water, several times the flow of the Amazon River, poured out of the gap and became known as the **Bonneville Flood.** The flood gouged out much of the Snake River Canyon and left behind fields of giant boulders called "melon gravel."

Buried Treasure

Northwest of Preston, **Malad City's** claim to fame is a nearby lost treasure stolen from a stagecoach which was traveling the famed Gold Road from Utah to Montana. The bandits had to hide their loot, and legends have it still out there somewhere. In 1890, Glispie Waldron reported spotting an iron door covering a cave. He tied his coat to a tree to mark the spot but could not find it again. The tale gives fresh vigor to modern-day treasure hunters who try their luck at finding the iron door.

Oxford Slough

Oxford Slough Wildlife Production Area is near Oxford, south of Downey off County Hwy. D1. The slough, which is managed by the U.S. Fish and Wildlife Service as part of the National Wildlife Refuge System, is a popular spot to watch wading birds like the white-faced ibis, black-crowned night heron, and snowy egret. Tundra swans also pass through here and rest during their migrations to and from breeding grounds.

PRACTICALITIES

Accommodations

Preston is the major population center in the area. Accommodations include the **Deer Cliff Inn,** tel. 852-0643, off Hwy. 91 at 2106 N. Deer Cliff Rd. in the Cub River Canyon. The inn has four cabins for $28-32. **Plaza Motel,** tel. 852-2020, has rooms for $30-43. Malad lodgings include the **Village Inn Motel,** tel. 766-4761, with rooms ranging $39-51.

Camping

The Caribou National Forest **Malad Ranger District,** tel. 766-4743, at 75 S. 140 E, maintains several campgrounds in the area. A favorite is the **Dry Canyon Campground** southeast of Malad. North of Malad is the **Summit Campground.** The **Curlew Campground,** near Stone Reservoir, has about a dozen sites designed for RVs. Electrical hookups are planned for the campground, but are not in place yet. Call for an update.

Events

Preston's most entertaining undertaking is the **Worm Creek Opera House Summer Theater,** which offers melodramas with all the primping and vigor of the old-timey shows. Preston's other main events include the **Preston Night Rodeo** held in late July each year, and the **Idaho Festival of Lights,** from Thanksgiving to New Year's, which includes fireworks and a parade. Malad's main event is the **Old Fashioned Fourth of July Celebration.** Franklin holds an annual **Idaho Day Celebration** the last weekend of June.

Recreation

The **Preston Golf Club,** tel. 852-2408, offers nine holes for visitors who like to chase the little white ball around. It is located at 1215 N. 800 E.

Malad is surrounded by eight reservoirs from five to 45 minutes away. The reservoirs are stocked with trout and produce some big ones. **Daniels Reservoir** northwest of town along Elkhorn Rd. is a favorite. **Pleasantview Reservoir** just to the west off St. John Rd. is another popular escape, as is **Deep Creek Reservoir.**

Information

Preston Chamber of Commerce, tel. 852-2703, is located at 70 S. State. The **Malad Chamber of Commerce,** tel. 766-4160, is located at 57 Bannock St.

BLACKFOOT AND VICINITY

Blackfoot occupies the confluence of the Snake and Blackfoot rivers near I-15 north of Pocatello. Intrepid fur-trapper Donald Mackenzie named the area for Indians whose name he intrepreted to mean black foot. First a stage stop, then a rail stop, and later an important station, Blackfoot (the town) was founded in 1879. In 1880 Blackfoot narrowly lost a bid to become Idaho's capital. Today the town serves as the Bingham County seat.

Blackfoot is one of Idaho's major potato-growing centers and claims the title "Potato Capital of the World." The russet Burbank potato developed by Luther Burbank thrives in the volcanic soils and climate of the upper Snake River Plains. Most of the dark green irrigated fields west and north of Blackfoot are planted in potatoes. Idaho's license plates proclaimed "Famous potatoes" for many years until legislators grudgingly bowed to public pressure to add "Scenic Idaho," striking a balance of sorts with a twin-motto plate. In Blackfoot, residents proclaim the potato the world's most popular vegetable. There's no specific world peace platform built on potatoes. But take a larger view. If both renowned broccoli-hater George Bush, and Bill Clinton, husband to no-peas-please Hillary Clinton, can agree to love spuds, might the rest of the planet be far behind?

SIGHTS

World Potato Exposition

The World Potato Exposition, tel. 785-2517, occupies the sturdy **Union Pacific Depot** at N. Main and W. Idaho, which was built by the Oregon Short Line. The exposition operates May-September. Admission is free but donations are requested to help spread the word about spuds. Signs along I-15 near town have lured nonresident tourists with the promise "Free Taters for Out-of-Staters." The museum itself sells potato ice cream and houses the world's largest potato chip. A video takes a potato's eye view of the industry. Other displays focus on antique potato-growing equipment and Peruvian artifacts from the ancestral home of the spud, perfected on the volcanic plains of Idaho. Outside its door is a massive Idaho baker, that is, alas, concrete.

Fort Hall Indian Reservation

East and south of town, the Fort Hall Indian Reservation, tel. 233-1525, is the headquarters of the Shoshone-Bannock tribes of Idaho. The reservation for the Boise and Bruneau Shoshones was established by proclamation in 1867. The Fort Hall bands of Bannock and

giant spud outside the Potato Expo

Shoshone were included in 1869. In June 1900, the reservation's size was reduced and much of it opened for settlement. A land rush followed in 1907. The Shoshone-Bannocks are Idaho's biggest tribe, with more than 3,000 members on the reservation.

Bingham County Historical Museum

This museum, housed in a lava rock home built in 1905, maintains a collection of pioneer artifacts. It is located at 190 N. Shilling.

PRACTICALITIES

Accommodations And Food

Riverside Inn, tel. 785-5000, has rooms for $30-48, at 1229 Parkway, and the **Y-Motel,** tel. 785-1550, has rooms for $20-30, at 1375 S. Broadway.

Blackfoot restaurants range from **Arctic Circle** (burger joint), at 814 S. Broadway and 900 W. Bridge, to the venerable **Colonial Inn,** tel.

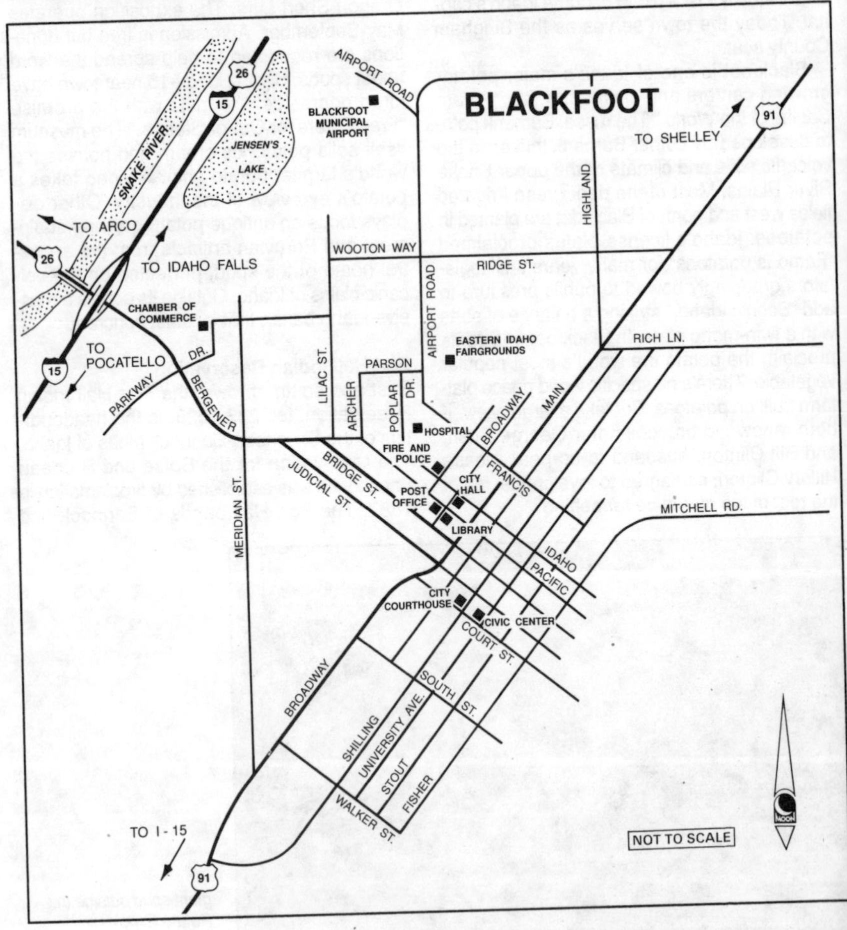

785-1390, at 659 S. Ash. **Latejanita,** tel. 785-4522, at 620 Bridge, and **Melina's Mexican Food,** tel. 785-3525, at 321 N.W. Main, represent Blackfoot's Mexican offerings. **Stan's Restaurant,** tel. 785-3110, at 465 N.W. Main provides family dining. Pizza is a major part of Blackfoot cuisine: **Little Caesars,** tel. 785-0040, is at 1355 Parkway Dr.; **Mr. Pizza,** tel. 785-3785, is at 125 N.W. Main; and **Pizza Hut,** tel. 785-6330 is at 1355 Riverside Plaza.

Events

The biggest event of the year in Blackfoot is the **Eastern Idaho State Fair,** held each year in early September. The spectacle includes horse racing, a carnival, and top country singers. Other events in past years have ranged from cookie contests to the state armwrestling championship. Fair information is available through the chamber of commerce or by writing Eastern Idaho State Fair, P.O. Box 250, Blackfoot, ID 83221. Another big draw each year is **Blackfoot Pride Days** in early June.

Recreation

Blackfoot City Golf Course, tel. 785-9960, is located at 3115 Teeples Drive. It is known widely for its challenging 18-hole course.

The **Snake River,** downstream from the mouth of the Blackfoot River, is a popular spot to float and watch nature go by. Popular boat ramps include the Tilden and Porterville bridges and the Blackfoot Railroad Bridge. A heron rookery in the cottonwoods along this stretch of river is popular with birders. Biologists ask boaters to stay in their boats while passing by the nests. The **Blackfoot River and Blackfoot Reservoir** are popular fishing spots for trout, while **Jensen's Grove Park** along the Snake River is a popular spot for picnicking and water-based activities, including water-skiing.

Information And Services

The **Blackfoot Chamber of Commerce,** tel. 785-0510, offers information about the area at P.O. Box 801, Blackfoot, ID 83221.

Police services in Blackfoot are provided by the **Blackfoot City Police,** tel. 785-1235, and the **Bingham County Sheriff,** tel. 785-4440, at 501 N. Maple Street. **Bingham Memorial Hospital,** tel. 785-4100, is located at 98 Poplar Street.

IDAHO FALLS AND VICINITY

Idaho Falls has grown to be Idaho's third-largest city on a diverse economic base that includes the Idaho National Engineering Laboratory's substantial workforce, other industries, medical care, education, and agriculture. The city began as Taylor's Bridge when J.M. Taylor built a toll bridge across the turbulent Snake River in 1865. The name was changed to Eagle Rock shortly afterward and again to Idaho Falls on Aug. 26, 1891.

SIGHTS

Parks

Idaho Falls, like Lewiston and Boise, prides itself on its riverine location. The **Idaho Falls Greenbelt** stretches about a mile along the river from the Broadway Bridge to the Hwy. 20 Bridge. The city boasts 40 parks, all managed by its **Parks and Recreation Department,** tel. 529-1480.

Tautphaus Park serves as the base for the **Idaho Falls Zoo,** tel. 529-1470, which includes a cat house with three species of big cats, an otter exhibit, monkeys, zebras, buffalos, exotic birds, pot-bellied pigs, and miniature zebu. Closed in winter.

Scenic walking and biking routes are the main attractions at **Eastbank, Westbank,** and **Freeman parks,** along Science Center Drive. A half-mile oval track on 400 acres at **Russett Noise Park,** 6.5 miles west along Hwy. 20, gives dirt-bikers and snowmobilers a playground. **Sand Creek Park and Rodeo Grounds** covers 150 acres along Hitt Road. The **Idaho Falls Recreation Center** at 520 Memorial Dr. has a gun range, gymnasium, racquetball courts, and weight and game rooms. **Lincoln Park** along Lincoln Rd. has tennis courts, picnic shelters, baseball diamonds, playground equipment, and a concession stand.

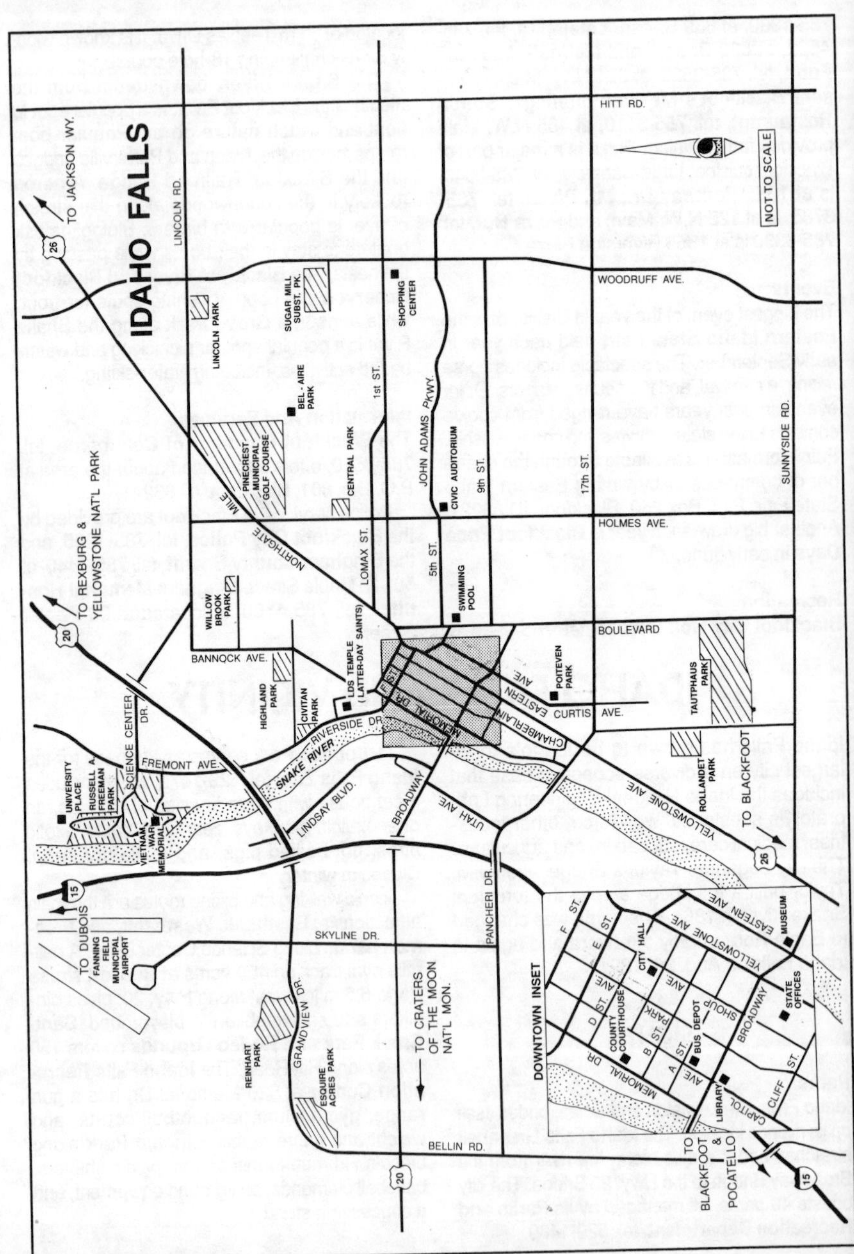
IDAHO FALLS
NOT TO SCALE
HITT RD.
WOODRUFF AVE.
HOLMES AVE.
BOULEVARD
SUNNYSIDE RD.
17th ST.
9th ST.
5th ST.
JOHN ADAMS PKWY.
1st ST.
LOMAX ST.
LINCOLN RD.
LINCOLN PARK
SUGAR MILL SUBST. PK.
SHOPPING CENTER
BEL - AIRE PARK
PINECREST MUNICIPAL GOLF COURSE
CENTRAL PARK
CIVIC AUDITORIUM
SWIMMING POOL
MILE
NORTHGATE
WILLOW BROOK PARK
BANNOCK AVE.
HIGHLAND PARK
LDS TEMPLE (LATTER-DAY SAINTS)
CIVITAN PARK
RIVERSIDE DR.
SNAKE RIVER
MEMORIAL DR.
F ST.
POITEVEN PARK
EASTERN AVE
CURTIS AVE.
CHAMBERLAIN
TAUTPHAUS PARK
ROLLANDET PARK
YELLOWSTONE AVE
TO BLACKFOOT
26
TO JACKSON WY.
TO REXBURG & YELLOWSTONE NAT'L PARK
20
SCIENCE CENTER DR.
FREMONT AVE.
UNIVERSITY PLACE
RUSSELL A. FREEMAN PARK
VIETNAM WAR MEMORIAL
LINDSAY BLVD.
BROADWAY
UTAH AVE
PANCHERI DR.
15
TO DUBOIS
FANNING FIELD MUNICIPAL AIRPORT
SKYLINE DR.
GRANDVIEW DR.
REINHART PARK
ESQUIRE ACRES PARK
TO CRATERS OF THE MOON NAT'L MON.
BELLIN RD.
DOWNTOWN INSET
F ST.
E ST.
D ST.
CITY HALL
COUNTY COURTHOUSE
PARK AVE
B ST.
A ST.
BUS DEPOT
SHOUP
EASTERN AVE
YELLOWSTONE AVE
MUSEUM
BROADWAY
STATE OFFICES
LIBRARY
CAPITOL
CLIFF ST.
MEMORIAL DR
TO BLACKFOOT & POCATELLO

Mormon Temple

The Church of Jesus Christ of Latter-day Saints built its **Idaho Falls Temple,** tel. 523-4504, at 1000 Memorial Dr., along the river. The visitor's center at the temple is open daily 9 a.m.-9 p.m. and features exhibits, videos, and artwork about Mormon history and culture.

Bonneville Museum

The Bonneville Museum, tel. 522-1400, at 200 N. Eastern Ave., is located in the Carnegie Library, built in 1916. The museum is operated by the Bonneville County Historical Society. It offers permanent displays about the area's natural history, early explorers and inhabitants, miners, and nuclear energy development. The museum also includes a walk-through facsimile of life in the earliest days of the city in its Eagle Rock U.S.A. exhibit. The **Fred Keefer Room** presents artifacts from the estate of an early pioneer.

Nuclear Reservation

Idaho Falls is the major base of employees for the **Idaho National Engineering Laboratories,** tel. 526-0111. "The site," as it's known in Idaho Falls, was created in 1949 as the National Reactor Testing Station, according to the U.S. Department of Energy, which oversees it. The site covers 890 miles of sagebrush and lava, chosen precisely because it was so isolated and unpopulated. The INEL and associated activities employ about 11,000 of Idaho Falls's residents. In all, the site holds 52 reactors.

The site recorded its first major significant achievement in 1951 when engineers first produced electricity with nuclear fission. The **Experimental Breeder Reactor No. 1,** tel. 526-2331, was the site of the experiments. EBR-1, as it's known hereabouts, is long since retired from active duty as a nuclear reactor but now serves to tell the nuclear story to visitors. The **visitor center** is along Hwy. 20-26, about 46 miles west of Idaho Falls toward Arco. The center is open daily 8-4 from Memorial Day to Labor Day. Visitors can see two nuclear reactors, a control room, remote handling devices for radioactive materials, Geiger counters, and other facets of the nuclear age. The center also offers guided tours.

After the EBR-1 development, the site became the stage for the BORAX III reactor, which in 1955 first supplied electricity to light Arco, 20 miles to the west. The Idaho National Engineering Laboratory undertook basic research on pressurized and boiling-water reactor prototypes.

INEL, out in the midst of all that desert, also is the birthplace of the nuclear Navy. The Idaho desert continues to serve as one of the stranger duty posts for U.S. Navy sailors as they learn to operate nuclear ship engines. INEL's main mission, however, is to provide research on reactor design and operation, and conduct related research. Much of the technical work to determine the cause and problems from the Three Mile Island nuclear accident in Pennsylvania was conducted here.

Craters Of The Moon National Monument

To the west of the Idaho National Engineering Laboratory is Arco and west from there is Craters of the Moon National Monument, tel. 527-3257 (P.O. Box 29, Arco, ID 83213). Its vast expanse of lava flows, cavelike lava tubes, and cinder cones has been likened to the lunar landscape. Despite the desolate appearance, Indian hunters ventured here after game. Ranchers, however, avoided the place and miners found little that would entice them enough to file a claim.

The weird country here was deemed unique enough to be declared a national monument in 1924, and today the monument encompasses 83 square miles. In 1970, Congress designated the southern portion of the national monument as the Craters of the Moon Wilderness.

The landscape here looks fresh because it is new, at least in geologic time. The lava flows began to erupt about 15,000 years ago and finished (for the time being at least) 2,000 years ago. A walk across the lava flows reveals two distinct varieties of the volcanic rock. The Hawaiians have been the world's experts on lava, and their language supplies the terms to distinguish the two basic kinds. *A'a* (pronounced ah-ah) lives up to its name. The jagged edges of this rubble can slit a shoe to ribbons in short order. *Pa'hoehoe* (pronounced pa-hoy-hoy) is as smooth and silken as its name. *Pa'hoehoe* lava is relatively fluid when it emerges, and it folds into ropy pleats as it hardens. *A'a* is more viscous, and moves slowly forward as a mass of jagged rubble as it is pushed out by the pressures below. When exploring the lava fields, the National Park Service warns visitors to stay on trails and refrain from climbing on spatter cones or monoliths.

The **visitor center** at the park entrance contains an informative set of displays, and shows a short video covering the park's volcanic history and features. A seven-mile loop road from here takes visitors to sites such as the **Devil's Orchard Trail,** the **Inferno Cone Viewpoint** trail, the **tree molds** trail, and the **Cave Area.** The Devil's Orchard Trail, recently improved with wheelchair access and new exhibits, winds through the weird lava formations that gave the trail its name. The Inferno Cone Viewpoint is one of the best spots to get a panorama of the entire volcanic landscape; the top of the cone offers a clear view to the southeast of the line of cinder cones marking the Great Rift—a series of fissures and cracks. Farther south along the loop, a turnoff leads to the trail to the tree molds, where hot lava surrounded, then hardened around ancient trees. Another trail near here heads southeast into the wilderness. Those planning to venture into the wilderness should note that the area has no water in summer and challenges the expert hiker and explorer. Special backcountry permits must be obtained at the visitor center for overnight trips into the area, and rangers offer advice about special precautions for travel there. Continuing counterclockwise around the loop road, visitors come to the Cave Area. A half-mile trail here takes visitors to Dew-

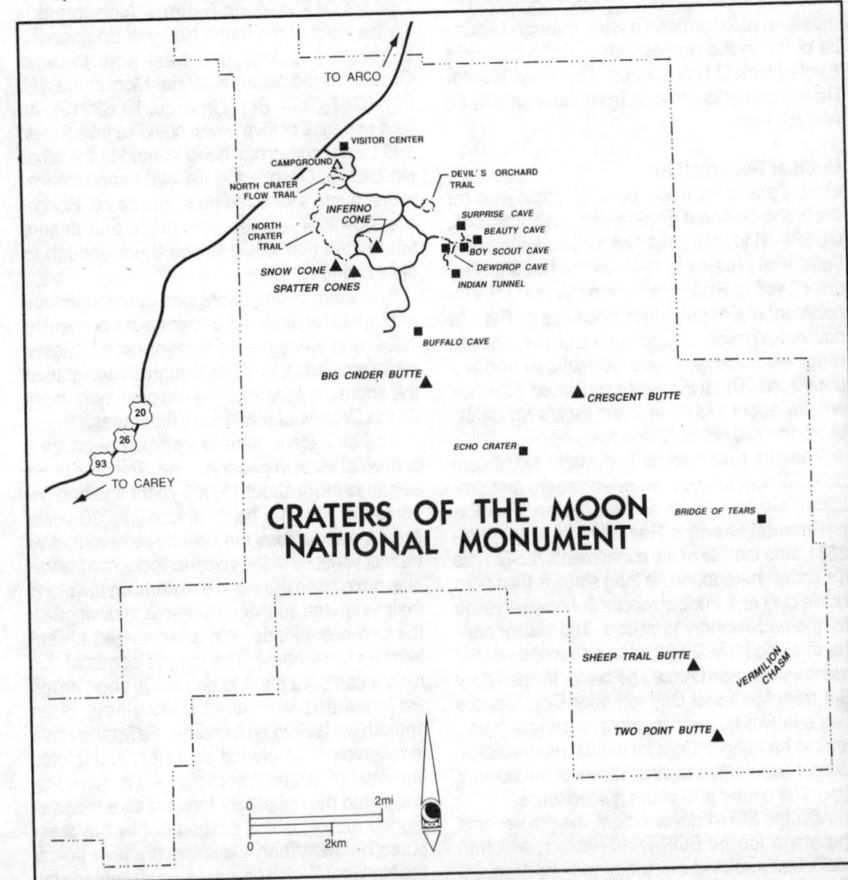

Rangers lead nature walks at Craters of the Moon National Monument.

drop, Boy Scout, Beauty, and Surprise caves, and the largest of these lava tubes, Indian Tunnel. You'll need to take your own flashlights into the caves. Be sure the batteries are fresh.

The campground at the park doesn't look like much at first. In July and August it seems all cinders and uninviting at best, particularly for tent campers. But for families with young children, the campground has some surprising attractions: the rocks themselves. Young children delight in being able to lift canteloupe-sized chunks of the light, porous lava, and enjoy exploring all the nooks and crannies of the lava flows. Caution is advised, of course, because a fall can leave some nasty scrapes. And rangers ask you to please leave all the rocks the way you found them. The park's campground is open year round. Rangers conduct guided walks during the day and present programs in the campground amphitheater in the evenings.

From May to October the campground has running water and there is a fee of $8 per night per site. The rest of the year, camping is free, but there is no running water. The visitor center is open year-round (except holidays), 8 a.m.-6 p.m. in summer, 8-4:30 in winter. During winter, the loop road into the park makes a starkly scenic trail for cross-country skiers and is groomed whenever snowpack is adequate.

Heise Hot Springs

Heise Hot Springs, tel. 538-7312, is open year-round near Heise, which is northeast of Idaho Falls near Ririe. The springs have been developed with swimming pools and a slide. The campground is well shaded with the tall cottonwoods that make the South Fork of the Snake a special place. The resort has a restaurant and play area for children. Admission to the pool is $4.50 for adults and $2.50 for children. An all-day pool pass is $5.50 for adults and $3.50 for children younger than 12. Water-slide rides are $5 for an unlimited pass or less for limited tickets. Swimsuits are available for rent as are towels.

RECREATION

Water Sports

The **Idaho Falls Aquatic Center,** tel. 529-1111, at 149 7th St., is an indoor pool open to the public. The center has eight 25-yard swimming lanes, a children's area, two diving boards, a second-floor observation area, and two hot tubs.

The **Snake River Whitewater Project** is an Olympic-class whitewater course being developed on an island 3.5 miles from the city center, near the city's northern power plant. The course is 38 feet wide and 1,908 feet long.

Golf

Idaho Falls has three municipal 18-hole golf courses: **Pinecrest,** tel. 529-1485, at 701 Elva; **Sandy Creek,** tel. 529-1115, at 5230 Hackman Rd.; and **Idaho Falls Country Club,** tel. 523-5757, at 11611 S. County Club Dr., a private course. Near Ririe is the par-29, nine-hole **Heise Hills Golf Course,** tel. 538-7327, at 5136 E. Heise, five miles northeast of Ririe off Hwy. 26. Greens fees at Heise Hills are $5 for nine holes and $9 for 18.

Skiing

Kelly Canyon Ski Area, tel. 538-6261, is 25 miles northeast of Idaho Falls and eight miles east of Ririe off Hwy. 26. Kelly Canyon has 870 vertical feet of skiing with four double chairs and a rope tow. The ski area is normally open Wed.-Sunday. Kelly Canyon has a day lodge and ski rentals.

Rental skis are available in Idaho Falls at **Idaho Mountain Trading Co.,** tel. 523-6679, at 474 Shoup Ave., and at **Solitude, The Mountain Shop,** tel. 523-7000, at 475 A.

The **Idaho Falls Ski Club,** tel. 529-0717, arranges outings for skiers to surrounding ski areas.

Fishing

The South Fork of the Snake River southeast of Idaho Falls is considered by many to be among the best in Idaho for big cutthroat and some very big brown trout. The biggest brown trout on record was taken from the South Fork in 1981. The 36.5-incher tipped the scales at 26 pounds, 6 ounces! The South Fork's fishing has spawned a thriving outfitting business with most fishing guides based out of Swan Valley. The **Idaho Fish and Game Department** maintains its Upper Snake regional office, tel. 525-7290, at 1515 Lincoln Road at Idaho Falls.

Camping

An excellent source of information about recreation on the national forests and public lands of southeastern Idaho is available in Idaho Falls at the **Eastern Idaho Visitor Center,** tel. 523-1012, operated by the BLM and the Forest Service. The center is located at 505 Lindsay Blvd. and can be reached by mail at P.O. Box 50498, Idaho Falls, ID 83405.

The South Fork and Palisades Reservoir along its upper reaches are the setting for one of the most concentrated strings of campgrounds in the **Targhee National Forest.** The Forest Service campgrounds along Hwy. 26 south of Swan Valley include **Palisades,** with seven campsites; **Big Elk Creek,** with 16 campsites and a boat ramp; **Falls,** with 48 campsites; and the largest, **Calamity,** with 62 campsites along the reservoir (closed for renovation in 1994). Other campgrounds are **Bear Creek,** with eight campsites; **McCoy Creek,** with 19; and **Hoffman,** with 20. For more information, call the national forest headquarters at 523-1412, or the **Swan Valley Ranger Station** at 483-3001.

Spectator Sports

The **TRAC** at Sandy Downs is located at St. Clair and York roads and features weekend pari-mutuel racing, horse shows, and rodeos.

The **Idaho Falls Braves,** tel. 522-8363, fill the summer nights with the joyous sounds of the national pastime at McDermott Field.

ACCOMMODATIONS AND FOOD

Motels

Motels in Idaho Falls include **Best Western Driftwood Motel,** tel. 523-2242, at 575 River Parkway, with rooms for $40-55; **Best Western Stardust,** tel. 522-2910, at 700 Lindsay Blvd., with rooms for $40-65; **Bonneville Motel,** tel. 522-7847, at 2000 S. Yellowstone, with rooms for $26-42; **Comfort Lodge,** tel. 523-2960, at 255 E St., where rooms go for $28-55; and **Evergreen Gables Motel,** tel. 522-5410, at 3130 S. Yellowstone, with rooms for $19-35.

Other motels include **Idaho Falls Super 8,** tel. 522-8880 or (800) 800-8000, at 705 Lindsay Blvd., which has rooms for $37-51; **Littletree Inn,** tel. 523-5993 or (800) 521-5993, at 888 N. Holmes ($54-69); **Motel 6,** tel. 522-0112, at 1448 W. Broadway ($30-43); **Motel West,** tel. 522-1112, at 1540 W. Broadway ($32-46); and **Ross Motel,** tel. 525-9958, at 343 C St. ($14 and up).

Other choices in Idaho Falls include **Shilo Inn,** tel. 523-0088 or (800) 222-2244, at 780 Lindsay Blvd., which has all minisuites for about $105; and **Quality Inn,** tel. 523-6260, at 850 Lindsay Blvd., with rooms for $44-50.

Arco area motels include **D.K. Motel,** tel. 527-8282 or (800) 421-3287, at 316 S. Front, with rooms for $23-43; **Lazy A Motel,** tel. 527-8263, with rooms for $25-35; **Lost River Motel,** tel. 527-3600, at 405 Highway Dr., with rooms for $27-45 and RV sites for $5; and **Riverside Motel,** tel. 527-8954, with rooms for $25-49.

Bed And Breakfast Inn

Little Bush Inn, tel. 529-0567, ranks as the only bed and breakfast in Idaho Falls. It's at 498 Maple St., five minutes from downtown. The inn's two rooms rent for $40 s, $50 d, which includes a full breakfast.

Campgrounds

In addition to the Forest Service campgrounds listed above, several privately owned campgrounds are available in the area. The **Idaho Falls KOA,** tel. 523-3362, is at 1440 Lindsay Blvd. and has 180 camp spaces for $12-16 a night. Others include **Shady Rest Campgrounds,** tel. 524-0010, at 2200 N. Yellowstone Hwy.; **Sunnyside Acres Park,** tel. 523-8403, at 905 W. Sunnyside Rd.; **Heise Hot Springs,** tel. 538-7944, $10-12 a night; and **Mountain River General Store,** tel. 538-7735.

Food

In Arco, restaurants include **Deli Sandwich Shop,** at 119 N. Idaho; **Golden West Cafe,** at 143 W. Era Ave.; **Lost River Drive-In,** at 520 W. Grand; **Mello-Dee Club and Steak House,** at 175 Sunset Dr.; and **Pickle's Place,** at 440 S. Front Street.

Idaho Falls restaurants encompass a variety rivaled only by Boise and include **Bonneville Restaurant and Lounge,** tel. 523-7987, at 410 Constitution Way; **O'Brady's Restaurant,** tel. 523-2132, at 1438 W. Broadway; **Jake's Steak and Fish House,** tel. 524-5240, at 851 Lindsay Blvd.; **The Sandpiper,** tel. 524-3344, at 750 Lindsay Blvd.; **Shilo Inn Restaurant and Lounge,** tel. 523-1818, at 760 Lindsay Blvd.; and **Stardust Restaurant and Lounge,** tel. 523-1865, at 680 Lindsay Boulevard.

Family or casual restaurants include **Babe's Bakery and Croissanterie,** tel. 523-5809, at 2099 E. 17th; **North Hiway Cafe,** tel. 522-6212, at 460 Northgate Mile; **Smitty's Pancake and Steak House,** tel. 523-6450, at 645 Broadway which offers good service and familiar food; and **Choices,** tel. 523-2131, at 1869 N. Yellowstone.

Chinese restaurants lead the parade of ethnic cuisine in Idaho Falls, including **Hong Kong Restaurant,** tel. 522-9914, at 1570 W. Broadway; **Paris Cafe,** tel. 523-5405, at 354 Broadway; **Chinese Garden,** tel. 522-6300, at 1646 E. 17th; and **Happy's Chinese Restaurant,** tel. 522-2091, at 549 Park Avenue. Mexican restaurants include **Garcia's,** tel. 522-2000, at 2180 E. 17th; **Mama Inez of Idaho Falls,** tel. 525-8968, at 344 Park Ave.; and **Mi Casa,** tel. 523-9381, at 235 Cliff.

Pizza restaurants include **Godfather's Pizza,** tel. 529-0553, at 1745 N. Yellowstone; **Papa Tom's Pizza,** tel. 523-6800 or 524-7272 for delivery, at 1830 Woodruff Ave.; and **Round Table Pizza,** tel. 529-5090, at 1680 E. 1st.

OTHER PRACTICALITIES

Entertainment And Events

Idaho Falls has a more diverse menu of entertainment than most of the state's communities. **Idaho Ballet Theatre,** tel. 522-3838, is located at 472 Park Avenue. The **Idaho Falls Opera Theatre,** tel. 523-0620, schedules two performances a year. **Idaho Falls Symphony,** tel. 529-1080, is based at Suite 101, 545 Shoup. Performances are held at the **Idaho Falls Civic Auditorium,** tel. 529-1396, at 501 S. Holmes Avenue. For a general overview of artistic events in the city, the **Idaho Falls Arts Council,** tel. 522-0471, keeps track.

The holiday celebrated with the most hoopla in Idaho Falls is the Fourth of July, with the **Settler's Festival,** a parade, and fireworks. The **War Bonnet Round-up,** the region's oldest annual rodeo, is held the first weekend in August.

Transportation

Idaho Falls Municipal Airport is located in the northwest portion of the city off I-15, Exit 119 at the north end of Skyline Drive. Idaho Falls is served by **Horizon Air,** tel. (800) 547-9308, and **Skywest,** tel. (800) 453-9417.

Bus lines include local service provided by **CART,** tel. 524-0090, which stands for Community and Rural Transportation. CART buses, based at 844 S. Mulligan Rd., follow fixed routes Mon.-Fri. 7 a.m.-5 p.m. Long-distance services include **Greyhound Bus Lines,** tel. 522-0912, at 2874 N. Holmes, and **Teton Stage Lines,** tel. 529-8036, at 1425 Lindsay Boulevard.

Car rentals at Municipal Airport are available from **Avis,** tel. 522-4225 or (800) 331-1212; **Budget,** tel. 522-8800 or (800) 527-0700; **Hertz,** tel. 529-3101; and **National,** tel. 522-5276. Other companies in town include **Broadway Ford,** tel. 525-8500; **Dollar,** tel. 524-1056; and **Practical Rent A Car,** tel. 529-5535.

Information And Services
The **Idaho Falls Chamber of Commerce,** tel. 523-1010, is located at 505 Lindsay Blvd. (P.O. Box 50498, Idaho Falls, ID 83405-0498). The **Idaho Falls Public Library,** tel. 529-1450, is located at the corner of Capital and Broadway streets. Police services are provided by the **Idaho Falls Police,** tel. 529-1200 or 911 for emergencies, at 605 N. Capital Ave.; and **Bonneville County Sheriff,** tel. 529-1200 or 911, at 585 N. Capital Avenue.

Idaho Falls hospitals include **Eastern Regional Medical Center,** tel. 529-6111, at 3100 Channing Way; and **Family Emergency Centers,** tel. 529-5252, at 1995 E. 17th, and tel. 525-2600, 250 S. Skyline Drive.

MARK MORRIS

pica

REXBURG AND THE TETON VALLEY

SIGHTS

Ricks College

Rexburg is home to **Ricks College,** tel. 356-2011, established in 1888 by the Church of Jesus Christ of Latter-day Saints. Founded a year earlier than the University of Idaho—the state's flagship university at Moscow—the college originally was intended as a haven for young Mormons persecuted for their political and religious beliefs. The college has since emerged as the largest two-year private college in the country with its enrollment of 6,500 students. Ricks graduates receive associate degrees and the college's specialties include agribusiness, office education, business and marketing, and emergency medical technology. Students sponsor several cultural groups, and the college's annual folk-dance festival draws international troupes.

Mormon Tabernacle

The Mormon Tabernacle, at 17 N. Center St., is listed on the National Register of Historic Places and stands as a major attraction in Rexburg with its gray stone walls and twin towers.

Famous Son

Rigby, between Idaho Falls and Rexburg along Hwy. 20, deserves at least a nod from visitors passing through for its role as the cradle of one of the century's most powerful forces: television. **Philo T. Farnsworth,** the inventor of the television camera, all-electric television, radar, and black light, grew up in Rigby. He held more than 300 patents when he died at age 64. Farnsworth was born Aug. 19, 1906, in Beaver, Utah, then attended Rigby High School in 1921. While there he studied the molecular theory of matter and electrons. In 1922, he invented and patented the practical basis for television, the cathode ray tube. A museum in Rigby commemorates Farnsworth's achievements, and signs along the highway proclaim Rigby to be the birthplace of television.

Spencer Opal Mines

Some 65 miles north of Idaho Falls along I-15 lie the **Spencer Opal Mines,** which are open May-September. The mines were discovered in 1948 by a pair of deer hunters and are the only commercial opal mines in the United States. The opals were formed by silica carried by hot water that fed geysers. The sequence of eruptions in the area left the opal in layers. Miners are charged $17.50 a day for up to five pounds of opal-bearing rock. Diggers who exceed the five-pound limit are charged $3.50 for each additional pound. Only diggers are allowed in the mining area. The mine is open for digging Sat.-Mon. 8:30 a.m.-4 p.m. A shuttle bus leaves the town of **Spencer** at 8 a.m. Miners must provide their own tools, and the company requires safety glasses. Other suggested tools include a rock hammer, three- or four-pound crack hammer, points and chisels, an eight- to 10-pound sledgehammer, bucket, spray bottle, gloves, and sturdy clothes and shoes. Diggers must bring their own drinks and lunch. The mine is headquartered at the Conoco gas station and trailer court, which is open daily 7:30 a.m.-8 p.m.

Museums

Some 25 miles east of Rexburg is the site of the **Teton Dam,** which caused a billion dollars in damages and devastated Sugar City and much of Rexburg when it collapsed June 5, 1976. Down a paved road is the desolate parking area built by the U.S. Bureau of Reclamation to let visitors see the majesty of man's work. What's left is a pyramidal section of dam, all that remains of the earth-filled core of the Teton Dam. The shoulder of the canyon is dotted with control towers, fences, and other reminders of what was once a major government installation. The **Teton Flood Museum** (also known as the Upper Snake River Valley Historical Museum), tel. 356-9101, at 51 N. Center in Rexburg, preserves memories of the disaster, as well as offering exhibits including the ship's bell from the U.S.S. *Rexburg,* rock and mineral displays, and a barbed-wire collection. Further information about the dam disaster is available at the damsite north of Hwy. 33 east of Rexburg.

St. Anthony Sand Dunes

One of Idaho's stranger and more fascinating areas is the St. Anthony Sand Dunes, north of Rexburg, which form part of a recreation area managed by the BLM at Idaho Falls, tel. 529-1020. The sand dunes cover about 15 square miles and are "live," meaning they are continually shifting and are not anchored in place by vegetation. The Idaho Fish and Game Department's **Sand Creek Wildlife Management Area,** tel. 624-7065, encompasses 15,000 acres in the area and is popular for camping, fishing, and hunting.

St. Anthony is also home to the **Fremont County Historical Society Museum.** The supervisor's office for the **Targhee National Forest,** tel. 624-3151, is located at 420 N. Bridge Street.

The Tetons

One of the West's most famous mountain ranges, the Teton Range, lies in Grand Teton National Park just a few miles across the Wyoming border. The Teton Valley of Idaho, with its towns of **Driggs, Victor,** and **Tetonia,** offers a seldom-seen view of the great peaks from the west. Idaho has designated Highways 31, 32, and 33 as the **Teton Scenic Route** from Idaho Falls north to Ashton. The Tetons are so dramatic partly because of their youth. The three granite peaks rose during the last nine million years, the geological record indicates, and they are still growing. The peaks we see today were chiseled by glacial ice during the last 250,000 years.

The valley west of the Tetons was known as **Pierre's Hole** by mountain men, who made it a favorite stomping grounds and rendezvous site from 1819 to 1840. The valley took its name from "Old Pierre" Tevanitagon, an Iroquois trapper for the Hudson's Bay Company. The 1832 Rocky Mountain Fair was held in the valley and ended with a running battle between the Gros Ventre Indians and the trappers and their allies. The valley was permanently settled in 1882. Driggs is home to the **Teton County Historical Museum** with its excellent collection of ranching artifacts. The storefront museum is located along Main Street.

BOB RACE

elk

PRACTICALITIES

Accommodations

Motels in Rexburg include **Best Western Cotton Tree Inn,** tel. 356-4646, at 450 W. 4th St., with rooms for $48-65; **Calaway Motel,** tel. 356-3217, at 361 S. 2nd W, with rooms for $24-35; **Rex's Motel,** tel. 356-5477, at 357 W. 4th S, with rooms for $24-36; and **Days Inn,** tel. 356-9222, at 271 S. 2nd W, with rooms for $39-54.

In St. Anthony, the **Weston Inn,** tel. 624-3711, at 115 S. Bridge, offers rooms for $45-58. **Green Canyon Hot Springs,** tel. 458-4454, at 2432 S. Canyon Creek Rd. near Newdale on Hwy. 33, has a campground ($6 tent sites, $7.50 sites with hookups; plus 10 cents per person).

Driggs offers **Best Western Teton West,** tel. 354-2363, with rooms for $42-58; **Pines Motel,** tel. 354-2774, at 105 S. Main, with rooms for $25-60; and **Larsen's Mobile Home Park,** tel. 354-2205, with 20 camping spaces. Near Driggs is **Teton Valley Lodge,** tel. 354-2386. Victor has the **Timberline Motel,** tel. 787-2772, with rooms for $29-43. The **Teton Valley KOA,** tel. 787-2280, has campsites for $16-21.

Food

Teton Valley restaurants include **Knotty Pine Bar and Restaurant,** tel. 787-2866, at 58 S. Main; **Timberline Bar and Cafe,** at 14 W. Center; and **Victor Steak Bank,** tel. 787-2277, at 13 S. Main, all in Victor. **Little Max's Cafe** is at 110 Main in

the "back" side of the Tetons near Driggs

Tetonia. In Driggs, eateries include **O'Rourkes Fine Food and Beer,** tel. 354-8115, at 42 Little Ave.; **Pierre's Rendezvous,** at 189 N. Main; **Teton Bakery and Cafe,** tel. 354-8116, at 68 N. Main; **Mike's Eats** at 10 N. Main; and **The Tree** at 12 N. Main. Mike's wins the author's vote as the winner in the cafe chic category. It features buffalo burgers, good coffee, and great pastries.

Rexburg restaurants include **Golden Corral Steakhouse,** tel. 356-9626, at 240 N. 200 East; **Golden Dragon,** tel. 356-9123, at 145 W. Main; **Gringo's Mexican Restaurant,** tel. 356-9400, at 23 S. Center; **JB's Big Boy Family Restaurant,** tel. 356-7722, at 150 W. Main; **Me 'N' Stan's,** tel. 356-7330, at W. Main and S. 2nd W; **PS Restaurant,** at 15 E. Main; and **TJ's Final Touch Restaurant,** tel. 356-3566, at 10 E. Main. Pizza and fast-food places include **Domino's Pizza,** tel. 356-9555; **Kentucky Fried Chicken,** at 27 W. Main; **McDonald's Restaurant,** at 175 E. 350 N; **Pizza Hut,** tel. 356-7811, at 163 W. Main; **Taco Time,** at 274 S. 2nd W; and **Wendy's Old Fashioned Hamburgers,** at 545 N. 200 East.

At Rigby are the **Country Diner,** tel. 745-7888, at 160 S. State; **Donae's Family Restaurant,** at 100 W. Main; and **Goldilocks Sandwich Shop,** at Bond City Mall.

St. Anthony restaurants include **Big J's Drive In** at 245 N. Bridge; **Chiz' Cougar Cave,** tel. 624-7633, at 245 N. 1st E; **Country Kitchen,** at 137 N. Center in Parker; **Lamplighter Restaurant,** tel. 624-3554, at 22 N. Bridge; and **Stardust Lounge,** tel. 624-7195, at 39 W. Main.

Events

St. Anthony's **Fishermen's Breakfast** kicks off the late-May opening of fishing season with free flapjacks. The major event of the entire Teton Valley is the **Budweiser Hot Air Balloon Festival,** during which more than 40 hot-air balloons typically lift off from Driggs in early July. A craft fair is also held. Rexburg gets into the events scene with its **Whoopee Days and Fourth of July Parade,** as well as the **Idaho International Folk Dance Festival,** held in late July and early August each year. Festival events include a street fair, rodeo, Western hoedown, and then the festival itself. Dancers have attended the festival from such diverse countries as China, Hungary, Austria, Soviet Union, France, Brazil, and India in past years. The major event in Driggs each year is **Pierre's Rendezvous Days** held the first week of August. The **Madison County Fair** is held at the fairgrounds in Rexburg in mid-August each year. Rigby is home to the **Jefferson County Fair** in mid-August as well. **Mud Lake Fair and Rodeo** gets rolling at Terreton 30 miles west in late August.

Golf

Targhee Village Golf Course, tel. 354-8577, is at Stateline and Cemetery roads in Driggs. In Rigby, **Jefferson Hills Golf and Recreation Center,** tel. 745-6492, is off Labelle Road. Rexburg offers **Teton Lakes Golf Course,** tel. 356-8140, along the Hibbard Highway. **Fremont**

County Golf Course, tel. 624-7074, is five miles north of town.

Information And Services

Information about the area is available from the **Rigby Area Chamber of Commerce,** tel. 745-6646; **Rexburg Chamber of Commerce,** tel. 356-5700, at 134 E. Main; **South Fremont Chamber of Commerce,** tel. 624-3494, at 110 W. Main; and **Teton Valley Chamber of Commerce,** tel. 354-2500.

Police services in the Teton Valley area are available from the **Driggs City Police** or **Teton County Sheriff,** both at tel. 354-2323 (911 in emergencies). **Rexburg City Police,** tel. 359-3000, at the Madison County Courthouse, or the **Madison County Sheriff,** tel. 356-5426, may be reached at 911 in emergencies. **St. Anthony Police,** tel. 624-4482, are located at 146 N. 2nd West. Emergency care is available at **Madison Memorial Hospital,** tel. 356-3691 or 911.

NORTH OF ASHTON

Ashton was named for a railroad engineer, but for most it marks the beginning, spiritually if not geographically, of that holy of holies of Idaho fishing waters, the **Henry's Fork of the Snake River.** The Henry's Fork is one of the top trout streams in the West. Anglers migrate here for the mayfly and stonefly hatches each spring. **Henry's Lake** and **Island Park** reservoirs also draw thousands of anglers each summer to fish for the big rainbow trout that thrive in these waters. The Henry's Fork is known for such landmarks as Upper and Lower Coffee Pot Rapids, Big Springs, and Box Canyon. The most fished stretch of the Henry's Fork is between Island Park Dam and Osborne Bridge. For the best chance at big fish, Box Canyon is preferred by many anglers. For first-time Henry's Fork anglers or those without a boat, hiring an outfitter here is probably a good idea.

SIGHTS

Big Springs, Mesa Falls

Big Springs wells up northeast of Island Park about 30 miles north of Ashton off Hwy. 20, and supplies most of the flow for the Henry's Fork from then on. The Targhee National Forest maintains a campground at Big Springs and a place to observe the big rainbow trout that flourish there. The major attractions along the Henry's Fork are Upper and Lower **Mesa Falls,** both east of Ashton along Hwy. 47. The falls are a mile off the highway along Forest Service Rd. 295. The beautiful and scenic upper falls drop 114 feet from a wall of rock. Several visitors have gone over them, so be careful. The Idaho Parks and Recreation Department and U.S. Forest Service joined forces recently to lessen the hazard. A beautiful boardwalk now parallels the edge of the canyon and offers dramatic vantage points to see the upper falls at their best. The lower falls drop 65 feet. A turnout, dubbed Grandview, is along Hwy. 47 several hundred feet above the river.

Harriman State Park

Harriman State Park, tel. 558-7368, also north of Ashton, is one of the most popular recreational parks in the Idaho parks system. The rich meadows along the Henry's Fork of the Snake River here were bought up by Oregon Shortline Railroad officials in 1902 for "Railroad Ranch," a cattle ranch and vacation retreat. The Oregon Shortline was a subsidiary of the Union Pacific, which built the line to haul visitors to West Yellowstone, Montana. The magnates who bought the land included Solomon Guggenheim of New York and Charles Jones. Edward H. Harriman bought one of the five shares in the ranch in 1908. He died before he could see it. His wife, Mary, brought their three youngest children, Carol, Averell, and Roland, to the ranch in 1911.

The ranch was a working one. Cowboys tended cattle in the lush meadows along the river and in the surrounding hills. Fall meant roundup time, when the hands and guests would join forces to herd the cattle to the railhead or ranch proper from their summer pastures. During the long, silent winters, the hands would tend the stock and cut ice from Silver Lake for the next summer. They also shoveled a lot of snow—6-10 feet—from the cabin roofs to keep them from collapsing.

In 1961, Roland Harriman and Gov. Robert E. Smylie signed an agreement giving the Harrimans life estates in the ranch, but promising its future to the people. The gift had several conditions, one of which was the formation of a professional park service to oversee it. In 1965, the Idaho Legislature approved the creation of the Idaho Parks and Recreation Department. In 1977, the ranch was transferred to the state with the Harrimans as witnesses. The park was opened to the public in 1982.

The ranch holds several of the old barns and sheds, as well as a cluster of cabins built by the previous owners to house the working hands. Several of the cabins are available for inspection, and a bunkhouse, built in 1978, is available for rent from the Parks Department. The park is one of only two in the state parks system with a stable on the grounds.

The park protects a dozen miles of the Henry's Fork shoreline and is popular with fishermen. Some 16,000 acres surrounding the ranch have been designated as the **Harriman Wildlife Refuge,** which shelters a wealth of species ranging from moose to bald eagles, ospreys, elk, sandhill cranes, and endangered trumpeter swans.

Upper Mesa Falls on Henry's Fork

Henry's Lake State Park

Henry's Lake is one of Idaho's biggest high-country lakes, covering 6,200 acres at an elevation of 6,427 feet. The lake's rich waters grow big trout—brook trout to five pounds, rainbows and cutthroat-rainbow hybrids several pounds bigger still. Each summer, rainbows or hybrids (cutbows to some) have been caught that top eight pounds. Needless to say, the state park here is about fishing for the most part. The park offers a shoreline campground with well-developed access to the lake. Henry's Lake is on the way to Yellowstone National Park for the many visitors who choose to enter its western gate at West Yellowstone, Montana, just over Targhee Pass.

The lake's name and that of the river that flows from it commemorate Maj. Andrew Henry, who explored the area in 1810, four years after the Lewis and Clark Expedition returned east. Henry built a winter post that year near St. Anthony to the south. In 1868, Gilman Sawtell founded the first ranch in the valley, on the lake's west shore near Staley Springs.

Henry's Lake would be a shallow wetlands similar to Grays Lake were it not for a dam near its outlet, which raised the lake's depth to an average of 12 feet. The rainbow trout that now capture anglers' attention apparently didn't enter the lake until about 1900 and naturally hybridized with the native Snake River cutthroats. The hybrids are still popular, although the Idaho Fish and Game Department has taken the chance out of the fishes' pairings. So prized are hybrids now that the state agency heat shocks the eggs to alter their chromosomes, rendering the fish sterile. Like steers, the new hybrids grow heavier and stronger.

Wildlife, including white pelicans, tundra and trumpeter swans, deer, and moose make frequent visits to the park. A developed nature trail stretches northeast from the park. The **Henry's Lake Fish Hatchery,** tel. 558-7202, along the lake's northern shoreline, is open to visitors by appointment during most of the summer. Call to make arrangements.

The Henry's Fork of the Snake River reflects the sky at the Millionaire's Hold in Harriman State Park.

Other Points Of Interest

The **Johnny Sack Cabin** at Island Park was built by a German immigrant along the banks of Big Springs in 1939. The cabin is open during July and August to show off the elegant inlaid flooring and hand-carved furniture within. The **Hess Museum,** tel. 652-3987, in Ashton, preserves relics of early settlement in the area.

PRACTICALITIES

Motels And Condos

Motels in Ashton include the **Four Seasons Motel,** tel. 652-7769, with rooms for $28-50 at 112 Main; **Log Cabin Motel and Trailer Park,** tel. 652-3956, at 1001 E. Main St., with rooms for $23-47; and **Rankin Motel,** tel. 652-3570, with rooms for $20-38.

The town of Island Park is the major lodging center along Henry's Fork. Motels in the area include **A-Bar Motel,** tel. 558-7358, with rooms for $32-50; **Aspen Lodge,** tel. 558-7407, with rates of $50-60; **Mack's Inn Resort,** tel. 558-7272, in the town of Mack's Inn, with rooms for $35-70; and **Sunset Lodge,** tel. 558-9941, along Henry's Lake with rooms for $20-35.

Condominiums are available through the **Island Park Village Resort,** tel. 558-7502, along Hwy. 20 a mile north of Mack's Inn, with 65 units ranging $120-175.

Bed And Breakfast Inn

Jessen's Bed and Breakfast and RV Park, tel. 652-3356, is a mile and a half south of Ashton along Hwy. 20 and offers three B&B rooms for $40.

Guest Ranches

Island Park and the surrounding area are home to several guest ranches, which in general means ranches with cabins for rent. Activities range from horseback riding to fishing or cross-country skiing. **Elk Creek Ranch,** tel. 558-7404 (summers), has eight rooms for around $50 a night; **Lucky Dog Retreat,** tel. 558-7455, has five cabins for $37-70; **Pond's Lodge,** tel. 558-7221, has 18 cabins for $40-70; **Staley Springs Lodge,** tel. 558-7471, has 15 rooms or cabins for $55-90 and campsites with full hookups for $17 a night; and **Wild Rose Ranch,** tel. 558-7201, has 12 rooms or cabins, and campsites.

Campgrounds

Commercial campgrounds along Hwy. 20 include **Island Park KOA,** tel. 558-9973, with 50 campsites, and **Valley View Trailer Park,** tel. 558-7443, with 55 campsites for $10 a night (for two adults; additional adults $2 per day) including water, power, and sewer hookups and shower privileges. **Jessen's Bed and Breakfast and RV Park,** tel. 652-3356, is a mile and a half south of Ashton along Hwy. 20 and offers 20 campsites with full hookups for $14.

Food

Restaurants include **Trails Inn Restaurant,** tel. 652-9918, at 213 Main in Ashton; **Chalet Restaurant,** tel. 558-9953, at Last Chance; **Island Park Lodge,** tel. 558-7281, at Island Park; **Pond's Lodge,** tel. 558-7221, at Island Park; **Lucky Dog Retreat,** tel. 558-7455, along Big Springs Rd.; **Valley View Truck Stop and Cafe,** tel. 558-7282, near Henry's Lake; and **Yale Creek Restaurant,** tel. 558-7991, at Island Park.

Events

The major events in the area are Ashton's **Fourth of July Celebration** and Island Park's **Wild Horse Stampede** each August.

Recreation

Ashton offers golfers the 18-hole **Aspen Acres Golf Club,** tel. 652-3524. In Island Park, golfers have the nine-hole **Island Park Golf Club.**

Island Park has more cross-country skiing trail systems than anywhere else in Idaho, with the possible exception of Sun Valley. **Harriman State Park,** 20 miles north of Ashton along Hwy. 20, offers 21 miles of marked trails and 10 miles of groomed trails. **Fall River Ridge Park 'n' Ski Area** is 10 miles east of Ashton along Cave Falls Rd. off Hwy. 47. The seven miles of trails thread through rolling hills, meadows, and forests of lodgepole pines and aspens. **Bear Gulch and Mesa Falls,** seven miles northeast of Ashton along Hwy. 47, offers a trail to view the spectacular Upper and Lower Mesa falls. The nine-mile trail is recommended for intermediate and advanced skiers because of a steep climb in the first mile. North of Island Park Ranger Station, along Hwy. 20 near Pond's Lodge Resort, is the **Brimstone and Buffalo River Trail System,** which covers nine miles of trails with scenic views of Box Canyon, Buffalo River, and Island Park Reservoir. The 2.6-mile trail along Buffalo River starts at the **Island Park Ranger Station,** tel. 559-7301.

Information And Services

Information about the region is provided by the **Ashton Chamber of Commerce,** tel. 652-3987, at 604 Main St.; and **Island Park Area Chamber of Commerce,** tel. 558-7448. Police services are provided by the **Fremont County Sheriff,** tel. 624-4482. In Ashton, emergency help is available by dialing 911.

CENTRAL IDAHO

Idaho's rugged **Sawtooth Mountains** reach into the high blue skies of central Idaho. Their name comes from an observer's belief that their profile resembled the view down the length of a crosscut saw with its sharp teeth slightly offset. The **Sawtooth National Recreation Area** here is Idaho's best-known destination for those who love clean granite spires and sapphire strings of mountain lakes.

Tucked away in the expanses of high meadows and lonely canyons are the remnants of mining booms that went bust, as well as flourishing guest ranches that form the foundation of the state's emerging tourism economy. **Stanley** has won a reputation as one of the last unsullied cow towns on the tourist trail. The "Stanley Stomp," the Sawtooth Valley's celebration of Saturday night, has attracted the attention of national newspapers and magazines.

The **Salmon River** is the silvery thread that stitches this part of Idaho together. Beginning at the foot of the Sawtooths and running 420 miles to its confluence with the Snake River, it's the nation's longest river that starts and ends in the same state. Raft trips can range from a day's float to a sojourn of more than a week, beginning on the Middle Fork and emerging from the state's wild heart at Riggins near the western border.

The Salmon as a playground or a respite from civilization would have seemed odd to the members of the Lewis and Clark Expedition. As the expedition's first taste of the lands west of the Contintental Divide, the Salmon's rugged watershed turned them back to find a safer route to the Pacific Ocean.

The mountains rebuffed the first explorers but drew in the next wave, miners who valued the bare rock for its hidden riches. They built towns like Bonanza and Custer only to relinquish their hold when the veins of silver and gold pinched out. Modern mining efforts to extract molybdenum and other minerals fell victim to economic difficulties. But cattlemen still make their living from the land as they have for generations, and loggers find their livelihoods here, too, although in shrinking numbers. The business that has boomed the most in recent years has been tourism, whether based on rafting, fishing, or backcountry pack trips.

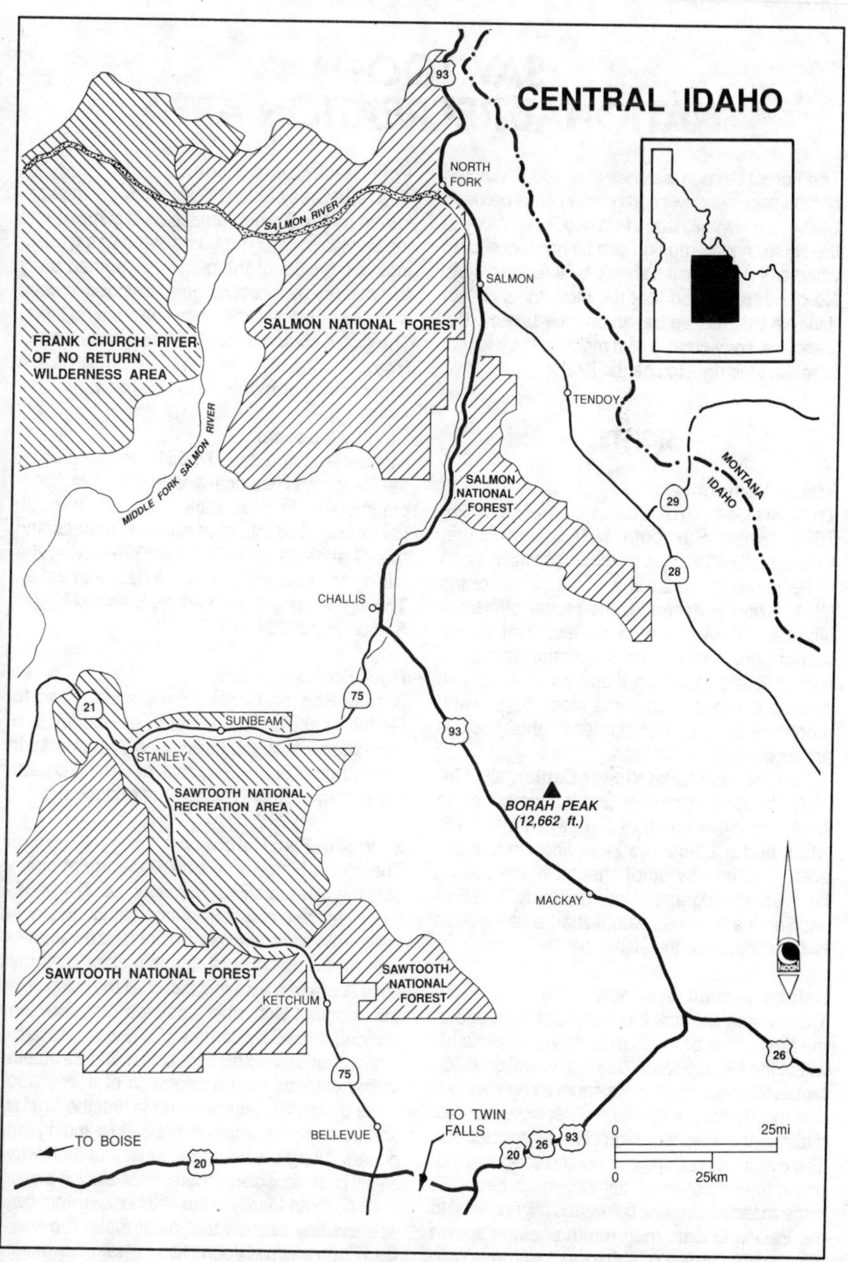
CENTRAL IDAHO
93
NORTH FORK
SALMON RIVER
SALMON
SALMON NATIONAL FOREST
FRANK CHURCH - RIVER OF NO RETURN WILDERNESS AREA
MIDDLE FORK SALMON RIVER
TENDOY
MONTANA
IDAHO
29
SALMON NATIONAL FOREST
28
CHALLIS
75
21
SUNBEAM
93
STANLEY
SAWTOOTH NATIONAL RECREATION AREA
BORAH PEAK
(12,662 ft.)
MACKAY
MOON
SAWTOOTH NATIONAL FOREST
SAWTOOTH NATIONAL FOREST
KETCHUM
26
75
TO TWIN FALLS
BELLEVUE
TO BOISE
20
20
26
93
0
25mi
0
25km

SAWTOOTH NATIONAL RECREATION AREA

The Forest Service watches over 765,000 acres of mountain meadows and granite peaks between Stanley on Hwy. 75 and the Wood River Valley to the south. A long-running debate has focused on whether the Sawtooths should be a national park. No one has argued that the mountains do not deserve that mantle based on their beauty. But Idahoans, sometimes a slim majority, have fought to retain their right to use the land.

SIGHTS

Visitor Centers

The **Sawtooth NRA Visitor Center,** tel. 726-7672 (write: Sawtooth NRA, Star Route, Ketchum, ID 83340), is located eight miles north of Ketchum in the southeastern corner of the NRA. Open year-round, the center offers exhibits about area wildlife, an excellent collection of books and other information about the region, and numerous displays. Visitors can pick up audio-tour cassette tapes here. Tape recorders that plug into cigarette-lighter sockets are also available for loan.

The **Redfish Lake Visitor Center,** tel. 774-3376, is open summers and is located in the NRA five miles south of Stanley. It offers exhibits and a 20-minute slide show about the area. The nearby amphitheater is the setting for evening programs Wed.-Saturday. The Forest Service has also established a self-guided **nature trail** near the visitor center.

Galena Summit Overlook

The Galena Summit Overlook provides one of the best views of the Sawtooth Valley available within the NRA. Galena Summit, elevation 8,752 feet, is 23 miles north of Ketchum along Hwy. 75. The road to the summit from either side is as dramatic as the view, which qualifies as spectacular. The overlook contains some interesting material about the migration of salmon, which begin life in the meadow streams below and migrate west to the Pacific Ocean, then return again to spawn after a river journey of 900 miles, each way.

Pole Creek Guard Station

The Pole Creek Guard Station has been maintained by the Forest Service as a glimpse into the service's past. The guard station's log buildings are typical of the outposts manned early this century by forest rangers assigned to keep watch over the federal lands surrounding them. The guard station is located three miles east of Hwy. 75 along the Pole Creek Rd., which is just a few miles north of Galena Overlook.

Stanley Museum

Stanley Museum, tel. 774-3517, is operated by the Sawtooth Historical and Interpretive Association, and is open daily from July through Labor Day. The museum holds an entertaining mix of artifacts, many of them preserving the mining and ranching past of the Sawtooth Valley. The log building served as the Stanley Ranger Station from 1934 to 1971.

Rock Shelter

Across Redfish Creek from the side road to Redfish Lake six miles south of Stanley is a rock shelter that has been used by hunters for thousands of years. The rock overhang is near the entrance station across the bridge.

Sawtooth Fish Hatchery

The Idaho Fish and Game Department operates the Sawtooth Fish Hatchery, tel. 774-3684, mainly to raise chinook salmon, although steelhead—the seagoing relatives of rainbow trout—also find a place here. Idaho's clear streams once supplied a third to a half of all the chinook in the bountiful Columbia's salmon runs. But the chinook, prized by commercial and sports fishermen, have fallen on hard times. The Sawtooth Valley chinook face a migration of nearly 900 miles down the Salmon River to first the Snake and then the Columbia rivers before finding the ocean. Along the way they must find their way safely past eight giant federal hydroelectric dams.

Until about March in the hatchery, visitors can see the tiny salmon that must make the seaward journey. The young fish migrate downriver

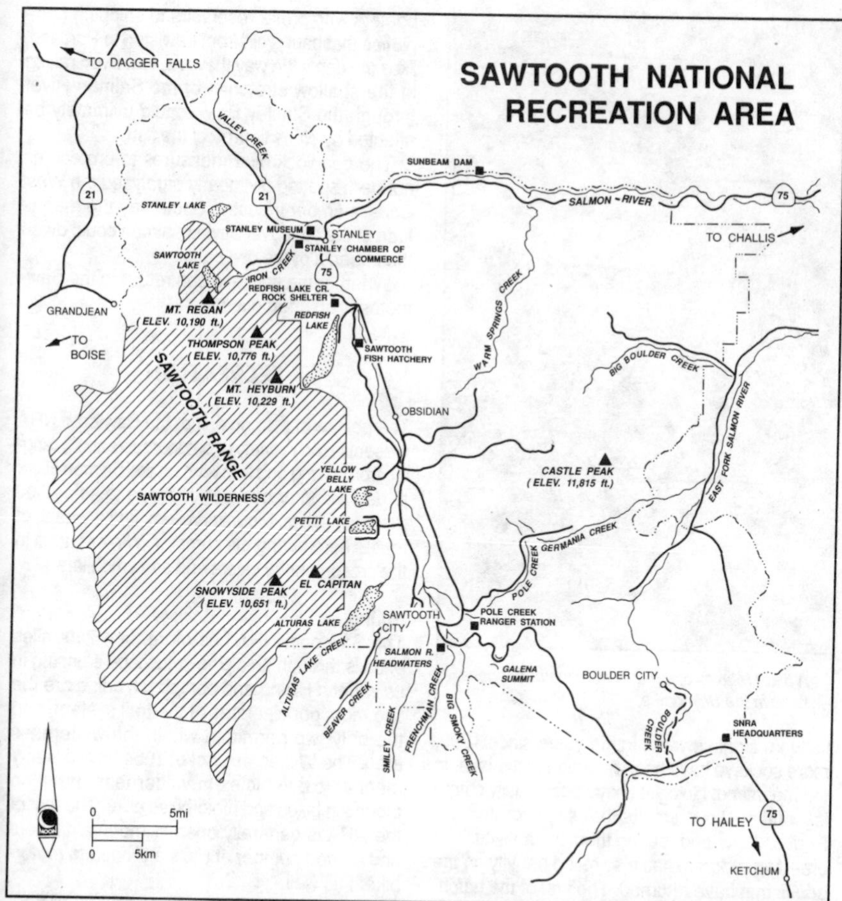

with the rising tide of runoff, the flood of snowmelt that swells the rivers each spring. As the young salmon, known as smolts, are completing their journeys to the sea, the adult salmon are migrating back upriver against the current from it. The big salmon begin arriving about June and are ready to spawn in August and September.

Redfish Lake Salmon

One sad note should be made here for those who find the Snake River salmon wonderful and mysterious. Redfish Lake in the Sawtooths was named for the sockeye salmon, the prized red salmon of commercial fishermen and diners alike. The large alpine lakes here once supported thousands of sockeyes. In 1989, only two sockeyes made the journey back to Idaho waters. In 1990, none did.

Federal and state officials launched a major effort to revive the sockeye run, beginning with listing the fish as an endangered species in 1991. The National Marine Fisheries Service and Idaho Fish and Game Department now raise the last remnants of the Salmon River's sockeye runs in hatchery tanks at Eagle and Seattle. Each year's supply of sockeye eggs is split between the two to ensure that a power outage, disease, or some other disaster couldn't wipe out the remaining

A hiker relaxes along the shoreline of Imogene Lake in the Sawtooths.

fish in a single sweep. In the years since 1990, more sockeye have been returning to the lake. In the meantime, biologists have been busily catching wild sockeye smolts that still migrate from Redfish Lake and rearing them in captivity. The breeding program has also relied heavily on the adults that have returned. The first of the hatchery-reared sockeye smolts were released into the shallows of Redfish Lake in 1993 to begin the perilous migration to the ocean. If fortune smiles, the sockeye run should begin to show signs of revival in 1995.

The Endangered Species Act protection for the sockeye and threatened species status for the Snake River's chinook runs has touched off a Northwest-wide debate. Traditional uses of the land such as grazing and logging already have been affected by the salmon measures. Many more undoubtedly will be. The Army Corps of Engineers balks at dramatically changing its operations of the lower Snake River hydroelectric dams. And a platoon of interests, ranging from boaters who prefer reservoirs to shipping companies that haul grain from Lewiston to Portland, likes the dams the way they are, too. Even rafting in the shallow stretches of the Salmon River through the Stanley Basin could ultimately be affected by plans to protect the fish.

The deadlock over measures to protect the northern spotted owl nearly paralyzed the West Coast's timber industry. Some say the magnitude of the fight over saving salmon could dwarf the impacts of the owl battle.

Whether the sockeye can return to the Sawtooths is an open question.

RECREATION

The politics of salmon aside, the Sawtooth NRA presents a rich variety of outdoor recreation, ranging from rafting and kayaking on the Salmon River to day-hiking or backpacking trips to some 300 mountain lakes. Mountain bikers find a wealth of routes here during the summer. Winter brings in the cross-country skiers and snowmobilers.

Hiking

The Sawtooth NRA has more than 750 miles of trails through an alpine landscape stunning in its variety. Hiking and horseback riding are the two most popular uses of the trail system, and the only two permitted within the wilderness area. The Wilderness Act of 1964 prohibits any mechanical vehicles in wilderness, banning mountain bikes and motorbikes alike. The rest of the NRA is generally open to mountain bikers and a good number of trails are open to motorbikers as well.

Hiking is the way most backcountry visitors choose to see the area. As a broad generality, the easier trails are the most heavily used. Some of the favorites include the 5.2-mile **Hell Roaring Creek Trail,** which takes hikers from the Salmon River westward to Hell Roaring Lake—a serene pool at the base of the ridge lofting the Finger of Fate. The lake is a popular destination for day-hikers and remote enough for backpackers. Another popular day-hike is the **Fishhook Creek Trail,** which begins at the Redfish Lake Trailhead and stretches three miles. Both trails are passable in summer and fall.

For spring hiking, the best bets are south of Galena Summit. Popular in the spring is the five-mile trek to **Prairie Creek Lakes** from the Prairie Creek Trailhead north of NRA heaquarters. An easy (despite a stiff elevation gain) route for hikers is the six-mile **Boulder Basin Road.**

For a summer hike near Galena Summit, the 1.2-mile stretch from **Galena Summit to Titus Lake** is rated as easy despite its share of heights. It starts at a trailhead just west of the pass at 8,700 feet and ends at 9,100 feet elevation. The trailhead is off the south side of the highway at the point of the last switchback before the summit when heading north. An alternate route takes hikers up Titus Creek. Its trailhead is just across the highway from the Galena Lodge.

In the White Cloud Mountains, easy hiking routes for backpackers include the **Williams Creek Trail,** which stretches seven miles from its start near Obsdian south of Stanley, and the 16.5-mile route from **Livingston Mill to Castle Divide.**

Horseback Riding

To discover the reason why many of the trails through the Sawtooths or any other of Idaho's mountains are laid out as they are, clamber aboard a horse. The ups and downs of the trails become dramatically less taxing. **Mystic Saddle Ranch,** tel. 774-3311, offers trail rides lasting from an hour and a half to all day at reasonable prices, about $20-50. An overnight pack trip is also available that routes riders to 11 lakes, through two canyons, and over a mountain pass. The **Idaho Rocky Mountain Ranch,** tel. 774-3544, also offers horseback riding six miles south of Stanley.

Rafting

Several outfitters offer guided trips on the Salmon River near Stanley during the summer. **White Otter Adventures,** tel. 726-4331, 726-8818, or 838-2406 during the summer, provides half-day or full-day trips on the upper Salmon. Clients may choose between the semi-wild rides aboard rafts or wilder rides aboard inflatable kayaks. Prices start at about $40 per person for half-day trips for groups of eight or more to $70 for full-day trips, including a dinner of steak or chicken. The Stanley-based **Triangle C Ranch,** tel. 774-2266, offers day-trips for about $60. The 12-mile float trip includes a Dutch-oven lunch prepared along the way. The trips are run May-September. The Triangle C also offers three- to six-day float trips on the nearby Middle Fork of the Salmon River.

Rental rafts are available from **White Otter Adventures,** tel. 726-4331, which maintains a base at Sunbeam Village east of Stanley along Hwy. 75. Raft rentals start at about $50 a day. Inflatable kayaks are also available, starting at $25 a day. **Sawtooth Rentals,** tel. 774-3409, is based at Stanley and offers rafts for about $15 per person. Inflatable kayaks are also available for $25 s or $35 d.

Mountain Biking

The Sawtooth NRA is Idaho's most scenic destination for mountain bikers. The area's mining history has also left much of the area laced with primitive roads that are often little more than two indistinct tracks marking the passage of a few vehicles sometime in the distant past. Such a prescription is enough to perk up most mountain bikers. The wilderness may be off limits to mountain bikers, but the vast majority of the NRA is not wilderness.

Some of the most heavily favored haunts for mountain bikers are along the dirt or gravel roads near the major lakes on the east side of the wilderness area proper. The roads are the easiest to travel and the easiest to reach. Another favored realm for backcountry bikers is the upper **Wood River Valley** to the south of Galena Summit. **Boulder City** is an easy day ride that is within the skills of nearly all bicyclists with fat tires on their machines.

The White Cloud Mountains on the east side of the Sawtooth Valley offer the wildest and least-crowded playground to mountain bikers. A wealth of trails and what pass for roads weave their way among the light-colored mountains here. A couple of adventuresome roads worth considering lead eastward from the Sawtooth Valley. **Fourth of July Creek Road** crawls upward into the White Clouds and onto the shoulder of Blackman Peak at elevation 10,307. **Germania Creek Road** heads north and upward toward 10,519-foot Washington Peak. Bikers can reach Germania Creek Rd. via the historic Pole Creek Guard Station. On both treks to higher elevations, bikers should carry plenty of water, stay hydrated, and avoid overexertion. The price of too much fun is a headache that is better avoided.

Cross-country Skiing

The Sawtooth NRA draws most of its visitors during the summer months. That doesn't mean winter is without its charms. The valley itself presents an impressive array of options for those aboard skinny skis. The hills within and without the wilderness draw a hardy band of adventurers who like the winter solitude. The cross-country skiing trails in the valley are pretty much self-operated. If Redfish Lake sounds like a great destination, don't expect to find groomed trails to take you there. A skier *will* find a snowed-in road to lead the way, and the most-popular destinations often have tracks cut by other visitors.

Busterback Ranch was once the heart of Nordic skiing in the Sawtooth Valley but has since been converted to a private residence. The lodge and its trail system are history. The Sawtooth Ski Club, the Blaine County Recreation District, and the Forest Service did pick up some of the slack by grooming trails in the Sawtooth Valley and at Galena Lodge. To find out about current conditions, skiers can call 726-6662. More information about trail details, both summer and winter, is available from the Recreation District, tel. 788-2117.

PRACTICALITIES

Lodging

It's tempting to call **Redfish Lake Lodge,** tel. 774-3536 or 726-3241 during the off season, the hallowed ground for Sawtooth Valley accommodations. The historic lodge on the shore of what for many embodies Idaho's mountain beauty is where conservationists gather annually to recharge their batteries. But in the Sawtooth Valley, you can hardly find a doorway or a window that doesn't open onto a stunning view. Still, the lodge, which operates from Memorial Day to late September, has its ranks of loyalists who will brook no other. Motel rooms range $40-90 and cabins $80-195. An off-season deal is available from late May to mid-June and from mid-Sept. to closing that features three nights for the price of two on Sunday, Monday, or Tuesday check-ins.

If Redfish is one standard for many visitors, the other in the Sawtooth Valley is the **Idaho Rocky Mountain Ranch,** tel. 774-3544, with nine cabins and 19 rooms for $70-250. Rocky Mountain Ranch, like the Railroad Ranch (now Harriman State Park), was developed by another Eastern industrialist who fell in love with Idaho's beauty. In Stanley, the list of venerables must also include the **Stanley Hotel,** tel. 774-9947, with rooms for $24-54. The rooms upstairs in the historic lodge will accommodate up to two. Baths are shared and are at the end of the hall. Next to the hotel is a more conventional motel with baths in the rooms.

Other Sawtooth lodgings include **Danner's Log Cabin Motel,** tel. 774-3490, with nine cabins for $32-48; **McGowan's Resort,** tel. 774-2290, with rooms for $45-70; and **Mountain Village Lodge,** tel. 774-3661 or (800) 843-5475, with rooms from $40 in the winter to $55 in the summer for singles. Additional occupants are $5 apiece. New in town and next to the Mountain Village is the **Creekside Lodge,** tel. 774-2213 or (800) 523-0733, with 14 kitchenettes for $42-57. Also in the valley are the **Redwood Motel,** tel. 774-3531, with rooms for $33-44; **Sessions Lodge,** tel. 774-3366, with rooms for $25; **Smiley Creek Resort,** tel. 774-3547, with cabins for $25 with a showerhouse and shared bath, or lodge rooms from $65; **Triangle C Ranch,** tel. 774-2266, with cabins for $40-50; and **Valley Creek Motel and RV Park,** tel. 774-3606, with rooms for $30-45 during the winter, $45-60 during summers. Campsites are available for $15 a night with hookups. The motel also rents a three-bedroom house for $100 a night.

One of the newer lodgings in lower Stanley is **Jerry's Motel,** tel. 774-3566, which offers riverside rooms for $38-55 winters, $45-60 after June 1 for the summer season.

Camping

With the Sawtooth NRA in the valley, finding a campsite poses more of a problem in the choices available than in the lack thereof. The NRA maintains 29 campgrounds, most of them in the Redfish Lake and Salmon River areas. The Forest Service has relinquished the idea of first-come, first-served in seven of the campgrounds. Campers may now plan in advance through the **National Forest Recreation Resevations** by calling (800) 280-2267 (that's 280-CAMP). The national booking agency charges a $6 fee for making reservations. A three-night stay at an $8-a-night campsite, for example, would cost $24 for the campsite and $6 for the reservation fee.

Campgrounds with spaces that may be reserved include **Easley,** 13 miles north of Ketchum; **Boulder View,** 13.5 miles north of Ketchum; **Glacier View Campground** and **Point Campground,** both in the Redfish Lake complex six miles south of Stanley; **Elk Creek Campground,** 10 miles west of Stanley off Hwy. 21; **Sheep Trail Campground,** nine miles west of Stanley off Hwy. 21; and **Trap Creek Campground,** 15 miles west of Stanley off Hwy. 21.

Other popular campgrounds, where sites are first-come, first-camped, include **Wood River** and **North Fork** campgrounds along the Big Wood River at the southeastern fringe of the NRA. The biggest clusters of campgrounds and other interesting sights occupy the valleys with the big lakes. Alturas Lake offers three popular campgrounds: **Alturas Inlet, Smokey Bear,** and **North Shore.** Redfish Lake and Little Redfish Lake offer **Chinook Bay, Mountain View, Redfish Outlet, Mount Heyburn,** and **Sockeye** campgrounds.

The northwestern corner of the NRA is also a popular camping destination. **Stanley Lake Inlet, Lakeview,** and **Stanley Lake** campgrounds are all in the area. **Grandjean** is west of Hwy. 21 on the northwestern flank and is one of the most remote developments in the region.

A concentration of campgrounds and sites rivaling Redfish Lake provides a haven for campers along the Salmon River east of Stanley. Campgrounds here include **Salmon River, Riverside, Mormon Bend, Basin Creek, Dutchman Flat, Upper O'Brien, Lower O'Brien, Snyder Springs,** and **Holman Creek.**

Food

Restaurants in the Stanley area include the **Idaho Rocky Mountain Ranch,** tel. 774-3544, which pretty well sets the standard with its historic dining room, serenades, and excellent meals. Reservations are required. The **Kasino Club,** tel. 774-3516, specializes in prime rib, lamb, seafood, and pasta—from $5 for burgers to $18 for prime rib. The **Knotty Pine Restaurant** offers cafe dining and groceries. **Mountain Village Restaurant, Saloon and Dancehall,** tel. 774-3371, offers breakfast through dinner. **Sawtooth Hotel,** tel. 774-9947, specializes in sourdough pancakes and other unique Stanley offerings.

Events

Sawtooth Mountain Mamas Arts and Crafts Fair draws as many as a hundred artists and craftsmen to Stanley during the third week of July. The celebration includes old-time fiddlers, a barbecue, and a pancake breakfast.

Transportation

Charter aircraft companies operating from **Stanley Airport** include **McCall And Wilderness Air,** tel. 774-2221 or (800) 992-6559, and **Stanley Air Taxi,** tel. 774-2276 or (800) 225-2236. Options include a half-hour aerial tour of the Sawtooths and an hour flight over that range and the nearby White Clouds. Prices per person begin at $30. Flights from Stanley typically begin in April or May when the snow melts off the airstrip near town.

Rental cars are available from Mountain Village Lodge, tel. 774-3661. It offers free pick-up at the Stanley Airport.

Information And Services

The **Stanley-Sawtooth Chamber of Commerce,** tel. 774-3411, is at P.O. Box 8, Stanley, ID 83278. Emergency services are available by dialing 911 for fire and ambulance or (800) 523-1537 for the **Custer County Sheriff.** Also In Stanley is the **Salmon River Emergency Clinic,** tel. 774-3565.

THE GOLD COUNTRY

The first party of miners made its way into the Stanley Basin and the headwaters of the Salmon River in 1863. A party led by John Stanley found the gold following a riotous Independence Day celebration in 1863. Frank Coffin, one of the celebrants, told of the miners polishing off a 10-gallon keg of whiskey as part of the festivities at Warrens Diggings, northeast of present-day McCall.

About 75 men were ready to accompany Stanley's prospecting party south. ". . . But we couldn't of course get out of town until we got through the whiskey," recalled Frank Coffin. "We had a lot of trouble getting out of town. I fell off my horse two or three times, and every time I fell off we'd go back and take another drink."

The miners headed south and east, finding color in remote basins. But the isolation and the fear of Indians kept the party moving. The party dwindled to 10 before crossing the Sawtooths. In the upper reaches of the Salmon River, the miners found a large band of Indians drying redfish, or sockeye salmon, and decided to head south for the Boise Basin mines. A.P. Challis was a member of the prospecting party and later returned to search the area more thoroughly. A town is named for him today.

Within a decade, prospectors had combed the upper Salmon country, discovering small but often rich deposits of placer gold along the streams. The Yankee Fork of the Salmon River showed the most promise when William Norton found a rich vein of ore in 1875. His ledge of golden ore became the foundation for the Charles Dickens Mine near Bonanza, Idaho. The following summer, a trio of miners found another rich and more extensive vein. The lucky miners founded the General Custer Mine, named after none other than George Armstrong Custer, who had made a serious error in judgment that summer along the Little Bighorn River in nearby Montana Territory.

The attraction of the mines and the steady work they offered drew a rising tide of humanity into the steep valley of the Yankee Fork. Mining persisted as the main occupation in the area for nearly a century before yielding to recreation as the area's major source of excitement (and revenue).

SIGHTS AND RECREATION

Sunbeam Dam

For travelers following the Salmon River along Hwy. 75, the Sunbeam Dam 12 miles east of Stanley provides a jarring reminder of the area's past as a mining mecca. The dam was built in 1910 to produce electricity for the Sunbeam Mill upriver along the Yankee Fork. The dam, now a breached crescent of concrete, is blamed for decimating the sockeye salmon run that gave Redfish Lake its name. The dam was breached in 1934 but the run of sockeyes, now listed as an endangered species, never fully recovered from the Sunbeam Dam and other changes along their 900-mile river route to the sea.

Land Of The Yankee Fork State Park

Like the Sunbeam Dam, several sites north of Hwy. 75 from the town of Sunbeam are part of Idaho's Land of the Yankee Fork State Park, tel. 838-2459. Park headquarters is based at the intersection of Highways 75 and 93 south of Challis. It's open year-round, with staff stationed up the Yankee Fork at Custer during the summer. The History Awareness Center holds displays about the progress of human endeavor in the Yankee Fork country and can help visitors decide whether they want to try the Old Toll Road, a scenic trek that requires a high-clearance vehicle. The park operates much like the Nez Perce National Historical Park to the north does: roads link its major sites which are scattered from the Yankee Fork to Challis. Most of the sites included in the park are overseen by other public agencies, mainly the U.S. Forest Service.

The park was created by the Idaho Parks and Recreation Commission in 1989 to recognize central Idaho's mining history. The historic sites that form the focus for the park include the ghost towns of Bonanza, the Yankee Fork Dredge, Custer, and the rugged old toll road that links the Yankee Fork country to Challis across a stretch of scenic high country. The park pulls together information about some of Idaho's best-known ghost towns, tangible links to a colorful past.

Bonanza

Bonanza, the town that once rivaled Custer as a Yankee Fork center of culture and commerce, had one amenity its sister boomtown didn't: a cemetery. **Boot Hill Cemetery** above the Bonanza Guard Station holds some of the most colorful characters from Yankee Fork's past. Bonanza was the first of the Yankee Fork towns, established in 1877. Gold had been discovered along Jordan Creek just upstream along the Yankee Fork seven years earlier by prospectors Sylvester Jordan and Dudley B. Varney. Their find prompted the Yankee Fork gold rush. Bonanza peaked in 1881, then fell victim to major forest fires in 1889 and 1897 before becoming a ghost town after 1911 when the last major mine closed.

Yankee Fork Gold Dredge

The Yankee Fork holds one of Idaho's most unusual museums, the floating Yankee Fork Gold Dredge. The dredge's devastation is readily apparent along much of the lower Yankee Fork. Piles of sterile gravel line the road where the giant dredge literally turned the valley floor upside down. Dredging began in 1939 after the Snake River Mining Co. found enough gold in test samples to justify a major investment. The company commissioned the Bucyrus-Erie Co. to build the massive machine, which was shipped by train to Mackay and by truck to the Yankee Fork. Assembled in 1940, it's 112 feet long, 54 feet wide, and weighs 988 tons. The dredge's 64-foot-high profile dominates the roadside eight miles north from the highway.

The dredge operated from 1940 to 1952, its 71 specially cast iron buckets systematically rearranging the valley floor to sift the gold from the soil and rock. It was shut down in 1953 for the last time. In its 12 years of operation, the dredge mined 6,330,000 cubic yards of gravel along 5.5 miles of valley, sifting from it more than $1 million in gold and silver. Idaho business magnate J.R. Simplot owned the dredge for most of its working life and later donated it to the Forest Service. A nonprofit group, the Yankee Fork Gold Dredge Association, formed to restore the dredge and keep its history alive. Guides have been drawn from the families of dredgemen who operated the giant machinery and remembered its past first-hand. The group offers tours of the dredge 10 a.m.-5 p.m. during the summers.

Custer

Custer Museum, like the gold dredge, originated through the efforts of those who remembered the past and were willing to devote their efforts to preserving its remnants. In the case of Custer, two of the most notable were Tuff and Edna McGown, who once lived and worked in

The Yankee Fork gold dredge recalls the days when men turned the valley upside down for a few ounces of precious metal.

the area while life still lingered in the town. The museum preserves an extensive collection of mining artifacts, ranging from heavy iron-mine equipment to clothing and everyday items. The museum's collection recalls the busiest days of Custer, from the town's founding in 1878 to its virtual demise in 1911 when the last mine closed. Behind the restored schoolhouse that houses the collection is the grave site of the three daughters of Nels and Maria Johnson. The girls died the night of Feb. 2, 1890, when an avalanche swept down from the slopes above, demolishing their house and carrying their souls to glory.

The largest structure in the immediate area was the General Custer Mill. Capable of processing 900 tons of ore monthly with its 30 stamps, the mill was built in 1880 to process gold ore from the General Custer Mine. By 1888, it had produced $8 million worth of gold from that mine alone. The mill fell victim to cost accounting in 1904 and was demolished in the 1930s.

The best way to recall the town's past is by taking a walking tour of the townsite, past the jailhouse, destroyed by fire in 1964 by a careless smoker; the blacksmith shop; and Dr. Charles Kirtley's Empire Saloon, which still offers refreshments, although tamer ones. Still lingering is the McKenzie Home, built in 1880 and occupied for nearly 30 years. The log cabin with its curved archway was one of Custer's elegant homes. A ways downstream was McKenzie's Livery Stable, where horses were boarded for $1.50 a day and horse-trading prospered. Near Custer's southwestern corner was the bawdy house where whores with kind hearts lived—according to the historical record, they sometimes helped the town's poor families. Next door was the Deardon and McGown Mercantile.

Other points of interest include the former locations of Burton's Rooming House and the Thompson Dance Hall. Sandwiched between the dance hall and the Casto and McGee Saloon was the carpenter shop of Judge J.F. Davis, who lived in Custer and Bonanza for 30 years. Davis's specialty along the Yankee Fork was coffins. A pine coffin and an outer box of rough boards cost $30. Finally, there's a log cabin once owned by Charlie Raine, who worked a small mine but never struck it rich.

Historic Drive

The **Custer-Challis Wagon Trail,** which is also known as the Old Toll Road, offers today a glimmer of what it was like to be a miner traveling across central Idaho's rugged mountains a century ago. The old wagon road was built as a toll road in 1879 for $30,000 under a territorial charter issued to Alex Toponce. Toponce and Co. ran a stagecoach line from Challis to the Yankee Fork twice weekly. Passengers paid $8 for a 35-mile, bone-jarring ride from Challis to Bonanza. The route provided the link for freighters and travelers between Custer and the Yankee Fork mines and Challis to the northeast. The road is considerably improved since then. In 1933 the Civilian Conservation Corps rebuilt the road and christened it the Custer Motorway. It is still not suitable for RVs or cars towing trailers, but it is passable for those piloting passenger cars or other vehicles with good clearance and calm dispositions. The views are tremendous. The historic sites along the way include Fanny's upper and lower holes, small valleys where stage stops were built. The old toll gate stood atop the Mill Creek Summit west of Challis. The route stretches 38 miles from Custer to Challis. Travelers planning to explore along the route should allow at least half a day.

Sunbeam Hot Springs

Sunbeam Hot Springs is a half mile west or upstream along Hwy. 75 and the main branch of the Salmon from the Yankee Fork. The springs are developed into pools but are noncommerical.

Recreation

The Forest Service has designated the **Knapp Creek-Loon Creek Trail** as one of two national recreation trails in Challis National Forest. The trailhead on the western edge is north of Stanley near Cape Horn. The Loon Creek trailhead is northwest of Bonanza. The Loon Creek side of the trail passes through some small meadows before winding up a narrow valley clothed with lodgepole pine and marked by alpine terrain near its headwaters. The trail crosses over the headwaters of Loon Creek at 8,600 feet, providing a stunning view of the 10,000-foot Tango Peaks. Near the trail is a cluster of high mountain lakes, including Knapp Lakes, Tango Lakes, Fish Lakes, and Cabin Creek Lakes. All are easy to reach and can provide excellent fishing.

PRACTICALITIES

Accommodations

Along the Yankee Fork, **Sunbeam Village,** tel. 838-2211, provides the only lodging. Just off Hwy. 75, the village has been a popular tourist destination for decades, a place where one could unwind in scenic surroundings, catch a few fish, and take life easy. The rise of commercial rafting along the main Salmon has livened things up considerably, but the charm remains. The village offers log cabins for rent for $45-70 and campsites for around $12. **Torrey's Burnt Creek Inn,** near Clayton east along Hwy. 75, has rooms for $31-48 and campsites.

Dude Ranch

The **Diamond D Ranch,** tel. 336-9772, is also located in the Yankee Fork country, northwest of Custer along Loon Creek at the fringe of the Frank Church–River of No Return Wilderness. Rates range $400-645 a week. Tom and Linda Demorest have owned and operated the family-oriented ranch for over 40 years. They offer great fishing, guided pack trips, gold-panning, volleyball, and softball . . . something for everyone. But if you just want to come and do nothing at all, that's fine with them too. For more information write P.O. Box 35, Stanley, ID 83278 (summer) or P.O. Box 1555, Boise, ID 84701 (winter).

Campgrounds

The Challis National Forest staff operates campgrounds throughout the Yankee Fork country. All are at high elevation, ranging from 5,600 to 8,000 feet. The higher the elevation, the shorter the camping season (some would say sweeter, too). In general the camping season runs from June to September. Campers can inquire about conditions at the **Challis National Forest Supervisor's Office,** tel. 879-2285, along Hwy. 93 at the north edge of Challis or at the **Yankee Fork Ranger Station,** tel. 838-2201, near Clayton along Hwy. 75. Just north of Hwy. 75 are the **Blind Creek, Flat Rock,** and **Pole Flat** campgrounds. Farther upstream along the Yankee Fork is the **West Fork** campground. Near Custer are the **Custer No. 1, Greylock,** and **Eightmile** campsites. To the east of the Yankee Fork is the **Mill Creek Campground,** along the old toll road near Challis. The campground was the focus of a recent renovation project that paved its road and rebuilt its pullouts to make them more accessible for campers. The campground is west of Challis and is reached by travelling along the Garden Creek Road. North of Bonanza is the **Tin Cup Campground,** along Loon Creek near the edge of the Church Wilderness. One of the national forest's most popular camgrounds is also about as far from Challis's headquarters as visitors can get. The **Boundary Creek Campground** is a popular departure point for rafters on the Middle Fork of the Salmon and lies northwest of Stanley.

Food

The **Sunbeam Cafe,** tel. 838-2260, is along the Salmon River east of Stanley at Sunbeam Village. The cafe offers sandwiches for about $5. Its more ambitious dinner menu varies but generally offers entrees for $7-15.

Services

The Challis-based **Custer County Sheriff,** tel. 879-2232, provides emergency services in the area.

MACKAY AND VICINITY

South of Challis toward Arco, Hwy. 93 parallels the Lost River Range that juts up on its eastern shoulder. The slopes are bare; these mountains are too new, too arid to hold much life. Mackay is at the center of an open landscape where ranchers still operate much as they did 100 years ago, and farmers must stick to the river valleys to earn a livelihood.

The miners who ventured into the Lost River country in the late 1800s have left little more than a legacy of names. The object of interest was copper ore that had been discovered in the White Knob Mountains west of the valley. In 1901, John Mackay, who found the Comstock Lode near Virginia City, Nevada, founded the town of Mackay as a copper smelter town. The ore didn't prove to be rich enough, however, and the smelter was moved elsewhere, but Mackay hung on. Other mines in the White Knobs continued to yield copper until 1930.

SIGHTS

Borah Peak

The Lost Rivers are notable for their beauty and for holding Borah Peak, Idaho's tallest mountain at 12,662 feet. These mountains rise abruptly from the tumbled valley with mass and power, forming pillars strong enough to prop up the broad Western sky. A road to the base of Borah Peak leaves the highway 18 miles north of Mackay near Dickey, a former townsite now marked by a surviving ranch.

Borah Peak gained more notoriety on Oct. 28, 1983, when a massive earthquake struck central Idaho. The great quake, which measured 7.3 on the Richter scale, dropped the valley floor nine feet and raised the peak six inches. The earthquake created a fault line that stretches 15 miles along the mountain's base, a six- to 10-foot-high scarp that ripped open in a matter of seconds, according to witnesses. Challis suffered the most damage from the earthquake when falling masonry killed two children on their way to school. In 1990, the Idaho Legislature required state officials to review school construction plans for earthquake resistance. The monetary damage was estimated at $12 million. The ground movement shifted the flow of water in the Lost River Valley.

Research since the quake shows that visitors probably don't need to spend a lot of time worrying about a repeat. The last quake along the same part of the fault was 6,000-8,000 years ago.

The Lost River Range near Mackay holds Borah Peak, Idaho's highest mountain.

Grand View Canyon

Twenty miles by highway north of Borah Peak (and 14 miles south of Challis) is the Grand View Canyon. The highway slips into the canyon and follows it, twist for twist, down through geologic time. The canyon is most notable for its tight fit for modern traffic.

Museums

The **Lost Rivers Museum** in Mackay preserves artifacts from the the area's mining and ranching heritage. The museum is in the old Methodist Church, which now stands next to the Mackay Library at 320 Capitol Avenue. The museum is on the National Register of Historic Places and is open Saturday and Sunday 1-5 p.m. or by appointment; call 588-2669. Mackay is also home to the **Centennial Native American Gallery,** which houses a collection of Indian artwork and artifacts. The gallery is open weekends.

PRACTICALITIES

Accommodations

Lodging choices in Mackay are limited. Motels in town include the **Wagon Wheel Motel and RV Park,** tel. 588-3331, with 15 rooms for $26-48 and campsites from $6. The **White Knob Motel and RV Park,** tel. 588-2622, has six rooms to $45 and 21 campsites from $3.50 ($10 with full hookups). Campers will find **Marinac's River Park Campground,** tel. 588-2296, with sites for $10.50 a day.

Food

Restaurants in Mackay start with **Amy Lou's Steak House,** tel. 588-9903, along Hwy. 93, which offers sandwiches and more substantial dinners including steak, seafood, and Mexican dinners on Sunday with entrees $6-12. **Ken's Club and Steakhouse,** tel. 588-9983, is in Mackay and specializes in prime rib and steak with entrees from $7.50 to $18.

Events

The event in Mackay is the **Mackay Rodeo,** which is held the fourth weekend in June each year and bills itself as "Idaho's Wildest Rodeo." Besides rodeo, other events during the weekend include a cowboy polo tournament and buffalo barbecue. In August, the **Custer County Fair and Horse Show** are held. In mid-September, Mackay sponsors its annual **Free Barbecue,** which stretches back to 1923. The event draws thousands to Mackay and functions as a reunion for Lost River Valley residents.

Information And Services

Lost River Valley Chamber of Commerce, at P.O. Box 209, Mackay, ID 83251, provides information about the area. The **Custer County Sheriff,** tel. 588-2676 (911 in emergencies), maintains an office at 203 S. Main.

CHALLIS AND VICINITY

Challis draws its name from Alvan P. Challis, who surveyed the townsite when the city was founded in 1878. A.P., as he was known, was on the Stanley expedition, one of the first mining parties to explore the Sawtooths and Stanley Basin for gold. The town has functioned as a mining supply center for more than a century and as the home base for generations of ranchers. The ranchers and farmers form the largest crowd, but Challis still has mining in its blood.

SIGHTS

North Custer Historical Museum

Challis is home to the North Custer Historical Museum, which preserves Indian, ranching, and mining artifacts.

Visitor Center

Land of the Yankee Fork State Park maintains a headquarters at the junction of Highways 75 and 93 just south of town. The visitor center offers information about the historical park, which consists of sites scattered through the backcountry (see "Land of the Yankee Fork State Park," under "The Gold Country," above). The center itself contains displays about the area's mining history and settlement.

Morgan Creek Road

Eight miles north of Challis, Morgan Creek Rd. takes off northeast of Hwy. 93. The valley is a favored winter range for elk, mule deer, pronghorn, and bighorn sheep from November to May. During the summer, a cacophony of songbirds can be heard along the stream. Some of the more colorful inhabitants are lazuli buntings, yellow warblers, northern orioles, and Brewer's blackbirds.

Challis National Forest

The Challis National Forest, tel. 879-2285, is headquartered along Hwy. 93 near Challis. The forest encompasses 2.5 million acres and is laced with 1,600 miles of trails, 1,000 miles of fishing streams, and 250 lakes.

PRACTICALITIES

Accommodations

Motels in Challis include the **Challis Lodge and Lounge,** tel. 879-2251, along Main Street with 19 rooms for $26-40; **North Gate Inn,** tel. 879-2490, along Hwy. 93 at the north end of town, offering 56 rooms for $32-47; and **The Village Inn,** tel. 879-2239, with 54 rooms for $26-48 along Hwy. 93 at the south edge of town.

Camping

Campgrounds in the Challis area include **Challis Hot Springs,** tel. 879-4442, three miles south of town along Hwy. 93, then five miles east. The campground has a hot-springs-heated swimming pool that carries a charge of $3.50 for swimmers 12 and older and $2.50 for younger ones. Its 27 campsites rent for $8.50-10.50, depending on the season. Another private campground is the **Valley RV Park,** tel. 879-2393, with 30 spaces from $13.50. Public campgrounds in the Challis area include **Bayhorse Campground,** operated by the BLM along the Salmon River, eight miles south of Challis. **Bayhorse Lake Campground** is operated by the Forest Service eight miles west of Hwy. 75 along Forest Service Rd. 051. Eight miles north of Challis along Hwy. 93 is the turnoff for **Morgan Creek.** Five miles up Morgan Creek is another BLM campground. Ten miles north of Challis along Hwy. 93 is the **Spring Gulch Campground.**

Food

Restaurants in Challis include **Antonio's,** tel. 879-2210, at 5th and Main, with a menu of pizza and pasta, and prices of $3-15; **Challis Lodge and Lounge,** tel. 879-2251, with steaks for $7 and $9; and **Y-Inn Cafe,** tel. 879-4426, along Main St., which specializes in steaks, hamburgers, and sandwiches but adds chicken and other items and keeps the crowd happy with prices ranging $5-19.

Events

In Challis the fun doesn't officially start until the **Little Britches Rodeo** hits town at the end of

May. **July 4th** is a big day with a parade, water fights, and fireworks.

Information And Services

Information about the Challis area is provided by the **Challis Chamber of Commerce,** tel. 879-2771, at P.O. Box 1130, Challis, ID 83226. Police services are provided by the **Custer County Sheriff,** tel. 879-2232, at the county courthouse.

SALMON AND VICINITY

The city of Salmon sticks tight to its heritage as a ranching and logging town. All the same, the rising tide of outfitters and their clients, river-runners, and other outdoor adventurers who descend on the town are hardly a new phenomenon either. Mountain men the likes of Joe Meek, Jim Bridger, Kit Carson, Donald Mackenzie, Peter Skene Ogden, and a brigade of other famous names have spent time in the Salmon River Valley.

Modern Salmon is a city in transition. Timber is still part of the town's economy, subject as it has been and will always be to the vagaries of the market. Ranching suffers the same mood swings, depending on swings in the supply and demand for red meat. Recreation has its shifting currents, too, although the rise of Salmon as a fun town appears steadier than the growth of the other businesses.

SIGHTS

Lemhi County Historical Museum

Lemhi County Historical Museum, which is located at Main and S. Terrace streets, offers a display of Indian artifacts gathered by a grocer. Another display recounts the history of gold mining in the area, including the 1866 discovery of gold at Leesburg, the first find in Lemhi County. Also on display is a collection of Oriental art gathered during the 1920s. The museum is open May-Oct., Mon.-Sat. 10 a.m.-5 p.m.

Leesburg

In 1866, five miners from Montana struck gold along Napias Creek west of the Salmon River. Confederates prevailed on the naming of the new settlement, calling it Leesburg. Within a short while, the meadows were covered with white canvas tents to house the 3,000 residents. Nearly 100 businesses opened in the new settlement, including a newspaper, saloons, liveries, hotels, mercantiles, and restaurants.

Leesburg is little more than a few dilapidated log cabins and a cemetery these days. But being in Leesburg is about the next best thing to having lived in the 1800s. Imagine riding an ore wagon or a horse into Leesburg. The turnoff to the ghost town is at Shoup, six miles south of Salmon along Hwy. 93. If it's been raining, a 4WD and experience driving on slick roads will be required. If the visit is made during the dry days of summer, a passenger sedan and cautious driving will be enough to succeed. From the Shoup Bridge, take Williams Creek Rd. just shy of 14 miles to Williams Creek Summit, where there's a four-way intersection. Take the road that heads straight and down into Mocassin Creek, which spills into Napias Creek. At the bridge over Napias Creek, turn right. The last six miles to Leesburg are difficult driving and require caution.

Historic Trail

The Salmon River earned the reputation as a one-way river during the early years of exploration. The name River of No Return has become synonymous with the Salmon because boaters who went downstream, if they survived, could not return, by river at least. That's all changed now with jetboats, of course, but the river did form the only obstacle fearsome enough to repel the Lewis and Clark Expedition.

The Corps of Discovery entered Idaho's Salmon River country across the Continental Divide from Montana on Aug. 12, 1805. The pass they crossed, Lemhi Pass, is a popular drive during dry weather. The turnoff for the pass from Hwy. 28 is at Tendoy, 20 miles south of Salmon. During that initial foray into Idaho, Capt. Meriwether Lewis made contact with a band of Shoshone. Needing horses, he persuaded them to return with him to the other side of the mountains. Once there, the chief of the Shoshone band found that the expedition's guide, Sacajawea, was his sister, who had been kidnapped. Two weeks later the entire expedition entered the

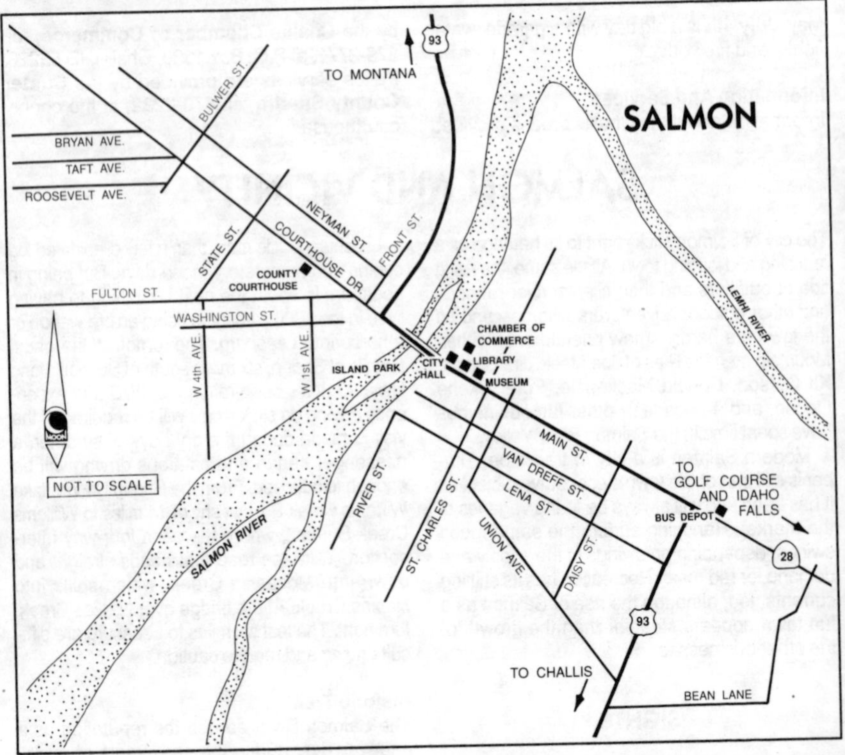

Salmon River Valley. Finding the river impassable, they left Idaho again for Montana in early September. The expedition headed north into Montana before turning west at Lolo Creek for its crossing of the northern Nez Perce Trail.

Historic Fort

Tendoy, the jumping-off point for Lemhi Pass, is also the home of the first attempt at irrigated agriculture in Idaho. In 1855, a party of 100 Mormons dispatched from Salt Lake City by Brigham Young built a fort here. The fort was more religious than military, however, and lasted but three years before Indian troubles forced them south again. An old adobe wall with a plaque telling of its place in history stands on the Muleshoe Ranch near Tendoy. The site is reached from a gravel road that heads east south of the main ranch entrance. Take the next gravel road north to see the site of Fort Lemhi behind the ranch buildings.

Battleground

Two miles south of the site of Fort Lemhi in a narrow valley was the site of a celebrated battle between mountain men and the fierce Blackfoot people. The mountain men, led by Finan McDonald, won when they set fire to a brush field the Indians were fighting from.

RECREATION

Public Lands

The Salmon area is rife with public lands and the opportunities for recreation they present. For more information about road conditions, trails, campgrounds, rivers, and lakes, contact the **Salmon National Forest,** tel. 756-2215, or the **BLM's Salmon District,** tel. 756-5400. Both are located south of town along Hwy. 93. The Salmon National Forest also serves as a major clearinghouse of information about the 2.3-million-acre **Frank Church–River of No Return Wilderness** which protects the wild heart of Idaho. The Church Wilderness is the biggest chunk of wilderness in the lower 48 states.

Golf

The **Salmon Valley Golf Club,** tel. 756-4734, offers a nine-hole course to linksters. The par-72, 6,434-year course is located a mile east of town on Hwy. 28. Greens fees for 18 holes are $10 weekdays, $12 weekends (nine holes is $2 less). Cart and club rentals are available.

River-running

Outfitters based in Salmon specialize in everything from steelhead fishing to birdwatching; river-running trips can last less than a day on calm waters to a week on some of Idaho's most exciting whitewater. Salmon is also a base for backcountry horse trips.

Idaho-based outfitters offering trips on the main Salmon include **Aggipah River Trips,** tel. 756-4167; **Idaho Adventures,** tel. 756-2986; **Kingfisher Expeditions,** tel. 756-4688; **Northwest River Expeditions,** tel. 865-2534; **Salmon River Lodge,** tel. 756-3033; **Silver Cloud Expeditions,** tel. 756-6215; **Warren River Expeditions,** tel. 234-7361; and **Wilderness River Outfitters,** tel. 756-3959, with five- and six-day trips ranging from $955 to $1700. **Twin Peaks Ranch,** tel. 894-2290, also offers short floats on the river.

For visitors who want to see the river more quickly and like the idea of a hard-hulled boat beneath them, Salmon-based jet-boat outfitters include **Eakin Ridge Outfitters,** tel. 756-2047; **Rusty Gore's Salmon River Jet Boat and Float Trips,** tel. 756-4550; **Idaho Adventures,** tel. 756-2986; **Northwest River Expeditions,** tel. 865-2534; **Salmon River Boat Tours,** tel. 865-2512; and **Salmon River Lodge,** tel. 765-3033.

Outfitters who specialize in horse-packing trips into the backcountry near Salmon include **Chamberlain Basin Outfitters,** tel. 756-3715; **Eakin Ridge Outfitters,** tel. 756-2047; **Magnum Outfitters,** tel. 756-4868; **Salmon River Lodge,** tel. 756-3033; **Stanley Potts Outfitters,** tel. 788-4584; **Twin Peaks Ranch,** tel. 894-2290; and **Gillihan's Lodge,** tel. 365-5384.

Skiing

Wilderness River Outfitters, tel. 756-3959, offers an adventure for Nordic skiers. The company maintains a series of backcountry huts for cross-country skiers. The company offers three- and five-day trips at prices ranging from $450 to $750, which include accommodations and Missoula shuttle.

Downhill skiers will find **Lost Trail Ski Area,** tel. (406) 821-3211, 42 miles north of Salmon along Hwy. 93. The ski area has 1,200 vertical feet of skiing and offers ski rentals and day care.

Fishing

The town of Salmon was named for the river, which was named for its fish runs. It should be no surprise that fishing is still important here. Steelhead runs in Idaho waters have dramatically improved in recent years, and Salmon has enjoyed the bounty. Fishing guides here are as plentiful as the fish.

Kingfisher Expeditions, tel. 756-4688, offers a range of trips beginning with single day outings for $65 and ranging up to six-day Middle Fork trips for $1,100. **Aggipah River Trips,** tel. 756-4167, offers a three-day Middle Fork outing for $750. Their four-day trip on the Lower Salmon is $500 and the company's grand tour is a five-day steelhead-fishing trip based at lodges along the river for $1,500.

Other outfitters include **Silver Cloud Expeditions,** tel. 756-6215, offering fall steelhead-fishing outings and summer rafting trips; **Idaho Adventures,** tel. 756-2986; and **Salmon River Boat Tours,** tel. 865-2512. **North Fork Guides,** tel. 865-2534, is located halfway between Gibbonsville and Salmon along Hwy. 93 and offers rafting and fishing trips for a half-day to six days ranging in price from $55 to $900. **Salmon River Lodge,** tel. 756-3033, offers four-day rafting trips on the main Salmon for $650 or $900 for six days. A half-day jet boat trip is $65 per person with a minimum of four or $95 per person for a full day outing. The lodge also operates as a bed and breakfast for $50 a night with meal rates $8 for breakfast, $7 for lunch, and $15 for dinner.

Bicycling

Wilderness River Outfitters, tel. 756-3959, offers a five-day mountain-biking excursion along the historic Magruder Road across central Idaho from Conner, Montana, to Red River, Idaho, for $650. A combination trip featuring three days in the bicycle saddle and three days in a raft on the Salmon River below the road is also available.

The price includes the use of mountain bikes and a support van as well as all meals. **Rendezvous Sports,** tel. 756-4495, offers suggestions for bicycle tours in the Salmon area. The store also offers rafting and camping equipment and information. **Lemhi Bicycles,** tel. 756-2666, is located at 322 N. Saint Charles St. in Salmon.

Outdoor Gear

Adventure Boats and Spokes, tel. 756-6477, is located at 511 Main in town. **All Season Sports,** tel. 756-4904, is located at 109 S. Center and offers hunting, fishing, and camping equipment.

PRACTICALITIES

Bed And Breakfasts

Heritage Inn Bed and Breakfast, tel. 756-3174, at 510 Lena St., specializes in historic decor. Its rates are $25-39, which include an expanded continental breakfast. **Smith House Bed and Breakfast,** tel. 756-2121, is along the Salmon River and features nearby hiking, fishing, and other outdoor pursuits. Rates are $35-54.

Guest Ranches

Guest ranches and resorts in the Salmon area offer a variety of activities ranging from fishing to horseback riding. **Broken Arrow,** tel. 865-2241, charges $25 for cabins for singles or doubles, $5 for additional guests. Camping fees range from $5 for one or two tenters and $2.50 per head for additional campers; RV spots $12 with hookups. The resort also offers a restaurant with Mexican and basic American fare from steaks to prime rib with prices ranging $6-12. Broken Arrow is open mid-May to mid-November. The resort has a trout pond stocked by the Idaho Fish and Game Department. It's available for free use by guests and the public. The resort also helps guests book backcountry, rafting, hunting, or fishing trips.

Twin Peaks Ranch, tel. 894-2290 or 756-3696, has weekly rates from $960 in original cabins to $1,285 per person in deluxe accommodations. Prices include all meals and activities, which range from horseback riding, hiking, and target shooting to rafting. Nightly rates are available Sept. 16-May 30. **Williams Lake Resort,** tel. 756-2007, has rooms and cabins for $25-85, a restaurant, boat rentals, and tackle for anglers, and the **Red Dog Saloon.** Other guest-ranch lodgings are available through **Happy Hollow Vacations,** tel. 756-3954 ($490 per person per week); **Magnum Outfitters,** tel. 756-4868; and **Salmon River Lodge,** tel. 756-3033, with rates of $35-100.

Motels

Motels in the Salmon area include **Motel Deluxe,** tel. 756-2231, 112 S. Church, with rooms for $28-35; **River's Fork Inn,** tel. 865-2301, 20 miles north of Salmon; **Stagecoach Inn Motel,** tel. 756-4251, along Hwy. 93 north of town with rooms along the river or the highway for $41-53; **Suncrest Motel,** tel. 756-2294, at 705 S. Challis with rooms starting at $26-34, depending on the season; and **Wagons West Motel,** tel. 756-4281, 503 Hwy. 93 N, with rooms for $35-54.

Campgrounds

Private campgrounds in the Salmon area include **Heald's Haven Campground,** tel. 756-3929, with 22 campsites from $7; and **Salmon Meadows Campground,** tel. 756-2640, with 65 campsites for $10-15. Public campgrounds near Salmon include **Cougar Point,** in the Salmon National Forest 17 miles southwest of town along Forest Service Rd. 60021; **Iron Lake,** also in the Salmon National Forest 46 miles southwest of town; **Wallace Lake,** 22 miles by road northwest of town in the national forest; and **Williams Lake,** a BLM campground 11 miles southwest of Salmon.

Food

Salmon has a healthy selection of restaurants. **Shady Nook,** tel. 756-4182, specializes in steak and seafood along Hwy. 93 north of town and has its own art gallery and trophy room. **River's Fork Inn,** tel. 865-2301, has steaks, seafood, prime rib, and sandwiches along the river. **Union Ave. Depot,** tel. 756-2095, prides itself on the largest steaks in Lemhi County and the greatest variety of pasta. **Granny's Steakhouse,** tel. 756-2309, at 1403 E. Main St., offers charbroiled steaks and burgers with fresh pies and cinnamon rolls. The **28 Supper Club** is five miles south of Salmon along Hwy. 28 and offers steaks cut to order, chicken, and seafood. **Salmon River Coffee Shop,** tel. 756-3521, offers breakfast, lunch, and dinner menus. The **Smoke House Cafe,** tel. 756-4334, at 312 Main St., is open 24 hours and features omelettes.

North Fork Lodge, tel. 865-2412, is a roadside cafe featuring a full menu and specializing in barbecued ribs, sandwiches, and pies.

Pizza has its place in Salmon at **Last Chance Pizza,** tel. 756-4559, at 605 Lena, and **Garbonzos Pizza,** tel. 756-4565, along Hwy. 28 at the east edge of town. The **Burnt Bun,** tel. 756-2062, at 516-1 Challis, is a popular takeout and burger cafe. **Johnny B's Family Restaurant,** tel. 756-2254, at 507 Main, is open daily 6 a.m.-11 p.m. **Salmon River Inn,** tel. 756-3643, at Main and Andrews streets, is a popular spot to wet your whistle and usually features live music.

Transportation

The **Salmon Airport** is five miles south of town along Hwy. 93. It serves as a major departure point for backcountry flying services including: **Alpine Air Service,** tel. 756-4200; **Salmon Air Taxi,** tel. 756-6211; and **Wilderness Aviation,** tel. 756-4713.

Information And Services

The **Salmon Valley Chamber of Commerce,** tel. 756-2100, is located at 200 Main St., Suite 1, Salmon, ID 83467. **Salmon City Hall,** tel. 756-3214, is located at 200 Main Street. The **Lemhi County Sheriff,** tel. 756-4201, at 206 Courthouse, provides emergency services in outlying areas and the **Salmon Police Department,** at 200 Main St., provides services in town—same phone number as the sheriff. Salmon is home to **Steele Memorial Hospital,** tel. 756-4291, at 811 Main.

BOOKLIST

DESCRIPTION AND TRAVEL

Alt, David D., and Donald W. Hyndman. *Roadside Geology of Idaho.* Missoula, MT: Mountain Press Publishing Co., 1989. A milepost guide to the state's geology with detailed accounts of why Idaho looks the way it does.

Beckwith, John A. *Gem Minerals of Idaho.* Caldwell, ID: The Caxton Printers Ltd., 1972. More rocks, but such beauties. A surprising look at how rich Idaho is in gems.

Bluestein, Sheldon. *Hiking Trails of Southern Idaho.* Caldwell, ID: The Caxton Printers Ltd., 1981.

Brooks, Charles E. *The Henry's Fork.* New York: Nick Lyons Books, Winchester Press, 1986. The West's (and Idaho's) most revered trout stream provides the focus for a celebrated outdoor writer.

Carrey, John, Ace Barton, and Cort Conley. *The Snake River of Hells Canyon.* Cambridge, ID: Backeddy Books, 1978. The most comprehensive guide to the canyon's history and rapids. Ace Barton was a Hells Canyon pioneer; his mother discovered the Bartonberry.

Carrey, John, and Cort Conley. *The Middle Fork—A Guide.* Cambridge, ID: Backeddy Books, 1992. Another worthy effort in preserving the past and providing a workable river-running guide to the Middle Fork of the Salmon River.

Carrey, John, and Cort Conley. *River of No Return.* Cambridge, ID: Backeddy Books, 1978. The river-runner's guide to the Salmon River, including a healthy dose of history.

Conley, Cort. *Idaho for the Curious.* Cambridge, ID: Backeddy Books, 1982. The comprehensive guide to Idaho's history, mile-by-mile along the state's highways. A must for those who want to know more about Idaho.

Exploring Idaho's High Desert. Boise: Challenge Expedition Co., 1988. A passport providing free passage to some of Idaho's most unusual sights.

Fisher, Vardis, ed. *Idaho: A Guide in Word and Picture.* New York: Oxford University Press, Inc. 1950. A Depression-era look at a great untamed state. Now in a revised form, this book manages to offer fresh perspectives more than 40 years after it was written.

Franzwa, Gregory M. *Maps of the Oregon Trail.* St. Louis: The Patrice Press, 1990. Provides locations and historical descriptions of the Oregon Trail's route west.

Fuller, Margaret. *Trails of the Frank Church–River of No Return Wilderness.* Edmonds, WA: Signpost Books, 1987. Fuller is the modern chronicler of much of Idaho's remote and wonderful trails.

Fuller, Margaret. *Trails of the Sawtooth & White Cloud Mountains.* Edmonds, WA: Signpost Books, 1979. Detailed accounts of excursions available in Idaho's most dramatic mountains.

Gnass, Jeff. *Idaho: Magnificent Wilderness.* Englewood, CO: Westcliffe Publishers, 1988. One of America's top wilderness photographers focuses on Idaho.

Green, Randall. *Idaho Rock, A Climbing Guide to the Selkirk Crest and Sandpoint Areas.* Seattle: The Mountaineers, 1987. Sketches mountain-climbing routes in some of the Panhandle's most scenic areas.

Hendrickson, Borg, and Linwood Laughy. *Clearwater Country!* Kooskia, ID: Mountain Meadow Press, 1989. Traces the history of the Clearwater River and surroundings from Missoula, Montana, to Lewiston, Idaho.

Huser, Verne. *River Running.* Chicago: Regnery Press, 1975. A nuts-and-bolts approach to how to run a river.

Landers, Rich, *Ida Rowe Dolphin and the Spokane Mountaineers.* Seattle: The Mountaineers, 1987. Overall, one of the best guidebooks to northern Idaho adventures south to the Clearwater country.

Linkhart, Luther. *Sawtooth National Recreation Area.* Berkeley: Wilderness Press, 1988. This ranks as the best overall guide to the history and terrain of the Sawtooths.

Loftus, Bill. *Idaho State Parks Guidebook.* Lewiston, ID: Tribune Publishing Co., 1989. A comprehensive look at Idaho's state parks system.

Maughan, Jackie Johnson. *The Hiker's Guide to Idaho.* Helena, MT: Falcon Press Publishing Co., 1984. Details a smattering of hikes across the state with an intensive focus on central Idaho.

Mitchell, Ron. *50 Eastern Idaho Hiking Trails (And Trouting Retreats).* Boulder, CO: Pruett Publishing, 1979. An outdoor writer lets some secrets slip.

Moser, Don. *The Snake River Country.* New York: Time-Life Books, 1974. A beautifully illustrated natural history of the Snake River and its surroundings.

North Idaho Hiking Trails. Boise: Challenge Expedition Co., 1982. A guide to some of the north's best hiking trails.

Perry, John, and Jane Greverus Perry. *The Sierra Club Guide to the Natural Areas of Idaho, Montana, and Wyoming.* San Francisco: Sierra Club Books, 1988. A listing of parks and places to get out and observe wildlife.

Rabe, Fred W., and David C. Flaherty. *River of Green and Gold.* Moscow, ID: Idaho Research Foundation, 1974. A look at the St. Joe River from Coeur d'Alene Lake upstream to its stony headwaters.

Stone, Lynne. *Adventures in Idaho's Sawtooth Country.* Seattle: The Mountaineers, 1990. Sixty-three adventures in the Sawtooths for mountain bikers and hikers.

Watson, Lewis, ed. *Idaho's Top 30 Fishing Waters.* Rupert, ID: Idaho Outdoor Digest, 1989. Thirty experts tell what they know about Idaho's most famous waters and how to fish them.

Watters, Ron. *Ski Trails and Old Timers' Tales in Idaho and Montana.* Moscow, ID: Solstice Press, 1978. Historical anecdotes accompany good descriptions of Idaho's cross-country skiing areas.

HISTORY

Ashworth, William. *Hells Canyon, The Deepest Gorge on Earth.* Hawthorne, 1977.

Beck, Richard J. *Famous Idahoans.* Moscow, ID: self-published, 1989. Thumbnail sketches of great Idahoans celebrate a past few residents recall.

Boone, Lalia. *Idaho Place Names, A Geographical Dictionary.* Moscow, ID: University of Idaho Press, 1988. Supplies the historical background about how the state's towns and features got their names.

Brown, Mark H. *The Flight of the Nez Perce.* New York: Capricorn Books, 1971. Another telling of the 1877 Nez Perce War and Chief Joseph's struggle to maintain his tribe.

Earl, Capt. Elmer. *Hells Canyon: A River Trip.* Lewiston, ID: Elmer Earl, 1990. A Snake River boatman's account of the history of the river canyon.

Jordan, Grace. *Home Below Hells Canyon.* Lincoln, NE: University of Nebraska Press, 1954. The engaging account of a family's life in the gorge. Len Jordan was later elected governor of Idaho and a U.S. Senator.

Josephy, Alvin M. *Chief Joseph's People and Their War.* Yellowstone Library and Museum Association, 1964. A look at the Nez Perce during the era of their 1877 struggle against an encroaching civilization.

Just, Rick. *Idaho Snapshots.* Meridian, ID: Radio Idaho, 1990. Vignettes of some of Idaho's most interesting history, present-day characters, and issues.

The Nez Perce Indians and the Opening of the Northwest. Lincoln, NE: University of Nebraska Press, 1977. Historical perspective about the Northwest's most famous tribe and their influence on white settlement.

Oppenheimer, Doug, and Jim Poore. *Sun Valley, A Biography.* Boise: Beatty Books.

Parker, Rev. Samuel. *Journal of an Exploring Tour.* Moscow, ID: University of Idaho Press, 1990. Reprint of an 1842 account of a pioneering missionary's journey across the unsettled reaches of the Rockies and Idaho.

Peterson, Harold. *The Last of the Mountain Men.* New York: Scribners, 1969. The story of Sylvan Hart, a.k.a. Buckskin Billy, a throwback to the 19th century who persisted into the mid-20th along the River of No Return.

Satterfield, Archie. *The Lewis & Clark Trail.* Harrisburg, PA: Stackpole Books, 1981. A light account of the Lewis and Clark Expedition's travel across the West.

Wright, William H. *The Grizzly Bear,* Lincoln, NE: The University of Nebraska Press, 1909. A narrative by a hunter and naturalist who pursued the grizzly across north-central Idaho and grew to respect the great bear.

MISCELLANEOUS

Idaho Secretary of State. *Idaho Blue Book.* Boise: Office of the Secretary of State, 1990. All the facts and figures about how Idaho's government works.

McCunn, Ruthanne Lum. *Thousand Pieces of Gold.* New York: Dell Publishing Co., 1981. The biography of Polly Bemis, a Chinese girl sold into slavery who married miner and merchant Charlie Bemis in the pioneer gold mining town of Warrens, Idaho. They later homesteaded along the Salmon River.

Maclean, Norman. *A River Runs Through It and Other Stories.* Chicago: University of Chicago Press, 1976. A modern bible of fly fishing's spiritual side with an engaging account of the Forest Service in Idaho's Bitterroots in 1919.

Moore, Rob, ed. *Field Guide to Outdoor Erotica.* Moscow, ID: Solstice Press, 1988. An Idaho-focused account of alternative recreation in wild places.

INDEX

Page numbers in **boldface** indicate the primary reference to a given topic. *Italicized* page numbers indicate information in captions, special topics, charts, illustrations, or maps.

N

O

XYZ

ABOUT THE AUTHOR

Bill found Idaho by serendipity. After two years at the University of Hawaii's Manoa campus, he was eager to travel to the Mainland. In 1975, the National Student Exchange Program and a year at the University of Idaho offered a chance to explore a state he'd never visited before—and one that he hasn't left since for more than a few weeks at a stretch.

After completing a degree in zoology and journalism, Bill signed on with Moscow's *Idahoan* newspaper. In 1982, the *Lewiston Morning Tribune* hired him as a sports copy editor and outdoor writer. Since then he's enjoyed the cream of Idaho's outdoor world—walking, skiing, riding horses, and mountain biking into the wild corners of the state. The Outdoor Writers Association of America honored the *Tribune's* Outdoors section as the best in the nation from 1987 to 1990.

Bill wrote the *Idaho State Parks Guidebook* as part of the *Tribune's* celebration of the Idaho Centennial in 1990. He has also worked as an outdoor columnist for the Associated Press and as Idaho editor for *Western Outdoors* magazine.

Bill enjoys his status as an Idahoan because it is a state where almost everyone is on a first-name basis with the mayor, maybe a Congressman, or the governor. Bureaucrats there become next-door neighbors and likable folks after 5 p.m.

Bill and Kelli, his wife, are raising two native Idahoans, Bob and Kate. They live in Genesee, a farming community at heart which also serves as a roost for commuters from nearby Moscow and Lewiston.

THE METRIC SYSTEM

1 inch = 2.54 centimeters (cm)
1 foot = .304 meters (m)
1 mile = 1.6093 kilometers (km)
1 km = .6124 miles
1 fathom = 1.8288 m
1 chain = 20.1168 m
1 furlong = 201.168 m
1 acre = .4047 hectares
1 sq km = 100 hectares
1 sq mile = 2.59 square km
1 ounce = 28.35 grams
1 pound = .4536 kilograms
1 short ton = .90718 metric ton
1 short ton = 2000 pounds
1 long ton = 1.016 metric tons
1 long ton = 2240 pounds
1 metric ton = 1000 kilograms
1 quart = .94635 liters
1 US gallon = 3.7854 liters
1 Imperial gallon = 4.5459 liters
1 nautical mile = 1.852 km

To compute centigrade temperatures, subtract 32 from Fahrenheit and divide by 1.8. To go the other way, multiply centigrade by 1.8 and add 32.

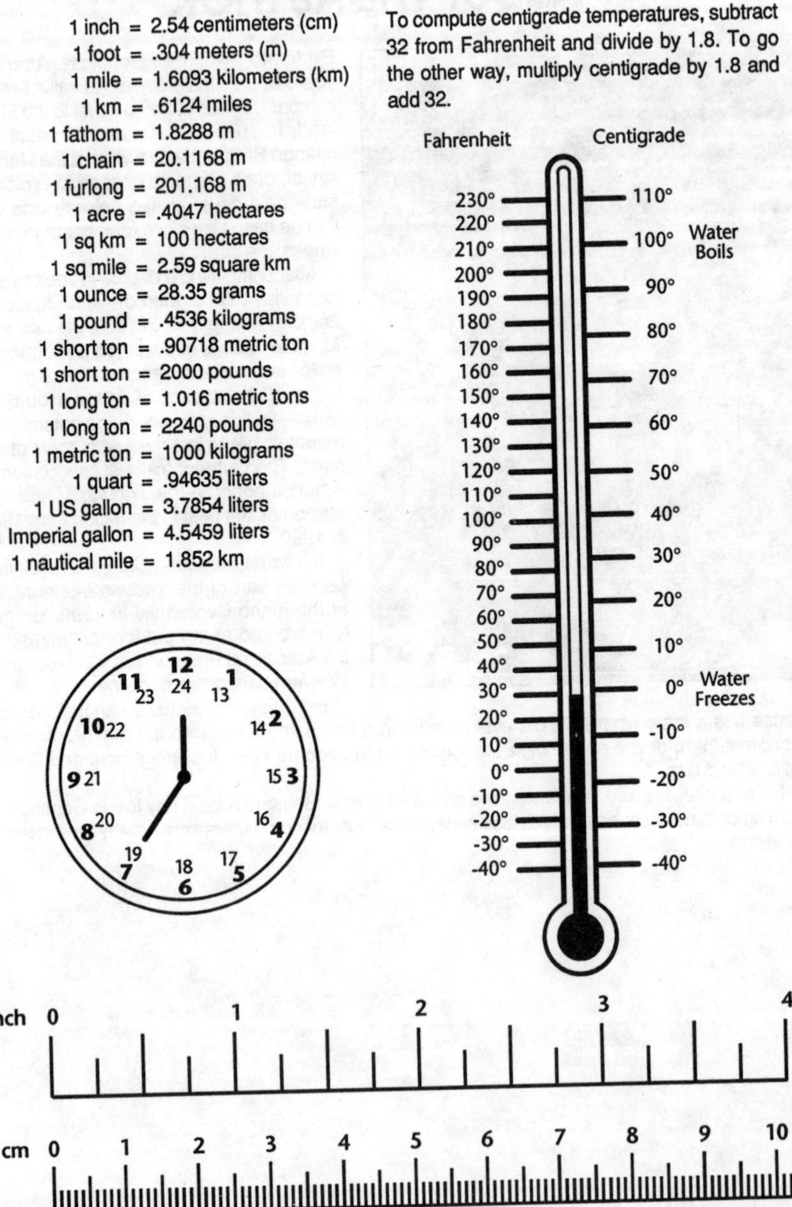

MOON HANDBOOKS—THE IDEAL TRAVELING COMPANIONS

Moon Handbooks provide travelers with all the background and practical information he or she will need on the road. Every Handbook begins with in-depth essays on the land, the people, their history, arts, politics, and social concerns—an entire bookshelf of introductory information squeezed into a one-volume encyclopedia. The Handbooks provide accurate, up-to-date coverage of all the practicalities: language, currency, transportation, accommodations, food and entertainment, and services, to name a few. Moon Handbooks are ideal traveling companions: informative, entertaining, and highly practical.

To locate the bookstore nearest you that carries Moon Travel Handbooks or to order directly from Moon Publications, call: (800) 345-5473, Monday-Friday, 9 a.m.-5 p.m. PST.

THE PACIFIC/ASIA SERIES

BALI HANDBOOK by Bill Dalton
Detailed travel information on the most famous island in the world. 428 pages. **$12.95**

BANGKOK HANDBOOK by Michael Buckley
Your tour guide through this exotic and dynamic city reveals the affordable and accessible possibilities. Thai phrasebook. 214 pages. **$10.95**

BLUEPRINT FOR PARADISE: How to Live on a Tropic Island by Ross Norgrove
This one-of-a-kind guide has everything you need to know about moving to and living comfortably on a tropical island. 212 pages. **$14.95**

FIJI ISLANDS HANDBOOK by David Stanley
The first and still the best source of information on travel around this 322-island archipelago. Fijian glossary. 198 pages. **$11.95**

INDONESIA HANDBOOK by Bill Dalton
This one-volume encyclopedia explores island by island the many facets of this sprawling, kaleidoscopic island nation. Extensive Indonesian vocabulary. 1,000 pages. **$19.95**

JAPAN HANDBOOK by J.D. Bisignani
In this comprehensive new edition, award-winning travel writer J.D. Bisignani offers to inveterate travelers, newcomers, and businesspeople alike a thoroughgoing presentation of Japan's many facets. 950 pages. **$22.50**

MICRONESIA HANDBOOK: Guide to the Caroline, Gilbert, Mariana, and Marshall Islands
by David Stanley
Micronesia Handbook guides you on a real Pacific adventure all your own. 345 pages. **$11.95**

NEW ZEALAND HANDBOOK by Jane King
Introduces you to the people, places, history, and culture of this extraordinary land. 571 pages. **$18.95**

OUTBACK AUSTRALIA HANDBOOK by Marael Johnson
Australia is an endlessly fascinating, vast land, and *Outback Australia Handbook* explores the cities and towns, sheep stations, and wilderness areas of the Northern Territory, Western Australia, and South Australia. Full of travel tips and cultural information for adventuring, relaxing, or just getting away from it all. 355 pages. **$15.95**

PHILIPPINES HANDBOOK by Peter Harper and Evelyn Peplow
Crammed with detailed information, *Philippines Handbook* equips the escapist, hedonist, or business traveler with thorough coverage of the Philippines's colorful history, landscapes, and culture. 600 pages. **$17.95**

SOUTHEAST ASIA HANDBOOK by Carl Parkes
Helps the enlightened traveler discover the real Southeast Asia. 873 pages. **$21.95**

SOUTH KOREA HANDBOOK by Robert Nilsen
Whether you're visiting on business or searching for adventure, *South Korea Handbook* is an invaluable companion. Korean glossary with useful notes on speaking and reading the language. 548 pages. **$14.95**

SOUTH PACIFIC HANDBOOK by David Stanley
The original comprehensive guide to the 16 territories in the South Pacific. 740 pages. **$19.95**

TAHITI-POLYNESIA HANDBOOK by David Stanley
All five French-Polynesian archipelagoes are covered in this comprehensive guide by Oceania's best-known travel writer. 235 pages. **$11.95**

THAILAND HANDBOOK by Carl Parkes
Presents the richest source of information on travel in Thailand. 568 pages. **$16.95**

THE HAWAIIAN SERIES

BIG ISLAND OF HAWAII HANDBOOK by J.D. Bisignani
An entertaining yet informative text packed with insider tips on accommodations, dining, sports and outdoor activities, natural attractions, and must-see sights. 350 pages. **$13.95**

HAWAII HANDBOOK by J.D. Bisignani
Winner of the 1989 Hawaii Visitors Bureau's Best Guide Award and the Grand Award for Excellence in Travel Journalism, this guide takes you beyond the glitz and high-priced hype and leads you to a genuine Hawaiian experience. Covers all 8 Hawaiian Islands. 879 pages. **$15.95**

KAUAI HANDBOOK by J.D. Bisignani
Kauai Handbook is the perfect antidote to the workaday world. Hawaiian and pidgin glossaries. 236 pages. **$9.95**

MAUI HANDBOOK by J.D. Bisignani
"No fool-'round" advice on accommodations, eateries, and recreation, plus a comprehensive introduction to island ways, geography, and history. Hawaiian and pidgin glossaries. 393 pages. **$14.95**

HONOLULU-WAIKIKI HANDBOOK: The Island of Oahu by J.D. Bisignani
A handy guide to Honolulu, renowned surfing beaches, and Oahu's countless other diversions. Hawaiian and pidgin glossaries. 360 pages. **$14.95**

THE AMERICAS SERIES

ALASKA-YUKON HANDBOOK by Deke Castleman and Don Pitcher
Get the inside story, with plenty of well-seasoned advice to help you cover more miles on less money. 460 pages. **$14.95**

ARIZONA TRAVELER'S HANDBOOK by Bill Weir
This meticulously researched guide contains everything necessary to make Arizona accessible and enjoyable. 445 pages. **$16.95**

BAJA HANDBOOK: Mexico's Western Peninsula including Cabo San Lucas by Joe Cummings
A comprehensive guide with all the travel information and background on the land, history, and culture of this untamed thousand-mile-long peninsula. 362 pages. **$15.95**

BELIZE HANDBOOK by Chicki Mallan
Complete with detailed maps, practical information, and an overview of the area's flamboyant history, culture, and geographical features, *Belize Handbook* is the only comprehensive guide of its kind to this spectacular region. 263 pages. **$14.95**

BRITISH COLUMBIA HANDBOOK by Jane King
With an emphasis on outdoor adventures, this guide covers mainland British Columbia, Vancouver Island, the Queen Charlotte Islands, and the Canadian Rockies. 381 pages. **$15.95**

CANCUN HANDBOOK by Chicki Mallan
Covers the city's luxury scene as well as more modest attractions, plus many side trips to unspoiled beaches and Mayan ruins. Spanish glossary. 257 pages. **$13.95**

CENTRAL MEXICO HANDBOOK: Mexico City, Guadalajara, and Other Colonial Cities by Chicki Mallan
Retrace the footsteps of Cortés from the coast of Veracruz to the heart of Mexico City to discover archaeological and cultural wonders. 391 pages. **$15.95**

CATALINA ISLAND HANDBOOK: A Guide to California's Channel Islands by Chicki Mallan
A complete guide to these remarkable islands, from the windy solitude of the Channel Islands National Marine Sanctuary to bustling Avalon. 245 pages. **$10.95**

COLORADO HANDBOOK by Stephen Metzger
Essential details to the all-season possibilities in Colorado fill this guide. Practical travel tips combine with recreation—skiing, nightlife, and wilderness exploration—plus entertaining essays. 416 pages. **$17.95**

COSTA RICA HANDBOOK by Christopher P. Baker
Experience the many wonders of the natural world as you explore this remarkable land. Spanish-English glossary. 574 pages. **$17.95**

IDAHO HANDBOOK by Bill Loftus
A year-round guide to everything in this outdoor wonderland, from whitewater adventures to rural hideaways. 282 pages. **$14.95**

JAMAICA HANDBOOK by Karl Luntta
From the sun and surf of Montego Bay and Ocho Rios to the cool slopes of the Blue Mountains, author Karl Luntta offers island-seekers a perceptive, personal view of Jamaica. 230 pages. **$14.95**

MONTANA HANDBOOK by W.C. McRae and Judy Jewell
The wild West is yours with this extensive guide to the Treasure State, complete with travel practicalities, history, and lively essays on Montana life. 427 pages. **$15.95**

NEVADA HANDBOOK by Deke Castleman
Nevada Handbook puts the Silver State into perspective and makes it manageable and affordable. 400 pages. **$14.95**

NEW MEXICO HANDBOOK by Stephen Metzger
A close-up and complete look at every aspect of this wondrous state. 375 pages. **$14.95**

NORTHERN CALIFORNIA HANDBOOK by Kim Weir
An outstanding companion for imaginative travel in the territory north of the Tehachapis. 765 pages. **$19.95**

NORTHERN MEXICO HANDBOOK: The Sea of Cortez to the Gulf of Mexico
by Joe Cummings
Directs travelers from the barrier islands of Sonora to the majestic cloud forests of the Sierra Madre Oriental to traditional villages and hidden waterfalls in San Luis Potosí. 500 pages. **$16.95**

OREGON HANDBOOK by Stuart Warren and Ted Long Ishikawa
Brimming with travel practicalities and insiders' views on Oregon's history, culture, arts, and activities. 461 pages. **$15.95**

PACIFIC MEXICO HANDBOOK by Bruce Whipperman
Explore 2,000 miles of gorgeous beaches, quiet resort towns, and famous archaeological sites along Mexico's Pacific coast. Spanish-English glossary. 428 pages. **$15.95**

TEXAS HANDBOOK by Joe Cummings
Seasoned travel writer Joe Cummings brings an insider's perspective to his home state. 483 pages. **$13.95**

UTAH HANDBOOK by Bill Weir
Weir gives you all the carefully researched facts and background to make your visit a success. 445 pages. **$14.95**

WASHINGTON HANDBOOK by Archie Satterfield and Dianne J. Boulerice Lyons
Covers sights, shopping, services, transportation, and outdoor recreation, with complete listings for restaurants and accommodations. 419 pages. **$15.95**

WYOMING HANDBOOK by Don Pitcher
All you need to know to open the doors to this wide and wild state. 495 pages. **$14.95**

YUCATAN HANDBOOK by Chicki Mallan
All the information you'll need to guide you into every corner of this exotic land. Mayan and Spanish glossaries. 391 pages. **$15.95**

THE INTERNATIONAL SERIES

EGYPT HANDBOOK by Kathy Hansen
An invaluable resource for intelligent travel in Egypt. Arabic glossary. 522 pages. **$18.95**

MOSCOW-ST. PETERSBURG HANDBOOK by Masha Nordbye
Provides the visitor with an extensive introduction to the history, culture, and people of these two great cities, as well as practical information on where to stay, eat, and shop. 260 pages. **$13.95**

NEPAL HANDBOOK by Kerry Moran
Whether you're planning a week in Kathmandu or months out on the trail, *Nepal Handbook* will take you into the heart of this Himalayan jewel. 378 pages. **$12.95**

NEPALI AAMA by Broughton Coburn
A delightful photo-journey into the life of a Gurung tribeswoman of Central Nepal. Having lived with Aama (translated, "mother") for two years, first as an outsider and later as an adopted member of the family, Coburn presents an intimate glimpse into a culture alive with humor, folklore, religion, and ancient rituals. 165 pages. **$13.95**

PAKISTAN HANDBOOK by Isobel Shaw
For armchair travelers and trekkers alike, the most detailed and authoritative guide to Pakistan ever published. Urdu glossary. 478 pages. **$15.95**

STAYING HEALTHY IN ASIA, AFRICA, AND LATIN AMERICA
by Dirk G. Schroeder, Sc D, MPH
Don't leave home without it! Besides providing a complete overview of the health problems that exist in these areas, this book will help you determine which immunizations you'll need beforehand, what medications to take with you, and how to recognize and treat infections and diseases. Includes extensively illustrated first-aid information and precautions for heat, cold, and high altitude. 200 pages. **$10.95**

TIBET HANDBOOK: A PILGRIMAGE GUIDE
by Victor Chan
This remarkable book is both a comprehensive trekking guide to mountain paths and plateau trails, and a pilgrimage guide that draws on Tibetan literature and religious history. 1104 pages. **$30.00**

MOONBELTS

Made of heavy-duty Cordura nylon, the Moonbelt offers maximum protection for your money and important papers. This all-weather pouch slips under your shirt or waistband, rendering it virtually undetectable and inaccessible to pickpockets. One-inch-wide nylon webbing, heavy-duty zipper, one-inch quick-release buckle. Accommodates traveler's checks, passport, cash, photos. Size 5 x 9 inches. Black. **$8.95**

New travel handbooks may be available that are not on this list.
To find out more about current or upcoming titles,
call us toll-free at (800) 345-5473.

IMPORTANT ORDERING INFORMATION

FOR FASTER SERVICE: Call to locate the bookstore nearest you that carries Moon Travel Handbooks or order directly from Moon Publications:

(800) 345-5473 • Monday-Friday • 9 a.m.-5 p.m. PST • fax (916) 345-6751

PRICES: All prices are subject to change. We always ship the most current edition. We will let you know if there is a price increase on the book you ordered.

SHIPPING & HANDLING OPTIONS: 1) Domestic UPS or USPS first class (allow 10 working days for delivery): $3.50 for the first item, 50 cents for each additional item.

Exceptions:

- **Moonbelt** shipping is $1.50 for one, 50 cents for each additional belt.
- Add $2.00 for same-day handling.
- UPS 2nd Day Air or Printed Airmail requires a special quote.
- International Surface Bookrate (8-12 weeks delivery): $3.00 for the first item, $1.00 for each additional item. Note: Moon Publications cannot guarantee international surface bookrate shipping.

FOREIGN ORDERS: All orders that originate outside the U.S.A. must be paid for with either an International Money Order or a check in U.S. currency drawn on a major U.S. bank based in the U.S.A.

TELEPHONE ORDERS: We accept Visa or MasterCard payments. Minimum order is US$15.00. Call in your order: (800) 345-5473, 9 a.m.-5 p.m. Pacific Standard Time.

ORDER FORM

Be sure to call (800) 345-5473 for current prices and editions or for the name of the bookstore nearest you that carries Moon Travel Handbooks • 9 a.m.–5 p.m. PST
(See important ordering information on preceding page)

Name: ______________________ Date: ______________

Street: ______________________________________

City: ______________________ Daytime Phone: ______________

State or Country: ______________ Zip Code: ______________

QUANTITY	TITLE	PRICE

Taxable Total ______

Sales Tax (7.25%) for California Residents ______

Shipping & Handling ______

TOTAL ______

Ship: ☐ UPS (no PO Boxes) ☐ 1st class ☐ International surface mail

Ship to: ☐ address above ☐ other ______________________

Make checks payable to: **MOON PUBLICATIONS, INC.** P.O. Box 3040, Chico, CA 95927-3040 U.S.A. We accept Visa and MasterCard. **To Order**: Call in your Visa or MasterCard number, or send a written order with your Visa or MasterCard number and expiration date clearly written.

Card Number: ☐ **Visa** ☐ **MasterCard**

☐☐☐☐ ☐☐☐☐ ☐☐☐☐ ☐☐☐☐

Exact Name on Card: ______________________

expiration date: ______________________

signature ______________________

W94-95

WHERE TO BUY THIS BOOK

BOOKSTORES AND LIBRARIES:
Moon Publications Handbooks are sold worldwide. Please write our sales manager for a list of wholesalers and distributors in your area that stock our travel handbooks.

TRAVELERS:
We would like to have Moon Publications Handbooks available throughout the world. Please ask your bookstore to write or call us for ordering information. If your bookstore will not order our guides for you, please write or call for a free catalog.

MOON PUBLICATIONS, INC.
P.O. BOX 3040
CHICO, CA 95927-3040 U.S.A.
TEL: (800) 345-5473
FAX: (916) 345-6751

TRAVEL MATTERS

Travel Matters is Moon Publications' quarterly newsletter. It provides today's traveler with timely, informative travel news and articles.

You'll find resourceful coverage on:

TRAVEL MATTERS

Ecotourism: Trojan Horse Or Savior Of The Last, Best Place?

- **Money**—What does it cost? Is it worth it?
- **Low impact travel**—tread lightly travel tips
- **Special interest travel**—cultural tours, environmental excursions, outdoor recreation, adventure treks, and more
- **Travel styles**—families, seniors, disabled travelers, package and theme tours
- **Consumer reviews**—books, language aids, travel gadgets, products, and services
- **Facts and opinions**—reader's letters and Moon Handbook author news
- **Moon Handbook booklist**—the latest titles and editions, and where and how to purchase them

To receive a free copy of *Travel Matters*, write Moon Publications Inc., P.O. Box 3040, Chico, CA 95927-3040, or call toll-free (800) 345-5473, Monday–Friday, 9 a.m. – 5 p.m. Pacific Standard Time.